The Handbook of
ETHICAL RESEARCH
With
ETHNOCULTURAL
POPULATIONS & COMMUNITIES

The Handbook of
ETHICAL RESEARCH
With
ETHNOCULTURAL
POPULATIONS & COMMUNITIES

Edited by

JOSEPH E. TRIMBLE • CELIA B. FISHER
Western Washington University   Fordham University

SAGE Publications
Thousand Oaks ▪ London ▪ New Delhi

For information:

Sage Publications, Inc.
2455 Teller Road
Thousand Oaks, California 91320
E-mail: order@sagepub.com

Sage Publications Ltd.
1 Oliver's Yard
55 City Road
London EC1Y 1SP
United Kingdom

Sage Publications India Pvt. Ltd.
B-42, Panchsheel Enclave
Post Box 4109
New Delhi 110 017 India

Printed in the United States of America

Library of Congress Cataloging-in-Publication Data

Trimble, Joseph E.
The handbook of ethical research with ethnocultural populations
and communities / Joseph E. Trimble, Celia B. Fisher.
  p. cm.
Includes bibliographical references and index.
ISBN 0-7619-3043-4 (cloth)
  1. Ethnic groups—Research—Handbooks, manuals, etc. 2. Ethnology—
Research—Handbooks, manuals, etc. 3. Ethnopsychology—Research—
Handbooks 4. Anthropological ethics—Handbooks, manuals, etc.
I. Fisher, Celia B. II. Title.
GN495.4.T75 2005
305.8′0072—dc22   2005008158

This book is printed on acid-free paper.

05   06   07   08   09   8   7   6   5   4   3   2   1

Acquisitions Editor:	Jim Brace-Thompson
Editorial Assistant:	Karen Ehrmann
Production Editor:	Diane S. Foster
Copy Editor:	Robert Holm
Typesetter:	C&M Digitals, (P) Ltd.
Proofreader:	Joyce Li
Indexer:	Jeanne R. Busemeyer
Cover Designer:	Janet Foulger

Contents

Acknowledgments

In the late 19th century, Lone Man (isna la wican), a Teton Siouan spiritual leader, is thought to have said, "I have seen that in any great undertaking it is not enough for a man to depend upon himself." The conceptualization, organization, preparation, and writing of this handbook depended on the commitment, cooperation, and dedication of a number of scholars from a variety of academic disciplines who either are contributors to the writing of chapters or friends and colleagues who provided thoughtful guidance, criticism, and commentary along the way. We want to use this special occasion to express our profound gratitude to those kindred spirits because as Lone Man appropriately stated, we could not have produced this handbook without them.

We are grateful to our talented and thoughtful contributors. Thank you all for your assistance, persistence, wisdom, and your well-written chapters. You were patient and understanding as we persisted in our efforts to get every aspect of the review and final draft process completed in great form. You returned e-mail messages and telephone calls promptly, sought advice from us on how to improve your chapter, and cooperated in every phase of the writing and review process. We are blessed to have you as colleagues in this important topic of inquiry and exploration.

Our special thanks and appreciation are extended to our dear friend and colleague, James Brace-Thompson, our senior editor at Sage Publications. Jim met with us over dinner in Chicago in August 2002 where we carefully laid out our book concept and plan. His enthusiasm for our proposal was apparent in the first 15 minutes. He has retained that level of excitement, encouragement, and commitment throughout the course of preparing and submitting the manuscripts, and without his support the handbook may not have materialized. Karen Ehrmann, our production assistant at Sage Publications, was extremely helpful in providing us with the materials we needed to expedite the production process as well as handle the many details associated with contracts and the handling of the production phase of the book. Indeed we are indebted for her careful attention to detail and, most important, her kind and gentle manner.

Joseph wishes to extend his gratitude to his graduate research assistants at Western Washington University. Ryan Dickson, MA, read through every chapter in detail with a careful eye to manuscript formatting, grammar, and composition. Janice Brendible, MEd, a Tsimshian Alaska Native from Metlakatla, Alaska, pored over every chapter and provided us with insightful comments, in part based on her experiences with outside researchers who frequented her village and her knowledge on the ethical conduct of research with ethnic communities in general. Their commentary, suggestions, and observations challenged us and thus helped us make this handbook better.

Molly Trimble and Gary Fisher have shared the ebb and flow of our frustrations and enthusiasm for the handbook from the moment we decided to embark on our venture. They have been with us as we poured out our thoughts and annoyances over the many aspects associated with the long writing and production process. Their loving spiritual encouragement and wisdom kept us focused.

—Joseph E. Trimble
Bellingham, WA

—Celia B. Fisher
New York, NY

Preface

Ultimately, we learned that it is essential to include members of the participating communities in the decision making regarding research methodologies (including limits of confidentiality), the meaning ascribed to research questions and participant responses, and the analysis and interpretation of the resulting data. Without community involvement in each of these steps, it is clear that any results are questionable at best, and harmful to the communities at worst.

—Gerald V. Mohatt and Lisa R. Thomas

In this volume, psychological scientists examine the changing face of America and address the change head-on as it affects research design. Soon the people of America will be better described as America's people of color. In 1980, African Americans made up 11.5% of the U.S. population, Latino/Latinas were 6.4%, Asians made up 1.5%, and Native Americans 0.6% (U.S. Bureau of the Census, 1983). By the year 2000, African Americans rose to be 12.1%, Latino/Latinas nearly doubled to 12.6%, Asian Americans rose to 3.6%, and American Indians and Alaska Natives increased to 0.7%. Although European Americans increased by only 8% between 1980 and 2000, in contrast Asian Americans increased by 190%, Latino/Latinas went up 143%, African Americans gained 30%, and American Indians and Alaska Natives increased by 46% (Social Science Data Analysis Network, 2004). These populations, once known as ethnic minorities, are destined to become the majority. As they grow, they bring their own special cultural characteristics such as beliefs, language systems, traditions, customs, worldviews, and values. These special characteristics must be acknowledged and understood by scholars planning research with such populations.

As ethnic populations gain in importance to scholars, the traditional approaches to responsible science demand review, reevaluation, and revision. The authors correctly contend that research with ethnocultural populations requires a paradigm shift in how social science is conducted if the research is to be considered ethical by participants reflecting the multicultural mosaic.

This is an inspiring and challenging book to read: It is sometimes confrontational and often blunt about the inadequacy of common approaches to scientific validity and human subjects protections that are steeped in traditionally accepted European American standards. The authors draw upon wisdom earned through their years of personal experience conducting ethnocultural research to challenge long-standing interpretations of ethical principles and epistemological assumptions in social science. They raise difficult questions of the role of investigator-participant-community power, control, and authority in strengthening or undermining scientific validity. They challenge the reader to reframe the concept of expert as it relates to informed consent and assessment of scientific value as a bidirectional dialogue between investigator and participants. Their honesty in sharing case studies of their research ethics efforts and failure will cause readers to reflect on the adequacy of current perspectives on scientific objectivity and of maintaining a neutral-observer role. Overall, the message is consistently given: designing culturally valid ethical procedures for research involves adopting a new perspective, one that derives from the ethnic groups themselves rather than one that starts from prior assumptions of what constitutes human values of respect, care, and justice. This is a groundbreaking volume that offers concrete information for scholars wishing to conduct research that is culturally appropriate, ethically defensible, and scientifically sound. The authors bring their special experience and expertise to address specific populations such as immigrants and refugees, the elderly, vulnerable adolescents, African Americans, American Indians, Asian Americans, and Hispanic/ Latin(a)o Americans. In addition, authors present useful information regarding research when a community is the target, when archival documents are used, or when the setting is the juvenile justice system or a developing country.

The book provides revisions to mainstream thinking about research design, data collection, analysis, and interpretation of results to assure culturally meaningful and ethically sound outcomes. Included are discussions regarding gaining access and earning credibility, weighing the value of a selective sampling instead of a randomized sampling procedure, defining incentives in a collectivistic culture, obtaining valid informed consent, selection of instruments with relevant norms, assuring translation/conceptual/ metric equivalence, and interpreting data within the proper cultural context. Also discussed are certain ethical dilemmas such as the following:

- Whether to remain objective or become a participant in the sociopolitical structure of the people or community being studied
- Whether to maintain a neutral role or permit the research activity to be by its very nature an agent of change
- Whether to proceed when the study benefits only the researcher or offer sustainable benefits to the community, group, or individuals under study
- Whether to view the researcher as the sole authority in design of the research or include community members in all aspects of the design

This volume is truly a must read and will take its place as an essential resource for anyone involved with ethnocultural populations and communities.

—Richard M. Suinn

Professor Emeritus,
Colorado State University
1999 President of the
American Psychological Association

REFERENCES

Mohatt, G. V., & Thomas, L. R. (in press). Ethical dilemmas in doing participatory research with Alaska Native communities. In J. Trimble & C. B. Fischer (Eds.), *The handbook of ethical research with ethnocultural populations and communities.* Thousand Oaks, CA: Sage.

Social Science Data Analysis Network. (2004). *United States population by race.* Retrieved October 2004, from www.censusscope.org/us/chart_race.html

U.S. Bureau of the Census. (1983). *1980 census of population.* Washington, DC: Government Printing Office.

Our Shared Journey: Lessons From the Past to Protect the Future

JOSEPH E. TRIMBLE

CELIA B. FISHER

> *The principle that underlies problems of ethics is respecting the humanity of others as one would have others respect one's own. If field [researchers] genuinely feel such respect for others, they are not likely to get into serious trouble. But if they do not feel such respect, then no matter how scrupulously they follow the letter of the written codes of professional ethics, or follow the recommended procedures of field (research) manuals, they will betray themselves all along the line in the little things.*
>
> —Ward H. Goodenough

In this quote, the longtime cultural anthropologist Ward Goodenough (1980, p. 52) points to two important components of field-based research: building and establishing trust and valuing and practicing respect with the host community and the respondents. These two components are essential to the conduct of responsible research with any community or pool of respondents. The quote's theme, however, implies that there are some researchers who are not sensitive to the lifeways and thoughtways in communities where they conduct research. Most field-based researchers are conscientious, sincere in their respect for their host communities, and sensitive to ethnocultural worldviews; a few are not. Good intentions, however, are not enough to ensure research involving ethnocultural communities is conducted in ways that reflect respect for human dignity and appreciation of community values. With rare exceptions, current professional standards and federal regulations for the protection of research participants fail to provide the guidance needed to achieve the responsible conduct of ethnocultural research. The stakes are especially high for members of minority ethnic groups, who need culturally validated mental health services to redress current health disparities but who are also most vulnerable to personal and group harms that can arise when traditional ethical research practices do not adequately protect their rights and welfare (Fisher, 1999).

Goodenough's words speak to the core theme of this handbook: the responsible and ethical conduct of research involving ethnocultural populations. Interest in social research with ethnocultural groups has been increasing dramatically, particularly in psychology. As contact with social scientists has increased, so have the concerns of many ethnic communities about research in general and the presence of investigators in their communities. The rising community concerns, accompanied by the emergence of community-based research review committees, present extraordinary challenges for researchers, challenges that are only beginning to be fully and seriously acknowledged at methodological, procedural, and conceptual levels. The most important challenge, though, is the responsible conduct of researchers while they are in the field, especially as it is reflected in the relationship they establish with their respondents (American Psychological Association, 2002; Cassell & Jacobs, 1987; Fisher, 1999; Fisher & Wallace, 2000).

HISTORICAL OVERVIEW

Research with ethnocultural populations has a long and rich history in the annals of the behavioral and social sciences in the United States, with its beginnings dating back to the mid- to late 19th century. A case in point concerns the long, rich history of research with American Indians and Alaska Natives. Interest in compiling ethnographic materials on American Indians began in 1877 with the geographical and geological survey of the Rocky Mountain region. Some of the earliest ethnographic collections from this period are the diaries of John Wesley Powell recounting his exploration of Colorado and study of the region's Indians. Three volumes printed under authority of special resolutions of Congress had been completed by 1879. Then in that year, the United States government through the Smithsonian Institute established the Bureau of American Ethnography to sponsor and publish research on American Indians and Alaska Natives. Lasting from 1879 to 1965, the bureau published thousands of pages of quality anthropological and archaeological research on a huge variety of subjects in the form of bulletins and annual reports.

From 1879 to the present, countless numbers of graduate students and academicians in anthropology collected data and compiled thousands of reports and publications dealing with the ethos of most Indian tribes and many Alaska Native villages. It is very likely that the rapid emergence of anthropology as a recognized academic discipline in part can be attributed to the massive amount of information conducted on the Americas' aboriginal people. Indeed, the career development of many cultural anthropologists was the result of their ongoing, lifelong studies with one or two tribes. Consequently, over the decades, well-intended researchers found their way to Indian and native communities, consorted with tribal leaders and their informants, conducted their research, snapped countless photos, recorded sacred songs, and documented rituals and ceremonies, many of which were forbidden to be witnessed by outsiders; then they left, in many instances never to be heard from again.

Increases in Ethnocultural Research Citations

The historical record shows that the North American Indian and Alaska Native is probably the most studied ethnic minority group in the United States. Several significant and comprehensive bibliographies have been published in the past four decades that reflect the extensive nature of the social and behavioral science literature on America's aboriginal people. In 1957, Dockstader compiled and published an extensive list of 3,684 theses and dissertations that dealt with American Indians dating back to 1890. Hodge (1976) published a comprehensive annotated bibliography listing 2,600 books and articles dealing with contemporary American Indian issues and topics; many of the cited articles are unpublished. Martin and O'Leary (1990) cite over 25,000 books and articles that describe the traditional culture and lifeways of North American Indians; about 1,700 citations deal with archaeology and another 500 focus on medical care. In 1981, Kelso and Attneave published an extensive bibliography of 1,363 citations dating back to 1930 on North American Indian mental health (Kelso & Attneave, 1981). The citations include articles covering many academic disciplines, not just psychology. Trimble and Bagwell in 1995 edited a bibliography of psychological and behavioral articles on North American Indians and Alaska Natives published from 1967 to 1994; most of the 2,328 citations published by over 3,000 behavioral and social scientists are presented in abstract or summary form (Trimble & Bagwell, 1995).

In 1988, the American Psychological Association (APA) began publishing an annotated bibliography series focusing on diverse ethnic populations. The series topics include African Americans, African American males, Hispanics, Asians, and, as mentioned above, North American Indians. The citations referenced in the special volumes provide ample testament to the fact that interest in conducting research with ethnic and racial populations is increasing rapidly; the trends are likely to increase in coming years as more and more interest is devoted to the field.

The bibliographic series documents a notable increase in citations in *PsycINFO* on all ethnic minority groups. Citations referencing African Americans increased from less than 2,063 in the 1960s to 10,382 in the 1990s. Research with Latino populations also showed a remarkable increase, from only 22 references in the 1960s to 3,720 in the 1990s. References on Asian Americans

grew from 17 citations in the 1960s to 1,360 in the 1990s, and for American Indians and Alaska Natives from 203 to 1,434 during the same period. As can be appreciated, the increase in citations referencing research related to racial and ethnic minorities is a reflection of a maturing of psychology as a science discipline for all members of society. The rapid growth of interest and levels of research activity must be tempered by an awareness of the ethical implications of efforts involving groups with whom most investigators have little familiarity.

COMPLAINTS AND CONCERNS FROM THE FIELD

The need for this book emerged from the voices of many community people across the country who have become highly vocal about the problems some researchers create for their villages, neighborhoods, and communities. More and more ethnic communities are becoming concerned about the presence of outside researchers; many are intolerant and unforgiving of past research efforts. The so-called safari-scholar era has come to an end and "data mining" is no longer acceptable. More now than ever, ethnocultural leaders demand that research occur in their communities under their direction and control. Researchers should be prepared to collaborate with communities, share results that have practical value, and accept the conditions imposed by the community in gaining access to information and respondents (Fisher et al., 2002).

Most researchers in the biomedical and social and behavioral sciences are acutely aware of the circumstances surrounding the infamous U.S. government Tuskegee Syphilis Study when, from 1932 to 1972, medical treatment for syphilis was withheld from 600 poor African American male research participants from rural Alabama (see Jones,

1993). Even the most basic ethical practices common to today's human research studies were absent: Participants were never given the option to terminate their participation in the study, were misinformed that they were participating in a study to examine "bad blood," and were induced to cooperate with free medical exams, meals, and burial insurance.

Details of the study were first published in a 1970s news story that led to an immediate call for action and an explanation from the U.S. Public Health Service. The federal government established an ad hoc committee to review the charges and allegations. At the end of the inquiry and investigation, the committee overwhelmingly concluded that the study was unethical and that it must be stopped. This prompted Public Law 93-348 calling for the establishment of the National Commission for the Protection of Human Subjects of Biomedical and Behavioral Research. In 1979 the commission published recommendations, known as the Belmont Report, that served as the basis for revised federal regulations published in the Federal Register in 1979 and subsequently revised several times resulting in the current Code of Federal Regulations Title 45-Part 46, Protection of Human Subjects (45 CFR 46), effective as of 1991 (U.S. Department of Health and Human Services, 2001). The Belmont Report laid out three general ethical principles that continue to govern human subjects research: *beneficence,* which is the maximization of benefits for science, humanity, and research participants and avoidance or minimization of risk or harm; *respect,* which is the obligation to protect the autonomy and privacy rights of participants; and *justice,* representing the obligation to ensure the fair distribution among persons and groups of the costs and benefits of research. A year later the National Association for the Advancement of Colored People (NAACP) filed a lawsuit against the federal agency on behalf of the study participants and their

families; $9 million was awarded to the participants and their familial descendants. Twenty-five years later President Bill Clinton issued a formal apology. Many scholars and civil rights activists wonder why it took so long.

Undoubtedly the Tuskegee Syphilis Study is one of many instances in which scientists have exploited historically oppressed groups, ostensibly to advance an understanding of the human condition (Inbrahim & Cameron, 2005). One would believe that the outcomes of the Tuskegee study would serve as a warning to those who would abuse participants and deny them their rights; that does not appear to be the case. Consider the significance and importance of the headlines in a February 2004 Arizona newspaper that read, "Havasupai file $25M suit vs. ASU" (Hendricks, 2004). In the story, the journalist summarizes the research circumstances that prompted 52 Havasupai tribal members to file the lawsuit and provides a status report on the suit's developments. Briefly stated, between 1990 and 1994, researchers from Arizona State University collected from the 52 tribal members blood samples that were to be used to study the correlates of diabetes. Tribal members eventually learned that the blood samples had been used for purposes other than those they agreed to in signing the human subjects consent forms. The ASU researchers had used the samples to study schizophrenia, inbreeding, and factors that could explain human migration patterns.

Consider, too, the chilling, controversial allegations that riled cultural anthropologists, bioethicists, and segments of the public in 2000 following the frightening and disturbing charges made by the journalist, Patrick Tierney (2000), in his book, *Darkness in El Dorado: How Scientists and Journalists Devastated the Amazon.* After devoting several years to investigating how research was conducted among the Yanomami people along the Ecuador-Brazil border, Tierney claimed that a few notable researchers were involved in dreadful biological experiments and that field-based ethnographic data was fabricated to support long-standing socio-biological theories about aggressive behavior. Tierney's allegations fanned the flames of debate among anthropologists and ethicists. According to Miller (2001), e-mail messages "ignited a swift and furious debate that left scholars with nowhere to go for information but online" (p. 1). Eventually the American Anthropological Association (AAA) convened an expert panel to investigate the allegations and concluded that "the book contains numerous unfounded, misrepresented, and sensationalistic accusations about the conduct of anthropology among the Yanomami. These misrepresentations fail to live up to the ethics of responsible journalism even as they pretend to question the ethical conduct of anthropology" (American Anthropological Association, 2002, p. 1). Additionally and not surprisingly, Venezuela's Office of Indigenous Affairs issued a moratorium on research with and among their indigenous populations. Authorities for indigenous affairs in Brazil and Ecuador have issued similar moratoriums.

To illustrate the breadth of community concerns and problems with researchers, the American Indian Law Center (1999) compiled a list of 15 major complaints expressed by Indian and native tribal groups. Here is a sample of some of the allegations and charges:

> Individual Indian people have been persuaded to participate in research in which they did not fully understand the nature of the risk to their health and safety; research was conducted which did not respect the basic human dignity of the individual participants or their religious and cultural beliefs; researchers have been interested in our people as an "isolated" or "pure" gene pool to be used for laboratory purposes, demeaning the dignity of the

people and the community; researchers have sought and published sensitive religious and cultural information, in some cases destroying its efficacy by publication; researchers have taken cultural information out of context and, as a result, have published conclusions that were factually incorrect; researchers have sensationalized community, family, and individual problems and released publications heedless of their impact on our community's legitimate political and social interests; (and) despite promises at the outset that research would benefit our community, researchers have failed or refused to follow through on promised benefits [and] to share preliminary results with the community or give the community an opportunity to participate in the formulation and recommendations of a final report. (pp. 1–2)

Informed Consent

There are numerous complaints flowing from the troubled voices of other ethnic minority communities across the United States. Consider, for example, the cultural implications of the federal law that requires researchers to have study participants complete an informed consent form. In some ethnocultural communities, especially those with high proportions of recently immigrated members, study participants may not understand the reason behind the use of consent forms, the technical words and scientific jargon used to describe aspects of the forms, the flow and length of the sentences and paragraph structure, and the implications if they refuse to sign. Furthermore, the readability indexes of most consent forms have been demonstrated on average to be three grades higher than one would expect for the typical study participant (Brainard, 2003). In some instances, when consent forms are translated into other languages, the English meaning of terms and the sentences do not accurately translate into words and sentences found and used in the native language of the participants. Furthermore, some researchers have experienced interpretation difficulties with participants who are not literate or whose reading comprehension levels are too low to understand consent forms (Gostin, 1995). In some ethnocultural communities, as suggested by Deloria (1980), "informed consent is somewhat akin to firing the warning shot immediately before the fatal bullet is sent on its way" (p. 270). A related problem arises when community participants erroneously believe that signing an informed consent form abrogates their right to withdraw from a study or issue a complaint about procedures or postexperimental reactions (Fisher, 2002).

Ownership of Data

Community members often question the ownership of research findings and the protocol developed to collect the information. In effect, they are asking who owns the data when the study is completed. Is it the sole property of the researcher? Does the community research advisory board or committee have the final say on how the data is used, where it is eventually stored, and how it will be used in scientific report writing? We raise these concerns because many community review boards now require that the data should reside with them and that they provide oversight on its future regardless of the circumstances. Jaarsma (2002) addresses some of these problems and pitfalls as they relate to use of ethnographic information; however, many of the conclusions could easily be generalized to include data of any form provided by community participants. Fisher et al. (2002) also highlight the ethical challenge of identifying persons who can best represent research-relevant concerns of prospective participants. Ensuring that community consultation reflects the needs of those within the community who will actually participate in the research requires

an understanding of the social structures and relationships that define a community (Weijer & Emanuel, 2000). Differences in the immigration and socialization histories of members of different ethnic and cultural groups may contribute to differences in the risks and benefits of the proposed research. There can also be instances when interests of the larger community are incompatible with the best interests or research goals of vulnerable groups within the community (Macklin, 1999). For example, individuals with addictive disorders may wish to participate in substance abuse research in the hope that it will result in immediate or future remedies, but nonaffected members of the community may reject the trial out of concern about group stigma (Fisher et al., 2002).

Mistranslation and Ethnic Gloss

Members of minoritized groups who participate in research have good reason to be suspicious about the way their responses are disseminated in the press and scientific publications, as often the findings are twisted and distorted to the extent that the "true and authentic" information is obscured through interpretation (Foulks, 1989; Monberg, 1975; Norton & Manson, 1996). There is considerable concern emerging among community representatives and research scholars about the way ethnic groups are represented in research findings. As observed by Deloria (1980), more often than not there are considerable problems associated with the "mistranslation" of research outcomes. Use of measures to label respondents under group categories such as socioeconomic status, levels of acculturation, geographic locale, and ethnic and racial identification place participants in artificially constructed subgroups ostensibly for purposes of analysis and teasing out of differences among groupings.

Often research findings are cast in either-or categories (high acculturation vs traditionalism, high ethnic identity vs low ethnic identity) as though such categorizations are accurate and genuine representations of the way people live their lives in their communities (Deloria, 1980). Too often ethnic groups are described using broad "ethnic glosses" or simplistic panethnic labels such as *Hispanic* or *Asian* (Fisher, Jackson, & Villarruel, 1997; Trimble, 1991). Such terms obscure unique cultural differences within different ethnocultural communities, like Puerto Rican and Chicano under the label *Hispanic* and Japanese and Chinese under the label *Asian,* and become a sorting device that has little to do with the deep cultural influences that guide a group member's thought, feelings, and behavior (Trimble, 1991; Trimble & Dickson, 2005).

Heath (1978) argues that "categories of people such as those compared under the rubric of 'ethnic groups' are often not really meaningful units in any sociocultural sense" and that "the ways in which people define and maintain the social boundaries between or among self-identified categories are often far more important and revealing of sociocultural dynamics" (p. 60). Use of broad-brushed categories to describe study participants is an insult to the dignity and richness of the cultural fabric of their ethnocultural communities. Those who develop a culturally sensitive scientific ethic must also be wary of "ethnic gloss." A "one-size-fits-all" approach to ethnocultural research ethics will result in more harm than good when assessment of research risks and benefits, the development of informed consent and confidentiality procedures, and the identification of community partners are not informed by the specific characteristics, values, and hopes of those who will be directly involved a study or immediately affected by the dissemination of research results (Fisher, 2002).

ETHNOCULTURAL ETHICS: AN EMERGING FIELD

Complaints from ethnocultural communities and research participants, as well as those from concerned researchers and scholars, have led to the publication of several reports and research guides. The publications are complete with statements of the problems associated with the abuse of ethnocultural populations, typically followed by a set of recommendations concerning culturally resonant, field-based research protocols and ethical considerations. In 1987, for example, Cassell and Jacobs edited a seven-chapter special publication of the American Anthropological Association, titled *Handbook on Ethical Issues in Anthropology.* The purpose of the small book was to improve and advance the ethical considerations in anthropological research and practice and encourage self-reflection on the ethics and moral thoughts and actions that bear on one's conduct in the field.

There are other similar publications worthy of recognition, although they do not fully represent the rich and inspirational literature that exists on the topic. In 2000, the American Psychological Association's Council of National Psychological Associations for the Advancement of Ethnic Minority Interest (CNPAAEMI) released a 21-page brochure drawing attention to the cultural inappropriateness of the methodologies of much of the research occurring in ethnic minority communities and the negative impact it was having on participants. Brochure contributors outlined a series of thoughtful procedures and guidelines for conducting, interpreting, and disseminating culturally relevant research. In 2004, Castellano with the assistance of numerous aboriginal people from Canada published a lengthy journal article proposing "a set of principles to assist in developing ethical codes for the conduct of research internal to the Aboriginal community or with external partners" (2004, p. 98). Eight principles are carefully laid out calling for the appropriate and enforceable protection of aboriginal peoples' interest in research ventures, highlighting the rights of aboriginal people as the true owners of the information they provide for researchers and researchers' obligation to consider in their research plans the aboriginal peoples' struggles for self-determination.

The themes and recommendations expressed in most publications—certainly in the ones described above—on the topic are consistent. Carey (2003) best summarizes these themes when he calls for a "symbiotic approach" in forming community partnerships for the purpose of research, whatever form it takes.

> Community-based research projects that allow local people to define and lead the research agenda, provide an excellent model for symbiotic relationships between scholars and research populations. This approach challenges the researcher because she will not have complete control over the project, but in most cases these results provide unique data that would otherwise have been unavailable to researchers. (p. 107)

The National Conference on Research Ethics for Mental Health Science Involving Ethnic Minorities

The handbook builds on the contributions described above, but the immediate impetus for it was the involvement of the editors and many of the contributors in the groundbreaking conference, Research Ethics for Mental Health Science Involving Ethnic Minority Children and Youth, sponsored by the Fordham University Center for Ethics Education, the Child and Adolescent Consortium of the National Institute of Mental Health, and the Science and Public Policy Directorates of the American Psychological Association (Fisher et al., 2002). The

conference, held at Fordham University, convened a group of 50 national leaders in bioethics, multicultural research, ethnic minority mental health, and community advocacy to produce a living document to guide ethical decision making for mental health research involving ethnic minority children and youth. The conference was propelled by the ethical urgency to ensure that recent government initiatives to stimulate research on health disparities in racial and ethnic minority communities (U.S. Public Health Service, 2001) would not lead to the unintended consequences of group stigmatization, exploitation, and harm that has occurred throughout the history of medical and mental health research involving ethnic minority communities in the United States (Caplan, Edgar, & King, 1992; Darou, Hum, & Kurtness, 1993; Foulks, 1989; Harris, Gorelick, Samuels, & Bempong, 1996; Jones, 1993; Norton & Manson, 1996; Trimble, 1989). As in this volume, the conference attendees shared with each other their personal experiences and struggles as ethnic minority and majority scholars striving to work with ethnocultural communities to design and implement scientifically valid and ethically appropriate research. Many of us participating in this groundbreaking discourse among ethnocultural science stakeholders saw a need to extend the ethical discourse to research involving a broader range of populations.

THE GOAL OF THIS BOOK

This volume contains 17 chapters distributed among four sections addressing (1) Foundations of Ethnocultural Research and Research Ethics; (2) Research Ethics Challenges Involving Diverse Ethnocultural Groups; (3) Socially Sensitive Research Involving Ethnocultural Families and Communities; and (4) The Rights and Responsibilities of Individuals, Communities, and Institutions. Chapter authors are distinguished and well-known researchers in the social and behavioral sciences, education, medicine, and psychiatry with extensive experience working in collaboration with ethnocultural populations.

The goal of this handbook is to produce a comprehensive document to encourage ethical decision making for social and behavioral science research that reflects the unique historical and sociocultural reality of ethnic and racial groups. The book explores and summarizes key ethical and research issues and provides guidance based on personal experience to the following questions:

- What steps can be taken to incorporate a cultural perspective to the evaluation of research risks and benefits?
- How can investigators develop and implement respectful informed consent procedures in diverse cultural and language communities?
- What needs to be considered when constructing culturally sensitive confidentiality and disclosure policies?
- What are ethical pitfalls and successful approaches to engaging in community and participant consultation?

Each section incorporates as background a summary of leading research and scholarship on these issues framed within the authors' personal failures, challenges, and successes in the dynamic process of creating a multicultural research ethics.

The primary audiences for the handbook include upper division undergraduate students, graduate students, researchers, research policy planners and developers, program officers at private and federal funding agencies, knowledgeable community leaders, and institutional review boards. The multiple disciplines of the chapter authors (anthropology, education, medicine, psychiatry, psychology, public policy, social work) and real-world expository style of each chapter make the handbook's contents accessible to a broad range of disciplines and levels of research experience.

OVERVIEW OF THE CHAPTERS

Part I: Foundations of Ethnocultural Research and Research Ethics

Part I begins with Celia Fisher and Kathleen Ragsdale's innovative model for guiding ethical decision making across diverse populations, "Goodness-of-Fit Ethics for Multicultural Research." This ethic calls for investigators to approach research ethics involving ethnic minority and other potentially vulnerable populations within an ethics framework that conceptualizes participant respect and protections in terms of the goodness-of-fit among the specific research context and the unique characteristics of the participant population (see also Fisher, 2003a, 2003b, 2005; Fisher & Masty, in press). According to the authors, framing research risks and benefits "as a product of both experimental design and participant attributes shifts judgments regarding ethical procedures away from an exclusive focus on assumed participant vulnerabilities to (a) an examination of those aspects of the research setting that are creating or exacerbating research vulnerability and (b) consideration of how the design and ethical procedures can be modified to best advance science and participant and social welfare" (Fisher & Ragsdale, this volume). Goodness-of-fit ethics can help investigators guard against institutional and scientistic biases that often single out ethnic minority populations as posing "unique" and "difficult" ethical problems that have an unfortunate history of resolution by bending ethical requirements. The authors illustrate the application of this framework in a very personal case study on Ragsdale's experiences studying the lives of sex workers in Belize.

In the chapter that follows, John Fantuzzo, Christine McWayne, and Stephanie Childs recount their experiences in scientist-community collaborations from the viewpoint of the scientist and community advocate. Among the numerous lessons gathered from their work is the importance of respecting and learning from the voices of those who say no to research. Their experiences exemplify their pioneering four-step, partner-based transactional model for addressing participant rights and investigator responsibilities.

In the final chapter of this section, Nancy Busch-Rossnagel takes us on a personal life journey working with Latino/a populations that led her to challenge her early training in institutional scientistic assumptions about the benefit of intervention research to the children and families it is intended to serve. Along this journey, her partnership with Latino/a communities helped her develop an ethic of "first do not harm" that should be a moral guide for all those concerned with ensuring that the design, implementation, and outcome measures for development-promoting interventions avoid societal bias, reflect community values, and merit participant trust.

Part II: Research Ethics Challenges Involving Diverse Ethnocultural Groups

Part II of this volume includes six groundbreaking chapters on ethical risks and remedies for research with distinct ethnocultural populations. The section begins with Scyatta Wallace's personal reflections and empirical findings from her work on cultural contributions to risk and resilience in African American youth. Her chapter illustrates the importance of incorporating participant perspectives in the design of ethical procedures.

Tim Noe, Spero Manson, Calvin Croy, Helen McGough, Jeffrey Henderson, and Dedra Buchwald provide an all-too-rare insight into the voices of American Indians involved in research. Among the numerous contributions of the chapter is its identification of a challenge intrinsic to work with American Indian and other communal cultures: recognizing that the dominant discourse in biomedical ethics is individualistic and, therefore, incomplete in many cultural settings that value group decision making.

In the chapter that follows, Gerald Mohatt and Lisa Thomas bring the reader into the culture of experience that insiders and outsiders bring to participatory research conducted with Alaska Native communities and show how these different cultural perspectives can be joined in the development of responsible research practices.

Challenges to the ethical conduct of research with Asian and Pacific Islander American populations are detailed through the extensive experiences of Jean Lau Chin, Jeffery Scott Mio, and Gayle Y. Iwamasa. In their chapter, the authors demonstrate the importance to ethics-in-science decision making of understanding linkages among the common and unique historical, political, immigration, language, geographic, and cultural experiences and characteristics of the diverse cultural groups making up the continuously changing Asian and Pacific Islander demographic landscape in the United States.

Felipe Castro, Rebeca Rios, and Harry Montoya examine issues in the design of methodologically rigorous research studies within the context of developing ethically responsible community-based intervention programs for Hispanic populations. The authors propose that researchers create a balance between science and community culture in order to conduct research that is respectful of the lifeways of Hispanics and those of other ethnic minority people. They argue that the product of successful university-community cooperation is the development of a new genre of hybrid research studies that successfully integrate science and culture in a manner that optimizes scientific rigor, coupled with cultural sensitivity to local community needs.

In the last chapter of this section, Dina Birman gives illuminating examples of the multiple ethical dilemmas encountered in her work with immigrants and refugees. Her chapter looks at the bidirectional relationship of research ethics to immigration policy: its ability to be unduly influenced by, and unduly influence, policies that will have direct effects on the lives of those coming to the United States to escape poverty and persecution.

Part III: Socially Sensitive Research Involving Ethnocultural Families and Communities

Although one might argue that all research involving racial and ethnic minorities is socially sensitive, the focus of this section is on the most vulnerable within historically oppressed ethnocultural populations. The part begins with a chapter by Katherine Elliott and Anthony Urquiza in which they discuss the need for ethical and responsible research examining the risks and benefits of child welfare services (CWS) policies and procedures, the results of which could better inform policy decisions and contribute to improved care for the safety and welfare of children. The need for CWS outcome research is most compelling for policies involving ethnic minority children and families.

The next chapter by Ana Mari Cauce and Richard H. Nobles focuses on the ethical dilemmas navigated during Cauce's pioneering research involving both parenting practices of African American youth transitioning from junior to senior high school and risk and resilience in a multicultural sample of homeless youths. Among the numerous ethical challenges Cauce faced were distinguishing community from participant needs,

reflecting on the potentially stigmatizing effect of the research on participants and their ethnocultural groups, balancing obligations toward parental authority and adolescent autonomy, and protecting youth who have no adult guardians.

Susan Krauss Whitbourne, Joshua Bringle, Bobbie Yee, David Chiriboga, and Keith Whitfield introduce the reader to the unique ethical issues encountered when conducting research involving minority elders. This chapter illustrates how issues of individual autonomy, family responsibility, and cultural values toward life and death are perhaps no more central than in the study of ethnocultural populations in later life.

Fred Beauvais's chapter uncovers ethical challenges that emerge when prevention researchers enter ethnocultural communities as outsiders. The chapter highlights the special responsibilities faced by external investigators in attempt to influence the course of development in cultural populations, especially those experiencing the trauma of a wave of youth suicide or substance use. Beauvais's chapter also addresses the persistent problem of sustaining effective prevention programs within communities once research is completed.

Anthropologist Merrill Singer and his colleague Delia Easton describe the many personal and professional challenges faced by investigators conducting ethnographic research on drug use and HIV/AIDS in ethnic minority populations in the United States and abroad. The authors delve into the moral dilemmas that arise when researchers immerse themselves in the natural social and geographic "space" of research participants, gain access to the private thoughts and behaviors, interact with their neighbors and families, are present during occasions of community celebration and remorse, and are privy to, and sometimes observe participants engaged in, illegal activities.

Part IV: The Rights and Responsibilities of Individuals, Communities, and Institutions

The chapters in Part IV raise research ethics concerns rarely heard by nonethnic minority researchers. In their groundbreaking chapter, Copeland Young and Monica Brooker draw upon their experiences at the Murray Research Center's Diversity Archive to articulate perhaps for the first time a uniform approach to identifying and resolving ethical challenges that arise in archival research from stored data involving communities of color. Their chapter addresses the ethical implications of data preservation and use through three critical debates: primary versus secondary data analysis, individual versus community protection, and qualitative versus quantitative data.

Janet Helms, Kevin Henze, Jackquelyn Mascher, and Anmol Satiani draw upon Janet Helms's theory of White identity development to raise ethical challenges for ethnic majority scientists working with ethnocultural populations. One of the most difficult challenges is to recognize the institutionalized, privileged status of White Americans in science and society at large and build upon that recognition in ways that create fair, unbiased, and respectful research designs and ethical procedures.

In the last chapter in the form of a coda, Joseph E. Trimble and Gerald V. Mohatt emphasize the importance and significance of the moral and virtuous character of researchers, why they must be considered in establishing community partnerships, and how one's character may influence the overall success of the research venture. "Doing good well," as recommended in the first chapter by Celia B. Fisher and Kathleen Ragsdale, implies that the researcher and the team are virtuous people and embody values and beliefs that community members and research participants find acceptable. Framing their chapter according to six primary virtuous ethics, the authors point out that respect and trust, for example, may have different meanings and expression across cultural groups. Their meaning for researchers may not coincide with their meaning within the worldview of a culture different and foreign to the outsider. Learning the deep cultural meaning of what constitutes trust and respect, therefore, requires the researcher to spend time with the community. One will soon discover that community members will put the researcher through a sequence of tests to assess the researcher's level of commitment to working closely with them and learning about their cultural ways. Also, they introduce the concept of relational methodology. *Relational methodology* means that one takes the time to nurture relationships, not merely for the sake of expediting the research and gaining acceptance and trust but because one should care about the welfare and dignity of all people.

OUR SHARED JOURNEY: LEARNING FROM THE PAST TO PROTECT THE FUTURE

Ethical planning for science, involving constantly changing patterns of ethnocultural diversity, requires flexibility and sensitivity to the contextual challenges and concerns of each ethnic group and research problem (U.S. Public Health Service, 2001). The points for consideration raised in this book are not intended to serve as regulation, policy, or absolute prescriptions for research ethics practices. Rather, the goal is to assist stakeholders in the responsible conduct of research—investigators, funding agencies, and institutional review boards, research participants, ethnocultural communities—in identifying key ethical crossroads and in developing culturally sensitive decision-making strategies.

It is not easy to write about ethics. It requires self-reflection and an ability to recognize and share with others personal values, errors of judgment, and lessons learned along the path toward the respectful and responsible conduct of research. We are grateful to our contributors for the courage and generosity they have demonstrated in their remarkable chapters. We hope this volume provides encouragement and support for our fellow scientists as we all continue on this journey toward establishing a research ethic that reflects the values and merits the trust of ethnocultural populations.

REFERENCES

American Anthropological Association. (2002). *Preface for El Dorado Task Force papers.* Retrieved March 16, 2005, from www.aaanet.org/edtf/final/preface.htm

American Indian Law Center. (1999). *Model tribal research code: With materials for tribal regulation for research and checklist for Indian health boards* (3rd ed.). Albuquerque, NM: Author.

American Psychological Association. (2002). Ethical principles of psychologists and code of conduct. *American Psychologist, 57,* 1060–1073.

Brainard, J. (2003, January 17). Study finds research consent forms difficult to comprehend. *Chronicle of Higher Education,* p. A21.

Caplan, A., Edgar, H., & King, P. (1992). Twenty years later: The legacy of the Tuskegee Syphilis Study. *Hastings Center Report, 22,* 29–38.

Carey, D. C. (2003, September). Symbiotic research: A case for ethical scholarship. *NEA Higher Education Journal,* pp. 99–114.

Cassell, J., & Jacobs, S. (1987). *Handbook on ethical issues in anthropology, 23* [Special publication of the American Anthropological Association]. Retrieved March 16, 2005, from www.aaanet.org/committees/ethics/toc.htm

Castellano, M. B. (2004, January). Ethics of aboriginal research. *Journal of Aboriginal Health,* 98–114.

Council of National Psychological Associations for the Advancement of Ethnic Minority Interests. (2000, January). *Guidelines for research in ethnic minority communities.* Washington, DC: APA.

Darou, W. G., Hum, A., & Kurtness, J. (1993). An investigation of the impact of psychosocial research on a native population. *Professional Psychology: Research & Practice, 24,* 325–329.

Deloria, V. (1980). Our new research society: Some warnings for social scientists. *Social Problems, 27*(3), 265–271.

Dockstader, F. J. (1957). *The American Indian in graduate studies: A bibliography of theses and dissertations.* New York: Museum of the American Indian, Heye Foundation.

Fisher, C. B. (1999). Relational ethics and research with vulnerable populations. *Reports on research involving persons with mental disorders that may affect decision making capacity* (Vol. 2, pp. 29–49). Rockville, MD: Commissioned papers by the National Bioethics Advisory Commission.

Fisher, C. B. (2002). Participant consultation: Ethical insights into parental permission and confidentiality procedures for policy relevant research with youth. In R. M. Lerner, F. Jacobs, & D. Wertlieb (Eds.), *Handbook of applied developmental science* (Vol. 4, pp. 371–396). Thousand Oaks, CA: Sage.

Fisher, C. B. (2003a). A goodness-of-fit ethic for informed consent to research involving persons with mental retardation and developmental disabilities. *Mental Retardation and Developmental Disabilities Research Reviews, 9,* 27–31.

Fisher, C. B. (2003b). A goodness-of-fit ethic for child assent to non-beneficial research. *American Journal of Bioethics, 3*(4), 27–28.

Fisher, C. B. (2005). Clinician-parent communication during pediatric cancer trials: SES, ethnicity and goodness-of-fit. *Journal of Pediatric Psychology, 30,* 231–234.

Fisher, C. B., Hoagwood, K., Boyce, C., Duster, T., Frank, D. A., Grisso, T., et al. (2002). Research ethics for mental health science involving ethnic minority children and youths. *American Psychologist, 57,* 1024–1040.

Fisher, C. B., Jackson, J., & Villarruel, F. (1997). The study of African American and Latin American children and youth. In W. Damon (Series Ed.) & R. M. Lerner (Vol. Ed.), *Handbook of child psychology* (Theoretical models of human development, Vol. 1, 5th ed., pp. 1145–1207). New York: Wiley.

Fisher, C. B., & Masty, J. K. (in press). A goodness-of-fit ethic for informed consent to pediatric cancer research. In R. T. Brown (Ed.), *Handbook of pediatric psychosocial oncology.* New York: Oxford University Press.

Fisher, C. B., & Wallace, S. A. (2000). Through the community looking glass: Reevaluating the ethical and policy implications of research on adolescent risk and psychopathology. *Ethics & Behavior, 10,* 99–118.

Foulks, E. F. (1989). Misalliances in the Barrow Alcohol Study. *American Indian and Alaskan Native Mental Health Research, 2*(2), 17.

Goodenough, W. H. (1980). Ethnographic field techniques. In H. C. Triandis & J. W. Berry (Eds.), *Handbook of cross-cultural psychology* (Methodology, Vol. 2., pp. 39–55). Boston: Allyn & Bacon.

Gostin, L. O. (1995). Informed consent, cultural sensitivity, and respect for persons. *Journal of the American Medical Association, 274,* 844–845.

Harris, Y., Gorelick, P. B., Samuels, P., & Bempong, I. (1996). Why African Americans may not be participating in clinical trials. *Journal of the National Medical Association, 88*(10), 630–634.

Heath, D. B. (1978). The sociocultural model of alcohol use: Problems and prospects. *Journal of Operational Psychiatry, 9,* 55–66.

Hendricks, L. (2004, February 28). Havasupai file $25M suit vs. ASU. *Arizona Daily Sun,* p. A1.

Hodge, W. (1976). *A bibliography of contemporary North American Indians: Selected and partially annotated with a study guide.* New York: Interland.

Inbrahim, F. A., & Cameron, S. C. (2005). Racial-cultural ethical issues in research. In R. T. Carter (Ed.), *Handbook of racial-cultural psychology and counseling* (Vol. 1, pp. 391–413). Hoboken, NJ: Wiley.

Jaarsma, S. R. (Ed.). (2002). *Handle with care: Ownership and control of ethnographic materials.* Pittsburgh, PA: University of Pittsburgh Press.

Jones, J. H. (1993). *Bad blood: The Tuskegee syphilis experiment* (Rev. ed.). New York: Free Press.

Kelso, D., & Attneave, C. (Eds.). (1981). *Bibliography of North American Indian mental health.* Westport, CT: Greenwood.

Macklin, R. (1999). Moral progress and ethical universalism. In R. Macklin (Ed.), *Against relativism: Cultural diversity and the search for ethical universals in medicine* (pp. 249–274). New York: Oxford University Press.

Martin, M., & O'Leary, T. (1990). *Ethnographic bibliography of North America* (4th ed. supplement 1973–1987). New Haven, CT: HRAF.

Miller, D. W. (2001, September 12). Academic scandal in the Internet age: When a furor broke out in anthropology, e-mail was more powerful than peer review. *Chronicle of Higher Education*, p. A14.

Monberg, T. (1975). Informants fire back: A micro-study in anthropological methods. *Journal of the Polynesian Society, 84*(2), 218–224.

Norton, I. M., & Manson, S. M. (1996). Research in American Indian and Alaska Native communities: Navigating the cultural universe of values and process. *Journal of Consulting and Clinical Psychology, 64*, 856–860.

Tierney, P. (2000). Darkness in el Dorado: How scientists and journalists devastated the Amazon. New York: W. W. Norton.

Trimble, J. E. (1989). Malfeasance and foibles of the research sponsor. *American Indian and Alaska Native Mental Health Research, 2*, 58–63.

Trimble, J. E. (1991). Ethnic specification, validation prospects, and the future of drug use research. *International Journal of the Addictions, 25*(2A), 149–170.

Trimble, J., & Bagwell, W. (Eds.), (1995). *North American Indians and Alaska Natives: Abstracts of psychological and behavioral literature, 1967–1995* (Bibliographies in psychology, No. 15). Washington, DC: APA.

Trimble, J. E., & Dickson, R. (2005). Ethnic gloss. In C. B. Fisher & R. M. Lerner (Eds.), *Encyclopedia of applied developmental science* (Vol. 1, pp. 412–415). Thousand Oaks, CA: Sage.

U.S. Department of Health and Human Services. (2001, August). *Title 45 Public Welfare, Part 46, Code of Federal Regulations, Protection of Human Subjects*. Washington, DC: Author. (Original work published in 1991)

U.S. Public Health Service. (2001). *The surgeon general's mental health supplement on culture, race and ethnicity*. Washington, DC: Author.

Weijer, C., & Emanuel, D. J. (2000). Protecting communities in biomedical research. *Science, 289*, 1142–1144.

Part I

FOUNDATIONS OF ETHNOCULTURAL RESEARCH AND RESEARCH ETHICS

CHAPTER 1

Goodness-of-Fit Ethics for Multicultural Research

CELIA B. FISHER

KATHLEEN RAGSDALE

All medical and public-health researchers would like a magic bullet that would make research undeniably ethical. But there is no magic bullet. There is only the complex and difficult process of linking research in resource-poor settings to the services demanded by poor people.

—Paul Farmer, "Can Transnational Research Be Ethical in the Developing World?"

In this chapter, we discuss the dynamic nature of ethnic minority status and the unique challenges and opportunities this concept presents for scientists engaged in the ethical practice of research. Next, we discuss goodness-of-fit ethics (GFE) as a model for ethics-in-science decision making (Fisher, 2004). We then discuss the concept of co-learning and its role in the process of developing GFE, using case studies to illustrate particular points. We close with a discussion of "doing good well" as a concept that involves reframing traditional power dynamics associated with behavioral science in such a way that individual participants, their communities, and researchers are actively involved in a dynamic process of mutual accommodation that also meets the requirements of the scientific process.

THE DYNAMIC NATURE OF ETHNICITY AND MINORITY STATUS

Ethnicity as a research variable is a dynamic construct continuously challenged, expanded, and revised within an ever changing socio-political landscape. This fluid definitional environment requires cultural and ethical competence to ensure the responsible conduct of research with ethnic minority populations in the United States and abroad. Ethnic minority populations are challenging venues within which to conduct research for reasons including historical and contemporary stigmatization, cultural attitudes regarding individual autonomy and communal responsibility, within-group cultural variation, immigration history, language, acculturation-related issues, and multiethnic heritage (Fisher, Jackson, & Villarruel, 1997). Such challenges highlight the question, "What is ethnicity?" In this chapter we define ethnicity as a collective identity based on the shared cultural heritage of a social group. Typical markers of ethnicity, which vary across groups, include dress, language, foodways, religious and traditional practices, common ancestry, and/or geographic origin (Ragsdale, 2004). We draw an important distinction between the concept of ethnicity and the concept of race, in that *race* is not a scientific construct but a social construct used to classify individuals based on phenotypic variation (Fisher et al., 1997; Gould, 1981). We also draw a distinction between ethnic status and minority status. Whereas minority status is often conferred on a subordinated or marginalized social group by the dominant culture, ethnic status is a claim made by a particular collective body to a designated social identity (Eller, 1999; Ragsdale, 2004). In the next section, we draw on examples from the United States in order to illustrate the fluidity of ethnicity and minority status.

Contemporary Prejudice and Changing Demographics in the United States

Members of minority and ethnically marginalized populations experience multiple incidents of actual and perceived discrimination on an individual level from peers and on an institutional level from health care providers, educators, shopkeepers, social service providers, educators, police and security personnel, and others (Chun, 1995;

Demo & Hughes, 1990; Essed, 1991; Fisher, Wallace, & Fenton, 2000; Gaertner & Dovidio, 1986). The contemporary experience of institutionalized discrimination within the United States is deeply embedded within the historical groundwork of European conquest. Long before the United States existed as such, it was a multiethnic society. Individual members of indigenous populations conquered by Spanish, French, and English colonizers were assimilated into the dominant culture with varying "success," often through institutions such as slavery, the church, intermarriage, and educational systems. Later, enslaved peoples of African descent were conscripted as field labor for agricultural exports. Still later, poverty-stricken foreign nationals (such as Asian workers imported to build the transatlantic rail system) were allowed into the United States as a form of cheap labor during the industrial revolution. By the end of the 20th century, the experience of transnational integration had accelerated with the expansion of the global economy, communication technologies, and transportation. In the contemporary United States, economic migrants from Mexico and other Central American countries perform the manual labor that many U.S. nationals will not. In addition, political refugees from around the world are granted asylum in the United States, and lotteries allow other foreign nationals to immigrate to the country.

Although members of diverse ethnic groups may have shared experiences with historical and contemporary racism, groups may experience discrimination differently. This can be traced back to earlier U.S. political and social policies regarding peoples of non-European ethnicity, as well as issues of resistance and accommodation to dominant U.S. culture (Dublin, 1996; Gould, 1981; Ragsdale, 2004). For example, Cubans arrived en masse to the United States as political refugees beginning in the early

1960s. Those Cubans who settled in Miami, Florida, developed an enclave community that wields considerable political and economic dominance in Miami-Dade County (Portes & Stepick, 1993). In contrast, Haitians who arrived en masse to the United States as political refugees in the early 1980s have continued to experience social, economic, and political marginalization in Miami (Stepick & Foner, 1998; Stepick, Grenier, Castro, & Dunn, 2003). The divergence in discrimination experienced across ethnic groups can often be attributed to racial/ethnic stereotyping, which can be both positive and negative. For example, a high-status African national who has recently migrated to the United States may be confronted with racial/ethnic prejudice—and an accompanying loss of social status—based solely on ascribed characteristics that members of the dominant culture associate with his or her skin tone. The African national's first experiences with racial discrimination in the United States may be a cause of intense culture shock, especially if this experience was previously unknown to the person (see Mathabane, 1990; Ogbaa, 2003). Publicized threats to members of one's cultural group can also result in personal anxiety. The racial profiling that resulted in the 1999 police slaying of Amadou Diallo, an unarmed Guinean immigrant, exemplified the distal effects of institutional racism (Diallo, 2003). On the other hand, the generally positive stereotyping of Asians immigrants within the United States has been associated with academic achievement among some Asian youth in the U.S. educational system (Lowe, 1996).

Other factors that can mediate differential experiences of discrimination include characteristics unique to a particular ethnic enclave, such as internalized cultural attitudes that shape beliefs, decision making, and behavior (Ogbaa, 2003; Ragsdale, 2004). Despite the divergence

in discrimination that ethnic groups often experience, they also may share many unique similarities as minority populations operating within a dominant society. These can include issues related to acculturation, assimilation, immigration status, and stigmatization that result in discrimination in housing, banking, educational opportunities, and health disparities (Fisher et al., 1997). Another factor that may increase the complexity of understanding how and why various ethnic groups experience marginalization differentially is that second- and third-generation ethnic minority members often have quite different experiences associated with language acquisition, cultural assimilation, and social adjustment to dominant U.S. culture than do first-generation immigrants.

GOODNESS-OF-FIT ETHICS (GFE) AND CO-LEARNING

Fisher has called for investigators to approach research ethics with vulnerable populations within an ethics framework that conceptualizes participant respect and protections in terms of the goodness-of-fit among the specific research context and the unique characteristics of the participant population (Fisher, 2003a, 2003b; Fisher & Masty, in press). Conceptualizing research risks and benefits as a product of both experimental design and participant attributes shifts judgments regarding ethical procedures away from an exclusive focus on assumed participant vulnerabilities to (a) an examination of those aspects of the research setting that are creating or exacerbating research vulnerability and (b) consideration of how the design and ethical procedures can be modified to best advance science and participant and social welfare.

The GFE framework is especially important in addressing institutional and scientific

6 | FOUNDATIONS OF ETHNOCULTURAL RESEARCH AND RESEARCH ETHICS

biases that often single out ethnic minority populations as posing "unique" and "difficult" ethical challenges, which can only be resolved by bending ethical requirements. For example, a situation of placing the burden of vulnerability on the participant population rather than the investigative procedures can emerge when developmental scientists argue that IRBs should permit waiver of parental permission for lower-income minority populations because of the expected low permission rates. These requests are often based on the erroneous assumption that such populations are uncaring or lack the education to understand the value of the research (Fisher et al., 1997). The reality is that ethnic minority parents often refuse to permit their children to participate in research because they distrust the motives of the researchers, do not believe the research goals will benefit their communities, are fearful that the research will further stigmatize their children, or are concerned that confidentiality breaches will lead to unnecessary government intrusion (Fisher, 2002, 2004; Fisher & Wallace, 2000).

Correcting Ethnic Bias and Misperceptions

The GFE framework for research with ethnic minority populations presents an opportunity to correct biases and misperceptions. The GFE model, like the multicultural competence model (Sue et al., 1998), assumes that adequate ethical decision making requires more than slight modifications to traditional ways of conducting science. It requires critical reflection about potential modifications in research goals and design, which can enhance scientific validity, participant protections, and social value. In order to apply the GFE model to studies involving waiver of parental permission, for example, the developmental scientist would be required to explore (a) which aspects of the research

aims, designs, or recruitment procedures are "misfitted" to the values, fears, and hopes of the specific ethnic parent population and (b) how the design, aims, or recruitment procedures could be modified to produce a study that fit the requirements of population-sensitive science as well as methodologically sound science.

Research vulnerability as a relational concept. In the GFE model, research vulnerability is reduced when research procedures are fitted to participant characteristics (Fisher 2003a, 2003b, in press). In order to accomplish this, at the inception stage of research protocols, investigators should ask themselves the following questions: (a) What are the special life circumstances that render participants more susceptible to research risk? (b) Which aspects of the research design, implementation, or dissemination may create or exacerbate research risk? and (c) How can research and ethical procedures be fitted to participant characteristics to reduce vulnerability? (Fisher, 2003b; Fisher & Masty, in press)

When research involves ethnic minority populations, life circumstances that increase participants' research vulnerability can include a combination of demographic characteristics such as language, education, minority and immigration status, disparities in health and health care opportunities, socioeconomic status, cultural assumptions about gender roles and attitudes toward authority, ethnic identity, and racial mistrust. In addition, other social or health risks may be layered on top of ethnic/cultural life circumstances, such as addiction, comorbid mental health disorders, illegal behavior, health risks (including diagnosed and undiagnosed conditions), social stigma, and membership in a violent social network. In order to establish the boundaries of GFE, such variables must be given careful consideration in toto rather than on a piecemeal basis.

GFE AND THE SCIENCE ESTABLISHMENT

The traditional science establishment has endorsed a set of values by which investigators and the public can evaluate the responsible conduct of research. When embodied in federal regulations and professional codes of conduct, these largely Eurocentric, rational-deductive, libertarian conceptions of the good (Prilleltensky, 1997) become moral premises that resist cultural challenges (Fisher, 1999). Chief among these is the utilitarian philosophy that the morally right action is the one that produces the most pleasing consequences (Mill, 1861/1957). Applied to ethics-in-science decision making, when a conflict between scientific rigor and participant welfare arises, the investigator's obligation to a small group of research participants may be superseded by her or his responsibility to produce reliable data that can potentially provide future benefits to members of society at large or to the participants' particular social group. Utilitarianism thus encourages a value structure in which potential benefits of science to society can receive higher moral priority than concrete and measurable risks to research participants.

Drawing on established works on research ethics (Beauchamp, Faden, Wallace, & Walters, 1982; Freedman, 1975; Rosenwald, 1996; Veatch, 1987), Fisher (1999) identified a set of unchallenged assumptions based on traditional views of science:

- Knowledge gathering is a fundamental and unconditional good.
- Knowledge generated by the scientific method is and should be value free.
- Scientists are entitled to use humans as material for their pursuits.
- Respect, beneficence, and justice are guiding moral principles for ethical decision making in human subjects research.
- Cost-benefit analysis is an acceptable basis for deciding how to prioritize these moral

principles and for guiding ethical decision making.

- Informed consent is the primary means of ensuring participants are not victims of an imbalance in favor of greater risks than benefits.
- The right to make autonomous decisions regarding research participation is dependent on the ability to weigh the risks and benefits of the experimental procedures.
- Principles of beneficence and justice can be subordinated to the principle of autonomy reflected in informed consent policies.
- The absence of harm justifies the absence of benefits if it leads to scientifically valid information.
- Science-in-ethics decision making is the province of those with professional authority, be it scientists, bioethicists, IRB members, or policy makers (Fisher, 1999, p. 36).

Challenging Traditional Scientific Assumptions

Investigator contact with the constantly shifting demographic landscape of the United States and the increasingly influential voice of ethnic minority scholars and participant communities is creating a sea change in traditional scientific value assumptions. As exemplified by the contributions to this volume, social and behavioral scientists increasingly acknowledge that the pursuit of knowledge is neither as personally value-free nor unaffected by external forces (such as the priorities of funders) as previous generations of scientists often assumed (see also Altman, 1995). The important gains that have been made within ethics-in-science decision making confirm that the reevaluation of the costs and benefits of conducting research is an ongoing process. For example, although cost-effectiveness and cost-benefit analyses have merit in particular public health arenas (Haddix, Teutsch, & Corso, 2002), their application is controversial when scholars and practitioners adopt an ultrautilitarian and noncontextualized stance (MacQueen, 2004; Pinkerton, Johnson-Masotti, Derse, & Layde, 2002).

The GFE model moves multicultural ethics further by posing several interrelated questions about these value premises (Fisher, 1999; Greenfield, 1994; Markus & Kitayama, 1991; Parham, 1993; Triandis, 1990): (a) Do the values embodied in current professional codes and federal regulations reflect the moral visions of different ethnocultural groups recruited for research participation? (b) Do scientists and participant groups have different conceptions of research risks and benefits? and (c) Is the value placed on the control and manipulation of variables compatible with the values, collectivity, and harmony characteristic of many ethnocultural populations?

To ensure the responsible conduct of research, these questions require that investigators give careful consideration to the different cultural lenses through which they and research participants view the ethics of research involving ethnic minority populations. Indeed, one of the important gains in multicultural research ethics is the movement toward incorporating participant perspectives in the evaluation of research risks and potential benefits (Cassell, 1982; Fisher, 2002, 2004; Fisher & Wallace, 2000; Melton, Levine, Koocher, Rosenthal, & Thompson, 1988). Co-learning is the GFE process through which participant perspectives are incorporated into the identification of ethical issues and construction of ethical procedures (Fisher, 1999, 2002).

Co-Learning: The Process of Goodness-of-Fit Ethics

The GFE model views scientist and participant alike as moral agents joined in partnership to construct ethical procedures that contribute to research designs reflecting social value and scientific validity as well as the principles of justice and care (Fisher, 1997, 1999, 2000). The GFE process of co-learning assumes that ethical decision making is deficient when it occurs in the absence of discourse illuminating the cultural lens through which the participant population views the research. Co-learning is grounded in the principle of respect. It assumes that both investigator and participant populations come to the research enterprise as experts: The investigator brings expertise about the scientific method and the extant empirical knowledge base, and prospective participants and their community representatives bring expertise about the fears and hopes toward, and value that they place on, the prospective research (Fisher, 1999, 2000).

Investigators can use co-learning procedures to share with prospective participants their views on how and why it is important to apply the scientific method to examine questions of societal import and to debates underlying areas of current ethical concern. In turn, the prospective participants, their families, and community representatives can apply their moral perspectives to critique the scientific and social value of a proposed study and share with investigators the value orientations guiding participant and community reactions to the planned procedures (Fisher, 1999, 2000; Fisher & Wallace, 2000). When co-learning is soundly grounded and correctly implemented within a moral framework of respect, ethical procedures emerge that reflect a mutual accommodation to the values of science and the values of the cultural community in which the science will be conducted.

Similar in many ways to the principles underlying participatory research (MacQueen, 2004; Nichter, 1984; Weeks, Schensul, Williams, Singer, & Grier, 1995), in the GFE process of co-learning, to be a stakeholder does not assume that scientists and participants share equally in the risk and benefits of research or that they share the same rights, status, and privileges. For example, investigators often have the benefit of more social capital than do participants in terms of education, wealth, and access to power and opportunities (Fisher, 1999, 2000). As stakeholders in a research protocol, however, investigators are dependent on research communities to fulfill recruitment goals and produce empirically valid knowledge of social value. Although research participants and the communities to which they belong may benefit from study participation, the nature of conducting research is such that the benefits that accrue to participants can rarely be measured using the same yardstick as that used to measure the benefits that accrue to investigators. Participant stakeholders may receive increased income through participant incentives, benefit from receiving current knowledge about the strengths or vulnerabilities of their population motivating the research, or increase their understanding of research methods (and thereby increase their ability to be better informed consumers of scientific reports as well as community advocates).

The experience of co-learning and mutual accommodation between investigators and participants as process for developing GFE is essential in multicultural research. Rather than compromise, co-learning is a dialectic that creates something new from stakeholders' participation in a relational process. Co-learning provides the essential knowledge base from which investigators can identify research methods and ethical procedures that fit the needs and values of the participant population. Even as scientists have a responsibility to produce research grounded within accepted scientific practice, they are also required—and ethically compelled—to protect participant autonomy and confidentiality. As a dialectic process, co-learning calls for the development of ethical procedures that facilitate and build on mutual accommodation in order to accomplish these goals. For example, when engaged in research among vulnerable populations of diverse cultural background, investigators must recognize that social norms regarding deference to authority often vary across ethnicity, generation, socioeconomic status, and assimilation status (Fisher, in press; Fisher & Masty, in press; Kodish et al., 2004). Additionally, participants from multicultural backgrounds often must cope with language barriers, lack of experience in regard to asserting their rights within a clinical setting, and the perception that the delivery of future health care services is contingent on their research participation (Fisher et al., 2002; Fisher & Masty, in press).

In the sections that follow, we describe a series of ethical challenges and solutions that exemplify the value of goodness-of-fit co-learning with minority and vulnerable populations in a resource-poor nation.

ETHNOCULTURAL RESEARCH ETHICS IN THE DEVELOPING WORLD: TOURISM AND SEX WORK IN BELIZE

Much of GFE has dealt with studies conducted in the United States, yet proactive engagement in GFE is equally crucial when social and behavioral scientists from developed countries conduct international research in less developed and/or resource-poor nations (Benatar & Singer, 2000; Farmer, 1999, 2002). When international research involves official buy-in, approval, cooperation, or collaboration with national and local governmental agencies in host countries, consideration of the goodness-of-fit between Western research ethical practices and participant characteristics may require increased attention. Just as when scientists conduct studies in domestic settings, international researchers must be alert to the possibility that study findings may be used by governmental agencies to justify the implementation of social policies that further marginalize vulnerable populations. When conducting research among participants in developing countries, the "potentially exploitative nature of research" (Benatar & Singer, 2000, p. 825) should be given careful consideration by investigators. In light of this caveat, the following examples are meant as illustrative rather than exhaustive. The examples are derived from concerns raised during a study conducted by Kathleen Ragsdale (the study's principal investigator [PI] and second author of this chapter) and Jessica Anders in Belize, Central America (Ragsdale & Anders, 1998; Ragsdale & Anders, 1999).

Cultural and Economic Context of Sex Work in Belize

Formerly known as British Honduras until it gained independence in 1981, Belize is a small multicultural and multiethnic country wedged between Mexico and Guatemala, yet has the longest barrier reef in the Western Hemisphere. Like many Caribbean and Central American countries faced with catastrophic economic restructuring and faltering agriculture and manufacturing export industries (Safa, 1995), Belizean national development strategies have focused on tourism as a way to pump dollars into its cash-poor economy (Mahler & Wotkyns, 1993; SPEAR, 1993). Although tourism can bring in needed foreign currency to developing nations, it often differentially affects men and women due to the fact that "experiences with processes of economic growth, commercialization, and market expansion are determined by both gender and class" (Sen & Grown, 1987, p. 25; see also Levy & Lerch, 1991; McClaurin, 1996). Women working in the tourism sector often have fewer economic options than men. Economic opportunity for

many poor women is restricted to low-skilled jobs in the tourism industry, such as domestic service or street vending (Richter, 1995). As is often the case in many Caribbean and Central American countries, the growth of tourism in Belize has also increased women's involvement in sex work as a way to meet their basic economic needs (Kane, 1993; Kempadoo, 1999; Ragsdale & Anders, 1999). Although Belizean law does not prohibit sex work, it is illegal to operate a brothel in the country (U.S. Department of State, 2004); however, enforcement of this law is practically nonexistent. For example, one of the most well-known brothels in the Belize City area operates openly on the main highway that connects the city and the international airport.

To investigate the nature and scope of sex work and tourism in Belize, Ragsdale and Anders conducted multimethod research in 1998 at three field sites in the following order: Belize City, Orange Walk Town, and Ambergris Caye. Due to time and budget constraints, the investigators conducted 1 month of intensive research at each site to gain a rapid assessment of conditions under which women engaged in sex work, as well as sex tourism's embeddedness within the tourism sector. The ethical challenges emerging at the three study sites will be used to illustrate GFE and co-learning as reflective and organic processes. In particular, we will describe ways in which conditions unique to each site caused the investigators to adapt different strategies appropriate for each site (Bernard, 1995; Fisher, 1999, 2002).

Case I. Voice of Community Members: Competing Frameworks in Belize City

There is increased awareness that giving the community voice is a vital key to GFE in research. Yet investigators who are not prepared for the reality of how rival discourses operate in multicultural settings may unexpectedly find themselves faced with negotiating the social terrain of competing groups who, in sincere attempts to ameliorate disparities, seek to push a particular agenda or claim proprietary rights to data (Fisher et al., 1997). In this section, we describe how Ragsdale and Anders arrived in Belize City to begin collecting data on the nature of tourism and the sex trade in Belize only to find that both governmental and nongovernmental organizations (NGOs) had particular agendas that they wanted the investigators to address.

Contacting key informants. As Belize City is the first destination for most tourists entering the country of Belize, Ragsdale and Anders began their research efforts by visiting various governmental agencies located in the city, including the Department of Women's Affairs, the Ministry of Health, and the Ministry of Justice. They also visited NGOs, including the Belize Organization for Women and Development (BOWAND), the Belize Family Life Association (BFLA), representatives of the Peace Corps, and the Society for the Promotion of Education and Research (SPEAR). Key informants from the community at large who had contact with tourists and/or brothel workers were also contacted, including volunteer workers, tourism operators, bar and club owners, taxi drivers, security guards, and police officers. Governmental, NGO, and community sources gave conflicting advice about the safety of entering brothels to conduct research. After weighing these reports, the investigators made plans to visit the most prominent brothel operating in the Belize City area; however, the wisdom of this decision was challenged a few days before the planned visit when the local newspaper reported that a client at the brothel had shot a security guard in the face. On receiving this news, the PI cancelled the trip, deciding that it was too

dangerous for the investigators to enter the brothel.

Cultural stigma. Based on discussions with governmental, NGO, and community informants, the investigators confirmed that, as expected, there was much stigma associated with involvement in female sex work. In particular, at that time in Belize City there was a general perception that HIV/AIDS was a problem only among migrant sex workers and an associated assumption that limited health and research resources—such as represented by the presence of the investigators—should be directed toward more immediate concerns of permanent residents, such as domestic violence. Somewhat unexpectedly, the investigators also found that there was stigma attached to female investigators conducting research related to sex work. Among most key informants in Belize City, the investigation of sex work by female researchers was generally perceived as unusual—although in some cases it was deemed risqué or aberrant—when measured against traditional gender norms for Belizean women.

Confidentiality. Through discussions with contacts in Belize City, the investigators also learned that issues of confidentiality are exacerbated in this small and resource-poor country. For example, Belize has an estimated population of 250,000 (U.S. Department of State, 2004), and therefore the inhabitants of this small nation generally distrust claims of truly anonymous testing. The potential for stigmatization associated with being HIV-positive inhibits and delays HIV testing for many Belizeans and non-Belizeans who would otherwise like to know their HIV status. This is especially true for migrant women engaged in sex work in the country, for, although sex work is legal, the stigmatizing perception that female sex workers (FSWs) are carriers of sexually transmitted infections can deter such women from HIV testing.

Lessons learned. A primary lesson learned during this phase of the research is that investigators working in international settings must be able to fit not only ethical procedures but the research questions and methods as in-country conditions dictate. Ragsdale and Anders initially planned to spend approximately 2 weeks in Belize City making contact with key gatekeepers among governmental agencies, NGOs, and community members in order to gain an overall impression of the current state of tourism and sex work in Belize. The investigators then planned to travel directly from Belize City to the tourist destination of Ambergris Caye to conduct the primary part of the research project; however, during discussions among key informants in Belize City, the investigators learned that a considerable number of brothels operated openly in Orange Walk Town, which was located 66 miles from Belize City. According to several sources, the brothels serviced the local community as well as truck drivers and tourists on their way to Mexico. During this process, the investigators also discovered that freelance sex work (Kempadoo, 2001), commonly referred to as "streetwalking," was practically nonexistent in Belize. Although the investigators heard anecdotal reports of a handful of discrete escort services frequented by local businessmen and wealthier tourists, sex work is primarily conducted on brothel premises.

The multisourced co-learning consultations described above highlighted obstacles to brothel recruitment and study implementation embodied in community suspicions, intergroup conflict surrounding the goals of the research, and stigma associated with the investigators' gender. Ragsdale and Anders spent an extra 2 weeks in unsuccessful attempts to gain access to brothels in Belize

City. During those 2 weeks, it became increasingly clear that the investigators would have to sacrifice time spent at another site in order to build the community connections necessary to overcome the barriers of entering Belize City brothels. Yet Ragsdale and Anders were realistic in their evaluation that increased rapport building might not guarantee access to any brothel within the vicinity of the city. Therefore, rather than risk spending limited research time on recruitment efforts that might not prove productive, the investigators decided to move to a more promising site of data collection. As mentioned earlier, Ragsdale and Anders had initially decided that Ambergris Caye would be their second and final field site; however, after their consultations with key informants in Belize City, they felt compelled to investigate Orange Walk Town's potential as a field site before traveling on to Ambergris Caye.

Case 2. Vulnerable Populations and Research Challenges: Brothel Sex Workers in Orange Walk Town

The second phase of the pilot study was conducted among brothel-based FSWs in Orange Walk Town, Belize. The town was of particular interest because of Orange Walk's geographic location on a major highway that connects Belize City to Chetemal, Mexico. This transportation corridor brings long-haul truckers and tourists through the town, which had approximately 10 brothels in operation at the time of the study. In the following example, we use the investigators' experiences to illustrate how they identified circumstances of particular vulnerability for a sample of FSWs voluntarily engaged in sexual labor in Orange Walk Town.

Nature of the problem. With the advent of the HIV/AIDS pandemic in the 1980s, much biomedical and behavioral research that focused on women involved in sex work reinforced negative stereotypes by implicating female sex workers (FSWs) in the heterosexual transmission of HIV while downplaying the role of clients and domestic partners in unsafe sexual practices (Farmer, 1999; Vanwesenbeeck, 2001). In addition, the focus on HIV transmission associated with female sexual labor overshadowed more contextualized examinations of the economic, social, and health risks faced by impoverished women engaged in voluntary sex work. For example, many FSWs are the sole economic provider for their children, aging parents, or younger siblings, yet fear the loss of community respect and/or family support should the source of their remittances be discovered (Ragsdale & Anders, 1998, 1999). Consequently, impoverished FSWs often seek to safeguard their anonymity by migrating to foreign host countries in order to decrease the likelihood that their engagement in sex work will be reported back to members of their home communities. While continuing to support their dependents, migrant FSWs are physically and emotionally separated from their communities and families. As a further safeguard, migrant FSWs often purposefully distance themselves from social interactions with those who live in the host communities in which they work.

International migration can place FSWs—especially undocumented workers—in conditions where they are vulnerable to coercion by immigration officials, police, pimps, brothel owners, and clients in the host country. Vulnerability can be further increased when migrant FSWs have little education and/or do not speak the language of the host country. The social invisibility of women engaged in sexual labor, such as the migrant brothel-based sex workers discussed in this example, can also affect their vulnerability, even as it makes such hidden populations difficult to locate, access, and recruit to participate in studies (Singer, 1999). Yet the paucity of holistically grounded research on the

socioeconomic conditions faced by FSWs increases the difficulty of developing socially responsive policies that facilitate the delivery of services and foster advocacy for impoverished women and their children. Although it is critical to address global issues of sexual trafficking (Butcher, 2003), it is also important for researchers and policy makers to be aware that even among women who "voluntarily" engage in sex work, "the lines between autonomy and coercion [are] neither rigid nor always easily discernible" (Kempadoo, 2001, p. 53).

Research overview. In Orange Walk Town, the investigators verbally administered a face-to-face semistructured survey to 33 brothel workers who were legal migrants from the adjacent countries of El Salvador, Guatemala, and Honduras (Ragsdale & Anders, 1999). Participant responses, although not audiotape-recorded, were recorded as close to verbatim as possible on each survey. The Institutional Review Board of the University of Florida approved the consent procedures, which included informing participants of the sexually sensitive nature of the research, their right to refuse to answer any question, and their right to terminate the interview at any time. All participants lived on brothel premises, and the interviews were conducted on-site at each brothel. The majority of participants planned to return to their home country in the near future (less than 1 year from the date of the interview). The Orange Walk brothels accessible to the investigators employed between one and eight FSWs at the time of the study. It was from this prospective sample of 35 women that Ragsdale and Anders ultimately recruited 34 respondents. One prospective participant, the only Belizean national in the study, declined to be interviewed on the grounds that she served drinks but did not engage in sex work. Another participant had to terminate her interview shortly after it began when one of her regular clients arrived unexpectedly at the brothel. Therefore, the final sample of 33 women represented approximately 73% of the estimated 45 brothel-based FSWs in Orange Walk Town.

Ethical challenges to transnational research. Working in the developing world can present unexpected challenges when conducting research among vulnerable populations. In the town of Orange Walk, potential obstacles the investigators faced included unanticipated language barriers, the possibility of coerced participation from FSWs by brothel owners on behalf of governmental health officials, having to use a guide/interpreter appointed by the minister of health, inability to access participants off brothel premises in order to conduct interviews, personal safety issues while on brothel premises, and data safety monitoring. These potential obstacles are discussed in further detail below.

Language barriers and government-appointed interpreters. Although the official language of Belize is English, the investigators discovered that monolingual Spanish speakers predominated among the local Orange Walk population, including the migrant brothel workers in the sample. Although Anders was completely bilingual, Ragsdale's more limited Spanish language abilities required her to conduct interviews with the participants using the services of an interpreter. Through NGO contacts made while in Belize City, Ragsdale and Anders located an Orange Walk–based volunteer HIV-prevention worker fluent in Spanish to act as an interpreter; however, following a meeting in Belize City, the country's minister of health appointed a Ministry of Health worker to be the official interpreter for the investigators. The Ministry of Health worker was an HIV outreach worker whose responsibilities included visiting Orange Walk Town brothels to educate FSWs on safer sex

(including correct and consistent condom use) and other sexual health issues. He was comfortable and articulate discussing sexually sensitive topics, yet had no enforcement obligations or reporting duties associated with his position as a Ministry of Health worker. Thus, not only did he know most of the brothel owners and FSWs, but there was no risk that he would disclose to authorities personal information disclosed during the course of recruitment.

The investigators had reservations, however, about accepting the "offer" of an interpreter, based on the appointee's status as a Ministry of Health worker. As the meeting with the minister of health proceeded, it became clear that declining the offered services would have meant canceling the project in Orange Walk Town, with the strong implication that Ragsdale and Anders could be barred from conducting research elsewhere in the country. The investigators speculated that this tactic was a maneuver to gain a measure of surveillance over the researchers' data collection activities. They also speculated that this tactic was a way to ensure the personal safety of the investigators while on brothel premises in order to avoid the possibility of an incident that could have negative political ramifications for the country. The ethical dilemma of conducting research using a Ministry of Health–appointed interpreter, as opposed to one freely chosen by the investigators, was further complicated by the fact that the appointed interpreter was male. When conducting sexually sensitive research, it has become standard practice that field staff and participants be matched according to relevant sociodemographic characteristics, such as language and gender. That Anders was fluent in Spanish and female had a positive effect on rapport building and information exchange between the researcher and her interviewees; however, on their arrival in Orange Walk, Ragsdale and Anders quickly became aware that the Ministry of Health–appointed interpreter was an excellent gatekeeper, as he was well-known among the local FSWs and brothel owners in his capacity as a HIV-prevention outreach worker. The health worker became the liaison between the brothel owners and the investigators and was instrumental in facilitating the cooperation of the owners in allowing the investigators to access the brothels.

In his role as an HIV-prevention outreach worker, the health worker was also a skilled and experienced facilitator of discussions related to sexually sensitive topics. He was on a friendly basis with the participants, who displayed no discomfort discussing sex work–related issues within his presence. The cheerful banter between the health worker and the participants attenuated—but did not dismiss—the asymmetrical power dynamics between the research investigators, the interpreter, and the participants. The health worker proved to play an indispensable role as the gatekeeper between the brothel owners and the investigators, as well as between the participants and the investigators. He was also an excellent key informant who facilitated the investigators' understanding of brothel system organization in Orange Walk Town. Because he was a known and trusted entity, Ragsdale and Anders had access to 8 of the estimated 10 brothels operating in the town. The high level of success in accessing brothels in Orange Walk Town stood in sharp contrast to the investigators' unsuccessful efforts to safely access brothel premises in Belize City. Unaccompanied by a gatekeeper, the investigators were unable to gain permission from any Belize City brothel owner to gain access to brothel premises in order to recruit potential participants who engaged in sex work. The researchers also found that the stigma of conducting an investigation among sex workers was markedly reduced in Orange Walk. The reasons for this may have been twofold: (a) the Ministry

of Health worker's role as gatekeeper added legitimacy to the investigators' presence on brothel premises, which was suspect on the grounds that they were non-Belizean, female researchers and (b) the investigators lived with a well-respected host family within the Orange Walk Town community, a senior member of which was a local health care provider.

Coercion. The investigators carefully considered the multiple issues of potential coercion in this particular setting. For example, after having approved a study, governmental officials in some countries may pressure brothel owners to cooperate. In turn, brothel owners may pressure brothel workers to participate. This was not the case in Belize. Ragsdale and Anders accompanied the health worker when he initially approached the brothel owners, who displayed no concern in response to the request to interview FSWs. This is probably due to the fact that sex work is legal in Belize and the health worker had no direct authority over the brothels; however, this raised the issue of monitoring the safety of sensitive data, a concern the investigators faced near the end of the study, which will be addressed below.

A related ethical concern faced by the investigators was whether conducting interviews on the premises would be perceived as coercive by the participants. Contrary to Ragsdale and Anders's expectations, discussions with the participants indicated that they perceived their involvement in sex work to be voluntary and the brothel environment to be relatively noncoercive. For example, unlike standard practices in more coercive brothel systems (Cwikel, Ilan, & Chudakov, 2003; Reed, 2001), participants in Orange Walk Town could refuse sex with any client at their own discretion, a right that the participants stated they exercised regularly. In another example of how the Orange Walk Town brothel system deviated from more coercive brothel environments, the partici- pants were able to limit the amount and kind of sex activity in which they engaged with clients. In fact, most participants stated that they limited their engagement in sex work to one or two clients per night. Participants also reported that their *duenos* (brothel owners) did not retain their passports as a punitive or coercive measure to control the movement of the brothel workers. In fact, participants were free to move from brothel to brothel at will, and several respondents reported that they had worked at three or more different brothels in Orange Walk Town. The lack of an overtly coercive brothel environment was pivotal to Ragsdale and Anders's decision that it was ethically feasible to conduct the interviews on-site.

A third ethical concern was how to appro- priately demonstrate the investigators' appre- ciation of the time participants gave the interview. Budget constraints did not allow for monetary compensation to participants. Therefore, the process of co-learning was used to guide the investigators' selection of nail polish as a culturally appropriate token of appreciation for the respondents. The young women who took part in the study did not have easy access to these types of "extras." Participants received a gift of sev- eral bottles of nail polish and appreciated the opportunity to choose their own favorites among several color options. In the process of co-learning, the investigators also were informed by participants that taking part in the study had helped to alleviate the intense boredom associated with brothel life.

Confidentiality and data monitoring. Fitting confidentiality procedures to the culture of small or closed communities is particularly challenging in international settings (Fisher et al., 2002; Simons & Williams, 1999). In small developing countries, anonymity may be difficult to maintain, and the consequences of disclosure or participant identification

may raise serious safety issues. A breach of confidentiality can damage reputations and the social networks on which participants and their families may depend. For example, it is quite common for persons living in small countries to know many fellow inhabitants personally, by reputation, or through kin, social, and political networks. Therefore, many FSWs migrate to foreign countries, not only to earn more but to ensure their anonymity. For Ragsdale and Anders's population, the risk of a breach of confidentiality was low because the migrant sex workers did not gen- erally interact with the local population. Through co-learning, the investigators identi- fied that although the participants reported occasional local clients, their primary clients were transient long-haul truckers traveling the route from Belize City to the border of Mexico.

To safeguard the study population's anonymity, the investigators were careful not to approach participants in public venues, but only on brothel premises. Although par- ticipants did not perceive that there was a high level of stigmatization associated with sexual labor in Orange Walk, they stated that they personally felt ashamed of their involvement in sex work and, there- fore, rarely left brothel premises. As men- tioned earlier, participants said they were not restricted to brothel premises, as evi- denced by their ability to relocate from brothel to brothel; yet they did not often frequent the shops in Orange Walk.

Following informed consent describing the nature of the study and their rights as subjects of research, the participants were administered a semistructured survey in Spanish. The nature of the survey was such that there was no risk that the Ministry of Health appointee, in his dual role as Ragsdale's mandated interpreter and a governmental health worker, would discover information he otherwise would not have known, which might place the brothel workers at risk; however, it is important to consider the potential ramifications regarding confidentiality if the participants had been members of the host community rather than members of a migratory, transnational population that was not well integrated into community life. For example, how might this status difference have affected the issue of confidentiality posed by the mandated use of the health worker to conduct sexually sensitive research in a place were anonymity is difficult to maintain? According to the respondents, participants who migrated for the purpose of sex work believed that moving to Belize was one way to ensure that their involvement in female sex work remained unknown in their home countries.

Although such theoretical considerations are important, the investigators were faced with a far less theoretical dilemma after receiving a surprise announcement. Near the end of the data collection phase, Ragsdale and Anders were informed that highly placed governmental officials had made a unilateral decision that the Ministry of Health had proprietary rights to the survey data. This incident highlighted the fact that investigators who seek to contribute to knowledge about problems faced by stigmatized populations must be aware that the generation and dissemination of knowledge is not always value-free when addressing socially sensitive or emotionally charged issues (Fisher, 2002; Fisher & Wallace, 2000). The investigators decided that it was ethically untenable to turn over the primary data. They chose not to respond to the request and, inexplicably, were not asked to do so again; however, in her role as PI, Ragsdale had the surveys and informed consents carried out of the country by a trusted person as a further safeguard to ensure that the data would not be confiscated at a future date.

Research in populations of low literacy. According to Benatar and Singer (2000),

pivotal to the performance of ethically grounded research is "obtaining meaningful informed consent in the subjects' home tongue and with an understanding of their world view or value system" (p. 825). The participants in Orange Walk Town were administered informed consent in Spanish, which included informing respondents of their right to refuse to answer any question and to terminate the interview at any time. Ragsdale's interpreter initially tried to rush through the consent process. The PI was adamant that each prospective respondent be fully informed of her rights as a participant, and the Ministry of Health interpreter complied. As stated earlier, two prospective participants exercised their right to terminate the survey.

As Fisher and Wallace (2000) emphasize, "face validity is crucial if communities are to accept social policy proposals based on research" (p. 106). Engagement in co-learning is an important procedure to assure face validity. Through the process of co-learning, Ragsdale and Anders discovered they had to clarify or substitute particular survey terminology to assure the survey questions were appropriate to the population. Such modifications were tied not simply to English-to-Spanish translation but to the unique colloquialisms of the brothel workers. For example, most Orange Walk Town participants were unfamiliar with the Spanish medical term *sexo vaginal* (vaginal sex), which they referred to in lay language as *sexo normal* (normal sex). A goodness-of-fit approach also sensitized the investigators to language that might be insulting or distressful among already stigmatized or marginalized participants (Fisher, 2002). Sensitive to the historical misuse of stigmatizing language to pathologize women who engage in sex work as aberrant, Ragsdale and Anders adjusted the survey term *sex worker* to be more reflective of the participants' worldview. Although most participants did not find the unfamiliar term *trabajadora del sexo* (sex worker) offensive, they referred to themselves as *muchachas* (girls). Ragsdale and Anders adopted their use of the term *muchacha* as a sign of respect during all interactions and in subsequent publications (Ragsdale & Anders, 1998, 1999). Although a seemingly small linguistic change, the use of this term was an important signifier to the participants that the investigators did not view the women as aberrant. In the process of co-learning, the investigators also identified that (in contrast to much of the literature on women engaged in sexual labor) no participant referred to herself or a coworker as a *prostituta* (prostitute). In fact, participants described this term as nearly as offensive and derogatory as the slang term *puta* (whore).

Case 3. Participants as Experts: Locals and Tourists on Ambergris Caye

Ambergris Caye, Belize, was a town of particular interest to Ragsdale and Anders because of its social geography. The barrier reef offshore the resort island is one of the primary venues used to attract international tourists to Belize. The investigators had anticipated that, due to its prominence as a tourist attraction, Ambergris Caye would also have a brothel system in place as is typical of similar resort areas throughout the Caribbean (Kempadoo, 1995).

Contacting key informants. After arriving on Ambergris Caye, the investigators sought to make contact with governmental, NGO, and health care providers; however, due to the island's small population, as well as its proximity to Belize City (via water taxi or airplane), the investigators found that such resources were not readily available. Instead, Ragsdale and Anders spoke with community representatives, including tour operators, hotel owners, bartenders, taxi drivers, boat captains, business owners, hotel and restaurant workers, other local residents, and tourists. These key informants noted that brothel work was not typical on the island. Through firsthand observation, the investigators confirmed that the well-established brothel system that existed in Orange Walk Town did not operate on Ambergris Caye. For example, there was only one bar operating on the caye that employed a single FSW.

During this period of initial discovery, the investigators also found that their status as researchers was not recognized by key informants in the manner in which it had been in Orange Walk Town. Most residents of Ambergris Caye initially viewed the investigators as another pair of single tourist women visiting the small resort island rather than researchers exploring the connections between tourism and sex work in Belize. Therefore, the investigators again had to adjust their methods of data collection in order to accommodate the local conditions at the new field site of Ambergris Caye.

Ethical challenges to inquiry as research conditions change. Based on the unexpected discovery that there was not a population of sex workers from which to draw a sample, Ragsdale and Anders evaluated the feasibility of developing a new survey to explore the nature of sexual interactions between tourist and local populations on the island. The option of developing a new survey was dismissed as unfeasible given (a) the research time frame of 1 month at the site, (b) the expense and/or limited access to necessary technology available on the island to develop a new survey and consent form for IRB submission (such as exorbitant user fees for computers and international phone service), and (c) the time constraints involved for IRB approval after a new consent form had been developed and submitted to the University of Florida. Given these very real constraints, Ragsdale and Anders decided to use their limited time at the field site to conduct preliminary interviews and make observations that would become the basis for later research questions. Drawing on ethnographic models of knowledge elicitation (Bernard, 1995; LeCompte & Schensul, 1999), Ragsdale and Anders were able to build rapport with locals and tourists to obtain a holistic snapshot of the complexity of sexual exchanges between the inhabitants of Ambergris Caye and the tourists who migrated to the island to take advantage of its sun, sand, barrier reef, and other amenities.

Co-learning and community perspectives. The multimethod approach adopted by Ragsdale and Anders fit well into the normative life on the small island, where friendly and informal social relationships are prized. Many of the permanent residents on the caye quickly came to know that the investigators were there to conduct preliminary data collection on the nature of sex exchanges between local and tourist populations and were happy to assist by contributing their observations. The investigators, however, found that most informants felt the process of conducting formal interviews was cold, artificial, and unfriendly; and therefore, informants resisted this method of data collection. Local residents would not only poke good-natured jokes at the researchers when they appeared with their notebooks but would fail to arrive for scheduled interviews. As a way to adjust to local conditions and assimilate more appropriately into the culture on Ambergris Caye, Ragsdale and Anders began to appear without their notebooks. Instead, the investigators brought paper and pen tucked into their pockets for more unobtrusive note taking, which informants found acceptable. The investigators found that rich and descriptive conversations often ensued when they would informally stop by to "hangout and chat" with an informant at his or her place of employment or home. Ragsdale and Anders often shared

meals and conversation with locals who became friends and acquaintances, and the investigators began to be assimilated into normal work activities, such as helping to "collect the door" at live band performances, rolling silverware with a waitress, folding brochures for a dive shop owner, watching a jewelry shop for a friend, and looking after small children. In order to access the more transient population of tourists constantly arriving and leaving, Ragsdale and Anders made observations and contact with male and female tourists at bars, restaurants, and nightclubs. They struck up conversations with tourists at these venues, as well as on the beachfront and other venues regularly frequented by tourists on Ambergris Caye.

Co-learning as an avenue to research questions. As stated earlier, Ragsdale and Anders conducted preliminary research on Ambergris Caye based on a month of intensive interactions with locals and tourists on the island, far too short a time to make any hard-and-fast research conclusions. Rather, during the time spent on the caye, the investigators were able to make an important conclusion: There was little evidence that either organized sex tourism such as exists in Southeast Asia (Troung, 1990) or the organized brothel systems that exist in some Caribbean countries (Kempadoo, 1995) was established in Belize at the time of the study. Due to the lack of a population of brothel workers to whom the survey could be administered, the time spent on Ambergris Caye became a preliminary exploration of potential questions of research. Through observation, dialogue, and elicitation among permanent residents on the island (locals) and transient populations (tourists), Ragsdale and Anders were able to establish that tourists often engaged in sexual risk behavior with fellow tourists and local residents on Ambergris Caye (Ragsdale, 2000). This finding provided the groundwork for research conducted by

Ragsdale on the sexual risk behavior of single female tourists while on vacation in Costa Rica (Ragsdale, 2002).

GOODNESS-OF-FIT ETHICS: DYNAMICS OF DOING GOOD WELL

The GFE model holds that respectful relationships among investigators, prospective participants, and the community at large are instrumental to fulfilling the obligation to conduct scientifically valid and responsible research that serves to protect participant rights and welfare. In this final section, we discuss the GFE model applied to an understanding of investigator-participant power relationships.

Reframing the Discourse of Power

Goodness-of-fit ethics recognizes that, although power asymmetry is intrinsic to most research involving human subjects, relationship power is a fluid commodity that is constantly negotiated and renegotiated (Fisher, 1997, 1999).

> Those who seek greater symmetry in power relationships emphasize that each party must derive something out of the relationship and be able to exercise discretionary control over the resources prized by the other (Goodin, 1985). However, these resources must be used to enhance, not compromise, the ethical and scientific integrity of experimentation. (Fisher, 1999, p. 45)

A cornerstone of the GFE model calls for "investigators engaged in the critical task of generating the information on which . . . services, public opinion, and policies . . . will be based" to actively engage themselves in the "formidable responsibility of ensuring that their procedures are scientifically sound, culturally valid, and morally just" (Fisher et al., 2002, p. 1025). This may not be an easy task, as scientists can be unwilling or unable to actively engage in the difficult and personally challenging self-reflection necessary to lay an ethics-in-science foundation conducive to co-learning (Fisher, 2000). In turn, co-learning requires that investigators, who have often spent years training to become recognized as experts in a particular field of study or discipline, actively reframe discourses of power and hierarchy that may have afforded them special or privileged status, as investigators seek to achieve a more inclusive research environment.

The exercise of inclusion, especially when the needs and desires of community members do not easily fit into an investigator's research agenda, calls for vigilance to assure participant sensitive research. Although the dynamic nature of conducting human subjects research does not lend itself to "cookie cutter" solutions to sound ethics-in-science practices (Fisher, 2004; see also Hoagwood, Jensen, & Fisher, 1996), the goal of achieving GFE when designing and implementing research among vulnerable populations is attainable. Fisher and Wallace (2000) recommended several steps for achieving GFE to enhance problem identification through co-learning activities, such as focus groups. These include (a) creating an equitable environment in which all participants are encouraged to explore the multifaceted aspects of the topic under discussion, (b) interpretation of the discourse in a manner that recognizes the dynamic nature of ethical deliberation within individual participants and the multiplicity of views among participants, and (c) a determined effort to avoid simplistic interpretations of participant views (e.g., a procedure is either right or wrong). Applying this approach allows for "in-depth analysis of individual perspectives that can challenge current ways of thinking about ethics-in-science issues and point to new directions of moral awareness and scientific inquiry" (Fisher & Wallace, 2000, p. 102).

Goodness-of-Fit Ethics and Multicultural Research

Members of ethnic minority or otherwise marginalized communities are often understandably skeptical about the presumed benefits and/or merit of policy-driven research based on past personal experience and observation as well as historical misuse of scientific findings. The call for investigators to be proactively engaged in GFE will increase the identification of best practices in human subjects research as it simultaneously acts to increase trust of research among ethnic minority communities and their members.

The development and evaluation of culturally appropriate co-learning procedures to ensure goodness-of-fit in the ethical conduct of social and behavioral research is a dynamic and ongoing process. Although there is a growing body of qualitative research on ethics-in-science decision making involving ethnic minority populations, the transferability of such knowledge is less well understood. The aim of goodness-of-fit inquiry is not to document participant perspectives that can or should dictate specific research designs or ethical practices in other ethnic minority populations. Rather the purpose is to provide models of ethical procedures reflective of specific participant group perspectives that can challenge current ways of thinking about ethics-in-science issues and point to new directions of moral awareness and scientific inquiry for multicultural research.

REFERENCES

Altman, D. G. (1995). Sustaining interventions in community systems: On the relationship between researchers and communities. *Health Psychology, 14,* 526–536.

Beauchamp, T. L., Faden, R. R., Wallace, R. J., & Walters, L. (1982). Introduction. In T. L. Beauchamp, R. R. Faden, R. J. Wallace, & L. Walters (Eds.), *Ethical issues in social science research* (pp. 3–39). Baltimore: Johns Hopkins University Press.

Benatar, S. R., & Singer, P. A. (2000, September 30). A new look at international research ethics. *BMJ 2000, 321,* 824–826.

Bernard, H. R. (1995). *Research methods in anthropology: Qualitative and quantitative approaches* (2nd ed.). Walnut Creek, CA: AltaMira.

Butcher, K. (2003). Confusion between prostitution and sex trafficking. *Lancet, 361*(1973), 1983.

Cassell, J. (1982). Does risk-benefit analysis apply to moral evaluation of social research? In T. L. Beauchamp, R. R. Faden, R. J. Wallace, & L. Walters (Eds.), *Ethical issues in social science research* (pp. 144–162). Baltimore: Johns Hopkins University Press.

Chun, K. (1995). The myth of Asian American success and its educational ramifications. In D. Nakanishi & T. Nishida (Eds.), *The Asian American educational experience* (pp. 95–112). New York: Routledge.

Cwikel, J., Ilan, K., & Chudakov, B. (2003). Women brothel workers and occupational health risks. *Journal of Epidemiology and Community Health, 57,* 809–15.

Demo, D. H., & Hughes, M. (1990). Socialization and racial identity among Black Americans. *Social Psychology Quarterly, 53,* 364–374.

Diallo, K. (2003). *My heart will cross this ocean: My story, my son, Amadou.* New York: One World/Ballantine.

Dublin, T. (1996). *Becoming American, becoming ethnic: College students explore their roots.* Philadelphia: Temple University Press.

Eller, J. D. (1999). *From culture to ethnicity to conflict: An anthropological perspective on international ethnic conflict.* Ann Arbor: University of Michigan Press.

Essed, P. (1991). *Understanding everyday racism: An interdisciplinary theory.* Newbury Park, CA: Sage.

Farmer, P. (1999). *Infections and inequalities: The modern plagues.* Berkeley: University of California Press.

Farmer, P. (2002). Can transnational research be ethical in the developing world? *Lancet, 360*(9342), 1266.

Fisher, C. B. (1997). A relational perspective on ethics-in-science decision making for research with vulnerable populations. *IRB: Review of Human Subjects Research, 19,* 1–4.

Fisher, C. B. (1999). Relational ethics and research with vulnerable populations. *Reports on research involving persons with mental disorders that may affect decision-making capacity* (Vol. 2, pp. 29–49). Commissioned Papers by the National Bioethics Advisory Commission, Rockville, MD.

Fisher, C. B. (2000). Relational ethics in psychological research: One feminist's journey. In M. Brabeck (Ed.), *Practicing feminist ethics in psychology* (pp. 125–142). Washington, DC: APA.

Fisher, C. B. (2002). Participant consultation: Ethical insights into parental permission and confidentiality procedures for policy relevant research with youth. In R. M. Lerner, F. Jacobs, & D. Wertlieb (Eds.), *Handbook of applied developmental science* (Vol. 4, pp. 371–396). Thousand Oaks, CA: Sage.

Fisher, C. B. (2003a). A goodness-of-fit ethic for informed consent to research involving persons with mental retardation and developmental disabilities. *Mental Retardation and Developmental Disabilities Research Reviews, 9,* 27–31.

Fisher, C. B. (2003b). A goodness-of-fit ethic for child assent to non-beneficial research. *American Journal of Bioethics, 3*(4), 27–28.

Fisher, C. B. (2004). Ethics in drug abuse and related HIV risk research. *Applied Developmental Science, 8,* 90–102.

Fisher, C. B. (2005). Commentary: SES, ethnicity and goodness-of-fit in clinician-parent communication during pediatric cancer trials. *Journal of Pediatric Psychology, 30*(3), 231–234.

Fisher, C. B., Hoagwood, K., Boyce, C., Duster, T., Frank, D.A., Grisso, T., et al. (2002). Research ethics for mental health science involving ethnic minority children and youths. *American Psychologist, 57,* 1024–1040.

Fisher, C. B., Jackson, J., & Villarruel, F. (1997). The study of African American and Latin American children and youth. In W. Damon (Series Ed.) & R. M. Lerner (Vol. Ed.), *Handbook of child psychology: Vol. 1. Theoretical models of human development* (5th ed., pp. 1145–1207). New York: Wiley.

Fisher, C. B., & Masty, J. K. (in press). A goodness-of-fit ethic for informed consent to pediatric cancer research. In R. T. Brown (Ed.), *Handbook of pediatric psychosocial oncology.* New York: Oxford University Press.

Fisher, C. B., & Wallace, S. A. (2000). Through the community looking glass: Re-evaluating the ethical and policy implications of research on adolescent risk and psychopathology. *Ethics & Behavior, 10,* 99–118.

Fisher, C. B., & Wallace, S. A., & Fenton, R. E. (2000). Discrimination distress during adolescence. *Journal of Youth and Adolescence, 29,* 679–695.

Freedman, B. (1975). A moral theory of informed consent. *Hastings Center Report, 5,* 32–39.

Gaertner, S. L., & Dovidio, J. F. (1986). *Prejudice, discrimination, and racism.* Orlando, FL: Academic.

Goodin, R. E. (1985). *Protecting the vulnerable.* Chicago: University of Chicago Press.

Greenfield, P. M. (1994). Independence and interdependence as developmental scripts: Implications for theory, research, and practice. In P. M. Greenfield & R. R. Cocking (Eds.), *Cross-cultural roots of minority child development* (pp. 1–37). Hillsdale, NJ: Lawrence Erlbaum.

Gould, S. J. (1981). *The mismeasure of man.* New York: W. W. Norton.

Haddix, A. C., Teutsch, S. M., & Corso, P. S. (Eds.). (2002). *Prevention effectiveness: A guide to decision analysis and economic evaluation* (2nd ed.). New York: Oxford University Press.

Hoagwood, K., Jensen, P. S., & Fisher, C. B. (1996). Towards a science of scientific ethics in research on child and adolescent mental disorders. In K. Hoagwood, P. Jensen, & C. B. Fisher (Eds.), *Ethical issues in research with children and adolescents with mental disorders* (pp. 3–14). Hillsdale, NJ: Lawrence Erlbaum.

Kane, S. C. (1993). Prostitution and the military: Planning AIDS intervention in Belize. *Social Science & Medicine, 36*(7), 965–979.

Kempadoo, K. (1995). *Prostitution, marginality and empowerment: Caribbean women in the sex trade.* Paper presented at the International Workshop, Women on the Threshold of the XXI Century, University of Havana, Cuba.

Kempadoo, K. (Ed.). (1999). *Sun, sex, and gold: Tourism and sex work in the Caribbean.* Boulder, CO: Rowman & Littlefield.

Kempadoo, K. (2001). Freelancers, temporary wives, and beach-boys: Researching sex work in the Caribbean. *Feminist Review, 67,* 39–62.

Kodish, E., Eder, M., Noll, R. B., Ruccione, K., Lange, B., Angiolillo, A., et al. (2004). Communication of randomization in childhood leukemia trials. *Journal of the American Medical Association, 291,* 470–475.

LeCompte, M. D., & Schensul, J. J. (1999). *Analyzing and interpreting ethnographic data.* Walnut Creek, CA: AltaMira.

Levy, D. E., & Lerch, P. B. (1991). Tourism as a factor in development: Implications for gender and work in Barbados. *Gender & Society, 5*(1), 67–85.

Lowe, L. (1996). *Immigrant acts: On Asian American cultural politics.* Durham, NC: Duke University Press.

MacQueen, K. (2004). Bioethics and anthropology: A call for partnership. Retrieved December 2, 2004, from www.medanthro.net/stand/overview/index.html

Mahler, R., & Wotkyns, S. (1993). *Belize: A natural destination* (2nd ed.). Santa Fe, NM: John Muir.

Markus, H. R., & Kitayama, S. (1991). Culture and the self: Implications for cognition, emotion, and motivation. *Psychological Review, 98*(2), 224–253.

Mathabane, M. (1990). *Kaffir boy in America.* New York: Free Press.

McClaurin, I. (1996). *Women of Belize: Gender and change in Central America.* New Brunswick, NJ: Rutgers University Press.

Melton, G. B., Levine, R. J., Koocher, G. P., Rosenthal, R., & Thompson, W. C. (1988). Community consultation in socially sensitive research: Lessons from clinical trials of treatments for AIDS. *American Psychologist, 43,* 573–581.

Mill, J. S. (1957/1861). *Utilitarianism.* New York: Bobbs-Merrill.

Nichter, M. A. (1984). Project community diagnosis: Participatory research as a first step toward community involvement in primary health care. *Social Science and Medicine, 19*(3), 237–252.

Ogbaa, K. (2003). *The Nigerian Americans (the new Americans).* New York: Greenwood.

Parham, T. A. (1993). White researchers conducting multicultural counseling research: Can their efforts be "mo betta"? *Counseling Psychologist, 21,* 250–256.

Pinkerton, S. D., Johnson-Masotti, A. P., Derse, A., & Layde, P. M. (2002). Ethical issues in cost-effectiveness analysis. *Evaluation and Program Planning, 25,* 71–83.

Portes, A., & Stepick, A. (1993). *City on the edge: The social transformation of Miami.* Berkeley: University of California Press.

Prilleltensky, I. (1997). Values, assumptions, and practices: Assessing the moral implications of psychological discourse and action. *American Psychologist, 52,* 517–535.

Ragsdale, K. (2000). *Don't leave home without it: Tourist women, sexual risk and condom use.* Paper presented at the Annual Meeting of the Society for Applied Anthropology, San Francisco, CA.

Ragsdale, K. (2002). *Tourist women balancing temptation and HIV risk in Costa Rica.* Gainesville: University Press of Florida.

Ragsdale, K. (in press). Ethnocentrism. In Y. Jackson (Ed.), *Encyclopedia of multicultural psychology.* Thousand Oaks, CA: Sage.

Reed, K. D. (2001). A tale of two cities: Brothel-based female commercial sex work, spread of HIV, and related sexual health care interventions in India, using Bombay and Delhi as examples. *Journal of Family Planning and Reproductive Health Care, 27,* 223–227.

Richter, L. K. (1995). Gender and race: Neglected variables in tourism research. In R. Butler & D. G. Pearce (Eds.), *Change in tourism: People, places, processes* (pp. 71–91). London: Routledge.

Rosenwald, C. G. (1996). Making whole: Method and ethics in mainstream and narrative psychology. In R. Josselson (Ed.), *Ethics and process in the narrative study of lives* (Vol. 4, pp. 245–273). Thousand Oaks, CA: Sage.

Safa, H. I. (1995). *The myth of the male breadwinner: Women and industrialization in the Caribbean.* Boulder, CO: Westview.

Sen, G., & Grown, C. (1987). *Development, crises, and alternative visions: Third World women's perspectives.* New York: Monthly Review Press.

Simon, R. I., & Williams, I. C. (1999, November). Maintaining treatment boundaries in small communities and rural areas. *Psychiatric Services 50,* 1440–1446. Retrieved March 18, 2005, from http://ps.psychiatryonline.org/cgi/content/full/50/11/1440

Singer, M. (1999). Studying hidden populations. In J. J. Schensul, M. D. LeCompte, R. T. Trotter, E. K. Cromley, & M. Singer (Eds.), *Mapping social networks, spatial data, and hidden populations* (pp. 125–191). Thousand Oaks, CA: AltaMira.

SPEAR. (1993). *SPEAReports 9, Globalization and Development: Challenges and Prospects for Belize.* Belize: Author.

Stepick, A., & Foner, N. (1998). *Pride against prejudice: Haitians in the U.S.* Boston: Allyn & Bacon.

Stepick, A., Grenier, G., Castro, M., & Dunn, M. (2003). *This land is our land: Immigrants and power in Miami.* Berkeley: University of California Press.

Sue, D. W., Carter, R. T., Casas, J. M., Fouad, N. A., Ivey, A. E., Jensen, M., et al. (1998). *Multicultural counseling competences: Individual and organizational development.* Thousand Oaks, CA: Sage.

Triandis, H. C. (1990). Cross-cultural studies of individualism and collectivism. In J. Berman (Ed.), *Nebraska Symposium on Motivation, 1989* (pp. 41–133). Lincoln: University of Nebraska Press.

Troung, T. D. (1990). *Sex, money and morality: The political economy of prostitution and tourism in South East Asia.* London: Zed Books.

U.S. Department of State. (2004). *Country reports on human rights practices: Belize.* Washington, DC: Department of State. Retrieved March 21, 2005, from www.state.gov/g/ drl/rls/hrrpt/2004/41749.htm

Vanwesenbeeck, I. (2001). Another decade of social scientific work on sex work: A review of research 1990–2000. *Annual Review of Sex Research, 12,* 242–89.

Veatch, R. M. (1987). *The patient as partner.* Bloomington: Indiana University Press.

Weeks, M. R., Schensul, J. J., Williams, S. S., Singer, M., & Grier, M. (1995). AIDS prevention for African-American and Latina women: Building culturally and gender-appropriate intervention. *AIDS Education and Prevention, 7*(3), 251–263.

CHAPTER 2

Scientist-Community Collaborations

A Dynamic Tension Between Rights and Responsibilities

JOHN FANTUZZO

CHRISTINE MCWAYNE

STEPHANIE CHILDS

> The methods and theories of social science are not being produced by computers but by men and women; and for the most part, by men and women operating not in laboratories but in the same world to which the methods apply and the theories pertain. It is this which gives the whole enterprise its special character. Most social scientific research involves direct, intimate, and more or less disturbing encounters with the immediate details of contemporary life, encounters of a sort that can hardly help but affect the sensibilities of the persons who practice it. And, as any discipline is what the persons who practice it make it, these sensibilities become as embedded in its construction as do those of an age in its culture.
>
> —Clifford Geertz, *Available Light: Anthropological Reflections on Philosophical Topics*

We are at a propitious moment in the United States for the effective application of developmental science to meet the urgent needs of vulnerable children. National statistics indicate that approximately one in six children in the United States is living in poverty (National Center for Children in Poverty [NCCP], 2004). Poverty is associated with a host of risk factors, particularly for children living in disadvantaged urban areas. These include exposure to repeated and long-term stressors that threaten development, such as neighborhood crime, inadequate housing, and poor nutrition (Garbarino, 1995). Exposure to these stressors during early stages of development increases children's risk for psychological adjustment problems that can have a long-term impact over the life course (Knitzer, 2000). Unfortunately, young children (ages 0–5) evidence the highest prevalence rates of poverty compared with other age groups. Two of every five young children in the United States are living in low-income families (NCCP, 2004). Furthermore, Black and Latino children are disproportionately more likely to live in families with low income. National statistics from 2002 indicate that 58% of Black children and 62% of Latino children lived in low-income families compared with 25% of White children (NCCP, 2004).

Increased national attention to the early childhood years has put this period of life in the spotlight as a critical time for developing skills that children need to be successful in school. Three recent National Research Council reports—*Eager to Learn* (2001), *Neurons to Neighborhoods* (2002), and *Preventing Reading Difficulties in Young Children* (1998)—establish the significance of early experiences on later development and the effects that these experiences have on school achievement. The heightened attention to children's early development covers a range of topics, including early brain development and the impact of experience, the purposes and content of early childcare (National Institute of Child Health and Human Development Early Child Care Research Network [NICHD], 2002), the cognitive and social development of the child, the meaning and import of early literacy, and the role of the family and social context.

As a result of this increased attention, debates about social responsibility toward the quality of life and welfare of young children have now entered the public square. We have awakened to the risks attendant upon our long-term neglect of young children's welfare. Finally the nation is appreciating how much the well-being of young children is tied to our national well-being. This important awareness creates an urgent mandate to develop effective interventions for vulnerable, low-income children. This mandate in turn generates a "tall order" for scientists, practitioners, and policy makers to advance inquiry in a context of urgent knowing. Major policy action, like the No Child Left Behind Act of 2002 (U.S. Department of Education, 2004) and the sharp political debates on the effectiveness of Head Start, our nation's largest program for low-income young children (Zigler & Styfco, 2004), call for rigorous evaluation and evidence-based practices to justify public investment. Needless to say, these mandates focus our attention on the significance of the issues, but they are insufficient to produce the necessary evidence. What we need are models and effective methods that are both scientifically valid and relevant to the communities that they are designed to benefit. The purpose of this chapter is threefold: First, we will outline some of the ethical tensions inherent in the more traditional modus operandi of conducting research with ethnocultural populations; second, we will present a partnership-based, transactional model, which we propose better addresses the ethical issues related to conducting research with diverse populations; and third, we will present a case study to illustrate the application of this model.

THE APPLIED DEVELOPMENTAL SCIENCE PERSPECTIVE

Applied developmental scientists have advanced developmental models to guide research design and program development for vulnerable young children (Bronfenbrenner & Morris, 1998; Lerner, Fisher, Weinberg, 2000). These models reflect an overall developmental-ecological perspective that emphasizes the "whole child;" it places high value on child competencies, contexts, contributors, and various courses or pathways of development. Competencies of the whole child, not disorders or deficiencies, are core to this developmental perspective. This perspective seeks to understand human development in terms of changes in the multiple domains of child functioning over time. Here, development is understood by looking at the central tasks that children are expected to perform as a function of their age and culture. These tasks require children to bring to bear their language, cognitive, emotional, social, and motor competencies to meet major developmental challenges. Studying what constitutes competent performance in these areas of functioning for diverse groups of children and considering how this development occurs along various pathways (courses) across time is the major focus of this approach (Fisher, 1993; Fisher & Lerner, 1994, 2004).

Context and Spheres of Influence

In this approach, context plays an important role in determining the course of development. Context is the larger sphere in which development takes place. Interaction with context is what affects how and when children manifest psychological competencies and, to varying degrees, the content of these competencies. Context includes spheres of influence that create the expectations for performance and, hence, have an impact on the child throughout development. Various influences can alter the course of development creating different pathways for children attempting to adapt within their context. These spheres of influence, or systems, can in various ways enhance or impede development. Overall, multiple influences and multiple areas of functioning combine to shape the course of a child's development, resulting in adaptive or maladaptive patterns of child behavior (Cicchetti & Toth, 1997).

Embedded in these natural spheres of influence are important persons who are major contributors to children's development (i.e., family members, peers, teachers, and community leaders). These individuals can promote directly children's acquisition of developmental competencies. Partnering with key natural contributors is essential to promoting beneficial, systemwide change for children. Recognizing the key contexts and key contributors to children's development informs the collection of quality information about children's competencies and ultimately leads to establishing beneficial connections to enhance development at multiple system levels. This approach has at its core the importance of beneficial connections and dynamic transactions to children's well-being. Therefore, understanding how applied developmental scientists foster connections and disconnections with natural contributors is essential to this approach.

Disconnection and Disengagement

Substantial gaps exist in our understanding of appropriate and effective methods for identification and treatment of the early needs of vulnerable populations of children who are currently underserved by our traditional service delivery systems (National Advisory Mental Health Council's Workgroup on Child and Adolescent Mental Health Intervention Development and Deployment [NAMHC], 2001). These gaps are evidenced by disproportionately poor access to services, inability to sustain involvement in services (high attrition), the relative ineffectiveness of traditional intervention protocols, and concerns about the conduct of research for low-income, minority populations (Fisher et al., 2002). These realities foster disconnection and disengagement for community participants and may cause them to seriously question the motives of the service and research institutions seeking their involvement.

ETHICAL PRINCIPLES AND APPLIED DEVELOPMENTAL SCIENCE RESEARCH

A closer examination of the traditional modus operandi of conducting applied research will help us gain a better understanding of the processes that might impede forming beneficial scientist–community participant connections with our most vulnerable groups of children and families (Fantuzzo & Mohr, 2000). Central to the ethical conduct of research with human participants are three fundamental principles: beneficence, respect for autonomy, and justice (National Commission for the Protection of Human Subjects of Biomedical and Behavioral Research [National Commission], 1979). Beneficence calls for researchers to seek the best interest of the participant community; respect for autonomy mandates responsiveness on the part of researchers to the informed choices of the participants; justice prohibits any undue burden or hardship to participants as a result of their involvement as participants in research. Institutional review boards in U.S. university/research institutions are required to apply federal guidelines and requirements to ensure that these principles are upheld (Department of Health and Human Services, 2001). The traditional process for advancing a major research agenda requires researchers to provide a priori documentation to their IRB that their research methods comport with these principles; however, we believe that the traditional application of these principles falls short of the spirit of these ethical standards and impedes forming productive relationships with low-income, minority communities. Inherent in these principles is, first and foremost, showing respect for dignity of each individual and the culturally distinct groups of individuals involved in our research. This involves a process that truly considers, takes heed, shows interest, and regards what is important to diverse groups of research participants.

Lines of Authority and Power

University institutional review board (IRB) approval and grant funds awarded to researchers, at the outset, tend to set up lines of authority and power that are more likely to be unilateral and unidirectional. This unidirectional process is illustrated in Figure 2.1. The process is based on the initial motivation, ideas, investments, and resources that are generated by the researchers. University researchers use their credentials and position to present their ideas for peer review to obtain grants to conduct the research. Funded grants provide researchers with rights, responsibilities, and resources to conduct their research. Once funds have been secured, the researchers present their research agenda to potential participants. For the research agenda to proceed, a single consent interaction between the researcher and participants is required: a "Yes, I will participate in your study." After the researcher (or more typically the researcher's assistant) has secured a sufficient number of *yes* responses from the participant community to provide ample statistical power to conduct the research, research methods are implemented typically by a team of research assistants. Data are collected from participants across a battery of measures, and cases are retained for analyses if participants have completed all the measures or have not dropped out of the study. This data collection process customarily involves some financial exchange to compensate *yes* participants for their time spent completing the data collection protocol. Required reports on the progress of the research are periodically submitted to the grant sponsor and the IRB at the conclusion of the project, and results are typically shared with the scholarly community and possibly local agencies serving the community of participants.

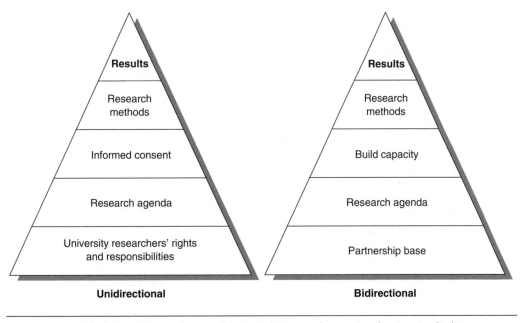

Figure 2.1   Traditional Versus Partnership-Based Approaches to Conducting Applied
Developmental Research

Limitations of Informed Consent

In this series of steps, a single informed consent transaction is the primary point of contact that defines the nature of the research/participant relationship in the research process (see Figure 2.1). The problem is that this single transaction might represent a number of false assumptions made by the university researchers and the IRB, who are generally not members of the participant community involved in the research. For example, it is assumed that (a) the investigator's informed consent statement reflects a comprehensive understanding of the participants' context and anticipates the full range of participant concerns about the investigator and the investigator's research agenda; (b) the residual *yes*'s represent a sufficient vote of confidence in the research agenda and trust that the research will result in genuine benefits for the larger participant community to sanction the research in their community (or institution in the case of the

practitioners); and (c) the individuals who have said yes have no remaining reservations or concerns about their involvement; that is, there are no latent unresolved *no*'s in the *yes* group.

What is missing from this standard sequence and essential to forming a genuine connection/partnership with the community of participants is a process that respects the voices of the *no* members of the community. The above sequence only represents *yes* respondents and therefore does not constitute an interaction with the full community of potential participants. *No* members of the community are those who evidence various overt and covert distancing actions that threaten the validity of the research findings (e.g., low participation rates, incomplete protocols, attrition rates, and lack of fidelity in following intervention protocol (NAMHC, 2001). The empirical fact is that historically there have been a disproportionate number of *no*'s from research participants representing economically disadvantaged and politically marginalized groups in our society (Fantuzzo & Mohr, 2000). These *no*'s challenge the assumptions of the standard operating procedure and call our attention to the significance of cultural, socioeconomic, and political gaps that separate researchers, practitioners, and citizens. These gaps provide a reasonable cause for potential participants' mistrust and tension about research in their community and the use of the resulting research findings by educators, clinicians, and government. Moreover, as was pointed out above, it may be false to assume that a one-time signature on an informed consent document represents the complete resolution of all latent *no* points of resistance for *yes* community participants.

Case example. A recent study of Head Start research partnership conducted by Lamb-Parker and colleagues (Lamb-Parker, Greenfield, Fantuzzo, Clark, & Coolahan, 2000) documented the importance of responding to *no* resistance of community participants to a university-initiated, research agenda. In this study, Head Start community partners and university researchers from over 60 different research projects were surveyed regarding a host of variables relevant to the partnership process. These included (a) the formation, maintenance, and the focus of the partnership, (b) community partners' level of participation in the research, (c) overall satisfaction with the partnership process, and (d) the perceived value of the research findings and products. They compared respondents whose projects had a high level of shared decision making with respondents whose projects had a low level of shared decision making. The results revealed that projects that minimized the role of community participants in decision-making activities and failed to make participants' rights and sensitivities a high priority early on in the research project were associated with a less successful implementation of the research

agenda. In addition, it was found that high shared decision making during the early phases of a project was associated with high levels of involvement for Head Start staff (e.g., in the recruitment procedures, data collection, data analysis, and interpretation of research findings). Researchers and community partners who spent less time in identifying and processing participant resistance in the first year of their project reported more major barriers to implementing the research methods in subsequent years and significantly less successful research projects than those who made the community participants' *no*'s their first priority.

Providing a genuine voice. What the above case demonstrates is that a process that does not provide the *no*'s with a genuine voice in the research agenda and method may threaten the validity and relevancy of the research. The concerns of the *no*'s genuinely embody the spirit of the guiding ethical principles: beneficence, autonomy, and justice. The fundamental reality is that the participant is the primary source of confirmation of the beneficence, autonomy, and justice of their involvement in the research. Too often, these principles can become esoteric in a political and academic atmosphere that encourages quick turnaround and precludes a focus on a true partnership-driven scientific process; however, it is evasive to claim that institutional and societal pressures are the major impediments to a partnership-based approach. There is a more fundamental tension that exists between scientists and participants. Here we have very different perspectives on what is most important in the conduct of research. In general, during the conduct of research, the community cares most about maximizing the immediate relevance of the research, whereas the scientist cares most about maximizing the rigor of the methods. The scientist insists that applied research cannot be relevant unless it is rigorous; the community participant insists that research cannot be rigorous and truly efficacious unless it is relevant.

Recognition of this dynamic tension is necessary for actualizing the kind of ethical scientific inquiry that takes into account issues of justice, autonomy, and beneficence. From the practitioner-community perspective, the scientist must respect their autonomy (voice), work toward justice, and in partnership, transform resources into beneficial outcomes that serve the community in meaningful ways. Billions of dollars in research grants are awarded each year in our country, and research scientists have an ethical responsibility to the community to account for and effectively use those resources. From the scientist perspective, research is often a slow, methodical process that cannot promise immediate answers. It must be considered within a larger body of knowledge and must maintain certain scientific standards to ensure validity. So, how do we conceptualize a balance between the rights and responsibilities of both scientists and communities within a partnership-based framework?

A MODEL FOR ADDRESSING THE TENSIONS BETWEEN RIGHTS AND RESPONSIBILITIES

Central to a partnership-based approach is the recognition that dynamic transactions between developmental scientists and community participants provide the foundation for rigorous and relevant scientific inquiry. Two-way transactions can yield two major benefits to the research process: First, they can surface the real *no*'s and *yes*'s of the participant community; second, they can identify the rights and responsibilities of the researchers and the participant community and provide a context for negotiating a genuine research partnership. These influential exchanges increase the likelihood of

conducting valid research that is maximally useful for improving the lives of vulnerable children and their families. Figure 2.1 shows the contrast between a more traditional unidirectional approach and a partnership-based, bidirectional approach to applied research.

Our conceptualization of partnership-based research evokes a scientist-community transactional model analogous to our understanding of child-environment transactions within a developmental-ecological and applied developmental science model (Cicchetti & Toth, 1997; Fisher et al., 1993). Similar to the dynamic interactions that occur between children and their environment over the course of development, the development of scientist-community collaboration involves ongoing, bidirectional influences (Fisher, 1999, 2002). These transactions generate variations in the quality of partnership outcomes. These outcomes, then, alter pathways toward future positive or negative transactions between community participants and scientists. Responsive and competent collaborations produce rigorous and relevant research; insensitive and incompetent exchanges yield invalid results that are not germane to real, community problem solving or meaningful scientific discovery. Rigor and relevance are, therefore, a direct function of the quality of the transactional relationships between scientists and community participants.

Research conducted in partnership involves a process in which researchers and community participants are willing to assert their rights with one another, to yield their rights when appropriate, and to accept their responsibilities to achieve beneficial outcomes. As discussed in the previous section, an imbalance between rights and responsibilities can jeopardize the validity and the ethical conduct of applied developmental research. Therefore, a useful and productive research modus operandi must be understood in terms of how to create a beneficial balance between the rights and responsibilities of scientists and

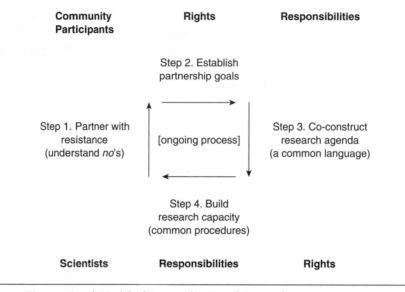

Figure 2.2 Transactional Model of Partnership-Based Research

community participants. The following presents a four-step approach designed to strike this beneficial balance. Figure 2.2 illustrates the sequence of steps in this approach and the dynamic tensions between the rights and responsibilities of university researchers and community participants.

Step 1: Partner With Resistance

A transactional model, in contrast to a unidirectional one, does not initiate the research process with an assertion of the researchers' expertise and rights to conduct a fixed research agenda (Figure 2.1). Instead, it begins with the goal of establishing a genuine partnership between the researchers and the participant/practitioner community. It is at this beginning point that applied developmental scientists have the opportunity to yield their initial rights and privileges to conduct research and assume their responsibility to encourage the participants to assert their rights regarding the real or perceived ways in which they believe that the research agenda threatens the well-being of their community.

At the outset is the fundamental recognition that partnership must begin by first seeking to identify the substantive *no*'s of the participant community, both visible and invisible, as well any significant ambivalence within the *yes* participants, a process that Fantuzzo and Mohr (2000) described as "partnering with resistance." This approach involves temporarily suspending the initial research agenda and gaining an understanding of the *no* responses. Understanding begins with an acknowledgement that participants may have many valid reasons for resisting or rejecting participation in a specific research agenda. Recognition and respect for those reasons is the antecedent to dialogue about the questionable merits of the research from the participants' perspective.

Efforts to partner with resistance can uncover a number of reasonable concerns. Major concerns may include beliefs about the stigma associated with various research methods. We have found that specific measures and procedures have been experienced by community members as confusing, offensive, impractical, disrespectful, threatening, or useless. Many of the *no* participants in our research, when given the opportunity, have shared that they fear a unilateral process that assumes the participant community does not have anything substantial to contribute to the conceptualization of a study, its methods, or the interpretations of the findings.

Within this approach, scientists accept responsibility for taking steps toward true partnership by recognizing the rights of the participant community to say no. This respect for the community participants' rights is designed to prevent the possibilities of injustice during the course of research, violation of participants' autonomy, and invalid results. By taking steps to understand community resistance, scientists are afforded an opportunity to partner with it. They are, in essence, assuming the responsibility for likely injustices and indignities as a cause of their work and creating a context for the possibility of a dynamic, two-way dialogue.

Step 2: Establish Partnership Goals for the Research

The principal aim of this second step is to build trust within the context of respectful, two-way dialogue that can lead to the articulation of a common purpose. By acknowledging participant rights and by listening to participants' perspectives about research in their communities and the problem under study, scientists open the door for relevant inquiry to occur. Building on knowledge obtained from the participants' communication of specific points of resistance (*no*'s), the researchers continue, in a respectful, nondefensive manner, to learn more about the community's concerns for its young children and to identify connections between these concerns and their research interests. These exchanges can provide valuable information from the participant community about barriers and resources that are unknown to the

researcher. The researchers also have an opportunity in these exchanges to share their rationale for pursuing the research questions and their commitment to improving the lives of children through scientific inquiry. The trust and understanding that are made possible by these exchanges provide a context to move beyond the *no*'s to truly informed *yes*'s who help the community understand the potential power and benefit of quality research. These foundational partnership exchanges can lead to what is represented in Figure 2.2 as step 2: establishing a common purpose for scientific inquiry. This overarching, co-constructed purpose can then be formulated into specific objectives that meet the goals of both sets of partners. This reciprocal and respectful dialogue, which is the aim of this step, creates an opportunity for the community to direct the research resources and expertise that the scientists bring to the partnership to the development of beneficial service for their own members.

Step 3: Co-Construct the Research Agenda

In the first two steps, the researchers yielded their rights to unilaterally implement their research agenda and exercised their responsibility to understand the community's real resistance to research (step 1 *no*'s) and their genuine needs for relevant research (step 2 *yes*'s). The common purpose that comes out of these first two steps serves as the partnership base to co-construct a specific research agenda. The questionable research methods (e.g., culturally insensitive and inappropriate measures and procedures) and major gaps (e.g., neglected needs or community strengths and resources that were overlooked) identified in steps 1 and 2 can now inform a more responsive and productive set of exchanges about the research agenda.

In this third step of our transactional approach, it is the community participants' turn to yield their rights to control the research and to exercise their responsibility to understand from their research partners the *do*'s and *don't*'s (*yes*'s and *no*'s) of what constitutes quality research. In the context of respectful, two-way transactions, the community participants recognize the expertise and experience that the researchers bring to the research process. At this point, the researchers share their knowledge about what methods result in the highest-quality research. The researcher introduces important concepts that define the quality of research and dictate the essential *how*'s of research methods (e.g., reliability and validity of measures, random assignment of participants in randomized field trials, implications of small sample size). Through these communications, the community partners learn about the significance of various aspects of the research process, and based on this shared understanding, the partners begin to create a common language about the research methods that are necessary to achieve their common purpose.

The community participants at this stage in the process provide the researchers with an opportunity to voice their *no*'s and *yes*'s about the research methods. The community participants also accept the researchers' right to say no to aspects of a research agenda that they believe would threaten the internal and external validity of the research and impede achieving the common purpose for the research. The success of this step is dependent on honest and trusting negotiations of rights and responsibilities of the partners, which are recognized as necessary to achieve their common purpose.

Step 4: Build Research Capacity for Ongoing Investigation

A partnership foundation and active two-way exchanges are necessary to establish a rigorous and relevant research agenda, but they are not sufficient. Community/researcher partnerships must build the necessary capacity to address the inappropriate methods or gaps in the research knowledge base that have been identified by the partnership process. Once again the participant community must yield to the expertise and resources of the scientific community. It is here that the researchers assert their knowledge about how researcher measures and methods are developed. It is the researchers' responsibility to use the common language that was developed in step 3 to guide respectfully the development of necessary procedures. For example, where there are no measures empirically validated for the community, new measures can be co-constructed and tested in partnership. Where there is a need for an intervention (or a culturally appropriate intervention component), partners can develop it together. Here, having a common language facilitates the design and testing of common procedures that are necessary to achieve the partners' common purpose.

In these last two stages, it is important to note that the rights and responsibilities of the community participants and researchers are still in dynamic tension. Although the community is yielding its rights out of responsibility to produce rigorous research to benefit the community, it is not abdicating its rights. The community always reserves its rights to say no. By accepting responsibility to proceed in partnership, they are temporarily bracketing their rights, just as the scientists are doing in the first two steps of this partnership process. This bracketing will continue only insofar as the partnership does not violate the community's autonomy or sense of justice as it seeks to produce beneficial outcomes for children and families. After capacity for rigorous and relevant scientific inquiry is built, if the scientist betrays the community's initial trust and is no longer responsive to the partnership, the cycle is broken and the research ceases being productive. Conversely, if the research partnership has integrity (i.e., a common purpose, common language, and common procedures have been adhered to), the expected trajectory of the transactional relationships is positive and the cycle will continue. Such a cycle of productive transactions is now in place, not only to complete one project successfully but to foster and sustain a dynamic learning community to address a host of relevant concerns.

THE PARTNERSHIP-BASED TRANSACTIONAL MODEL: CASE ILLUSTRATIONS

The following section provides case illustrations of the partnership-based transactional model described above. The illustrations demonstrate the significant tension and resistance that existed between university researchers and parents and between university researchers and teachers in a large, urban Head Start program. Moreover, they show how this model seeks to balance the rights and responsibilities of applied developmental scientists and community participants to maximize scientific rigor and relevance.

Our two partnership-building examples took place within the context of a large research grant designed to investigate questions regarding the social and emotional development of urban, African American, Head Start children. To conduct this research, we planned to collect data on children's social and emotional development from key informants (parents and teachers) using popular, standardized behavioral rating scales approved by our IRB.

Step 1: Partnering With Resistance

At the start of our research, we were following the traditional modus operandi: We formed questions, successfully competed for funding, and began recruiting participants. We were moving forward with a perception that the approved research reflected the best interests of the community of participants and that all involved were interested in advancing *our* research agenda to improve Head Start. Our background and significance section detailed well the manifold risk factors that adversely affect poor, urban, Head Start children. Our agenda was straightforward: We needed to know more about the nature of these problems and the pathogenic processes that resulted in preschool dysfunction.

As we proceeded, our perception of our beneficent research mission was challenged in many ways. These challenges represented various expressions of both visible and invisible resistance to our research agenda. Research assistants set up tables outside of Head Start classrooms to review measures with potential participants and to seek signatures on a one-page informed consent document. Once parents signed the document, they were asked to complete a packet of assessments in exchange for a small sum of money to compensate them for time spent. Based on parental consent, teachers were approached and also given assessment packets to complete for a monetary exchange. Some parents came to the tables; many parents passed by. A few parents looked at some of the measures and were upset and asked intense questions about who was going to see this information and if it was going to be shared with the government. Standard confidentiality statements were repeated, but these parents were not satisfied. The tension generated by the parental mistrust of the research agenda caused the parent leadership to strongly discourage other parents from participating in our project. During this process, the teachers looked on but did not offer any helpful translation to parents to defend the merit of our research agenda.

At the core of the parents' visible resistance was one of our proposed child measures of emotional and behavioral functioning: the Child Behavior Checklist (Achenbach, 1991). This measure is a widely used checklist of psychiatric symptoms associated with children's mental disorders. Both parent and teacher groups used this measure to make their case against our larger research agenda. Through the eyes of the parent members of the low-income, African American communities we were entering, research team members were privileged outsiders—predominantly White, middle-class scientists—coming to study poor Black children and document the deficiencies and dysfunctions of the disadvantaged. Through the eyes of the teachers working in these communities, we were coming into the community to label children with psychiatric problems. They believed that we knew nothing about children's home, neighborhood, and classroom contexts and that despite our level of ignorance, we were entering the community to diagnose the children, to find fault with their families and the larger Head Start program, and then leave them with nothing useful when we were done with our study. Their considerable mistrust of our motives and methods brought us to a critical point: Do we take the *yes* participant responses we had collected thus far and complete our research as proposed, or do we pursue the *no*'s and seek to understand the nature of the resistance. Because the *no*'s were more representative of the population than the *yes*'s, we decided that it was more scientifically credible to temporarily suspend our research agenda and seek a dialogue with both sets of *no* participants. The research team members asked the Head Start administration for support to initiate two sets of dialogues to understand the resistance, one with parents through the Head Start Policy Council and one with a representative group of teachers. At this point, we informed our grant project officer of our decision and indicated that we needed to change our proposed timeline. We realized that the burden was on us to communicate clearly to our project officer that altering our timeline was an act respecting our Head Start community participants (i.e., taking heed and carefully considering their concerns) and therefore was intended to protect the scientific integrity of our study.

Elicit and respond to parent concerns. The Head Start Policy Council appointed a committee of parents to meet with the research team to review the measures that parents found offensive. From the outset, the committee expressed very strong negative reactions to the deficiency/pathological nature of a number of the measures. They found some of our questionnaires to be overly negative, depicting Head Start children in a stereotypical way that emphasized aggression and deficiencies, ignoring children's strengths. Committee members informed us that many Head Start parents lived in neighborhoods where residents had seen the Department of Human Services remove children from homes because of reported child and family problems. Therefore, they relayed that parents are suspicious of outsiders asking questions about matters of family or child functioning and are more likely to refuse to participate or to provide us with misinformation by giving what they perceived to be socially desirable responses.

These initial discussions about our chosen measures surfaced more general fears associated with research involvement and led to a broader discussion of their many negative feelings and misunderstandings about the goals and objectives of research projects. It soon became apparent that the prevailing sentiments in the community toward research were extremely negative. Parents and community advocates described past experiences as research "subjects," whereby researchers took data from the community but offered nothing in return. This is a common complaint among numerous ethnic minority communities in the United States, particularly on American Indian reservations and in Alaska Native villages; to guard against exploitation, numerous tribes and native villages have their own internal, tribally controlled IRBs. These outsiders, the parents explained, had no appreciation of the challenges they faced or the strengths they demonstrated in the face of those challenges.

These meetings served as the crucible for researcher-citizen partnership. Although the parents' resistance was somewhat daunting, we recognized that the intensity of their feelings was an indication of the depth of their concern for the children and families in their community and their account of injustices associated with research. We saw this passion as strength. We acknowledged the fears expressed and conveyed to the committee that our primary commitment was not to a preconceived research agenda but to working with them to create a relevant, shared, just research agenda that would benefit children and their families. We listened to the concerns of our community counterparts and responded by inviting them to work with us as research partners, not subjects. Inviting the community members to be partners transformed the unilateral threat they originally resisted into an opportunity to foster beneficial changes for the community. The emotion underlying their resistance could now energize their active participation in the subsequent phases of a partnership process; however, we had much work to do to counter misperceptions of research.

Partner with teacher resistance. Working with a representative group of teachers also surfaced resistance toward our initial research agenda and particularly toward the measures of child behavior. We discovered that teachers' responses to the rating instruments were reflective of a variety of concerns for the children in their classrooms. If we were to obtain accurate information regarding children's social and emotional functioning, we needed partnership relationships with this key group as well.

As with parents, we set up various meetings with Head Start teachers. During our initial meetings with them, teachers voiced significant concerns about the children with emotional and behavioral problems in their classroom. They felt that measures that label children were not developmentally appropriate and therefore not helpful. Next, the teachers drew our attention to the injustices in the special needs referral system in this large, urban school district Head Start program (Fantuzzo et al., 1999).

In partnership with this teacher group and the Head Start administration, two assessments were conducted to examine system-wide practices. The first studied the nature of children's problems formally referred by teachers for special needs services. According to this assessment, all referred children evidenced speech and language difficulties, with 70% identified as having speech-only difficulties and 30% of children displaying both speech and behavior problems. A second assessment was conducted to determine the validity of this referral process by independently surveying teachers regarding the nature and prevalence of children's difficulties. They were asked to nominate children in their classrooms who evidenced the greatest needs. This assessment revealed the opposite of the referral study. Findings indicated that 70% of children identified demonstrated emotional and behavioral problems, whereas only 30% evidenced emotional and behavioral problems with accompanying speech and language difficulties. These findings clearly indicated that the program's current system was biased in favor of identifying children as having speech and language difficulties and against identifying children as having emotional and behavioral problems. These results match national studies documenting underreporting of children's emotional and behavioral problems in early childhood programs (Yoshikawa & Knitzer, 1997).

In order to better understand this apparent resistance to reporting, we conducted exploratory, open-ended interviews with a representative group of teachers (Lutz, Fantuzzo, & McDermott, 2002). These interviews revealed that there were several reasons for this phenomenon of underreporting. These reasons included dissatisfaction with the system, concern with labeling children, concern with family reactions to labeling, problems attributed to classroom context, and concerns about the negative reflections on the teacher. Through substantial discussion with teachers, we learned that they were overwhelmed by the demands placed on them, that they felt unsupported to meet the needs of children in their classroom evidencing emotional and behavioral difficulties. Also, they indicated that the mental health services available to them were extremely difficult to access, and when they were able to access services, the interventions were not relevant to their work in the classroom. Therefore, they concluded that it was not beneficial to identify students ("label" them) if there was no relevant information produced to inform classroom intervention. We learned that teachers were filling out the instruments in a manner that effectively hid the children, masking children's real difficulties with a more socially acceptable problem, one for which services were currently being provided. Therefore, teachers' reactions to our proposed research were embedded within a larger systems context. Our research agenda threatened to exacerbate the resistance to identifying children having difficulties.

Responding to both parent and teacher *no*'s within this context demanded that we take the Child Behavior Checklist (CBCL) off the table. Through our extended conversations and rather intense exchanges with both groups of participants, we learned of parent and teacher feelings about our original research protocol. Parents expressed outright anger. For parents, the CBCL elicited such negative reactions that either they would refuse to participate or they would give false information to protect their children from misuse of information. Teachers' reactions were more subtle; they reluctantly agreed to complete the measure and then responded in ways that rendered the data invalid for a variety of reasons. For teachers, the CBCL was very similar to the screening instrument they had been using and would elicit the same kind of biased reporting that would lead to misdiagnosis. Of course, the logical outcome of both of these responses to the measure was information with questionable validity. Here, we realized that it was our responsibility as researchers to yield our rights to conduct scientific investigation in the name of relevance and validity. We recognized that responsibilities are not unidimensional. For example, it was necessary but insufficient to satisfy the requirements of the university institutional review board. The key to conducting ethical research within this community was to acknowledge the real resistance and be willing to respond to the genuine concerns of key informants in this project: Head Start parents and teachers. Our responses were important but insufficient to advance the research agenda. We needed to invite parents and teachers to help us form a co-constructed research agenda.

Step 2: Establishing Partnership Goals

In the previous step, we listened to and valued the perspectives of both participant groups as they questioned our motives and research practices. They shared the indignities and injustices that they had experienced in the past. Through these exchanges, they began to move from *no* assertions about research to questions regarding how research might be beneficial. It was at this critical point that we had the opportunity to invite the participant groups to consider constructing with us a genuine *yes* research agenda, an agenda that was designed to address research questions that were relevant to both the participant and scientific communities. These dialogues resulted in a recognition of what each set of partners had to contribute to a rigorous and relevant inquiry process designed to benefit Head Start children.

Because the concrete focus of the resistance for both parents and teachers was the proposed measures of children's social and emotional development, our initial discussions were about real issues regarding the availability of quality measures that were developmentally and culturally appropriate for minority Head Start children. The parents wanted to participate in a process that helped parents and teachers learn more about the strategies that socially competent children use to "get along" with their peers and build friendships and, conversely, what specific types of behaviors isolate children from play and friendships. The teacher participant group wanted to know how children adapt (or fail to adapt) to the daily routine challenges and demands of their preschool classrooms. They wanted to develop a better understanding of how children respond appropriately and inappropriately to common, daily classroom situations. They also wanted to learn ways that classroom situations could be altered to enhance preschool children's positive adjustment to the demands of the classroom learning environment.

We were very excited about these goals. Not only were they authentic expressions of the participant community, they also identified genuine gaps in the scientific knowledge base. Much of the measurement available was not developed for diverse Head Start populations of children (Fantuzzo & Mohr, 2000). Therefore, these exchanges helped us identify a common purpose for our collaboration that was worthwhile for both sets of partners. We collectively decided that we would work to create sensitive measures that were valid for Head Start children, measures that could inform improved practices and policies.

Step 3: Co-constructing a Research Agenda

Within the dynamic tension between rights and responsibilities that pervades the partnership process, the voices of community participants were instrumental in shaping a relevant, common purpose (steps 1 and 2). Now the expertise of the scientists was needed to guide co-construction of a rigorous research agenda. At this point, our common purpose was to construct culturally and developmentally appropriate, psychometrically sound measures of child functioning to inform Head Start practice. Steps 1 and 2 were essential in identifying the relevant *what*'s of the partnership-based research. Through step 3 and step 4, we focused on the *how*'s of the research. How do we proceed to use state-of-the-art methods to develop the most scientifically precise measurement that will yield the most valid information about diverse groups of low-income, minority children? At this phase in the process, community participants yielded their rights to unilaterally control the research process and recognized the scientists' expertise in measurement. The scientists responded by bringing their skills and knowledge of scale development to the fore. This involved identifying the necessary steps of a scientifically credible process and describing these steps in ways that provided a clear rationale for the community participants; this rationale had to make clear how the scientific process would support the participants' rights (beneficence, autonomy, and justice).

The primary purpose of this step was to co-construct the research process that the partners would follow to develop culturally sensitive measures for low-income, minority children. To accomplish this purpose, a set of guidelines for scale development was introduced to both sets of participants that was designed specifically to be responsive to cultural and child development issues. A workshop format was used with teachers and parents to share these guidelines and to create a common language with which we could carry out the research agenda.

Measurement development in partnership. We introduced a process for measurement development that was selected to maximize transactions between researchers and culturally diverse community participants (Gaskins, 1994). According to Gaskins there are at least five phases of the research process that are necessary to ensure cultural validity for any study that has as its focus a group of which the researcher is not a member. These are a hypothesis-generating phase, a category-generating phase, a measure-generating phase, a quantitative data–generating phase, and an interpretation-generating phase. The first phase involves learning about children's development within that culture and establishing partnerships with adult members of the culture to determine their perceptions of development. In the next phase, partners generate categories based on an understanding of the culture. Subsequently, measures are developed that reflect cultural norms and expectations. Once the information is collected with these measures, the final phase involves interpretation. Gaskins' recommendations for conducting research are consistent with ethological research methods, which have also been endorsed for studies involving minority preschool children (Pellegrini, 1992). An ethological approach is based on detailed, inductively derived descriptions of children's behavior in their

natural context rather than solely on existing theory and categorical systems that, largely, do not include nonmainstream groups (Pelligrini, 1992).

After discussing broadly the phases involved in constructing new measurement, we explained to partners in more detail what each phase would entail. During the hypothesis-generating phase, the focus is on content and cultural validity. In other words, the aim is to ensure that the content of the measure will have meaning for the cultural group and be relevant to the constructs the investigators intend to study. In this case, ethological methodology involves a preliminary step of unstructured observation during which a descriptive base of typical behavior patterns is compiled. Because ethological methods promote the inductive description and categorization of behaviors and minimize the extent to which preconceived, culture-laden conceptualizations are imposed on the phenomena of interest, they are a sensible first step to conducting research with understudied populations (Pelligrini, 1992). It is crucial at this phase to identify the important behaviors as they occur in relevant contexts (i.e., home and school); and as Gaskins points out, "One must look at the way children develop within the culture to be studied and the way that the adult members of that culture view development and socialization" (p. 317). We agreed that this process must be engaged in by both Head Start teachers and parents to ensure that the behaviors actually mean what the researchers and participants think they mean. We explained that at this phase, it is important to devote significant effort to first describing the phenomena of interest without making judgments about the categorization of children's behaviors. Then, after sufficient observations are conducted, partners can enter the category-generating phase. During this phase of the instrument development process, "categories are related to meaningful distinctions" among young children

(Gaskins, 1994, p. 320). This is the place where adaptive and maladaptive behaviors are distinguished. In our partnership process, teachers and parents would help us identify which observable behaviors were deemed as helpful or not helpful for children in a situation (which behaviors seemed to work for children and which did not). We then explained that after relevant categories are identified, representative behaviors can be sampled from each of the identified domains. These categories would eventually become the foundation for the development of our new measurement tools.

With respect to Gaskins' next phase, the measure-generating phase, we outlined that the goal is to generate an actual measure of the phenomenon of interest that is culturally unbiased, based on the above procedures. The behaviors thought to be representative of the identified domains are sampled from the above categories and translated into specific items. We would have to work together to ensure that these items are clear, understandable, nonoffensive, and take into consideration literacy levels of future participants. Efforts also would need to be made to prevent redundancy and create an appropriate response format for the respondents. The resulting combination of our co-constructed items and assurances should result in a culturally sensitive measure of the social and emotional development of young, low-income children.

During the last two phases, quantitative data–generating and interpretation-generating phases, efforts are aimed at "breaking up a unified whole into meaningful parts" (Gaskins, 1994, p. 321) and making sense of the findings. We explained that this necessarily involves subjecting the set of co-constructed items to a series of empirical tests to assure that the hypothesized dimensions (categories) are useful. For measurement development, this would involve two main activities: ensuring construct validity and assessing predictive validity. In our investigation of children's social and emotional development, we knew it would be important to determine if our co-constructed measure actually measured something meaningful. We had to explain to our partners the necessity of certain rigorous and time-consuming data collection/statistical methods to determine this (e.g., factor analysis). We discussed the importance of assessing underlying constructs, ensuring that the item sets we created actually were related in a meaningful way. We highlighted the need for large samples to uncover behavioral dimensions reliably. We also introduced teachers and parents to important terms that are used to describe the psychometric integrity of a scale. For instance, we explained why internal consistency of a scale was important and the significance of establishing the concurrent and predictive validity of a scale.

Step 4: Build Research Capacity for Ongoing Investigation

With a common purpose and a common language, we were ready to develop and validate measures for each participant group (common procedures). Our purpose for parents was to develop a behavioral rating scale that could be used by teacher and parents to provide good information on the adaptive and maladaptive behaviors that children show in their play interactions with peers in the school and home context. After a careful search of the research literature available in the early 1990s, we found that the supply of psychometrically sound preschool measures was very limited (Bracken, 1987).We identified existing measures that focused on competencies and conducted investigations to examine their appropriateness for use with Head Start children. We found some to be not valid (Fantuzzo, McDermott, Manz, Hampton, & Burdick, 1996, for African American Head Start children and others to not have comparable parent and teacher versions (Manz, Fantuzzo, & McDermott, 1999). Therefore, we decided in partnership to co-construct a new behavior-rating measure of children's social competence with parent and teacher versions: the Penn Interactive Peer Play Scale (PIPPS; Fantuzzo et al., 1995).

Development of the PIPPS. The research process outlined in step 3 guided the PIPPS's development. We obtained permission to videotape a variety of natural play sessions in Head Start. Videotapes were used by groups of parents, teachers, and researchers to identify relevant categories of behaviors that were associated with successful and unsuccessful peer play interactions. Behaviors were subsequently placed into either adaptive or maladaptive categories. Partners sampled behaviors from these categories to be included in the PIPPS. Then, peer play behaviors were selected if they could be observed in both home and school settings. The next step involved carefully developing the items and response format for the measure to ensure that they would have comparable meaning for the respondents. Incorporating teacher and parent input into each stage of development of this measure was intended to heighten researchers' sensitivity to meaningful cultural expressions contained within children's play and to assess play in a child's most predominant contexts, at home and in school. This step increased the likelihood of developing a common language that parents, teachers, and researchers could use to describe children's functioning.

After a 32-item measure was developed and field tested, partners collected data across a large representative sample of Head Start children, and factor analytic methods were used to uncover naturally emerging behavioral categories. Many studies since the measure's creation have documented its effectiveness for identifying children's strengths and needs during play with their peers, both at home and at school. These dimensions of peer play have demonstrated high reliability and strong validity, showing that they relate meaningfully to school readiness competencies (Fantuzzo, Sekino, & Cohen, 2004).

Development of the ASPI. Now we turn to our instrument development with our teacher partners. One of the major criticisms teachers had of widely used measures of emotional and behavioral adjustment was that they asked them to report on children's outward and inward states out of context. The teacher participant group wanted to know how children adapt (or fail to adapt) to the daily routine challenges and demands of their preschool classrooms. They wanted to develop a better understanding of how children respond, appropriately and inappropriately, in the context of common, daily classroom situations.

In our partnership discussions, we were guided by the teachers' assertions that measures need to describe children's responses to actual classroom situations as can be observed routinely by early childhood educators. Moreover, they stated that children's difficulties adjusting to the classroom should be determined through comparison with children who are ethnically and culturally similar. Both of these requirements were difficult to meet, given the available assessment technology. The most commonly employed assessment instruments for identifying children's social and emotional adjustment are psychiatric symptom checklists, such as the CBCL (McDermott, 1993), which we had discarded after our initial dialogue with parents and teachers. This type of measure has been criticized in the literature as inappropriate for use with Head Start children because it is illness-oriented, identifies children's behavior out of context, and requires teachers to infer children's internal thoughts or feelings (McDermott, 1993; Sherrod, 1999). Such information does not clarify whether the symptomatic behavior is isolated to specific circumstances or whether it is pervasive across varied situations. As we learned and others have experienced, teachers tend to underreport children's needs using this type of assessment for a variety of reasons (Mallory & Kerns, 1988; Yoshikawa & Knitzer, 1997).

We identified an alternative approach to child assessment developed by McDermott (1993). This approach requires teachers to report on adaptive and maladaptive behaviors of children observed across multiple routine classroom situations. In partnership, we agreed to test this method in Head Start and developed the Adjustment Scales for Preschool Intervention (ASPI; Lutz, Fantuzzo, & McDermott, 2002). Teachers and special needs coordinators in Head Start selected both the routine classroom situations and the adaptive and maladaptive behaviors associated with these situations. For example, a common routine situation in an early childhood classroom is "circle time." Circle time is a teacher-directed, large-group learning activity. Adaptive behaviors in this context include sitting quietly, paying attention, and keeping hands to oneself, whereas maladaptive behaviors include talking out of turn, disturbing neighbors, kicking feet, and gazing around the room. Next, our partners helped us script the language of the items so that children's behavior was described in the language of classroom teachers rather than clinical psychologists. The ASPI asks for teachers to report on behaviors that are readily observable within routine classroom situations, thus reducing the need for teachers to make inferences regarding children's internal mediating psychological processes. Moreover, the ASPI defines children's emotional and behavioral problems by the pervasiveness of difficulties across classroom situations rather than by the frequency or intensity of psychiatric symptoms. Several validity studies have since provided evidence that the ASPI is indeed reliable and valid for use with Head Start children (e.g., Fantuzzo, Bulotsky, McDermott, Mosca, & Lutz, 2003). This partnership process resulted in a measure that accurately identifies children with emotional and behavioral needs and that is more sensitive to teacher concerns about reporting.

Because of the commitments of both researchers and participants, we now have empirically tested measures with cultural relevance to study the social and emotional development of children in urban Head Start programs and to inform culturally responsive and developmentally appropriate intervention. Our collaborations continue. We continue to study the measures that have been created and to build new measurement and intervention capacity within the local program. There still exists a dynamic tension between the scientists and the participants, as both sets of partners seek a balance asserting and yielding rights and taking responsibility. The pursuit of relevance and rigor has become a joint commitment. This joint commitment has gone far beyond a single study and has evolved into a robust, learning community.

CONCLUSION

As indicated in Figure 2.2, the partnership process is ongoing and continues as long as the community participants trust that the scientists (a) have the best interest of the community participants at the core of the research, (b) are prepared to yield their rights to the voices of community participants regarding real or perceived inequities and injustices, and (c) are willing to build capacity to address participants' research questions.

The transactional approach illustrated in this chapter is built on a foundation of trust. Genuine partnership is possible only when sufficient trust has been established among all of the stakeholders in the partnership process: researchers, administrators, frontline staff (i.e., teachers and caseworkers), the recipients of services (i.e., parents), and concerned members of the community at large. This requires going beyond just recognizing participant-community resistance to understanding the implications of the resistance for partnership activity. Stakeholders' resistance should be viewed not as a bane or threat to the research process but as a valuable and appropriate manifestation of their commitment to protecting the interests of their particular group. Therefore, the first step in our model is to identify the substantive *no*'s and work to understand the sources of resistance.

Next, the partnership process should be grounded in an exchange of information that allows each group of stakeholders to voice its needs and expectations with respect to the prospective collaboration (*yes*'s). Researchers should attempt to understand the community's needs and respond to them by incorporating expressed concerns into the partnership agenda. This activity, in effect, involves connecting with the *yes*'s, who might have previously belonged to the *no* group but who also might still have some strong reservations about the research. The objective of this process is for the partnering groups to form and articulate a shared commitment to a constructive plan of action that addresses each group's concerns and therefore has a greater likelihood of being implemented successfully. By working through the participant community's fear and apprehension regarding research in the context of trust, researchers can gain an understanding of where participants see existing gaps and what they would like to see research accomplish in response to these identified needs.

Whereas in the first two steps of our model the researchers are yielding to the rights of the participant community, the latter two steps require that the participant community yield to the rights of the researchers to carry out credible scientific inquiry. They must learn about what research can accomplish and the methods that are necessary to answer co-constructed questions and then be willing to assume responsibility and participate in the actual work.

From a partnership-based perspective, scientists must yield their initial rights as investigators and recognize the rights of participants to legitimize their right to conduct scientific investigation. This leads to a process of ongoing negotiation that ultimately provides for shared responsibility and embodies the three guiding ethical principles of respect for autonomy, justice, and beneficence. Therefore, partnership is not just a means to an end; it is an end in itself. Research resulting from such an understanding and commitment is much more likely to be responsive to the needs of the participant community, aligning research, policy, and practice in a contextually appropriate way. Researchers committed to a partnership-based research agenda continue to work with their partners to create and maintain a common purpose, common language, and common procedures through uncommon collaboration.

REFERENCES

Achenbach, T. M. (1991). *Child behavior checklist.* Burlington: University of Vermont.

Bracken, B. A. (1987). Limitations of preschool instruments and standards for minimal levels of technical adequacy. *Journal of Psychoeducational Assessment, 5,* 313–326.

Bronfenbrenner, U., & Morris, P. (1998). The ecology of developmental processes. In W. Damon & R. Lerner (Eds.), *Handbook of child psychology* (pp. 993–1028). New York: Wiley.

Cicchetti, D., & Toth, S. L. (1997). Transactional ecological systems in developmental psychopathology. In S. S. Luthar, J. A. Burack, D. Cicchetti, & J. R. Weisz (Eds.), *Developmental psychopathology: Perspectives on adjustment, risk, and disorder* (pp. 317–349). New York: Cambridge University Press.

National Commission for Protection of Human Subjects of Biomedical and Behavioral Research. (1978). *The Belmont Report: Ethical principles and guidelines for the protection of human subjects research.* (DHEW Publication No. (OS) 78–0012). Washington, DC: Government Printing Office.

Department of Health and Human Services. (2001, August). Title 45 Public Welfare, Part 46, *Code of federal regulations, protection of human subjects.* Washington, DC: Government Printing Office.

Fantuzzo, J., Bulotsky, R., McDermott, P., Mosca, S., & Lutz, M. N. (2003). A multivariate analysis of emotional and behavioral adjustment and preschool educational outcomes. *School Psychology Review, 32,* 185–203.

Fantuzzo, J. W., McDermott, P., Manz, P. H., Hampton, V. R., & Burdick, N. A. (1996). The Pictorial Scale of Perceived Competence for Young Children: Does it work with low-income urban children? *Child Development, 67,* 1071–1084.

Fantuzzo, J., & Mohr, W. (2000). Pursuit of wellness in Head Start: Making beneficial connections for children and families. In D. Cicchetti, J. Rapapport, I. Sandler, & R. Weissberg (Eds.), *The promotion of wellness in children and adolescents* (pp. 341–370). Washington, DC: CWLA Press.

Fantuzzo, J., Sekino, Y., & Cohen, H. (2004). An examination of the contributions of interactive peer play to salient classroom competencies for urban Head Start children. *Psychology in the Schools, 41,* 323–336.

Fantuzzo, J., Stoltzfus, J., Lutz, M. N., Hamlet, H., Balraj, V., Turner, C., et al. (1999). An evaluation of the special needs referral process for low-income preschool children with emotional and behavioral problems. *Early Childhood Research Quarterly, 14,* 465–482.

Fantuzzo, J., Sutton-Smith, B., Coolahan, K. C., Manz, P. H., Canning, S., & Debnam, D. (1995). Assessment of preschool play interactions behaviors in young low-income children: Penn Interactive Peer Play Scale. *Early Childhood Research Quarterly, 10,* 105–120.

Fisher, C. B. (1999). Relational ethics and research with vulnerable populations. *Reports on research involving persons with mental disorders that may affect decision-making capacity* (Vol. 2, pp. 29–49). Commissioned Papers by the National Bioethics Advisory Commission. Rockville, MD.

Fisher, C. B. (2002). Participant consultation: Ethical insights into parental permission and confidentiality procedures for policy relevant research with youth. In R. M. Lerner, F. Jacobs, & D. Wertlieb (Eds.), *Handbook of applied developmental science* (Vol. 4, pp. 371–396). Thousand Oaks, CA: Sage.

Fisher, C. B., Hoagwood, K., Boyce, C., Duster, T., Frank, D. A., Grisso, T., et al. (2002). Research ethics for mental health science involving ethnic minority children and youths. *American Psychologist, 57*(12), 1024–1040.

Fisher, C. B., & Lerner, R. M. (1994). *Applied developmental psychology.* Mahwah, NJ: Lawrence Erlbaum.

Fisher, C. B., & Lerner, R. M. (2004). Introduction. In C. B. Fisher & R. M. Lerner (Eds.), *Encyclopedia of applied developmental science.* Thousand Oaks, CA: Sage.

Fisher, C. B., Murray, J. P., Dill, J. R., Hagen, J. W., Hogan, M. J., Lerner, R. M., et al. (1993). The national conference on graduate education in the applications of developmental science across the life span. *Journal of Applied Developmental Psychology, 14,* 1–10.

Garbarino, J. (1995). *Raising children in a socially toxic environment.* San Francisco: Jossey-Bass.

Gaskins, S. (1994). Integrating interpretive and quantitative methods in socialization research. *Merrill-Palmer Quarterly, 40,* 313–333.

Geertz, C. (2000). *Available light: Anthropological reflections on philosophical topics.* Princeton, NJ: Princeton University Press, p. 23.

Knitzer, J. (2000). *Using mental health strategies to move the early childhood agenda and promote school readiness.* New York: National Center for Children in Poverty.

Lamb-Parker, F., Greenfield, D. B., Fantuzzo, J. F., Clark, C., & Coolahan, K. C. (2000). Shared decision making in early childhood research: Foundation for successful community-university partnerships. *NHSA Dialog, 3,* 234–257.

Lerner, R. M., Fisher, C. B., & Weinberg, R. A. (2000). Towards a science for and of the people: Promoting civil society through the application of developmental science. *Child Development, 71,* 11–20.

Lutz, M., Fantuzzo, J., & McDermott, P. (2002). Multisituational measures of the emotional and behavioral adjustment problems of low-income preschool children. *Early Childhood Research Quarterly, 17*(3), 338–355

Mallory, B. L., & Kerns, G. M. (1988). Consequences of categorical labeling of preschool children. *Topics in Early Childhood Special Education, 8,* 39–50.

Manz, P., Fantuzzo, J., & McDermott, P. (1999). The parent version of the preschool social skills rating scale: An analysis of its use with low-income, ethnic-minority children. *School Psychology Review, 28,* 493–504.

McDermott, P. A. (1993). National standardization of uniform multisituational measures of child and adolescent behavior pathology. *Psychological Assessment, 5,* 413–424.

National Advisory Mental Health Council's Workgroup on Child and Adolescent Mental Health Intervention Development and Deployment. (2001). *Blueprint for change: Research on child and adolescent mental health.* Washington, DC: Author.

National Center for Children in Poverty. (2004). Low income children in the United States. [Document available at www.nccp.org/media/cpf04-text.pdf]

National Institute of Child Health and Human Development Early Child Care Research Network. (2002). Early child care and children's development prior to school entry: Results from the NICHD study of early child care. *American Educational Research Journal, 39,* 133–164.

National Research Council. (1998). *Preventing reading difficulties in young children.* Washington, DC: National Academy Press.

National Research Council. (2000). *From neurons to neighborhoods: The science of early childhood development.* Washington, DC: National Academy Press.

National Research Council. (2001). *Eager to learn: Educating our preschoolers.* Washington, DC: National Academy Press.

Pelligrini, A. (1992). Ethological studies of the categorization of children's social behavior in preschool: A review. *Early Education and Development, 3,* 284–297.

Sherrod, L. R. (1999). A commentary on "Head Start and mental health: An argument for early screening and intervention" by Edward G. Feil. *NHSA Dialogue, 2,* 412–415.

U.S. Department of Education. (2004). *No Child Left Behind Act.* [Document available at www.ed.gov/nclb/landing.jhtml#]

Yoshikawa, H., & Knitzer, J. (1997). *Lessons from the field: Head Start mental health strategies to meet changing needs.* New York: National Center for Children in Poverty.

Zigler, E., & Styfco, S. J. (Eds.). (2004). *The Head Start debates.* Baltimore: Paul H. Brookes.

CHAPTER 3

First, Do No Harm

Culturally Centered Measurement for Early Intervention

NANCY A. BUSCH-ROSSNAGEL

First, do no harm! This fundamental principle guiding federal regulations and organizational standards for research protections is often taken for granted by psychologists and others involved with the evaluation of early interventions. Members of the academy assume that intervention research is beneficial, if not directly to research participants, at least for society as a whole, which supposedly draws on our data to improve services for children and families. My experience in research with Latinos, however, has suggested that we need to reexamine this assumption. When conducting research involving ethnic minority populations, we need to keep the goal of "First, do no harm" in mind at every stage of the research process from the design selected for the project through the instrument development to the dissemination of the results.

The premise of early intervention is that we can make a difference in children's lives. In my case, that basic premise was established in the summer of 1965 when I participated as an aide in what I thought was just another one of my mother's preschool programs. Perhaps some of you recognize that summer of '65 was anything but "just another preschool program." Yes, I was one of those bright-eyed, idealistic individuals participating in the first summer of Head Start. And I just knew that the program would change the lives of those young children forever.

That involvement as a Head Start volunteer probably shaped my choice of psychology as a major and after my master's, led to my first job as a head teacher in a laboratory preschool in Canada. There I saw in practice what I learned in theory in graduate training: that basic theory and research provide hypotheses about how, when, and where to intervene. I started a toddler program in the preschool and, remembering the importance of maternal involvement in my Head Start experience, started a mothers' program as well.

But being in Canada taught me another lesson. In exploring early intervention programs for its children living in poverty, Canada was determined to learn from America's successes and failures (Ryan, 1972). That is where I first heard about program evaluations and the infamous Westinghouse Report (Westinghouse Learning Corporation,

1969). This report was an evaluation of the effectiveness of Head Start and suggested that summer programs like the one in which I participated really did not make that much difference in children's lives.

I went to a conference to learn more about Canada's early intervention programs and was shocked to learn that an intervention had actually been terminated because the preliminary data analysis suggested that the children in the intervention scored lower on measures of competence than the controls. Today, the public has more experience with intervention trials being stopped, but in those days, no one ever stopped a scientific study!

This intervention into an intervention occurred at about the same time as other results (Susan Gray's studies at Peabody and the Perry Preschool Project of David Weikart) were showing that my earlier optimistic assumption was right: Early intervention can make a difference (Bronfenbrenner, 1975). But we need to temper that optimism with the realization that the difference might be negative. Thus, when I left Canada to complete my doctorate, I was convinced that to do no harm required rigorous program evaluation as a component within early interventions.

THE FALLACY OF RELYING ON CLASSIC PSYCHOLOGICAL EXPERIMENTAL DESIGN

Most program evaluations rely on traditional research design paradigms, with the experimental method being the gold standard with which all other designs are compared (McCall & Green, 2004). Experimental studies have three characteristics: theory-driven hypotheses, random assignment of participants to intervention or control groups, and consistency or uniformity of the intervention. Indeed, many of the criticisms of the Westinghouse Report focused on the design

of the study, particularly emphasizing that the study did not utilize random assignment to form the control and experimental groups and that the Head Start programs themselves were not uniform across or within programs.

The classic experiment is a powerful tool and the only way to establish causality. When an attempt is made to apply it to many of the basic questions of human development, however, its limitations become apparent. For example, if we are interested in sex differences, we can't randomly assign sex to research participants. For researchers like me interested in ethnic minority groups, culture and ethnicity are particularly problematic for random assignment. A research design in which culture or ethnicity is the independent variable with which the dependent variables of behavior are expected to covary will only be a "pseudo experiment" unless the project involves the manipulation of culture or ethnicity, perhaps through a simulation.

We rarely use simulations to enable random assignment of ethnicity to children and families, but culture or ethnicity is often used as an independent variable to examine the population generalizability of tests or previous research results (Busch-Rossnagel, 1992). Research conducted to examine population generalizability can yield two results: significant differences between the groups or no significant group differences. The finding of no significant group differences is essentially meaningless because it is a test of the null hypothesis.

The finding of group differences is potentially problematic. Ethnicity is so confounded with other variables such as language use, childrearing attitudes, social economic status, and so on, that we really do not know how to interpret a significant difference between ethnic groups. Consider for example the results of a study by Luis Laosa (1980) who observed differences between Chicana and Anglo mothers' teaching behaviors. When he controlled for differences in educational level of the two groups of mothers, the ethnic group difference disappeared. Thus, when we equate naturally occurring cultural or ethnic groups with the groups that are formed by random assignment in an experiment and draw conclusions about group differences, we run the risk of doing harm by reporting ethnic differences that are likely the result of a confounded variable. These differences often turn into stereotypes about ethnic minorities rather than correct ascriptions of cultural influences on parental approaches to their children's education.

CHARACTERISTICS OF RESEARCH ON LATINOS

In the early '90s, I thought I was poised to begin an intervention study with Latino families. Through the Hispanic Research Center at Fordham, I had been exposed to the demographic profile of Puerto Rican and Dominican families in the Bronx and was concerned about the educational attainment of children in these families. Remembering my experience in Head Start, I sought to use my training in life span development to modify the parenting practices of Latino families to influence their children's development. Trying to expand my knowledge of early childhood socioemotional development to include educationally at-risk Latino children, I started reading more deeply in the literature on Latino families with the goal of developing theory-driven hypotheses for the intervention study (the second characteristic of experimental research, McCall & Green, 2004). Rather than creating experimental hypotheses, I quickly learned that the field of development psychology knew little about Latinos, in general, and even less about their parenting practices and their children's academic success.

Research Inclusion and Representation

I did a context analysis of developmental literature to assess the representation of Latinos (Busch-Rossnagel, 1992). At that time, *Developmental Psychology* and *Child Development* were the two leading journals in the field. In the years 1988, 1989, and 1990, most of the authors did not report the ethnicity of the participants. When the authors did report ethnicity, only 6% of the articles in *Developmental Psychology* and 8% of the articles in *Child Development* included **any** Latinos. Examining the issue of *Developmental Psychology* with the greatest percentage of articles including any Latinos, the percentage of Latinos in all the samples combined was .004% of all research participants in the journal issue, at a time when Latinos represented almost 10% of the population and were the fastest growing ethnic minority!

Inclusion in research is not necessarily representation. How valid were the studies including Latinos? In April 1990, *Child Development* published a special issue devoted to ethnic minority children that included seven empirical studies with Latinos. These seven studies, however, did not report the percentage of participants tested in Spanish versus English, although Latinos are often characterized as a linguistic minority (Marín & Marín, 1991). Six of the seven studies used lower- or lower middle-class subjects, but less than half recognized the possible confounded relationship between ethnicity and socioeconomic status. I concluded that the literature was not helpful in providing the necessary foundation theory–driven hypotheses. So, instead of an intervention, I proposed to embark on a longitudinal study of mastery motivation in Puerto Rican and Dominican families.

A CULTURALLY CENTERED APPROACH TO MASTERY MOTIVATION

Mastery motivation is defined as the impetus to achieve and improve one's skills in the absence of any physical reward. The mastery of the environment seems to be the reward in itself. Another way of thinking about mastery motivation is "stick-to-itiveness" (Busch-Rossnagel, 1997). This motivation to act on the environment is a primitive biological endowment, but research has also suggested that aspects of mastery motivation can be acquired. The contingency between the child's action and the outcome produces pleasure in the child, and awareness of the contingency increases motivation. The acquisition process is also social. The encouragement of others provides information about successes and becomes internalized as development occurs. The child who does not receive praise for independent acts will be less likely to develop internal self-praise and thus will continue to be dependent on external sources of motivation (Busch-Rossnagel, Knauf-Jensen, & DesRosiers, 1995).

A Rationale for Studying Mastery Motivation in Latinos

Why do I think mastery motivation is a concept worth investigating? I believe that mastery motivation will help us understand children's success in school. Individuals succeed in school and other endeavors, not just because of cognitive or social abilities but also because they have high levels of achievement motivation, and mastery motivation has been linked with achievement motivation (Dweck & Elliott, 1983). Within a more proscribed age period, research in toddlerhood has shown that mastery motivation will predict later cognitive abilities (Yarrow, Klein, Lomonaco, & Morgan, 1975). Achievement motivation and cognitive abilities are good predictors of school success. Thus, if we can influence levels of mastery motivation, we should be able to foster children's success in school.

This issue of school success is particularly intriguing for ethnic groups in this country. In particular, Latinos have a lower level of school achievement than other ethnic minority groups (U.S. Bureau of the Census, 2001), and this level of achievement is at odds with the value placed on education in the traditional Latino cultures (Fracasso & Busch-Rossnagel, 1994). Indeed, *No te lo puede quitar nadie* ("No one can take that from you") is a saying frequently repeated to children when urging them to pay attention to their studies.

Although my goal is to be able to use understanding of mastery motivation to improve the school success of Latinos, that is not why I originally chose Latinos as a population for the study of mastery motivation. Indeed, work on differing levels of school achievement, or even differing levels of mastery motivation across ethnic groups, would be exactly the type of pseudo experiment that is fatally flawed and potentially harmful because of its lack of internal validity due to the potential confounds between ethnicity and other variables such as education (Busch-Rossnagel, 1992). Instead, what I hope to articulate in this chapter is an example of how I believe research with differing ethnic or cultural groups should be conducted.

I involved samples of Puerto Ricans, Dominicans, and Mexicans in the United States and in their native countries to study mastery motivation, not only to provide a foundation for early intervention with these populations but because the Latino cultures represent a *contrast* to the predominant European American culture of our society. Specifically, the predominant Anglo-American culture has been characterized as an individualistic culture, one that emphasizes independence and the separation from relationships such as family, community, and clan. In contrast, Latino cultures are seen as collectivistic or interdependent with an emphasis on familial and communal relatedness (Triandis, Bontempo, Villareal, Asai, & Lucca, 1988). In terms of mastery motivation, the contrast between the child's independent efforts to learn, which have characterized most of mastery motivation research, and the possibility of cooperative attempts may open up new avenues for educational interventions heretofore ignored in the majority culture

Domains of Mastery Motivation

The question of cultural differences in individual versus collective or independent versus interdependent effort influenced my conceptualization of mastery motivation to include multiple domains for expression of mastery motivation. The first domain is *object-oriented persistence*. Most of the work done on mastery motivation has focused on children working by themselves to explore and use a toy. Examples of mastery motivation in this domain would be learning to put pieces in puzzles or finding out how a toy CD player worked. The method used to measure motivation is to quantify the child's persistence in working on a moderately difficult task and their pleasure while doing so, particularly noting smiles or claps when a solution was achieved. This is the individualized approach to mastery motivation (MacTurk, Morgan, & Jennings, 1995).

The notions of mastery motivation can be expanded to include not only actions with toys or objects but also actions directed toward people, or motivation within the second domain, *social mastery motivation*. What we term social mastery motivation can be indexed by the child's attempts to initiate, maintain, and influence interactions with others (Busch-Rossnagel, 1997). I am intrigued by the idea that social mastery motivation may be more compatible with collective cultures than object-oriented persistence.

In my thinking on mastery motivation, I added a third domain, that of *self mastery motivation*. This conceptualization is the result of looking at the literature in mastery motivation within the context of the six dimensions of self-concept (DesRosiers & Busch-Rossnagel, 1998). The motivational component of self-concept, termed self-assertion, is behaviorally expressed through autonomy, or the child's independent effort. Such autonomy is a key component of the definition of object-oriented mastery motivation. The emotional dimension of self-concept, first appearing between 27 and 36 months, is termed self-evaluation, of which pride and shame are operational expressions. The positive affective expression of object-oriented persistence is sometimes called pride, and the operational definition of *pride* and *shame* from either perspective requires comparison of an outcome with an achievement standard. Pride results from success in meeting a standard, whereas shame occurs when the standard is not met. The social dimension of self-concept is self-regulation, or compliance. The development of self-regulation, as expressed by compliance with requests and social norms, may confound the measurement of social mastery motivation.

The Developmental Nature of Mastery Motivation

In addition to exploring multiple domains, my approach stresses the developmental nature of mastery motivation (Busch-Rossnagel, 1997). These developmental changes occur both across and within the age periods. I am interested in the toddler period, which I operationalize as being from 15 to 42 months. During this period, there are probably three different phases and two transitions of mastery motivation. The first transition occurs between 17 and 22 months and involves a change from exploration and preference for novelty (the first phase) to a preference for challenging tasks and goal-directed activity, coupled with pleasure for success or frustration and sadness at failure (the second phase). The second transition, occurring between 32 and 36 months, involves the mastery of sequential, multipart tasks, the acquisition of standards, and pride when those standards are achieved and shame when they are not (the third phase). The focus on the age period from 15 to 42 months is designed to allow the examination of both of these transitions. I am particularly interested in transitions because they probably hold the key to understanding influences on mastery motivation and ultimately to any interventions that might be suggested by this work.

The Socializing Environment

This emphasis on transitions highlights a third characteristic of my approach to mastery motivation, namely the importance of the socializing environment. The socializing environment includes mothers and other caregivers who affect the context of the child's attempts at mastery (Busch-Rossnagel et al., 1995). I have identified three dimensions of the socializing environment related to mastery motivation. One dimension contains the *inanimate objects* that might be seen in the provision of appropriately stimulating toys. The second dimension, the affective nature of the interaction in the caregiver-child dyad, is termed *emotional communication* and seen in smiles and praise. The third dimension, the didactic or *instrumental interchanges* in the dyad, has been operationalized by contingent responses, specific feedback, and demonstrations. Each of these variables has been shown to affect the development of mastery motivation during

the toddler years in European American samples.

Thus, there are three characteristics of my approach to mastery motivation: multiple domains, developmental changes, and the importance of the socializing environment. Much of this approach still remains at the abstract level because of the limitations in operational definitions of key constructs such as social mastery motivation and the socializing environment, and this lack of measures is particularly problematic for Latino populations.

DEVELOPMENT OF MEASURES OF MASTERY MOTIVATION FOR LATINO POPULATIONS

A decade ago, when I thought I was ready to undertake a study of mastery motivation in Latino children and families, I was lucky that the National Institute of Child Health and Human Development (NICHD) issued a call for studies on normative development in ethnic minority children. As I prepared the grant, however, I realized that new culturally centered instruments were needed before I could embark on a longitudinal study. Fortunately, I was able to convince the study section reviewers of this as well (Busch-Rossnagel, 1998).

The aims of the grant were chosen to provide a basis for the development of culturally centered measures. We started with the simple identification of child behaviors desired by Puerto Rican and Dominican parents (aim 1) and of the childrearing used by these Latino parents to achieve those child behaviors (aim 2). This information formed the basis for our instrument development efforts to fit the concepts of our model. As seen in Figure 3.1, the developmental contextual model of our research proposes that culture influences the socializing environment, which in turn influences the

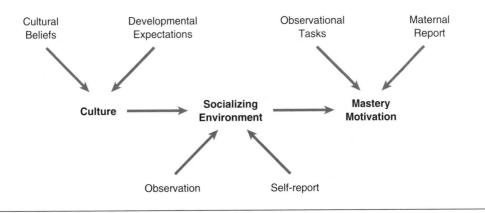

Figure 3.1   Developmental Contextual Model of Research

development of mastery motivation in children. Each construct in the model (culture, socializing environment, and mastery motivation) was to be assessed by two measures (one observational, one self-report when possible), so the other aims of the grant were to develop culturally centered measures of culture and the socializing environment (aim 3), and mastery motivation (aim 4). This next section of this chapter will discuss the development of the measure of the Socializing Environment Questionnaire (SEQ) as an example of these instrument development efforts.

Focus Groups as a Substitute for Ethnography

At the time the grant started, I had just completed the review of the socializing environment for mastery motivation, which identified the three dimensions just discussed (inanimate objects, emotional communication, and instrumental interactions). Most researchers in such a situation would have focused their instrument development efforts on those three dimensions. Please remember, however, that I critiqued the developmental literature because the samples do not often include minorities. For mastery motivation,

I had to question whether conclusions from middle-class European American families with nonworking mothers who have the time to participate in longitudinal research studies will generalize to lower-class families from collectivistic cultures. Specifically, the review that identified the three dimensions was not based on research with Latinos, so I didn't know whether the three dimensions adequately characterized the Latino socializing environment. Thus, I needed to start my work on instrument development at a more basic, descriptive level.

One approach to description of the socializing environment would be ethnography or participant observation in which a researcher immerses herself in the daily life of the setting she is trying to understand. This approach yields detailed observations of parenting practices but is very time-consuming. I substituted focus groups for these lengthy ethnographic techniques. In these endeavors, I was fortunate that Fordham has a diverse student body, with Latinos being the predominant ethnic minority group. The team for the research grant included several graduate and undergraduate students who were bilingual and bicultural, being Puerto Rican, Dominican, Cuban, Argentine, and Mexican in family heritage.

First steps. As a first step, we talked to Latino mental health providers to get vignettes of children's behaviors that were related to socioemotional development. Then, we asked focus groups of Latino mothers and grandmothers to respond to these vignettes. Do you see these behaviors in your children? What other similar behaviors do you see? The vignettes were refined after more discussion with Latino mental health providers, and after some preliminary focus group discussions, we chose six domains of development associated with mastery motivation: object-oriented persistence, social mastery with adults, social mastery with peers, autonomy, pride, and compliance. This is an example of a vignette describing low social mastery with peers: *Ana is a 3½-year-old girl who plays by herself most of the time. Her parents try to get her to play with other children, but often she simply goes back to playing by herself with her favorite toy.*

Coding and creating culturally centered measures. The next focus groups used vignettes in these six areas and asked parents how they would respond to these behaviors. We also asked whether these were desirable behaviors. After the tapes of the focus group discussions were transcribed (and translated, if necessary), content analysis was performed on the statements. This coding revealed statements about behaviors the mothers and grandmothers reported using, what they had seen other parents do, child behaviors that they desired, and childrearing values.

The statements about desired child behaviors and values were used to create measures of the culture; the statements parents made about their own behaviors and about the behaviors of other parents were used to develop the SEQ. The coding of the content analysis showed that six specific behaviors accounted for approximately 50% of the statements parents made about their own behaviors. These were directives (14%),

compliance (10%), tolerance (9%), help (8%), explanations (8%), and bargaining (5%). The statements made by the focus group participants about the behaviors of other parents again included a high percentage of directives (17%), but the rest of the behaviors were different. These statements were coded as referring to physical punishment (11%), verbal punishment (9%), negative physical interventions (8%), and refusals (9%). Obviously, we had a little impression management going on in the discussions, but the inclusion of behaviors likely to be seen as negative in the discussion of *other* parent behaviors suggested that the focus group discussions served the purpose of eliciting an adequate sample of possible parenting behaviors for inclusion in an instrument to assess the socializing environment.

In creating the SEQ, we used these most frequently cited behaviors from both the parents themselves and for other parents as the first set of parenting behaviors. The focus group discussions thus led us to create a test blueprint (see Figure 3.2) that assessed nine parent behaviors within the six domains of socioemotional development. For the six domains, we refined 18 vignettes from the focus groups and then asked graduate students to assess the content validity of the domains, using the index of item-objective congruence. The two vignettes with the highest indexes were selected for each domain; these indexes ranged from .75 to .98 for the 12 vignettes.

The next step was to create response items to tap each of the parenting behaviors for each vignette, for example a bargaining response to an autonomy vignette. When possible, we used specific wording from the focus groups to create the initial set of items. Using the mothers' own words demonstrated our commitment to the mothers as partners in the research process—and when we took the instruments back to the centers for the mothers to debrief the mothers, they often recognized their own wording.

Test Blueprint for SEQ

	Object	Social-Adults	Social-Peers	Autonomy	Pride & Shame	Compliance
Directive						
Explain						
Bargain						
Threat						
– Physical						
Punishment						
+ Physical						
Patience						
Compliance						

Figure 3.2   Test Blueprint for the Socializing Environment Questionnaire

Creating Instruments in Two Languages

Because we were working with populations in which English was often a second language and we wanted to be able to collect data in the country of origin, we needed to have measures available in both English and Spanish. The easiest way to do this is with a simple translation, done by an individual with fluency in both languages.

Translation is not an exact process, so the process often includes having a number of bilingual individuals undertake the translation to achieve a consensus. Unfortunately, the result is likely to be phrases in the second language that are not true to the intent of the English measure because of the lack of precision in the original English version. Another problem is that the most precise words are often less commonly used in everyday interactions, so their use in a psychological measure increases the reading level, and the difficulty, of the measure.

A second way of approaching translation is through the process of *back translation,* which is also known as double translation. For example, to create a Spanish version of an English measure, a bilingual person first translates the English version into Spanish, and this Spanish translation is then translated back into English by a second bilingual person. This completes the back, or double, translation. The back translation (which is in English) is compared with the original English text. If the two versions are different, the Spanish version is altered to more closely approximate the original English. The altered Spanish version is then subjected to another back translation to English.

Back translation through several iterations is usually seen as the best practice to develop linguistically equivalent versions of measures. Because only the Spanish version is modified, however, and the English version is not changed, back translation has limitations. When the original English measure is standardized and cannot be modified without jeopardizing the psychometric information gathered on the standardized measure, then iterative back translation must suffice to protect the standardization.

When both versions of the instruments are being developed simultaneously, a better option is available. This is the process of *decentering* (Werner & Campbell, 1973). On the surface, the process of decentering is the same as the iterative process of back translation. The difference is that when comparing versions, either the Spanish or the English version may be modified to enhance the match between the two. When discrepancies exist between the two versions, researchers can discuss the intent of the item, rewrite the item for clarification, and then translate and back translate again.

In this way, each round of translation informs the development process for both versions of the questionnaire and often has the effect of clarifying the focus of the items. Decentering is likely to affect the development of a measure because it clarifies the linguistic boundaries of the constructs and thus is likely to lead to culturally centered measures. In the case of the SEQ, these items were subjected to the decentering process to create English and Spanish versions simultaneously. The decentering process continued through several iterations until the final result is equivalent versions in both Spanish and English.

After decentering, we gave both the Spanish and English versions to try-out subjects; some of these individuals were fluent in both Spanish and English and responded to both versions of the questionnaire. Examination of these preliminary data suggested that the Spanish-English equivalence was pretty good but that parents didn't differentiate between negative physical interventions and physical punishments or between parent compliance and tolerance. We collapsed these behaviors, so seven parental response categories remained.

Reliability and Validity of the SEQ

Using a different set of expert raters, we examined the content validity of these items (parenting behaviors in response to a vignette describing child behavior), again using the index of item-objective congruence. It is interesting to look at the responses with the lowest and highest indexes, which were both for a positive physical intervention. The lowest index was to a vignette describing autonomy, which was as follows: *Blanca is a 3-year-old who is always doing something and looks for every opportunity to be involved in everything that is going on. For instance, last night when the family was getting ready to have dinner, Blanca insisted on bringing the dishes to the table, saying, "I do it." Blanca seemed to enjoy this activity although her parents had to wait a while longer to sit down to eat.* The positive physical response was *Hand her just her own plate to bring to the table,* and this response was confused with other parenting behaviors, such as patience or bargaining.

The highest index involved the following social mastery with peers vignette: *Marcos is an only child who loves to watch his three cousins play and pulls his mother to come closer to the group of playing kids. However, Marcos will not join in the play even though his cousins are about the same age. His parents are not sure of what to do.* The response was *Start to play with his three cousins so that Marcos will follow.* The index was 1.0, so the raters clearly saw this as a positive physical intervention. What the variability in indexes within domains suggests is that some responses don't fit every domain. For example, we had trouble thinking of physical punishment responses to the social mastery vignettes.

Seventy-five of the 84 item-objective indexes were above .70, and the medians were above .75 (see Table 3.1). Based on this additional evidence for the content validity of

Table 3.1   Validity and Reliability of the SEQ

Parental Response	Item-Objective Congruence (Median)	Coefficient Alpha	2-Week Stability
+			
Directive	.89	.61	.67
Explain	.82	.70	.61
Bargain	.83	.76	.83
Threat	.78	.74	.76
Punishment	.88	.75	.72
Positive physical intervention	.88	.57	.61
Patience/ Compliance	.94	.65	.64

the SEQ, we proceeded to obtain preliminary reliability evidence with this version of the SEQ (Garcia & Busch-Rossnagel, 1996). Our participants for this reliability study were 90 mothers with toddlers between the ages of 15 and 48 months from New York City and Los Angeles. Most of the participants were Latinas (59), but we also included Anglos, African Americans, and Asian Americans. The median level of education was less than a high school diploma.

We collected two types of reliability, internal consistency and 2-week test-retest stability. As seen in Table 3.1, the coefficient alphas ranged from .57 to .76 for the seven parenting behaviors. Sixteen of the 19 mothers also completed the SEQ 2 weeks later. For this small sample, the correlations between time 1 and time 2 ranged from .61 to .83 across the seven parenting behaviors.

One notable aspect of these reliability data is that the alphas and the stability coefficients are fairly similar. Alphas are usually higher than stabilities, suggesting that we still have some work to do on internal consistency. Considering that the test blueprint examined the seven parent behaviors across the six domains of mastery motivation, we are still somewhat uncertain about the

appropriate scales for reducing the data. Our examination of the focus group responses showed us that parents said that their behavior would differ depending on the domain. For example, parents cited more use of directives and bargaining in the domain of object-oriented persistence, whereas physical interventions were used in the social mastery domain. Thus, we probably should not be collapsing parenting behaviors across all domains of child mastery motivation, as we are here.

Parenting Clusters

Instead, there are probably ways that the parent behaviors could be collapsed. To examine this possibility, we conducted a study of the similarity of the behaviors using multiple dimension scaling (Kline & Busch-Rossnagel, 1997). The participants in this study were either child development specialists ($N = 13$) or parents of preschool children ($N = 17$). The stimulus pairs of the seven parenting behaviors were developed using the Ross ordering method (Ross, 1934), which balances both time and space effects. The total number of stimulus pairs was 21, and four versions of the questionnaire were developed to overcome the effects of fatigue. After reading definitions of the seven parenting behaviors, each participant was asked to indicate the degree of similarity of the two parenting items making up the stimulus pair.

The similarity data were analyzed using nonmetric, multidimensional scaling, and the results suggested three clusters. The first cluster, labeled *negative parental power,* consisted of threats and physical punishments, which might be considered instances of negative emotional communication, which was one dimension of the socializing environment identified in the review (Busch-Rossnagel et al., 1995). Bargains, explanations, and tolerance also formed a cluster and were interpreted as *child-centered behaviors.* Directives and positive physical interventions were grouped together and labeled *positive parental assertion.* These last two clusters were closer together than to negative parental power, and thus these two groups might be two ends of the continuum of instrumental interchanges.

These results highlighted the fact that the questionnaire did not examine the provision of inanimate objects as a dimension of the socializing environment. This omission resulted from the use of the mother's responses in the focus groups as the structure for the test blueprint. The mothers only rarely mentioned providing toys or other objects as a parenting behavior in the focus group discussion of parenting behavior. The contrast between these mothers' responses and the marketing of "educational" toys to enhance child development is striking to me, and I would like to explore it further.

CONCLUSION

By describing in depth the development of this one measure, I hope that I have illustrated what I consider the measurement foundations for intervention programs with ethnic minority groups. First, do no harm in evaluating interventions by utilizing culturally appropriate measures to evaluate the effects of your intervention. This often means developing your own culturally or community-centered measures. Valid instrumentation is necessary, but not sufficient for culturally centered intervention evaluations. Do not rely on pseudo experiments using ethnic minority status as an independent variable in program evaluations because of the confounding of ethnicity with other variables. To achieve valid cultural centering, collaborate with community stakeholders and potential participants at all phases of the intervention, especially during the instrument development. Perhaps what is unique about our instrument development efforts is that we go back to the centers where we did our focus groups to ask the mothers to assess our instruments, to tell us whether they think we have captured their behaviors. In effect we are asking for their evaluation of the face validity of our instruments, a type of validity perhaps not very important from the vantage point of psychological science but clearly an issue when it comes to how individuals respond to research situations.

When I finally get to the point of doing an intervention, I anticipate that I will also be asking the mothers for their reactions with the intention of refining the interventions to fit the mothers' interests and needs. This continued collaboration is the heart of my model of culturally centered research and intervention. In this way, we see the mothers not as subjects, or even participants, but as partners who can join with us in understanding and enhancing children's socioemotional development. Perhaps this is the true legacy for me of that Head Start summer so long ago.

REFERENCES

Bronfenbrenner, U. (1975). Is early intervention effective? In B. Z. Friedlander, G. M. Sterritt, & G. E. Kirk (Eds.), *Exceptional infant: Vol. 3. Assessment and intervention* (pp. 449–475). New York: Brunner/Mazel.

Busch-Rossnagel, N. A. (1992). Commonalities between test validity and external validity in basic research on Hispanics. In K. F. Geisinger (Ed.), *Psychological testing of Hispanics* (pp. 195–214). Washington, DC: APA.

Busch-Rossnagel, N. A. (1997). Mastery motivation in toddlers. *Infants and young children, 9*(4), 1–11.

Busch-Rossnagel, N. A. (1998, January). *Development in Puerto Rican and Dominican Toddlers.* Final report to National Institute of Child Health and Human Development (HD30590). (Available from the author)

Busch-Rossnagel, N. A., Knauf-Jensen, D. E., & DesRosiers, F. S. (1995). Mothers and others: The role of the socializing environment in the development of mastery motivation. In R. H. MacTurk & G. A. Morgan (Eds.), *Mastery motivation: Origins, conceptualizations and applications* (pp. 117–145). Norwood, NJ: Ablex.

DesRosiers, F. S., & Busch-Rossnagel, N. A. (1998). Self-concept in toddlers. *Infants and Young Children, 10*(1), 15–26.

Dweck, C. S., & Elliott, E. S. (1983). Achievement motivation. In P. H. Mussen (Ed.), *Handbook of child psychology: Vol. 4. Socialization, personality and social development* (pp. 643–692). New York: Wiley.

Fracasso, M. P., & Busch-Rossnagel, N. A. (1994). Parents and children of Hispanic origin. In M. P. Procidano & C. B. Fisher. (Eds.), *Contemporary families: A handbook for school professionals* (pp. 83–98). New York: Teachers College Press.

Garcia, N., & Busch-Rossnagel, N. A. (1996). *Assessing the socializing environment for mastery motivation: Development of a parenting behaviors measures for Latino mothers.* Bronx, NY: Fordham University, Department of Psychology.

Kline, M., & Busch-Rossnagel, N. A. (1997). *Applying multidimensional scaling to parenting behaviors.* Bronx, NY: Fordham University, Department of Psychology.

Laosa, L. M. (1980). Maternal teaching strategies in Chicano and Anglo-American families: The influence of culture and education on maternal behavior. *Child Development, 51,* 759–765.

MacTurk, R. H., Morgan, G. A., & Jennings, K. D. (1995). The assessment of mastery motivation in infants and young children. In R. H. MacTurk & G. A. Morgan (Eds.), *Mastery motivation: Origins, conceptualizations and applications* (pp. 19–56). Norwood, NJ: Ablex.

Marín, G., & Marín, B. V. (1991). *Research with Hispanic populations.* Newbury Park, CA: Sage.

McCall, R. B., & Green, B. L. (2004). Beyond the methodological gold standards of behavioral research: Considerations for practice and policy. *Social Policy Report, 18*(2), 2–19.

Ross, R. T. (1934). Optimum orders for the presentation of pairs in the method of paired comparisons. *Journal of Educational Psychology, 25,* 375–382.

Ryan, T. J. (1972). *Poverty and the child.* New York: McGraw-Hill Ryerson.

Triandis, H. C., Bontempo, R., Villareal, M. J., Asai, M., & Lucca, N. (1988). Individualism and collectivism: Cross-cultural perspectives on self-ingroup relationships. *Journal of Personality and Social Psychology, 54*, 323, 338.

U. S. Bureau of the Census. (2001). *The Hispanic population: Census 2000 brief* (121st ed.). Washington, DC: United States Department of Commerce. Retrieved April 14, 2004, from www.census.gov/prod/2001pubs/c2kbr01–3.pdf

Werner, O., & Campbell, D. T. (1973). Translating, working through interpreters and the problem of decentering. In R. Naroll & R. Cohen (Eds.), *A handbook of method in cultural anthropology* (pp. 398–420). New York: Columbia University Press.

Westinghouse Learning Corporation. (1969). *The impact of Head Start: An evaluation of the effects of Head Start on children's cognitive and affective development* (Executive Summary). Athens, OH: Westinghouse Learning. (ERIC Document Reproduction Service No. ED036321)

Yarrow, L. J., Klein, R. P., Lomonaco, S., & Morgan, G. A. (1975). Cognitive and motivational development in early childhood. In B. Z. Friedlander, G. M. Sterritt, & G. E. Kirk (Eds.), *Exceptional infant: Vol. 3. Assessment and intervention* (pp. 491–502). New York: Brunner/Mazel.

Part II

RESEARCH ETHICS CHALLENGES INVOLVING DIVERSE ETHNOCULTURAL GROUPS

CHAPTER 4

Addressing Health Disparities Through Relational Ethics

An Approach to Increasing African American Participation in Biomedical and Health Research

SCYATTA A. WALLACE

How good does it feel to reach out to other Black people? And if you don't get paid for it, would you do this research for free? If you're gonna reach out to Black people, reach out with your heart, not your mind. Remember, always stay true to what you do to help us because every bit of it helps.

—11th grade student

Disparities continue to persist in the life expectancy and health status of racial and ethnic minority populations in the United States. Health disparities are particularly striking for African American populations. For example, rates of infant mortality, homicide, cancer, cardiovascular disease, and HIV/STDs are significantly higher for African American populations compared with Whites (National Center for Health Statistics, 2004). Many strategies have been implemented to address these disparities, including increasing the number of African American participants in biomedical and behavioral health research (Corbie-Smith, Thomas, & St. George, 2002; Eastman, 1996); however, efforts to increase African American participation in health research have been met with few improvements.

Relational ethics is an approach that may have utility in increasing the participation of African Americans in health research. Relational ethics recognizes the contextual nature of ethical judgments and the need to understand this context through scientist-participant dialogue (Fisher, 1997, 1999). Relational ethics draws on a mutual and respectful exchange of information between the researcher and the prospective community under study to ensure that the values, hopes, and concerns of participants will be reflected in the design, implementation, and interpretation of research. Through a relational ethics approach, participants learn how the scientific method can be applied to improve the health status of individuals and communities while investigators learn about community expectations that may facilitate or impede research (Fisher, 1999, 2002). Relational ethics takes into consideration participant historical memories, attitudes toward research, and notions of ethical principles.

This chapter challenges researchers to consider using a relational ethics approach when designing, implementing, and evaluating biomedical and behavioral health studies. It begins with a history of African American experiences with health research and continues with a discussion of current African American attitudes toward the scientific process. This is followed by considerations of ethical principles that guide health research from an African American point of view. Community consultation is presented as a tool to assist relational ethics decision making.

THE LEGACY OF AFRICAN AMERICANS AND HEALTH RESEARCH

African American populations have had many negative experiences with health research. Medical and scientific history in the United States has a dark past when it comes to the professions' involvement in and support for racist social institutions. Theories developed by the medical and scientific community were used to perpetuate stereotypes proposing the racial inferiority of African Americans (Guthrie, 1998). These scientific theories and studies were often used as justification for the mistreatment and misuse of African Americans during slavery and the Jim Crow period (Guthrie, 1998; Shavers-Hornaday et al., 1997).

Historical records document that slaves often found themselves as subjects of medical experiments. Slaves could not refuse to participate because the state considered them property (Savitt, 1982). An example of this type of experimentation is the case of Dr. J. Marion Sims, the father of modern gynecology. Between 1845 and 1849, he used slave women to develop an operation to repair vesicovaginal fistulas. These women underwent up to 30 painful and dangerous operations without anesthesia. Only after his experiments with the slave women proved successful did he attempt the procedure with anesthesia on White women volunteers (Gamble, 1997).

Misuse of African Americans continued after slavery ended. Due to the Jim Crow status of African Americans, they did not have the power to protect the graves of their dead. Harris, Gorelick, Samuels, and Bempong (1996) report that southern Blacks became a prime source for medical school dissection experiments and autopsy specimens. They list accounts of African Americans expressing the hope to die in the summer months when dissection classes were not in session. Fry (1984) notes that according to folklore in African American communities, students of medicine stole cadavers from which to learn about bodies. The legend was that unsuspecting Black people would be kidnapped, usually at night, and taken to hospitals to be killed and used in experiments.

The Tuskegee Syphilis Study has been cited as a pivotal event marking African American negative perceptions of the purpose and benefit of medical research (or lack thereof). The Tuskegee Syphilis Study of untreated syphilis in the Negro male ran from 1932 to 1972. It was the longest nontherapeutic study in medical history. This study was conducted by U.S. Public Health Service in Alabama with over 600 African American men (399 subjects and 201 controls). The participants in the study were never informed that they had syphilis, and when penicillin became the standard of care, the men were prevented from receiving treatment. It is estimated that up to 100 men in the study died as a result of untreated syphilis (Jones, 1993).

CURRENT PERCEPTIONS OF HEALTH RESEARCH

A relational ethics approach takes this historical memory of the African American community and uses it to guide decision making in the design and conduct of health research. Relational ethics also considers the current context in which African Americans understand and view health research. Recent studies have documented that African Americans lack knowledge about the purpose of research, they fear exploitation by researchers, and they mistrust the scientific process (Corbie et al., 2002; Fisher & Wallace, 2000; Freimuth et al., 2001).

Lack of Familiarity

A lack of familiarity with health research may be a product of the fact that many African Americans receive health care in settings that are less disposed to conduct research studies, such as emergency rooms or neighborhood clinics. Freimuth et al. (2001) conducted focus groups with 60 African American men and women (mean age 37). The data indicated that the distinction between treatment, prevention, and research was blurry for participants. Relational ethicists realize that many African Americans have no previous conception of research and implement extensive educational efforts to increase their familiarity with the scientific process. This involves providing lay-friendly information about study development, including identification of research questions, trial design, and data interpretation. Researchers following a relational ethics approach

discuss in detail with prospective participants the responsibilities of both researchers and participants (Fisher, 1999, 2002).

Fear of Exploitation

In addition to not fully understanding the research process, data reveals that African Americans fear they will be exploited by researchers and research institutions. Corbie-Smith et al. (2002) conducted a survey study with 1,000 African American and White adults. Results indicated that African Americans were more likely than Whites to state that someone like them would be used as a guinea pig without his or her consent, that physicians often prescribed medications as a way of experimenting on people without consent, and that their physicians had given them treatment as part of an experiment without their permission. In the study by Freimuth et al. (2001), participants were particularly fearful of invasive research procedures. As one participant stated, "I might do it if it's research where they're taking something like fluid samples from me. But if it's injecting anything, no" (p. 804).

Group Stigmatization

African Americans also fear how research will affect social reactions to their ethnic group. Fisher and Wallace (2000) conducted a series of focus groups with 46 parents and 55 high school students from diverse ethnic communities. Respondents commented on the injustice of focusing exclusively on inner-city and minority populations when studying health risk behaviors. Both adults and teens expressed concern that such studies would stigmatize minority communities and promote racial prejudices. The view that researchers exploit participants and focus on issues that do not serve the communities they study hinders participation in health research (Gil & Bob, 1999). A relational ethics approach works with prospective participants to identify and prioritize research projects that the community feels are noteworthy. Investigators attuned to the values and attitudes of African American participants can also apply relational ethics to verify their interpretations of the data with the community to ensure that the results do not unduly cause harm.

Cultural Mistrust

Current research shows that African Americans mistrust biomedical and health studies. Sengupta et al. (2000) conducted a survey study of 301 African American adults examining factors affecting their participation in AIDS research. Results indicated that nearly two thirds agreed that "Blacks were suspicious when research is done in their communities." More than half did not believe that the U.S. government's involvement in AIDS research has been beneficial to the African American community. In another survey study, African Americans were more likely than Whites to report mistrust in research organizations and less likely to deny the existence of conspiracies related to efforts to adversely affect the health of African Americans (Armstrong, Crum, Rieger, Bennett, & Edwards, 1999).

As previously mentioned, African American communities mistrust health research based on historical experiences of misuse in biomedical and health research. In addition, they have experienced multiple barriers within the health care system in general. Many African American patients encounter mistreatment in health settings and with health professionals (Freimuth et al., 2001; Institute of Medicine, 2002). Relational ethics acknowledges that African Americans view research within the context of contemporary racism, urban legends, and mistrust in society at large (Shavers-Hornaday et al.,

1997). Relational ethics strives to demonstrate the trustworthiness of research. This involves revealing humanistic qualities in the researcher and the research process. A relational ethics approach is transparent with the motives and intentions of the research, making every effort to design studies that incorporate the values of the population under study. This approach may engender greater trust in research as well as the belief that research can result in a substantive benefit to the community (Casas & Thompson, 1991; McNeilly et al., 2000).

AFRICAN AMERICAN NOTIONS OF ETHICAL PRINCIPLES IN HEALTH RESEARCH

Researchers have an obligation to design studies that exemplify the ethical principles of beneficence, justice, and respect outlined in the Belmont Report by the National Commission for the Protection of Human Subjects (National Commission for the Protection of Human Subjects of Biomedical and Behavioral Research, 1978). Relational ethicists choose to weigh how these principles translate to various cultures (Dickens, 1997).

Beneficence

Beneficence is defined as maximizing good outcomes for science, humanity, and the individual research participants while avoiding or minimizing unnecessary risk, harm, or wrong. African Americans may differ from investigators in their perceptions of participant and community research risks and benefits (Fisher, 1999). In the study conducted by Fisher and Wallace (2000), participants questioned whether research would ultimately benefit their community. They stated that no matter how many studies are conducted, problems would still exist if researchers continue to ignore contextual factors such as discriminatory policies and sociopolitical institutions that influence their lives. Relational ethics proposes that researchers work to make sure their studies result in tangible, direct, indirect, short-term, and long-term benefit to the communities under study (Casas & Thompson, 1991). Therefore, care is taken to assure that risk and benefits weighed in ethical decision making include those identified as important to the community.

Respect

The principle of *respect* focuses on protecting participant autonomy, with courtesy and respect for individuals as persons. This principle includes the mandate that individuals have the right to refuse participation in research and should be provided disclosure of the nature of research participation. Because participation in research may be an alien concept for many African Americans, it may be more difficult for them to fully comprehend the various components of the research process (Fisher et al., 2002; Miskimen, Marin, & Escobar, 2003). For example, in the study by Freimuth et al. (2001), many participants listed difficulty understanding study consent forms. As one person stated, "You sit there and you read it but you don't necessarily understand what you're reading when you sign the paper" (p. 802). In addition, participants thought that providing consent was the equivalent of "signing away your rights," and the process was designed primarily to protect researchers from any legal responsibility (see also Fisher, 2002). Researchers using a relational ethics approach develop consent procedures that clearly state in a jargon-free manner the rights, obligations, and privileges to which these communities are entitled regarding research participation (Casas & Thompson, 1991). A relational ethics approach adapts the informed consent process to mirror the cultural values of African American populations. Given that biomedical and behavioral health study designs are often very complex, one such strategy to increase participant comprehension is to develop explanations about the research process and procedures in visual form. Another strategy is to include family members in the consent process because health decisions among African Americans are often made by consensus (Miskimen, Marin, & Escobar, 2003).

Justice

The principle of justice ensures reasonable, nonexploitative, carefully considered procedures, as well as the fair administration and distribution of costs and benefits among persons and groups. This can be compromised when the interests and goals of research are directed solely by the biomedical and behavioral health community. A small fraction of biomedical and health research is dedicated to studies that affect poor and vulnerable communities. The "10/90" gap refers to the fact that only 10% of the $70 billion spent on health research and development by private and public sectors is used for research into 90% of the world's health problems (Berlinguer, 2004). A lack of research on issues affecting the African American community and limited participation of this population in health studies prevents these communities from fully benefiting from treatment outcomes (Miskimen et al., 2003). Considering the interests of diverse communities is a form of procedural justice that is a priority in relational ethics. In addition, relational ethics works to increase participation in research studies to ensure fair distribution of costs and benefits.

COMMUNITY CONSULTATION AS A TOOL IN RELATIONAL ETHICS: AN EXAMPLE WITH AFRICAN AMERICAN YOUTH

An important resource in relational ethics is community consultation. Community consultation is a procedure that appears to be responsive to many of the ethical concerns that have arisen in biomedical and behavioral health research (Melton, Levine, Koocher, Rosenthal, & Thompson, 1988). The primary purpose of community consultation is to enlist potential participants as partners in solving the ethical dilemmas posed in designing research. A pilot study was conducted by the author to illustrate how community consultation can be utilized to inform health risk research involving African American youth. Specifically, the study explored how prospective research participants perceive the ethical dimensions of adolescent violence and drug use surveys. The sample included 48 African American high school students (mean age 15.93, SD 1.64). Twenty-six percent of the sample was male and 74% female. Sixty-two percent lived in two-parent households (i.e., married or living together), and 37% lived in single-parent homes (i.e., never married or divorced). This subset of youth were participants in a larger survey study examining parent, peer, and cultural factors associated with youth attitudes toward drug use and violence (Wallace, 2000).

African American Youth Attitudes Toward Parental Permission

Youth completed the informed consent procedures subsection of the Ethics for Adolescent Research Questionnaire (Fisher, 2003). Results with this sample of African American youths demonstrated that teens value parental rights and responsibilities when considering parental permission

procedures in health risk research. Sixty percent of students agreed that parent permission should be required before asking teens questions about violence or drug use. Sixty-nine percent agreed that parent permission is important so that parents can help their child if they are upset after being in a health risk survey study, and 54% agreed that parent permission was important because parents are better able to know if being in a study would hurt their child. These findings are consistent with Fisher's (2003) findings that African American youth were more likely to value parental involvement in research participation decisions than Hispanic, East and South Asian, and non-Hispanic White youth.

In this pilot study, the African American adolescents demonstrated an ability to balance their respect for parental authority with appreciation of their own emerging autonomy and maturing decision-making abilities. Eighty-five percent agreed that teens are old enough to make their own decisions about whether or not they should answer questions about violence or drug use, and 77% stated that teens have the right to decide for themselves whether they want to answer violence or drug use questions. Fifty-three percent stated that teens would worry that their parents would start asking them questions about violence or drug use if parent permission is required to participate in the research. African American youth gave several explanations for why it might be appropriate to waive parental permission under some circumstances. For example, many teens (43%) felt that parents receiving permission forms would misconstrue the purpose of the study and think that their teen was selected because he or she was known to exhibit violent behavior or use drugs. This response signifies the need for researchers to further educate parents about the purpose and design of studies. Moreover, 50% agreed that teens are more likely to tell the truth about violence or drug use if their parent does not know about the study. Eighty percent of the African American youth did not think their parents would be angry if they found out their teen was in a survey study about violence or drugs without parental permission. Despite this, 64% agreed that researchers should always get parent permission before a teen can participate in a health risk survey.

The majority of teens favored items endorsing parental permission requirements. Therefore, investigators working with African American youth need to consider whether a decision made by researchers to waive parental permission may inadvertently communicate a lack of respect for the cultural values of the population under study. These results highlight the importance of community consultation prior to study development and implementation. It illustrates community consultation as a relational ethics method to assist in understanding the views of prospective African American research participants.

CONCLUSION

The quotation at the beginning of this chapter from an African American research participant underscores the complexities of the communities' perspectives on biomedical and behavioral health research. Many African Americans feel committed to addressing the needs of their community. African Americans recognize the value of research (Freimuth et al., 2001), and their desire to help their community through participation in health research has been documented (Sengupta et al., 2000). There is an undertone of suspicion, however, that biomedical and health research will not be done for the "right" reasons. There is the feeling that the research will be conducted with only the agenda of individual investigators and research institutions and not with the good of the African American community in mind. In addition, unfamiliarity

with the scientific process and historical experiences of mistreatment serve to perpetuate mistrust of research and hinder participation in biomedical and health-related studies.

It is not in the best interests of researchers to gloss over these issues or to downplay their resonance with African Americans. Relational ethicists are proactive in addressing scientific mistrust. They work to decrease the power differential between the participant and the researcher by building relationships between the African American community and research establishments. Relational ethicists espouse the values of significant involvement and functional relevance, which call for members of the group under study to have a central role in the entire research process and dictate that studies promote the expressed needs and perspectives of the study population (Bowman, 1991). Relational ethicists use community consultation prior to beginning recruitment efforts to determine community conceptions of the ethical principles that guide the research process, to deliberate risk and benefits, and to enhance participants' understanding of research procedures, including informed consent (Fisher, 1997, 1999; Freimuth et al., 2001; McNeilly et al., 2000). Community consultation is a tool for relational ethicists and does not substitute for the decision making of researchers (Fisher, 1997). It does, however, situate the researcher within the context of the community and allow researchers to make decisions while considering the cultural lens of the population under study (Fisher & Wallace, 2000). It has the potential for meriting the trust of African Americans in research, increasing their knowledge of the scientific process, and improving participation rates in biomedical and behavioral research. Thus, a relational ethics approach to biomedical and health research may help to decrease the disparities that currently exist in health outcomes for African American populations.

REFERENCES

Armstrong, T. D., Crum, L. D., Rieger, R. H., Bennett, T. A., Edwards, L. J. (1999). Attitudes of African Americans toward participation in medical research. *Journal of Applied Social Psychology, 23,* 552–574.

Berlinguer, G. (2004). Bioethics, health, and inequality. *Lancet, 364,* 1086–1091.

Bowman, P. (1991). Race, class, and ethics in research: Belmont principles to functional relevance. In R. L. Jones (Ed.), *Black psychology* (3rd ed., pp. 747–766). Berkeley, CA: Cobb & Henry.

Casas, J. M., & Thompson, C. E. (1991). Ethical principles and standards: A racial-ethnic minority research perspective. *Counseling and Values, 35,* 186–195.

Corbie-Smith, G., Thomas, S. B., St. George, D. M. (2002). Distrust, race, and research. *Archives of Internal Medicine, 162,* 2458–2463.

Dickens, M. (1997). Research ethics and HIV/AIDS. *Medicine and Law, 16,* 187.

Eastman, P. (1996). NCI hopes to spur minority enrollment in prevention and screening trials. *Journal of the National Medical Association, 267,* 954–957.

Fisher, C. B. (1997). A relational perspective on ethics in science decision making for research with vulnerable populations. *IRB: A Review of Human Subjects Research, 19*(5), 1–4.

Fisher, C. B. (1999). Relational ethics and research with vulnerable populations. *Reports on research involving persons with mental disorders that may affect decision-making capacity* (Vol. 2, pp. 29–49). Commissioned Papers by the National Bioethics Advisory Commission (NBAC), Rockville, MD.

Fisher, C. B. (2002). Participant consultation: Ethical insights into parental permission and confidentiality procedures for policy relevant research with youth. In R. M. Lerner, F. Jacobs, & D. Wertlieb (Eds.), *Handbook of applied developmental science* (Vol. 4, pp. 371–396). Thousand Oaks, CA: Sage.

Fisher, C. B. (2003). Adolescent and parent perspectives on ethical issues in youth drug use and suicide survey research. *Ethics & Behavior, 13,* 302–331.

Fisher, C. B., Hoagwood, K., Boyce, C., Duster, T., Frank, D., Grisso, T., et al. (2002). Research ethics for mental health science involving ethnic minority children and youths. *American Psychologist, 57*(12), 1024–1040.

Fisher, C. B., & Wallace, S. A. (2000). Through the community looking glass: Reevaluating the ethical and policy implications of research on adolescent risk and psychopathology. *Ethics & Behavior, 10*(2), 99–118.

Freimuth, V. S., Crouse-Quinn, S., Thomas, S. B., Cole, G., Zook, E., & Duncan, T. (2001). African Americans' views on research and the Tuskegee Syphilis Study. *Social Science and Medicine, 52,* 797–808.

Fry, G. (1984). *Night riders in black folk history.* Knoxville: University of Tennessee Press.

Gamble, V. (1997). Under the shadow of Tuskegee: African Americans and health care. *American Journal of Public Health, 87,* 1773–1778.

Gil, E. F., & Bob, S. (1999). Culturally competent research: An ethical perspective. *Clinical Psychology Review, 19*(1), 45–55.

Guthrie, R. V. (1998). *Even the rat was white: A historical view of psychology.* Boston: Allyn & Bacon.

Harris, Y., Gorelick, P. H., Samuels, P., & Bempong, I. (1996). Why African Americans may not be participating in clinical trials. *Journal of the National Medical Association, 88,* 630–634.

Institute of Medicine. (2002). *Unequal treatment: Confronting racial and ethnic disparities in health care.* Washington, DC: National Academy of Sciences.

Jones, J. (1993). *Bad blood: The Tuskegee syphilis experiment* (2nd ed.). New York: Free Press.

McNeilly, M., Musick, M., Efland, J. R., Baughman, J. T., Toth, P. S., Saulter, T. D., et al. (2000). Minority populations and psychophysiologic research: Challenges in trust building and recruitment. *Journal of Mental Health and Aging, 6*(1), 91–102.

Melton, G. B., Levine, R. J., Koocher, G. P., Rosenthal, R., Thompson, W. C. (1988). Community consultation in socially sensitive research. Lessons from clinical trials of treatment for AIDS. *American Psychologist, 43*(7), 573–581.

Miskimen, T., Marin, H., Escobar, J. (2003). Psychopharmacological research ethics: Special issues affecting U.S. ethnic minorities. *Psychopharmacology, 171,* 98–104.

National Center for Health Statistics. (2004). *NCHS data on racial and ethnic disparities.* Atlanta, GA: Centers for Disease Control and Prevention.

National Commission for Protection of Human Subjects of Biomedical and Behavioral Research. (1978). *The Belmont Report: Ethical principles and guidelines for the protection of human subjects research.* (DHEW Publication No. (OS) 78–0012). Washington, DC: Government Printing Office.

Savitt, T. L. (1982). The use of Blacks for medical experimentation and demonstration in the Old South. *Journal of Southern History, 48,* 331–348.

Sengupta, S., Strauss, R. P., DeVeillis, R., Crouse-Quinn, S., DeVeillis, B., Ware, W. B. (2000). Factors affecting African American participation in AIDS research. *Journal of Acquired Immune Deficiency Syndromes, 24,* 275–284.

Shavers-Hornaday, V. L., Lynch, C. F., Burmeister, L. F., Torner, J. C. (1997). Why are African Americans under-represented in medical research studies? Impediments to participation. *Ethnicity and Health, 2*(1/2), 31–45.

Wallace, S. A. (2002). Cultural resilience: An examination of parent, peer, and cultural factors associated with Black teenage attitudes towards delinquency and substance use (Doctoral dissertation, Fordham University, 2002). *Dissertation Abstracts International, 63,* 592.

CHAPTER 5

In Their Own Voices

American Indian Decisions to Participate in Health Research

Tim D. Noe

Spero M. Manson

Calvin D. Croy

Helen McGough,

Jeffrey A. Henderson

Dedra S. Buchwald

Investigators conducting studies in American Indian communities confront unique ethical challenges due to the community context of their research, the methods of inquiry they employ, and the potential implications of their findings. The consequences with respect to unethical and/or culturally insensitive research practices in this special population have proven to be enormous, both for researchers and the communities. Consequences range from lawsuits against researchers, charging that they infringed on the rights of Native communities, to research findings being used to stigmatize Native communities and to undermine their economic vitality.

AUTHORS' NOTE: The preparation of this manuscript was supported by U26 94 00002 (J. A. Henderson, PI), P30 AG15292 (S. M. Manson, PI), P01 MH 42473 (S. M. Manson, PI), P01 HS10854 (S. M. Manson, PI), and P60 MD000507 (S. M. Manson, PI).

For example, consider the recent legal battle between researchers at Arizona State University (ASU) and the Havasupai tribe. The tribe's lawsuits allege that researchers from ASU and other institutions used DNA for studies without proper consent. This conflict has resulted in a moratorium on biomedical research on the Havasupai reservation, depriving this and other communities from discoveries that have the potential to address their health concerns (Dalton, 2004). The accused researchers adamantly deny any wrongdoings, but the case illustrates the sensitivities associated with conducting genetic research on American Indian populations and the subsequent ethical and legal considerations.

Also take into account the early references of the hantavirus pulmonary syndrome as "Navajo flu," which resulted in stigmatization of the Navajo communities. Furthermore, consider the well-known example of the Barrow Alcohol Study in which the premature press release of the limited results of a survey conducted among a largely Inupiaq community led to sensational headlines in leading eastern U.S. newspapers that characterized Barrow as a city of alcoholics. Consequently, the city's Standard & Poor's bond rating dropped dramatically, precluding financing for numerous important community projects and dramatically undermining their economic development.

Critiques of the conduct of research in American Indian communities date to the work of Vine Deloria, a Lakota social scientist over 30 years ago (Deloria, 1969). He asserted that researchers "derive all the benefits and bear no responsibility for the ways in which their research is used" (Deloria, 1991, p. 457). Deloria (1995) subsequently expanded his argument to include the scientific process as a whole, questioning not only the manner in which scholars pursue their research among Native people but the very nature of the questions they ask and the tools they employ in searching for answers.

NEED FOR COMMUNAL DISCOURSE

Recent attention to racial and ethnic disparities has generated a flurry of dialogue relating to the need for different approaches to the conduct of research in minority communities. There is a growing literature on this topic specific to American Indians (Byers & Hubbard, 1997; Macaulay et al., 1999; Norton & Manson, 1996), which has been fueled, in turn, by similar concerns in the more general professional codes and federal regulations regarding scientific conduct (Fisher et al., 2002).

Literature on the ethics of research with Indian and Native people has long emphasized the need for such efforts to be collaborative and based on partnerships with Indian and Native people (e.g., Attneave, 1989; Mohatt, 1989; Norton & Manson, 1996). Based on what he calls "communal discourse," the approach of Foster and his colleagues (1998, 1999) recommends building, in powerful ways, on the collaborative and culturally specific approach that characterizes the best of contemporary cultural anthropology (e.g., Lassiter, 1997). Recognizing that the dominant discourse in biomedical ethics is individualistic and therefore incomplete in many cultural settings that value group decision making (Blackhal, Murphy, Frank, Michel, & Azenl, 1995; Christakis, 1992; Gostin, 1995; Juengst, 1998), these authors recommend consultation and the development of a research design in collaboration with well-recognized and locally influential social units like extended families. This process is conceived of as a necessary supplement to the requirements for individual consent on one hand, and tribal approval on the other, as it involves consultation beyond the individual but at a level less general than the recognized tribal authorities. This communal discourse can alert researchers to culturally specific understandings of risk and can point the way to mutually satisfactory solutions to many of these potential problems (e.g., Foster, Bernsten, & Carter, 1998; Foster et al., 1999).

These additional recommendations may strike many researchers as onerous. But in light of the concerns about research that have developed in many Indian and Native communities (e.g., Harry, 1999), this kind of collaboration may very well be essential to securing tribal approval. Moreover, it promises to yield important ethical, legal, social, and institutional lessons that can only emerge from consideration of the particularities of local cultural context. For example, the work of Foster and colleagues provides us with important insight into what some of the culturally specific concerns of Indian communities might look like, for example the effects of recruitment strategies that do not consider local social units, questions about the appropriate disposal of bodily products, and concerns about the appropriateness of certain types of research studies (Foster et al., 1999).

IMPORTANCE OF PARTICIPATION IN RESEARCH

Despite such concerns, research continues to play a dominant role in establishing the benefits of specific interventions and procedures. Thus, another central ethical concern for health researchers is to increase the proportion of racial and ethnic minorities in research. Although investigators have tried to increase the representation of minorities in health research, especially in response to the 1993 National Institutes of Health (NIH) requirement to include women and minorities (Hohmann & Parron, 1996), the

scientific progress embodied in the results of such research is not shared equitably among all segments of the American population. In order to do so, we must better understand potential participants' decision-making processes regarding participation in clinical and public health investigations.

Of course, given the tremendous cultural variability that characterizes American Indian communities, no one research project can hope to describe the full range of issues in diverse Indian communities for diverse kinds of health-related research projects. Investigators can, however, anticipate specific issues surrounding the participation of American Indian and Alaska Native communities in health research and thus better understand potential participants' decision-making processes regarding participation in clinical and public health investigations.

Historically, few American Indians have taken part in research studies and little has changed in the last decade. Notably, the Institute of Medicine has recently encouraged participation in research as one strategy to eliminate the health disparities experienced by American Indians (Institute of Medicine, 2002). Yet, little is known about the involvement of American Indians in health research (Macaulay et al., 1999; Manson, Garroutte, Goins, & Henderson, 2004), and only one study on recruitment of American Indians into epidemiologic research and one study on cancer trials has specifically addressed their recruitment and retention (Stoddart et al., 2000). This latter study described several barriers experienced by American Indians such as the cultural distinctiveness of individual tribes, coping with participants' family orientation, and determining how potential participants obtain care. In addition, many American Indian communities are rural and impoverished, circumstances that pose additional difficulties in recruitment and retention (Lewis et al., 1998).

In this chapter, we present a recent study in which we collaborated with three northern plains tribes to determine their likelihood of participating in health research. Specifically, we asked, "What factors influence participation in health research among American Indians?" We were particularly interested in ascertaining the extent to which respondent age, gender, education, cultural affiliation, tribal status, and prior experience with research may interact with such critical elements as attributes of the investigator, the institution conducting the study, the subject matter under investigation, and the study design itself.

In response to the ethical concerns about the conduct of research in Native communities and the need for a collaborative research process and to more actively engage American Indians in health research, we sought to move beyond broad recommendations for a process of community consultation. We hoped to identify, in more specific ways, factors likely to operate at the level of individual members' concerns regarding research and their decision to participate or not in health research. It was our assumption that the results would inform critical next steps in framing and pursuing culturally relevant, locally meaningful health research in Native communities, for without well-grounded empirical findings to guide us, future conversations about these matters are likely to be plagued by abstract claims that will forestall the constructive education of prospective investigators, of community participants, as well as the knowledge acquisition process in general.

This effort is the first large-scale, systematic, empirical inquiry into factors affecting the participation of American Indians in health research. Although past efforts—largely case studies and policy statements—have provided important insights into the broader forces that influence the research process, we have until now lacked empirical corroboration.

METHODS

Setting and Sample

This study used a one-point-in-time survey of students registering for coursework at three tribal colleges/universities (TC/Us). TC/Us are analogous to historically Black colleges and represent the major postsecondary educational opportunity for most American Indian students interested in associate- and baccalaureate-level preparation. The study population consisted of all undergraduate and graduate students who enrolled for formal coursework at three, rural, reservation-based, northern plains TC/Us during scheduled registration periods. The pool of potential respondents at site 1 was 400, site 2: 218, and site 3: 800. Based on previous research experience in these communities, we anticipated a participation rate greater than 75%. Data collection occurred during three successive registration periods: spring 2003 (January 6–10) at site 1; fall 2003 (August 25–September 5) at site 2; and spring 2004 (January 5–9) at site 3.

Measurement Approach

Study vignettes. Based on our extensive experience in research among American Indian and Alaska Native communities, we drafted a set of vignettes (hypothetical research studies) designed to capture factors that may influence an American Indian's decisions about engaging in research activities. These vignettes were discussed at length by a group of 10 American Indian investigators in the context of a postdoctoral fellowship program. We then prepared questions that might be productively asked of respondents regarding key features of each hypothetical study. The vignettes and questions subsequently were compiled in survey form.

To assess respondents' likelihood of participating in research, the survey asked about their willingness to participate in four hypothetical studies (vignettes): a focus group, an exploratory genetic study, a behavioral intervention, and a clinical drug trial. Following are the vignettes used in the survey.

Study number 1. You are being asked to participate in a study about health in your community. This study will use group interview discussions, called "focus groups," where community members meet in groups of 6–8 people to talk about issues. The focus group will take about 2 hours of your time. The questions in the focus group will include asking about your personal opinions and experiences.

Study number 2. You are being invited to participate in a study to see if certain genes contribute to health. You will be interviewed about your health and asked to have a blood test. You will also be asked to give blood that will be used to find out whether you have certain types of genes. Researchers suspect that some of these genes may be involved in health. To see if this is true, researchers will compare the genes in people who have health problems with those who do not. Data collection for the study will take about 2 hours of your time.

Study number 3. You are being invited to participate in a study testing how changes in behavior might affect your health and the health of your community. Half of the people who agree to participate in the study will be assigned to a new treatment that emphasizes changing their behavior. The other half will be in a group that only receives information about health. The treatment group will participate in 5 weekly 2-hour support group sessions. Following those first 5 weeks, there will be weekly follow-up sessions with an educator for an additional 5 weeks. The decision about who gets in the treatment group and who gets only the informational materials will be made randomly, as in flipping a coin. The study will require 10 sessions over a period of 6 months

for all participants, totaling 15 hours of your time. All the study visits, treatments, and follow up will be provided free of charge.

Study number 4. You are being invited to participate in a study that is testing an experimental drug for a problem that is common in your community. This experimental drug may be better than anything on the market, but researchers need to complete this study to find out. People who agree to be in the study will get either the experimental drug or a drug that is currently approved. The decision about who gets the experimental drug and who gets the current drug will be made randomly, as in flipping a coin. The study will require 10 research visits over a period of 6 months. All the study visits, treatments, and follow up will be provided free of charge.

Presentation of each vignette was followed by 34 questions. The first question asked about respondents' likelihood of participating based solely on the information contained within the vignette. The second question asked respondents to imagine that they were a parent of a teenager and to rate how likely they would be to allow their son or daughter to participate in the hypothetical study. Thirty-two questions then followed about the respondents' likelihood of participating when an additional piece of information about the study was provided. The additional-information questions sought to assess the degree to which the following contributed to their likelihood of participation: respondent and investigator attributes, institutional characteristics, the subject under investigation, type of community involvement, type of information use, compensation and benefits, and perceived risks. Respondents answered how likely they were to participate by choosing a response alternative ranging from 1 to 5, where 1 indicated "I definitely would not participate" and 5 indicated "I definitely would participate." Thus, each respondent provided, in total,

34 indications of his/her probability of participation.

Focus-group work to ensure comprehensibility and relevance of survey. After the draft survey was completed, focus groups were conducted in each TC/U community with the goal of reviewing the survey for cultural relevance and comprehensibility. Focus-group work proceeded in five distinct steps: working with TC/U's administrators to identify, recruit, and hire a local TC/U liaison, who was a tribal member and well-established in the community; identifying and recruiting focus-group members; arranging for facilities and scheduling focus groups; conducting focus-group discussions; and revising and finalizing the survey based on focus-group feedback.

All focus-group discussions were audiotaped, transcribed, and supplemented by extensive staff notes. Recommendations were then used to revise the survey and finalize it prior to data collection at each site.

Typical focus-group feedback included revision of language to increase comprehensibility (e.g., changing *scenario* to *situation*) and cultural sensitivity (e.g., deemphasizing potential conflict by changing *problem* to *issue*). In addition, the focus groups believed it would be important to ask respondents to imagine they were being asked to participate in each situation, so the preamble to each scenario was modified to include, "Imagine you are being asked to participate . . ."

Data Collection

At each site, the TC/U liaison gained institutional approval and arranged for a booth in the registration area during the semester enrollment period. Booths were positioned in areas clearly visible to registrants. As students registered for classes, they were asked if they would like to complete a survey. Potential respondents were informed that the survey was designed to determine what factors influence whether or not someone participates in health research. They also were informed that they would receive a 60-minute phone card for completing the survey. The survey was self-report in nature, anonymous, and required approximately 20 to 25 minutes to complete.

Analysis

The data were pooled from the three sites to comprise four data sets, one for each vignette. We calculated the percentages of respondents by their demographic characteristics, by their likelihood of participation, and by whether they would allow their teenage son or daughter (if applicable) to participate in each of the four hypothetical studies. Next, we used logistic regressions to determine how the attributes of each hypothetical study influenced respondents' personal likelihood of participation. Each observation represented an answer to each of the 33 questions about the respondent's likelihood of participation; thus, the data file for each logistic regression contained 33 observations for each survey respondent. The dependent variable for each observation was a variable wherein 1 indicated that the respondent said she or he probably or definitely would participate, given the additional information about the study; 0 denoted that the respondent did not choose either of these responses. The independent variables were coded 1 or 0 to indicate which piece of additional information had been read by the respondent, plus each respondent's demographic background data was coded as $1/0$. Indicator variables were also included to identify site membership.

Logistic regressions were population average models for correlated data because the values of the dependent variable were correlated across observations. As discussed by Hosmer and Lemeshow (2000), this modeling approach adjusts the standard errors of the logistic regression coefficients to reflect correlations within clusters. The variables that indicated the type of information given were cluster-specific covariates because their values varied across observations within each cluster; the demographic independent variables did not vary within each cluster.

Statistical tests were conducted to examine the resulting logistic regression coefficients. The Stata (StataCorp, 2003) output for the *p* values of the coefficients' *Z* scores was reviewed to assess whether the coefficients were significantly different from 0. Potential interactions were examined between the site variable and the remaining independent variables: namely, respondent characteristics, research institution, community involvement, salience, compensation/benefits, and information use.

We also tested three interactions with age (age X years lived on the reservation, age X previous participation in research, age X having children), which were the most likely confounds of relevant exposure. To judge whether the odds ratios (*OR*s) varied across the scenarios, the 99% confidence intervals were examined for overlap.

RESULTS

The participation rate was 82% (site 1 = 80%, site 2 = 100%, and site 3 = 66%). Table 5.1 summarizes the demographic and social characteristics of the sample. The mean age was 33.6; 33.5% were male, and 92.1% of the students were American Indian. The sample was primarily rural, having spent on average of almost 23 years living on or near a reservation. Nearly a third had previously participated in research.

As shown in Table 5.2, respondent characteristics did not consistently influence the odds of participating in the four hypothetical studies after reading only the vignette. Site 1 and site 3 respondents were more likely to

participate in the drug study than respondents from site 2. The odds of participation increased by a factor of 1.1 for every year of age for the focus group, genetic, and behavior intervention vignettes. Respondents with an associate or higher degree were less likely to participate in the drug study than were people with only a high school or less education. No significant interactions were detected for site or age and variations by site are noted at the bottom of Table 5.2.

Research Institution

Research conducted by a tribal college or university increased the odds of participation for all four hypothetical studies with the exception of the drug study at site 3. These factors had a significantly greater positive effect for the focus-group vignette. Similarly, a study conducted by a national organization increased the odds of participation for all studies. In contrast, if the study was conducted by the federal government, the likelihood of participation decreased across all types of studies with the exception of the drug study at site 2.

Community Involvement and Salience

Table 5.2 also illustrates that community involvement generally increased the odds of participation. Community involvement in developing a study and having an American Indian as the lead researcher substantially increased likelihood of participation for almost all vignettes. The notable exception to increasing the odds of participation was that community involvement in data collection actually decreased the odds of participation in the genetic study. Also, community involvement in developing the study was not significant for the genetic study.

The salience, or relevance, of the study's substantive focus to the community also had a dramatic impact on participation. Factors

Table 5.1   Descriptive Characteristics of Respondents by Site

| | Site 1 | | Site 2 | | Site 3 | | Site 4 | |
| | $n = 891–1,031$[1] | | $n = 258–306$[1] | | $n = 170–208$[1] | | $n = 463–517$[1] | |
	% or Mean	99% CI	% or Mean	99% CI	% or Mean	99% CI	% or Mean	99% CI
Age, mean years	33.6	32.7–34.6	32.7	30.9–34.4	36.5	34.1–38.8	33.1	31.8–34.4
Male, %	33.5	29.8–37.4	33.7	26.8–41.0	35.6	27.2–44.6	32.6	27.4–38.2
Racial/Ethnic Affiliation, %								
American Indian	92.1	89.6–94.1	94.4	90.2–97.3	90.9	84.5–95.3	91.1	87.4–94.0
White	9.6	7.4–12.2	10.5	6.4–15.8	9.1	4.7–15.5	9.4	6.3–13.1
Spanish	2.4	1.4–4.0	2.3	0.7–5.5	1.4	0.2–5.2	2.9	1.3–5.4
Black	1.1	0.4–2.2	0.7	0.03–3.0	1.0	0.05–4.4	1.4	0.4–3.3
Marital Status, %								
Never married	48.0	44.0–52.2	49.8	42.2–57.4	43.1	34.2–52.4	49.1	43.3–54.9
Married	26.6	23.1–30.3	26.3	20.3–33.4	27.5	19.8–36.2	26.4	21.5–31.8
Widowed	3.0	1.8–4.6	2.7	0.9–6.1	4.9	1.9–10.2	2.4	1.0–4.7
Divorced	16.8	13.9–20.0	15.5	10.5–21.6	20.6	13.8–28.8	16.0	12.0–20.6
Separated	5.6	3.9–7.7	5.7	2.8–10.1	3.9	1.3–8.9	6.1	3.7–9.4
Has Children, %	73.9	70.2–77.3	70.3	63.1–76.9	77.2	68.8–84.3	74.7	69.4–79.5
Education, %								
High school graduate or less	23.2	19.9–26.8	29.2	22.7–36.3	29.8	22.0–38.6	17.0	13.0–21.7
Some college but no degree	45.5	41.5–49.6	45.9	38.5–53.4	37.5	29.0–46.6	48.6	42.8–54.3
Associate or higher degree	31.3	27.6–35.1	24.9	18.8–31.8	32.7	24.6–41.6	34.4	29.1–40.0
Residence, mean years								
Lived on or near a reservation	22.9	21.8–24.1	23.1	21.0–25.3	26.2	23.2–29.1	21.6	20.1–23.1
Lived in an urban area	16.0	14.8–17.2	17.6	15.2–19.9	16.8	13.6–20.0	15.1	13.6–16.6
Ever Worked in Health Care, %	29.4	25.8–33.2	28.0	21.6–35.2	33.3	25.1–42.3	28.6	23.6–34.1
Ever Been in Research Study, %	31.0	27.3–34.8	29.8	23.2–37.0	17.9	11.6–25.7	36.9	31.5–42.6

NOTE:
1. n based upon variances in characteristic and amount of missing data; CI = confidence interval

Table 5.2 Odds Ratios and 95% Confidence Intervals for Influences on Research Participation by Study Type

	Focus Group	Genetic Study	Intervention	Drug Study
Respondent Characteristics	OR (CI)	OR (CI)	OR (CI)	OR (CI)
Site 2 Tribal college or university	1.0[1-]	1.0[1-]	1.0[1-]	1.0[1-]
Site 1 Tribal college or university	0.8 (0.6–1.1)	0.9 (0.7–1.4)	0.9 (0.6–1.3)	1.4 (1.0–2.2)[2]
Site 3 Tribal college or university	0.9 (0.7–1.2)	0.9 (0.6–1.3)	0.9 (0.7–1.3)	1.4 (1.0–2.1)[2]
Age	1.1 (1.0–1.1)[2]	1.1 (1.0–1.2)[2]	1.1 (1.0–1.2)[2]	1.0 (.09–1.1)
Male	0.9 (0.7– 1.1)	0.9 (0.7–1.1)	0.9 (0.7–1.2)	1.3 (1.0–1.8)[2]
American Indian race/tribal affiliation	1.0 (0.7–1.6)	1.0 (0.6–1.7)	1.4 (0.8–2.4)	1.2 (0.7–2.1)
Never married	1.0[1-]	1.0[1-]	1.0[1-]	1.0[1-]
Married/cohabitating	0.9 (0.7–1.1)	1.0 (0.7–1.3)	1.1 (0.8–1.4)	1.0 (0.7–1.3)
Widowed/divorced/separated	1.0 (0.8–1.3)	1.0 (0.7–1.3)	1.1 (0.8–1.5)	1.0 (0.7–1.5)
High school or less education	1.0[4]	1.0[4]	1.0[4]	1.0[4]
Some college but no degree	1.0 (0.8–1.4)	0.9 (0.7–1.3)	1.0 (0.7–1.4)	0.8 (0.6–1.1)
Associate or higher college degree	1.0 (0.7–1.4)	0.8 (0.5–1.1)	1.0 (0.7–1.5)	0.6 (0.4–1.0)[3]
Years lived on reservation	1.0 (1.0–1.0)	1.0 (1.0–1.0)	1.0 (1.0–1.0)	1.0 (1.0–1.0)
Has children	1.0 (0.8–1.3)	1.0 (0.7–1.4)	0.9 (0.6–1.2)	0.9 (0.6–1.3)
Been in a research study	1.1 (0.8–1.4)	1.1 (0.8–1.5)	1.1 (0.9–1.5)	1.1 (0.8–1.5)
Worked in health care	1.1 (0.9–1.4)	1.2 (0.9–1.6)	1.1 (0.8–1.5)	1.0 (0.7–1.4)
Research Institution				
State university	1.4 (1.1–1.7)[4]	0.7 (0.6–.8)[4]	0.8 (0.7–1.0)[3]	0.9 (0.8–1.0)[2]
Tribal college or university	2.4 (1.9–3.0)[4]	1.3 (1.0–1.5)[4]	1.3 (1.1–1.5)[4]	[5]
Federal government	0.4 (0.3–.5)[4]	0.4 (0.3–.5)[4]	0.5 (0.4–.6)[4]	[6]
Private health care provider	0.9 (0.7–1.1)	0.8 (0.7–1.0)[3]	0.9 (0.7–1.0)[2]	1.1 (0.9–1.2)
Tribal government	0.9 (0.7–1.1)	0.7 (0.5–.8)[4]	0.8 (0.7–1.0)[3]	[7]
National organization	2.4 (1.8–3.0)[4]	1.7 (1.4–2.1)[4]	1.8 (1.5–2.1)[4]	[8]
Office run by researchers	0.9 (0.7–1.2)	0.7 (0.6–.8)[4]	0.9 (0.7–1.0)[2]	1.0 (0.8–1.1)
Community Involvement				
Developing study	1.8 (1.4–2.2)[4]	1.0 (.8–1.2)	1.2 (1.0–1.4)[3]	1.3 (1.1–1.5)[4]
Collecting data	1.6 (1.3–2.0)[4]	0.8 (.7–1.0)[3]	1.1 (.9–1.3)[3]	1.3 (1.1–1.5)[4]
Interpreting data	1.3 (1.0–1.6)[3]	1.0 (.8–1.2)	1.2 (1.0–1.5)[3]	1.4 (1.1–1.6)[4]
Researcher is American Indian	3.3 (2.5–4.3)[4]	1.5 (1.3–1.9)[4]	1.7 (1.4–2.1)[4]	1.7 (1.5–2.0)[4]
Salience				
Personal experience with topic	2.1 (1.6–2.7)[4]	1.5 (1.2–1.8)[4]	1.5 (1.2–1.8)[4]	1.6 (1.4–1.9)[4]
Addresses serious community problem	4.0 (3.0–5.4)[4]	1.9 (1.6–2.4)[4]	2.2 (1.8–2.7)[4]	2.0 (1.6–2.3)[4]
Research brings money to community	4.1 (3.0–5.4)[4]	2.2 (1.8–2.7)[4]	2.4 (1.9–3.0)[4]	2.3 (1.9–2.7)[4]
Study about lactose intolerance	1.2 (1.0–1.6)[2]	1.1 (.9–1.3)	1.3 (1.1–1.6)[3]	1.8 (1.5–2.1)[4]
Study about cancer	3.3 (2.5–4.4)[4]	2.3 (1.8–2.9)[4]	2.5 (2.0–3.1)[4]	3.0 (2.5–3.6)[4]
Study about diabetes	4.6 (3.4–6.3)[4]	2.7 (2.1–3.4)[4]	2.9 (2.3–3.6)[4]	3.2 (2.6–3.9)[4]
Study about depression	3.0 (2.3–3.9)[4]	2.2 (1.7–2.7)[4]	2.4 (2.0–3.0)[4]	2.8 (2.3–3.4)[4]
Study about alcoholism	3.2 (2.4–4.2)[4]	2.2 (1.7–2.7)[4]	2.5 (2.0–3.1)[4]	2.8 (2.3–3.4)[4]
Compensation/Benefits				
Study leads to new treatment/service	3.0 (2.3–3.9)[4]	2.3 (1.9–2.9)[4]	2.2 (1.8–2.7)[4]	2.3 (1.9–2.7)[4]
No compensation	0.8 (0.6–1.0)[2]	0.7 (0.5–0.8)[4]	0.8 (0.6–0.9)[4]	0.8 (0.7–1.0)[2]
Immediate compensation	2.3 (1.7–2.9)[4]	0.7 (0.5–.8)[4]	1.9 (1.5–2.3)[4]	0.8 (0.7–1.0)[2]
Feedback about results	1.6 (1.2–2.0)[4]	1.4 (1.1–1.7)[4]	1.5 (1.2–1.8)[4]	1.7 (1.4–2.0)[4]

(Continued)

Table 5.2 (Continued)

	Focus Group	Genetic Study	Intervention	Drug Study
Risks				
Risk of physical harm	0.1 (0.1–0.2)[4]	0.1 (0.1–1.2)[4]	0.2 (0.1–0.2)[4]	0.2 (0.1–0.2)[4]
Risk of emotional harm	0.1 (0.1–0.2)[4]	0.1 (0.1–0.2)[4]	0.1 (0.1–0.2)[4]	0.2 (0.1–0.3)[4]
Results discriminate against family	0.1 (0.0-0.1)[4]	0.1 (0.0–0.1)[4]	0.1 (0.1-0.1)[4]	0.2 (0.1-0.2)[4]
Results discriminate against tribe/race	0.1 (0.0-0.1)[4]	0.1 (0.0–0.1)[4]	0.1 (0.1-0.1)[4]	0.2 (0.1-0.2)[4]
Information Use				
Risk of broken confidentiality	0.1 (0.0–0.1)[4]	0.1 (0.0–0.1)[4]	0.1 (0.1–0.1)[4]	0.2 (0.1–0.2)[4]
Data anonymous	2.1 (1.6–2.6)[4]	1.0 (0.9–1.3)	1.1 (0.9–1.3)	1.1 (0.9–1.4)
Researchers use medical records	0.3 (0.2–0.4)[4]	0.3 (0.2–0.4)[4]	0.4 (0.3–0.5)[4]	0.6 (0.5–0.7)[4]
Data only used for specific problem	0.6 (0.5–0.8)[4]	0.6 (0.5–0.8)[4]	0.8 (0.7–1.0)[4]	0.9 (0.8–1.1)
Data used to answer new questions	1.2 (0.9–1.5)	1.0 (0.9–1.3)	1.2 (1.0–1.4)[2]	[9]

NOTES:

1. This category was the reference group
2. Odds ratio differs from 1.0 at $p < 0.05$
3. Odds ratio differs from 1.0 at $p < 0.01$
4. Odds ratio differs from 1.0 at $p < 0.001$

Odds ratios varied across sites for the following items:

5. Site 1 [1.2 (1.0–1.6)][2]; Site 2 [1.4 (1.1–1.9)][3]; Site 3 [1.1 (.9–1.3)]
6. Site 1 [0.8 (.6–1.0)][2]; Site 2 [0.8 (.6–1.2)]; Site 3 [0.6 (.4–.7)][4]
7. Site 1 [0.8 (.6–1.1); Site 2 [1.2 (.9–1.6); Site 3 [0.7 (.6–.9)][4]
8. Site 1 [1.6 (1.2–2.0)][4]; Site 2 [2.2 (1.7–2.9)][4]; Site 3 [1.6 (1.3–2.0)][4]
9. Site 1 [1.5 (1.2–2.0)][4]; Site 2 [1.1 (0.8–1.5)]; Site 3 [1.3 (1.1–1.6)][3]
OR = odds ratio; CI = confidence interval

associated with salience increased the odds of participation more than any other element of study design. The largest ORs were observed when the research addressed a serious problem in the community, the research could bring money to their community, or the study was about cancer, diabetes, depression, or alcoholism.

Compensation, Benefits, and Risk

For all scenarios, the odds of participation were significantly higher if new treatments or services might emerge from the research. Compensation also increased participation in the focus-group and intervention vignettes. Conversely, perceived risks decreased the odds of participation more than any other design element. As shown in Table 5.2, potential physical and emotional harm, as well as possible personal or racial discrimination, precipitated dramatic declines in likely participation in all vignettes.

Information Use

Risk that confidentiality might be broken significantly decreased participation for all vignettes. This possibility was among the most potent factors that decreased participation. Conversely, keeping information anonymous increased the likelihood of participation only in the focus-group study. Additionally, using study results to answer new, future questions increased likelihood of participation for the intervention study and the drug study, but only for sites 1 and 3.

DISCUSSION

The literature on participation of racial and ethnic minorities in health research has focused primarily on barriers to participation and strategies to increase their involvement (Curry & Jackson, 2003). Several themes have emerged from this literature that focus on individual characteristics and attitudes toward research, as well as investigator characteristics, study design, and type of sponsoring institution (Levkoff, Levy, & Weitzman, 2000). Individual characteristics that may reduce involvement in research include health behaviors such as delaying medical care or underutilizing preventive care, which may inhibit willingness to enroll in studies; a sense of fatalism (Swanson & Ward, 1995); doubts about the benefits of participation (Areán & Gallagher-Thompson, 1996; Levkoff et al., 2000; Swanson & Ward, 1995); and beliefs that certain types of health research will reflect negatively on participants and their families (Levkoff et al., 2000) Our results, however, did not provide strong support for respondent characteristics as key variables affecting the odds of participating in health research for American Indians. The only exception was age, where the odds of participation increased by a factor of 1.1 for every year of age for the focus group, genetic, and behavioral studies. One explanation may be that older participants are more aware of the value of the results of health research and the relatively low risk of these types of studies.

Obstacles to successfully engaging diverse groups in health research have also been associated with investigators' failure to gain trust and establish credibility with the population of interest (Areán & Gallagher-Thompson, 1996; Corbie-Smith, Thomas, Williams, & Moody-Acres, 1999; Norton & Manson, 1996), with ineffective communication of the study's rationale and relevance (Brawley & Tejedam, 1995; Gavaghan,

1995; Manson et al, 2004; Shavers, Lynch, & Burmeister, 2002), and with investigator biases (Swanson & Ward, 1995). In this regard, we found that research led by an American Indian investigator significantly increased the odds of participation across all four types of studies. Likewise, the salience of the research strongly and positively increased participation. For example, if respondents perceived the research would address a serious problem in their community, such as diabetes or cancer, or if the study would bring money into the community, the odds of participating increased markedly.

Perceptions of sponsoring institutions may also be associated with the likelihood of participating in research (Gorelick, Harris, Burnett, & Bonecutter, 1998; Shavers et al., 2002; Unson, Dunbar, Curry, Kenyon, & Prestwood, 2001). Universities often are viewed as elitist and not commited to the welfare of minority communities (Curry & Jackson, 2003), have inadequate resources for effective outreach, lack support for investigators from diverse backgrounds, and support policies for the conduct of research that are perceived as burdensome (Unson et al., 2001). Furthermore, tensions between academic health centers and community health agencies may lead to assumptions that the benefits of research do not outweigh the costs (Curry & Jackson, 2003). This is exacerbated by minority groups' limited access to health care provided in academic medical settings, thereby reducing opportunities to learn about and enroll in clinical studies (Shavers et al., 2002).

Consistent with this literature, we observed that the type of institution conducting the hypothetical studies significantly affected the likelihood of participation among our respondents. Studies conducted by a TC/U or national organization generally increased participation significantly across all four hypothetical studies, but not for site 3, for the drug study. Conversely, if the study was conducted by the federal government, the odds of participation generally decreased with the only exception being site 2, for the drug study.

One of the most important observations derived from actual research experience emphasizes the benefits of building partnerships with minority communities to improve participation in research (Gorelick et al., 1998; Manson et al., 2004; Norton & Manson, 1996). These efforts embrace educating communities about the value of research, a commitment by investigators to give something back to the community, removal of cultural barriers to participation, cultural sensitivity among research staff, community involvement in research design and study execution, trust and connection with the community, and involvement of minority researchers (deBrey & Gonzalez, 1997; Norton & Manson, 1996; Ory, Lipman, Barr, Harden, & Stahl, 2000; Paskett, DeGraffinreid, Tatum, & Margitic, 1996; Saunders, 1995; Swanson & Ward, 1995; Thompson, Neighbors, Munday, & Jackson, 1996; Vollmer et al., 1998; Whelton et al., 1996). In our study, engaging the community in developing the study and collecting the data generally increased the odds of participation, as did involving them in understanding the results. The only exception was for the genetic study for the factors of community involvement in developing the study and collecting the data, which did not significantly increase the odds of participation. This particular finding is consistent with a recent focus-group study that found that research on behavioral genetics has little social value for participants and that individuals labeled as genetically at risk may be ostracized or discriminated against (Fisher & Wallace, 2000). Furthermore, participation was positively influenced if the information from the study would be used in the future

to answer new questions (significant for the intervention study and the drug study for site 1 and 3), addressed a serious problem in the community, brought money to the community, or was led by an American Indian investigator.

This study has several limitations. First, vignette-based research is an established form of qualitative research (Finch, 1987; Hughes, 1998), yet it may not adequately capture all relevant variables. Second, the TC/U student population undoubtedly overrepresented younger, more educated members of the local community, although these students were older (mean age = 34 years) than those typically found in other higher education institutions (National Center on Education Statistics, 2000). Third, our response rates were generally good, but the lowest rate (66%) was a function of numerous, geographically decentralized registration sites at the largest TC/U that could not be fully covered by project staff. On the other hand, virtually no one who was approached refused. Fourth, the anonymous nature of the survey precluded our ability to characterize the differences between participants and nonparticipants. Last, only three closely related tribes were included in this study. Given these limitations, our findings, despite being from among the largest of tribes, cannot be generalized to the entire American Indian population, the nonstudent local community, older individuals, or urban American Indian populations.

CONCLUSION

Given valid concerns about the ethical conduct of research in Native communities and the need for a participatory research process and the need to increase participation of American Indians in health research, we sought through this study to engage in a process of community consultation to identify, through the voices of Native community members, concerns regarding research and factors likely to influence the decision to participate or not in health research. It was our assumption that the results would inform critical next steps in framing and pursuing culturally relevant, locally meaningful health research in Native communities.

This study is the first large-scale, systematic, empirical inquiry into factors affecting the participation of American Indians in health research. Although past efforts— largely case studies and policy statements— have provided important insights into the broader forces that influence the research process, we have until now lacked empirical corroboration. Our findings document key factors influencing study participation, thereby identifying approaches that might increase participation of American Indians in health research. Many factors significantly increased the odds of participation, including having

the study conducted by a tribal college/ university or national organization, involving the community in study development, having the research led by an American Indian, addressing serious health problems, bringing money into the community, providing new treatments or services, compensation, anonymity, and using the information to answer new questions. Decreased odds of participation were observed if results could lead to discrimination against one's family, tribe, or racial group, lack of confidentiality, and if physical harm was possible. These findings demonstrate that paying close attention to institutional sponsorship, investigator attributes, community involvement, potential risks and benefits, and how results will be used is essential when conceptualizing, designing, and implementing successful health research efforts with American Indian populations.

REFERENCES

Areán, P., & Gallagher-Thompson, D. (1996). Issues and recommendations for the recruitment and retention of older ethnic minority adults into clinical research. *Journal of Consulting and Clinical Psychology, 64,* 875–880.

Attneave, C. L. (1989). Who has the responsibility? An evolving model to resolve ethical problems in intercultural research. *American Indian and Alaska Native Mental Health Research, 2*(3), 18–24.

Blackhall, L. J., Murphy, S. T., Frank, G., Michel, V., & Azen, S. (1995). Ethnicity and attitudes toward patient autonomy. *Journal of the American Medical Association, 274,* 820–825.

Brawley, O., & Tejedam, H. (1995). Minority inclusion in clinical trials issues and potential strategies. *Journal of the National Cancer Institute, 17,* 55–57.

Byers, T., & Hubbard, J. (1997). The Navajo Health and Nutrition Survey: Research that can make a difference. *Journal of Nutrition, 127*(10 Suppl.), 2075S–2077S.

Christakis, N. A. (1992). Ethics are local: Engaging cross-cultural variation in ethics for clinical research. *Social Science and Medicine, 35,* 1079–1091.

Corbie-Smith, G., Thomas, S., Williams, M., & Moody-Acres, S. (1999). Attitudes and beliefs of African Americans toward participation in medical research. *Journal of General Internal Medicine, 14,* 537–546.

Curry, L., & Jackson, J. (2003). Recruitment and retention of diverse ethnic and racial groups in health research: An evolving science. In L. Curry & J. Jackson

(Eds.), *The science of inclusion: Recruiting and retaining racial and ethnic elders in health research* (pp. 1–7). Washington, DC: Gerontological Society of America.

deBrey, V. N., & Gonzalez, V. M. (1997). Recruiting for arthritis studies in hard-to-reach populations: A comparison of methods used in an urban Spanish-speaking community. *Arthritis Care Research, 10,* 64–71.

Dalton, R. (2004). When two tribes go to war. *Nature, 430,* 500–502.

Deloria, V., Jr. (1969). *Custer died for your sins. An Indian manifesto.* New York: Avon.

Deloria, V., Jr. (1991). Commentary: Research, Redskins, and reality. *American Indian Quarterly, 15,* 457.

Deloria, V., Jr. (1995). *Red earth, white lies.* New York: Scribner.

Finch, J. (1987). The vignette technique in survey research. *Sociology, 21,* 105–114.

Fisher, C. B., Hoagwood, K., Boyce, C., Duster, T., Frank, D. A., Grisso, T., et al. (2002). Research ethics for mental health science involving ethnic minority children and youths. *American Psychologist, 57,* 1024–1040.

Fisher, C. B., & Wallace, S. A. (2000). Through the community looking glass: Reevaluating the ethical and policy implications of research on adolescent risk and psychopathology. *Ethics & Behavior, 10*(2), 99–118.

Foster, M. W., Bernsten, D., & Carter, T. H. (1998). A model agreement for research in socially identifiable populations. *American Journal of Human Genetics, 63,* 696–702.

Foster, M. W., Sharp, R. R., Freeman, W. L., Chino, M., Bernsten, D., & Carter, T. H. (1999). The role of community review in evaluating the risks of human genetic variation research. *American Journal of Human Genetics, 64,* 1719–1727.

Gavaghan, H. (1995). Clinical trials face lack of minority group volunteers. *Nature, 373,* 178–191.

Gorelick, P. B., Harris, Y., Burnett, B., & Bonecutter, F. J. (1998). The recruitment triangle: Reasons why African Americans enroll, refuse to enroll, or voluntarily withdraw from a clinical trial. *Journal of the National Medical Association, 90*(3), 141–145.

Gostin, L. O. (1995). Informed consent, cultural sensitivity, and respect for persons. *Journal of the American Medical Association, 274,* 844–845.

Harry, D. (1999). Tribes meet to discuss genetic colonization. *Anthropology Newsletter, 40*(2), 15.

Hohmann, A. A., & Parron, D. L. (1996). How the new guidelines on inclusion of women and minorities apply: Efficacy trials, effectiveness trials, and validity. *Journal of Consulting and Clinical Psychology, 64,* 851–855.

Hosmer, D. W., & Lemeshow, S. (2000). *Applied logistic regression.* New York: John Wiley.

Hughes, R. (1998). Considering the vignette technique and its application to a study of drug injecting and HIV risk and safer behavior. *Sociology of Health and Illness, 20,* 381–400.

Institute of Medicine. (2002). *Unequal treatment: Confronting racial and ethnic disparities in health care.* Washington, DC: National Academy Press.

Juengst, E. T. (1998). Groups as gatekeepers to genomic research: Conceptually confusing, morally hazardous, and practically useless. *Kennedy Institute of Ethics Journal, 8,* 183–200.

Lassiter, L. E. (1997). "Charlie Brown": Not just another essay on the gourd dance. *American Indian Culture and Research Journal, 21*(4), 75–103.

Levkoff, S., Levy, B., & Weitzman, P. (2000). The matching model of recruitment. *Journal of Mental Health and Aging, 6,* 29–38.

Lewis, C. E., George, V., Fouad, M., Porter, V., Bowen, D., & Urban, N. (1998). Recruitment strategies in the women's health trial: Feasibility study in minority populations. *Controlled Clinical Trials, 19,* 461–476.

Manson, S. M., Garroutte, E. M., Goins, R. T., & Henderson, P. (2004). Access, relevance and control in the research process: Lessons from Indian country. *Journal of Aging and Health, 16,* 58S–77S.

Macaulay, A. C., Gibson, N., Freeman, W. L., Commanda, L. E., McCabe, M. L., Robbins, C. M., et al. (1999). Participatory research maximizes community and lay involvement. *British Medical Journal, 319,* 774–778.

Mohatt, G. V. (1989). The community as informant or collaborator? *American Indian and Alaska Native Mental Health Research, 2*(3), 64–70.

National Center on Education Statistics. (2000). *Enrollment in public secondary education 1999-2000.* Washington, DC: Author.

Norton, I. M., & Manson, S. M. (1996). Research in American Indian and Alaska Native communities: Navigating the cultural universe of values and process. *Journal of Consulting and Clinical Psychology, 64,* 856–860.

Ory, M., Lipman, P., Barr, R., Harden, J., & Stahl, S. (2000). A national program to enhance research on minority aging and health promotion. *Journal of Mental Health and Aging, 6,* 21–23.

Paskett, E. D., DeGraffinreid, C., Tatum, C. M., & Margitic S. E. (1996). The recruitment of African-Americans to cancer prevention and control studies. *Preventive Medicine, 25,* 547–553.

Saunders, E. (1995). Recruitment of African-American patients for clinical trials: The ALLHAT challenges. *Journal of the National Medical Association, 87,* 627–629.

Shavers, V., Lynch, C., & Burmeister, L. (2002). Racial differences in factors that influence the willingness to participate in medical research studies. *Annals of Epidemiology, 12*(4), 248–256.

StataCorp. (2003). Stata Statistical Software: Release 8.0 [Computer software]. College Station, TX: Stata.

Stoddart, M. L., Jarvis, B., Blake, B., Fabsitz, R. R., Howar, B. V., Lee, E. T., et al. (2000). Recruitment of American Indians in epidemiologic research: The strong heart study. *American Indian and Alaska Native Mental Health Research, 9,* 20–37.

Swanson, G., & Ward, A. (1995). Recruiting minorities into clinical trials: Toward a participant-friendly system. *Journal of the National Cancer Institute, 87,* 1747–1759.

Thompson, E. E., Neighbors, H. W., Munday, C., & Jackson, J. J. (1996). Recruitment and retention of African American patients for clinical research: An exploration of response rates in an urban psychiatric hospital. *Journal of Consulting and Clinical Psychology, 64,* 861–867.

Unson, C., Dunbar, N., Curry, L., Kenyon, L., & Prestwood, K. (2001). The effects of knowledge, attitudes, and significant others on decisions to enroll in a clinical trial on osteoporosis: Implications for recruitment of older African-American women. *Journal of the National Medical Association, 93,* 392–401.

Vollmer, W. M., Svetkey, L. P., Appel, L. J., Obarzanek, E., Reams, P., Kennedy, B., et al. (1998). Recruitment and retention of minority participants in the DASH controlled feeding trial. *Ethnicity & Disease, 8*(2), 198–208.

Whelton, P. K., Lee, J. Y., Kusek, J. W., Charleston, J., DeBruge, J., Douglas. M., et al. (1996). Recruitment experience in the African American study of kidney disease and hypertension (AASK) pilot study. *Controlled Clinical Trials, 16,* 17S–33S.

CHAPTER 6

"I Wonder, Why Would You Do It That Way?"[1]

Ethical Dilemmas in Doing Participatory Research With Alaska Native Communities

GERALD V. MOHATT

LISA R. THOMAS

> *It is really good information for the people. I wish more would participate. They would learn a lot but it is up to them.*
>
> —Alaska Native Elder, after participating
> in a health research project (2004)

GOALS OF THIS CHAPTER

Our chapter will examine ethical issues that are tied to methodological decisions that may inadvertently violate the cultural values and sociolinguistic and social interactional rules that organize life in Alaska Native communities. At a deeper level, such decisions may also violate the symbolic cultural system that structures both values and sociolinguistics

(Erickson, 1975; Mohatt & Erickson, 1981). We will utilize the People Awakening Project as a case example to illustrate many of the dilemmas faced by university-based researchers and to show how these dilemmas have been negotiated. The specific point of departure for our approach is the belief that research is not fully ethical if it violates the fundamental values of a cultural group. This implies that most research is *more or less*

AUTHORS' NOTE: The study was funded by National Institute of Alcohol Abuse and Alcoholism and the National Center for Minority Health Disparities of the National Institutes of Health (RO1 03 11446 A2A). We would like to thank the NIAAA staff who supported us throughout this project, including Drs. Jan Howard, Suzanne Heurtin-Roberts, Marcia Scott, and Judith Arroyo. We want especially to thank all of the many participants who agreed to be interviewed.

ethical rather than either ethical or not ethical. There are certainly those who engage in potentially unethical research that violates the principles outlined in the Belmont Report, and it is necessary to sanction such conduct; however, we consider judgments of ethics to be more dimensional and continuous than categorically right or wrong. Therefore, we will explore the question of what defines and supports research that is ethical in indigenous or minority cultures.

We propose that within any investigator's assumptions about the process of constructing research procedures there exists a fundamental ethical dilemma: How do we ethically and effectively balance sound scientific inquiry with the specific needs involved in doing research in ethnically and culturally diverse communities whose values, worldviews, and meanings attached to specific experiences may be profoundly different from those held by the majority community from which current research practices evolved? Our research takes place in complex social interactions embedded within diverse communities, not in labs with animals, or even in labs with participants drawn randomly from a subject pool. Such interactions appear in our methods of recruitment and the procedures of our methodology. Convincing an individual or community to participate in the project is fundamental to the research enterprise. It is this process that is laden with assumptions that may or may not make sense cross-culturally and which we found ourselves negotiating throughout our project in order to honor our commitment to conduct ethically sound participatory research with Alaska Native communities.

BACKGROUND

For over a quarter of a century, issues related to informed consent and participant protection from harm have dominated ethical

discourse on the responsible conduct of research. In 1979 in what became known as the Belmont Report, the National Commission for the Protection of Human Subjects of Biomedical and Behavioral Research identified the principles of autonomy, beneficence, and justice as the moral ideals to which all research ethics should aspire. These principles formed the basis of federal regulations and scientific codes of conduct that require investigators to design studies that protect against harm by adequately minimizing research risks, maximizing potential research benefits, protecting confidentiality, and ensuring that participation is voluntary.

As important as the Belmont principles are to rightly practiced science, they do not necessarily speak to ethical issues that must be addressed when participants are members of communities that are ethnically and culturally different from those of the researchers (American Psychological Association [APA], 1993; Bernal & Scharron-del-Rio, 2001; Council of the National Psychological Associations for the Advancement of Ethnic Minority Interests [CNPAAEMI], 2000; Fisher et al., 2002). As researchers working in ethnocultural communities, we need to ask ourselves if the questions we pose are important and relevant to the communities in which we work and if the communities (research participants) share our research goals. For example, are the research questions we ask relevant to the experiences of these communities and are the community members, therefore, motivated to participate in research because it represents their concerns? When working with culturally diverse communities, understanding, respecting, and aligning ourselves with the needs, goals, and values of our participants is essential. Making concerted efforts to understand community perspectives on research becomes even more important when we acknowledge that the majority of researchers are not members of the communities they seek to study.

NEED FOR COLLABORATIVE RESEARCH MODELS

Past research efforts with Native people have rarely asked for their collaboration or contribution in the design, conduct, analysis, and interpretation of research. Fortunately, some pioneering efforts are beginning to emerge (see Fisher & Ball, 2002; Mohatt et al., 2004, for examples of approaches to working with American Indian and Alaska Native communities). Failure to use a collaborative approach often results in published data with scant useful feedback to the communities of concern, as well as intentional or unintentional exploitation of community knowledge, a process called "colonizing" by Smith (1999). There is increasing evidence that investigator-community collaborations are likely not only to result in research that is appropriate, relevant, and respectful but to produce results that are accurate and effective (Edwards, Jumper-Thurman, Plested, Oetting, & Swanson, 2000; Fisher & Ball, 2002; Parker-Langley, 2002; Rowe, 1997). Significant work remains to be done, however, in studying the differential benefits of collaborative research and in sorting out the complex issues that define when, how, and by whom it can be used (Trickett & Espino, 2004).

The last decade has witnessed the emergence of ethical guidelines for research involving ethnically and culturally diverse communities, in general (APA, 1993; CNPAAEMI, 2000; Fisher et al., 2002), and for research with American Indian and Alaska Native communities specifically (Alaska Native Science Commission [ANSC] 2001a, 2001b; CNPAAEMI, 2000). Besides the inclusion of community collaboration in the research process, these guidelines also advocate for Native *ownership* of research process, data, and outcomes.

CULTURAL SENSITIVITY

Emphasis on understanding context in community work becomes even more important as community psychologists work cross-culturally (Bernal & Scharron-del-Rio, 2001; Hall, 1997; Panigua, 1998; Sue, 2001). A growing awareness of the need for researchers to attend to ways culture influences the choice of research questions, methods, and interpretations (Allen & Walsh, 2000; Malgady, 1996; Matsumoto, 1994; Montero, 1994; Orlandi, Weston, & Epstein, 1992) shapes the research process or various research paradigms (Chataway, 1997; Santiago-Rivera, Morse, Hunt, & Lickers, 1998; Tandon, Azelton, Kelly, & Strickland, 1998). In addition, our experience highlights the imperative that researchers closely attend to *their own* values and beliefs when they are shaped by a Western scientific paradigm if their research is to meet the highest of ethical standards.

ALASKA: THE UNIQUE CONTEXT OF OUR RESEARCH

Alaska Natives, though often viewed from outside Alaska as a single group, comprise over 225 federally recognized tribes that are also separate villages scattered throughout rural Alaska. These tribes represent the major cultural groups: in the north, the Inupiaq; in the interior, the Athabascan; in the southwest, the Yup'ik and Cup'ik; in the south and west along the coast and Aleutians, the Aleut and the Alutiiq; and to the southeast, the Tlingit, Haida, and Tsimshian. Each group engages in unique subsistence economies, cultural practices, and rituals. Linguistically, the indigenous languages can differ as much as English and Chinese, in that they represent entirely distinct language families. Within groups, significant linguistic diversity also exists; for example, there are at least 11 recognized regional dialects of Athabascan.

Though almost half of Alaska Natives reside in urban centers, the majority live in widely dispersed rural villages where they are typically the majority ethnic group and vary in population from 10 to approximately 700 (U.S. Census Bureau, 2002). These villages rarely have road access and can be several hours from urban centers by boat or small plane. Much of the cash economy work is limited to education, health care, and government, with some seasonal employment opportunities in commercial fishing, construction, firefighting, tourism, and natural resources management. The majority of rural residents maintain a subsistence way of life through hunting and gathering, which provides the major portion of their diet as well as being culturally and spiritually significant. Distance and isolation are factors in the maintenance of a distinct cultural identity during a period of recent and rapid social transition.

Tribal groups and communities vary in how they monitor research in their communities and allow access to community members by researchers (gatekeeping). Most Alaska Native health corporations have ethics or human studies committees who utilize the university or Indian Health Service for the approval of an institutional review board (IRB); however, in many places, these committees or agencies may function like an IRB. All Alaska Native communities require village approval, local ethics and corporate board approval, and IRB approval prior to researchers beginning a project. Some regions require the approval of a regional health corporation or regional nonprofit corporation prior to engaging in the local approval process. Once approval is given, there is the expectation that progress reports and a final report will be provided to the participating communities and/or sponsoring Native agencies. In some regions, ethics boards will also require review of any abstract, presentation, or publication of research by a local board, and in some villages research will only be approved if the researcher agrees not to publish the results.

AUTHOR BACKGROUNDS

The authors of this chapter come from different cultures. Both are trained in psychology. G. Mohatt is European American, with a rural French, Irish, and German ethnic heritage, and raised in the rural Midwest. Dr. Mohatt left that area to live on the Rosebud Sioux, Sicangu Lakota reservation in South Dakota in 1968 and then moved to Alaska in 1983 where he has continued to work within indigenous communities. Mohatt has worked in Native communities as an educator, researcher, and clinician. His work with Native people deeply affected the value he places on family and a sense of place and community. He learned to speak Lakota, the western dialect of the Sioux Nation, and realized that our worldview is structured by language.

The other author, L. Thomas, is Tlingit and was raised in rural northwestern United States. Her father was raised in a small village in southeast Alaska and was subjected to both the strengths of this upbringing and the challenges: loss of resources and rights to live and practice cultural traditions and lifestyles, oppression and hostility based on racism and stereotyping, and rapid introduction to different (European American, Western, Christian) cultural norms and experiences. Therefore, Dr. Thomas was raised "in the middle ground," with both Tlingit and Western values and norms. She has worked with Native communities as a consultant, researcher, and clinician since 1987.

Having set the context for our discussion— including a brief description of the background for these ethical issues, the unique opportunities and challenges in doing collaborative research in cross-cultural and multicultural settings, and the importance of researcher/author perspectives—we offer our experiences in a recent study conducted in Alaska, the People Awakening Project.

WORKING THROUGH ETHICAL DILEMMAS: A CASE STUDY

We feel that the dilemmas described above, as well as the dilemmas discussed below, relate to the fundamental issues of choice and participation in the research process. Do the processes and procedures that are currently considered the scientific "gold standards" closely enough resemble the ways Native communities seek knowledge and construct meaning such that we can comfortably assert that there exists active and full consent to participate at all levels in the research? This question leads to some very practical issues that both of us confronted in the context of the People Awakening Project, which we offer as a case example.

People Awakening

Within the evolving and innovative approach of ethically aligning research with the concerns of the participating community, the People Awakening project (PA) was conceived as a collaborative relationship between Alaska Native community members and university-based scientists. As a collaborative process, the PA project was developed over a 4-year period into a study intended to identify potential protective and resiliency factors among Alaska Natives who recover from, or do not abuse, alcohol, using an approach grounded within an Alaska Native cultural worldview (Hazel & Mohatt, 2001).

The approach drew from community psychology perspectives that attend to the context of community (Sarason, 1971), emphasize empowerment (Rappaport, 1987; Wallerstein, & Bernstein, 1994), and utilize participatory action research approaches (Fals Borda, 2001; Gaventa, 1988). This community-focused approach moved away from interacting with participants as objects of representational knowledge to building equal community-investigator partnerships working together to shape and construct the research questions, methods, interpretations, and conclusions. This collaborative process imbues knowledge (or results) with the meanings ascribed to these results by the participants. It is intended to build *conscientization* (Friere, 1970), wherein knowledge is *emancipatory* (Fals Borda, 2001) and generated in a process of empowering communities.

In the first phase of the PA project, we completed 101 life history interviews of Alaska Natives who either were lifetime abstainers ($n = 15$), non–problem drinkers ($n = 28$), or had been sober for 5 or more years ($n = 58$). Recruitment procedures made extensive use of Alaska Native coresearcher consultants who nominated individuals for participation, with permission of the nominee. Interviewers were Alaska Native students, non-Native students, and Native and non-Native university researchers who traveled to participants' communities or, at participants' preference, interviewed them away from their home village to protect participant privacy (e.g., some participants were interviewed at the university). Participants were offered a $25 honorarium, though some declined, considering their story a gift to their communities. Interviews were conducted in a setting of the participant's choice and preferred language. Interviews were recorded digitally and transcribed verbatim or translated, in cases of indigenous language. Interviewees were given opportunity to review transcripts and/or recordings for accuracy. In phase two of the study, we constructed quantitative measures for the variables hypothesized from our qualitative analysis of the life histories to be protective factors (for those who never had a drinking problem) or recovery factors (for those who had recovered from an alcohol abuse problem).

A key mechanism of coresearcher involvement in this study was the Alaska Native Coordinating Council (ANCC), which included Alaska Natives from all regions, and the Alaska Native cultural groups participating in the project (see above for a listing of these cultural groups). Council members had grassroots activism and personal or work experience with Native sobriety or alcohol programs. These coresearchers did not function merely as an advisory panel; they engaged in planning and decision making at each juncture of the research process through an annual ANCC face-to-face meeting and periodic audio conference meetings. PA also employed Alaska Native research staff, field research staff, and cultural consultants, all of whom participated in our decision making, thus providing the project with ongoing cultural auditing. Our research team believes that working in this collaborative manner and infusing our research process with local knowledge and guidance supported our overall goals and strengthened the project; however, bringing such a varied group of people to the table also provided opportunities for conventional aspects of the research project to be challenged, bringing up numerous ethical issues and dilemmas, which we present below.

ETHICAL DILEMMAS IN PARTICIPATORY RESEARCH: RESOLUTIONS AND LIVING WITH TENSIONS

1. Does a common ground exist? Is the issue defined and understood similarly by the researcher and the community or population targeted for the study?

The PA project originated out of a number of questions posed by Alaska Natives: Why do some Alaska Natives not become alcoholic? How does this happen? What strengths does this sobriety reveal? Having a clear set of questions provided by the community of concern to which one can respond as a researcher is a luxury. As researchers, how often do we offer potential research questions to the communities in which we intend to work and engage in a dialogue to determine if they are relevant to the community under study? It might appear that if one has this luxury (i.e., the opportunity to collaborate with the participating community at this stage of the research process), no dilemma would exist; however, the situation was more complex than this. The ANCC (the group of sobriety leaders from the Native community described earlier) began to meet and discuss the aims and methodology with the university-based researchers, and our first dilemma became apparent: Did we share a common point of departure (i.e., did we have a shared understanding of the issues to be studied)?

Shared Understanding of the Goals of Research

Two events illustrate this dilemma. First, many of us found ourselves defining resilience in terms of the *absence* of problem drinking rather than the *presence* of sobriety and would frame the question similarly: How did people not have a problem? We found our focus gradually began to shift from strengths and resilience-based questions (e.g., what might protect people from alcohol abuse, or which traits in an individual and events in an individual's life might be related to them choosing to live a well life?) to questions directed toward identifying and assessing risk. Continually, one member or another of our planning group would ask why we so frequently talked about problems and sickness. Should we, indeed could we, shift our attention and language so that we reframed our questions to emphasize resilience? We agreed, but old habits die slowly, and this dilemma remained an issue to be navigated. Negotiating and renegotiating this fundamental question was the only way that we could create enough of a common ground from which we could focus on resilience, protective factors, and recovery processes. It took nearly 2 years prior to grant application to ensure that all members of the collaborative work group felt we shared the same point of departure and the same overall goals. The group did share a commitment that at the end of this planning process we would not write a grant for a project that would pathologize Native people, as much of the current literature suggests has been done. This process required that everyone (ANCC and university-based researchers) viewed each other as equals and that we seriously considered each person's opinion. If we had failed at this point, we could have at best moved forward to ask the wrong questions and at worst engaged in unethical and irresponsible research that might harm the communities.

We were also challenged early by the second dilemma. The issue was raised regarding whether we would study non–problem drinkers and whether we would accept into the sample individuals who had 5 or more years of recovery but were now non–problem drinkers. After much discussion, the group agreed that non–problem drinkers would be appropriate and important as a category for study. In fact, recent studies have pointed out that challenging what has been referred to as the firewater myth, which posits that all Native people are vulnerable and at-risk for becoming alcoholic, is an important issue to address (LaMarr, 2004); however, the ANCC remained concerned about how non–problem drinking would be defined and whether we would encourage drinking if we studied non–problem drinkers. This forced us to think thoroughly about how we would define

non–problem drinking and how we would present this issue to the communities in which we would be working. One member of the council cautioned us against including "the one black-eyed people," or those who might be considered by the community to be inappropriate due to their unacknowledged problem use of alcohol. Her discussion of this phenomenon encouraged the council to define nonproblem status in terms of negative consequences associated with drinking rather than by only frequency and amount drank. Obviously, this question is a controversial and sometimes troubling one and drew intense discussion. Issues such as whether the spirit of alcohol was good or evil, whether we might be interpreted as encouraging people to try to hang onto drinking and fool themselves, and whether we might lose our credibility because we would be seen as encouraging people to drink, although we knew that the results were devastating to the Alaska Native community. We faced the ethical issue of the potential impact of our study on communities. Rather than simply viewing the questions as scientific inquiry meant to contribute to the literature, we tried to balance scientific rigor with social responsibility and to challenge research conventions in order to appropriately and ethically work in a Native community. In the end, because these discussions highlighted the potential negative impact on the community, we chose not to include those who were in recovery from alcohol abuse but were currently non–problem drinkers. Many of us believed that it would be useful to include individuals who drank responsibly after having abused alcohol because so little is known about this group: Do they, in fact, exist, and how can they continue to drink without associated harmful consequences? Although we argued this point, we always found ourselves returning to the fundamental issue of how the PA project would affect the community, the ethical principle on which we would base many of our decisions. We finally agreed that including a group that had resolved alcohol abuse by responsible drinking was scientifically very important, but the ethical considerations of pursuing it outweighed trying to answer it.

In summary, in the discussions of both resilience versus pathology and whether to include non–problem drinkers, the ethical framework was necessarily expanded to include the community in addition to the individual. We could not simply consider the potential risk and benefits of research on the individual but rather needed to consider the effect on the entire community in order to define our research questions and goals and to determine our sample. This was critical to resolving the ethical question posed earlier: Do the researchers and the community from which the participants would come share the same goals for the research? Achieving a consensus regarding these overall goals was a painstaking process in which we worked collaboratively to understand and respect the differences of perspectives between community members and university researchers.

2. Do we share the same goals for each step of the research process?

This second ethical dilemma became apparent when, as a group, we had to choose from a myriad of proposed methodologies to study the research questions that we had collaboratively constructed. In addition, we were acutely aware of the issue facing all researchers: What was going to be fundable and what might not be fundable by NIH/NIAAA? Indeed, could we even develop a proposal that would represent the shared goals of our group and have a successful review in the NIH study section? This brought the pragmatic into the discussion. If research that has successfully negotiated a more ethical point of departure, as described above, is to remain aligned with the ethical standards of the community (ANSC 2001a, 2001b), it must match a set of scientific methods to the

community's culture or utilize the methods of investigation of the culture.

The ethical dilemmas we faced at this point focused on two issues: research approach (i.e., qualitative vs quantitative) and sampling methods. In our situation, the methodology that fit was narrative, or qualitative, in nature. Life histories of individuals that allowed participants to tell their stories in a manner that was natural and acceptable to them might be more likely to maximize choice and minimize coercion. Therefore, in order to work ethically in these communities, we faced balancing the more appropriate methodologies for this project (qualitative in design, purposive sampling) with those more conventional, and therefore more likely to be funded, methodologies (quantitative, random sampling).

Although the ANCC made it clear that random sampling for such a study (sobriety process in Alaska Natives) would be unacceptable as well as unsuccessful in recruiting participants, we were also informed by consultants with much NIH study section experience that a nonrandom strategy would have a difficult time in a grant review study section. Additionally, the ANCC informed us that using an instrument-based approach to exploring the research questions would also be less likely to capture the truth, to elicit meaningful information from the participants. As both researchers and culturally competent psychologists, we had to ask ourselves which would guide us: integrity to the goals and values of the community or these more conventional and accepted research methodologies. Once again, we turned to the wisdom of our ANCC for guidance.

Research Design

We met as a collaborative team to determine whether to offer only a qualitative approach or to use a set of mixed methods, with the first phase being qualitative and the subsequent phase being more quantitative in nature, involving measurement development and pilot testing. Throughout this process of negotiation, some of the team wanted to be practical and said that we should do what is necessary to obtain the funding because of the potential benefits of the knowledge generated to Alaska Native communities. This approach, therefore, considered both what might be best for the participants and what might be most useful for the communities. In this context, the issue was not simply what was expedient but meant that we must explore the pros and cons for the community if we decided to include a quantitative design. In the end, we decided to include measurement development and piloting of a set of quantitative instruments because researchers and the communities lacked a set of measures of protective or recovery factors that were emically derived and tested for linguistic and cultural equivalence. We knew that treatment programs currently used instruments that may not relate to the lives of Native people and that prevention programs needed measurement tools to identify factors that might be protective and to measure their effects. Good cross-cultural science and honoring the goal of contributing to the community came together, and we appeared to again have achieved a level of convergence between methodology and cultural values of the ANCC. Yet we still faced the process of negotiating the issue of sampling.

Sampling

In phase one, we agreed to propose a purposive convenience sample for the life histories. Word of mouth, advertising, radio shows, television shows, and newspaper articles brought us more volunteers than we could interview; however, in phase two we proposed a random sampling strategy for measurement development. We had randomly selected villages stratified by size and were going to randomly select households and request participants who fell into our preestablished sobriety and age categories. One of the researchers developed a method using a Rolodex with house numbers and a door-to-door method of contacting those who were to be sampled; however, this caused a sharp dispute among the research team members. Our local coordinator in rural Alaska, as well as other members of the research team, felt that this strategy for sampling would violate the community's culture because the door-to-door visiting would appear intrusive and coercive. The sense was that we might be perceived as attempting to convince individuals to participate by focusing on the benefits of the research and that it was difficult to say no to someone standing at the door or in one's home. In fact, from a culturally grounded perspective, this sampling strategy might be considered coercive, as community values might make it difficult to say no to a researcher presenting at a potential participant's home. The ethics of research require that an individual's decision to participate be as unpressured and free as possible (i.e., not coerced).

Given the nature of rural Alaska communities, however, many on the list of potential participants would not have phones and could not be contacted in a less intrusive method. We explored ideas about using bulk mail to these households. We discussed other forms of randomization that were quasi-experimental, given that we already had a unit of randomization at the community level rather than the individual level and convenience sampling as the procedure within the community. Although we had randomized by community, it did not solve either the methodological or the ethical problem because we still had to decide how to recruit individual participants. We stumbled without resolution. Finally, at one point, the first author asked the team to begin the process of going door to door in order to try the method with the Rolodex and house-to-house contacting. The research team agreed to try it but found it intrusive, if not coercive. The field researchers felt it was unethical because *we* decided who should be included rather than offering it to everyone and then agreeing to interview all those who chose to enroll. This sort of exclusion is a violation of community values in most Alaska Native communities.

Following many discussions and deep division, the first author decided over the objections of some of the team to return to a purposive sample. It was difficult to abandon random sampling, but there was a point at which the ethical considerations discussed above superseded the methodological issue. The conflict within the team about this approach revealed an ethical issue that we would face in attempting to implement a more conventional random sampling design at the household level in Alaska Native communities.. This reflected ethical issues that we would face in attempting to implement a more conventional sampling procedure in Alaska Native communities. In addition, other important issues had to be taken into consideration in this process. As described earlier, research in Alaska must contend with the following: large geographical distances between the university and the communities in question; the impact of subsistence lifestyles, cultural values, customs, and traditions on availability of participants; rules regarding inclusion and exclusion; and the nature and parameters of confidentiality when working in small, isolated communities. Clearly, the ethical dilemmas faced at this stage were complex and required an immense amount of negotiation among the team members and the communities.

Importance of Acceptance Into the Community

One approach that we did not try in PA but are attempting in another study is to set a goal of enrolling 70 to 80% of eligible participants and continue to recruit until that goal is attained. This does not resolve the complex issues of recruiting individuals from Native communities; however, it appears that if one couples this type of sampling with locating a field researcher full-time in the participating community, and also has other researchers from the team continually visiting the community, a relationship may develop that allows people in the community to learn about the project and, just as importantly, the researchers. Additionally, trained volunteers from the community and/or members of the research team can visit homes in the community and discuss the project without it seeming coercive. This could provide the potential participant more freedom to decline or agree to participate in the project. This strategy then becomes more inclusive rather than exclusive and fits the kinship nature of indigenous communities because the research team develops stronger relationships with the people.

Although the PA project could not support a field researcher in each community, we tried to solve this dilemma by hiring research staff who were trained and who possessed the communication skills to negotiate in a culturally appropriate manner. We continually examined and discussed these issues so that we could attend to any potential ethical problems. At the most fundamental level, our experience demonstrated that the most appropriate and effective solution is to allow researchers to take the time to become embedded in, and accepted by, communities so that the questions and methods used in the research project emerge from the community. If this type of relationship is achieved between researchers and Native communities, the potential exists for what Erickson (1975) called "shared co-membership" (e.g., we hunt or sew or have children of the same ages or went to the same school). He found that in cross-cultural dyads that had high shared co-membership (e.g., in our case, being Alaska Native, speaking the same indigenous language, having attended the same high school, being mothers, being former/current basketball players), individuals of the minority culture and the majority culture felt freer to identify conflict and resolve it. Our experience is that when the community begins to identify our researchers as part of their community, with shared interests and increased co-membership, individuals within the communities will begin to feel more comfortable to choose to participate or not in a research project.

Perhaps an example of enhancing shared co-membership and addressing potential challenges in participatory research would be helpful. During the first year of funding, we had a 3-day meeting with the coordinating council, the ANCC. One of the investigators presented the results of instrument development that occurred in our pilot study, describing the measurement tool (coping) and its factor structure. After the first intensive day, the second author, L. Thomas, shared a taxi with three of the council members. The ride was curiously quiet for the first few minutes, at which point the council members looked at each other and said, "We didn't understand a word of what you guys were saying," referring to the technical research terms used to describe the measurement development process. Thomas queried them about what had not made sense to them and then contacted Mohatt and the presenter and told them about the problem. The presenter was not defensive, decided on a method of explaining factor analysis, and then went over the presentation again so the council could assist in determining what the best factor solution was and how to name the factors. Many of the council were women who shared the practice of a traditional craft and thus had felt a level of co-membership with Thomas as an Alaska Native woman, which they did not have with the other investigators. They were comfortable

disclosing to her that they had not understood the discussion and wanted to participate in a fully informed manner. This example illustrates how critical it is to form a team that allows community members to share their lack of knowledge, concerns, and disagreements. One can have very culturally competent researchers, but the project needs to have a culturally inclusive and competent team or organization. Members should have an investment in the well-being of the communities and a sense of co-membership in important aspects of the values and activities of the community in order to provide proper venues for this kind of exchange of information.

We did not achieve this level of shared co-membership in the PA project in all situations. Due to financial and time restraints, we could not place long-term field researchers in the communities in which we were working. Although the research team was successful in developing and sustaining relationships built on trust and the communities endorsed the goals of PA, we were rarely able to spend significant amounts of time in our participating communities. We simply did not have the funding to place people within each village or to have local researchers who reside in the participating communities in order to develop these types of reciprocal relationships. We also discovered that, although somewhat more advantageous, having a regional coordinator who could be located a bit closer to the communities than Fairbanks (University of Alaska Fairbanks was the site of the PA project) did not solve the issue. That person and the project staff could (and did) struggle with the tension between how a local person can be a scientist, field worker, and a community member. Therefore, this issue was not entirely resolved.

In summary, our experience indicated that in order to conduct research in American Indian/Alaska Native communities that is ethical, appropriate, relevant, respectful, and effective, many issues regarding methodology must be addressed. These include negotiating a research design that both explores the research questions and respects the population of interest. Similarly, sampling procedures that provide sound scientific parameters and are acceptable to the values and context of the community must be worked out. As mentioned, in the process of negotiating these issues, it became apparent to the PA staff that these ethical dilemmas must be resolved, which requires building trusting relationships over a lengthy period of time.

3. Are the proposed methodologies not only "scientifically sound," but culturally appropriate, relevant, and respectful? Are the measurement instruments asking the appropriate questions? Are these questions and the responses given by the participants understood similarly by both the researchers and the participants?

Other issues also became apparent throughout the PA project, challenging our understanding of research as both scientific and ethical. Specifically, from which perspective does the question become scientific and ethical? As we discuss below, when the potential exists for differences in worldview, values, and meaning between the research team and the community in question, many ethical dilemmas emerge.

Confidentiality and Native Worldviews

The issue of confidentiality, for example, is problematic and presents a significant ethical dilemma: confidentiality versus respect for cultural norms. In many Native cultures, not identifying yourself, your family, your homeland, and so forth is not acceptable; however, from a Western scientific perspective, we are required to maintain a maximum distance

between researchers and research subjects. We are required to ensure that the participant's identifying information is protected and that confidentiality is ensured at every juncture of the research process. In fact, participants are not identified by name, family, clan, or homeland but rather by subject number; and, as researchers, we consider this the ethical gold standard; however, for a Native person, this might appear unethical.

For example, at the guidance of our ANCC, PA participants were originally asked if they wanted to be identified as participants and/or have their story published with their names included. We received objections from some of the IRBs that had to review and approve our methods and consent forms prior to beginning the project. The IRB members felt that if we offered this as an option, we could be perceived as encouraging participants to agree to identify themselves, therefore reducing their freedom to assent or decline confidentiality; however, when we discussed dropping this option and informing participants that we would destroy the data 5 years after completing the research (per current research convention), elders in the communities protested, stating that they could not imagine why they would tell their story if it would *not* be shared with others and would be destroyed. Thankfully, after giving feedback to the IRB, PA was able to receive permission from the IRB to continue with a protocol that included a consent form giving multiple options to participants regarding degree of confidentiality.

This example illustrates that the issues of cross-cultural variation with respect to confidentiality must be carefully considered and negotiated between researchers, communities, and institutional review boards charged with protecting research participants from harm. Additionally, it underscores the fact that researchers and IRBs need to discuss assumptions to ensure that they are not culturally bound to a European American individualistic ethos of privacy.

Use of Standardized Instruments

A second ethical dilemma we faced regarding research methodology involved the use of measurement and instrumentation in psychological research. When we do cross-cultural psychological research with measurement instruments, do we really know how the participant perceived our research questions and what kinds of meaning they may have attached to the questions when they responded? Do we know what their answer means? That is, how do we, as researchers, interpret their responses? For example, PA developed a measure of coping and adaptation that asked participants to indicate factors most important to them in the process of their becoming sober or never developing a problem with alcohol. We had worked collaboratively with our council to develop a set of potential ways of coping that were important to Alaska Natives in support of sobriety and wellness. For example, the council indicated that Native dancing, spirituality, subsistence activities, counseling, and AA were important factors that contributed to wellness in Alaska Native people. The participants were asked to respond to this measure using a five-point Likert scale ranging from *not at all important* to *very important* regarding whether or not each item helped them become sober or never develop a problem with alcohol.

As we tested this instrument in the field, interviewers reported that they were often confused by the responses of participants. For example, a Native elder who never engaged in Native dancing and was deeply Christian and did not believe that people should engage in Native dancing rated it as very important. We would repeat this question, per the protocol, with the instructions: "How important is this *for you?*" This elder, however, would repeat his response, "very important." This issue regarding responses that were difficult to interpret came up consistently, so we queried our respondents about it. They told us that these things were important for sobriety even if they were not important in their own personal lives or even if they did not engage in the activity themselves. They said that if they thought of these items as important to the tribe, or to their family or community, they would endorse the item as important. Although some participants had no problem with this, it appeared that the more linguistically traditional the person was, and more embedded within their community, the more likely it was that they would respond to an item with the tribal group or community as the referent rather than themselves. We realized that our methods assumed that we expected people to switch into a Western individualistic perspective to answer the questions rather than maintain their collectivist orientation.

This raised an ethical question for us: Should we persist in using this instrument and analyze the data to see how it worked statistically or drop the measure from the protocol and the analysis until we could both understand our participants' perspectives and find a better way to ask the questions? It became clear that by continuing to use this instrument, we might be doing harm to the communities in which we were working by presenting results that we truly did not understand. We decided to drop the measure.

Understanding One's Data

This raises a related and very critical issue: understanding one's data. This includes making sure that one discusses and understands the limitations of the data and accurately presents the meaning of the data. If we had not asked our participants for their input regarding the coping instrument, we would never have known that the responses we were obtaining were not addressing the question that we asked, *as we understood it*. Even if we had successfully run statistical analyses that demonstrated certain consistent patterns, we would not have been able to accurately interpret it *as our participants meant it*.

Through this process of understanding the meaning of confidentiality and understanding the problematic differences of meaning inherent in standardized instruments in PA, we came to acknowledge and resolve another ethical dilemma: Who should participate in the analysis and interpretation of data? We learned that it is essential to include members of the community in this process either as focus groups or as a coordinating or advisory council, as the PA project did. Additionally, the mechanism for having community involvement in the analysis and interpretation is variable and in dire need of further exploration. Using our data as an example, we must consider if it is appropriate for (a) conventional interpretation strategies (i.e., the researchers), (b) Alaska Native persons, nontribal specific to interpret all Alaska Native data, or (c) only Inupiat to interpret Inupiat data, Tlingit and Haida to interpret Tlingit and Haida data, and so on. This is an interesting query, as to date only European Americans interpret data collected from European American subjects. Would the analysis and interpretation change at all if the analysis and interpretation were done by non–European American researchers? This dilemma demands further exploration: As scientists, what are the critical factors we need in order to ensure that we have adequately understood, analyzed, interpreted, and represented the data from one group or from another?

The PA project attempted to resolve this issue in two ways: by directly involving participants from the communities in the analysis process and by requiring that the research team be multiethnic, multicultural, and cross-disciplinary. Our sense is that the most

important method that we utilized to address the issue of appropriate strategies for interpreting our data was for the participants themselves to engage in interpretation. We achieved this by mailing to the appropriate participant some of the transcripts and our reflections and notes on the interpretations we were making of the life stories they had shared. Then we followed up with a phone call to allow the participant to provide feedback to us regarding the accuracy of our interpretation. Members of our council were also participants in this phase of the analysis and engaged in extensive interpretation and analysis at two separate meetings devoted to this process. This enlisted the participants as coresearchers to help frame the interpretation (Hall, 1981; Mohatt et al., 2004). Unfortunately, it was impossible to check our interpretations of every life history with every participant. Had we triangulated our interpretations of the qualitative and quantitative results with non-Native and Native members of the team, our outside consultants and ANCC, and with all of the participants, we might have further resolved any ambiguity about the truth of our inferences. The dilemma that we often faced was how to do all of the steps we considered ethical and important when we had limited time and resources. Our resolution was to try to do part of what we considered ideal by contacting some of the participants with our reflections and interviewing them about what they thought about our interpretations, even if we could not recontact all participants.

In addition, PA had members on the research team who represented each of the five cultural groups in the study, as well as from other tribal and nontribal backgrounds. Although analysis was guided by the principal investigator, collaborating investigators, and project director, the entire team participated in analysis and interpretation. This meant that we were able to include in our analysis input from team members with significant experience in the tribal communities, allowing us to more completely ground our interpretation in the context of our participants. Our position in PA was that interpreting the data was best done with a variety of perspectives. Although this did not satisfy everyone as a pure enough approach, it appeared to be the most appropriate and effective manner in which to resolve this ethical dilemma.

In summary, we faced numerous ethical dilemmas as we navigated between conventional research practices and the complex issues that come into play with cross-cultural research. Ultimately, we learned that it is essential to include members of the participating communities in the decision making regarding research methodologies (including limits of confidentiality), the meaning ascribed to research questions and participant responses, and the analysis and interpretation of the resulting data. Without community involvement in each of these steps, it is clear that any results are questionable at best and harmful to the communities at worst.

4. **What is our responsibility for dissemination of the research results, not just in peer-reviewed journals but also in venues that stakeholders and our participants will utilize?**

Clearly, one of the goals of research is dissemination of important findings, with the accepted route of dissemination being peer-reviewed journals. The PA team was obviously motivated to publish results in this manner; however, one of the major criticisms of research in Native communities is that researchers do not share the results with the communities from which the data was collected. Rather, convention dictates that the data is stored in locked file cabinets under researcher control to be destroyed at the completion of the research. As mentioned

earlier, however, PA was ethically bound by our participants to share our data and our results with the Alaska Native community. The PA team shared this belief, and remained committed throughout the project to disseminate information resulting from the project with the Alaska Native communities across the state in a variety of formats.

PA published an annual newsletter with information about the progress of the project, information about the research team, nonidentifying information about the participants (unless participants wished to be identified), and information about the trends that were emerging in the data. These newsletters were mailed to individuals and service providers across the state of Alaska. In addition, various team members did oral presentations, which provided similar information to the newsletters, to communities, health agencies, Native organizations, and corporations. Also, because the PA grant provided no funding for these types of dissemination, we found ourselves seeking alternative sources of support from, in particular, other departments at the University of Alaska Fairbanks and Alaska Native agencies.

Finally, we wanted to develop a report in a form that would provide a tool for the individuals and service providers in Alaska Native communities. At the time of this chapter, we are preparing a CD-ROM and a booklet of excerpts of the life histories to send with a lay version of our final report to NIAAA. This CD-ROM and booklet will also go to each participant and each tribal corporation. The CD-ROM allows a person to read or listen to the life histories on a computer and can be navigated, allowing for a search in the life histories by tribe, gender, sobriety category, or the heuristic model that we developed from the life histories describing what protects people from developing a problem with alcohol or supports their recovery. The booklet has short excerpts of the life histories, and each one that was included was approved by the participant. These life histories are inspiring and useful for prevention and treatment programs. Although we have not received funding to disseminate the CD or the booklet, we have shared these resources, and tribal groups are now contacting PA and inviting us to speak or provide training in the PA model to them.

The National Institutes of Health (NIH) has begun to develop model programs that take dissemination at the community level seriously. Community-responsive interventions to reduce cardiovascular risk in American Indians and Alaska Natives will fund four projects to reduce cardiovascular risk factors among Alaska Natives and American Indians. They were developed in consultation with tribes and call for early collaboration, a year of planning and measurement development, 2 years of intervention, and a year of analysis followed by dissemination. Researchers are required to partner in the projects. When more of NIH funding is structured in this manner, we will more easily address the issue of responsibility to disseminate and return to the community.

SUMMARY

A Conversation

LRT: The ethical dilemma in doing research with Native communities, for me, begins with the whole idea or concept of research as conventionally defined. This is a two-part issue. First, the fundamental context and purpose of research can be viewed as problematic. That is, why do research? Research, as practiced by scientifically trained psychologists, is primarily embedded in the values of a Western, individualistic, Judeo-Christian, Caucasian society.

Second, assuming we can reasonably come to some point of consensus about the appropriateness of conducting research, we must then address the specific issues encountered in each step of the research process as presented above.

GVM: I agree that it appears to me that we get into trouble when we don't examine our goals and epistemology.

LRT: To me, these unexamined goals reflect this conflict, and it is fundamentally a cultural conflict. It is a conflict that I deeply feel as a Native researcher and includes a number of challenges:

- Identifying and isolating particular responses (behaviors, emotions, cognitions) for study
- Giving these responses some sort of value, either neutral or relative
- Controlling these responses, as well as other characteristics, so that the response can be somehow measured, eliminated, increased, manipulated, and so forth
- Interpreting these responses, as well as any changes that occur after manipulating or controlling, and assigning potential meanings and relationships
- Making an assumption that because standardized methodologies and statistical analysis suggest a particular result, this result exists regardless of the fact that the worldview, value systems, context, and so on may be entirely different for the participants who are responding to the research questions than for the researchers. This brings a complexity to the point raised earlier in this chapter regarding the alignment of research questions: Are the *responses* given to a particular research question understood and interpreted similarly by the researcher and the participant?

GVM: This last one you mention I face a lot, and we tried to deal with it in PA. Maybe we were able to do some good adaptations of methods and instruments, but were we careful enough? I agree that the measurement instruments we used have never been scrutinized for cultural equivalence and validity in indigenous contexts. We just simply don't know if they work in the same manner, if they have the same factor structure, if the response sets make sense, and if we have established validity for them within the population we study. I have been told by colleagues that if we had to do this, research would come to a halt because no one has the time or money to do this and the agencies don't typically fund it. So we use instruments that may or may not have established cross-cultural construct validity. Some examine the instruments to see how well they work across cultural groups, and others do not. This appears to me to increase our likelihood of both false negatives and false positives; but most fundamentally, we will not know what we have proved or discovered. This has always made me wary of claims made by research within cross-cultural settings.

LRT: This raises for me the question of deep cultural structures and philosophy. I don't believe that these goals and this process are consistent with an indigenous approach to life, which may or may not be individualistic, Judeo-Christian, and Caucasian, and, therefore, may be something entirely different. Look at the work of Dauenhauer and Dauenhauer (1987),

Dombrowski (2001), Emmons (1991), Goldschmidt and Haas (1998), Hope (2000), Joles and Oozeva (2002), and Nelson (1983). Many traditional Native people or communities would not isolate behaviors, emotions, or cognitions and assign values to them, measure them, manipulate them, and interpret the results. Rather, many Natives believe in the connectedness of life, as an interesting balance between the autonomy of the individual and the importance of the community or collective. That is, they would not presume to isolate and identify behaviors, thoughts, or feelings with the intent to intervene in some manner. Additionally, I find it startling that we are discouraged from pursuing good scientific inquiry because of the costs and difficulties associated with it!

GVM: For sure! We saw that a lot in PA. For me this is the critical area of our dilemma. The work of research that we described is often like an "as if" experience. If I move one way, I violate a fundamental principle of the Western science, and if I move in another way, I feel as if I am not fully telling the truth to the participants about what the measurement instruments or methodology can tell them. For example, when I tell the participants the results of their blood glucose test, it is fairly clear, and the measure makes cross-cultural sense; however, when I tell a person about body/mass-index (BMI), then it is much more ambiguous because it has not been clearly validated for most indigenous groups. When I move back into social science, my measurement instruments have typically never been scrutinized for construct validity, linguistic and cultural equivalence, and other forms of validity for Native people. This leads to a higher level of ambiguity, leaving me with a fundamental dilemma of potentially stating a result that is not valid. In fact, in many cases, I have found that the questions I am asking are not at all understood in the same way by indigenous participants. Although we have limitations sections, I don't recall *ever seeing one* that says we don't know if the measurement instrument is valid for this population but we used it anyway because it is all we have. We must be honest about our uncertainties with the communities and clear about what we have learned or are likely to learn.

LRT: Historically, the canon of Western science has set the burden of proof regarding the appropriateness of current research practices with ethnic minority communities and those that advocate for them. I believe this burden should shift to the researchers to prove that the current conventional, standardized methodologies are accurate and appropriate rather than assume that they are unless indicated otherwise.

GVM: I think another good example that we discussed and that illustrates this burden is sampling. I believe that random sampling procedures violate a fundamental principle of every indigenous group with whom I have worked. It assumes that a statistical or mathematical rationale should determine whom we talk to or with whom we intervene. It is exclusive rather than inclusive (that is, selects only a certain number of participants rather than invites everyone to participate). Without such a statistical structure, the canons for establishing proof and generalizable knowledge are assumed to be violated. Conversely, this statistical structure assumes that we will find out what is most important to characterize the group that we are studying if we sample in this manner, and that mathematics, a linguistic system, gives us the right to establish a shared trait of a group or the shared result of an intervention. Within an indigenous context, however, one looks for proof and generalizeable knowledge by *selective* sampling of those who have the knowledge that fits the question. In this contextual framework, we would study how people recover from alcohol abuse by selecting exemplary models to illustrate and share their knowledge or by selecting elders with significant wisdom. We should not, and really could not, decide whether it applies to others, but would rather provide the communities with the discovered knowledge and information so that each individual can choose to use the information and knowledge discovered by the research. Appropriate application of results, therefore, would be left up to each person to decide. I don't think that most indigenous groups assume that they could say x or y applies to another individual or group in any normative manner. If one were to do so, it would violate a rule and value not to speak for others or stand in the place of the other.

LRT: As I said above, we, as indigenous people, do not value knowledge that is without a context or a relationship to people and places. To isolate participants' behaviors, responses, and choices from family, community, culture, land, and lineage is to potentially take all the meaning, perhaps the truth, out of the data.

GVM: I agree with the idea but also know that many researches are aware of the importance of context and do not want to decontextualize themselves or the community. My recent experience in the field indicates how critical the relationship of the researcher to the village is. It takes a lot of time for a village to know you and trust you as initial outsider. Also, for me, then, this issue of recruiting that we discussed has significant cultural issues. In my work as a researcher, I persuade in subtle and not so subtle ways. I market a study for its benefits. I encourage participation in my study. My indigenous field assistants typically ask me to send a non-Native to do recruitment because they say that they are more assertive. When we explore this, they tell me that their values influence their resistance to "push others, to interfere." We do not try to coerce; we try to only lay out the potential benefits and leave it to each individual to choose. In one tribal context, a healer said that if anything bad happens after we persuade another, then it becomes our responsibility. Human choice is never to be violated or played with; to do so becomes a fundamental ethical violation.

LRT: Yes, it takes courage and conviction, as well as commitment to sound science, to challenge the conventions for research in which we have been trained. This very issue, potential for coercion, provides an example of differences in worldview. As discussed earlier, a random sampling strategy, employed by outsiders to the community, would likely be viewed by many indigenous communities as both exclusive and dangerous because not all members of the community would be included, and there would be no evidence of co-membership on the part of the researchers and therefore no sense of protection from harm.

GVM: What we have been trying to communicate is that research is about knowledge and expanding knowledge. When our procedures do not elucidate the unique worldview of indigenous people, then I think that we are distancing ourselves from truth, and our ethics will become problematic. Since I learned Lakota, I have been fascinated by how Native people construct knowledge and whether how I interpret and make sense of what I am told differs fundamentally from what they have told me. Ethical guidelines indicate clearly that in a cross-cultural study (in which there exist differences between the culture of the researchers and the culture of the community in question), individuals from the culture or community of the participants should participate in data analysis and interpretation and that this should constitute one of the norms for culturally appropriate research. Without such involvement, the opportunities to build emic meanings are diminished. Without the emic in cross-cultural research, we lack an ethical and scientific foundation to know when we have discovered something new; however, it is unfortunately more complex than simply attending to the ethnicity of the researchers and the participants. It is necessary to build a critical set of feedback loops that will allow constant questioning and affirming what the responses to our interview questions, surveys, or measurement instruments mean. Personally, I would like to learn the language of the group with whom I am working in order to have some idea of their epistemology. But my sense is that those of us not from the community in which we are doing the research must work to establish a relationship that is similar to a kinship relationship. To work with trust, to have Native people entrust their knowledge to us, we must see our research participants as relatives. It is relatives that receive our greatest trust and to whom we can entrust our honest opinions, attitudes, and our knowledge. As the elder whom we quoted earlier said, "Choice is the bedrock of participation." My experience of how Native families develop children and how hunters prepare for a hunt is they prepare well and think out their choices. This takes time, and research based on this way of learning and functioning takes time.

LRT: Absolutely. As I stated earlier, I am startled, even discouraged,

that we are not trained as psychologists and researchers in a manner that encourages, better yet requires, us to adapt our research methodologies to the various and unique settings in which ethnically and culturally diverse communities and individuals exist. To be prohibited from doing so because of associated costs and increased complexity is unthinkable! As both a Native woman and a psychologist, I am excited by the challenges that negotiating cross-cultural research presents. I believe that I am challenged to become both a better scientist and a better scholar of indigenous and ethnically diverse communities. I am also challenged to understand who I am, what my values and worldviews are, and how they affect my work as a clinician and a researcher. I am encouraged by projects such as People Awakening, by the commitment you and your research team demonstrated throughout the collaborative research process. There are wonderful people doing important work similar to this, and they should be acknowledged, applauded, and learned from. As we both have mentioned, we are all connected: to each other, to the land, to our ancestors, and to our children and all the children to come. That is powerful medicine that, rather than being viewed as "noise in the data," can inform, clarify, and strengthen our work as culturally competent and culturally grounded psychologists and scientists.

NOTE

1. This is a question that would often come up in our PA meetings, phrased in different ways: Why would you say it that way? This just can't be translated? Isn't there a better way to ask this or find a participant? The question was always, *Are there better ways than Western science has devised?* (or perhaps, a better way to skin the proverbial cat?)

REFERENCES

Alaska Native Science Commission. (2001a). Code of research ethics. Retrieved March 23, 2005, from www.nativescience.org/html/Code%20of%20Research%20Ethics.html

Alaska Native Science Commission. (2001b). Guidelines for respecting cultural knowledge. Retrieved March 23, 2005, from www.nativescience.org/html/guildlines_cultural.htm

Allen, J., & Walsh, J. A. (2000). A construct-based approach to equivalence: Methodologies for cross-cultural/multicultural personality research assessment. In R. H. Dana (Ed.), *Handbook of cross-cultural and multicultural personality assessment* (pp. 63–86). Mawah, NJ: Lawrence Erlbaum.

American Psychological Association Office of Ethnic Minority Affairs. (1993). Guidelines for providers of psychological services to ethnic, linguistic, and culturally diverse populations. *American Psychologist, 48*(1), 45–48.

Bernal, G., & Scharron-del-Rio, M. R. (2001). Are empirically supported treatments valid for ethnic minorities? Toward an alternative approach for treatment research. *Cultural Diversity and Ethnic Minority Psychology, 7*(4), 328–342.

Chataway, C. (1997). An examination of the constraints on mutual inquiry in a participatory action research project. *Journal of Social Issues, 53,* 747–766.

Council of National Psychological Associations for the Advancement of Ethnic Minority Interests. (2000). *Guidelines for research in ethnic minority communities.* Washington, DC: Author.

Dauenhauer, N. M., & Dauenhauer, R. (1987). *Haa shuká, our ancestors: Tlingit oral narratives.* Juneau, AK: Sealaska Heritage Foundation.

Dombrowski, K. (2001). *Against culture: Development, politics, and religion in Indian Alaska.* Lincoln: University of Nebraska Press.

Edwards, R. W., Jumper-Thurman, P., Plested, B. A., Oetting, E. R., & Swanson, L. (2000). Community readiness: Research to practice. *Journal of Community Psychology, 28*(3), 291–307.

Emmons, T. G. (1991). *The Tlingit Indians* (F. de Laguna, Ed.). Seattle: University of Washington Press.

Erickson, F. (1975). Gatekeeping and the melting pot: Interaction in counseling encounters. *Harvard Educational Review, 45,* 44–69.

Fals Borda, O. (2001). Participatory (action) research in social theory: Origins and challenges. In P. Reason & H. Bradbury (Eds.), *Handbook of action research.* London: Sage.

Fisher, P. A., & Ball, T. J. (2002). The Indian family wellness project: An application of the tribal participatory research model. *Prevention Science, 3*(3), 235–240.

Fisher, C. B., Hoagwood, K., Boyce, C., Duster, T., Frank, D. A., Grisso, T., et al. (2002). Research ethics for mental health science involving ethnic minority children and youths. *American Psychologist, 57*(12), 1024–1040.

Gaventa, J. (1988). Participatory research in North America. *Convergence, 21,* 19–28.

Hall, B. L. (1981). Participatory research, popular knowledge and power: A personal reflection. *Convergence, 14,* 6–17.

Freire, P. (1970). *Pedagogy of the oppressed.* New York: Continuum.

Goldschmidt, W. R., & Haas, T. H. (1998). *Haa aani, Our land: Tlingit and Haida land rights and use* (T. R. Thorton, Ed.). Seattle: University of Washington Press; Juneau, AK: Sealaska Heritage Foundation.

Hall, C. I. J. (1997). Cultural malpractice: The growing obsolescence of psychology with the changing U.S. population. *American Psychologist, 52,* 642–651.

Hazel, K. L., & Mohatt, G. V. (2001). Cultural and spiritual coping in sobriety: Informing substance abuse prevention for Alaska Native communities. *Journal of Community Psychology, 29*(5), 541–562.

Hope, A. (2000). On migrations. In A. Hope, III & T. F. Thorton (Eds.), *Will the time ever come? A Tlingit sourcebook* (pp. 23–33). Fairbanks: Alaska Native Knowledge Network, Center for Cross-cultural Studies, University of Alaska Fairbanks.

Joles, C. Z., & Oozeva, E. M. (2002). *Faith, food and family in a Yupik whaling community.* Seattle: University of Washington Press.

LaMarr, J. C. (2004). Firewater myth: Fact of self-fulfilling prophecy. In S. H. Stewart & P. J. Conrad (Chairs), *New developments in prevention and early intervention for alcohol abuse in youth.* Symposium conducted at the meeting of the Research Society on Alcoholism, Vancouver, BC; Austin, TX: Research Society on Alcoholism.

Malgady, R. G. (1996). The question of cultural bias in assessment and diagnosis of ethnic minority clients: Let's reject the null hypothesis. *Professional Psychology: Research and Practice, 27*(1), 73–77.

Matsumoto, D. (1994). *Cultural influences on research methods and statistics.* Pacific Grove, CA: Brooks/Cole.

Mohatt, G. V., & Erickson, F. (1981). Cultural differences in teaching styles in an Odawa school: A sociolinguistic approach. In H. Trueba, H. P. Guthrie, & K. Au (Eds.), *Culture and the bilingual classroom.* Rowley, MA: Newbury Press.

Mohatt, G. V., Hazel, K., Allen, J. R., Stachelrodt, M., Hensel, C., & Fath, R. (2004). Unheard Alaska: Participatory action research on sobriety with Alaska Natives. *American Journal of Community Psychology, 33*(3), 267–277.

Montero, M. (1994). Consciousness raising, conversion, and de-ideologization in community psychosocial work. *Journal of Community Psychology, 22*(1), 3–11.

National Commission for Protection of Human Subjects of Biomedical and Behavioral Research. (1978). *The Belmont Report: Ethical principles and guidelines for the protection of human subjects research.* (DHEW Publication No. (OS) 78–0012). Washington, DC: Government Printing Office.

Nelson, R. K. (1983). *Make prayers to the raven.* Chicago: University of Chicago Press.

Orlandi, M. A., Weston, R., & Epstein, L. G. (Eds.). (1992). *Cultural competence for evaluators: A guide for alcohol and other drug abuse prevention practitioners working with ethnic/racial communities*. Rockville, MD: Department of Health and Human Services.

Panigua, F. A. (1998). *Assessing and treating culturally diverse clients: A practical guide* (2nd ed.). Thousand Oaks, CA: Sage.

Parker-Langley, L. (2002). Alcohol prevention programs among American Indians: Research findings and issues. In *Alcohol use among American Indians and Alaska Natives: Multiple perspectives on a complex problem* (No. 37, pp. 111–140, NIH publication No. 02–4231). Washington, DC: Department of Health and Human Services.

Rappaport, J. (1987). Terms of empowerment/Exemplars of prevention: Toward a theory of community psychology. *American Journal of Community Psychology, 15*(2), 121–144.

Rowe, W. E. (1997). Changing ATOD norms and behaviors: A Native American community commitment to wellness. *Evaluation and Program Planning, 20*, 323–333.

Santiago-Rivera, A., Morse, G. S., Hunt, A., & Lickers, H. (1998). Building a community-based research partnership: Lessons from the Mohawk Nation of Akwesasne. *Journal of Community Psychology, 26*, 163–174.

Sarason, S. B. (1971). *The culture of schools and the problem of change*. Boston: Allyn & Bacon.

Smith, L. T. (1999). *Decolonizing methodologies: Research and indigenous peoples*. New York: Zed Books.

Sue, D. W. (2001). Multidimensional facets of cultural competence. *Counseling Psychologist, 29*(6), 790–821.

Tandon, S. D., Azelton, L. S., Kelly, J. G., & Strickland, D. A. (1998). Constructing a tree for community leaders: Contexts and processes in collaborative inquiry. *American Journal of Community Psychology, 26*, 669–696.

Trickett, E. J., & Espino, S. L. (2004) Collaboration and social inquiry: Multiple meanings of a construct and its role in creating useful and valid knowledge. *American Journal of Community Psychology, 34*, 1–71.

U.S. Census Bureau. (2002). *American Indian and Alaska Native tribes in the United States: 2000*. Retrieved March 23, 2005, from www.census.gov/population/www/cen2000/phc-t18.html

Wallerstein, N., & Bernstein, E. (1994). Introduction to community empowerment, participatory education, and health. *Health Education Quarterly, 21*, 141–149.

CHAPTER 7

Ethical Conduct of Research With Asian and Pacific Islander American Populations

JEAN LAU CHIN

JEFFERY SCOTT MIO

GAYLE Y. IWAMASA

Former President Jimmy Carter tells of a speech he delivered in Japan in 1981.[1] He wanted to begin his speech with a humorous story and chose one that never received much laughter; however, it had the advantage of brevity because it was to be translated into Japanese. After he told the story, there was uproarious laughter from his Japanese audience. At the end of his speech, President Carter went up to the interpreter and said, "Please tell me how you translated my humorous story."

The interpreter said, "Well, President Carter, I just tried to do the best job I could."

President Carter insisted, "No, I need to know exactly how you translated it," but again the interpreter avoided answering directly.

After several times, President Carter insisted as strongly as he could, "It is very important to me that you tell me *exactly* what you said!"

The interpreter's face turned red, he cast his eyes downward, and said, "What I said was 'President Carter just made a joke and it is your duty to laugh.'"

This humorous anecdote identifies some interesting cross-cultural phenomena. The "duty to laugh" ordered by the Japanese interpreter identifies compliance behavior associated with politeness and respect for authority common in Asian cultures. Such behaviors and the values they represent are likely to confound the conduct of research and interpretation of research results among Asian populations in the United States.

The present chapter will provide a brief historical overview of research involving Asian and Pacific Islander American (APIA) populations, introduce some principles to guide researchers, and identify some major issues in the ethical conduct of research with APIA populations. Several case studies will illustrate these ethical challenges. With the changing demographics and growing diversity of this country's population, the implementation of culturally competent research has ethical implications for the responsible conduct of science.

HISTORICAL FACTORS IN RESEARCH WITH ASIAN AND PACIFIC ISLANDER AMERICAN POPULATIONS

Data and research on APIA populations is simply lacking. The absence of empirically valid knowledge has perpetuated the stereotype of APIA populations as the model minority. This erroneous assumption is particularly dangerous when it supports the belief that the APIA population has few of the major health problems. Epidemiological research or datasets on population trends typically omit APIA populations because they are too small, classified as "Other," or lumped together as one APIA ethnic group. This phenomenon was most blatant in the task force report of the secretary of Health and Human Services on Black and minority health (Heckler, 1985) in which Asian Americans were declared healthy because they did not show significant problems compared with Whites on six major mortality and morbidity indicators, thus reinforcing the "model minority myth." Not included among the indicators were the high rates of tuberculosis and hepatitis B among APIA groups or the disproportionately high site-specific rates of liver and esophageal cancer. The report set policy for the next decade in the United States that severely and adversely affected APIA populations in the allocation of resources. The report failed to recognize the diversity of ethnic groups within the APIA population and the differential patterns in health status among APIA groups and in comparison with the White population (Chin, 2000). Methodological problems included inadequate sampling techniques, which raise additional ethical issues of over-generalization.

COMPARATIVE AND DEFICIENCY APPROACHES

Research conducted on APIA populations is often comparative with Whites and guided by a population deficiency approach (Fisher et al., 2002). Earlier comparative and deficiency-oriented research typically resulted in stereotypical and negative images of Asian Americans. For example, Asian Americans were frequently described as less dominant, aggressive, and autonomous (Fenz & Arkoff, 1962), more introverted (Meredith & Meredith, 1973), less verbal (Lesser, Fifer, & Clark, 1965), and more alienated (Sue, 1973) than their Caucasian counterparts.

Health services research typically found that APIA populations underutilize services, had poor access to care, and received poorer quality services due to language, cultural, and financial barriers (Kaiser Commission on Medicaid and the Uninsured, 2000). In most APIA populations, more than 50% are foreign born; therefore, English as a second language and cultural factors contribute significantly to utilization of services. Culturally specific and language-appropriate services are typically inadequate; these are compounded by the higher rates of poverty among immigrant populations. Bimodal distributions within the APIA population tend to skew the results when different Asian and Pacific Islander groups are lumped together in many research designs (Lin-Fu, 1993). These findings typically use a comparative approach in which APIA populations are compared with Whites as the norm; in doing so, APIAs are found to be deficient. To counteract misinformation produced by such designs, there is a growing trend toward looking within populations to identify population needs. Both the surgeon general's report (U.S. Department of Health and Human Services [USDHHS], 2001) and the Zane and Takeuchi (1993) book use such a strength-based approach to identify population trends, examine health problems, and identify intervention strategies.

Ethical Dilemma: Unintended Consequences of Traditional Design Assumptions

The use of a comparative methodology is common in research designs to replicate instruments within a different language or replicate research findings involving different ethnic/cultural groups. In comparative designs, APIA groups typically fare poorly because they are viewed as "more than or less than" the normative group (i.e., White middle-class or Western groups). The assumption that studies with ethnic minority populations are only legitimate if a White comparison group is included has traditionally dictated evaluation criteria for grant and editorial review boards. The dilemma for APIA researchers is whether to conform to these criteria to ensure their work is funded or published in peer reviewed journals or to defend the validity of research designs that use more appropriate within-group comparisons. A further dilemma is that although conformity to the comparative-study standard runs the risk of adverse interpretations and distortions of the data from Western perspectives, failure to conform to the standard may result in smaller studies conducted in the absence of external funding and in the publication of APIA within-group designs in less prestigious journals, which in turn perpetuates the omission of APIA populations from the general literature.

As Tatum (1997) indicated, when we are immersed in racism, it is in the air that we breathe. Therefore, we cannot recognize our own contributions to racism when we are just acting according to community standards. Common practices that might be considered racist from a different perspective often go unnoticed because we are merely applying the common practices. Korchin (1980) discussed how a research article of his involving an African American population was rejected because the research standard implicitly suggested that Whites were necessary as the basis for comparison when studying non-Whites. "In the opinion of one consulting editor, the study was 'grievously flawed'— there was no White control group" (p. 263). As Korchin questions, "What would happen, might we suppose, if someone submitted a study identical in all respects except that all subjects were White? Would it be criticized because it lacked a Black control group?" (p. 263). As Ridley (1989, 1995) would say, this is an example of covert, unintentional racism. It is unintentional because the consulting editor was probably not intending to be racist, but it is covert because such unintentional racism generally occurs outside of most people's awareness.

DIVERSITY WITHIN APIA POPULATIONS

Although APIA populations are discussed as a group, their rich diversity includes many ethnicities and countries of origin. Groups included in the general classification of the APIA population are East Asians, Southeast Asians, South Asians, and Pacific Islanders. Each of these broad classifications has different subgroups. East Asians are generally considered to be those of Chinese, Japanese, and Korean descent. Even within the Chinese classification, Chinese immigrants and refugees to the United States typically are from Hong Kong, Taiwan, east mainland China, or Vietnam. Those from the western regions of China actually have more in common with South Asians and Middle Easterners and typically have not emigrated to the United States. Religious influences differ across groups with Taoism, Confucianism, and Buddhism being more common among Chinese and Japanese immigrants and with Christianity being more common among Korean immigrants.

Southeast Asians include those from Vietnam, Cambodia, Laos, and Myanmar/Burma. Many from this region have been strongly influenced by Catholicism as a vestige of French colonization. South Asians typically include those from India, Pakistan, Bangladesh, Sri Lanka, Nepal, Bhutan, and the Maldives. Major religious influences in these countries are Hinduism, Islam, Christianity, Sikhism, and Buddhism. The greatest variation comes from the Pacific Islander populations, which include those from the Philippines, Malaysia, Indonesia, Samoa, Fiji, Hawaii, Tahiti, Guam, and many other island nations. There are those who argue that Hawaiians are native people. Some of the dominant religions in these island nations are Islam, Catholicism, Christianity, and indigenous religions.

Although Pacific Islanders are often categorized together with Asian Americans, there has been controversy over whether or not they should be considered a separate group; Native Hawaiians, for example, will argue that they are not immigrants to the United States. Filipinos also have had a history of sometimes being included under the Asian American label and sometimes not. This inclusion/exclusion has been both imposed and self-defined, as at times Filipinos have been included for purposes of the census and also for political power, and at other times Filipinos have insisted that they should be considered a different classification because of some markedly different racial and historical backgrounds (Espiritu & Omi, 2000). In addition to country of origin, regional differences, and differences in spirituality and religion, one must also consider differences in

the various languages, cultural practices and traditions, gender roles, socioeconomic status, and sexual orientation.

Within Group Differences

It is imperative that we as a profession take multicultural issues seriously. Fisher et al (2002) proposed a set of guidelines for research with ethnic minority children and youths. For example, they warn about the need to take into account within-group differences. Many researchers may simply compare Whites with APIA populations; however, as most multicultural researchers would point out, there is more within-group variation than between-group differences (Iwamasa & Yamada, 2001; Paniagua, 1998, 2001; Samuda, 1998; Sue & Sue, 2003). In addition to variation in ethnicity and country of origin within APIA subgroups, one must also consider issues of immigration and/or acculturation experiences, socioeconomic status, and educational attainment. A group composed of immigrants and refugees will be different from fourth-generation participants. If studying refugees, the effects of discrimination in their country of origin, the trauma of their experiences in detention camps, the discrimination encountered in the United States, and the sociopolitical history of immigrant groups nationwide will affect the variables of interest. Finally, when studying APIAs, researchers must consider the increasing number of biracial and multiracial individuals who do not fit into one ethnic category.

Principles for the Ethical Conduct of Research and Respect for Within-Group Differences

The American Psychological Association (APA) first developed 10 ethical principles to guide research with human participants in 1973 (American Psychological Association

[APA], 1973), soon after the Tuskegee Study hearings in which African Americans involved in a longitudinal study of the natural course of syphilis sponsored by the Public Health Service were deceived and denied treatment (Jones, 1993). In this research, the government had garnered the support of local community leaders such as African American researchers from Tuskegee Normal and Industrial Institute (now, Tuskegee University) and church ministers. Over 600 African Americans were recruited, and as many as 161 may have died as a result of their untreated syphilis (Sue & Sue, 2003; Williams, 1974). Although the study led to new federal regulations and APA guidelines for the protection of human research participants, none of these principles addressed ethnic minority issues.

It was not until 1981 that the APA ethical principles mentioned issues relevant to ethnic minority groups (APA, 1981). For example, psychologists were prohibited from engaging in or condoning illegal or inhumane practices and required to abide by existing laws against discrimination; however, the principle of "do no harm" reflected in these early principles is not equivalent to proactive efforts to "do good" by becoming culturally competent (Casas, Ponterotto, & Gutierrez, 1986). The APA Ethics Code, revised in 1992 and then again in 2002, includes principles and standards that offer greater protection and justice for ethnic minority groups (APA, 1992, 2002; Fisher, 2003). Principle E of the APA Ethics Code (APA, 2002) on Respect for People's Rights and Dignity states that psychologists need to be aware of cultural, individual, and role differences, including those due to race, ethnicity, national origin, and religion.

Sue and Sue (2000) proposed three guidelines for designing culturally valid research using APIA populations. First, researchers should understand the context within which the APIA populations under study reside.

Researchers need to seek consultation with individuals in the community or who have expertise with the populations under investigation. Within APIA populations, sociopolitical histories are contextual variables that need to be considered in research designs. For example, Chinese immigrants from Taiwan, Hong Kong, and mainland China bring very different experiences and worldviews because of their respective histories under a nationalist government, British colonial rule, and a communist government. Second, researchers should recognize the diversity within APIA populations and decide when it is necessary and significant to disaggregate data by subgroups. Aggregation of groups may be appropriate for broad topics such as individualism and collectivism, but it may not be for topics such as the effect of racism on immigration experiences when experiences will vary with sociopolitical histories, countries of origin, and periods of immigration. Third, when comparing APIA populations with non-APIA populations, differences should not be interpreted as deficiencies on the part of the APIA group.

Knowledge about group differences can provide a useful context for hypothesis testing. Knowing that a person belongs to a group may help to target a domain (e.g., interdependence) relevant to cultural differences. For example, the assumption that an infant's inability to leave her mother to play independently in a new situation reflects insecure attachment may not be accurate for those cultural groups in which interdependence is encouraged, as in Asian cultures (Vereijken & Riksen-Walraven, 1997). Orientation to one's mother is common in interdependent cultures, whereas orientation to the environment is common in independent cultures (Rothbaum, Weisz, Pott, Miyake, & Morelli, 2000). In such cases, culturally specific definitions of secure and insecure attachment are needed.

In another example, thalassemia is a genetic blood disorder with a 15% carrier rate in Chinese and Southeast Asian groups (compared with 1% in the White population); the disorder requires regular blood transfusions and results in shortened lifespan. A child has a 50% chance of acquiring the disease when both parents are carriers of the gene. The senior author found that rates of decisions made by couples in which both were carriers to proceed with their pregnancy were high. They based their decisions on the cultural value to carry on the family line and their fatalistic view that a normal child would be born if it was their fate. These differences in worldview need to be incorporated into research design.

Cultural competence: An ethical essential. Cultural competence is essential to the ethical conduct of research, not only with APIA populations but with all multicultural populations (Chin, 2002; Fisher, 2003). Culture is integral to all interpersonal interactions and communication. According to the surgeon general's report on mental health (USDHHS, 2001), culture matters! The emphasis on cultural competence as an ethical essential suggests that researchers must acquire skills to enable them to conduct research that produces valid information and offers legitimate protections to the populations being studied. Research design, implementation, and interpretation that fail to take into account the unique cultural values, expectations, and interpersonal interactions of participant populations will lack the scientific validity necessary to produce beneficial knowledge and the protections necessary to avoid individual and group harms. Cultural competence requires training and experience in the skills needed to design research that values the differences, strengths, and diversity within the populations being studied. This means being able to take the other's perspective in designing research questions, using indigenous expertise

to interpret research results, and avoiding bias. It also means going beyond awareness and sensitivity to the acquisition of skills.

For a long time, people have been aware of the difficulties in transferring research methods and generalizing research results across cultures (Campbell & Naroll, 1972; Kobben, 1952; Mio, 1999). Among the first researchers to discuss such matters were van der Bij (1929, cited in Kobben, 1952) and Steinmetz (1898–1899, cited in Kobben, 1952). To determine the degree to which generalities of human behavior could be made across cultures, these investigators proposed statistical methods and reasoning to test such generalizations (Reynolds, 1999; Sue & Sue, 2003). A fundamental problem in this early research was the failure of researchers to step outside their own worldviews in generalizing about groups from other cultures. It was not until 1973 that psychologists at the APA Vail summit recommended that individuals be aware of cultural differences in the science and practice of psychology (Hall, Iwamasa, & Smith, 2004; Mio & Awakuni, 2000).

RESISTANCE TO MULTICULTURALISM: INTENTIONAL AND UNINTENTIONAL

Although cultural competence is an ethical essential, multiculturalism is the assertion that our training, research, and practice operate in a context of multiple cultures and with diverse populations. Sue et al. (1998) documented a history of resistance to multicultural issues in psychology, both intentional and unintentional. Resistance is defined by the failure to recognize bias and the tendency to challenge the legitimacy of multiculturalism. This resistance was first expressed in claims about the generalizability or universality of psychological theories to all populations. It was followed by claims that current research methods could not address cultural differences if they did exist and that standards were absent to define how research with diverse populations was to be conducted. Although ethical standards and multicultural guidelines were proposed for cross-cultural research and diverse populations (Sue et al., 1982; Sue, Arredondo, & McDavis, 1992), they were criticized for lack of specificity. The guidelines were alternately criticized for both lacking specificity and being too complex and detailed. Other criticisms claimed that the effectiveness of multicultural competencies was too difficult to measure without addressing the similar difficulties in the conduct of "traditional" methods of research about treatment outcomes. The resistance to multiculturalism next took the form of delay in implementing the multicultural competencies and standards until they were developed for other groups, such as the elderly, women, the physically challenged, and gay and lesbian populations. The most recent phase of resistance has been more confrontational in claiming that the requiring of cultural competence training or embracing of multiculturalism is a form of reverse discrimination. This form of resistance has been criticized as disguised racism in modern form (Gaertner & Dovidio, 1986; Jones, 1997; McConahay, 1986; Mio & Awakuni, 2000; Sears, 1988).

For APIA populations, covert forms of racism take the form of "model minority" myths, and overt forms of racism include anti-Asian legislation limiting immigration and access to economic opportunities. In research, this resistance took the form of excluding APIAs as an underrepresented population in the U.S. National Institute of Mental Health (NIMH) under the National Institutes of Health (NIH) in its Research Supplements for Underrepresented Minorities Program (http://grants.nih.gov/grants/guide/pa-files/PA-01-079.html). Originally

announced in 1989, this program was established to address the need to increase the number of underrepresented minority scientists participating in biomedical research and the health-related sciences. NIH has continued its efforts to establish a diversified workforce by increasing the number of individuals from underrepresented racial and ethnic groups actively participating in biomedical research. In addition, in more recent years, it has become increasingly clear that there is a serious health care disparity among minority groups in this country. The NIH recognizes the need to expand research opportunities for minority scientists to help eliminate health disparities. APIAs were initially declared by NIMH to be ineligible as candidates for the purpose of this announcement until the National Asian Pacific American Families Against Substance Abuse (NAPAFASA) advocated eliminating this biased definition. Underrepresented minority students and investigators are now defined as individuals belonging to a particular ethnic or racial group that has been determined by the grantee institution to be underrepresented in biomedical, behavioral, clinical, or social sciences.

In graduate research training, this type of intentional resistance has been manifested in reluctance to include multicultural topics as required course content in psychology graduate programs or as an area of emphasis on comprehensive examinations (Mio & Awakuni, 2000). Iwamasa (2001) called this attitude the "cultural-diversity-is-a-special-topic" problem. Holders of this view either do not consider themselves as possessing cultural characteristics or assume that their cultural values and perspectives are the "right" ones. Consequently, they marginalize the study of cultural diversity to those whose personal characteristics "qualify" them to be "culturally diverse."

Myers (2002) describes another type of resistance: failure to recognize that science is not purely objective. "Scientists do not simply read the book of nature. Rather, they interpret nature, using their own mental categories" (Myers, 2002, pp. 9–10). Myers further discussed how the language we use to describe a phenomenon or observation necessarily reflects our own values and biases. Insurgents engaging in attacks against the power structure may be characterized as "freedom fighters" or "terrorists" depending on whether one supports the cause or is against it. From a multicultural perspective, proponents would be characterized as culturally competent, supporting multiculturalism, or advocates for social justice and the elimination of bias, whereas those against the concept might say these same individuals have identity problems, are subjective, or practice soft science. Such labels and characterizations are often imposed on ethnic minority individuals by White scientists in the name of "objective reality" without acknowledging that they are engaging in racism or are resistant to multicultural perspectives.

Acknowledgment of racial bias. As Hall and colleagues (2004) pointed out, scientists need to be aware of their tendency to study only those issues of interest to them and to interpret data in a manner favorable to their own biases. Gilbert (1998) indicated that this is especially important when scientists are unaware of such biases or deny their existence. Researchers may attempt to ignore the sociocultural context within which their biases take place (Iwamasa, 1997). Scientific interpretations that fail to take into account cultural context lack meaning, and such interpretations are tantamount to committing "cultural malpractice" (Hall, 1997).

For example, in his review of Diener and Suh's (2000) edited book on subjective well-being around the world, Mio (2003) questioned the validity of authors' conclusion that subjective well-being was higher and more consistent across individualistic societies

than collectivistic (primarily Asian) societies. Mio pointed out that measures used were biased toward an "achievement of personal goals" individualistic definition of subjective well-being, whereas well-being is related to interpersonal connections in collectivistic societies. In a particular sense, subjective well-being may not even be a relevant term to study in collectivistic/Asian societies.

There are many instances of unintentional and covert resistance and bias (i.e., racism) that have been institutionalized within the field of psychology and in research. Cultural competence helps to ensure that researchers address their biases and avoid adverse consequences for the populations being studied. Researchers need to acquire the skills to enable them to recognize these biases, develop research methods that are responsive to cultural difference, and avoid distorting the interpretation of data about the populations being studied.

CULTURAL EQUIVALENCE OF MEASURES

In instances where psychologists desire to determine the generalizability of scientific knowledge, the most convenient method is to use an existing measure of a construct and apply it to a new sample, that is, different ethnic group; however, different worldviews and language held by APIA cultures compared with Western cultures will result in significant differences in measuring that construct. Given the high rate of immigrants within the APIA populations, the sampling of non-English-speaking populations and the use of culturally appropriate instruments is essential to the ethical conduct of research with APIA populations. Principle C, Professional and Scientific Responsibility (APA, 2002), draws attention to the need for psychologists to adapt their methods to needs of different populations; this is most evident in the use of culturally appropriate assessment instruments.

Equivalence guidelines. Sue, Kurasaki, and Srinivasan (1999) have described four psychometric criteria to consider when adapting and selecting measures for comparing ethnic groups and differences within groups when studying APIA populations: (a) translation or language equivalence, (b) cultural and socioeconomic equivalence, (c) conceptual equivalence, and (d) metric equivalence. Translation or language equivalence refers to the nature of the questions being asked when conducting research using instruments that are translated from English. Do the translated terms have the same meaning in the other language? All translated research instruments need to be back translated into English to ensure that alteration in meaning of the terms has not occurred. Translations need to be done by bilingual speakers taking into consideration the difficulty level of the terms between the two languages and colloquial terms associated with geographic regions. Validity coefficients need to be reported between the two instruments. The internal validity of a study can be affected when researchers use translated scales.

Cultural equivalence refers to socioeconomic and other contextual factors that may influence the meaning of terms or constructs used in a measure (Sue et al., 1998). Conceptual equivalence is concerned with the meanings of terms used in a study and the relevance of a construct in a particular cultural group. For example, Sue and Sue (2000) suggest that *good decision* may mean different things in Western versus Asian cultures. In Western cultures, a *good decision* generally means that one makes an independent decision that is not unduly influenced by others; however, in Asian cultures, a *good decision* generally means that the decision is best for the collective group, not necessarily that it is best for the self. Similarly, Triandis

et al. (1986) found that the meaning of the term *self-reliance* differed across individualistic and collectivistic cultures. In individualistic cultures, *self-reliance* was related to the pursuit of one's own goals with a tinge of competition with others, whereas in collectivistic cultures, it was related to not wanting to burden the collective group, and competition was not related to the concept. Differences in meaning of terms across cultures may not be captured in translated instruments. Unless researchers address this issue, they commit an ethical violation in assuming cultural equivalence of terms and interpreting study results from a biased perspective.

Metric equivalence deals with the comparability of test scores across cultural groups. A test lacks metric equivalence if a specific score does not represent the same degree or intensity of the construct in different cultural groups (Knight & Hill, 1998). For example, on a 7-point Likert scale, a rating of 6 by a participant from one culture may not mean the same as a rating of 6 by someone from another culture? Western cultures, for example, may be more familiar and more comfortable in making such numerical assessments, whereas a Pacific Islander culture may not; moreover, they may be more familiar with qualitative methods of assessment. Some cultures may also be risk averse and tend to avoid using ratings at the extremes of the scale, so that a 6 in one culture may be equivalent to a 7 in another. In our research with Asian American groups, we found greater discomfort with Likert-format instruments and greater difficulty finding agreement with items on a Likert-formatted (ADD) scale (Iwamasa & Sorocco, 2002). Sue et al. (1998) recommends that multiple measures be used to determine the convergent validity of measures. Windle, Iwawaki, and Lerner (1987) and Nishimoto (1986), for example, used factor solutions to examine the metric equivalence of personality scales administered to Asian and non-Asian populations. In both studies, the factor solutions did not differ; however, the item composition and thus the factor meanings did vary.

Ethnic Membership

Social and behavioral science researchers rely on a variety of techniques and procedures to identify the ethnicity of populations recruited for research. Some researchers will ask respondents to check their ethnic background, and on the basis of that one item, they group data into "ethnic" categories. Others will select subjects on the basis of surnames or physiognomic appearances and then proceed to generalize results to the total ethnic or racial population. These procedures that use a singular, more visible and accessible domain to identify ethnicity are guilty of using an "ethnic gloss," that is, "an overgeneralization or simplistic categorical label of ethnic groups . . . that neglect the unique differences found among individuals in various cultures or groups" (Trimble & Dickson, 2005). Trimble identifies four domains of inquiry including (a) natality in which an emphasis is placed one's ancestral genealogy including those of the parents, siblings, and grandparents; (b) subjective identification in which the respondent provides a declaration of their own ethnic or racial identity or individual self-designation; (c) behavioral expressions of identity in which the respondent indicates their preferences for activities germane to their ethnic affiliation, such as foods, music, magazines, books, and so forth; and (d) situational or contextual influences in which the respondent indicates the situations that call for a deliberate expression of the ethnic affiliation, such as traditional ceremonies, interaction with family and peers, neighborhood gatherings, and so forth (Trimble, 2000). At a minimum, he argues for scales and measures to capture the essence of each domain to provide a full and complete profile or silhouette of one's identity.

Dialect differences. The importance of cultural equivalence of terms used in psychological measures has ethical implications when terms have different meanings for the researcher and participant. An example of such a difference between the Toisanese and Cantonese dialects within the Chinese language demonstrates the complexity of issues that need to be considered. Although speakers of these dialects can understand one another, terms used in one dialect may not be equivalent to those in another. For example, in her account of her experience, a Toisanese woman with a history of domestic violence talked about her husband coming into the room and "opening fire"; the Cantonese worker panicked and threatened to call the police because she heard this as the husband's assault with a dangerous weapon and wondered how the client could be so nonchalant in reporting the event until it was clarified that in the Toisanese dialect "open fire" means turning on the light (clinical vignette related by the senior author, 2004). On paper and pencil instruments or audiotape-recorded responses, such language differences could easily be misinterpreted.

SAMPLING: INCLUSION OF APIA POPULATIONS

Since 1994, the National Institutes of Health have required the inclusion of ethnic minority participants in funded research projects (Hohmann & Parron, 1996). For APIA populations, this regulation discourages investigators from simply omitting APIA participants because inclusion of such samples would confound the results; however, the simple inclusion of ethnic minorities in research projects is far from a guarantee of culturally competent and ethical research. Sue and Sue (2000) presented four guidelines with respect to sampling methodology: First, research samples need to include APIA populations. Difficulties in obtaining representative samples of APIA populations may result in sampling errors or results that cannot be generalized beyond the research sample. For example, studies on APIA populations using college samples may overrepresent individuals of Chinese descent, given their relative number on college campuses. Second, assessment instruments should be validated with APIA populations before they are used in studies. Third, instructions used to conduct the research should be understandable, recognizing that a study of elderly immigrants from rural areas, for example, cannot be written at a level appropriate for college students. Fourth, ethnic response sets may influence participants' responses to specific items or instruments and should be taken into account when interpreting one's results. This is related to a phenomenon of over-generalizing ethnic characteristics based on superficial characteristics (e.g., surname) described by Joseph Trimble as "ethnic gloss" (http://www.wwu.edu/~trimble; Trimble & Dickson, 2005).

Even when APIAs are represented in normative samples, ethical issues are raised. The Wechsler intelligence scales, for example, are one of the most common psychological instruments used to measure intellectual functioning and are well standardized. In the last renorming, the authors purported that because the scales now represent racial/ethnic populations to the degree that they exist within the United States, they are now valid for use with those groups. These general norms are not relevant for the interpretation of individual profiles within APIA populations because they are still only represented within the normative sample by just 3%. Clinical data collected by the senior author[2] found that Chinese children typically test within a 15-point difference between the performance and verbal scales, which is considered to be statistically different. In contrast to findings from other ethnic populations, the performance-verbal difference was not associated with verbal deficiency or nonverbal strength, as measured by academic performance.

Yu (1992, 1999; Yu & Lin, 1993) recommends oversampling as a method to obtain sufficient sample sizes for meaningful analysis and to correct for the low numbers of APIA populations in epidemiological studies. In addition, aggregating data on specific ethnic groups over several years is another way to ensure that sample sizes are large enough for analysis of APIA data on epidemiological studies; however, this is typically not done by national health statistic surveys because it is considered too costly or a violation of the integrity of the research design.

Combining disparate groups. Uehara, Takeuchi, and Smukler (1994) caution that combining disparate APIA ethnic groups may lead to erroneous conclusions, given the diversity within the APIA population. Whether by choice or necessity, however, mental health studies still typically consider Asian Americans as a single ethnic category rather than as separate ethnic groups. Few investigations have addressed the consequences of this practice. When treated as a single ethnic category in a multivariate linear regression model, Asian Americans are found to have a lower level of community functioning than their White counterparts; however, when different APIA ethnic groups are measured individually (e.g., Vietnamese, Japanese), only one of five Asian ethnic groups yielded a significantly lower level of functioning. Although the disaggregation of the Asian American ethnic category makes intuitive sense, there are pragmatic problems that make this practice difficult to execute. In community epidemiological studies, the large number of Asian ethnic groups and the geographic dispersion of these groups create a host of sampling issues that are time-consuming and costly for researchers.

CULTURALLY COMPETENT INTERPRETATION OF RESULTS AND COMMUNITY PARTICIPATION

Research conducted on ethnic minorities is often unrepresentative of ethnic minority communities (Fontes, 1998; Gil & Bob, 1999) because it is often driven by problem-oriented designs. Consequently, there is a tendency to overstudy those groups in lower socioeconomic categories. The term "ethnic minority" has often become a euphemism for socioeconomic disadvantage or psycho-pathology (Hall, 2001). Interpretation of results needs to consider these sampling biases and implications for overgeneralizations to the APIA population as a whole. Researchers using their own worldviews and biases in understanding the research may fail to recognize this phenomenon.

Ethical Dilemma

Researchers investigating APIA populations often build into their research projects funding for APIA consultants with ethnic group expertise. They often hire APIA team members to gain credibility within the community or in the recruitment of subjects. As consultants, their role becomes marginalized when they are excluded when it comes to interpreting the data or publishing the results. Furthermore, funds are often not available to pay for a more extensive role so that the consultant is faced with the dilemma of putting in the time with no compensation or allowing the potential for misinterpretation of results based on the worldviews of the principal investigators rather than that of the participants. Given the existence of bias and

differences in worldviews, the inclusion of the APIA community in the interpretation of the research results is ethically responsible. This could take the form of presenting results first to the participants or issuing a preliminary report to the community for public comment and correction before they are presented to the scientific community.

Researchers typically come into communities with a conception of what good research is and how it should be conducted. Their conception of a research design may not be consistent with how a community may want to or be able to implement a program resulting from the research. This becomes a negotiating exercise, which often arouses concerns about maintaining the integrity of the research design over the needs and expectations of the community. In 1974, a report on cross-cultural ethics to the APA Committee on International Relations in Psychology recommended that cultural acceptability of methods should be evaluated and that cultures in which research is conducted be respected. Collaboration with local researchers from that culture was recommended. Researchers were also encouraged to ensure that participants benefited from the research. Thus, research conducted on a community should involve the community and provide benefits to the community.

Principle E of the 1992 APA Ethics Code, Concern for Others' Welfare, indicated that psychologists must be sensitive to real and ascribed differences in power between themselves and others. Sensitivity to power disparity is a first step in preventing psychologists from exploiting research participants. The 2002 APA Ethics Code does not explicitly reference issues of power; however, it is explicit that boundaries of competence apply to populations as well as problem areas, in that psychologists are responsible for gaining competence in working with different populations. The APA Ethics Code also includes standards prohibiting bias, harm, and harassment based on race, ethnicity, and other factors (Fisher, 2003). The involvement of communities (as opposed to individuals) in the process of designing research projects often helps to draw on the power of community leaders to protect the rights of their communities. Given the high rates of non-English-speaking people within APIA communities, collaboration with community leaders is often integral to the ethical conduct of research. It is not uncommon for non-English-speaking APIA populations to rely on community leaders to interpret and approve requests from researchers coming into the community. Often these leaders have the trust of the community, and their approval will be met with willingness of the community to participate.

Ethical dilemma: Gatekeeper role. As the executive director of a large community health center serving the Asian community, the senior author found that she received requests at least monthly from researchers wishing to access the large pool of potential research participants served by the agency. It was also clear that her approval would carry a lot of weight to enable the research to be conducted. The dilemma was the frequent gatekeeper role in which she found herself. In addition to evaluating the merits of the research, she also needed to evaluate the volume of requests and weigh the merits of the research against the potential benefits to both the participants and the community. In one instance, she required that the researcher write a grant proposal to benefit the community before allowing him to conduct his own research.

Informed consent. The principle of informed consent presumes that individuals know about the consequences of the procedures being conducted as well as their potential harm. The consent form is intended to serve this purpose; however, ethical issues arise

because its use often shifts the burden of proof for "do no harm" from the researcher to the individual participant or community (Fisher et al., 2002). The current APA ethical standards (APA, 2002) explicitly require that psychologists obtain informed consent. Ethical research insists on appropriately signed informed consent before proceeding with a study on the assumption that the consent form identifies all known risks to enable the participant to make an informed decision about his or her participation in the study; however, there are factors within APIA communities that militate against this being true. Language factors may result in non-English-speaking participants relying heavily on translators to decide whether or not to participate in a study. Informed consent may be poorly translated, or not translated, such that the true intent of the study is not known. Last, participants may defer to the judgment of their community leaders in deciding the benefits of participation. Culturally competent procedures would require that all consent forms are adequately translated and measures taken to ensure there is a true understanding.

Ethical dilemma: Use of power. A Chinese-speaking participant was presented with an informed consent form for a health care option, which was translated and explained by a worker speaking the same language as the participant. After lengthy explanation and discussion, the participant then turned to the worker and said, "OK, tell me which option you think I should choose?" The dilemma occurs when non-English-speaking participants place their trust in the interpreter, and the interpreter must be aware of the inappropriate use of power to favor the recruitment of subjects in a study.

Community cooperation. Many communities have different traditions. Recognizing these traditions adds to the cooperation that one receives from these communities. For example, a Japanese tradition involves a concept called *omiyage*. This term means that when one visits someone else's home, it is traditional to give a gift showing one's appreciation for being welcomed into the home. Iwamasa and Sorocco (2002) honored this tradition when collecting data at a Japanese American senior citizen's center in Los Angeles. They brought gifts such as plants, flowers, art, and photography supplies to members of the center and staff to show their appreciation to these individuals for inviting them into the center for the purpose of conducting research.

Community benefits. With the recommendations to expand the diversity of research samples, APIA communities are increasingly pressed by researchers to provide access to research participants. Researchers frequently enter communities with promises of benefits in order to obtain subjects and then leave without delivering. This has resulted in community mistrust and an unwillingness to participate in future research, as noted by the experience of the senior author in running a community health center targeting the APIA community. Crossing community boundaries may result in an invasion of privacy and confidentiality, even when measures are taken to protect confidentiality of information and anonymity of participants.

Iwamasa and Sorocco (2002) collaborated with the staff at the senior citizen's center where they collected data. Although Iwamasa and Sorocco were interested in anxiety among elderly Japanese Americans, they asked the staff what they were interested in including in the study. The staff expressed interest in knowing what kinds of programs and services the senior citizens attended in the past for purposes of planning and grant writing. Thus, Iwamasa and Sorocco were able to include such questions in their data collection. The data were then used when the center applied for grants to help demonstrate the effectiveness of the center and the programs offered.

CONCLUSIONS: ETHICAL DECISION MAKING AND UNINTENDED CONSEQUENCES

Cultural competence is core to all decision making when conducting research. There must be a focus on skills and a process-oriented approach in the design and implementation of the study. Principles of strength-based methods, culturally appropriate measures, and adequate sampling, which take into consideration the diversity within APIA populations and the different worldviews between Asian and Western cultures, are essential.

In addition to benefits to individual research participants, community benefits must be considered, especially with regard to unintended consequences. Research *on* the community should *benefit* the community. The following are questions to guide researchers in defining these benefits:

- Why is the research question important to the population of interest?
- How will the results be used to benefit participants and the community?
- Are incentives or compensation for research participation respectful and fair?
- What follow-up is there once the research is completed?
- Who owns the data?

Research may affect policy and the allocation of resources. Without a consideration for the ethical conduct of research and the culturally competent interpretation of the results, even the best designed research may have adverse consequences because it favors Western ways of interpreting Asian behavior.

NOTES

1. We first heard this story when President Carter was a guest on the *Tonight Show* with Johnny Carson in the 1980s; however, we do not have a reference for this specific show.

2. Chin, J. L. Unpublished clinical data.

REFERENCES

American Psychological Association. (1973). *Ethical principles in the conduct of research with human participants.* Washington, DC: Author.

American Psychological Association. (1981). Ethical principles of psychologists. *American Psychologist, 36,* 633–638.

American Psychological Association. (1992). Ethical principles and code of conduct. *American Psychologist, 48,* 1597–1611.

American Psychological Association. (2002). *Ethical principles of psychologists and code of conduct.* Washington, DC: Author.

Campbell, D. T., & Naroll, R. (1972). The mutual methodological relevance of anthropology and psychology. In F. L. K. Hsu (Ed.), *Psychological anthropology* (pp. 435–463). Cambridge, MA: Schenkman.

Casas, J. M., Ponterotto, J. G., & Gutierrez, J. M. (1986). An ethical indictment of counseling research and training: The cross-cultural perspective. *Journal of Counseling and Development, 64,* 347–349.

Chin, J. L. (2000). Culturally competent health care. *Public Health Reports, 115,* 29–38.

Chin, J. L. (2002). Assessment of cultural competence in mental health systems of care for Asian Americans. In K. Kurasaki, S. Okazaki, & S. Sue (Eds.), *Asian American mental health: Assessment theories and methods* (pp. 301–314). New York: Kluwer Academic/Plenum.

Diener, E., & Suh, E. M. (Eds.). (2000). *Culture and subjective well-being.* Cambridge, MA: MIT Press.

Espiritu, Y. L., & Omi, M. (2000). "Who are you calling Asian?": Shifting identity claims, racial classifications, and the census. In P. M. Ong (Ed.), *The state of Asian Pacific America: Transforming race relations: A public policy report* (pp. 43–101). Los Angeles: LEAP Asian Pacific American Public Policy Institute and UCLA Asian American Studies Center.

Fenz, W., & Arkoff, A. (1962). Comparative need patterns of five ancestry groups in Hawaii. *Journal of Social Psychology, 58,* 67–89.

Fisher, C. B. (2003). *Decoding the ethics code: A practical guide for psychologists.* Thousand Oaks, CA: Sage.

Fisher, C. B., Hoagwood, K., Boyce, C., Duster, T., Frank, D. A., Grisso, T., et al. (2002). Research ethics for mental health science involving ethnic minority children and youths. *American Psychologist, 57,* 1024–1040.

Fontes, L. A. (1998). Ethics in family violence research: Multicultural issues. Family relations. *Interdisciplinary Journal of Applied Family Studies, 47,* 53–61.

Gaertner, S. L., & Dovidio, J. F. (1986). The aversive form of racism. In J. F. Dovidio & S. L. Gaertner (Eds.), *Prejudice, discrimination and racism* (pp. 61–90). Orlando, FL: Academic.

Gil, F. F., & Bob, S. (1999). Culturally competent research: An ethical perspective. *Clinical Psychology Review, 19,* 45–55.

Gilbert, D. T. (1998). Ordinary personology. In D. T. Gilbert, S. T. Fiske, & G. Lindzey (Eds.), *The handbook of social psychology* (4th ed., Vol. 2, pp. 89–150). New York: McGraw-Hill.

Hall, C. C. I. (1997). Cultural malpractice: The growing obsolescence of psychology with the changing U.S. population. *American Psychologist, 52,* 642–651.

Hall, G. C. N. (2001). Psychotherapy research with ethnic minorities: Empirical, ethical, and conceptual issues. *Journal of Consulting and Clinical Psychology, 69,* 502–510.

Hall, G. C. N., Iwamasa, G. I., & Smith, J. N. (2004). Ethical principles of the psychology profession and ethnic minority issues. In W. Donohue & K. E. Fergusson (Eds.), *Handbook of Professional Ethics for Psychologists: Issues, Questions, and Controversies* (pp. 301–318). Thousand Oaks, CA: Sage.

Heckler, M. M. (Ed.). (1985). *Report of the secretary's task force on Black and minority health: Volume 2. Crosscutting issues in minority health.* Washington, DC: Department of Health and Human Services.

Hohmann, A. A., & Parron, D. L. (1996). How the new NIH guidelines on inclusion of women and minorities apply: Efficacy trials, effectiveness trials, and validity. *Journal of Consulting and Clinical Psychology, 64,* 851–855.

Iwamasa, G. Y. (1997). Behavior therapy and a culturally diverse society: Forging an alliance. *Behavior Therapy, 28,* 347–358.

Iwamasa, G. Y., & Sorocco, K. H. (2002). Aging and Asian Americans: Developing appropriate research methodology. In G. C. N. Hall & S. Okazaki (Eds.), *Asian American psychology: The science of lives in context* (pp. 105–130). Washington, DC: APA.

Iwamasa, G. Y., & Yamada, A. M. (2001). Asian American acculturation and ethnic/racial identity: Research innovations in the new millennium: Introduction to the special issue. *Cultural Diversity and Ethnic Minority Psychology, 7,* 203–206.

Iwamasa, G. Y. (2001). What's the big deal about cultural diversity anyway? *Behavior Therapist, 24,* 212–214.

Jones, J. H. (1993). *Bad blood: The Tuskegee syphilis experiment* (Rev. ed.). New York: Free Press.

Jones, J. M. (1997). *Prejudice and racism* (2nd ed.). New York: McGraw-Hill.

Kaiser Commission on Medicaid and the Uninsured. (2000). *Health insurance coverage and access to care among Asian Americans and Pacific Islanders.* Retrieved December 2004, from www.kff.org

Knight, G. P., & Hill, N. E. (1998). Measurement equivalence in research involving minority adolescents. In V. C. McLoyd & L. Steinberg. *Studying minority adolescents.* Mahwah, NJ: LEA.

Kobben, A. J. F. (1952). New ways of presenting an old idea: The statistical method of social anthropology. *Journal of the Royal Anthropological Institute of Great Britain and Ireland, 82,* 129–146. Reprinted from *Readings in cross-cultural methodology,* pp. 175–192, by F. Moore Ed., 1970, New Haven, CT: HRAF Press.

Korchin, S. J. (1980). Clinical psychology and minority problems. *American Psychologist, 35,* 262–269.

Lesser, G., Fifer, G., & Clark, D. (1965). Mental abilities of children in different social class and cultural groups. *Monographs Social Research and Child Development, 30,* (Whole number 102).

Lin-Fu, J. S. (1993). Asian and Pacific Islander Americans: An overview of demographic characteristics and health care issues. *Asian American and Pacific Islander Journal of Health, 1,* 20–35.

McConahay, J. B. (1986). Modern racism, ambivalence, and the Modern Racism Scale. In J. F. Dovidio & S. L. Gaertner (Eds.), *Prejudice, discrimination and racism* (pp. 91–126). Orlando, FL: Academic.

Meredith, G., & Meredith, C. (1973). Acculturation and personality among Japanese-American college students in Hawaii. In S. Sue & N. Wagner (Eds.), *Asian-Americans: Psychological perspectives.* Ben Lomond, CA: Science and Behavior Books.

Mio, J. S. (1999). Holocultural method. In J. S. Mio, J. T. Trimble, P. Arredondo, H. E. Cheatham, & D. Sue (Eds.), *Key words in multicultural interventions: A dictionary* (pp. 141–142). Westport, CT: Greenwood.

Mio, J. S. (2003). Subjective well-being: An etic construct? [Review of the book *Culture and subjective well-being*]. *Contemporary Psychology: APA Review of Books, 48,* 195–197.

Mio, J. S., & Awakuni, G. I. (2000). *Resistance to multiculturalism: Issues and interventions.* Philadelphia: Brunner/Mazel.

Myers, D. G. (2002). *Social psychology* (7th ed.). New York: McGraw-Hill.

Nishimoto, R. (1986). The cross-cultural metric equivalence of Langner's 22-item index. *Journal of Social Service Research, 9*(4), 37–52.

Paniagua, F. A. (1998). *Assessing and treating culturally diverse clients.* Thousand Oaks, CA: Sage.

Paniagua, F. A. (2001). *Diagnosis in a multicultural context.* Thousand Oaks, CA: Sage.

Reynolds, A. L. (1999). Etic/emic. In J. S. Mio, J. T. Trimble, P. Arredondo, H. E. Cheatham, & D. Sue (Eds.), *Key words in multicultural interventions: A dictionary* (pp. 115–116). Westport, CT: Greenwood.

Ridley, C. R. (1989). Racism in counseling as an adverse behavioral process. In P. B. Pedersen, J. G. Draguns, W. J. Lonner, & J. E. Trimble (Eds.), *Counseling across cultures* (3rd ed., pp. 55–77). Honolulu: University of Hawaii Press.

Ridley, C. R. (1995). *Overcoming unintentional racism in counseling and therapy: A practitioner's guide to intentional intervention.* Thousand Oaks, CA: Sage.

Rothbaum, F., Weisz, J., Pott, M., Miyake, K., & Morelli, G. (2000). Attachment and culture: Security in the United States and Japan. *American Psychologist, 55,* 1093–1104.

Samuda, R. J. (1998). *Psychological testing of American minorities.* Thousand Oaks, CA: Sage.

Sears, D. O. (1988). Symbolic racism. In P. A. Katz & D. A. Taylor (Eds.), *Eliminating racism: Profiles in controversy* (pp. 53–84). New York: Plenum.

Sue, D. W. (1973). Ethnic identity: The impact of two cultures on the psychological development of Asians in America. In S. Sue & N. Wagner (Eds.), *Asian-Americans: Psychological perspectives.* Ben Lomond, CA: Science and Behavior Books.

Sue, D. W., Arredondo, P., & McDavis, R. J. (1992). Multicultural competencies/ standards: A pressing need. *Journal of Counseling and Development, 70,* 477–486.

Sue, D. W., Bernier, J. B., Durran, M., Feinberg, L., Pedersen, P., Smith, E., et al. (1982). Position paper: Cross-cultural counseling competencies. *Counseling Psychologist, 10,* 45–52.

Sue, D. W., Carter, R. T., Casas, J. M., Fouad, N. A., Ivey, A. E., Jensen, M., et al. (1998). *Multicultural counseling competencies: Individual and organizational development.* Thousand Oaks, CA: Sage.

Sue, D. W., & Sue, S. (2003). *Counseling the culturally diverse: Theory and practice* (4th ed.). New York: Wiley.

Sue, S., Kurasaki, K. S., & Srinivasan, S. (1999). Ethnicity, gender, and cross-cultural issues in clinical research. In P. C. Kendall, J. N. Butcher, & G. N. Hombeck (Eds.), *Handbook of research methods in clinical psychology* (2nd ed., pp. 54–71). New York: Wiley.

Sue, S., & Sue, D. W. (2000). Conducting psychological research with the Asian American/Pacific Islander population. In Council of National Psychological Associations for the Advancement of Ethnic Minority Interests (Ed.), *Guidelines for research in ethnic minority communities* (pp. 2–4). Washington, DC: CNPAAEMI.

Tatum, B. D. (1997). *"Why are all the Black kids sitting together in the cafeteria?" and other conversations about race.* New York: Basic Books.

Triandis, H. C., Bontempo, R., Betancourt, H., Bond, M., Leung, K., Brenes, A., et al. (1986). The measurement of etic aspects of individualism and collectivism across cultures. *Australian Journal of Psychology, 38,* 257–267.

Trimble, J. E. (2000) Social psychological perspectives on changing self-identification among American Indians and Alaska natives. In R. H. Dana (Ed.), *Handbook of cross-cultural and multicultural personality assessment* (pp. 197–222). Mahwah, NJ: Lawrence Erlbaum.

Trimble, J. E., & Dickson, R. (2005). Ethnic gloss. In C. B. Fisher & R. M. Lerner (Eds.), *Applied developmental science: An encyclopedia of research, policies, and programs* (pp. 412–414). Thousand Oaks: Sage.

Uehara, E. S., Takeuchi, D. T., & Smukler, M. (1994). Effects of combining disparate groups in the analysis of ethnic differences: Variations among Asian American mental health service consumers in level of community functioning. *American Journal of Community Psychology, 22,* 83–99.

U.S. Department of Health and Human Services. (2001). Mental health care for Asian Americans and Pacific Islanders. In *Mental health: Culture, race and ethnicity* (a supplement to Mental health: A report of the Surgeon General). Rockville, MD: Department of Health and Human Services, Office of the Surgeon General. (Available at www.mentalhealth.org/cre/ch5.asp)

Vereijken, C. M. J. L., & Riksen-Walraven, J. M. (1997). Maternal sensitivity and infant attachment security in Japan: A longitudinal study. *International Journal of Behavioral Development, 21*(1), 35–51.

Williams, R. L. (1974). The death of White research in the Black community. *Journal of Non-White Concerns in Personnel and Guidance, 2,* 116–132.

Windle, M., Iwawaki, S., & Lerner, R. (1987). Cross-cultural comparability of temperament among Japanese and American early and late adolescents. *Journal of Adolescent Research, 2*(4), 423–446.

Yu, E. S. H. (1999). Ethical and legal issues relating to the inclusion of Asian/Pacific Islanders in clinical studies. In A. C. Mastroianni, R. Faden, & D. Federman (Eds.), *The institute of medicine, women and health research* (Ethical and legal aspects of including women in clinical trials: Vol. 2. Workshop and Commissioned Papers, pp. 216–231). Washington, DC: National Academy Press.

Yu, E. S. H., & Liu, W. (1992). U.S. national health data on Asian Americans and Pacific Islanders: A research agenda for the 1990s. *American Journal of Public Health, 82,* 1645–1684.

Yu, E. S. H., & Liu, W. (1993). Methodological issues in studying the health of Asian/Pacific Islanders. In N. W. S. Zane, D. Takeuchi, & K. Young (Eds.), *Confronting critical health issues of Asian Pacific Islander Americans* (pp. 22–52). Newbury Park, CA: Sage.

Zane, N. W. S., Takeuchi, D., & Young, K. (Eds.). (1993). *Confronting critical health issues of Asian Pacific Islander Americans.* Newbury Park, CA: Sage.

CHAPTER 8

Ethical Community-Based Research With Hispanic or Latina(o) Populations

Balancing Research Rigor and Cultural Responsiveness

FELIPE GONZÁLEZ CASTRO

REBECA RIOS

HARRY MONTOYA

CHALLENGES IN BALANCING RIGOR AND CULTURAL RESPONSIVENESS

Overview

This chapter examines issues in the design of methodologically rigorous and ethically responsible research studies within the context of developing community-based intervention programs within Hispanic communities. The aim of such research is to create a balance between science and community culture in designing research that is respectful of the lifeways of Hispanics and of other racial or ethnic minority people. One important way to attain this balance is by establishing a collaborative and well-organized partnership between university scientists and community leaders. Although obtaining this balance may be quite challenging (Rawson, Martinelli-Casey, & Ling, 2002), the product of successful university-community collaboration is the development of a new genre of research, hybrid research studies that successfully integrate science and culture in a manner that both optimizes scientific rigor and cultural sensitivity.

Currently, few scientific research investigators have developed the cultural competence necessary for working effectively with people from various Hispanic cultures. At the same time, community advocates and leaders may lack adequate information regarding the potential risks and benefits of participating in community research. The current chapter examines cultural and ethical issues in program design that consider scientific and community imperatives for quality research. In addition, this chapter proposes strategies for integrating into community-based research with Hispanic populations. The purpose is to increase awareness among research investigators regarding major issues pertinent to successful collaborations with Hispanic communities in order to conduct effective community-based research. In addition, community leaders and advocates are encouraged to use this information to become familiar with research designs and to learn about ways to ensure that research initiatives in their communities are conducted under mutual agreements and for purposes that are beneficial to the entire community. Although the issues presented focus primarily on research with Hispanic communities, they may also be applied to research conducted with other ethnic communities.

This chapter is organized into six sections. After an introductory description characterizing broad demographic, contextual, and cultural issues that apply to the Hispanic population in the United States, the second and third sections present the scientific and community imperatives relevant to the conduct of research with Hispanics. The fourth section integrates the imperatives presented from the preceding two sections, and the fifth section presents strategies and approaches for the conduct of scientifically effective, and ethically responsible, community-based research with Hispanics. Finally, the sixth section offers some concluding thoughts.

The Hispanic Population of the United States

With a population of over 37.4 million as of March 2002, Hispanics constitute the largest racial/ethnic minority population in the United States (Ramirez & de la Cruz, 2003). Within this population, there exists considerable within-group variation that is based on several categories or dimensions of variability. These dimensions include: nationality (e.g., Mexicans, Puerto Ricans, Colombians), region (Mexican Americans of Southern California vs those from the Rio Grande Valley of Southern Texas), level of acculturation (low-acculturated monolingual Spanish speakers, high-acculturated monolingual English speakers, and bilingual/bicultural Hispanics), level of education (nonliterate school dropouts to highly educated college graduates with advanced degrees) (Balcazar, Castro, & Krull, 1995). Some dimensions like region are applicable to other subpopulations, whereas others (e.g., level of acculturation) are applicable specifically to Hispanic or other immigrant populations. The capacity to recognize, understand, and work effectively with respect to many forms of cultural diversity can be referred to as cultural competence. *Cultural competence* originally applied to the provision of health services, although it can also be applied to the conduct of culturally responsive research with diverse groups of Hispanics/Latina(o)s (Castro, Cota, & Vega, 1999; Orlandi, Weston, & Epstein, 1992; Resnikow, Soler, Braithwait, Ahluwalia, & Butler, 2000).

What Is Cultural Responsiveness?

Several critical issues require special attention in the conduct of scientific and culturally responsive research with Hispanic populations. A concept that is similar to cultural competence, *cultural responsiveness* refers to research designs and methodologies that adequately respect the local culture and effectively respond to critical cultural issues. Historical and intergenerational instances of racism occurring within the health care and research sectors have introduced lasting concerns among generations of minority individuals in the United States. A particularly extreme example of discriminatory research practices is the Tuskegee experiment, funded by the U.S. government, in which Black men with syphilis were observed without any form of treatment in order to examine the long-term effects of this disease. The resulting distrust toward researchers from this experience endures and may remain in the affected communities for several generations.

Accordingly, researchers must also be sensitive to political and social contexts that exist within a community of interest. For example, in southwest U.S. border states such as Arizona, the current trend toward the exclusion of undocumented Hispanic immigrants from basic human services brings with it a significant burden of mistrust that may easily be directed toward behavioral scientists. Ironically, this situation makes it difficult even for researchers who are dedicated to the well-being of immigrant groups to gain trust within such communities. In addition to experiences of racial discrimination, other cultural and language barriers experienced within the health care system may contribute to existing health disparities observed among minorities. Given that a growing proportion of the Hispanics in the United States are low-acculturated, monolingual Spanish speakers, it is particularly important that research investigators develop culturally responsive methods for working effectively with this subgroup. Thus, the rationale for the design and implementation of rigorous yet culturally responsive scientific research encompasses (a) the ethical imperative of social responsibility—protecting Hispanic and other minority communities from research-based abuse and disempowerment—and (b) the scientific imperative of enhancing intervention effectiveness by making interventions as potent as possible based on the use of scientifically based principles of prevention science (Castro & Garfinkle, 2003).

RESEARCH IMPERATIVES: STRONG SCIENCE FOR CLEAR INFERENCES

The Purpose of Research Design

The purpose underlying the design of scientifically rigorous research is to discover and test causal mechanisms that govern biological and social processes in order to inform the development of prevention and treatment interventions that promote health and well-being (Kellum & Longevin, 2003). Thus, scientific knowledge seeks to correctly identify and understand causal mechanisms of disease morbidity or mortality for the ultimate purpose of reducing health disparities and the burden of disease while also promoting wellness. Accordingly, to obtain an accurate understanding of these mechanisms, it is critical to develop well-designed scientific research studies having high scientific integrity and merit. By contrast, it has been demonstrated that poorly designed research studies offer no benefit to science or to the community (Fisher et al., 2002).

Model- and Evidence-Based Programs

The Substance Abuse and Mental Health Services Administration/Center for Substance Abuse Prevention (SAMHSA)/CSAP) has sponsored the National Registry of Effective Prevention Programs (NREPP), which as of 2002 had listed 44 model programs. These are prevention intervention programs that have been certified as tested and effective. These programs have been proven to work based on evidence that they have yielded the outcomes that they purported to produce when tested under rigorous study designs that typically consist of experimental–control group research designs. In addition, over half of these programs have been modified or adapted culturally to increase their relevance for use with members of certain special populations (Schinke, Brounstein, & Gardner,

2002). In fact, the adaptation of such model programs has become the rule rather than the exception. Program adaptation, or tailoring, is often needed to align original program goals and activities with the unique needs and preferences of specific communities or subgroups of participants; the goal is to eliminate sources of mismatch or cultural conflict while maintaining essential program components (Castro, Barrera, & Martinez, 2004).

What Works? Effect Size, Efficacy, and Effectiveness

The goal of effective program design is to demonstrate the ability to produce a desired outcome in terms of a measurable and desired intervention *effect size.* Effect size is used to measure intended health outcomes, as for example, a significant weight loss and related health benefits obtained from a weight reduction program. Programs that work are those that provide scientifically valid evidence of *efficacy,* a demonstrated program effect—that is, a significant intervention-related change on one or more relevant outcomes when examined under ideal, controlled conditions. In other words, efficacy trials involve research designs that demonstrate intended outcomes under ideal conditions. Beyond efficacy, a program may provide evidence of *effectiveness,* a demonstrated program effect, when the program is administered in an applied real-world setting such as a clinic or community as opposed to a laboratory or other controlled setting (Kellum & Longevin, 2003).

It should also be noted that a statement of efficacy should be of this form: "Program X is efficacious for producing Y outcomes for Z population." (Flay, Biglan, Boruch, Castro, Gottfredson, et al., 2005). Thus, measured program efficacy can differ across various health outcomes and, as examined, across different populations. For example, a prevention program developed and validated with White, nonminority adolescents from a suburban community may demonstrate high efficacy for that subpopulation but low efficacy with racial or ethnic minority adolescents from a rural community. A model program, such as to prevent cigarette smoking, is often developed and validated under ideal conditions with a White mainstream sample of youth; however, when it is then administered to a racial or ethnic sample of youth, this model may exhibit a loss of efficacy. That is, a model program that shows high efficacy but is later administered unchanged to a racial or ethnic sample may now yield low efficacy levels on a targeted outcome, such as rates of cigarette smoking, indicating that it does not work as well with the racial or ethnic group. This loss of efficacy would implicate the influences of certain cultural factors—such as level of acculturation or rurality—as factors that must be considered in the design of culturally effective prevention intervention programs for use within such racial or ethnic populations.

Recall that a program's effect size refers to the magnitude of change in preintervention to postintervention measurements of a specific health outcome. Conventional effect sizes for changes that are measured in standard deviation units are as follows: small = .30 SD, medium = .50 SD, and large = .80 SD (Cohen, 1988). The transfer and implementation of a prevention program from laboratory to community typically results in an erosion in effect size, as it becomes more difficult to produce relevant changes within a real-world environment. Thus, typically [Efficacy > Effectiveness]. This means that the transfer of a tested and effective program to a community setting typically yields a smaller program-related effect, that is, a lower "bang for the buck." This known erosion of efficacy raises significant ethical issues when delivering a tested and effective program to a new community or population of consumers. Under such conditions, the model program may not deliver what it promises to deliver.

Clinical Trials

The National Institutes of Health (NIH) Web site glossary defines a clinical trial as, "a prospective biomedical or behavioral research study of human subjects that is designed to answer specific questions about biomedical or behavioral interventions (drugs, treatments, devices, or new ways of using drugs, treatments, or devices)." Such clinical trials are used to investigate whether new interventions are "safe, efficacious and effective" (National Institutes of Health [NIH], 2002).

There are four phases (NIH, 2002) in testing intervention efficacy:

- Phase I: in a small group of people (about 80) for the first time to evaluate safety (e.g., safe dosage, side effects)
- Phase II: in a larger group of people to determine efficacy and further evaluate safety
- Phase III: in large groups of human subjects (from hundreds to thousands) by comparing the intervention with other standard or experimental interventions, monitoring side effects, and obtaining information on safe use
- Phase IV: after the intervention is marketed, to monitor effectiveness in the general population for information on adverse effects associated with widespread use

Randomization: Some ethical challenges. The strongest research design for ascertaining program effects (causality) is the randomized controlled clinical trial. Randomization is one of the fundamental procedures used in rigorous laboratory and scientific community-based research designs. Basically, randomization involves the unbiased assignment of individual participants or subjects to two or more groups. A randomized design allows

the conduct of data analyses that can yield clear and unambiguous results on the effects of an intervention that is applied within the experimental (intervention) group when compared against the no-intervention control group. Randomization ensures that the groups are equivalent before the intervention is administered by eliminating the influences of confounding, effects that otherwise introduce ambiguity in the results. Randomization allows us to attribute the observed outcomes to the effects of the intervention, for example, the medication, a psychotherapy treatment, or a community prevention intervention is said to produce the observed outcome.

A research design for a controlled clinical trial must have at least one comparison condition that does not receive the tested intervention (Flay et al., 2005). A strong research design allows causal statements regarding the effectiveness of the intervention program because of the *randomization* of participants into groups and the use of a *comparison condition,* a group that does not receive the tested intervention. A comparison group can consist of (a) no treatment, (b) usual care, (c) attention placebo, (d) a wait-list group, or (e) a best available alternative intervention (Flay et al., 2005).

Unfortunately, the use of a conventional experimental–control group design within a controlled clinical trial may raise ethical objections from some community leaders and activists, given that under this basic design the experimental (intervention) group receives the presumably beneficial intervention, whereas the control (or comparison) group receives no active intervention (either a placebo or no active intervention at all). From the perspective of research ethics, this experimental-control design "pits" good science against participant welfare, wherein it may be unethical to deny treatment in the control condition to a group of participants who are in need of that treatment

(Gil & Bob, 1999). Beyond this, some community activists consider randomization to be a form of manipulation that disempowers members of the local community and can harm those from the control group who are denied needed treatment.

Conversely, rigorous scientific studies such as randomized controlled clinical trials require randomization as an integral scientific design feature. In fact, NIH scientific review committees often regard research designs that lack randomization as weak and lacking in sufficient scientific merit to be worthy of receiving a competitive scientific merit score. Such proposed research studies are often not funded and cannot be conducted. This dilemma begs the question, "What can an ethical research investigator do to protect the welfare of Hispanic or other minority participants and also propose the strongest scientific research design for developing effective interventions?" After describing some community research imperatives in the next section, we attempt to tackle this dilemma.

COMMUNITY IMPERATIVES: RESEARCH THAT HELPS THE COMMUNITY

Rationale for Community Research

Should controlled clinical trials be conducted within racial/ethnic communities? From a community perspective, despite the challenges and potential burden imposed by methodological issues, there exist strong imperatives for conducting community-based research. In fact, it is worth noting that ultimately, scientific and community imperatives should pursue the same goal: to improve the quality of life, that is, to ease human suffering by using effective treatments or interventions. On the other hand, community advocates certainly have reasons

to raise questions regarding the conditions under which research is to be conducted within their own community. This section presents some potential benefits and risks of research as seen from a community perspective, along with examples that highlight the importance of establishing community partnership in research.

Communities can benefit a great deal from research, provided that it is conducted under conditions of a true partnership. Research data generated from such a partnership may be used for a wide variety of purposes, ranging from a needs assessment to data for influencing local policy, to data for improving public health outcomes. An important purpose for such research data is to identify new and important community needs. For example, a community coalition might test an emerging hypothesis that the community has developed increasing rates of uninsured children. This enhanced capacity to obtain valid needs assessment data can improve a community's capability to engage in strategic planning and establish priorities from among several competing health-related needs. The next step after identifying community needs is to use the observed data to demonstrate these community needs to legislators or policymakers for the purpose of influencing policies and accessing additional funding. Having "hard" data that accurately demonstrate community needs allows community advocates to take a more targeted, direct approach toward influencing local policy and accessing funds, as opposed to the use of anecdotal reports of alleged community needs. In addition to demonstrating need, research data may be useful in quantifying a community agency's positive impact on its service population. With diminishing public resources, the issue of an agency's sustainability and survival emerges as a recurring challenge. Research that gathers treatment outcome or evaluation data offers valuable information for sustaining important community programs that rely on public funding and the support of policymakers.

Another important design in which community members can observe the benefits of community-based research involves the comparison of an enhanced treatment to a standard treatment that is used as the control condition. In this design, a program intervention that meets an important need is introduced into the community as part of a research study. The preceding section described the possible negative ethical consequences of the use of pure no-treatment control groups in clinical research; however, research designs that utilize a standard treatment as a control condition may benefit participants in both the treatment and the comparison groups. In such a design, if community advocates and participants alike feel that their needs are being addressed and they appreciate feeling included in the research effort, the community as a whole benefits from both of the interventions administered under this design. The fifth section in this chapter on hybrid program designs further describes this use of such comparison and control groups.

Finally, community research is important to clarify the occurrence of racial or ethnic disparities in health and may be instrumental in improving health outcomes for Hispanics. Community research can be used to find better ways to identify and access the individuals who are at high risk for a given health outcome and to identify culturally specific (selective) prevention interventions that target specific subpopulations and specific conditions. The problem of racial and ethnic disparities in health and health care access has received considerable attention in recent years. In response, major initiatives have been developed to address these staggering disparities, as described in *Healthy People 2010*, a national set of health goals and objectives initiated in 2000.

Decreasing Health Disparities: The Case of Type 2 Diabetes Mellitus

Type 2 diabetes mellitus is now identified as a major public health epidemic within the United States and is a chronic degenerative disease that disproportionately affects Hispanics. Rates of diabetes mellitus have increased in the past decade in direct relation to increases in obesity and overweight status within the American population. In a recent study of lifetime risks of type 2 diabetes mellitus in the United States, the higher estimated lifetime risks for diabetes were observed among Hispanics: males 45.4% and females 52.5%, relative to 32.8% for White American males and 38.5% for White American females (Nayaran, Boyle, Thompson, Sorensen, & Williamson, 2003). Such high risks for losses in quality of life and life expectancy resulting from type 2 diabetes mellitus prompt a need for the design and implementation of efficacious prevention and treatment interventions that are culturally relevant for various Hispanics. Moreover, mental health comorbidities with diabetes, and the lack of a clear understanding and recognition of co-occurring such as depression, can further complicate health outcomes among Mexican Americans with type 2 diabetes (Black, Markides, & Ray, 2003). These psychosocial considerations should be incorporated into the design of potent and culturally relevant, community-based interventions that address diabetic morbidities among Hispanics. The case of type 2 diabetes in Hispanics represents a pertinent example of the need for partnerships between researchers and Hispanic communities to work toward improved public health outcomes in combating a chronic degenerative disease within a specific population, thereby contributing toward the reduction of racial and ethnic disparities in health.

Potential Risks of Community Research

Unfortunately, in the past, incompatible agendas—research investigator insensitivity to a community's cultural norms and mutual misunderstandings between researchers and community residents—have compromised the potential success of community-based research. In the worst cases, researchers have used data in a way that presents a community, its residents, and agencies in a very negative light. In addition to past abuses, misconceptions on the part of some community leaders or residents regarding scientific research methods and program designs for conducting rigorous community-based research have created a resistance and opposition to community-based controlled clinical trials. Fortunately, establishing a genuine partnership between community members and research staff can avoid misconceptions and negative consequences and can generate mutually beneficial community-based studies. Community advocates and researchers alike must establish a dialogue that clarifies the potential risks of poorly designed or culturally insensitive community-based research by avoiding insensitivity or exploitation while also dispelling misconceptions on the part of both researchers and community residents.

Research investigators who submit applications to conduct research studies within Hispanic communities do so for a variety of reasons. Some proposal writers may submit a research application based on a genuine desire to generate new scientific knowledge that helps the local Hispanic community to reduce health disparities. By contrast, some may submit a research application in order to secure a large research grant that infuses funds and resources into their own research organization. Clearly, this latter type of motivation is inconsistent with establishing a true community partnership. An entirely "top-down" planning orientation on the part of some research investigators discourages collaboration. This approach demands total investigator power and control over all decision making to the exclusion of input from community regarding their needs or wishes. For some research investigators, the power sharing implicit in investigator-community collaborations is a source of significant discomfort and resistance.

Even with the best of intentions, misconceptions on both sides can create difficulties in collaboration. On the part of the investigator, a lack of cultural competence impedes a true cultural understanding of the community. The researcher is not expected to know everything there is to know about a community, although the culturally competent researcher will have an attitude of openness to collaboration and the basic skills necessary to seek information from key informants from the local community. Misconceptions on the part of community members can also serve as barriers to an effective partnership as, for example, from a lack of understanding of core strategies and procedures needed to develop rigorous scientific research designs. Again, reducing such misconceptions requires effective communications.

An illustrative example of a university research team's failure to consult and establish a genuine community partnership demonstrates key points regarding the utility of university-community partnerships. In a small community within the southwestern United States, a local community coalition became upset with a team of university researchers for their failure to contact and consult with that coalition. These investigators unilaterally initiated and attempted to conduct a study of health care access within that community. These researchers neglected to create ties within that community to the extent that they even utilized advocates from the university rather than recruit advocates from the local community. The result was that this research team's work exerted a negative impact on the local community in several ways. Naturally, as community leaders and stakeholders became alienated from this research effort, these stakeholders withdrew their support and become wary of future collaborations. In addition, this coalition was especially upset by the lost opportunity for mobilizing their community resources and incorporating their cultural insights into the proposed research. This coalition's collective wisdom could have been incorporated into the design of the proposed research via the use of key informants and stakeholders who could have participated as knowledgeable partners who would ensure that the conceptual framework and data collection would be culturally congruent with local community needs and values. This example illustrates the fact that establishing a collaborative community partnership is essential in community-based health research, not only for the purpose of establishing good community relations but also to ensure the ecological validity of the entire study. Moreover, the investigators were unable to know how representative their data were in capturing true community needs, and their results were not accepted as valid by members of this local community.

INTEGRATING RESEARCH AND COMMUNITY IMPERATIVES

Reframing the Question

Should controlled clinical trials be conducted within racial or ethnic communities? Given the strong potential for research to contribute to scientific knowledge and to benefit communities, the question is not

whether controlled clinical trails should be conducted but rather *how*. To address the many health disparities affecting U.S. Hispanic populations, the delivery of tested and effective health interventions is absolutely necessary for the prevention and treatment of conditions such as type 2 diabetes mellitus in adult Hispanics, alcohol abuse in Hispanic men, cocaine dependence in young adult Hispanics, and other chronic degenerative diseases. The critical question is, "How can representatives of a racial or ethnic minority community be involved in the design and implementation of research studies that contribute to tangible and needed health benefits to Hispanic communities and also that advance science?"

This reframing of the critical question about the use of controlled clinical trials raises several key issues that must be addressed in order to find an integrated, culturally responsive and scientifically rigorous solution to this dilemma. The following issues must be considered in developing a viable solution to this critical question:

- Representation: Who will serve as authorized representatives of the local community (key informants, stakeholders, gatekeepers), and how will they serve?
- Participation in design and implementation: How will community needs and wants be voiced and incorporated, from the beginning and at every stage in the design and implementation of the proposed research and its intervention protocols?
- Tangible and needed benefits: What direct and useful benefits that improve the community's health and well-being will be provided to members of the participating community?
- Advancing science: What is the scientific and practical significance of this study in terms of the generalizability and/or factual knowledge that will be gained from the conduct of this study and as it may benefit of the local community?

Ethics and Cultural Competence in Research

There are several important issues involved in the conduct of ethical research with Hispanics. In addition to following general human subjects regulations for ethical practice, researchers must be culturally competent in order to effectively respond to culturally specific issues that apply to research and partnerships with Hispanic communities. Community stakeholders should be prepared to ask questions that assess the cultural competence of research investigators who wish to conduct research within the local community.

Ethical guidelines that govern all human subject studies involve (a) clearly informing prospective participants regarding the risks and benefits involved in participation, (b) recruiting participants without coercion or obligation, and (c) protecting participants from physical and psychological harm. Of course, researchers must also refrain from deception or otherwise misleading participants about the effects of the research on the individual or on the community and must also inform participants of their right to withdraw from the study at any time without penalty. This process of disclosure, called informed consent, is essential to uphold ethical procedures and relies on clear and effective communication. To ensure adequate communication, especially in cross-cultural situations, cultural competence in knowledge, attitudes, and skills is an essential element required of all research staff.

Even if some research staff come from the same ethnic or cultural group as that of the research participants, research investigators and members of the community who are hired as research staff (e.g., lay health workers, prevention specialists, etc.) still need to understand and acquire new cultural competence skills to fully understand and appreciate cultural nuances that exist within a given community (Castro, 1998). For monolingual, Spanish-speaking, or low-educated Hispanic participants, informed consent documents must be translated carefully and with equivalence in meaning in order to provide accurate, clear, and understandable information to the prospective participant. There is also a need to advise and educate members of the Hispanic community regarding the nature of the research study, its purpose, as well as the gains and limitations of research as relevant for members of the local Hispanic community.

Moreover, Hispanic community leaders, gatekeepers, and stakeholders should insist on a research team's commitment to safeguard the well-being of the local Hispanic community, as this research team would enter into a partnership with members of the local community. In order to ascertain whether researchers are culturally competent and genuinely qualified to work effectively within a local community, Hispanic leaders are advised to ask several important questions. Some questions to assess a research team's cultural competence and a commitment to a genuine partnership include the following:

- Why are you interested in conducting research within the local Hispanic community at this time?
- What is your track record in working in a culturally competent manner with Hispanic communities?
- Is the principal investigator willing to meet face-to-face with community leaders in the community as needed?
- Do you speak Spanish? If not, how will you communicate effectively with local Hispanics (Mexican Americans, Puerto Ricans, Cubans, etc.) in a culturally competent manner?
- Are you willing to issue a subcontract for the distribution of research funds within the local community and to hire community members as paid research staff who will hold important staff positions, such as projector director, lay health educators, interviewers, clerical staff, and others?

Infusing such culturally competent procedures into community-based research is essential for integrating ethical and research imperatives into a scientific project that also serves the needs of the local community.

Don't Make Decisions About Us Without Us

Community participation is a scientific, as well as an ethical imperative in working with Hispanic and other racial or ethnic minority communities. Some communities may be suspicious of programs developed and conducted by outsiders who in the past have not respected the needs and preferences of the local community (Montoya, 2003). To maintain cultural responsiveness in scientific community-based research, it is essential to ensure community participation in every stage of research program design and implementation.

Regarding community participation, a lack of community input and "buy-in" can result in low participation by local community residents, ultimately resulting in low program efficacy along with other adverse consequences that threaten the validity of the community study. As noted, as consumer participation dwindles, program effects will also erode toward zero. Conversely, approaches for enhancing program participation include promoting community ownership of the program and the use of the *principle of relevance* and the *principle of participation* (Frankish, Lovato, & Shannon, 1999). The principle of relevance invokes the need to "start where the people are," and the principle of participation emphasizes that the best learning occurs during experiences involving active participation by the learner. Creating opportunities for community involvement in program design and in implementation can enhance participation. Thus, the principle of relevance

and the principle of participation serve as key factors in the design and implementation of effective and ethical community-based research.

STRATEGIES FOR CULTURALLY RESPONSIVE SCIENTIFIC RESEARCH DESIGNS

Promoting Investigator-Community Partnerships

Community-based research benefits from working partnerships with community-based leaders and organizations in a culture of collaboration that involves an active partnership in conceptualization, design, implementation, and interpretation of study results (Flores, Castro & Fernández-Esquer, 1995; Minkler & Wallerstein, 2002). In fact, developing investigator-community collaboration is perhaps the most important strategy in developing a community research initiative. However, crafting viable community-university research partnerships is not easy and it takes time to develop true working partnerships, some of which may fail (Rawson et al., 2002). In developing such working partnerships, culturally responsive attitudes and approaches are important.

To illustrate, the following is an example of a successful partnership. Researchers from a local university and the state public health department were interested in conducting a study that examined factors in residents' perceptions and access to treatment within their own community. In this instance, the research team was conscientious from the start in involving people from the community and requested that community stakeholders help in planning the study and in gathering the data. Community members were pleased to be involved from the beginning in both the design process and in the implementation of the study. Problems caused by a lack of community involvement, such as alienation and lack of buy-in, were avoided, and both the community and the research team were satisfied with the end product.

This example illustrates the importance of community involvement from the beginning, and it honors the community's important request: "Don't make decisions about us, without us." The most important way to involve key community stakeholders is by reaching out to community advocates. Whatever can initially be done to involve and engage these people is critical. Community leaders are the people who can inform the research process, although they can also pose the greatest obstacles and barriers in trying to achieve a valid and useful research product. In getting started, the first step is to inquire about who in the community is working in the health issue in question and to obtain their participation in an atmosphere of respect and genuine interest in obtaining their advice. Although the potential exists to encounter resistance from certain individuals who may feel territorial about their own community, the best way to overcome such resistance is to develop and build a relationship with these individuals and to explain to them how the goals of the research coincide with the best interests of the local community.

Another strategy to establish successful working partnerships is to develop and maintain a proactive policy of inclusion regarding partnerships and collaboration. Successful agencies are proactive about notifying, inviting, and organizing community groups regarding various initiatives. Research projects may not only be initiated by research institutions but also by members of a local community group or coalition. Thus, this strategy applies to both community agencies and to university-based or other research institutions. In the initial stages of a research project, it is advisable to start immediately in

involving advocacy groups to serve as important allies in conducting a successful community-based study.

Finally, a positive attitude toward safeguarding the well-being of the local community, coupled with a mastery of scientific principles in research design, jointly contribute to the design of successful community-based research studies. Here, a balance is needed between the interests of community participants and those of scientific research investigators. This balance requires cultural competence on the part of the research investigator, along with a commitment towards promoting community health. The University of California's Universitywide Tobacco-Related Disease Control Program (TRDRP) provides an excellent operating model of a research infrastructure that promotes and supports university-community collaborative research projects (for information see www .trdrp.org).

Regarding issues of power sharing of research responsibilities and decision-making authority, an important distinction should be made between exercising scientific control over vital research procedures versus exercising authoritarian control over all aspects of the research study. To maintain the integrity of the research protocol for conducting rigorous scientific research, the research investigator, the project director, and project staff should implement the planned research protocol with high fidelity. A failure to do so may lead to procedural errors that compromise the quality of the research.

By contrast, a research investigator's insistence on exercising authoritarian, unilateral, and exclusionary decision-making control is inconsistent with the spirit of an investigator- community collaboration. The responsible quality control of the scientific aspects of a research protocol should not be confused with absolute and unilateral control over all project-related decisions. An approach that is consistent with the principle of participation involves the strategic assignment of project tasks to community stakeholders, an approach that is consistent with matching certain stakeholder competencies with project tasks. Responsible community leaders will not be experts in rendering scientific judgments about a project's scientific procedures, although it is useful to inform them of the science that underlies the study. By contrast, community stakeholders are capable of offering important information regarding local cultural customs and traditions and in making judgments about community-related political issues. Thus, community leaders and stakeholders can be delegated certain authority in deciding and presiding over certain project activities in congruence with the research project's specific aims, goals, and objectives. Such authority as delegated selectively to responsible community leaders builds community buy-in and promotes more active program participation.

Community Education About Research

In the spirit of promoting participatory social action research that brings researchers into partnerships with community leaders, research investigators should engage in community education outreach efforts regarding the methods and approaches of scientific research. As noted earlier, within some sectors of Hispanic and other racial or ethnic minority communities there exist various misconceptions, some of which may prompt suspicion and mistrust. A vague familiarity with known ethical abuses, or views that research often uses people as "guinea pigs," prompts an aversion to research or a suspicion of research investigators. Along these lines, among undocumented and low-acculturated Hispanic community residents, referring to research in Spanish translations as *una investigación* (an investigation) can prompt fears of deportation and concerns over the threat of legal sanctions against the participant. Providing community residents with information about well-established safeguards contained within conventional informed consent procedures will aid in clarifying the true nature of many research studies and in dispelling myths and misconceptions about ethically conducted scientific research.

Hybrid Program Designs

Given the frequent need for program adaptation to respond to the varying needs of diverse Hispanic or Latino communities nationally, the challenge still lies in making adaptations that increase program effects and not erode them. Haphazard programmatic changes that indiscriminately modify or eliminate program components or activities will likely erode a model program's effectiveness, not enhance it. A prevention intervention or treatment program should be adapted in direct correspondence with the specific cultural needs and preferences of prospective consumers, as well as in consultation with frontline program staff who have delivered the program, such as prevention specialists, *Promotoras* (lay health workers). In principle, designing programs that purposely build in adaptation and fidelity should yield higher levels of effectiveness that approach or even exceed original levels of efficacy established by the model program; however, needed still are empirical elaborations of preliminary guidelines for program adaptation that are aimed at maximizing model program effectiveness within the context of diverse populations (Backer, 2001). As noted previously, sources of potential community-related erosions in program efficacy can involve low consumer participation. Thus, within community settings, promoting, maintaining, and sustaining consumer participation in a prevention program is essential to maximizing program effectiveness.

Thus, a new generation of hybrid programs is needed. These hybrid programs would integrate adaptation and fidelity as core components of program design as these are incorporated into a two-phased approach: (a) initial and systematic adaptations to ground the program within the local cultural community and (b) fidelity of implementation with careful evaluation of implementation and outcomes. Thus, if research investigators are capable of successfully designing prevention and treatment programs that address a wide variety of programmatic goals and objectives, they should also be able to design prevention and treatment programs that explicitly build in community participation and program adaptation from the very beginning.

Furthermore, newly developed and innovative, as well as existing model intervention programs should be adapted under a collaboration that involves the program developer and a panel of local community representatives who are well acquainted with local community beliefs, customs, traditions, and values. The ultimate aim of such culturally informed research designs is still the development of a rigorous scientific prevention intervention that is also acceptable to scientific review committees. A related aim is to develop rigorous health research that is also culturally and ethically responsive to the unique needs and concerns of a local community. Along those lines, needed now is a series of controlled randomized trials of culturally enhanced programs (the enhanced intervention group), which are evaluated for program effectiveness against their original (or standard) prevention program (the comparison group). Within these studies, process evaluations may also be conducted to inform and refine the strategies and methods used in implementing these programs.

The Indigenous Outreach Model

The indigenous outreach (*Promotora*) health education model is a promising approach to health promotion and disease prevention that has been used to address the current epidemic of type 2 diabetes (Ramirez, Villareal, & Chalela, 1999). The use of lay health workers as outreach health educators offers a therapeutic relationship of trust and support that is especially relevant for conducting health research and interventions with Hispanic populations. This outreach model may build on the traditional Hispanic or Latino cultural values of *personalismo* (value of close, trusting relationships), *confianza* (intimate trust), and *respeto* (a deep respect). In addition, cognitive-behavioral approaches to behavior change, such as self-monitoring, role playing, cognitive restructuring, and problem solving have been endorsed by some Hispanic scholars as compatible with Hispanic cultural values and needs (Organista & Muñoz, 1998). The direct, concrete, and results-oriented nature of cognitive-behavioral methods has been described as a feature that is culturally compatible for health promotion with Hispanic clients. Thus, integrating the outreach and *personalismo* of the *Promotora* approach with the use of cognitive behavioral techniques can enhance health promotion efficacy for community-based prevention and treatment of diabetes and other chronic degenerative diseases.

Integrating the *Promotora* (culturally responsive outreach) and the cognitive-behavioral technologies can be accomplished via several steps. These include the following:

- Program manuals, which include a participant manual and a health educator manual
- Behavioral skills training for health educators (*Promotoras*)
- Skills role play for *Promotoras* and consumers
- Skills measurement via in-vivo assessments
- Design of randomized trials to evaluate program efficacy under ideal program delivery conditions
- Program adaptations for local delivery (fidelity-adaptation balance) to maximize

program relevance to local subpopulation needs and for applied setting effectiveness

In addition, in the manualized approach that integrates behavior change technology, the design of culturally relevant programs for Hispanics or Latinos should not ignore the importance of relationship issues. The distinction between relationship-focused versus curriculum-focused programs (McDonald, 2004) is useful in an initial appraisal of the cultural relevance of a prevention program as evaluated prior to adaptation. Relationship-oriented prevention programs appear to be more consumer friendly and relevant to the needs of certain populations, such as low-acculturated Hispanics or Latinos, American Indians or Native Americans, and other traditional or indigenous groups of racial or ethnic minority people. Programs that are more curriculum-focused in nature may be more effective in their use with certain traditional subpopulations, if such programs are adapted to include an enhanced focus on relationship building.

Social Participatory Merit Ratings

In the future, it would be useful to expand the current human subjects protection ratings regarding the inclusion of women, race or ethnicity, and children to include the participation of community representatives in the design and implementation of a proposed research study. As noted previously, sources for enhancing program participation are based on (a) promoting program ownership, (b) the use of the principle of relevance and the principle of participation (Frankish et al., 1999), and (c) consumer involvement in program design and in implementation. These program ratings would involve the usual rating categories of *acceptable, unacceptable*, or *not included*, that in this case would describe the extent to which members of a local community have been involved in the design and

future implementation of such a proposed study. Such ratings might be similar to the following:

- P1: Community included in both study design and implementation
- P2: Community included in study design only
- P3: Community included in program implementation only
- P4: No inclusion of community into the study design or implementation

The authors propose that such a rating system would mark an advance towards incorporating community collaboration into proposed community-based research.

CONCLUSIONS

In conclusion, several challenges face research investigators and prevention interventionists, as well as community leaders, challenges that involve finding ways to develop programs that are both scientifically effective and also culturally responsive to ethical community concerns. The most scientific approaches seek to maximize a program's impact in changing the adverse effects of a disease, such as preventing or reducing the effects of depression, HIV/AIDS, drug abuse, obesity, diabetes, and other major public health problems. By contrast, community leaders have expressed concerns over the development and implementation of interventions that are insensitive to local community needs, and these concerns should be aptly addressed in an atmosphere of respect and a spirit of collaboration.

In this chapter, we have attempted to demonstrate that scientific, cultural, and ethical concerns can be addressed simultaneously. Although the balance between community and research imperatives may be difficult to achieve, the basic agenda of communities and researchers alike is ultimately the same: to improve community health outcomes and to reduce health disparities. The key to a truly unified effort involves a clear and specific dialogue between research investigators and community leaders in an effort to design research initiatives—from the very beginning—in ways that are both scientifically sound and ethically responsive.

REFERENCES

Backer, T. E. (2001). Finding the balance: Program fidelity and adaptation in substance abuse prevention: A state-of-the art review. Rockville, MD: Center for Substance Abuse Prevention.

Balcazar, H., Castro, F. G., & Krull, J. L. (1995). Cancer risk reduction in Mexican American women: The role of acculturation, education, and health risk factors. *Health Education Quarterly, 22,* 61–84.

Black, S. A., Markides, K. S., & Ray, L. A. (2003). Depression predicts increased incidence of adverse health outcomes in older Mexican Americans with type 2 diabetes. *Diabetes Care, 26,* 2822–2828.

Castro, F. G. (1998). Cultural competence training in clinical psychology: Assessment, clinical intervention, and research. In A. S. Bellack & M. Hersen (Eds.), *Comprehensive clinical psychology: Sociocultural and individual differences* (Vol. 10, pp. 127–140). Oxford: Pergamon.

Castro, F. G., Barrera, M., & Martinez, M. (2004). The cultural adaptation of prevention interventions: Resolving tensions between fidelity and fit. *Prevention Science, 5,* 41–45.

Castro, F. G., Cota, M. K., & Vega, S. (1999). Health promotion in Latino populations: Program planning, development, and evaluation. In R. M. Huff & M. V. Kline (Eds.), *Promoting health in multicultural populations: A handbook for practitioners* (pp. 137–168). Thousand Oaks, CA: Sage.

Castro, F. G., & Garfinkle, J. (2003). Critical issues in the development of culturally relevant substance abuse treatments for specific minority groups. *Alcoholism: Clinical and Experimental Research, 27,* 1–8.

Cohen, J. (1988). *Statistical power analysis for the behavioral sciences* (2nd ed.). Hillsdale, NJ: Lawrence Erlbaum.

Fisher, C. B., Hoagwood, K., Boyce, C., Duster, T., Frank, D. A., Grisso, T., et al. (2002). Research ethics for mental health science involving ethnic minority children and youths. *American Psychologist, 57,* 1024–1040.

Flay, B., Giglan, A., Boruch, R. F., Castro, F. G., Gottfredson, D., Kellam, S., Moscicki, E. K., Schinke, S., Valentine, J. C., & Ji, P. (2005). Standards of evidence: Criteria for efficiency, effectiveness, and dissemination. *Prevention Science.* DOI: 10.1007/s11121-005-5553-y.

Flores, E. T., Castro, F. G., & Fernández-Esquer, M. (1995). Social theory, social action, and intervention research: Implications for cancer prevention among Latinos. *Journal of the National Cancer Institute Monographs, 18,* 101–108.

Frankish, C. J., Lovato, C. Y., & Shannon, W. J. (1999). Models, theories, and principles of health promotion with multicultural populations. In R. M. Huff & M. V. Kline (Eds.), *Promoting health in multicultural populations: A handbook for practitioners* (pp. 41–72). Thousand Oaks, CA: Sage.

Gil, E. F., & Bob, S. (1999). Culturally competent research: An ethical perspective. *Clinical Psychology Review, 19,* 45–55.

Kellum, S. G., & Longevin, D. J. (2003). A framework for understanding "evidence" in prevention research and programs. *Prevention Science, 4,* 137–153.

McDonald, L. (2004, May). Substance abuse prevention in Indian country: Adapting SAMHSA model programs for tribal communities: The FAST program. Presentation at the 12th Annual Meeting of the Society for Prevention Research, Quebec City, Canada.

Minkler, M., & Wallerstein, N. (2002). *Community-based participatory research for health.* San Francisco: Jossey-Bass.

Montoya, H. (2003, November 15). *Don't make decisions about us without us.* Presentation at the "Lifting the Lives of Latino Youth" summit, Phoenix, AZ.

Nation Institutes of Health. (2002, April 8). Instructions to reviewers for evaluating research involving human subjects in grant and cooperative agreement applications. Bethesda, MD: Author. Document available at http://64.233.179.104/search?q=cache:fachVIctYA8J:grants.nih.gov/grants/peer/hs_review_inst.pdf+Instructions+to+reviewers+for+evaluating+research+involving+human+subjects+in+grant+and+cooperative+agreement+applications&hl=en&ie=UTF-8

Nayaran, K. M., Boyle, J. P., Thompson, T. J., Sorensen, S. W., & Williamson, D. F. (2003). Lifetime risk for diabetes mellitus in the United States. *Journal of the American Medical Association, 290,* 1884–1890.

Organista, K. C., & Muñoz, R. F. (1998). Cognitive behavioral therapy with Latinos. In P. B. Organista, K. M. Chun, & G. Marín (Eds.), *Readings in ethnic psychology* (pp. 353–366). New York: Routledge.

Orlandi, M., Weston, R., & Epstein, L. G. (1992). *Cultural competence for evaluators: A guide for alcohol and other drug abuse prevention practitioners working with ethnic/racial communities.* Rockville, MD: Office of Substance Abuse Prevention.

Ramirez, A. G., Villareal, R., & Chalela, P. (1999). Community-level diabetes control in a Texas barrio. In R. M. Huff & V. Kline (Eds.), *Promoting health in multicultural populations: A handbook for practitioners* (pp. 169–187). Thousand Oaks, CA: Sage.

Ramirez, R. R., & de la Cruz, P. (2003). *The Hispanic population in the United States: March 2002* (Current Population Reports, P20–545). Washington DC: Census Bureau.

Rawson, R. A., Martinelli-Casey, P., & Ling, W. (2002). Dancing with strangers: Will U.S. substance abuse practice and research organizations build mutually productive relationships? *Addictive Behaviors, 27,* 941–949.

Resnikow, K., Soler, R., Braithwait, R. L., Ahluwalia, J. S., & Butler, J. (2000). Cultural sensitivity in substance abuse prevention. *Journal of Community Psychology, 28,* 271–290.

Schinke, S., Brounstein, P., & Gardner, S. (2002). *Science-based prevention programs and principles, 2002* (DHHS Pub No. (SMA) 03-3764). Rockville, MD: Center for Substance Abuse Prevention, Substance Abuse and Mental Health Services Administration.

CHAPTER 9

Ethical Issues in Research With Immigrants and Refugees

DINA BIRMAN

ETHICAL ISSUES IN RESEARCH WITH IMMIGRANTS AND REFUGEES

As is the case with much of social science, research on immigrants and refugees is not morally neutral. Immigration policies are hotly debated in our society. Supporters of immigration argue that immigrants benefit the country but may need special programs to assist them in their adjustment, whereas opponents suggest that immigrants drain resources that could be spent on other national priorities. Ethical issues are also involved in refugee admissions policies that may cause great suffering for those whose asylum claims may be denied, forcing them to return to their native country. Research on the experience and adaptation of immigrants and refugees is used to argue both sides of this debate, as illustrated in several articles in the journal *International Migration Review* (Abernethy, 1996; Carens, 1996; Gibney, 1996) that considered the pros and cons of immigration policies. The uses of this research place great responsibility on the researchers who study these populations, as the findings of their studies may be used to inform policies that have great impact on the lives of many people.

At the same time, defining ethical responsibilities for the researcher is complex when working with vulnerable populations and diverse cultures with distinctive and sometimes conflicting definitions of what is ethical. As a result, researchers confront ethical dilemmas that cannot be easily resolved with guidance from existing ethical principles and guidelines. The first type of ethical dilemmas may arise when researchers try to balance attention to humanitarian concerns with scientific rigor, such as when studying experiences of refugees in the midst of humanitarian crises (Leaning, 2001). Jacobsen and Landau (2003) describe the "dual imperative" faced by researchers who must balance their concerns about reducing suffering with their professional responsibility to produce research that meets the highest scientific standards. In order to address humanitarian concerns in such situations, researchers may compromise the research design and methodology. On the other hand, although ethical considerations must guide the research process, if studies make compromises with respect to the research design, findings will ultimately not be interpretable or useful to the groups being studied. For example, studies that do not employ control groups in order to provide treatment to all who need it or omit important questions from questionnaires out of concern for the respondents' reactions may fail to yield valid data, and the research effort will have been in vain. As Jacobsen & Landau (2003) suggest, ensuring scientific rigor in research on vulnerable populations is an ethical responsibility of the researchers because of the importance of the issues and the need for valid data that can inform intervention efforts.

The second type of ethical dilemmas in research with refugees and immigrants involves balancing potential differences in the ways *ethical* behavior is defined by the culture of the researcher and the research community versus the culture of the research participants. There are situations when cultural norms with respect to what is ethical may be contradictory, making *ethical* behavior, as defined by one culture, unethical in the other, and vice versa. Existing ethical guidelines do not provide sufficient guidance to help the researcher determine how to reconcile such conflicting perspectives.

The complexity of these dilemmas means that researchers studying refugee and immigrant populations must develop a sophisticated understanding of the underlying issues so that they can negotiate creative solutions to resolve them. The purpose of this chapter is to highlight the problems and complexities in acting ethically while conducting research with immigrants and refugees and to offer some suggestions for solutions to such dilemmas. Throughout, the chapter illustrates the points made with examples from the author's experience with research in immigrant and refugee communities from the former Soviet Union and Vietnam.

The chapter is organized as follows: First, a description of who are refugees and immigrants is offered to highlight the distinctive characteristics and needs of these populations

relative to other groups, such as ethnic minorities. Second, the chapter will outline ethical considerations and challenges that arise in conducting research with these groups. Inclusion of immigrants and refugees in research is highlighted as one critical ethical issue, and challenges faced by researchers who try to include these groups are discussed. Further, challenges involving ethical treatment of participants in research conducted across cultures are described. The chapter concludes with the suggestion that inclusion of cultural insiders on research teams is necessary to ensure that researchers act ethically. It is argued that because of the complexity of ethical considerations that arise in research with immigrant and refugee groups, broad ethical guidelines will never be sufficient to help resolve ethical dilemmas that arise in the course of research with culturally diverse and politically vulnerable populations. Rather, inclusion of cultural insiders on research teams can help create processes that can ensure discussion and negotiation of research approaches that result in ethical research.

WHO ARE THE IMMIGRANTS IN THE UNITED STATES?

Immigrant is a term used to describe foreign nationals who enter a country for purposes of permanent resettlement. In the United States, there are three broad categories of immigrants: (1) voluntary migrants who come to join relatives already settled in the United States or to fill particular jobs for which expertise may be lacking among U.S. nationals, (2) refugees and asylum seekers who enter the country to avoid persecution, and (3) and undocumented immigrants who enter the country illegally. It is currently thought that since the 1970s, the United States has been experiencing the largest migration wave in its history. Approximately

1 million immigrants enter the country for permanent resettlement each year, about 700,000 of them legally and an estimated 200,000 to 300,000 without legal documents, mostly from Mexico.

Among the legal immigrants, approximately 50,000 to 100,000 annually are refugees. The United Nations Convention Relating to the Status of Refugees (1951) defines *refugee* as a person who "owing to a well-founded fear of being persecuted for reasons of race, religion, nationality, membership of a particular social group, or political opinion, is outside the country of his nationality, and is unable to or, owing to such fear, is unwilling to avail himself of the protection of that country" (United Nations High Commissioner for Refugees, 1951, Article 2). Unlike refugees, immigrants are seen as continuing to receive the protection of their government were they to return home; however, refugees flee because of the threat of persecution and cannot return safely to their homes. The distinction between refugees and immigrants can be vague and tied to United States foreign policy. Some groups, including refugees from Somalia, Vietnam, and Jews and Evangelical Christians from the former Soviet Union, qualify for refugee status in the United States "based on their membership in a protected category with a credible, but not necessarily individual, fear of persecution" (United States Department of State, 2002).

Refugees, immigrants, and undocumented immigrants confront unique challenges in resettlement that have implications for conducting ethical research. For example, undocumented immigrants may fear being identified and may thus shy away from participation in research studies, particularly if research might lead to their identification by authorities. Refugees who have been granted asylum, on the other hand, do have the benefits of legal status and protection, but may *feel* vulnerable, based on their prior experiences (Yu & Lieu, 1986).

One of the main features of the current migration wave is its diversity. Unlike prior waves in U.S. history, the vast majority of current arrivals are not European. Mexicans continue to represent the largest immigrant group entering the United States. With the fall of Saigon in 1975, a large influx of Vietnamese refugees began to arrive, soon joined by migrations from Cambodia and Laos. Other countries from which immigrants came to the United States in large numbers since the 1970s include the Philippines, China, Taiwan, Korea, as well as other countries throughout Asia and Latin America. Current immigrant and refugee arrivals represent a diverse group, coming from more countries than ever before, with larger populations, such as Mexican, and small groups, such as the Hmong, continuing to enter the country. In addition, relatives of refugees who had arrived in the late 20th century continue to come to United States for permanent resettlement.

Several aspects of the diversity of immigrant groups are worth noting. First, immigrant and refugee experiences may overlap, but are not synonymous with experiences of ethnic and racial minorities. For example, on entering the United States, immigrants from East Asia and Africa experience themselves as racial minorities in their new country. On the other hand, some immigrants from Europe who may have been ethnic minorities in their countries of origin, such as Jews or Irish, on entering the United States experience themselves as "White" and have the possibility of blending in with the majority. Thus although all immigrants may experience difficulties with discrimination, acculturation, and maintaining ties to their culture of origin, immigrants who are also racial minorities in the United States may experience additional discrimination and prejudice. On the other hand, White immigrants share many aspects of experience with non-White groups, yet may be overlooked amidst concerns about addressing issues of minority groups.

Second, some of the immigrants have formed large ethnic enclaves whereas others have not. Some are members of groups that have large representation across different geographical locations in the United States, such as Mexican Americans who comprise the largest immigrant population across the United States and in many local communities. Other smaller groups have ethnic concentrations in specific regions, such as Polish immigrants in Chicago or Cuban immigrants in Miami. These immigrants have the option of settling within ethnic enclaves that maintain some infrastructure, including cultural institutions, events, agencies, and programs in the native language. This infrastructure provides opportunities to interact with others from similar backgrounds. On the other hand, other groups are relatively small, and even when small ethnic enclaves exist, they do not provide the types of resources that larger communities can sustain, such as native language television and radio programming, newspapers, or ethnic health service providers. The implication of these differences is that research with larger populations within ethnically concentrated communities confronts different issues than research with the smaller populations. Although public attention and often funding focuses on such larger groups, it is the smaller groups that may require greater resources in the context of fewer available experts who can address these issues.

Third, in addition to the complexity mentioned above, the current migration flow is continually changing, with new countries becoming sources of migration. This makes it difficult to anticipate the needs and characteristics of potential new migration waves and places researchers interested in these groups in the position of constantly confronting new languages, cultures, and circumstances. It is well known that, historically, immigrants from Europe have been a progressively smaller proportion of immigrants, declining from over 90% in the decade between 1901 and 1910 to about 15% in the years between 1991 and 2000 (U.S. Citizenship and Immigration Services [USCIS], 2003); in the last few years, European migration decreased from 16.5% of all immigrants in 2001 to 14.3% in 2003 (USCIS, 2003). At the same time, migration from a variety of countries in Africa has been on the rise in recent years, increasing from 5% in 2001 to almost 7% of all immigrants in 2003. With refugee admissions in particular, countries of origin of migrants change depending on political situations throughout the world, with time-limited migration waves resulting from wars in Southeast Asia, the Balkans, and Africa. This dynamic quality of the migration flow means that it is difficult to anticipate the needs of the newly arrived groups, and resources are rarely available to assist with resettlement and guide research with newly arrived refugee populations.

Finally, refugee and immigrant groups are characterized by tremendous diversity within ethnic groups. There are differences with respect to socioeconomic status, religion, and political views. As illustrated in the next section, some immigrant populations have varied ethnic subgroups within them, marking important differences in backgrounds, reasons for migration, and hopes for life in the United States. Further, acculturation differences between those who arrived in earlier waves and newer arrivals can create important differences in attitudes, values, lifestyles, and (indeed) perceptions of ethical issues in research.

Immigrants From the Soviet Union and Vietnam in the United States

Consider the case of Vietnamese and former Soviet émigrés, whose diversity and complexity illustrate the points made above. Both groups entered the United States largely as refugees fleeing communist countries. The migration of both groups has spanned the decades from the 1970s to today, and both groups are extremely diverse with respect to length of residence in the United States, socioeconomic status, ethnicity, religion, and status as refugee or immigrant.

Soviet migration. With respect to migration from the Soviet Union, approximately 700,000 have come to the United States for permanent resettlement since the early 1970s (USCIS, 2003), with approximately 550,000 having entered the country with refugee status. Former Soviet émigrés are diverse in a variety of ways. The U.S. government granted refugee status to ethnic Jews who were seen as seeking freedom from discrimination in the former Soviet Union. In the United States, some former Soviet Jews have integrated into the American Jewish community and have adopted religious practices that they were not able to engage in within the atheist Soviet state. The majority, however, are predominantly secular, and many have not become active members of American Jewish communities (Gold, 1992; Markus & Schwartz, 1984; Simon & Simon, 1982a, 1982b). In addition to Jews, some Evangelical Christians fleeing antireligious policies of the Soviet Union were also granted refugee status by the United States. Although the majority of Jews are urban and highly educated, Evangelical Christians are more likely to have less formal education and come from more rural areas. Since the breakup of the Soviet Union in 1991, an additional influx of approximately 150,000 has entered the United States holding immigrant visas. Although some of these immigrants are ethnic Jews, most are from the dominant ethnic groups of the former Soviet republics and include Russians, Ukrainians, Armenians, and others.

Vietnamese migration. The Vietnamese migration to the United States also began in the 1970s, with over 1 million arriving since the fall of Saigon in 1975 (SEARAC, 2003; USCIS, 2003). Many fled their home country involuntarily due to war and may have spent months or years residing in camps without any idea of where they would resettle (Rumbaut, 1991); however, in later years, with improvement of relations with Vietnam, an increasing number have come for reunification with family members living in the United States. Thus, current migrants are increasingly entering with immigrant rather than refugee status. Vietnamese refugees and immigrants also differ in the ways they left their country. Some fled on boats, spending long years in refugee camps in Thailand and the Philippines. More recently, others have been able to take direct flights to the United States. Although some suffered severe trauma and persecution, such as former South Vietnamese military officers who may have spent years in communist "reeducation camps," others were born into a country increasingly open and friendly to the United States.

As with the former Soviets, improvements in relations between the United States and Vietnam over the years have made it possible for some to come with immigrant rather than refugee status, further differentiating those who were resettled within the United States refugee resettlement program and those who arrived without such support. As with former Soviets, there are also important ethnic and religious distinctions among the Vietnamese. A large portion of the migrants are ethnic Chinese who were living in Vietnam but had maintained a distinctive language and culture. Many ethnic Chinese have assimilated into "Chinatowns" in the United States and have had a resettlement experience quite distinctive from other Vietnamese émigrés. Further, a large subset of the Vietnamese immigrants and refugees are Catholics, whereas others are Buddhists. Finally, the Vietnamese migration has also been economically diverse, ranging from rural migrants with low educational levels to others such as former military officers who are well educated.

Diversity and ethical issues. This kind of complexity and diversity in today's migration wave is important to understand when considering ethical issues in research with these groups. The experience of immigrants and refugees may or may not overlap with that of ethnic minority groups and require particular attention. For example, many Vietnamese refugees have lived through experiences different from those of Asian Americans, such as war-related trauma, postwar communist repression, and traumatic experiences during flight from Vietnam. At the same time, they share some experiences with Asian Americans in the United States, particularly as they relate to discrimination as members of a racial minority group. Former Soviets, on the other hand, are White and, it would seem, have the opportunity to assimilate easily. Yet they experience problems in adaptation and acculturation, including discrimination (Birman & Trickett, 2001a), that suggest a similarity to issues faced by non-White immigrants. Because of this diversity and the marginality of refuge and immigrant groups, it is particularly important to articulate ethical considerations with these populations in their own right.

INCLUSION OF IMMIGRANTS AND REFUGEES IN RESEARCH

One of the implications of the diversity of immigrant groups is that they are often not included as participants in research; however, including diverse refugee and immigrant groups in research samples *is* an ethical issue. Without studies that include these populations,

policy remains uninformed about their experiences and the effectiveness of medical and psychological interventions unknown. For example, it is National Institutes of Health (NIH) policy that all grant applications explain the extent to which they are including women, children, and minorities in their research. This requirement was precipitated by recognition that historically, much of medical and mental health treatment efficacy research included only adult White males, with little known about whether these treatments would be effective with minorities, women, and children (Hohmann & Parron, 1996; U.S. Department of Health and Human Services, 2001).

Similar dangers exist with respect to diverse migrant groups. Failing to routinely include refugees and immigrants in research samples runs the risk of perpetuating health care services that may be ineffective or harmful to these groups. As pointed out above, some of the migrant groups are subsumed within the classification of ethnic and racial minorities in the United States, but many are not. In addition, the experiences of recent immigrants and refugees are distinct from those of U.S.-born minorities. In the absence of policies advocating for specific inclusion of refugee and immigrant groups in research samples, it is likely that we will continue to know little about these populations and run the risk of imposing policies and interventions developed for other populations on them without attention to their particular circumstances and needs; however, it can be extremely challenging to identify and include these groups in research projects.

Challenges of Identifying Refugee and Immigrant Populations

Researchers can confront many difficulties trying to identify members of particular refugee or immigrant populations within a local community in order to develop an appropriate sampling frame. In most communities, there is an absence of specific data in many agency records that can be used to reliably identify populations of interest and select representative samples. For example, although statistics are kept on legal admissions to the United States, after immigrants and refugees are resettled, most institutions do not track immigrant status as a relevant demographic descriptor. Schools, for example, are not permitted to ask about immigrant status, making it difficult even to estimate the numbers of refugees versus immigrants attending schools in a particular district. Although data on racial/Hispanic make up of a school's students is readily available on most school Web sites, other information may only be obtained at the district or state level. Even then, only proxy variables, such as the language spoken in the child's home or the country of birth are available to deduce information on specifics of the immigrant or refugee background of the students. Refugees born in refugee camps outside their country of origin, or speaking languages that are common to several countries, are particularly difficult to identify through such data. For members of specific ethnic subgroups or African tribes, only information on country of birth or last residence may be available. Further, it is impossible from such information to distinguish immigrants from refugees arriving from the same country. Thus it may be impossible to identify members of particular ethnic groups or separate out students who come from war torn areas, and who may suffer from traumatic stress symptoms, from those whose parents came as economic immigrants and who do not need such services.

Sample Size

In the social sciences, the incentive structure for publishing in mainstream journals makes it important to collect relatively large and homogeneous samples in empirical work. In this context, variability with respect to culture is perceived as "noise" that makes it difficult to draw causal inferences from the data. Studies that include multiple ethnic subgroups must have sufficient participants in every cell to be able to conduct analyses that account for ethnocultural differences; however, the realities of most research projects prohibit such a focus and lead researchers either to concentrate on a single (generally larger) migrant group or to ignore specific cultural variation and use a broader category, such as Latino or Black to describe them. To reduce variability, studies either concentrate on collecting data from majority groups or oversample a preselected number of minority groups in order to gather enough of a sample size. As a result, populations that represent relatively small subgroups in the society either are not included in the majority of studies or are absorbed by larger categories. For example, Caribbean Blacks are grouped with African Americans, or European, first-generation immigrants are grouped with Anglo-Americans, although the phenomenology of their lives with respect to the research questions of interest may be quite distinct.

Public Health Interest

A related issue is that research funding mechanisms encourage an emphasis on populations of public health interest. Such interest is understandably focused on larger groups within the country. Although this is a worthy goal, it may inadvertently discourage research efforts with less prevalent groups that may also experience a great many difficulties and have few resources. This perspective reinforces the unintended biases of such policies as those of NIH mentioned above to limit the inclusion of immigrants and refugees in research samples.

Within-Group Diversity

Another consideration for researchers who are specifically interested in the migration experience is that the wide diversity within these migrant groups makes it difficult to even delimit the population of interest and thus determine sampling frames. We have struggled with this in our research with immigrants and refugees from among former Soviet and Vietnamese samples.

Case 1: Soviet refugees. With former Soviets, our sampling frame and definition of the population of interest has differed from study to study. In one research project for example, we were interested in how adolescents from the former Soviet Union were adapting to schools. The term *Russian* is frequently used to describe these adolescents by school administrators, resettlement organizations, and others, without always acknowledging that it may be inappropriate, given that many are ethnic Jews (and thus not considered Russian in the former Soviet Union) and others may be ethnic Ukrainians, Georgians, Byelorussian, and others; however, because all are Russian speaking and culturally Russian, this is the term used to designate them in the United States. The only way the county school system could identify these students was to give us a list of students whose native language was listed as Russian in the records (Birman, Trickett, & Buchanan, 2005). Our resulting sample was diverse; approximately 50% had arrived as refugees and 50% as immigrants. Further, approximately 50% (and 80% of those arriving with refugee status) identified themselves as Jews, but the rest did not. Consider the dilemma then of how to compare our findings with other studies with "this" population (however that is defined) in other locations. Would it be appropriate, for example, to compare our data with those of samples that are predominantly Jewish, or had refugee status? If the composition of the Russian population is different on multiple dimensions in every community, how can our data, or data collected in any community, be generalized to other communities?

In a study in a different community, our sample of Russian students attending a public high school was approximately 80% Jewish, with 100% of the respondents having reported arriving as refugees (Birman & Trickett, 2001a; Birman, Trickett, & Vinokurov, 2002). In a third study (Birman & Trickett, 2001b; Trickett, Birman, & Persky, 2004), we purposely sampled only those who arrived with refugee status, because the goal of the study was to understand the resettlement experiences of refugees, and the funding for the study came from the state refugee resettlement office. Consider the difficulty, however, in determining what population(s) these three different studies generalize to. It is no wonder many researchers overlook such complexity and settle for studies of groups that are easier to define!

Case 2: Vietnamese refugees. Similar issues emerged with Vietnamese refugees (Birman, Trickett, & Persky, 2003). This study was also conducted with funding from the refugee resettlement office, and thus we concentrated on those who arrived as refugees, not immigrants; however, because of difficulties in accessing the community, we used a snowball method that initially targeted a Vietnamese Catholic church, a location where many gathered and it was easier to spread the word. We were conscious of the fact that our data might be biased toward Vietnamese Catholics, a segment of the Vietnamese population who often tend to come from higher socioeconomic strata. Further, although we asked respondents on questionnaires to indicate whether they were ethnic Chinese, we found that almost no respondents answered yes to that question, although we knew that this is an important subsection of the Vietnamese community. We were not certain whether this bias in the sampling resulted from our overreliance on the Vietnamese church (ethnic Chinese are less likely to be Catholic), particular networks of our data collectors, or specific characteristics of the Maryland Vietnamese community. As was the case for other researchers of Vietnamese refugees elsewhere (Yu & Lieu, 1986), we could locate no data on the composition of the community with respect to these variables, making it impossible for us to assess the representativeness of our sample. Thus we have had to acknowledge that our sample is not pure and that any generalizations to Vietnamese refugees that we might draw from our study need to be made with all of these caveats.

Inclusion of Refugees and Immigrants in Research: Lessons Learned

As researchers, we are trained to ask whether our samples are representative of the population we are studying. In the two examples offered, however, the question becomes how we even define our population of interest. Is our population of interest refugees, immigrants, or all émigrés from Soviet Union and Vietnam resettled; and are we interested in those resettled in Maryland, the entire United States, or the northeastern region of the country? Even if we can determine the boundaries of our population of interest, no statistics are available to allow us to confirm whether or not our samples fit the particular population profile. These types of problems plague most studies of refugee and immigrant groups that most often draw samples of convenience. Yet few published reports of such studies acknowledge the possible limitations of their sampling methods, leading readers to draw implications and inappropriately generalize to the entire ethnic

group rather than a subgroup that the study represents. The ethics of this are treacherous, particularly when research is used to inform policy.

Although some may argue that this set of considerations makes it practically impossible to include diverse refugee and immigrant samples in research, ethically we cannot turn away from the challenge of doing so. By pretending that ethnic Chinese from Vietnam are not an important subgroup of Asian Americans, for example, we do not take away the variability associated with their experience; it's still there and may be an important factor in our research findings. By removing them from such samples in order to simplify the research design, we may be acting unethically by excluding them from research and making their lived experience invisible.

Our experience suggests that the sampling strategy must be determined by the research questions being asked. In one case, the purpose of our study (Trickett et al., 2004) was to document the adaptation of refugees resettled by the Maryland state resettlement services, and we were specifically interested in those with that legal status because they made use of specialized services and the research project was in part designed to evaluate the impact of these services; however, our findings from this study cannot be used to generalize to the population of émigrés from the former Soviet Union, a broader and more diverse population. On the other hand, if we were interested in the ways in which immigrants and refugees from the former Soviet Union and Vietnam come together to form ethnic communities that transcend these legal distinctions, we would have needed a different sampling frame. This was our approach in studying adaptation of all Russian-speaking students in Montgomery County Schools, regardless of their legal status or whether or not they identified as Jews (Birman et al., 2005).

An ethical approach to research is to insist on including the diversity of immigrant and refugee populations in research and to include questions about the variety of within-group variations in the research protocol. Researchers need to define and describe the specific population of interest and the ways in which their sampling strategies are intended to capture its particular segments. Most important, researchers bear an ethical responsibility to clearly outline the limitations of their sampling strategy and caution others against generalizing inappropriately to other segments of the refugee or immigrant group. In this way, others can learn about these populations and appreciate the limitations of the findings.

ETHICAL TREATMENT OF RESEARCH PARTICIPANTS IN RESEARCH ACROSS CULTURES

When research projects are conducted across cultures, researchers need to tailor ethical guidelines for the responsible conduct of research to the ways in which ethical issues are viewed by the culture of the community being studied. Cultures different from that of the investigator may have different perceptions of what issues constitute ethical dilemmas. Lack of familiarity with participant cultures poses particular challenges with respect to assessing research risk/benefits, procedures to obtain informed consent, determining appropriate incentives in research and avoiding coercion, and maintaining confidentiality.

Challenges in Determining What Is Ethical

Different cultures may have ethical codes that may be in direct contradiction to those of the culture of the researchers. For example, in many countries worldwide,

terminally ill patients are not told the truth about their medical condition, and doctors only reveal the seriousness of their health status to the family. This is done because of cultural assumptions that dying people would not want to know about their condition and that knowing may actually harm them by making them more likely to give in to depression, which can in turn worsen their health outcome (Levin & Sprung, 2003). On the other hand, in the individualistically oriented United States, the reverse is true. Doctors feel it is their duty to tell the truth to the patient, yet they are judicious about releasing information to others, even family members, unless the patient gives consent. Thus, if immigrants were involved in a research project, revealing to research participants that they have a terminal illness may be perceived as a right in one culture and an ethical violation in another.

When conducting research across cultures, most ethical guidelines (e.g. Tapp, Kelman, Triandis, Writsman, & Coelho, 1974) expect the researcher to act ethically according to the norms of both cultures involved. As illustrated in the example above, however, it may not be possible to honor both the culture of the researcher and the culture of the research participants. Our current ethical codes do not help us resolve such dilemmas. Researchers may feel that the only option to act ethically for them is to decide not to do the study. This, however, creates ethical dilemmas in their own right and can lead to exclusion of vulnerable populations from research.

Participant Rights

Barry (1988, cited in Davidson, 1999) described a particularly challenging situation while attempting to conduct studies of HIV infection in Tanzania. The problems arose as a result of the Tanzanian government's insistence that blood samples drawn for other purposes be used for research without the informed consent of the women who were to be tested and that donors not be informed of the blood test results. These research practices were deemed by the researchers to be in violation of the rights of donors and of regulations for research with human participants within the researchers' culture. Thus, the study did not proceed.

As Barry (cited in Davidson, 1999) points out, however, the ethical problems were not eliminated by the researchers' decision that the study should not proceed. "On the contrary, the researchers' insistence that the host culture apply ethical standards as stringent as those applied to research carried out within the developed country had the same public health outcomes that were associated with anonymous serum sampling and nondisclosure" (Barry, 1988, p. 1085, cited in Davidson, 1999). Specifically, there was no health promotion or medical treatment of persons testing HIV positive that could have resulted from conducting this research project. Further, the women who had HIV would have been no worse off had the research been conducted; they would not have been harmed by the study, and with or without the study, they would not learn about their HIV status. Negotiation of a long-term research and education plan might have contributed to prevention of HIV in the country, and collaboration with the Tanzanian government may have, over time, led to the researchers convincing them to follow Western-style research procedures. Thus ethical research practices involve attempting to negotiate a reasonable solution before deciding not to conduct the research project at all.

Informed Consent Procedures

Informed consent is a complex process when administered by researchers from one culture to research participants from another. The intent of informed consent procedures is to fully disclose to research participants all relevant aspects of the research study. The benefit of this process is to educate the research participants that laws and regulations govern the research process, holding the researchers accountable. On the other hand, some informed consent procedures can be so cumbersome that they may make it nearly impossible to engage refugees and immigrants as research participants.

Benefits of informed consent procedures. Informed consent procedures conducted by research teams can help educate the communities they study and prevent unethical practices. In our experience, some of the organizations that refugees encounter do not follow the kinds of ethical standards that university researchers are bound by. Thus, refugees may have had experiences that lead them to distrust researchers, questionnaires, and any assurances of confidentiality. Our research team was once contacted by someone who had participated in one of our research projects and had thus spoken to us about issues of informed consent. She was calling because she was concerned that her elderly relative was being asked to complete questionnaires on personal matters as part of a special recreational program at a social service agency; however, there was no explanation or consent form for the survey provided, and the surveys were not anonymous. Her experience participating in our research project led her to question procedures of this organization and raise awareness among others in the community about research ethics. Thus, carefully conducted informed consent procedures can have benefits beyond assuring the rights of participants in a particular research project.

Challenges resulting from informed consent procedures. In practice, however, informed consent procedures can also discourage members of communities from participating in research projects for a variety of reasons. The need to sign informed consent forms takes away the possibility of anonymous participation and may create great fears about loss of confidentiality. Further, the increasingly stringent expectations about complexity of consent forms on the part of university internal review boards may inadvertently create as many problems as they solve. Informed consent forms often resemble the kinds of small-print, lengthy, and legal-sounding documents and statements that consumers are frequently asked to sign in our society. They can leave the reader confused and worried that by signing, they may be giving up their rights to object or withdraw. Studies have shown that research participants perceive the informed consent process as intended to protect the researcher rather than the participant (Howard-Jones, 1982). Moreover, complex and legalistic consent forms can prove nearly impossible to translate into multiple languages, particularly for immigrants and refugees who have low levels of literacy in their own language.

For example, Yu & Lieu (1986) described great difficulties in obtaining signed informed consent from Vietnamese refugees whom they were surveying, even when they were perfectly willing to participate in the study. The prospective participants' fears stemmed from their perceptions of the threat of communism, as they believed that Vietnamese communist spies may come after them after learning that they willingly signed such a document. Subsequent to obtaining informed consent, these researchers report that one refugee discontinued the interview and asked for the form back so that she could destroy it, and another had 3 sleepless nights following the interview, fearing possible repercussions that might result from signing the form.

Informed consent: Lessons learned. In our research, we've learned that the informed consent process needs to be an important part of the research project, requiring budgeting of sufficient time and resources. Informed consent procedures need to be carefully crafted and may sometimes require extensive discussions with the research participants who may have no context within which to understand the purposes or process of research. We have tried to take an informal approach and explain our research in nontechnical ways, to the extent possible. These procedures have been extremely labor-intensive and time-consuming but have yielded excellent response rates.

For example, in our studies with Vietnamese and former Soviet émigrés, we sent out a letter, in English and in Russian/Vietnamese, to explain the reasons for the project. In this letter, we carefully explained our personal and professional interests in the project, revealing to research participants that some of us on the research team are ourselves from immigrant/refugee backgrounds and have a personal investment in collecting information on the migration experience. Bilingual and bicultural research assistants followed up the letter with a phone call and arranged for a time to meet with the prospective participants in their homes. The informed consent process was then explained during this meeting. Our explanations included describing the reason for the stringent rules and need for signatures and the professional sanctions that exist for the investigators if confidentiality is breached or approved procedures are violated.

It is interesting to note that in one case a woman who had refused to participate called the university IRB coordinator to explain that she did not want to participate in the study. Our sense was that she was checking to see if our project was legitimate. We were delighted that she did so because she learned that indeed, the phone numbers on the consent form did lead her to a high-level administrator in the university whose job it was to hold us accountable. We hoped that she would share her experiences with others in the community and that this would help us earn the community's trust.

In general, we've come to view participants challenging the informed consent procedures or refusing to participate as opportunities to learn about their concerns and improve our procedures. In the former Soviet community, for example, on several occasions participants who had been contacted by mail or phone called me to complain about the study and expressed strong feelings that we had no right to ask that their children be taken out of class to complete questionnaires. They did not trust that we were acting independently of the state agencies that fund refugee services.

In these situations, we've insisted on assuring them that they had every right not to participate, but when possible we also provided extensive explanations of our project and mailed a blank questionnaire to ask for their feedback. In other cases, we've contacted those who refused to participate, not to persuade them to change their minds but to ask them to help us understand why. These conversations have been extremely instructive, and we've adapted our procedures based on this feedback. In almost every case, we've found that people we contacted were extremely appreciative of being asked about their opinions and input, and in several instances these conversations ended in offers to help us recruit more participants for the study. These conversations have also served as a reminder of the importance of allowing the time and space in our interaction with potential research participants to explore their reservations and concerns and reassure them about our procedures. Thus, there is a need for researchers to treat informed consent as a critical process in its own right. The informed consent process needs to be a dialogue that can reassure the participants and provide opportunities for the research team to learn about and address participant concerns unanticipated by the research protocol.

Defining Incentives and Coercion in Culturally Diverse Situations

Another particularly complicated issue in research with immigrants and refugees involves cultural differences in determining what may constitute coercion. These issues require particular attention when, as is most often the case, power differentials exist between the researchers and the research participants. For example, when the research participants are undocumented aliens, they may want to avoid participation in research projects but may also not fully trust that they are free to decline participation. Refugees who are being held in refugee camps constitute a particularly vulnerable group, as their rights are substantially restricted, and to some extent they are a "captive" population. Thus, what constitutes voluntary participation in research projects, particularly when they are sponsored by powerful organizations, is not always clear (Fisher et al., 2002). In our own work with Vietnamese and former Soviet refugees, we have had several instances of differences with the communities with respect to what constitutes coercion. Two specific examples are offered below.

Case 1: Involvement of religious community leaders. In our research with the Vietnamese community, we collaborated with Mr. Nguyen (a fictitious name), a master's level psychologist of Vietnamese background, to identify the sample, translate and adapt measures, structure and coordinate data collection, and supervise the bilingual/bicultural research assistants who collected the data. We felt that he was an ideal choice because he had extensive training in psychology, firsthand knowledge and understanding of the Vietnamese language and culture, and was a leader commanding respect from the local community. We had discussed at length various procedures, including informed consent and ethical practices in conducting the study, and, in retrospect, we assumed that because of his master's level training in psychology and experience conducting his own research project for that degree, Mr. Nguyen's understanding of ethical concerns would be similar to ours. We were surprised to learn, however, that his perception of what was coercive differed from our more American or Western views.

We were planning to set up data collection in a Vietnamese church when Mr. Nguyen called us with what he thought was great news, that the priest was happy to help us with our project and was willing to describe and endorse this project during the services. In addition, Mr. Nguyen was particularly pleased that the priest was going to recommend that the $15 stipend that our research project was giving families in return for their participation be donated by the families to the church. Mr. Nguyen thought this was a great idea. He had been concerned in the past that many families were uncomfortable taking the money in return for participation, but he thought that this was a very palatable option for them. There would be no embarrassment involved in accepting the money, and they would feel that it would be a great honor to be able to do this for their church. Our own ethnocentric reaction was one of surprise that Mr. Nguyen, despite his level of training in psychology and some experience with research, did not perceive this procedure as unethical.

Mr. Nguyen was, in turn, surprised to learn that our perception of this arrangement was that it would be coercive and unethical. Our concern was that parishioners would feel that the priest's endorsement of the project meant that he expected them to become involved; and the suggestion to donate to the church the money that we were giving them for their participation seemed to take away their rights for reimbursement in return for their participation. After some discussions, Mr. Nguyen assured us that he would ask the priest not to speak to the congregation at all, and we continued with a more limited snowball data collection procedure.

Although we considered negotiating with the priest some other noncoercive process that would take advantage of his endorsement of our project, we were also humbled by our realization that we were outsiders to the church and community and would have little control over, or firsthand knowledge of, what actually would take place in the church. Because our lack of language facility made it impossible for us to participate in this process, because we were sure that other misunderstandings may take place, and because we were conducting the project from out of state, we decided not to risk colluding in potentially unethical behavior and chose a different participant recruitment strategy altogether. Under different circumstances, however, and with more time and resources, we might have considered working out an alternative process with the priest.

Case 2: Involvement of community organizations. The second situation occurred within the former Soviet immigrant community. Mrs. Katz (not her real name), a woman active in the community, agreed to help us with collecting data from former Soviet elderly. Mrs. Katz lived in a subsidized housing building with many other former Soviet elderly. She invited us to the party room in her building where she said that she would gather the Russian-speaking elderly. The incentive for research participation was $10 a person, which is a substantial sum of money for the refugee elderly, most of whom live on Supplemental Security Income (SSI). Thus, when she told us that she could gather as many as 50 people one evening, we were not surprised and collected the questionnaire data. Subsequently, we received a call from someone else in the Russian community who had heard that an elderly woman was very upset because she was denied the opportunity to participate in a research study and earn $10. On further investigation, it turned out that Mrs. Katz was the president of a community association in her building. We also learned that Mrs. Katz charged a membership fee of $7 to belong to her association. Apparently, she made the announcement in her building about the research project and said that this would be an opportunity for the participants to earn $10; however, only association members would be allowed to participate. Those who were not association members had to join the association but could use part of the money from the $10 research incentive to join at the time of the data collection. The woman who had complained did not want to join the association and was denied the opportunity to participate in our research project.

We were horrified to learn of this and proceeded to make every attempt to rectify the situation. We called Mrs. Katz and had a long discussion with her about the problem that she had created for us. Our efforts to protect the confidentiality of the research participants created a further problem because we did not have a list of names and contact information of those who participated. Although we obtained signed consent forms that we could use to decipher the participant names, we had promised them that their participation was confidential, and contacting them after the data collection, we thought, would ruin that trust. Mrs. Katz promised to call everyone who joined the association that evening (she told us there were very few) and offer to return the association fees. She also contacted the two people to whom she had denied the opportunity to participate, and we were able to include them in the study.

Although we felt confident that Mrs. Katz had acted unethically according to our standards (and were upset that she had not been truthful with us), from her perspective she took the opportunity to do something positive for her community: Create an association that would serve as an advocate for the members and garner resources on their behalf. Here, we learned the importance of extensive discussion about ethics with community organizations who help us in the research process. In retrospect, we had jumped on the opportunity to collect a large amount of data too quickly, and we should have looked into Mrs. Katz's background with others in the community who would have probably alerted us to the existence of her community organization.

Confidentiality

Issues of confidentiality can also pose difficulties in conducting research with immigrants and refugees. First, some communities are small, and members of the research team need to guard against inadvertently revealing information that they became privy to as a result of the study (Fisher et al., 2002). Having members of the community collect data can, in fact, be problematic because respondents may feel that fellow immigrants will not honor their promises of confidentiality. In Russian culture, for example, the word *privacy* doesn't exist, and many are unlikely to believe that professional ethics will truly prevent a researcher from gossiping. This is why it is a helpful strategy to explain to former Soviet émigrés that sanctions exist against the researcher when confidentiality is violated. Some researchers (e.g. Jacobsen & Landau, 2003) suggest that, to guard against this, research assistants collecting data must be proficient in the language of the refugees, but not from the same culture or community.

On the other hand, relationships within the ethnic community can be a great asset in the research. Ironically, it was through community gossip networks that we learned about the ethical violation involving data collection using Mrs. Katz. In our experience, working with an ethnic community over a long period of time provides multiple opportunities to demonstrate to others that we will not reveal information that was provided to us by participants as part of the data collection. Thus, in the long term, trust can be earned.

Case 1: Receipts for research compensation. Even when it is possible to develop an excellent reputation and community trust, other obstacles can emerge. In our study with former Soviets, we reimbursed families for their participation. The simplest process to do this was to pay cash for participation; checks would take some time to cut, and we did not want to risk the possibility that they would arrive late or not at all, which would violate the participants' trust; however, in return for the cash, the university required not only signed receipts from participants but also their Social Security numbers. Research participants were extremely uncomfortable with this process and felt that it completely undermined our assurances of confidentiality. They were concerned that because the study was being funded by the state office of refugee resettlement, we were interested in tracking private information about them by using their Social Security number. Former Soviet émigrés have good reason not to trust bureaucratic procedures, and we took their concerns seriously. In the end, we were able to convince the university to reconsider the rule, and they waved the Social Security number requirement. Nonetheless, this experience again reminded us of how much care needs to be taken to assure and protect confidentiality in these situations.

Ethical Treatment of Research Participants: Lessons Learned

It is perhaps an understatement that conducting research with people from different cultures, with different norms and definitions of ethical behavior, different experiences with research, and lack of trust of government organizations that fund research is tremendously challenging. The importance of ensuring protection of participant rights, guarding confidentiality, avoiding coercion, and creating extensive informed consent procedures cannot be overstated. These activities are labor-intensive and costly procedures and require a constant willingness to learn about and resolve unanticipated barriers and concerns. They must also be informed by a true understanding of the culture and community of the participants. The processes that are required to assure ethical treatment of research participants from diverse immigrant and refugee groups are in many ways identical to those required to successfully recruit these participants into research. Many have noted (e.g. Miranda, Azocar, Organista, Muñoz, & Lieberman, 1996) that minorities and immigrants are often reluctant to participate in research projects. We have viewed the process of ensuring that we engage in ethical research practices and the process of recruiting research participants as one and the same. The most important strategy in this process involves working with cultural insiders on the research team to ensure that understanding of the community and the culture informs the ways in which these aspects of the study are designed and implemented. This is the most important lesson learned, and the subject of the next section.

INCLUSION OF CULTURAL INSIDERS ON RESEARCH TEAMS

The ethical dilemmas described above arise out of cultural differences and power differentials between the investigators and research participants. The Tapp Report (Tapp et al., 1974), a landmark attempt to provide guidelines for ethical conduct of cross-cultural research, was developed by cross-cultural psychologists, primarily from the United States, but with extensive input from international colleagues and involvement of the American Psychological Association, the International Association for Cross-Cultural Psychology, and other organizations. Although it has been criticized more recently (Davidson, 1999) for being overly idealistic, the report represents the most comprehensive effort to date to provide ethical guidance to psychologists working in cross cultural situations. The advisory principles outlined in the report are directly relevant to research with immigrants and refugees.

The report outlines principles of responsibility within three broad areas: (a) to individuals and communities studied; (b) to collaborators and colleagues in the host community, and (c) to the scientific community to ensure scientific standards. The first and third sets of principles are echoed in the discussion above, as they involve the importance of attending to ethical treatment of research participants, maintaining scientific rigor in research design, and reporting of research findings with candor. The second area mentioned by the Tapp Report, however, is the focus of the remainder of this chapter and concerns the ways in which researchers must involve cultural insiders, or collaborators, from the host community in the research process.

The underlying assumption of the Tapp Report is that cross-cultural research can be conducted ethically *only when done in collaboration and partnership with members of the cultural communities being studied.* Thus, it is not enough for the investigator to develop cultural sensitivity and knowledge about the group of interest. Rather, ethical research cannot be conducted across cultures without involvement of members of the community being studied. In this vein, the Tapp Report suggests that involvement of members of the community on the research

team must be collegial and is most effective when the ethnic collaborators are professional peers to the principle investigator and thus also highly trained researchers. The Tapp Report cautions about the potential for exploitive relationships and goes even further to suggest that investigators are responsible for ensuring that involvement in the research project must be professionally beneficial for the cultural collaborators.

The notion that it is important to include members of the community being studied is generally accepted by most researchers and not new (Fisher et al., 2002); however, on closer inspection, the need to include cultural insiders on research teams raises several questions that have not yet been sufficiently explored in our field, particularly with respect to immigrant and refugee groups. The first question is who is qualified to be a true cultural insider and represent an immigrant community on the research team; the second is in what capacity does this cultural insider need to join the team.

I have conducted the research program on émigrés from the former Soviet Union described above as a cultural insider, having come to the United States as a Soviet Jewish refugee; however, I was an outsider to the Vietnamese community. My perspective on insiders and outsiders on research teams is shaped by these experiences. Seeing firsthand the relative advantages I had as a cultural insider, I have become convinced of the importance of seeking out ways to involve cultural insiders, to the extent possible, in the research enterprise.

Defining Cultural Insiders

I use the term *cultural insiders* to refer to persons who have knowledge of the language and familiarity with the culture of a particular group through their membership in that group. Although insiders in general have shared lived experience with persons whose lives they study (Bartunek, Foster-Fishman, & Keys, 1996; Bartunek & Louis, 1996; Chaitin, 2003; Griffith, 1998; Staples, 2000), *cultural* insiders have the additional advantage over outsiders because they have facility with the language and culture that allows them access to the cultural community, which can be extremely difficult to gain even by sensitive and knowledgeable outsiders.

Partial insiders. To some extent, a true cultural insider is an abstraction. The prior discussion of the complexity of defining the refugee and immigrant group may raise the question of whether it is possible to be a cultural insider at all. Social class, extent of acculturation, and religious and other differences can make people who are seemingly united by language and culture only *partial* insiders to each other's world in some situations (Griffith, 1998). In my case, for example, although I speak Russian and am familiar with Russian culture, I came as a Jewish refugee and may be perceived as an outsider by non-Jews. Many have written about the extent to which anyone is both an insider and an outsider when working within any community (Chaitin, 2003; Griffith, 1998). On the other hand, in immigrant and refugee communities, native knowledge of the language and culture creates a different degree and level of access than that available to sensitive and caring outsiders.

The insider identity. In the research context, the definition of who constitutes an insider rests on the extent to which the researcher identifies with the culture or community being studied. With a sense of identity, insiders experience the findings of the research as reflecting on them directly. Even in situations when members of my research team were only partial insiders in the former Soviet community, doors to participants' homes and community organizations were opened to us

when we were able to explain to them the ways the research touched on our lives personally. Further, not only did they understand that our study was designed to learn about *their* perspectives, but they also trusted that we had enough understanding of their experience to know what questions to ask to uncover the issues that concerned them the most. Most important, the participants understood that the bicultural members of the research team identified with the émigré community they were studying. As a result, the ways in which our study would portray members of the community would reflect on those of us on the research team who were Russian as well.

The cultural insider continuum. We have also found that it is useful to think of cultural insiders along a continuum. No one person can represent the entire community, as there are differences in perspectives and experiences within any community. Thus it is necessary to have a spectrum of community members involved with a research project. Our Vietnamese project may have benefited from involvement of multiple persons of Mr. Nguyen's stature who may have represented different segments of the émigré community. Access to multiple gatekeepers may have provided us with a better appreciation of differences within the community and forced us to be more sensitive to differences and peculiarities of various religious and other organizations and their leaders. In my case, I have been fortunate in working with other cultural insiders from the Soviet Union on shared research projects, people whose experience of migration and acculturation differed from mine. Through this work, we have found that although we shared a common language, country, and culture of origin, acculturation differences among us created an "acculturation chain" of experience, with people forming "links" between divergent perspectives of those who are more or less acculturated than others. Without such links, more acculturated persons may not fully understand the cultural perspectives of those who are newly arrived. Yet through these links, such group discussions among people at different places in their acculturation process can be very helpful when trying to understand cultural phenomena, design questions, or interpret findings. In this way, multiple perspectives on what constitutes ethical behavior or how to translate Western research practices into the immigrant culture can be discussed and alternative solutions determined.

This image of the acculturation chain can also be useful for outsiders working with an immigrant community. For example, in coming to know the Vietnamese community, we found it useful to begin our interviews with community members who were closer to us on the acculturation chain, that is, those who were more acculturated. Because they shared some cultural assumptions with us, they could explain to us the perspectives of those who were farther away from us along the acculturation continuum. Other members of the community on the researcher team can then serve as further links to different experiences that may be less accessible to those who are more acculturated.

Social networks. Another invaluable asset available to cultural insiders are the social networks within the ethnic community. Our research has confirmed the importance of ethnic social networks for both former Soviet and Vietnamese refugees, particularly adults. In fact, we have found that adults in both groups continue to have over 80% of their social contacts with members of their own ethnic group, even after many years in the United States (Trickett et al., 2004). Immigrant networks are also interesting because members of particular local communities within the

countries of origin are scattered across the United States in the process of resettlement. This phenomenon creates multiple and overlapping ethnic networks, as immigrants and refugees come to know others from their ethnic group who live near them in the United States but also maintain contact with close family and friends elsewhere in the country. The interwoven nature of immigrant networks makes them potentially broader, and membership in them can help provide tremendous access to multiple segments of the population. At the same time, it makes protection of confidentiality even more imperative.

Our ethnic social networks played a critical role in our experience with Mrs. Katz, described above. First, without insider status and personal connections (Mrs. Katz was the mother of a friend's friend), we would not have had access to these research participants, or at least it would have been difficult to earn their trust. Mrs. Katz made data collection on a large scale possible for us. At the same time, without social networks in the community, word would not have reached us that the ethical problem had occurred. It was through an acquaintance that I heard about what happened, who had heard it from someone else. Further, without insight into the culture, we might have become outraged and accused this important community member of egregious ethical violations when, in fact, she was acting in ways she felt were ethical. We learned to ask many questions about how data collection opportunities are being set up in future work to avoid such situations. On the other hand, although I have no reason to assume that anything unethical took place, I hate to think about what kinds of things we might be unaware of in our Vietnamese project. As an outsider to the Vietnamese community, I know that I am unlikely to hear what people in the community may be saying about our research project.

The Role of Cultural Insiders on Research Teams

Although there are many good reasons to include cultural insiders on a research team, the challenge remains how to do it in ways that result in their knowledge and experience truly reflecting on the research process. As the Tapp Report suggests, the best way to collaborate with cultural insiders is with professional colleagues who are themselves from the culture that we are studying. Yet the relative absence of scholars from many of the immigrant/refugee communities that we study can make that impossible. This suggests that one long-term solution to the problem of how to conduct ethical and competent research in immigrant and refugee communities is to encourage professional training opportunities for members of refugee and immigrant groups. As noted earlier, professional organizations need to acknowledge the importance of special efforts to recruit and retain in training programs not only minority group members but also members of refugee and immigrant communities who may or may not be from underrepresented minority groups in the United States. Only such specialized attention to training can create a corps of professionals who can be knowledgeable about particular immigrant groups and about the general issues that concern immigrant and refugee research.

When such collaboration is not possible, however, the task of the researcher becomes more complicated. Typically, researchers believe that they can include the insider perspectives on the research team by hiring members of the group being studied at different levels of the research project. In our Vietnamese study, we did just that. We had several highly qualified consultants who were well respected within the Vietnamese community assist us with every step of the process, including measure selection and translation, developing the sampling and data collection procedures, and interpreting the findings. We were also very fortunate to work with Mr. Nguyen who was trained within our field and oversaw all aspects of the data collection process. We have no reason to doubt that the interviewers that we hired to collect the data were sensitive to the research process and knowledgeable about the community. At the same time, in the end, there are countless ways in which we, those responsible for the design and implementation of the study, remain outsiders to the research process and the resulting data. This suggests to me that more is required in order to assure the true involvement of cultural insiders in the research process.

Unfortunately, existing structures, such as grant mechanisms, do not provide adequate opportunities to do that. In fact, most grants require that there be only one principal investigator, making it difficult for researchers to collaborate with each other, much less with community members. The only solution seems to be for researchers to carefully attend to these issues as they unfold in the research process, to be cognizant of their own limitations, to be constantly vigilant about issues in the communities they study, and to ensure that cultural insiders feel free to voice their concerns and explain their perspectives throughout the research process.

THE FUTURE OF RESEARCH ETHICS INVOLVING IMMIGRANTS AND REFUGEES

This chapter has outlined a large set of complexities in carrying out ethical research with immigrants and refugees. Reviewing the long list of issues and problems, one might conclude that it is much simpler not to do research with these groups! Yet as argued in this paper, this would not be an ethical stance. Rather, researchers must acknowledge and embrace the complexity of all groups in our society and include them in research projects.

A major theme of this chapter has been the notion that the level of complexity involved in doing research with diverse and vulnerable groups precludes the possibility that any code of ethics can fully anticipate and successfully resolve the multiple ethical dilemmas that arise in the course of doing this work. Researchers must be familiar with the ethical issues and concerns of the immigrant cultures. In addition, researchers must devote sufficient time and resources to engaging in a lengthy process of recruiting participants into the research project, obtaining truly informed consent, and assuring ethical treatment of participants.

We have learned to never underestimate possible differences in the ways that our perceptions of ethical issues differ from those of the community members. Only ongoing communication can unearth such differences and prevent potential ethical violations. Without such efforts, the researcher can remain naive about ongoing ethical issues; yet the fact that the researcher is unaware of an ethical violation does not mean that it isn't occurring.

Finally, such a process can only be successful if multiple cultural insiders are active and influential members of the research team. Further, it would be valuable for the field to learn more from the experiences of cultural insiders on the research teams, those persons who've been hired by researchers to help inform the research process. Perhaps insight into their experience can help us restructure the ways in which we organize the research process so as to ensure that they can help us, cultural outsiders, conduct ethical research in their communities.

REFERENCES

Abernethy, V. (1996). Environmental and ethical aspects of international migration. *International Migration Review, 30*(1), 132–150.

Bartunek, J. M., Foster-Fishman, P. G., & Keys, C. B. (1996). Using collaborative advocacy to foster intergroup cooperation: A joint insider-outsider investigation. *Human Relations, 49*(6), 701–733.

Bartunek, J. M., & Louis, M. R. (1996). *Insider/outsider team research.* Thousand Oaks, CA: Sage.

Birman, D., & Trickett, E. J. (2001a). Cultural transitions in first-generation immigrants: Acculturation of Soviet Jewish refugee adolescents and parents. *Journal of Cross-Cultural Psychology, 32*(4), 456–477.

Birman, D., & Trickett, E. J. (2001b). Psychosocial and work-related adaptation of Soviet Jewish refugees in Maryland. Retrieved September 9, 2004, from http://63.236.98.116/mona/pdf/project2.pdf

Birman, D., Trickett, E. J., & Buchanan, R. (2005). A tale of two cities: Replication of a study on the acculturation and adaptation of immigrant adolescents from the former Soviet Union in a different community context. *American Journal of Community Psychology, 35*(1-2), 87–101.

Birman, D., Trickett, E. J., & Persky, I. (2003). Psychosocial and work-related adaptation of adult Vietnamese refugees in Maryland. Retrieved September 9, 2004, from http://63.236.98.116/mona/pdf/vietnam2.pdf

Birman, D., Trickett, E. J., & Vinokurov, A. (2002). Acculturation and adaptation of Soviet Jewish refugee adolescents: Predictors of adjustment across life domains. *American Journal of Community Psychology, 30*(5), 585–607.

Carens, J. H. (1996). Realistic and idealistic approaches to the ethics of migration. *International Migration Review, 30*(1), 156–170.

Chaitin, J. (2003). "I wish he hadn't told me that": Methodological and ethical issues in social trauma and conflict research. *Qualitative Health Research, 13*(8), 1145–1154.

Davidson, G. R. (1999). Short-comings in cross-cultural research ethics: The Tapp et al. (1974) report revisited. In J. C. Lasry, J. G. Adair, & K. L. Dion (Eds.), *Latest contributions in cross-cultural psychology* (pp. 355–365). Amsterdam: Swets and Zeitlinger.

Fisher, C. B., Hoagwood, K., Boyce, C., Duster, T., Frank, D. A., Grisso, T., et al. (2002). Research ethics for mental health science involving ethnic minority children and youth. *American Psychologist, 57*, 1024–1040.

Gibney, M. (1996). A response to Carens and Weiner. Commentary. *International Migration Review, 30*(1), 198–202.

Gold, S. (1992). *Refugee communities: A comparative field study.* Newbury Park, CA: Sage.

Griffith, A. I. (1998). Insider/outsider: Epistemological privilege and mothering work. *Human Studies, 21*(4), 361–376.

Hohmann, A. A., & Parron, D. L. (1996). How the new NIH guidelines on inclusion of women and minorities apply: Efficacy trials, effectiveness trials, and validity. *Journal of Consulting and Clinical Psychology, 64*(5), 851–855.

Howard-Jones, N. (1982). Human experimentation in historical and ethical perspectives. *Social Science & Medicine, 16*(15), 1429–1448.

Jacobsen, K., & Landau, L. (2003). The dual imperative in refugee research: Some methodological and ethical considerations in social science research on forced migration. *Disasters, 27*(3), 185–206.

Leaning, J. (2001). Ethics of research in refugee populations. *Lancet, 357*(9266), 1432–1433.

Levin, P. D., & Sprung, C. L. (2003). Cultural differences at the end of life. *Critical Care Medicine, 31*(5 Suppl.), S354–S357.

Markus, R. L., & Schwartz, D. V. (1984). Soviet Jewish émigrés in Toronto: Ethnic self-identity and issues of integration. *Canadian Ethnic Studies, 16*(2), 71–87.

Miranda, J., Azocar, F., Organista, K. C., Muñoz, R. F., & Lieberman, A. F. (1996). Recruiting and retaining low-income Latinos in psychotherapy research. *Journal of Consulting and Clinical Psychology, 64*(5), 868–874.

Rumbaut, R. G. (1991). The agony of exile: A study of the migration and adaptation of Indochinese refugee adults and children. In F. L. Ahearn Jr. & J. L. Athey (Eds.), *Refugee children: Theory, research, and services: The Johns Hopkins series in contemporary medicine and public health* (pp. 53–91). Baltimore: Johns Hopkins University Press

Simon, R., & Simon, J. (1982a). The Jewish dimension among recent Soviet immigrants to the United States. *Jewish Social Studies, 44*(3-4), 283–290.

Simon, R., & Simon, J. (1982b). Some aspects of the socio-cultural adjustment of recent Soviet immigrants to the United States. *Ethnic and Racial Studies, 5*(4), 535–541.

Southeast Asian Resource and Action Center. (2003). *Americans from Cambodia, Laos and Vietnam: Statistics.* Retrieved September 9, 2004, from www.searac .org/sea_stats.2003.01.27.pdf

Staples, L. H. (2000). Insider/outsider upsides and downsides. *Social Work with Groups, 23*(2), 19–35.

Tapp, J. L., Kelman, H. C., Triandis, H. C., Writsman, L., & Coelho, G. (1974). Continuing concerns in cross-cultural ethics: A report. *International Journal of Psychology 9,* 231–249.

Trickett, E. J., Birman, D., & Persky, I. (2004). *Soviet and Vietnamese refugee adults and adolescents in Maryland: A comparative analysis.* Baltimore: Maryland Office for New Americans, Maryland Department of Human Services. Retrieved September 9, 2004, from http://63.236.98.116/mona/pdf/ project1.pdf

UN High Commissioner for Refugees. (1951). *Convention relating to the status of refugees.* Retrieved September 9, 2004, from www.unhcr.org/1951convention/index.html

U.S. Citizenship and Immigration Services. (2003). *2002 Yearbook of immigration statistics. Immigration by selected country of last residence.* Retrieved September 9, 2004, from http://uscis.gov/graphics/shared/aboutus/statistics/ybpage.htm

U.S. Department of Health and Human Services. (2001). *Mental health: Culture, race, and ethnicity: A supplement to mental health: A report of the Surgeon General.* Rockville, MD: Department of Health and Human Services, Public Health Service, Office of the Surgeon General.

U.S. Department of State. (2002). *Refugee admissions and resettlement policy.* Retrieved September 9, 2004, from http://fpc.state.gov/documents/organization/ 8047.pdf

Yu, E. S. H., & Lieu, W. T. (1986). Methodological problems and policy implications in Vietnamese refugee research. *International Migration Review, 20*(2), 483–502.

Part III

SOCIALLY SENSITIVE RESEARCH INVOLVING ETHNOCULTURAL FAMILIES AND COMMUNITIES

CHAPTER 10

Ethical Research With Ethnic Minorities in the Child Welfare System

KATHERINE ANN GILDA ELLIOTT

ANTHONY J. URQUIZA

> *Ethnocentric history serves no one. It only shrouds the pluralism that is America and that makes our nation so unique, and thus the possibility of appreciating our rich racial and cultural diversity remains a dream deferred.*
>
> —Ronald Takaki, *Strangers From a Different Shore*

For much of the 20th century, significant efforts have been made by the child welfare system (CWS) to protect children from the experiences of abuse and neglect. In pursuit of this goal, state agencies have conducted a wide array of interventions of varying invasiveness ranging from providing preventive psychoeducation in the form of public service announcements, to school safety/prevention programs, to removal of children from the care of their parents and placement in foster care. Although these interventions have had a considerable impact on children and families, there is a dearth of empirical evidence regarding the relative risks and benefits of specific child welfare policies, practices, and interventions. A significant amount of research has been conducted in the CWS; however, many of the most important decisions, such as whether or not to place children in foster care or allow them to stay with caregivers, continue to have limited empirical foundation. Thus, there is a tremendous need for research examining the risks and benefits of CWS policies and procedures, the results of which will better inform policy decisions and contribute to improved care for the safety and welfare of children. The need for CWS outcome research is most compelling for policies involving ethnic minority children and families.

Ethnic minority populations are disproportionately affected by the decisions and policies of the CWS (U.S. Department of Health and

Human Services [DHHS], 2002). Recent surveys indicate that African Americans, American Indians and Alaska Natives, and Latino American children and families are overrepresented in the CWS (DHHS, 2002). Concerns regarding the equity of placement decisions made by the CWS have been one reason why states have embarked on efforts to redesign significant portions of child welfare services and address the impact of culture on child maltreatment and child welfare decisions (Child Welfare Services Stakeholders Group, 2003; Cohen, Deblinger, Mannarino, & Arellano, 2001). Despite such efforts, the majority of research conducted in this setting has ignored both race and culture.

Conducting culturally informative empirical research in CWS settings is exceptionally challenging. In addition to developing culturally appropriate hypotheses, designs, and outcome measures, investigators must address constraints on data collection resulting from the often conflicting priorities of state and federal legislators, child welfare administrators, judges, social workers, both parents' and children's legal representatives, and families. In this chapter, we will identify several potential areas of conflict in the conduct of research involving ethnic minorities in the CWS. We will also provide recommendations for conducting ethically and socially responsible research with ethnic minorities within this context. Previous literature has addressed the ethical concerns in conducting research with ethnic minorities (Fisher et al., 2002; Nagayama Hall, 2001; Sue, 1999). Although some information will be drawn from these sources, this chapter will focus specifically on the conduct of research within the CWS.

HISTORICAL AND CONTEXTUAL FACTORS

Although the problem of child maltreatment began to receive increasing attention in the early 1900s, it was not until 1974 that the U.S. Congress passed the first Child Abuse Prevention and Treatment Act (CAPTA). This legislation allocated funds for child abuse prevention and treatment to be disbursed to states that agreed to conform to federal guidelines and regulations regarding child maltreatment. In subsequent years, CAPTA was amended to include provisions requiring states to adopt policies that would move children toward adoption and permanency planning. All 50 states adopted these guidelines, and most states enforce the federal regulations through state child welfare services, social services providers, and county and local child protection agencies.

The U.S. Department of Health and Human Services defines the CWS as services to promote the well-being of children by ensuring safety, achieving permanency, and strengthening families (DHHS, 2004). To accomplish these goals, laws, policies, and standards of practice have been established to guide CWS decisions. Included in these policies are primary obligations to protect children's physical safety and respect the rights of parents. Although there is little disagreement over these overarching principles, the interpretation and implementation of these principles vary widely. Decisions to provide supportive services, remove a child, place a child in foster care, or terminate parental rights are affected by a wide range of factors including laws, local CWS policies and procedures, media influences, community characteristics, and individual situational factors. All of these factors are subject to cultural influences.

For example, a case worker has the responsibility of taking action when there is evidence of child abuse; however, deciding when to take action is difficult given that the definition of abuse has been difficult to establish (Terao, Borrego, & Urquiza, 2001). The law provides a legal definition of child abuse, but this definition is subject to a range of interpretations. Furthermore, although the federal government mandates that states conform to federal guidelines, each state has its own definitions of child abuse and neglect (National Clearinghouse on Child Abuse and Neglect Information, 2004). In addition, local interpretations may be influenced by recent events (e.g., a high-profile child death due to maltreatment may influence social workers and agencies to employ a more stringent interpretation of abuse), by agency climate, or by individual case workers' values and educational or cultural background. Thus, a number of contextual factors may influence child welfare decisions.

Furthermore, the nature of the population demands that cultural similarities and differences be identified and addressed. Families referred to CWS are diverse in ethnicity, socioeconomic status, education level, and many other demographic variables that influence culture. Because of this, families present with a broad range of parenting values and practices. It is incumbent on the CWS system and the individuals that make up this system to maintain an awareness of these differences and to communicate acceptance of practices that are different but do not fulfill the legal definition of abuse.

To complicate matters further, although the express purpose of the CWS as described by DHHS is to contribute to the welfare of children and families, in practice there is often an adversarial relationship between families and the CWS. Although the CWS can supply much needed resources, assistance, and support, it is frequently in the position of imposing additional and often burdensome responsibilities on parents. There is often the implicit or explicit threat of loss of child custody if CWS requirements (as directed by the court) are not met. Caregivers, in turn, may have limited resources and face significant challenges in meeting the requirements imposed by their CWS case worker (e.g., traveling across town with small children,

on public transportation, to participate in required mental health treatment services). Thus, case workers may inaccurately perceive parents as noncompliant and uncooperative, and families may have distorted perceptions of case workers as demanding, unyielding, insensitive, and coercive. This conflict may result from a case worker's limited understanding or knowledge of family cultural characteristics (Terao et al., 2001) or from families' lack of understanding of the function of child protective services or caseworker roles and responsibilities.

The conduct of research in this milieu is especially challenging as the adversarial relationship may interfere with the researcher's ability both to conduct valid studies and to engage participants in research. For example, a researcher conducting a study to identify behaviors or attitudes that place families at risk for abuse may encounter difficulties recruiting participants and obtaining accurate data through self-report because of the participants' dislike and distrust of the CWS. Similarly, and perhaps more common in CWS research, parents may distort, that is minimize or underreport, characteristics of themselves or their children because they fear that disclosure may hinder their efforts at reunification. A pattern of such behavior may increase the risk of a Type II error.

In addition to these systemic contextual factors, research must take into account the specific historical experiences of ethnic minority participants. Personal or group histories of oppression, immigration, group stigmatization, and economic exploitation are common in many ethnic minority communities (Derezotes & Snowden, 1990). An awareness of the historical and sociopolitical experiences specific to the ethnic group studied is essential to the development of a culturally responsive approach to research.

For example, American Indian children have historically been discriminated against by child welfare agencies. In the early 1970s, it was estimated that approximately 25–35% of American Indian children were removed from their homes and 85% were placed in non-American Indian homes (Dietrich, 1982). As a consequence of these actions, a large number of children were raised in homes in which they had no contact with their cultural heritage and practices, and this resulted in an erosion of native cultures. The Indian Child Welfare Act (ICWA) of 1978 sought to address this by establishing stringent federal standards for the removal of American Indians from their homes and requiring states to enact policies that would promote the stability of American Indian families and the adoption of children into American Indian homes (National Clearinghouse on Child Abuse and Neglect Information, 2003). Many states' CWS organizations have been criticized, however, for their poor adherence to these guidelines (Belone, Gonzalez-Santin, Gustavsson, MacEachron, & Perry, 2002). In conducting research with American Indian children in the CWS, researchers should be aware of this history and the impact it might have on participants' receptivity to research, their willingness to participate, and their distrust of researchers and the CWS. All of these factors may affect the researcher's ability to recruit, retain, and establish trust with research participants.

Finally, a major issue facing researchers in the CWS is the differential representation of ethnic groups in the CWS. Data from the National Child Abuse and Neglect Data System (DHHS, 2002) has consistently indicated that African Americans are greatly overrepresented in the child welfare system. In addition, Native Americans and Latino/as are overrepresented, and non-Latino Whites and Asian Americans are underrepresented in the CWS System (DHHS, 2002). Since the identification of these discrepancies, federal legislation has been enacted to address this disproportionality. For example in 1978, policies were enacted under the aforementioned

ICWA to promote the stability of American Indian families and to establish minimum standards for the removal of American Indian children. In addition, the Multiethnic Placement Act, enacted in 1994, included several measures to facilitate permanency planning and adoption of ethnic minority children and provided funds for the recruitment of ethnic minority foster families.

A research roundtable recently convened by the U.S. Department of Health and Human Services (Courtney & Skyles, 2003) to investigate the causes of racial disproportionality in the CWS suggested that the causes are complex and may involve both "entry" and "exit" factors. That is, children from ethnic minority families enter the system more frequently (increased rate of entry) and remain in the system longer (slower rates of exit or placement in permanent homes). One major objective for CWS research is to identify the causes for these discrepancies (e.g., increased investigation of child abuse referrals for ethnic minorities vs substantiation rates), as well as develop and evaluate effective means for ameliorating these disparities.

CULTURAL CONSIDERATIONS IN THE ETHICAL CONDUCT OF CWS RESEARCH

In this chapter, we identify five specific areas of research that commonly present ethical dilemmas for investigators: informed consent, confidentiality, random assignment, validity of measurement tools, and interpretation of results. In each of these areas, researchers in any field may encounter ethical quandaries; this chapter will focus on those relevant to research with ethnic minority clients in the CWS. The following vignette illustrates some of the issues encountered.

Maria, a 27-year-old Mexican immigrant, was referred to an outpatient clinic for mental health services following a removal of her two children (ages 3 and 5 years) due to neglect. Maria was a victim of domestic violence and separated from her husband. Throughout her lifetime, she struggled with depression, but this became severe when she was living with her husband, precipitating her inability to adequately protect and care for the children. Her reunification plan indicated that she was required to obtain mental health services for problems related to her depression, counseling related to domestic violence, and parenting services to better manage her children (both of her children have been exposed to domestic violence and present with disruptive behavior problems such as aggression, defiance, and noncompliance).

During the initial intake appointment at a program to assist her in managing her children, she was asked to participate in a research study comparing two mental health treatments designed to decrease her children's behavioral problems and strengthen her parenting skills. She attended the initial intake appointment with both of her children, who were whining, constantly interrupting, and frequently fighting with each other. A research assistant began to talk with her about a research study and reviewed a consent form with her. Maria did not fully understand what her signature entailed; she was unfamiliar with the concept of research, and her English reading ability was poor. She knew from past experience that when she is rushed or anxious she needs to concentrate a lot to understand English, but she was too anxious to ask the research assistant to slow down or repeat herself. Fortunately, the research assistant spoke some Spanish and asked her if she would like to review the consent form in English or Spanish. She chose Spanish.

She did not understand some of the concepts explained on the consent form such as confidentiality and participant's rights but was reluctant to ask questions as she thought this would appear rude or disrespectful. Also, although she understood much of what was written on the Spanish-language version of the consent form, some of the concepts were still not quite clear (e.g., the Spanish-language translation of the concept of a "Bill of Rights" [*Derechos de los Sujetos Participantes de Experimentos*] did not quite make sense to her). Her social worker, however, told her that she would be required to come to this agency and participate in therapy. She felt very frustrated and rushed because her children kept interrupting. She worried that their behavior was getting worse in foster care, and she wanted them home with her, so she readily signed the consent form, hoping that this would help her regain custody of her children and fearing that being perceived as uncooperative might hinder reunification.

OBTAINING INFORMED CONSENT

Maria signed a document indicating that she consented to participate in a research study; however, it is doubtful that she truly provided informed consent. Informed consent requires that individuals have "received complete and effective information about the content and procedures of a study and can decide on the merits of participating voluntarily without extraneous compelling factors" (Heppner, Kivlighan, & Wampold, 1992, p. 97). Several factors hinder the acquisition of informed consent from ethnic minorities in the CWS.

Ensuring that participants are truly informed, given a lack of familiarity with research and language barriers, is challenging. It is improbable that Maria had a true understanding of the nature of the study, given her limited exposure to research, scientific procedures, and language barriers. Racial or ethnic minority individuals (especially those from other countries) may have limited experience with the concept or process of research. Although the procedures of the study are reviewed in the consent process, this may not be sufficient to ensure that people who are not familiar with research have an adequate understanding of the study and the nature of their participation.

Furthermore, ethnic minorities in the CWS are vulnerable to feeling coerced into participating in therapy. It can be reasonably argued that Maria's consent was gained, not because she truly wished to participate in the study but because she was concerned that she might be penalized if she did not. Although the researcher probably explained the voluntary nature of participation, the climate of the CWS is one in which refusal to participate in required services may lead to severe repercussions. Many services are mandated by the CWS, and the ethnic minority research participant may not clearly understand that the research is not mandated. Further, if the participant is mandated to receive clinical services and the research involves these clinical services, the participant may feel obligated to consent to the research to complete the case plan; that is, the distinction between what are required services and what is optional research may be blurred if these are the same activities, as in child abuse clinical interventions. She might fear that refusal to participate in the study will be noted in the case file and will be perceived unwillingness to cooperate. This perception is particularly deleterious in the child welfare setting, as the elements of coercion are extremely powerful (e.g., a juvenile court judge ordering services) and the stakes are very high (e.g., loss of parental rights). The threat of loss of child custody may be so egregious as to sway parents to consent to a number of activities with which they may feel uncomfortable or to which they would normally be opposed.

The perception of coercion may be exacerbated for ethnic minority participants by the existing sociopolitical climate. Many ethnic minority individuals and families experience discrimination based on race or ethnicity, both on an institutional and individual level. As noted above, on an institutional level, the overrepresentation of ethnic minority children in the CWS has been well documented (DHHS, 2002; Webb, Courtney, Jones Harden, & Jones, 2003). On an individual level, ethnic minority families may be the victims of overt racist acts (violent attacks, verbal harassment) or more insidious forms of racism such as discrimination in housing and employment. In the context of a discriminatory social environment, individuals often perceive a power difference between themselves and the majority culture. Clients with this perception of relative powerlessness may not feel they have a choice when presented with the option to participate in research. Obtaining true consent from individuals within the context of both institutional and individual oppression is both crucial and challenging.

In addition, cultural values may predispose clients to agree to participate in research despite experiencing doubts or reservations. For example, in the Latino culture, deference to authority is emphasized (Cuellar, Arnold, & Gonzalez, 1995). Authority figures are often those with a higher level of education, higher socioeconomic status, or males. When asked to provide informed consent by a person who is perceived to have authority, a Latino client may consent because of a cultural tendency to defer to individuals of higher status.

Finally, children in the CWS may be dependents of the court, and it often unclear who is legally authorized to provide consent. In practice, consent for participation in research has been incorrectly obtained from social workers, foster caregivers, kin caregivers, and noncustodial parents. If the child is a dependent of the court, consent should only be obtained from the judge, legal advocate (i.e., attorney), or the biological parent; however, often researchers do not have contact with these individuals to review consent forms and research procedures. For many ethnic minority participants, this task may be particularly challenging, given the increased prevalence of diverse caregiving arrangements in ethnic minority families. For example, for African American and Latino families, the use of extended family as primary caregivers is common (Atkinson, Morten, & Sue, 1993). These arrangements are often informal, although they may have been in place for years. Identifying the person who is capable of providing legal consent for research participation in these situations may be challenging. Further, in situations where children have been cared for by extended family for long periods of time, obtaining consent from biological parents may not be appropriate as biological parents may have had little contact with children or little interest in becoming involved with them. In this case, the primary caregiver, although not legally authorized, may ethically be a more appropriate person to provide this consent.

Because securing true informed consent for research may be particularly challenging with ethnic minority clients, it is the researcher's responsibility to ensure that clients understand the nature of the research and the extent of their participation. Further, the researcher must ensure that clients are fully aware of the voluntary nature of participation and of the alternatives to participation and are free from coercion. Finally, clients must be fully apprised of the distinction between their participation in research and their completion of case plan requirements. Although this task is daunting, a number of measures may be used to promote understanding of research consent as well as freedom from coercion. The following suggestions may improve the researcher's ability to obtain true informed consent.

An extended orientation to the nature of research may facilitate ethnic minority clients' understanding of the aforementioned aspects of participation. This orientation may be conducted in several ways. Many scholars have advocated for the establishment of a relationship with the community being studied prior to the commencement of the research project (Sue, 1999; Fisher et al., 2002). Urquiza and Wyatt (1994) recommend contacting individuals from the following groups to establish a community board: religious organizations, community family support centers, and organizations for new immigrants. Establishing a relationship with community members and organizations may serve to increase the researchers' rapport and credibility and allow researchers to provide information regarding the study to potential participants.

In addition, upon the initial intake for the study, several procedures may facilitate the process of obtaining informed consent. Sue, Fujino, Hu, and Takeuchi (1991) used a short informational video to orient clients to the therapy process. The results of their study indicate that presentation of the video prior to the start of treatment reduced attrition in therapy. Although this research focused on increasing client's understanding of the therapy process, a similar format may be used to orient clients to the nature of research. This format is beneficial in that it does not require a level of literacy and may be easier to understand than written consent forms.

Researchers should provide the participant with the choice of completing the forms and interview in English or their native language. Consent forms should undergo a translation process that ensures forms have translation and conceptual equivalence (Okazaki & Sue, 1995). For example, although it is fairly easy to translate the words "informed consent" into Spanish, it is more difficult to translate the meaning or concept into terms that are understood by individuals who are not familiar with research terminology.

Researchers may also consider spending additional time establishing a relationship with the participant. This serves to increase both researcher's credibility and client's trust. Principal investigators who take the time to meet clients and introduce the study to them instead of delegating this duty to research assistants may foster a sense of the legitimacy of the study. Further, taking time to develop rapport may ensure that clients feel comfortable asking questions and exercising their right to refuse to participate.

Finally, in this context, it is imperative that researchers clarify their role relative to the CWS. Clients must be informed of the nature and extent of information that will be shared between the researcher and CWS. Further, the role, if any, of the researcher in providing feedback regarding completion of CPS requirements must be made clear. Clients must understand that researchers do not make case decisions. The distinction between the roles and activities of the researcher and the social worker must be clearly explained. For example, if clients receive outpatient treatment as part of a research study and to fulfill a case requirement, it is likely that researchers will need to provide caseworkers with progress reports or other evidence of participation; however, it is less likely that the researcher will be responsible for making recommendations regarding case disposition or plan. The researcher must clarify the nature of this collaboration.

PROTECTING CONFIDENTIALITY

Protecting the participant's rights to confidentiality is another challenge for researchers in the CWS, particularly in light of mandated reporting requirements. Because families who have a child placed in protective custody often have difficulties with parenting, there is an increased likelihood that participants will reveal information in the intake interview that meets criteria for mandated reporting of child abuse. Moreover, the type of information requested for the purpose of research (e.g., surveys regarding parenting practices or abuse history) may elicit disclosures of abusive behavior that warrant an abuse report.

When CWS research involves participants of diverse backgrounds, determining whether or not a participant's disclosure warrants a child abuse report may be especially difficult given differences in parenting values and practices across cultures. A number of studies have suggested that people of different ethnicities differ in their beliefs of what constitutes abuse (Ahn, 1994; Fontes, 2001). For example, in a study conducted by Ahn (1994), half of the Vietnamese and a majority of the Korean participants found the practice of hitting children on the hand with a stick to be an acceptable form of discipline, but the majority of participants from other ethnic groups were opposed to this practice.

Similarly, researchers are likely to vary in their judgments of abusive behavior. When a study participant discloses behavior that may be interpreted as abusive, the researcher must take culture into account in forming a decision regarding whether to file a child abuse report. Behavior that is culturally normative may or may not constitute abuse. If members of the community sanction a particular behavior (e.g., hitting the hand with a stick, coining, etc.) the researcher should exercise extra caution in determining whether a child abuse report is warranted. A comprehensive guide for deciding when to report child abuse is outside of the scope of this chapter. The reader is referred to Terao, Borrego, and Urquiza (2001) for guidelines regarding abuse reporting with diverse cultural groups. Notwithstanding, researchers should, at a minimum, have an awareness of diverse parenting practices across cultural groups, especially in those groups that are being studied, and should obtain appropriate consultation.

Once it has been determined that a child abuse report is warranted and the report has been filed, the researcher must contend with the consequences of breaching confidentiality. Although participants receive information regarding mandated reporting requirements during the informed consent process, they often feel betrayed when the abuse report is filed (Fisher, 2003). They may perceive that they have agreed to participate in a study and then are penalized for their willingness to comply. This sense of betrayal may add to a general distrust for the CWS or the research institution and may lead the client to terminate services prematurely.

The foregoing concern regarding confidentiality for research participants in the CWS is applicable to participants of all ethnicities but may be exacerbated for ethnic minority individuals. In particular, participants who are undocumented may be subject to greater sanctions if confidentiality is breached. Undocumented individuals are at risk for deportation if criminal behavior is revealed to law enforcement. For example, in a study conducted by the current authors, during a counseling session, a research participant revealed that her husband had been sexually molesting her daughter. The family was deported a few weeks later. (It must be noted that the practice regarding deportation of individuals who are reported for child abuse is quite variable and dependent on several case-specific and sociopolitical factors.)

The possibility of deportation following a mandated child abuse report raises several ethical questions for the researcher. Most notable of these is balancing the obligation to "do no harm" with the ethical and legal obligation to report child abuse. Deportation most likely results in harm to the research participant and their family; however, the consequences of failing to report child abuse may also result in significant harm to the family. Given this dilemma, the current authors suggest that researchers fulfill their

ethical mandate to report the abuse, while engaging in proactive measures to minimize the negative consequences of this report. These measures may include collaborating with CWS administrators to create a protocol for reporting undocumented study participants and developing a plan to minimize harm caused by this report.

Concerns regarding the breach of confidentiality with research participants may extend to include the broader community. As noted above, ethnic minority research is often enhanced by the recruitment and involvement of community members in the development and implementation of studies. When the researcher makes a mandated child abuse report, the sense of betrayal experienced by families may be shared by the larger community (Fisher, 2003). Thus, members of the community who initially embraced and supported the research may react negatively when a member's participation in research leads to a child abuse report. This result has negative ramifications both for community members and for the current and future research endeavors. Community members may have increased distrust for academia and researchers and, more generally, "the system," which may discourage them from participating in research that may ultimately benefit the community. Further, the damage caused to this relationship may hinder the researcher's ability to conduct future studies with this community. Thus, the likelihood that mandated reporting situations will arise is increased when conducting research within the CWS, and the ramifications of these reports may be magnified for ethnic minority participants and communities.

Ethically addressing the issue of confidentiality requires researchers to collaborate with the CWS and adequately inform clients of their responsibility regarding confidentiality. At the outset of the study, researchers must identify the types of information that will be shared with the CWS, that is, describe the form of the disclosure (monthly or quarterly reports), the individuals to whom information will be provided (social workers, therapists, judges, legal advocates, etc.), and the information that falls under mandated reporting laws. To facilitate this, the researcher should establish a relationship with the CWS to ensure that requirements are well understood by both the researcher and the administration. In addition, given differing cultural interpretations of abuse, extra care should be taken to provide a clear and comprehensive definition of what constitutes abuse to participants. Examples of abusive and nonabusive behavior may be given to clarify this distinction.

Finally, the researcher bears responsibility for managing problems caused by the client's participation research. If the client's participation in a study results in disruption of his or her successful completion of the case plan, the researcher must collaborate with the case worker and legal representatives to minimize the harm caused by this disruption. For example, if the client terminates treatment prematurely, the researcher should work with the client and caseworker to ensure that the client has access to other mental health resources. Fisher and colleagues (2002) advocate for the identification of persons or organizations that will serve as referrals in the event that further services are required.

It is also the responsibility of the researcher to maintain ties with the community when research activities create conflicts with families. The creation of a community panel is a way to facilitate this. This panel, which acts as a liaison between the researcher and the community, could assist in constructing a culturally valid means of evaluating parenting behavior and identifying abusive situations. In addition, the community panel could assist in developing problem-solving strategies to best serve families following an abuse report.

ENSURING ADEQUATE CONTROL/COMPARISON CONDITIONS

In addition to considerations regarding informed consent and confidentiality, researchers must protect participants' rights to access appropriate treatment. This becomes particularly challenging when the research design involves random assignment to treatment and comparison groups. In conducting clinical trials research, random assignment to treatment, control, or wait-list control groups can be justified when there is "genuine uncertainty" (Roberts, Lauriello, Geppert, & Keith, 2001, p. 890) regarding which condition is most beneficial. In conducting research in the CWS, however, investigators are generally working with families at risk for engaging in family violence. To withhold treatment for research purposes or to provide a treatment that is thought to be inferior in its effectiveness is clearly unethical in these circumstances as it places the family at further risk. Further, because families in the CWS are often mandated to obtain treatment, the researcher may not have the flexibility to assign participants to a wait-list control group. The researcher must ensure that participants are not prevented from obtaining adequate treatment due to their participation in the research. To address this, the researcher may choose to use a comparison treatment or a "treatment as usual" (TAU) condition. Spirito, Stanton, Donaldson, and Boergers (2002) assert that the use of a TAU is justified, as the increased monitoring of the control condition may render this condition more beneficial than treatment as usual as implemented in the community.

Despite these options, the task of protecting participants' right to treatment becomes more complex when research involves ethnic minority participants, as there is frequently a dearth of services available to ethnic minority families. For example, if assigned to the

TAU condition, language minority participants may have difficulty obtaining treatment in their native language in the community. There are frequently lengthy waiting lists for obtaining bilingual services. Although clearly it is not the responsibility of the researcher to ensure that all CWS families are receiving appropriate services, once family members have been enrolled as participants, the researcher has an ethical duty to ensure that the participants are not hindered by their assignment to the comparison group. Because of the dearth of services available to ethnic minority and especially linguistic minority clients, the participant in the comparison condition may be harmed by their participation in the study unless the researcher ensures that an appropriate treatment is provided. Thus, random assignment for clinical trials in the CWS may pose significant challenges, especially when working with ethnic minority participants.

The researcher may address this concern in two ways. First, the researcher may establish a relationship with providers in the TAU condition. In this way, the researcher may closely monitor the types of services provided and the frequency of treatment received to ensure that the client is provided with adequate treatment. Alternatively, the researcher may eschew the "treatment as usual" condition and instead use a comparison condition conducted by research personnel to ensure that the treatment is adequate.

USE OF ASSESSMENT TOOLS

Another consideration in the ethical conduct of research with ethnic minority families in the CWS is the use of measurement devices for the collection of data. Mental health research often calls for the use of psychometric questionnaires and structured observations. These measurement tools have evidence for their validity with non-Latino White populations, but very few measures have data supporting their use with ethnic minority clients. For example, research with the CWS often makes use of psychometric measures to determine the individual's level of risk for engaging in family violence. Clinical elevations on these instruments may indicate that the person is more likely to engage in abusive behavior. The use of these questionnaires to determine the level of risk for ethnic minority individuals may be inappropriate if the measure has not been validated for the population (Urquiza & Wyatt, 1994).

Erroneous interpretation of scale elevations may not only reduce the validity of the study's results but also have negative consequences for the participant. Specifically, if other service providers (e.g., social worker, attorney, judge) have access to the results of these questionnaires, they may base their decisions in part on this data. If the service provider deems that the parent is at risk for engaging in family violence based on the erroneous interpretation of data obtained for the purpose of research, the participant may be harmed by their involvement in the research.

For example, many empirical studies have employed the Child Abuse Potential Inventory (CAPI; Milner, Gold, & Wimberly, 1986) to investigate caregivers' level of risk for engaging in abusive behavior; however, this measure has not been validated for use with ethnic minority groups. If, for example, a Latino American caregiver obtains scale elevations when administered this measure, it is unclear whether this indicates an increased risk for abusive behavior, as this scale has not been normed with a Latino American population. If the case worker for this caregiver is apprised of the results of the administration of this questionnaire, the case worker may mistakenly assume that the caregiver has a high potential for engaging in abuse and may choose to prolong or terminate reunification efforts. In the case of the use of the CAPI, these concerns are supported by evidence that Latino caregivers may express more "rigid" views in caregiving despite exhibiting relatively warm and permissive parenting behavior (Derezotes & Snowden, 1990). Thus, Latino caregivers may obtain scale elevations on the CAPI rigidity scale that lead to spurious interpretations of the caregiver's potential for engaging in abusive behavior.

Ensuring that the measures used for the study are valid is important both for the validity of the research and for the protection of participants' rights. Whenever possible, the investigator should strive to employ measures that are normed and validated for the population studied. When this is not possible, the researcher should ensure equivalence of measures. Okazaki and Sue (1995) suggest that translation, conceptual, and metric equivalence must be established to ensure validity of the assessment utilized. That is, measures must undergo a rigorous translation process, the concepts measured must be equal across assessments, and the scores must have the same value across ethnic groups (Trimble, 2005). This is especially important if results across groups are being compared. Prior to conducting statistical analyses, the researcher may also use statistical tests such as the split-half reliability coefficient to ensure that reliability of assessments is obtained within the population sampled. In addition, qualitative methods may be used to corroborate or disconfirm information acquired through quantitative measures. The researcher must take steps to ensure that the results of questionnaires are kept as confidential as possible within the context of mandated treatment.

ETHICAL INTERPRETATION OF STUDY RESULTS

The evaluation of the results of child welfare research must also attend to cultural variables as interpretations that are ethnocentric may lead to conclusions that are not only inaccurate but also harmful to the population studied. Psychological research on ethnic minority groups has often employed non-Latino White populations as the comparison group. This approach has led many researchers to employ a "deficit model" in interpreting study results (Urquiza & Wyatt, 1994). Within this paradigm, characteristics found in ethnic minority communities are viewed as deficient when compared with those in non-Latino White populations.

For example, Latino families evidence a high degree of family cohesion and connectedness (Hovey & King, 1996). In Anglo-American families, high degrees of cohesion have been associated with a level of enmeshment that is considered dysfunctional (Olson, Sprenkle, & Russell, 1979). If interpreted in this light, Latino families with high levels of cohesiveness may be mistakenly perceived as pathologically enmeshed and in need of services to decrease this interdependence. Although it may be true that elevated cohesiveness may indicate dysfunction in non-Latino White populations, it does not necessarily follow that this construct has the same meaning in ethnic minority populations. Researchers should exercise caution in interpreting results that may have a particular significance within non-Latino White populations and a different meaning for other groups.

The interpretation of results from an ethnocentric perspective in child welfare research is damaging when it leads to the development of recommendations and decisions that pathologize normative behavior in ethnic minorities and ignore cultural values and practices that serve as strengths to members of a community (Fisher et al., 2002). Furthermore, erroneous interpretations of study results may perpetuate the notion that child maltreatment is more common among ethnic minority communities.

To avoid biased interpretation of study results, the researcher should consult community experts and stakeholders and utilize both quantitative and qualitative data. Accuracy of data interpretation may be enhanced by consultation with individuals knowledgeable in the areas studied. Ideally, consultants would include individuals with expertise in child welfare issues and cross-cultural issues. Involving members from different groups in the consultation process will enrich the interpretation of results. Thus, the researcher may consider conducting focus groups with caseworkers, consumers (parents and foster parents), legal representation, and community leaders, as well as other researchers to assist in the process of interpretation. In addition to aiding in the interpretation of results, this collaboration may assist in developing interventions based on study results. Promoting the participation of a diverse group in study outcome evaluation may have the added benefit of increasing the stakeholder's commitment to intervention approaches that arise from the results of the investigation. Finally, data interpretation may be enhanced through integration of qualitative and quantitative data (Urquiza & Wyatt, 1994). By conducting open-ended interviews or focus groups with study participants, the research may gain insight into the true meaning of the results achieved.

CONCLUSION

As children continue to enter the CWS at high rates, the need for research in this area becomes increasingly compelling. Given the disproportionate number of ethnic minority families in the CWS, it is crucial that empirical work in this field address ethical dilemmas that arise in working with ethnic minorities. In both content and procedures, research in the CWS must include measures to increase cultural responsiveness. This entails conducting research that is relevant to ethnic minorities, using procedures that employ sensitivity to ethnic differences, and interpreting results in light of the realities of ethnic minority communities. In this chapter, we have identified ethical dilemmas most frequently encountered in these phases of research. This review is by no means exhaustive but may provide initial guidelines for researchers embarking on empirical study in the CWS.

REFERENCES

Ahn, H. N. (1994). Cultural diversity and the definition of child abuse. *Child Welfare Research Review, 1,* 28–55.

Atkinson, D. R., Morten, G., & Sue, D. W. (1993). *Counseling American minorities: A cross-cultural perspective* (4th ed.). Madison, WI: Brown & Benchmark.

Belone, C., Gonzalez-Santin, E., Gustavsson, N., MacEachron, A. E., & Perry, T. (2002). Social services: The Navajo way. *Child Welfare, 81*(5), 773–790.

Child Welfare Services Stakeholders Group. (2003). *CWS redesign: The future of California's Child Welfare Services: Final report.* State of California, Health and Human Services Agency, Department of Social Services.

Cohen, J. A., Deblinger, E., Mannarino, A. P., & Arellano, M. A. (2001). The importance of culture in treating abused and neglected children: An empirical review. *Child Maltreatment, 6*(2), 148–157.

Courtney, M., & Skyles, A. (2003). Racial disproportionality in the CWS. *Children and Youth Services Review, 25*(5), 355–358.

Cuellar, I., Arnold, B., & Gonzalez, G. (1995). Cognitive referents of acculturation: Assessment of cultural constructs in Mexican Americans. *Journal of Community Psychology, 23,* 339–356.

Derezotes, D. S., & Snowden, L. R. (1990). Cultural factors in the intervention of child maltreatment. *Child and Adolescent Social Work, 7*(2), 161–175.

Dietrich, G. (1982). Indian Child Welfare Act: Ideas for implementation. *Child Abuse and Neglect, 6,* 125–128.

Fisher, C. B. (2003). Adolescent and parent perspectives on ethical issues in youth drug use and suicide survey research. *Ethics & Behavior, 13*(4), 302–331.

Fisher, C. B., Hoagwood, K., Boyce, C., Duster, T., Frank, D. A., Grisso, T., et al. (2002). Research ethics for mental health science involving ethnic minority children and youths. *American Psychologist, 57*(12), 1024–1040.

Fontes, L. A. (2001). Introduction: Those who do not look ahead, stay behind. *Child Maltreatment, 6(2),* 83–88.

Heppner, P. P., Kivlighan, D. M., & Wampold, B. E. (1992). *Research design in counseling.* Pacific Grove, CA: Brooks Cole.

Hovey, J. D., & King, C. A. (1996). Acculturative stress, depression, and suicidal ideation among immigrant and second-generation Latino adolescents. *Journal of the American Academy of Child and Adolescent Psychiatry, 35*(9), 1183–1193.

Milner, J. S., Gold, R. G., & Wimberly, R. C. (1986). Prediction and explanation of child abuse: Cross-validation of the Child Abuse Potential Inventory. *Journal of Consulting and Clinical Psychology, 54*(6), 865–866.

Nagayama Hall, G. (2001). Psychotherapy research with ethnic minorities: Empirical, ethical, and conceptual issues. *Journal of Consulting and Clinical Psychology, 69*(3), 502–510.

National Clearinghouse on Child Abuse and Neglect Information. (2003). *Major federal legislation concerned with child protection, child welfare, and adoption.* Retrieved November 2004, from http://nccanch.acf.hhs.gov/pubs/otherpubs/fedlegis.pdf

National Clearinghouse on Child Abuse and Neglect Information. (2004). *Reporting procedures.* Retrieved April 5, 2005, from http://nccanch.acf.hhs.gov/general/legal/statutes/repproc.cfm

Okazaki, S., & Sue, S. (1995). Methodological issues in assessment research with ethnic minorities. *Psychological Assessment, 7*(3), 367–375.

Olson, D. H., Sprenkle, D. H., & Russell, C. S. (1979). Circumplex model of marital and family systems: 1. Cohesion and adaptability dimensions, family types, and clinical applications. *Family Process, 18,* 3–28.

Roberts, L. W., Lauriello, J., Geppert, C., & Keith, S. J. (2001). Placebos and paradoxes in psychiatric research: An ethics perspective. *Biological Psychiatry, 49,* 887–893.

Spirito, A., Stanton, C., Donaldson, D., & Boergers, J. (2002). Treatment as usual for adolescent suicide attempters: Implications for choice of comparison groups in psychotherapy research. *Journal of Clinical Child & Adolescent Psychology, 31,* 41–47.

Sue, S. (1999). Science, ethnicity, and bias: Where have we gone wrong? *American Psychologist, 54*(12), 1070–1077.

Sue, S., Fujino, D. C., Hu, L., & Takeuchi, D. T. (1991). Community mental health services for ethnic minority groups: A test of the cultural responsiveness hypothesis. *Journal of Consulting and Clinical Psychology, 59,* 533–540.

Takaki, R. (1998). *Strangers from a different shore: A history of Asian Americans* (p. 7). Boston: Bay Back Books.

Terao, S. Y., Borrego, J., Jr., & Urquiza, A. J. (2001). A reporting and response model for culture and child maltreatment. *Child Maltreatment, 6*(2), 158–168.

Trimble, J. E. (2005). An inquiry into the measurement of racial and ethnic identity. In R. Carter (Ed.), *Handbook of racial-cultural psychology and counseling: Theory and research* (pp. 320–359). New York: Wiley.

U.S. Department of Health and Human Services. (2002). *National Child abuse and Neglect Data System (NCANDS): Summary of key findings from the calendar year 2000.* Administration on Children, Youth, and Families. Washington, DC: Government Printing Office.

U.S. Department of Health and Human Services, National Clearinghouse on Child Abuse and Neglect Information. (2004). *How does the CWS work?* Retrieved from November 2004, from http://nccanch.acf.hhs.gov/pubs/factsheets/cpswork.cfm [Page no longer available]

Urquiza, A. J., & Wyatt, G. (1994). Culturally relevant violence research with children of color. *The APSAC Advisor, 7*(3), 1–20.

Webb, M. B., Courtney, M., Jones Harden, B., & Jones, B. (2003, March/April). *Children of color project.* Presentation at the Fourteenth National Conference of Child Abuse and Neglect, St. Louis, MO.

CHAPTER 11

With All Due Respect

Ethical Issues in the Study of Vulnerable Adolescents

ANA MARI CAUCE

RICHARD H. NOBLES

> *The United States government did something that was wrong, deeply, profoundly, morally wrong. It was an outrage to our commitment to integrity and equality for all our citizens.*
>
> —President Bill Clinton, from the apology for the
> Tuskegee Study, May 16, 1997

> *While mental disorders may touch all Americans either directly or indirectly, all do not have equal access to treatment and services. The failure to address these inequities is being played out in human and economic terms across the nation— on our streets, in homeless shelters, public health institutions, prisons and jails.*
>
> —U.S. Surgeon General Dr. David Satcher,
> *Mental Health: Culture, Race and Ethnicity*

There is little question but that scientific research with human populations has been responsible for both a great deal of good and a great deal of harm. Basic and applied research has played a major role in the development of medical, pharmacological, and psychotherapeutic treatments that have not only extended life but enhanced its quality. Human research has also helped us learn more about ourselves,

AUTHOR'S NOTE: A special thanks also to Yvette Lohr, lead interviewer on SHARP and ethical and moral compass for that study.

how we interact with each other and are affected by social conditions. Nonetheless, one of the most shameful incidents in American history, the Tuskegee Study (1932–1972), which allowed 399 poor African American sharecroppers to go untreated for syphilis, all too clearly illustrates what can occur when a biased interpretation of what constitutes the scientific "greater good" results in the callous disregard for marginalized and vulnerable populations.

Ethics codes developed by professional and/or governmental entities have been revisited many times since 1972, and institutional review boards (IRBs) have been instituted to ensure that society could reap the benefits of scientific discovery while ensuring that individual research participants would be protected from undue harm; however, even as ethics codes and IRB regulations are refined and tightened—some would say needlessly or overzealously so—a researcher's own moral compass continues to play a major role in how ethical concerns about human research are addressed in the lab or in the field. As such, we can learn much from each other as to how we grapple with and resolve ethical issues, an aspect of our work that is seldom described in our formal research papers.

This chapter will examine four crucial areas of ethical concern that are encountered in conducting scientific research with vulnerable populations: (a) setting the context for a respectful research relationship with the communities of those studied, (b) developing sensitive and appropriate consent procedures, (c) implementing appropriate confidentiality and disclosure policies, and (d) weighing the risk and benefits of a research study or program. The latter three concerns are standard ones that must be considered in virtually any research study; the first is especially important when working with vulnerable populations from lower-status communities that have historically lacked social and economic capital and access to political power.

In discussing these concerns, we will primarily draw from two research studies conducted in the first author's lab over the last decades: the Families and Adolescent Study of School Transitions (FASST) and the Seattle Homeless Research Project (SHARP). An additional theme running through this discussion is the concern for how to ensure that a program of research, where appropriate, adequately reflects the lives of those being researched.

FASST AND SHARP: TWO STUDIES OF VULNERABLE YOUTH

Adolescence is an especially critical developmental period, characterized by rapid biological, emotional, and social changes, including puberty, the culmination of identity development, and shifting roles in social interaction with same-sex peers, opposite-sex peers, and adults (Brooks-Gunn & Reiter, 1990; Feldman & Elliot, 1990). How an adolescent navigates these developmental demands has critical implications for the rest of his or her life. Mistakes and mishaps here, like early pregnancy or drug abuse, can set up troubles that may haunt youths for years to come.

Although navigating adolescence presents challenges for all youth, additional stressors related to ethnic minority status, poverty, and homelessness may intensify these already difficult demands. It is imperative that we learn more about how adolescents deal with these additional challenges if we are to develop programs that will adequately meet their needs. It is also important that we construct our research programs in a manner that takes into account their multiple vulnerabilities due both to age and their "one-down" status in society.

More complete descriptions of the research background and goals of the FASST and SHARP studies are provided elsewhere (see Mason, Cauce, Gonzales, Hiraga, & Grove,

1994; Mason, Cauce, Gonzales, & Hiraga, 1994; Cauce, Gonzales, Hiraga, Grove, & Ryan-Finn, 1996; Cauce et al., 1994; Cauce et al., 1998; Cauce et al., 2000, for fuller descriptions of each). For the purpose of this chapter, it is worth noting that both studies were designed, at least in part, in order to help us better understand factors related to risk or resilience among these youth. But although FASST was a more classic social science research project that involved observations and interviews without intervention, the second, SHARP, was an intervention study.

In FASST, our specific interest was in family practices that enhanced or interfered with adolescent development in the years of transition from middle school to high school. One question we were especially interested in was what level of parental control related to optimal adolescent adjustment. Although much research with White youth suggested that high levels of control, sometimes referred to as "authoritarian" parenting, was related to higher levels of externalizing behavior or conduct problems, those working with African American families and youth had suggested that relatively high levels of control might be more normative and play a more positive role for this population. It is also worth noting that this was one of the first studies to bring African American families into the lab for parent-child conflict interactions that was videotaped and coded.

Participants in FASST were 144 African American adolescents who were in either the eighth or ninth grade at the start of the study. They were, on average, 13.5 years old. Adolescents were primarily recruited through local area schools and through formal and informal community systems (e.g. churches, youth groups). For inclusion in the study, at least one parent or equivalent had to agree to participate as well. Families were primarily working class, but socioeconomically diverse. Most of the mothers were high

school graduates (91%), although a few had graduated from college (11%). When household income was examined, most families could not be categorized as poor (58% reported incomes above $20,000 in 1992 dollars), but relatively few reported incomes that would put them in the higher end of middle class (less than 20% reported incomes greater than $40,000). A subset of 57 mothers and daughters participated in the interaction phase of the study. Only daughters were included because resources were limited and we wanted to ensure that we retained appropriate power for subsequent analyses.

This study has been referred to by others as a study of at-risk youth, but in fact it was a normative sample. Family income of participants was on average lower than would be the case for a comparable study of White youth but nonetheless representative of local African American families. Although the sample was normative and not chosen to be "at-risk," participants are considered vulnerable by virtue of their status as minors. They are doubly vulnerable by virtue of being members of an ethnic minority group.

Participants in SHARP were 364 runaway, homeless, and street youth between the ages of 13 and 21. The majority (82%) were between the ages of 15 and 18, with a mean age of 16.4. Although the majority of the youth were White, a substantial number (40%) were of ethnic-minority background. Moreover, many have noted that homeless youth are a subculture in their own right. Although this view may stretch the definition of culture beyond the point at which we feel entirely comfortable, there are certainly ways in which this is the case. For example, street youth will sometimes refer to a "code of the streets" or a code of honor that they aspire to.

Whether one ascribes subcultural status to street youth or not, there is no question but that this is a multiply vulnerable population. Not only do they lack the protection of a familial or familial-like adult to look after their best interests, but previous research has suggested that a substantial number of these youth would have mental health problems of diagnosable proportions, most often depression and conduct disorder. In addition, a substantial number of these youth were expected to have experienced the violation of trust by an adult in the form of physical or sexual abuse. These expectations were more than met, with more than half (67%) of our SHARP sample qualifying for a mental disorder according to DSM III standards (41% met the criteria for conduct disorder, 28% met criteria for dysthymia or major depression, 5% met criteria for prodromal or residual schizophrenia), over half the sample (52%) reported that they had been physically abused prior to leaving their homes, and 60% of the girls and 23% of the boys reported that they had been sexually abused (Cauce et al., 2000).

It is important to note that the primary purpose of SHARP was to examine the efficacy of an intensive case management treatment model for meeting the needs of homeless youth (see Cauce et al., 1994, for a full description). In order to do this, a partnership was developed between the first author's research team at the University of Washington; YouthCare, a local social service agency serving runaway and homeless youth; and the State of Washington Division of Human and Social Services. YouthCare played the primary role in developing the intensive case management program, called Project Passage, and the UW played the primary role in developing the research and evaluation plan. The State of Washington's involvement was meant to ensure that funding for services would continue after grant funding ended. The National Institute of Mental Health grant that funded the project was obtained under a Public-Academic Liaison (PAL) program. So, although each of the partners brought special skills to the table, all major decisions were made in partnership.

In order to evaluate Project Passage, youth in this new "experimental" program were compared with those in treatment-as-usual, regular case management services through YouthCare. Both programs were housed at YouthCare's Orion drop-in center. Youths in the study were randomly assigned to one of the two case management treatment conditions. It is important to note that there was no equivalent of a placebo condition and that no youth was denied treatment as a result of study participation. Youth either received regular case management, the best treatment available prior to this study, or the new intensive case management, which was considered state of the art and more resource intensive, but that had yet to be evaluated with this population. Although we considered having a no treatment condition, we opted not to because of our ethical concerns about withholding treatment from a population with this level of need.

In sum, both of the case study projects that we will discuss involved vulnerable populations by virtue of their age and because they come from groups that have traditionally been marginalized by society, in one case because of their ethnocultural group, the other because of their housing status (or lack thereof). The vulnerability of these populations required us to take special care in constructing and conducting our studies. This care began in our work with each respective community.

SETTING THE RESEARCH CONTEXT: ESTABLISHING A RELATIONSHIP WITH THE COMMUNITY

Perhaps the major concern of ethics codes, and the IRBs who implement them, is the desire to protect individuals from any harm that might befall them as a result of research participation. This focus on the individual has, if anything, been emphasized in recent years. Indeed, although benefits to society at large have historically been taken into account when weighing the risks and benefits of a project, there is an increasing focus on the benefits that come directly to the individual participant.

The individualistic nature of most ethics codes is clearly in keeping with the individualistic nature of Anglo-American society. But, an individualistically oriented code may not do as well in protecting the interests of cultures or subcultures with more collectivist orientations. More specifically, U.S. ethnic minorities, whether African American, Latino American, Asian American, Native American, or Pacific Islander American, tend to hold values that place a great deal of importance on the good of the group (Boykin, 1986; Chun & Akutsu, 2003; Cauce, Domenech-Rodriguez, 2002). Collectivistic orientation has also been described as characteristic of street youth culture and has often been viewed as helping to protect these youth from the many exploitative adults who can so often be found surrounding them (Dachner & Tarasuk, 2002; Ruddick, 1996).

Dealing with research-related risks that may be posed at the group level, rather than at just the individual level, is especially important for ethnic minority adolescents and homeless youth because both have so often been portrayed in a manner that is stigmatizing. For example, ethnic minority youth are quite commonly portrayed by the media as gang members, perpetrators of violence, sexually promiscuous, or sexually irresponsible. Street youth are portrayed in a similar fashion, with the added stigma of being viewed as drug abusers and/or prostitutes. All too often scientific research has been conducted in ways that reify such portrayals and may be viewed as harmful to the larger communities that research participants come

from. For example, although the individual minority subjects who participated in the research described in the bell curve (Hermstein & Murray, 1994) may not have been individually harmed, the results reported have been seen by some as harmful to African Americans as a group.[1]

We do not believe that one should shy away from research that documents real problems that exist within minority, poor, or otherwise marginalized communities, but it certainly seems preferable to construct research programs in ways that provide a fuller portrayal of the populations studied. When research does focus on problems, dysfunctions, or weaknesses, it would also be preferable if such studies were to do so with at least some intention of playing a role in remedying or alleviating these problems.

Consultation with members of the communities from which populations will be recruited can help ensure that the larger research program not only fails to harm but also provides some benefits to these populations at the level of the group. This type of consultation has the added benefit of helping the researcher construct recruitment and retention procedures that are not only respectful but effective. The same is the case when it comes to developing effective research paradigms or instrumentation. For example, our work with African American mothers proved invaluable in the design of our coding system. And, without the endorsement of a homeless youth–serving agency, it is unlikely that we would have attained the high rate of participation (95%) that we achieved.

The active engagement of community members in the design and conduct of research is the hallmark of participatory community research (Jason, Keys, Suarez-Balcazar, Taylor, & Davis, 2002). A goal of this approach is to construct research programs, especially prevention and intervention studies, in a manner that empowers participants and their communities (Balcazar, Keys,

Kaplan, & Suarez-Balcazar, 1998). We cannot say that we fully embraced this methodology in our research, which was carried out well before key writings in this area appeared in press, but many of the basic tenants of this approach were present in our approach, at least in some prototype form.

Identifying the community in question can, of course, raise difficult issues. Although decision-making authority is sometimes clearly delegated to a specific group, as is often the case among specific Native American communities, there was no clear group for us to go to in setting the context for FASST. Moreover, in 1989 when FASST was first being conceptualized and implemented, the creation of community boards as consultants to research projects was rare, and we did not think to create such a board in any formal manner. Instead, we brought together a group of about a half dozen African American women, most of whom were mothers and most of whom were working in mental health or social service agencies to help us think through the project as a whole and to provide help with specific aspects of the project, especially the coding scheme for the mother-daughter interaction.

We were already sensitized to issues of stigmatization among African American youth and from the outset had decided not to focus exclusively on an at-risk population or exclusively on negative behavior. For example, outcome measures focused on self-esteem and school achievement in addition to problem behavior; but it was not until our conversations with our community advisory group that we were sensitized to the fact that African American parenting, especially mothering, was also often portrayed in terms that were overwhelmingly negative. This did not deter us from the original plan to examine how parenting, mostly mothering, was related to negative adolescent behaviors, like externalizing; but it did lead us to be more sensitive about describing the context in

which parenting took place, especially the burdensome task of parenting youths growing up in high-risk circumstances, including high-crime neighborhoods. We were so influenced by the stories these women told us that we used them to frame our findings on the relationship between parental control and externalizing in one of our most cited publications (Cauce et al., 1996). Advice from this informal advisory work not only helped us in interpreting our findings but really sensitized us to some issues that the mothers might be bringing to the study, and we believe we were better able to engage with our sample as a result of this.

In contrast to FASST, SHARP presents an example of the dilemma faced by researchers working with a multicultural sample of youth, perhaps the most common situation in psychological research today. Youth in our studies typically come from multiple ethnic backgrounds, and no one group of ethnocultural experts may make sense as a consultation group. To the degree that we initially engaged in conversations with members of ethnic minority communities about youth homelessness, many viewed it as a "White" problem, on occasion insisting that their (e.g., the African American, Latino, Asian American, or Native American) community had informal structures that served to keep their youth off the street; but although it was true that we had trouble identifying homeless Asian American youth, the proportions of other youth of color in our sample seemed to mirror their ethnic representation within Seattle.

It did not make sense to set up an advisory board along ethnocultural lines, but as noted previously, we not only sought consultation from, but worked in full partnership with, YouthCare, the largest agency in town solely dedicated to serving runaway, homeless, and street youth (see www.youthcare.org/ for a fuller description of the agency). Throughout the implementation of the research study, all key decisions were made by the principal investigator (first author of this paper), together with an advisory board that included the director of YouthCare, key clinical personnel from the agency, and representatives from the Washington State Department of Social and Health Services. Both agencies were partners in the study, and almost all key personnel, including the data analyst and all research interviewers, were housed in YouthCare and hired as YouthCare employees.

The involvement of YouthCare in every aspect of SHARP was critical, as we had negligible experience with homeless youth prior to this study. Although we did spend time at the agency talking to case managers and youth prior to developing the proposal that led to funding the study, there is no way that we could have garnered in this short time the type of insights and experience that staff had who had worked with these youths for years and, in some cases, decades. The involvement of YouthCare, and its personnel, ensured that the best interests of this vulnerable sample of youth would be given all due consideration at every step of the research process. It also ensured that the youth would be treated with all due respect.

Each of these studies called for a slightly different strategy for ensuring appropriate community cooperation and consultation. In SHARP, we worked with a community agency in full partnership. In FASST, our work was with community members, and the relationship was much more informal and best characterized as consultative. In both instances, however, community involvement was critical in setting the stage for the conduct of ethically appropriate and responsible research with these vulnerable youth. The importance of setting the stage will become abundantly clear as we focus our discussion on informed consent, confidentiality and disclosure, and the balance of risks to benefits.

MAKING SURE THAT YES MEANS YES: OBTAINING CONSENT FROM VULNERABLE YOUTH

There are a host of issues involved in making sure that vulnerable youth fully and completely consent, or assent, to research participation. Among the issues that have been raised are questions about whether youth from nonmainstream populations are familiar enough with research to know what they are consenting or assenting to. How easy or difficult is it for youth from a one-down position to say no to those who are viewed as authority figures (Fisher et al., 2002)? To what degree do promises of monetary reward provide a coercive environment, especially when youth lack monetary resources (Sieber, 1994; Macklin, 1989)?

Although these issues are legitimate ones for both FASST and SHARP, it is in the latter study that they were most salient. The required participation of at least one parent in FASST ensured that parental consent to adolescent participation was given under conditions in which parents were keenly aware of what such participation required. That is, in this study, not only were parents required to allow their children to participate in the study, answering questions, completing surveys, or engaging in interactions with research staff, but parents were required to themselves engage in similar procedures. In fact, the videotaped parent-child interaction—arguably the most sensitive procedure of all, in that it can elicit strong negative emotions—is one where the parent (mother) is there, sitting across from her child, with full authority to stop the interaction at any time. In this sense, we made the assumption that parents could and would protect their own children's best interests. Furthermore, the procedures of the study were such that parents were fully aware of what the research experience was like for their child, as procedures for parents and child closely paralleled each other.

Nonetheless, in recognition of the fact that the adolescents in our study were old enough to make independent judgments about their participation, assent from adolescents was also required for study participation. Assent forms were not only written in language that would be easy for adolescent to comprehend but were administered in person, and adolescents were given ample opportunity to ask questions about procedures before assenting.

In addition, both parents and adolescents were given the opportunity to withdraw from the study at any time. They were very clearly informed that if they withdrew from the study, even after the first question or two, they would keep the compensation given for participation ($20 for each participant). Thus, compensation may have played a role in adolescent or parent's decision to participate, but we hoped that the role of compensation receded as the study progressed. It is important to note, however, that although some participants refused to answer an isolated question here or there or left portions of questionnaires unanswered, we did not have anyone totally withdraw from the study. We would like to think that this is because the interview experience was largely positive. It is also possible that once parents and adolescents agreed to participate in the study, they felt a sense of responsibility to continue, even if aspects of the study made them uncomfortable. Nonetheless, when participants were given the opportunity to give us feedback about the study after it was over, not one parent or child reported that they felt coerced or uncomfortable at any point. To the contrary, every indication suggested that the general experience had been a positive.

Issues about coercion and consent were much more salient in SHARP because there were no parents to look after the best interests of our minor participants. Moreover, although the majority of our homeless participants were not ethnic minorities, their histories of abuse, the large number of youth with diagnosable mental disorders, and their glaring lack of access to even basic resources, including food and shelter, made them the more vulnerable population.

The role that homeless youth service providers and advocates played in the design and implementation of SHARP was important to ensure that our research agenda did not inadvertently override concerns for the well-being of youth participants. This was especially important because the lead researcher was, at the outset, not personally familiar with the population under study. The inherent danger in all studies, that research-related priorities may blind researchers to the best interests of study participants, is magnified in cases when the investigator may have limited knowledge of the specific vulnerabilities of the population under study.

Obtaining consent from the parents of runaway, homeless, or street youth is not feasible, as they are not an active part of youth's lives; and, given the histories of these youth, one cannot make the assumption that in most cases such parents would be able to protect their child's best interests or ensure their well-being. Therefore, it was especially important that we construct consent procedures in such a way that consent was maximally comprehensible and transparent to youth (youth who were unlikely to understand what research was about).

In SHARP, the challenge was to make sure that youths not only understood they would be asked painful questions—and that these questions would ask them to recall and speak about painful experiences—but to make sure that they also understood they were consenting to the possibility of being assigned to a treatment condition that some might view as intrusive, even if we believed it to represent a higher standard of care.

We did our best to ensure that youths were fully cognizant of every aspect of the study. Not only did we construct a consent form that was detailed and written at a fifth-grade level or below, but the basic aspects of the study were also explained orally to all participants by investigative team members. Moreover, details of the study were presented to all case managers and all key YouthCare staff so that they could accurately answer questions that a youth might ask in an informal context. The fact that all research interviewers were YouthCare, as opposed to University of Washington, employees also helped to create a context in which the well-being of youths was paramount and in which there was minimal possibility that interviewers might feel the need to coerce youths to participate. That is, even research interviewers were part of an organization dedicated to the welfare of homeless youth, not one where research was paramount.

Despite these safeguards, the fact that monetary incentives were involved could be said to create a coercive environment for these youths because lack of resources are such a major issue for them. In deciding on a payment structure ($25 for initial interview, $15 for follow-up interviews), we had numerous discussions between researchers and service providers at the advisory board level and between researchers and the Washington State and University of Washing IRBs[2] about what payment rate would be appropriate. On one hand, there was some initial pressure from the IRBs to keep payment artificially low, well below what we were paying in other adolescent studies, in order to ensure that money was not the sole reason that youths participated in our study. Although there is certainly something to be said for this line of reasoning, there was also something that we found perverse about paying someone less money because they were poor. In addition, paying homeless youth less for their time than we would other youth seemed to communicate that they were somehow less worthy or that their time was less valuable than the time of others. Although we don't

believe that we would have had fewer participants in our study had we paid less, if we had, it would have sent a message to youth and to staff that is contrary to everything that this research intervention team was trying to communicate.

Another problem was deciding the form in which to provide compensation. Fears were expressed by some that if we paid youth in cash, they would be tempted to go out and buy alcohol or drugs. Although, again, we found such arguments to imply less than a respectful attitude or a positive message for our participants, we did consider other alternatives. We were not able to come up with another feasible avenue for payment. Providing them with a check, as was suggested by one IRB, did not make sense, as few youths had bank accounts or would be comfortable taking a check to the bank. Gift certificates for food did not seem a good alternative because it would require multiple meals to equal the price of payment. In the end, we went with cash, trusting youths to make reasonably good choices about how to spend it.

When we asked youths during their last set of interviews how they had been spending their money, food was the single item mentioned most frequently. None mentioned spending study money on illegal drugs, and only a handful mentioned alcohol, but cigarettes were mentioned quite frequently. This would not have been our choice for what youths should do with their money, but we are quite confident that nobody started to use alcohol or drugs or began to smoke as a result of receiving money in exchange for their time. Instead, we think that if some youths spent their money on drugs, cigarettes, or alcohol, study payment at least saved them from an evening of panhandling or worse activities that they otherwise might have engaged in for the money.

An additional safeguard that we put in place to ensure that youth were not participating in the study under coercive circumstances was the requirement that at the start of each new major section of the interview, interviewers explicitly ask youth if they wanted to continue and remind them that they had already earned compensation if they decided to stop. Six youths (fewer than 3%) took us up on this option. All indications were that the vast majority of youth enjoyed their time with interviewers, although questions were on sensitive topics. In most cases, interviewers reported that youths seemed to be in no rush to end the interview and that many lingered for a while, conversing with the interviewer about the study or unrelated issues. Many asked about subsequent interviews and seemed eager for the next round. In fact, once the study was up and running, the buzz about it was remarkably positive, and it was not uncommon for youth to ask if they qualified for participation. In this vein, one more reason to construct sensitive and appropriate consent techniques is that such procedures are apt to help with recruitment and procedures. At times, the imperatives of good science and those of ethics run at cross-purposes, but often they are one and the same.

ESTABLISHING AND MAINTAINING TRUST: CONFIDENTIALITY AND DISCLOSURE

Issues about confidentiality are paramount during the adolescent years. Fear of disclosure of their private thoughts and fears is among the top reasons they give for failure to seek counseling or professional care, even when they have significant problems or are in need of treatment (Cauce et al., 2002; Cheng, Savageau, Sattler, & DeWitt, 1993; Ginsburg, Slap, Cnaan, Forke, Balsley, & Rouselle, 1995).

On the other hand, recent research has documented that a substantial number of teenagers believe that disclosure of problems in a research context constitutes the equivalent of a cry for help (Fisher, 2003). That is, youth often believe that when adolescents disclose problems on research questionnaires, they are doing so with the hope that the researcher will intervene to obtain help for them.

Issues about confidentiality and disclosure were relatively minor concerns in FASST. The sample was a normative one, so participation in the study could not be viewed, in and of itself, as stigmatizing. Moreover, although we did examine adolescent problems like depression and externalizing behavior, diagnostic scales were not used and adolescents were not asked about suicidal behavior. Thus, we were not in a position to identify problem youth with any certainty. Given the risks of labeling and stigmatization, especially for African American youth, we believed that the dangers of false positives (e.g. identifying as problematic youths without problems) outweighed any benefits that might come from identifying youth who might actually be in need.

Still, we did not want to ignore the legitimate needs of youths with problems. So, we instituted a series of procedures to maximize the chances that youth in need would seek help if appropriate. First, we developed a one-page list of resources in the community available to deal with youth experiencing psychological problems. This list included our own psychology department clinic, which provides reduced-fee psychological services. This referral list was provided to every adolescent or parent of an adolescent who asked questions about services or how to seek treatment.

Participant parents were especially likely to use the research opportunity to ask questions about treatment and how to obtain it. Every time an interviewer gave out the referral list, the parent and/or teen was also given the option of obtaining the help of a clinically licensed psychologist (the first author[4]) in deciding whether a referral might be appropriate. We did not keep track of how often this option was used, but we can recall speaking only to a handful of parents and no teens.

Midway through the study, parents and teens also received a newsletter that contained group-level information about teens' endorsement of items that could be viewed as symptoms of disorder. This newsletter also contained basic referral information. Thus, although we did not make any direct referrals to treatment, nor do we believe it was appropriate for us to do so, we did our best to facilitate effective treatment seeking among teens and parents who were concerned about problem behavior and interested in seeking help. At no point were we concerned about creating conditions that might increase treatment utilization. We did not view this as a serious threat to the validity of our research, although it was longitudinal in nature. Such concerns seemed misplaced in light of the fact that mere study participation might alter developmental trajectories.

Compared with those of FASST, the ethical dilemmas related to confidentiality and disclosure in SHARP were more vexing. Not only were we using diagnostic scales in SHARP, we also asked very detailed questions about suicidal ideation and behavior and about past and potentially ongoing sex with adults.

The latter two issues, suicide ideation and participation in exploitative relationships with adults, were ones we expected to deal with repeatedly. Detailed protocols for how to handle each were developed in consultation with YouthCare and with the Division of Child Protective Services, which is part of DSHS, one of our partners. Youths were told at the outset of the study during the consent stage that if during the course of the interview we became concerned about the possibility that they might hurt themselves or someone else, we would share the information

with their caseworker or seek immediate care. Youths were again reminded of this before beginning the section in which the suicide questions would be asked. In a similar vein, before asking youth about their previous or present history of sexual abuse or sex with adults, we reminded them that we would have to report any incident in which they gave us details about the perpetrator sufficient to identify them. In this sense, we tried to make sure that youth were very aware of the fact that we would, in effect, treat any communication about suicidal behavior as a cry for help. We also made it clear that if they gave us details about perpetrators of child abuse, this would be the equivalent of reporting it to authorities.

Reporting suicidal intent became routine in SHARP, with several dozen reports shared with caseworkers. In one case, when an interview took place during the evening and the adolescent appeared quite agitated, she was walked over to the closest emergency room where she was evaluated and held overnight. Although we never became aware of any youths attempting suicide during their time in the study, there were more than a few times when interviewers found it hard to walk away from youths, despite knowing that the youths were working with a case manager and receiving services.

One of the unexpected ethical (and practical) challenges we faced in this study was the need to develop a system of support for the interviewers. By the end of the first month, we had instituted twice-weekly meetings of the interview team when we discussed issues they might have faced while interviewing or ethical dilemmas they were still thinking over. These meetings often functioned as debriefing sessions during which interviewers had the opportunity to vent about the unfairness of the world and about the plight of victimized and homeless youth.

During the course of the study, we also made several dozen calls to Child Protective

Services to report incidents of previous child abuse. In virtually every case, however, there was not sufficient information to allow for a more complete investigation. Youth generally had no difficulty reporting that they had been abused but seldom provided enough detail for CPS to identify the perpetrator. When the perpetrator was the parent, reports had already been filed in all cases that we heard of. In fact, a third (33%) of all youths had been placed in foster care at least once, in almost all cases due to parental abuse or neglect.

We chose not to report youth's diagnostic status to case managers because they typically did their own psychological assessment as part of the intake process. In cases in which our assessment and that of case managers yielded different information, we were more confident in results obtained by the latter. Case managers also had the option of referring any youth for further psychiatric assessment when they were unsure about a diagnosis. In contrast, our diagnostic interviews were conducted by lay persons with no specialty training in mental health.

The fact that homeless youth were in case management helped to make potentially very difficult questions about disclosure much more mundane. And the fact that research interviewers and case managers were all members of the same staff, worked in the same building, and frequently interacted created an optimal environment, not only for communicating to youth that we all regarded their well-being as paramount but for making this a reality.[5] It would be hard to imagine how to conduct this particular study without developing a public-academic partnership.

TO STUDY OR NOT TO STUDY: WEIGHING THE RISKS AGAINST THE BENEFITS

Assuming that a study is unlikely to result in serious harm, the key ethical question that researchers ask themselves, and that IRBs will ask researchers, is are the benefits of the research likely to outweigh the risks? This is generally a question that is asked at the beginning of a project in making the decision about whether one should go forward. But, in this case, we will try to examine it in retrospect. The two studies we have described were conducted well over a decade ago. What was gained by the youths themselves? By the scientific community? By the therapeutic community? By the service provider community? What might have been lost, or what harm resulted to the youths? To their communities?

Not surprisingly, given that it was a normative sample and that no high-risk procedures were used, we are not aware of any negative consequences to youth or families that resulted from the FASST research. Youth overwhelmingly reported that they enjoyed spending time with the interviewers, despite being asked some questions that might be viewed as intrusive or negative. Although other studies have shown that youth themselves report that answering such questions on a survey might create distress (Fisher, 2003), it has been our experience throughout the years—and in the course of numerous studies, many of them with youth of color—that, at least in a face-to-face interview situation, whatever distress is generated is more than outweighed by the experience of having an adult give them undivided attention and really listen. In thinking about the benefits of research, we consistently underestimate how rare, and how validating, this type of experience is for young people, especially those who are vulnerable or have been marginalized. It is relatively rare in the course of an adolescent's life that an adult will just listen to them for an hour, never saying anything that is judgmental, offering unsolicited advice, or talking about what life was like when they were young.

In the FASST study, our interviewers, who were primarily college students, many of them students of color, reported instances when adolescents showed them their sketch pads or insisted on playing an instrument for them. Youths showed off their rooms to interviewers and bragged about their accomplishments. They complained about little sisters or older brothers and in one case about an abusive uncle, triggering a report to Child Protective Services. With that one exception, they did not reveal serious problems to our team of interviewers, but we did receive some questions from the youths about where they could find help if needed, questions that we gladly answered. Perhaps the most common area of questioning had to do with college. One unintended, or at least unplanned, benefit of this study was that it exposed adolescents to college-attending positive role models, and a significant number of youth took this opportunity to learn a little more about college life and how to best prepare for it.

The warmth that interviewers experienced in their interactions with the adolescents was also evident in their encounters with parents. The parents we interviewed, most of them mothers, seemed overwhelmingly pleased to be spending time talking to someone about their child or about their parenting. They also often asked our interviewers about college and what was needed to be accepted there and do well. Compared with the youths, parents were much more likely to take this opportunity to talk about their children's problems and seek advice. Although our interviewers were not in a position to make professional judgments, they were able to provide referrals and encourage the parents to follow them up. This was an added, and unplanned, benefit of the study.

Although this is not the kind of question that IRBs ask, or that is highlighted by ethics codes, perhaps the biggest risk posed by this study, which focused exclusively on African American youth, was that our research could reinforce negative views or stereotypes about them. Interestingly, this is a concern that

some parents also expressed in no uncertain terms. More than once we were asked, "Please, don't *just* say bad things" about our children or about our parenting. It was a message we took very seriously.

The FASST study yielded many publications, and it serves as one of the first short-term longitudinal studies to focus exclusively on African American youth. It was also one of the first to conduct a videotaped parent-child interaction with this population, a technique that had long been considered the gold standard in studies of White youth. It made methodological contributions by raising questions about how such interactions should be coded and suggesting that one should pay attention to the ethnicity of the interviewers (Gonzales, Cauce, & Mason, 1997), and it made contributions to our understanding of how parental control affects externalizing behavior (Mason, Cauce, & Gonzales, 1997) and school achievement (Gonzales, Cauce, Friedman, & Mason, 1996), suggesting that one cannot talk about optimal levels of control without taking into account the neighborhood context in which youth grow up. But the single event that made us feel most strongly that the benefits had outweighed the risks came during a talk the first author gave at UNC-Chapel Hill (based on work reported in Cauce et al., 1996). An African American woman in the audience, who described herself as the mother of a teenager and a junior high school teacher, approached the first author afterwards to thank her profusely and enthusiastically for "getting it right" and portraying African American mothers in a positive light rather than simply blaming them for the risks faced by their children. One of the most important and seldom mentioned benefits from survey or interview research is that when gotten right, it can give voice to sectors of the population who are seldom included in public conversations. Although we're sure there are many things we missed and might have done better, there is little doubt that when taken as a whole, this was an enterprise that produced much more good than harm.

As we've noted throughout, the risks involved in SHARP were more salient than those in FASST. As an intervention study, so also was the possibility of gain. To minimize the risks, we developed extensive protocols to deal with suicidal behavior and reporting of child abuse. We also very carefully structured our interviews so that, for example, following the section on child abuse, we asked more upbeat questions about plans for the future. Sections when youths were asked to report about potentially difficult past experiences were generally followed by questions that were more neutral or positive. We also trained our interviewers to look for signs of distress and fatigue and empowered them to end the interview or to skip to the next section of the interview if they believed that a youth seemed distressed.

What was more unexpected than the few interviews that were terminated was the length of others. Initial interviews had been structured to last about 60 minutes for each session, and interviewers were instructed to end the interview at about 90 minutes, even if sections had not been completed. During the piloting, we found that the latter was happening so often that we finally divided the interview into two parts, and it was still not unusual for them to last almost 90 minutes each. What took so long wasn't answering the questions themselves, but the chit-chat that was taking place throughout. In more cases than not, youths were enjoying their conversations with interviewers, and they were obviously working to prolong that contact.

Youths repeatedly expressed positive feelings about the study and the interview process, and there were no instances of which we were aware of harm befalling any of the participants as a result of our study. Still, case managers involved with the project did not always understand why we wouldn't try to intervene, on the spot, when a youth was showing obvious signs of depression, and they clearly would have preferred that they (the case managers) do the interviews instead of researchers. The job of the researcher was often portrayed within the agency as a relatively "cushy" one. At times, it was also portrayed as a heartless one, requiring the ability to walk away from youths that were in obvious need.

For the duration of our interview staff's time in the field, biweekly or weekly meetings were necessary (as we previously described), both to discuss the interviews and any issues that had come up and to bolster the morale of the interview team. Interviewers often found it hard to walk away from young people, not knowing if they had a place to stay that night. More than once an interviewer said they had been tempted to bring a street youth home. Knowing that the youths were receiving services wasn't always enough to allay the interviewers' anxieties about youths' well-being; and being portrayed, even teasingly, by clinical staff as heartless didn't help things.

Things did turn around about halfway through the process. Our lead interviewer, Yvette Lohr, wrote a short story called, "The Boy in the Polka Dot Pajamas" that she read to our interview team. In it, she spoke about a young boy she had interviewed repeatedly. Each time he seemed fairly distant, answering questions directly, but offering little in the way of elaboration. Unexpectedly and remarkably, during the third interview, he told Yvette that she was the first adult that he had ever trusted because "You didn't want anything from me." This revelation led to an extended conversation about treatment providers, their expectations, and about his hopes and dreams and future goals. There is no way of knowing whether this happened or not, but he agreed that he would be more open with his case manager and share with her some of what he had shared with Yvette.

We would reprint the story here but didn't keep a copy, and Yvette, still in her early 30s, has passed away. But the fact that Yvette, a very kind hearted person, came to believe in the power of nonintervention and *just* listening really helped to bolster the morale of our interview team. They came to see that in their own way, they were playing a role in making things better for the youths they were growing to care about so deeply. Like Yvette, we too have come to believe that for vulnerable youths who are marginalized and neglected, merely listening can have a curative function. Thus, what is often considered a risk (e.g., asking youth about sensitive issues, then just listening) is often a benefit.

In addition to whatever validation youths may have experienced from being listened to and heard, we were also able to provide more than a hundred youths with state-of-the-art case management services, services that would not otherwise have been available. Initially, even this had been a point of contention with the clinical case management staff. In the early stages of project design, they had lobbied hard to be able to pick which youth were assigned to intensive case management. They assumed it was the better program and that youth with more problems should be assigned to that condition. It was argued by some that to do anything less was unethical, or at least not altogether ethical.

It is easy to understand their point of view, and it took some convincing to help some of the case managers to understand that we shouldn't simply assume that more (treatment) was necessarily better. We're not quite sure that some were ever convinced. What they did come to realize was that the only thing that made the intensive case management services possible in the first place was the study. (YouthCare did not have the money to provide such services otherwise.) So if we did not have rigor in our design, nobody would have received intensive case management services.

In the end, our study suggested that youth in both types of case management, regular (treatment as usual) and intensive (the experimental condition), improved over the course of treatment in various domains, including mental health and housing status. There was also some evidence that, especially for girls, intensive case management led to a greater degree of improvement than regular case management. Case vignettes that describe the types of services that youths received and their response to treatment are provided elsewhere (see Cauce et al., 1994, 1998) and clearly illustrate the high level of immediate and responsive care that intensive case managers were able to give their clients. Such services included (a) providing a diary and writing material to young girls struggling with issues of self-esteem related to a history of abuse, (b) taking a group of urban boys on an outward bound–type program, or (c) simply helping youths find a bed in a local shelter.

Although validation and treatment were those benefits that most directly affected the participating youth, the community of homeless youth as a whole might have gained the most from the research findings themselves. Quite a number of publications have resulted from this study, and they have been cited extensively, not only by other researchers but in a host of policy papers. Closer to home, this research was cited in a series of public meetings and legislative hearings that led to the Hope Act, passed in 1999, championed by Jim Theofilis, one of the case management directors in our study. The Hope Act provided increased temporary residential placements and comprehensive assessments for homeless street youth under 18 (see www .wsipp.wa.gov/rptfiles/HOPEfinal.pdf).

We are certainly not unbiased observers, but it seems quite clear to us that despite considerable risks, SHARP was a study in which benefits greatly outweighed harm. All indications suggest that if there was harm, it was not serious enough to reach anyone's attention. By contrast, the benefits, both to the youths in the study itself and to the broader community of street youth, are quite apparent.

CONCLUSIONS

Almost all health and mental health status indicators suggest that poor youth and youth of color lag behind their White middle-class counterparts (Cauce et al., 2002). In order to begin to bridge this gap, we must not only continue but expand our efforts to conduct health and mental health research that focuses on these health disparities. Minority, poor, and other vulnerable communities' distrust of research and the motivation of researchers have been considered important barriers to such efforts (Corbie-Smith, Thomas, Williams, & Moody-Ayers, 1999; Poussaint & Alexander, 2000). More recently, some have argued that the tightening of ethical codes and IRB restrictiveness constitute yet another barrier (Azar, 2002; Mueller, 2004). Although addressing this second concern is beyond the scope of this paper, it is worth noting that to the degree that IRBs are tightening up on the research they approve, they may not be focusing on those risks that may be most salient to these vulnerable communities.

Ethical codes and IRBs generally focus their attention on the harms or risks that accrue to individual participants in research projects, with little or no attention given to community-level risk or harm. They also make at least some assumptions about participants in research that may not be true. For example, it is typically believed that study participants will experience discomfort and distress when asked questions about painful incidents in their lives (e.g., child abuse) or about distressing thoughts or problems (e.g., suicidal thoughts, about lying

or cheating). This is also an assumption made by some members of the public (Fisher, 2003); however, it has been our experience that many, perhaps most, individuals from marginalized groups welcome the opportunity to talk about themselves and their problems. Moreover, they find the nonjudgmental listening in which research interviewers are trained to be validating, producing more comfort than distress.

In contrast, one of the concerns we heard most often from participants, especially ethnic minorities, was fear for how they would be portrayed in research studies. They wondered whether the portrayal of their communities by researchers would be overwhelmingly negative and how might this affect them. This is not a concern that IRBs address, nor do we believe it is one that they can address, at least not effectively.

The underlying premise of this chapter is that we can, indeed that we must, carry out research that deals with sensitive issues with vulnerable populations. The cost of not doing so is too high. We've already seen some of the consequences that come from, for example, not using children as subjects in studies that look at the effectiveness of medication for depression and what can happen when women are excluded from studies on coronary health. We cannot develop competent and effective treatments for those communities most in need if we exclude them from our research.

The challenge is finding ways in which to conduct important, and sensitive, research while treating vulnerable populations and the communities they come from with all due respect. In this chapter, we have tried to illustrate some ways in which we have tried to do this in our research. The key, as we see it, is involving community members in as many phases of the study as possible, beginning with the study design. The creation of public-academic or university-community partnerships can go a long way toward addressing the kinds of ethical dilemmas most likely to be salient when working with poor and/or minority populations (see Suarez-Balcazar et al., 2002, for a discussion of important characteristics in such partnerships). These formal partnerships are especially important when conducting intervention research.

In lieu of official partnerships, even informal consultation with key community members or the conduct of focus groups with individuals similar to those who will be participating in the study can be extremely helpful. We do not believe that it would be especially useful or effective to mandate that all studies have community advisory boards.

We are not even sure that like-minded researchers would always agree as to the type of board or partnership that would be optimally desirable. What we do believe is that over time most researchers will find that in most cases, community advisory boards will be in their best interests and in the best interests of their research, not to mention the best interests of the participants. The best route for arriving at this goal is not through coercion but through dialogue. Too often we focus only on the results of our work and not on the process that has gotten us there. It is wonderful to have this opportunity to do the latter.

NOTES

1. This is used as an example because most of the readership is apt to be familiar with the bell curve; however, much of the research in this book actually came from databases that had not been expressly collected with the analyses that Hernstein and Murray (1994) had in mind.

2. Because of the involvement of UW researchers and the Washington State Department of Social and Health Services, the study had to be approved by two separate IRBs.

3. Each interview had between four and six sections.

4. Since then the first author has let her license expire because she is no longer a treatment provider.

5. We have not been able to recreate this relationship in some subsequent studies with this population.

REFERENCES

Azar, B. (2002). Ethics at the cost of research. *APA Monitor, 33,* 37–38.

Balcazar, F. E., Keys, C. B., Kaplan, D. L., & Suarez-Balcazar, Y. (1998). Participatory action research and people with disabilities: Principles and challenges. *Canadian Journal of Rehabilitation, 12,* 105–112.

Boykin, W. A. (1986). The triple quandary and the schooling of Afro-American children. In U. Neisser (Ed.), *The school achievement of minority children: New perspectives* (pp. 57–92). Hillsdale, NJ: Lawrence Erlbaum.

Brooks-Gunn, J., & Reiter, E. O. (1990). The role of pubertal processes. In S. S. Feldman & G. R. Elliott (Eds.), *At the threshold: The developing adolescent* (pp. 16–53). Cambridge, MA: Harvard University Press.

Cauce, A. M., & Domenech-Rodriguez, M. (2002). Latino families: Myths and realities. In J. Contreras (Ed.), *Latino youth and families facing the future* (pp. 123–147). New York: Basic Books.

Cauce, A. M., Domenech-Rodriguez, M., Paradise, M., Cochran, B., Shea, J. M., Srebnik, D., et al. (2002). Cultural and contextual influences in mental health help seeking: A focus on ethnic minority youth. *Journal of Consulting and Clinical Psychology, 70,* 44–55.

Cauce, A. M., Gonzales, N., Hiraga, Y., Grove, K., & Ryan-Finn, K. (1996). African American mothers and their adolescent daughters: Intimacy, autonomy, and conflict. In B. J. Leadbeater & N. Way (Eds.), *Urban girls: Resisting stereotypes, creating identities* (pp. 100–116). New York: New York University Press.

Cauce, A. M., Morgan, C. J., Wagner, V., Moore, E., Wurzbacher, K., Weeden, K., et al. (1994). Effectiveness of case management for homeless adolescents: Results for the three month follow-up. *Journal of Emotional and Behavioral Development, 2,* 219–227.

Cauce, A. M., Paradise, M., Embry, L., Morgan, C., Lohr, Y., Theopolis, J., et al. (1998). Homeless youth in Seattle: Youth characteristics, mental health needs, and intensive case management. In M. Epstein, K. Kutash, & A. Duchnowski (Eds.), *Outcomes for children and youth with behavioral and emotional disorders and their families: Programs and evaluation best practices* (pp. 1–37). Austin, TX: Pro-ed.

Cauce, A. M, Paradise, M., Ginzler, J. A., Embry, L., Morgan, C. J., Lohr, Y., et al. (2000). The characteristics and mental health of homeless adolescents: Age and gender differences. *Journal of Emotional and Behavioral Disorders, 22,* 45–63.

Cheng, T. L., Savageau, A. L., Sattler, T. G., & DeWitt, T. (1993). Confidentiality in health care. A survey of knowledge, perceptions, and attitudes among high school students. *JAMA, 269,* 1404–1407.

Chun, K. M., & Akutsu, P. D. (2003). Acculturation among ethnic minority families. In K. M. Chun, P. B. Organista, & G. Marin. (Eds.), *Acculturation: Advances in theory, measurement and applied research* (pp. 95–119). Washington, DC: APA.

Corbie-Smith G., Thomas S. B., Williams M. V., & Moody-Ayers, S. (1999). Attitudes and beliefs of African Americans toward participation in medical research. *Journal of General Internal Medicine, 14,* 537–46.

Dachner, N., & Tarasuk, G. (2002). Homeless "squeegee kids": Food insecurity and daily survival. *Social Science and Medicine, 54,* 1039–1049.

Feldman, S. S., & Elliot, G. R. (Eds.). (1990). *At the threshold.* Cambridge, MA: Harvard University Press.

Fisher, C. B. (2003). Adolescent and parent perspectives on ethical issues in youth drug use and suicide survey research. *Ethics & Behavior, 13,* 302–331.

Fisher, C. B., Hoagwood, K., Duster, T., Grisso, T., Frank, D. A, Macklin, R., et al. (2002). Research ethics for mental health science involving ethnic minority children and youth. *American Psychologist, 57,* 1024–1040.

Ginsburg, K. R., Slap, G. B., Cnaan, A., Forke, C. M., Balsley, D. M., & Rouselle, M. (1995). Adolescents' perceptions of factors affecting their decisions to seek health care. *JAMA, 272,* 1913–1918.

Gonzales, N., Cauce, A. M., Friedman, R. J., & Mason, C. A. (1996). Family, peer and neighborhood influences on academic achievement among African-American adolescents: One year prospective effects. *American Journal of Community Psychology, 24,* 365–387.

Gonzales, N., Cauce, A. M., & Mason, C. (1997). Interobserver agreement in the assessment of parental behavior and parent-child conflict: African American mothers, daughters, and independent observers. *Child Development, 67,* 1483–1498.

Herrnstein, R., & Murray, C. (1994). *The bell curve: Intelligence and class structure in American life.* New York: Free Press.

Jason, L. A., Keys, C. B., Suarez-Balcazar, Y., Taylor, R. R., & Davis, M. I. (2002). *Participatory community research: Theories and methods in action.* Washington, DC: APA.

Mason, C. A., Cauce, A. M., & Gonzales, N. (1997). Parents and peers in the lives of African American adolescents: An interactive approach to the study of problem behavior. In R. Taylor & M. Wang (Eds.), *Social and emotional adjustment and family relations in ethnic minority families* (pp. 26–51). Mahwah, NJ: Lawrence Erlbaum.

Mason, C., Cauce, A. M., Gonzales, N., & Hiraga, Y. (1994). Adolescent problem behavior: The effect of peers and the moderating role of father absence and the mother child relationship. *American Journal of Community Psychology, 22,* 723–743.

Mason C., Cauce, A. M., Gonzales, N., Hiraga, Y., & Grove, K. (1994). An ecological model of externalizing in African American adolescents: No family is an island. *Journal of Research on Adolescence, 4,* 639–655.

Macklin, R. (1989). The paradoxical case of payment as benefit to research subjects. *IRB: A Review of Human Subjects Research, 11,* 6.

Mueller, J. (2004, July). *Best practices: What perspective, what evidence?* Paper presented at the American Psychological Association symposium on Protecting Science and Academic Freedom from Institutional Review Boards, Honolulu, Hawaii.

Poussaint, A., & Alexander, A. (2000). *Lay my burden down: Unraveling suicide and the mental health crisis among African Americans.* Boston: Beacon Press.

Ruddick, S. (1996). *Young and homeless in Hollywood.* London: Routledge.

Satcher, D. (2001). *Mental Health: Culture, Race and Ethnicity.* Rockville, MD: Department of Health and Human Services, Center for Mental Health Services.

Sieber, J. (1994). Scientists' response to ethical issues in research. In W. R. Shadish & S. Fuller (Eds.), *The social psychology of science* (pp. 72–93). London: Guilford Press.

Suarez-Balcazar, Y., Davis, M. I., Ferrari, J., Nyden, P., Olson, B., Alvarez, J., et al. (2002). Fostering university-community partnerships: A framework and exemplar. In L. A. Jason, C. B. Keys, Y. Suarez-Balcazar, R. R. Taylor, M. Davis, J. Durlak, & D. Isenberg (Eds.), *Participatory community research: Theories and methods in action* (pp. 105–120). Washington, DC: APA.

CHAPTER 12

Ethical Research Dilemmas With Minority Elders

Susan Krauss Whitbourne

Joshua R. Bringle

Barbara W. K. Yee

David A. Chiriboga

Keith Whitfield

OPENING THEMES

Culturally responsive ethical concerns in research and practice are important but receive little attention in the empirical literature on ethnic minority elders. Much of the literature with minority elders cites anecdotal evidence drawn from post hoc observations by investigators or by implication from service delivery and practice. This is a significant gap in the research literature, yet little progress has been made, and the topic remains a fruitful avenue of research. The present chapter reviews a diverse set of literature from aging and ethnic minority, cultural competence research, and practice. The goal is to both inform and set forth a research agenda to address this gap in the scientific literature on ethical issues in research with ethnic minority elders.

Research and practice have been strongly influenced by the interface of three initiatives: cultural competence, health disparities, and the need to respect the privacy and dignity of patients (i.e., Health Insurance Portability and Accountability Act or HIPAA). Combined, these initiatives underlie most of the salient issues in an ongoing debate about ethics, aging, culture, and ethnicity. The debate itself can be framed by the following questions: Do aging researchers and service providers engage in ethics code interpretations, implementation, and practice that translate appropriately in specific cultural and situational contexts, across worldviews, and for ethnic subpopulations? Do differences in research and patient care expectancies of ethnic minority elderly participants, families, and ethnic communities vary by culture, age cohort, and social class? If age, culture, and race influence ethical dilemmas, how do researchers address these factors in their recruitment and retention, research designs, and methodologies? Tensions arising from this debate led to the development of the surgeon general's report "Mental Health: Culture, Race and Ethnicity, A Supplement to Mental Health: A Report of the Surgeon General" (U.S. Department of Health and Human Services, 2001).

GENERAL CONSIDERATIONS

In the scanty empirical research literature on ethical concerns for multicultural populations, there is little consensus, but many authors do suggest it is theoretically possible to identity a set of human values and ethical principles with universal application. The universality of certain human and ethical values is often obscured by different behavioral expressions of perceptual, cognitive, and emotional underpinnings that vary across cultures, ethnic or gender subpopulations, and situations (Killien et al., 2000; Yee, 1999a, 1999c, 2004). Even professionals are not immune to such influences; researchers and service delivery professionals have been found to interpret ethical codes quite differently because they view these codes through their own cultural and professional filters (Pack-Brown & Williams, 2003; Peterson, 1997).

Equally important in any scientific investigation with ethnic minority elderly populations is detection of important age and ethnic differences in application or interpretation of ethical principles that are distinct from universal ethical principles. For instance, culture has a powerful way of influencing an individual family's and ethnic community's interpretation of the world and more specifically, the conduct of research and its ethics. Culture has numerous domains, but one of the pivotal cultural domains has to do with the perceived and accepted role of the individual (i.e., locus and agent of behavior and decision making) as opposed to the focal role of the family or larger community.

Decision Making as a Collective Process With Minority Elders

The crux of research ethics with ethnic minority elders is whether potential research participants place more emphasis on their own role as an individual decision maker, as opposed to family decision making based on the collective good, reflective of multicultural family dynamics and social interactions in late life. Collectivists are said to subordinate their personal goals to those of their collectives (e.g., family, community). Individualists are said to be more detached from their collective and depend on interpersonal contracts; they feel autonomous, and their social behavior maximizes personal enjoyment. Triandis (1995) summarized the literature on collectivists as indicating that the latter (a) consider doing their duty as more important and rewarding than their own happiness, (b) may have difficulty making decisions quickly because consensus and group decision making about the best course of action is the expectation, (c) exhibit relatively large differences between private and public behavior, and (d) expect relationships to evolve over an extended period of time, and therefore long-term cultivation of relationships is expected to occur prior to expecting the relationships to produce immediate benefits for participants.

Applying this theoretical framework, it can be hypothesized that individuals who adhere to a more collectivistic worldview are likely to want to involve others in key decisions about health care or even participation in a research project To expand on this last point, the collectivist cultural characteristic found among the traditional members of multicultural populations regard the central role of the family unit, rather than the individual, as the central locus of decision making

(Chun & Akutsu, 2003; Santisteban & Mitrani, 2003). Almost twice as many minority elders as White elders live with other family members (Angel & Hogan, 2004), and family members may play a more active role in decision making for elderly relatives. Collectivist cultures may regard older adults as vulnerable and dependent members of their family much earlier in the elder's journey to the end of life. The family unit often becomes the decision-making body for research participation, providing consent for starting or stopping medical interventions and advanced directives compliance. Acculturation by family members may attenuate traditional behavioral expressions of these collectivistic family values, but surprisingly, some research suggests these collectivist values may linger three generations past the immigrant generation (Yee, Huang, & Lew, 1998).

The roles of stigma, self-disclosure, and privacy. The literature is just beginning to provide an understanding of the roles that stigma, self-disclosure, and privacy play in research participation, ethical research conduct, and vulnerable ethnic minority populations. The research on HIV/AIDS reveals a very powerful influence of stigma on testing and help seeking for these stigmatizing conditions. In collectivist cultures, stigma plays an even more powerful role in restricting willingness to reveal the stigmatizing condition and what individuals would consider private information to outsiders. The resulting shame and embarrassment reflects badly, not only on the individual in question but on the reputation of the whole extended family. Some cultures regard public acknowledgement of familial genetic diseases or mental illnesses to be problematic, avoiding this at all costs, even to placing a person's life at risk. Culturally identified sources of stigma, its disclosure, and potential violation of privacy are very powerful forces in willingness to

participate in research studies on such topics. The role of stigma and privacy in conduct of ethical research with minority elders must be examined more closely.

The role of culture in research on end-of-life issues. The end-of-life and death-and-dying decision-making literature provides other examples of how culture may influence research participation, service delivery, and ethics. Blackhall, Murphy, Frank, Michel, and Azen (1995) compared Mexican, Korean, African, and Caucasian Americans on patient autonomy and end-of-life interventions. These authors found that Mexican and Korean Americans were less likely than African and Caucasian Americans to believe a patient should be told about a metastatic cancer diagnosis. Truth telling about a terminal condition may be culturally driven by the notion that it would be stressful for dying patients and would hasten their deaths in contrast to the full patient disclosure that is mandated by ethical principles of research review boards in the United States.

There are a number of studies highlighting the influence of culture and end-of-life decision making. Mouton, Espino, and Esparza (2000) discussed ways in which religious beliefs and ethnic group history create certain preferences for end-of-life care among African Americans. Those authors found that racism decreased levels of trust, resulting in preference for life-sustaining measures even when these measures were futile or resulted in a poorer quality of life. By implication, African Americans may be leery of any research participation or experimental treatments other than those proposed by a trusted health care professional. Yeo and Hikoyeda (2000) suggested that Asian and Pacific Islander families made end-of-life decisions for their elderly relatives and that the family typically did not reveal a terminal status to their dying relative. Such an approach to family decision making may conflict with legal obligations that advanced directives be obtained prior to a crisis situation and that family consensus decision making be made in consultation with the elderly relative. Both from an ethical and cultural competence perspective, this latter recommendation might best take into account the acculturation level of family members and the family's willingness to reveal terminal status to their dying relatives. By implication, it is a culturally responsive research and practice strategy to consult Asian and Pacific Islander families about enrolling their family members as research subjects or when making major medical decisions.

Similarly, reporting on the Hispanic perspective, Talamantes, Gomez, and Braun (2000) documented the critical importance associated with the cultural values of *familismo* (family needs take precedence over individual needs), *personalismo* (trust building developed over time and based on mutual respect), *jerarquismo* (respect for hierarchy), *presentismo* (emphasis on the present, not on the past or future), and *espiritism* (belief in spirits that influence well-being, death, and dying). Hispanic cultural values should be incorporated into ethical practice in research and provision of services. Cultural norms and scripts in American Indian and Alaska Native tribes have influence over ethics, research participation, and consent for medical interventions among American Indian and Alaska Natives (Manson, Garroutte, Goins, & Henderson, 2004). We have just begun to understand how cultural tenets influence the outcomes from ethical dilemmas in research and service delivery for ethnic minority elders. There are more questions to be answered than there are answers for addressing the issue of how to conduct ethical research that is culturally responsive to the unique historical experiences of minority elders.

The remaining sections of the chapter present information on demographic issues, conceptual models, respecting differences, ethical guidelines, and future directions for minority research related to ethical issues. As we proceed, we will use the following case study to illustrate key points.

CASE STUDY

Mrs. Kim Jung, a 76-year-old, lives in a small college town in New England. She came to the United States from Korea nearly 30 years ago and was widowed 6 months ago. Mrs. Jung moved from a large metropolitan area to live near her children, both of whom work at the college. Prior to her retirement, Mrs. Jung was a full-time homemaker married to an owner of a small "mom and pop" convenience store. She came to this country with the equivalent of a 10th-grade education, but soon after arriving she took advantage of night school classes to achieve her general equivalency degree. These days Mrs. Jung attends daily activities at the local community center and enjoys participating in activities such as bridge and an occasional yoga class. On a few occasions, she has traveled with groups from the community center to area museums and theater performances. Her apartment is located in a low-rent building for older adults, and although she lives completely independently, she is assigned to a social worker in the community center. Lately, Mrs. Jung has noticed that it is more difficult for her to remember some of the information she needs to carry out her daily routines, such as taking her medications and paying her bills. She has started to suffer from insomnia, and in addition to hypertension, she suffers from arthritis, diabetes, and osteoporosis; however, Mrs. Jung prefers not to focus on her illnesses and instead attempts to maintain a cheerful disposition. Her social worker has begun to make inquiries about moving Mrs. Jung to an assisted living facility and has spoken to Mrs. Jung's children about finances and other practical arrangements related to the move. During an afternoon at the community center, Mrs. Jung is approached by a research assistant working in the psychology department of the local college who is seeking volunteers for a study on exercise and cognitive functioning in older adults. Mrs. Jung is interested in participating and eagerly signs the consent form stating that she is being asked to participate in a study on the effectiveness of exercise in promoting psychological functioning. If she is placed in the treatment group, she will learn to use an elliptical training machine and weight-lifting equipment and then be asked to complete 45 minutes of exercise per session, three times a week. If she is not placed in the experimental group, she will spend 45 minutes, three times a week, sitting alone in a lounge in the community center where she will occupy herself with sedentary activities. Tests of cognition will focus on attention and will be administered on a personal computer in the researcher's laboratory.

BACKGROUND ON THE OLDER POPULATION

The aging of the overall population is becoming a phenomenon that is difficult to ignore. On a daily basis, news organizations report the impact of changing demographics on health care, the economy, and lifestyles. In fact, the number of Americans over the age of 65 years grew from 3.1 million in 1900 (about 4% of the population) to 35.3 million in the year 2001, equaling 12.4% of the total U.S. population (U.S. Bureau of the Census [Census], 2003). The highest rate of increase within the 65 and older population is of the oldest-old, those who are 85 years of age and older. This age group is projected to increase from 4.4 million (1.5% of

the total U.S. population) to 8.9 million (2.5% of the population) by the year 2030 and even higher to 19.4 million by the year 2050 (4.8% of the population). Centenarians are the fastest growing of all older age groups. In 1990, it was estimated that there were 37,306 centenarians in the United States. By 2000, this number increased by 35% to 50,545 (Administration on Aging, 2001), and by 2050, there will be 1.1 million centenarians (0.3% of the population) (Census, 2003). These large increases in the 65 and older population are being driven by the movement of the baby boomers who are expected to continue to live into their 80s, 90s, and 100s and hence increase the numbers of very old individuals well into the 21st century (Minino, Arias, Kochanek, Murphy, & Smith, 2002).

Changes in Gender and Minority Distributions

Of relevance to this chapter is the fact that the demographic increases disproportionately reflect changes in gender and minority distributions. Partly as a result of reductions in maternal mortality that came about fairly early in the previous century, for many years more women than men have survived into later life. Currently women over the age of 65 account for about 59% of the total over-65 population. The gender gap widens for those in the 85 and over category, with 71% females and 29% males, and extends even further to 79% females of all those over 100 compared with 21% males (Krach & Veloff, 1999; Meyer, 2001). Thus, with each successively older group of individuals past age 65, the imbalance between females and males grows even greater. This disparity between the genders, however, is expected to diminish by the year 2030 when the baby boomers reach advanced old age. At that time, there will be 56% females and 44% males in the total over-65 population, and 64% females and 36% males among those over the age of 85 years (Census, 2001).

A demographic imperative and lifelong disparities provide a compelling argument for increasing research with ethnic minority elders and, hence, growing sensitivity to ethical issues with this population. The number of ethnic minority elders is projected to grow more rapidly than the number of non-Hispanic White elders over the next 50 years (Angel & Hogan, 2004). Ethnic minority elders will grow in percentage from 12.3% in 2000 to 14.1% in 2020 and to 18.3% of the elderly population in 2050. The number of Black elders is estimated to grow from 2.9 million in 2000 to 8.6 million in 2050. Other races, besides White and Black, are expected to grow from 984,000 in 2000 to 5.8 million by 2050. The Black elderly group was the largest minority population in 2000. Hispanic elderly was the next largest group in 2000 but will be the largest minority elderly group by 2030. Hispanic elders, of any race, are projected to climb most rapidly from 1.5 million in 2000 to 13.8 in 2050. There are 861,725 Asian elders, with the fastest rate of growth fueled by immigration. There were 43,802 Native Hawaiian and Pacific Islander elders in the 2000 censuses. The number of Asian and Pacific Islander elders is estimated to double between now and 2050. A large part of this phenomenal growth in the Asian and Pacific Islander elderly segment is graying baby boomers and additional new immigrants. In 2000, there were 259,663 Alaska Native and American Indian elders in the United States, and this number is expected to grow by slightly over 1.5%. Hispanic and Asian Americans who report more than two racial memberships will become an increasingly larger and more important segment of the elderly population. Although the numbers and proportion of minority elders are growing, there are many disparities in the quality

of their lives. Therefore, there is a great imperative to seek justice and increase the quality of research on this underresearched group of vulnerable elders.

Despite the increases in the population of older minority adults, there is remarkably little in the way of theory and research to examine ethical considerations in soliciting these individuals as research participants. As we explore these ethical considerations, our intent is not only to summarize the existing work, but also to contribute ideas to shape future work so that aging issues are adequately addressed in the context of discussing ethical issues in research with minority populations. Furthermore, although there is a long held myth that people become more similar as they age, in actuality the opposite is true. Neugarten, Havighurst, and Tobin (1968) pointed out many years ago that the increasing statistical variance associated with age in many standard psychological measures provides evidence that people become more distinct and less like others as they become older. Older adults are a highly diverse segment of the population in terms of their physical functioning, psychological performance, socioeconomic status, and lifestyle (Nelson & Dannefer, 1992). This fact makes even more pressing the need for research on older adults from diverse populations and will require that researchers more fully elaborate the appropriate procedures and controls to ensure that their rights are protected and respected.

Variations in Later Life in Health and Mortality by Race and Ethnicity

It is generally recognized that social and cultural aspects of race and ethnicity may continue to influence an individual's development in adulthood through the structure of a society and through the existence of systematic biases against people identified with that race (Whitbourne, 2005). For example, health problems and mortality rates are higher for African Americans than for Whites. Although these differences in health and mortality in part may be attributed to lack of opportunities for education, well-paying jobs, and adequate health care, it is thought that systematic discrimination also takes its toll on health by increasing the levels of stress experienced by African Americans (Clark, Anderson, Clark, & Williams, 1999).

The continuing influence of race and ethnicity is manifest, not only at the individual level but at the multiple levels of the family, community, and society. For example, people with certain cultural expectations may exhibit respect for older adults only through provision of personal caregiving because they may feel a greater sense of obligation to care for their aging parents and other frail family members. Aging is influenced by race and ethnicity through a variety of physiological functions, in part through genetic inheritance and through lifelong exposure via social class and educational strata or cultural habits and traditions. Finally, discrimination against people of certain ethnic backgrounds may serve the same function as race in limiting the opportunities for educational and occupational achievements.

Impact of Socioeconomic Status on Health

Along with race and ethnicity, socioeconomic status has a strong association with physical and mental health outcomes in later life. Race and socioeconomic status are clearly related, particularly for African Americans, who tend to have lower socioeconomic status. Attempts to partial out the contributions of these factors in the equation become very complicated (Clark et al.,

1999), particularly when age and gender are added to the mix. At the same time, it is now generally acknowledged that education is associated with greater access to information about health care and more opportunities to utilize effectively preventative measures. Consequently, it is thought that socioeconomic status contributes independently to the prediction of health and physical functioning in late adulthood.

Implications of Changing Demographics on Research With Minority Populations

A potential danger is that researchers may conclude that economic factors alone play the major role in understanding development in later adulthood. In addition to examining the impact of culture and social class, researchers should also take care to consider other sociocultural factors related to gender, race, and ethnicity when studying development and well-being in later life. Further, researchers must be alert to the varying levels of familiarity with research methods that older adults have, based on their own exposure to resources in the media, the scientific literature, and other outlets of public information. What seems commonplace to a researcher, such as the notion of a control group, may not be so obvious to older or limited English-speaking participants. Special efforts, accordingly, need to be made to ensure that older adults are informed in a language that they can understand about procedures to which they will be exposed. In our case study, Mrs. Jung has been asked to sign a consent form stating that she may or may not be placed in the exercise group. The research assistant must take care to explain that because this is an experimental study, Mrs. Jung may not be assigned to the exercise group and thus may not be involved in activity that could help her.

CONCEPTUAL MODELS IN UNDERSTANDING CROSS-CULTURAL RESEARCH

The research cited in this chapter thus far reflects several underlying models that either implicitly or explicitly guide researchers as they think about and investigate age, culture, race, and ethnicity. Cauce, Coronado, and Watson (1998) have identified three models often used in conceptualizing and interpreting results from cross-cultural research. These models, which to varying extents reflect oversimplifications or misinterpretations of underlying issues, are the (a) cultural deviance model, (b) cultural equivalence model, and (c) cultural variant model.

The cultural deviance model proposes that groups who exhibit shortcomings from group norms are considered deviant and inferior. Attributing various advantages or superior performance to certain cultural groups effectively blames other cultural groups for not having the same ideals, resources, attitudes, and beliefs as the majority culture. The cultural equivalence model proposes that superior socioeconomic status (SES) provides advantages that translate into superior performance. Placing culpability solely on SES, however, shifts responsibility and diverts critical attention from other factors such as culture, education, or discrimination history. The cultural variant model assumes that differences are adaptations to external forces and exemplify cultural resilience in the face of oppression. This third model by definition promotes an appreciation of between-group differences and challenges researchers to explore within-group heterogeneity.

Examples of each of these models can be found in the current literature. The cultural variant model is important not only for the design and interpretation of research but has useful applications in the translation of research into practice. The presentation of findings in a manner that accurately depicts the life circumstances of ethnic minority elders will reduce stereotypes, will be more informative, and will serve the public good of eliminating disparities in late life based on ethnicity, race, and gender.

RESPECTING DIFFERENCES IN A RESEARCH CONTEXT

Our knowledge about differences within and between cultural groupings can grow only to the extent that researchers make a concerted effort to include systematically ethnic minorities in the sample pool. This does not mean simply including numbers that reflect their group proportions in the population, because this process may not yield numbers and power that are sufficient to examine group differences. Indeed, including proportions representative of the population can simply mean compliance with institutional review board or federal guidelines. A valid test for appreciating group differences must be translated into specific research designs and methodologies that allow for testing such differences. For instance, if we need to know about immigrant Hispanic or Asian elderly, the majority of whom are limited English proficient, investigators must develop language-of-origin, culturally competent questionnaires and provide translators for conduct of face-to-face studies. It is not sufficient to obtain this information by oversampling Hispanic or Asian women in English language–only national surveys. English-speaking immigrant elders have distinct issues relative to their limited English counterparts. Pursuit of such an important goal does not necessarily require the costly solution of dramatic increases in sample size, because in some cases it may actually be more appropriate to conduct qualitative analyses in order to understand properly how a behavior or issue may be experienced in a specific ethnic minority elderly group.

Factors Involved in Studying Aging Ethnic Minority Populations

Culturally appropriate studies provide researchers with an opportunity to examine more properly phenomena that are embedded or connected to culture. Such studies must take into consideration a number of factors that may be taken for granted in studies of the majority population, paying particular attention to recruitment strategies, design, instrumentation, analyses, and interpretations. Recruitment of minorities has perhaps received the most recent attention of these factors. Lack of attention to the lifestyle and views of cultural groups driven by historical experiences, in particular, has led to difficulty in recruiting older minority participants into clinical research studies (Curry & Jackson, 2003). Some of the current difficulty in recruitment efforts of African Americans, for example, comes from the latter group's awareness of past research that was poorly designed, or, in the case of the infamous Tuskegee Syphilis Study, clearly unethical (Bowman, 1991; Gamble, 1993). Another example is an unintended breach of privacy in the use and storage of genetic materials in large electronic databases that contained data codes that could be linked to village, tribe, and location, or to specific families in American Indian communities (Burhansstipanov, Bemis, & Dignan, 2002).

Although there are now safeguards in place to protect subjects in human experimentation, these measures have not erased the concern and fear among many African Americans and other minorities that their rights will be abrogated for the sake of medical research (Gamble, 1993). This fear of medical research and mistrust of medical researchers has contributed to the low participation rates and subsequent underrepresentation of minorities, especially African Americans, in clinical trials (King, 1992; Smith, 1991; Svensson, 1989). The legacy of experimental procedures without consent, or data use that goes beyond the purpose stated in the original consent, continues today. Another ethical briar patch comes from research in developing countries where smaller costs of clinical trials research draw drug companies to large pools of potential subjects, lured to participate by the prospect of medical care and financial incentives without fully understanding the implications and risks of participation in drug-testing clinical trials.

Examples of Culturally Appropriate Methods

There have been advances in considering ethically appropriate methods for recruiting older minorities. For example, Unson, Dunbar, Curry, Kenyon, and Prestwood (2001) conducted a comparison of different strategies and suggested that scientists need an appreciation of the cultural, historical, and social factors that influence older African Americans during recruitment efforts and in their responses to the research protocol. They also suggested that password-protected computer strategies could be used so that sensitive data could be removed from public use files and compiled as larger aggregated files. The experiences of other researchers suggest the critical importance of researchers becoming involved in the communities they study and demonstrating their personal valuation of the community and its residents. Holkup, Tripp-Reimer, Salois, and Weinert (2004) successfully used a community-based, participatory action–based approach when conducting an intervention with a group of Native Americans that included elders. Enhancing true partnerships with the community and collaborative research are a more direct approach to enhance significantly the ethical conduct of research with ethnic minority elders.

Importance of Considering Strengths of Aging Minority Populations

The concerns voiced by ethnic minorities also arise from problematic and biased conclusions generated from investigators unfamiliar with the ethnic community. For example, conclusions from much of the past research on African Americans do not reflect the strengths that African Americans possess but rather focus only on the differences from Caucasians. These differences may be presented as deviations from some normative standard for aging, largely developed on White, middle-class elderly populations. The interpretation of findings and study hypotheses are often not theory driven, nor do they accurately or sufficiently encompass the complex interrelationships among social, psychological, and biological factors that contribute to the human conditions as experienced by African Americans. Unson et al. (2001) examined the perceptions and attitudes toward research, particularly the cost/benefit thinking that African American women may use to decide if they will participate in clinical research. Such an approach identifies the factors needed to understand what may motivate potential subjects to participate and what information must be given to develop trust between researchers and African American subjects.

Not only is there concern from participants, but there are scientific issues concerning the most appropriate methodological approaches that will lead to the advancement and ethical conduct of research on older minorities. King (1992) writes that due to racism in American society, there are strong beliefs in scientific writing about the superior status of Caucasians and the inherent inferiority of African Americans. Furthermore, examinations of racial differences between African Americans and Caucasians are likely to be studied in a manner that burdens rather than benefits African Americans.

The discussion in the remainder of this section considers issues dealing with three common procedural challenges: those regarding the recruitment and locating of subjects, the willingness of potential participants to participate, and instrumentation. We also bring up once again the role of federal regulations as they apply to the ethics of caring and studying individuals with limited English proficiency.

Recruitment and Location Problems

A problem common in research with the elderly, but one magnified when studying minorities, is that our recruitment efforts often ignore those who are in greatest risk: the invisible minorities who fall through the cracks of standard recruitment efforts. Studies of African Americans and Asian subgroups often rely on religious organizations and local community or cultural groups for names of potential participants. As another example, studies of the homeless are unlikely to include many Hispanics because there is some evidence that they are unlikely to be found in the same area as homeless Anglo and African Americans (e.g., Conroy & Heer, 2003). For such reasons, recruitment and location are pivotal issues that should be addressed if the goal is an accurate representation of the population of interest. Fortunately, there resources available that can facilitate this effort.

For the researcher unfamiliar with the specific ethnic minority elderly population of interest, it may be helpful to obtain an overview of where participants live. As noted earlier, this is particularly important when studying older minorities because not only are there fewer minorities than the majority population in most geographic areas, but also the density and proportions of elders are often markedly lower than that found in non-Hispanic Whites. As a start, one can examine tables created by the American

Factfinder Web site (http://factfinder.census .gov). This Web site can map geographic area concentration by age and by such racial and ethnic categories as people who are White alone, non-Hispanic White alone, Black or African American alone, American Indian or Alaskan Native alone, Native Hawaiian and Other Pacific Islander alone, Asian alone, persons who are some other race alone, persons who are Hispanic or Latino and of any race, and various combinations of the preceding. Maps can be generated and "zoomed" from the national to the state level and street level. These maps can be modified to display concentrations, not only by age but more specifically by income and gender. Hence, it can be useful to identify areas to target for face-to-face interviews or even as a first step in identifying telephone exchanges.

One ethical issue that may arise is what to do when the most cost-effective sampling strategies will clearly omit certain sectors of an ethnic group. For example, in face-to-face interviews, it is most cost-efficient (i.e., cheaper) to sample in areas where there are high concentrations of the targeted population. The researcher may need to consider whether sampling only in higher-density areas will systematically omit groups of interest, such as rural and disadvantaged elders who may be at particular risk or need. It may create a biased sample. For example, those in ethnic enclaves may be more recent immigrants and less acculturated than their more geographically dispersed counterparts. For example, Mexican American elders are more readily found in urban and suburban areas than in the thinly populated farmlands of the Southwest, but the former generally have fewer barriers to health care than their rural counterparts. Any sampling strategy that systematically omits minority elders (e.g., resident in low-density areas, undocumented, homeless) should be recognized as a limitation for publication because otherwise policy and service decisions may be miscast.

On a more positive note, Bureau of the Census data can also provide information, per census track, on mean income, education, age, and ethnic/racial diversity. Not only can such information be valuable in identifying fruitful areas for recruitment, but if coupled with Census Bureau tract data, this information could be used to examine neighborhood context factors that may be extremely important in the lives of individuals. At least one study of Mexican American elders has found such contextual information to be associated with self-reported health (Patel et al., 2003).

An additional advantage of collecting census tract information for larger samples is that this can allow the researcher to calculate, on the basis of data from subjects within each census tract, estimates of neighborhood characteristics that go beyond those made available by the bureau. For example, in one 3,050 study of Mexican American elders, it was possible to use subject-provided data aggregated at the tract level to make estimates of average levels of linguistic acculturation in the 209 census tracts included in the study and then to evaluate how average acculturation by tract interacted with personal acculturation (Chiriboga, 2004).

Both uses of census tract information may be especially important in the study of immigrant populations, for whom the immediate cultural context may create or ease access problems. In ethnocultural research, the absence or omission of such information means obtaining only half the story or, worse, obtaining a garbled story, especially because foreign-born elders are often dependent on family members and the community gatekeepers for assistance with health care needs. Mrs. Jung, the subject of our case study, is sufficiently fluent in English to take courses in American night school, partially in consequence of the fact that she is able to avail herself of a full array of services, including not only community programs but those of the local social services department.

Those whose sampling frames cover regional or state or national areas must confront the near impossibility of being able to work with local groups as a means of improving acceptance rates. Local recruitment strategies can take advantage of the research team's knowledge of the way in which various groups are distributed residentially, as well as of their ongoing partnerships and linkages with various groups. Partnerships are a key element: local community groups often feel that researchers from the local university make a big fanfare of the importance of the proposed work; but after data is collected, investigators never return with study findings or help the community remedy issues related to the study. In the case of Mrs. Jung, the research assistant's acceptance by the staff of the community center was facilitated by the fact that the sponsoring college had the reputation in local ethnic communities as interested and invested in the elderly's well-being.

Unfortunately, laying the groundwork for community acceptance may take years of dedicated involvement. If the researcher is unknown and has not won the trust and respect of the community, even the most compelling study can be stymied. This lack of legitimacy can be counteracted if the researcher establishes a partnership with someone who has spent the necessary time and energy or if the researchers are clearly members of the ethnic minority group of interest. We have already noted an additional strategy that involves including community members as partners. In general, however, it is often the case that the most successful partnership efforts have been established through mutual engagements with ethnic communities prior to proposing and conducting specific research studies. Hence, successful subject recruitment is often a blend of the opportunistic and goal-specific, and places a premium on flexibility.

For example, a student of one of the authors wanted to examine how effective a specific meals-on-wheels program was for African American and Hispanic American elders. After obtaining permission from the local director of senior citizens' programs, he met with the drivers about the best way of recruiting subjects. The consensus was that the best way would be to ride around with the drivers and have them introduce him to the older clients as the food was being delivered. When done in such a way that the clients did not feel coerced to participate, that is that meal deliveries might be threatened, this turned out to be an effective way of overcoming any reluctance or suspicion on the part of the meal recipient. It also helped that the student was Mexican American, spoke Spanish, and many of the faculty in the host department had worked closely with minority programs in the local community for over a decade and as a result had established a deep level of trust and mutual respect.

Using organizational and agency lists to solicit subjects may be an efficient recruitment strategy for older minority adults but may create unintended biases in the sample and the study findings. For example, a number of studies have used religious associations as an efficient means of recruiting African American and Hispanic elders because both groups often have strong religious orientations. This, however, can lead to systematic bias in the sample because not all members of either ethnic group are going to be members of a church or organization, and nonparticipants in organizations may be most at risk. Obtaining sufficient numbers is not the whole story, and the ethics of research suggest that every effort should be made to include the diversity within an ethnic elderly population.

The nonrepresentativeness of research samples is important even when conducting pilot studies. For example, one colleague solicited a sample of Korean American elders by using the relatively close-knit community to enhance her ability to recruit a larger, more diverse sample. She started with ministerial groups, an approach often taken with researchers seeking access to the African American community, but used these groups as a source of information about individuals known in the community but not active churchgoers. She has also worked closely with several senior citizens programs that deal extensively with Korean Americans where she arranged to make a presentation or to have information about the study included in newsletters and other publications. Demonstrating the need to take a multistrategy recruitment approach, she also met with Korean shop owners and got many to agree to hand out questionnaires with stamped, self-addressed return envelops and also worked closely with several physicians who have agreed to hand out questionnaires to clients aged 60 and over. If Mrs. Jung had lived in the area, she would have surfaced as a churchgoer, participant in the local community center, and possibly through the health services and grocery shops as well. (Grocery store owners may even have known Mrs. Jung personally because she and her husband used to own a convenience store!)

One of the advantages of this multigroup recruitment strategy is that it increased the heterogeneity of respondents in the sample. For example, those subjects who received questionnaires from the grocery stores appear to be lower on religiosity than those recruited through the several participating churches. Although this may seem obvious, it underscores the point that although recruiting from churches may be an effective recruitment strategy, it also may lead to systematic biases in the study sample. Use of multiple recruitment strategies can help minimize some of the obvious biases, but researchers should acknowledge the limitations of their samples in publications and should remain vigilant to potential sample biases. For example, some sampling lists may lump members of diverse Asian or Hispanic ethnic groups together (e.g., Medicare and Medicaid lists), whereas others may approach the level of refinement manifest by the U.S. Census, which for 2000 included 19 ethnic/racial categories. Using multiple lists may expand the diversity of the final sample and help enhance identification of potential participants, something especially important in studies of older ethnic persons who may be in low concentrations (and numbers) throughout the community and more likely "invisible," or keeping a low profile due to immigration issues or language barriers.

Willingness to Participate

Various populations may distrust research efforts, regardless of how well intended. We have already mentioned the continuing distrust of medical and other forms of research engendered by the infamous studies of African Americans conducted at Tuskegee. Although these historical examples have generated continuing distrust, there may be other reasons for the lack of research acceptance and cooperation by ethnic minority elders, as Freedman (1998) found in the African American community. Less publicized is the unwillingness of ethnic minorities to participate in interviews that may seem to be obscure and meaningless or which might be interpreted as yet another attempt to sell products (feelings that are shared by non-Hispanic Whites as well). The fear of discovery in people who have come to the United States illegally is also a major barrier. Fears of community stigmatization may come from a lack of trust in the investigator's and research staff's ability and willingness to keep highly private information confidential. It is crucial to provide intensive ethics and privacy training to all research staff to ensure the confidentiality and privacy of data. One leak of information violates ethical codes and can wreak immediate havoc by ruining the ability to recruit ethnic minority elders and members of the larger community for years to come. A beneficent and culturally competent reputation in the community is everything, and investigators must go to great lengths to earn and develop a track record worthy of this reputation. As important in any relationship, investigators must do everything to maintain that relationship.

In the face of such problems, some researchers go to rather extreme efforts to motivate participation, including financial rewards and help in processing health-services forms, transportation, and the like. Generally, however, researchers report that use of bilingual data gatherers (preferably from the same culture and social class as the participant), clear and freely provided information about the study, clear benefits to self and/or society, and establishing a sense of trust can break down barriers to participation that often are greatest among older minorities (Levkoff & Sanchez, 2003; Napoles-Springer et al., 2000; Spring et al., 2003). For the older members of minority groups, publicly expressed support from respected elders of the minority community may be beneficial.

Instrumentation

The technique of back translation has been recognized for some time (Brislin, 1970) and is only the first step toward developing an instrument with cultural equivalence (Fisher et al., 2002). The team or panel method (Arnold & Matus, 2000) may contribute to developing the precision of assessment by involving a variety of translators and researchers of differing backgrounds in the development and testing of the instruments. In developing a Spanish version of a depression scale with greater rigor, Cuellar, Roberts, and Bastida (2002) used back translations, a panel approach, compared the internal reliability of Spanish and English versions,

correlated scores with another measure of depression, and evaluated evidence of convergent and divergent validity.

Even with such rigorous instrumentation efforts, researchers should be cautious when using a particular measure developed in a specific ethnic minority subgroup with anticipated samples that may differ greatly from the educational or acculturation levels of the original sample (National Research Council, 2004). An early warning of potential lack of equivalence can be found in resulting factor structures. Consider for example the popular Center for Epidemiologic Studies Depression Scale (CES-D). Although the initial research (Radloff, 1977) indicated a four-factor solution for the CES-D, countless studies of ethnic minority groups have found two-, three-, and five-factor solutions, and even the four-factor solutions, often with discrepancies from Radloff's solution (Long-Foley, Reed, Mutran, & DeVellis, 2002; Miller, Markides, & Black, 1997). Sometimes differences can be subtle. Posner, Stewart, Marin, and Perez-Stable (2001) reported that a four-factor solution fit Latinas but not Latinos, that is, men but not women. And, although factor structures of younger and older minorities—or even younger and older non-Hispanic Whites—have rarely been compared, in one of the very few such comparisons, structural differences in error variance were reported across the three generations in a study of Mexican Americans (Liang, Van Tran, Krause, & Markides, 1989).

Federal Regulations

Being sensitive to the values of minority elders is clearly an ethical concern and represents an instance in which ethically driven research results in better research products and better conformity with federal regulations. The Department of Health and Human Services (DHHS) Office of Minority Health (OMH), for example, has developed

14 standards for culturally and linguistically appropriate services (CLAS). These standards, although designed for provision of services to those with limited English proficiency, are also appropriate for research studies involving older adults of minority status. Four of them are mandated for any agency or program receiving federal funds, with the remainder either constituting suggested "guidelines" or, in one case, a recommendation. Of the four mandated standards, two are of particular relevance to those working with minority elders, especially the foreign born and those who live in households where English is not spoken. A significant proportion of the Hispanic and Asian American elderly report having difficulty with English communication. Even when English skills appear sufficient, certain disorders may adversely affect or diminish English ability when English is a second language among frail minority elders. English may not be the preferred language in discussion of sensitive matters or emotionally laden content. There may be no words in English to precisely describe certain emotions or conditions that are indigenous to another culture.

Standard 4. "Health care organizations must offer and provide language assistance services, including staff and interpreter services, at no cost to each patient/consumer with limited English proficiency at all points of contact, in a timely manner during all hours of operation (Office of Minority Health, 2001, p. 10)." This standard suggests the need for researchers to identify situations where bilingual staff should be available during the recruitment phase of research and at the telephone number listed on the human subjects form.

Standard 6. "Health care organizations must assure the competence of language assistance provided to limited English proficient patients/ consumers by interpreters and bilingual staff. Family and friends should not be used to provide interpretation services (except on request by the patient/consumer)" (Office of Minority Health, 2001, p. 12). This standard suggests that researchers must provide high-quality bilingual staff who demonstrate linguistic and dialect competence and gender and generational compatibility as important criteria. Differences in literacy in the written language of origin or English may also create serious barriers because a large majority of older minorities have a history of being disadvantaged with regard to educational opportunities.

Although not mandated, something that should guide any human research enterprise is the sentiment that consumers should receive "effective, understandable, and respectful care that is provided in a manner compatible with their cultural health beliefs and practices and preferred language" (Office of Minority Health, 2001, p. 7). Respect and consideration can go a long way toward making the research enterprise a collaborative scientific partnership to enhance the human condition.

ETHICAL GUIDELINES AND THEIR APPLICATION TO OLDER ADULTS

We have only begun to understand how worldview, culture, acculturation, and situational variables influence ethical dilemmas' outcomes for research and service delivery (Yee, 1999b). Any ethics discussion should fully examine how culture influences physical or mental health literacy, and for medical decision making, how English proficiency influences the process of gaining informed consent for research participation and the provision of advanced directives. This section reviews the major features of ethical guidelines and shows how they apply to research with minority elders.

Issues Related to Informed Consent

An essential feature of most ethical guidelines is the need to obtain the full informed consent of the respondent or the respondent's legal representative. In general, an informed consent form presents as much information about a study as possible to its research participants. In many cases, specific obstacles to obtaining informed consent are encountered when conducting research with older adults. Many research programs with older adults are focused on those who are impaired in some way. Broadly, older adults can be experiencing medical illnesses, cognitive impairment, or emotional disturbances. Older adults with medical illnesses may be unable to give informed consent to participate in a research study. Researchers studying older adults with medical illnesses should document the process of obtaining informed consent and pay special attention to the medical processes that the medically ill older adult may be navigating in order to avoid any undue strain for the patient. Although the institutional review board (IRB) will make judgments about whether procedures are too invasive or uncomfortable for a medically ill population, the researcher should be sensitive to the comfort and privacy of their patients and potential research participants.

Impact of cognitive impairment and linguistic barriers. Another important barrier to informed consent is the inability of potential participants to understand fully what is being asked of them. Cognitive impairment or linguistic barriers may contribute to this inability of research participants to be fully informed. To improve access to services, the Department of Justice and the federal government have determined that special linguistic accommodations are necessary for limited English proficient populations (www.usdoj.gov/crt/cor/lep/hhsrevisedlepguidance.html). These guidelines were developed to improve access

to federal services by limited English proficient people. In the ethics arena, limited English proficient patients and research subjects provide special challenges that must be met in order to address the informed consent requirements in research and medical/service decision making. This is particularly true for older adults who are more likely to have lower levels of education, research, and health literacy challenges. They may also have sensory deficits that make it even more difficult for them to hear or see the explanations of the research in consent forms and other related materials.

Reasonable accommodations (e.g., translations of written materials for larger linguistic populations in the community to on-site or phone translators) must be made to address the needs of limited English proficient people. Unfortunately, although linguistic accommodation is a basic necessity, it is not a sufficient condition to ensure that potential subjects and recipients of services are fully informed about possible risk of research services and procedures in which consent is solicited. The empirical literature has just begun to explore how limited English proficiency (Li, McCardle, Clark, Kinsella, & Berch, 2001), health, and research literacy interact with culture and race to influence research and service delivery ethics among multicultural and diverse elderly populations.

The preceding discussion of informed consent, recruitment problems, and other issues and vulnerabilities underscores the fact that although inclusion of minority elders may seem a reasonable goal, such inclusion raises numerous questions and methodological challenges. Returning to the case example, the question is whether Mrs. Jung really understands, for example, that although she signed up for a study of exercise and cognitive functioning, she may, in fact, be assigned to a sedentary control group. And how will she react to the potentially threatening task of having to use a computer, especially in an unfamiliar location where she may feel vulnerable? Linguistic proficiency does not seem to be a current issue, but with increasing memory loss and dementia, there may be a regression in the ability to use the more recent language acquired, and Korean translations may then become an issue. The number of potentially threatening medical conditions needs to be taken into account, and although she may be physically able to participate in the exercise program, she should be given specific information about the study's risks as well as benefits. Relying on her own self-report for this information may be problematic because she prefers not to focus on her illnesses. Therefore, the researchers will need to take steps to obtain more detailed medical information without invading her rights to privacy.

Guidelines to approaching older impaired adults. Researchers should approach older adults with cognitive impairments and/or emotional disturbances with caution. Older adults with these conditions may not be able to provide informed consent for themselves, and special care should be taken when enlisting participants for research studies on these conditions. When older adults' ability to give informed consent is, or may be, compromised, then it is important for researchers to consult with their participants' family members as well as their local IRB. Conditions that warrant special attention include, but are not limited to, progressive dementia, delirium, mood disorders, and psychotic disorders. Additionally, an older adult with cognitive impairments may be able to make an informed decision. The ability to make decisions includes the ability to communicate a choice, the understanding of the nature and consequences of the choice, and the ability to manipulate information in regard to that choice and to reason consistently with previously expressed values and goals (Pellegrino, 2000).

Older adults in nursing homes and hospitals. In addition to special conditions, particular settings warrant attention. Specifically, researchers working with nursing home residents and/or hospital patients should be aware of those populations' vulnerabilities. For example, they may be unable to exercise judgment in giving informed consent. When dealing with older adults in nursing homes and hospitals, researchers must ensure that individuals do not in any way feel that their ongoing treatment is contingent on research participation. Finally, it is important to note the individual circumstances of potential research participants as well as the contextual features listed above. The families of Hispanic residents, for example, may feel guilt about institutionalizing an elder, something that goes against the tradition of valuing the family (*familismo*) and as a consequence have greater resistance to allowing any kind of study participation (Williams, Tappen, Buscemi, Rivera, & Lezcano, 2001). Researchers should consider many more factors than just artificial categories such as chronological age when approaching older adults in health facilities as potential research participants for informed consent.

Previous research highlights a number of important issues to consider when soliciting informed consent from older research participants. Older individuals with lower educational backgrounds and poorer vocabularies may not comprehend and retain consent information as well as older adults with higher education levels and better vocabularies (Taub, Kline, & Baker, 1981). Although age should not be used as sole criterion to determine whether an older adult is able to give informed consent, Taub, Baker, and Sturr (1986) found that older adults may not retain consent information as well as younger individuals, and comprehension of consent information was found to be poorer in older adults. Even simplifying the information presented did not help them understand the research materials (Taub, 1980). More recent research, however, points out that respondents with mild to moderate dementia may understand an informed consent procedure. Buckles and colleagues (2003) showed that all individuals with very mild dementia and 92% of participants with mild dementia, as well as two thirds of those with moderate symptoms, understood their informed consent procedure by scoring 80% or better.

Should an older adult refuse to participate in research or refuse a particular invasive treatment, it is essential that researchers and medical personnel respect those wishes. If a patient understands the choice and its consequences, then a choice either to not participate or to refuse a specific treatment must be honored (Mueller, Hook, & Fleming, 2004).

Researchers may face circumstances in which a potential research participant is legally not able to give informed consent, necessitating that consent must be obtained from powers of attorney or other legal substitutes. When dealing with populations who are unable to grant informed consent, it is important to note that competency has five key components. Incapacity may be partial or complete. Incapacity is a legal term; it is not a medical or a psychological term. Incapacity should be supported by evidence of an increase in functional impairment over time. Incapacity should include the idea that the respondent could suffer substantial harm personally or financially due to the existing condition. Finally, incapacity should not be based solely on descriptive or diagnostic labels.

Surrogate consent. When seeking potential research participants, researchers may also need to address surrogate management. Before an individual becomes incompetent, a power of attorney may have been drafted. A power of attorney, however, is a document that grants a person or institution power or authority to act on one's behalf. Presence or absence of such a document can obviously

affect decisions regarding the research participation of those who are incompetent. Another condition affecting research participation of older adults is guardianship. This is a legal arrangement made after a person has become incompetent and can be partial or complete depending on the older adult's condition. Under guardianship, powers and authorities are taken from the older adult and given by the court to a guardian. Built into this arrangement is a monitoring process. The state requires guardians to report to the court annually on the care they provide. Thus, decisions regarding research participation must be made by the proxy decision makers for the older adult. Although Mrs. Jung has not signed away her power of attorney, she has nevertheless begun to show some signs that her cognitive abilities may be slipping. Her case raises the consideration of whether or not a person at her level of cognitive functioning should be able to give her consent for this study, a study that may present risks to her health. On the other hand, if she is assigned to the treatment group, and the treatment is beneficial, it may help her to overcome some of the mild cognitive deficits she is currently experiencing.

In studies conducted on Alzheimer's disease, researchers typically use the "double consent" method: obtaining consent from both the individual, who may lack decision making capabilities, and a surrogate, who may lack legal authority (Kim & Karlawish, 2003). This has become a questionable procedure, and there are new legal developments in states to address how to involve those with cognitive impairments in research. As there are no explicit federal guidelines for research participation, experimenters should consult state laws, approach a potential participant's guardian(s), and be sensitive to research participants who appear frightened, confused, or unwilling to participate. Within the literature, Buckles et al. (2003) recommend that by the moderate dementia stage, as assessed by the Clinical Dementia Ratings Scale, a caregiver should be included in the informed consent process, based on their findings of informed consent process comprehension. Even if not part of the legal process, including family members is a particularly important consideration with minority elders because the family may resent people who are essentially strangers involving their loved one in any research without their permission (Williams et al., 2001). This is especially true if the family members perceive no real benefit coming from the participation.

Withholding of Treatment

Ethical dilemmas occur when investigators withhold treatment in clinical trials as designed by the scientific study. The withholding of treatment via placebo or substandard treatment runs counter to the patient's expectations of their medical doctors and nurses. In traditional cultures, doctors and health professionals were trusted because they bore a great responsibility for ensuring the patient's health and well-being. A fundamental premise of the Hippocratic Oath is to "do no harm" and the physician knows best. Patients and their families expect the health professional to have the elder's best interest at heart and treat the elder's condition with the most effective and safest treatments available. Investigators and medical researchers abide by a different set of rules and may not be able to live up to these expectations because "standard" research protocols and designs mandate how the scientific enterprise is conducted (Killien et al., 2000).

In general, many patients and their families are unfamiliar with clinical trials, distinct clinical trial phases, and the varying outcomes for those who participate in these trials. The complexities of clinical trials are difficult to understand fully when explained in English to English-speaking people in Westernized cultures; translation validity and understanding of a translation by limited English proficient people are critical to the proper conduct of research. Cognitive, cultural, and emotional factors should be incorporated in such studies of health and research literacy for multicultural elderly populations and their families.

Under community conditions where a level of standard care was extremely low (e.g., low rate of recognition and treatment of depression in primary care clinics), investigators chose to raise the minimal level of care to a higher level, as seen in the PROSPECT study (Degenholtz, Parker, & Reynolds, 2002), a randomized, controlled trial that attempted to prevent suicide in the elderly. Through the process of screening in the study, depression may have been detected among the control sample. In order to maintain ethical standards in carrying out this research project, investigators chose to raise the floor of typical care and educate community primary care physicians so that they could detect depression in their elderly patients. The same ethical argument could be made regarding improvement of the minimal levels of care, (i.e., absent, substandard levels) in community control comparison groups (e.g., improving access to basic screening or elimination of stereotyping, which influences quality of care or research participation).

DIRECTIONS FOR FUTURE RESEARCH

As the introduction to this chapter indicates, research on the ethical conduct of research on ethnic minority elders is scanty, and much of what we know comes from ancillary literature on other populations. Having said this, however, we have indications that the answer to the question, "Do gerontological researchers and service providers engage in ethics code interpretations, implementation, and practice that translate appropriately in specific cultural and situational contexts, across worldviews, and for ethnic subpopulations?" appears to be "not yet." Research has yet to determine how ethics code interpretation, implementation, and practice translate across cultural and ethnic, age, and situational contexts; and when they are translated appropriately, we need to know what are their direct and indirect implications for reducing disparities among minority elders.

In response to the question, "Do differences in research and patient care expectancies of ethnic minority elderly participants, families, and ethnic communities vary by culture, age cohort, and social class?" the answer appears to be "yes," but we only have preliminary suggestions about how researchers should address. And "If age, culture, and race influence ethical dilemmas, how do researchers address these factors in their recruitment and retention, research designs, and methodologies?" Although the state of the literature on ethical research issues among minority elders is currently unsatisfactory, there are some research ethics safeguards that should be implemented immediately which could help address this question.

Need to Recognize Multifactorial Variables

First, recognition of multifactorial variables (e.g., culture, acculturation, and immigration; age and age cohorts; race and ethnic experiences; socioeconomic and education levels) should be the norm in accounting for differences, or universal findings (verification of the null hypothesis) should be acknowledged in all avenues of research dissemination. Second, there must be a cultural shift and creation of a scientific norm that supports respecting differences in the research context. This scientific norm of respect should be translated into scientific research strategies to address the unique ethnic minority elderly sampling issues, research methodologies, and development of culturally competent, responsive, and valid research instruments for specific populations of ethnic minority elders. Third, federal agencies and federal policies guiding ethnic minority elderly research grants need to provide extra financial incentives to address these unique research and ethic issues in research designs, as well as monitor progress to close disparities for minority elders.

Challenges for the Future

The application of concepts presented in this chapter will increase the general understanding of research for the public and should enhance the ability of researchers to recruit more ethnically diverse elderly samples and to conduct ethical and informed research. The interplay of historical events, age cohort effects, ethnicity, and acculturation/immigration history creates unique and complex ethical concerns for research participation. Ultimately, these issues present an important scientific challenge that we hope will be addressed by future researchers.

REFERENCES

Administration on Aging. (2001). *A profile of older Americans: 2001.* Washington, DC: Author. (www.aoa.dhhs.gov/aoa/stats/profile/2001/2.html)

Angel, J. L., & Hogan, D. P. (2004). Population aging and diversity in a new era. In K. E. Whitfield (Ed.), *Closing the gap: Improving the health of minority elders in the new millennium.* Washington, DC: Gerontological Society of America.

Arnold, B. R., & Matus, Y. E. (2000). Test translation and cultural equivalence methodologies for use with diverse populations. In I. Cuellar & F. A. Paniagua (Eds.), *Handbook of multicultural health* (pp. 121–136). San Diego, CA: Academic.

Blackhall, L. J., Murphy, S. T., Frank, G., Michel, V., & Azen, S. (1995). Ethnicity and attitudes toward patient autonomy. *Journal of the American Medical Association, 10,* 820–825.

Bowman, S. L. (1991). Race, class and ethics in research: Belmont principles to functional relevance. In R. L. Jones (Ed.), *Black psychology* (3rd ed., pp. 747–766). Berkeley, CA: Cobb & Henry.

Brislin, R. W. (1970). Back translation for cross-cultural research. *Journal of Cross-Cultural Psychology, 1,* 185–216.

Buckles, V. D., Powlishta, K. K., Palmer, J. L., Coats, M., Hosto, T., Buckley, A., et al. (2003). Understanding of informed consent by demented individuals. *Neurology, 61,* 1662–1666.

Burhansstipanov, L., Bemis, L. T., & Dignan, M. (2002). Native American recommendations for genetic research to be cultural respectful. *Jurimetrics, 42,* 149–157.

Cauce, A. M., Coronado, N., & Watson, J. (1998). Conceptual, methodological and statistical issues in culturally competent research. In M. Hernandez & M. R. Isaacs (Eds.), *Promoting cultural competence in children's mental health services.* Baltimore: Paul.

Chiriboga, D. A. (2004). Some thoughts on the measurement of acculturation among Mexican American elders. *Hispanic Journal of Behavioral Sciences, 26,* 274–292.

Chun, K. M., & Akutsu, P. D. (2003). Acculturation among ethnic minority families. In K. M. Chun, P. B. Organista, & G. Marin (Eds.), *Acculturation: Advances in theory, measurement and applied research.* Washington DC: APA.

Clark, R., Anderson, N. B., Clark, V. R., & Williams, D. R. (1999). Racism as a stressor for African Americans: A biopsychosocial model. *American Psychologist, 54,* 805–816.

Conroy, S. J., & Heer, D. M. (2003). Hidden Hispanic homelessness in Los Angeles: The "Latino paradox" revisited. *Hispanic Journal of Behavioral Sciences, 25,* 530–538.

Cuellar, I., Roberts, R. E., & Bastida, E. (2002). The DSM Scale for Depression-26 (DSD-26)-Spanish version: Application to Hispanic elders. *Journal of Mental Health and Aging, 8,* 161–175.

Curry, L., & Jackson, J. (Eds.). (2003). *The science of inclusion: Recruiting and retaining racial and ethnic elders in health research.* Washington, DC: Gerontological Society of America.

Degenholtz, H. B., Parker, L. S., & Reynolds, C. F. (2002). Trial design and informed consent for a clinic-based study with a treatment as usual control arm. *Ethics and Behavior, 12,* 43–62.

Fisher, C. B., Hoagwood, K., Boyce, C., Duster, T., Frank, D. A., Grisso, T., et al. (2002). Research ethics for mental health science involving ethnic minority children and youths. *American Psychologist, 57,* 1024–1040.

Freedman, T. G. (1998). Why don't they come to Pike Street and ask us? Black American women's health concerns. *Science and Medicine, 47,* 941–947.

Gamble, V. N. (1993). A legacy of distrust: African Americans and medical research. *American Journal of Preventive Medicine, 9,* 35–38.

Holkup, P. A., Tripp-Reimer, T., Salois, E. M., & Weinert, C. (2004). Community-based participatory research. *Advances in Nursing Science, 27,* 162–175.

Killien, M., Bigby, J. A., Campion, V., Fernandiz-Repollet, E., Jackson, R. D., Kagawa-Singer, M., et al. (2000). Involving minority and underrepresented women in clinical trials: The National Centers of Excellence in Women's Health. *Journal of Women's Health & Gender-Based Medicine, 9,* 1061–1070.

Kim, S. Y., & Karlawish, J. H. (2003). Ethics and politics of research involving subjects with impaired decision-making abilities. *Neurology, 61,* 1645–1646.

King, P. A. (1992). The dangers of difference. *Hastings Center Report, 22,* 35.

Krach, C. A., & Veloff, V. A. (1999). *Bureau of the Census, current population reports, Series P23–199RV. Centenarians in the United States* (No. P23–199RV). Washington DC: Government Printing Office.

Levkoff, S., & Sanchez, H. (2003). Lessons learned about minority recruitment and retention from the Centers on Minority Aging and Health Promotion. *Gerontologist, 43,* 18–26.

Li, R. M., McCardle, P., Clark, R. L., Kinsella, K., & Berch, D. (2001). *Diverse voices: The inclusion of language-minority populations in national studies: Challenges and opportunities.* Washington, DC: National Institute on Aging, National Institute of Child Health and Human Development, National Center on Minority Health and Health Disparities.

Liang, J., Van Tran, T., Krause, N., & Markides, K. S. (1989). Generational differences in the structure of the CES-D Scale in Mexican Americans. *Journal of Gerontology: Social Sciences, 44,* S110–S120.

Long-Foley, K., Reed, P. S., Mutran, E. J., & DeVellis, R. F. (2002). Measurement adequacy of the CES-D among a sample of older African-Americans. *Psychiatry Research, 31,* 61–69.

Manson, S. M., Garroutte, E., Goins, R. T., & Henderson, P. N. (2004). Access, relevance, and control in the research process. *Journal of Aging and Health, 16* (5 supplement), 58S-77S.

Marin, G., & Gamba, R. J. (2003). Acculturation and changes in cultural values. In K. M. Chun, P. B. Organista, & G. Marin (Eds.), *Acculturation: Advances in theory, measurement and applied research.* Washington, DC: APA.

Meyer, J. (2001). *Age 2000: Census 2000 brief.* Washington, DC: Bureau of the Census.

Miller, T. Q., Markides, K. S., & Black, S. A. (1997). The factor structure of the CES-D in two surveys of elderly Mexican-Americans. *Journals of Gerontology Series B: Social Sciences, 52,* S259–S269.

Minino, A. M., Arias, E., Kochanek, K. D., Murphy, S. L., & Smith, B. L. (2002). *Deaths: Final data for 2000. National vital statistics reports* (Vol. 50, no. 15). Hyattsville MD: National Center for Health Statistics.

Mouton, C. P., Espino, D. V., & Esparza, Y. (2000). Attitudes toward assisted suicide among community-dwelling Mexican Americans. *Clinical Gerontologist, 22,* 81–92.

Mueller, P. S., Hook, C. C., & Fleming, K. C. (2004). Ethical issues in geriatrics: A guide for clinicians. *Mayo Clinical Proceedings, 79,* 554–562.

Napoles-Springer, A. M., Grumbach, K., Alexander, M., Moreno-John, G., Forte, D., Rangel-Lugo, M., et al. (2000). Clinical research with older African Americans and Latinos. *Research on Aging, 22,* 668–691.

National Research Council. (2004). *Eliminating health disparities: Measurement and data needs.* Panel on DHHS Collection of Race and Ethnicity Data, Committee on National Statistics. Washington, DC: National Academies Press.

Nelson, E. A., & Dannefer, D. (1992). Aged heterogeneity: Fact or fiction? The fate of diversity in gerontological research. *Gerontologist, 32,* 17–23.

Neugarten, B. L., Havighurst, R. J., & Tobin, S. S. (1968). Personality and patterns of aging. In B. L. Neugarten (Ed.), *Middle age and aging: A reader in social psychology* (pp. 173–177). Chicago: University of Chicago Press.

Office of Minority Health. (2001). *National standards for culturally and linguistically appropriate services in health care* (final report). Washington, DC: Department of Health and Human Services. Retrieved October 2004, from www.omhrc.gov/omh/programs/2pgprograms/finalreport.pdf

Pack-Brown, S. P., & Williams, C. B. (2003). *Ethics in a multicultural context.* Thousand Oaks, CA: Sage.

Patel, K. V., Eschbach, K., Rudkin, L. L., Peek, M. K., Markides, K. S., & Eschbach, K. (2003). Neighborhood context and self-rated health in older Mexican Americans. *Annals of Epidemiology, 13,* 620–628.

Pellegrino, E. D. (2000). Decisions to withdraw life-sustaining treatment: A moral algorithm. *Journal of the American Medical Association, 283,* 1065–1067.

Peterson, P. (1997). *Culture centered counseling interventions: Striving for accuracy.* Thousand Oaks, CA: Sage.

Posner, S. F., Stewart, A. L., Marin, G., & Perez-Stable, E. J. (2001). Factor variability of the Center for Epidemiological Studies Depression Scale (CES-D) among urban Latinos. *Ethnic Health, 6,* 137–144.

Radloff, L. S. (1977). The CES-D Scale: A self-report depression scale for research in the general population. *Applied Psychological Measurement, 1,* 385–401.

Santisteban, D. A., & Mitrani, V. B. (2003). The influence of acculturation processes on the family. In K. M. Chun, P. B. Organista, & G. Marin (Eds.), *Acculturation: Advances in theory, measurement and applied research* (pp. 121–135). Washington DC: APA.

Smith, M. D. (1991). Zidovudine. Does it work for everyone? *Journal of the American Medical Association, 266,* 2750–2751.

Spring, M., Westermeyer, J., Halcon, L., Savik, K., Robertson, C., Johnson, D. R., et al. (2003). Sampling in difficult to access refugee and immigrant communities. *Journal of Nervous and Mental Disease, 191,* 813–819.

Svensson, C. K. (1989). Representation of American blacks in clinical trials of new drugs. *Journal of the American Medical Association, 261,* 263–265.

Talamantes, M. A., Gomez, C., & Braun, K. L. (2000). Advance directives and end-of-life care: The Hispanic perspective. In K. L. Braun, J. H. Pietsch, & P. L. Blanchette (Eds.), *Cultural issues in end-of-life decision making* (pp. 83–100). Thousand Oaks, CA: Sage.

Taub, H. A. (1980). Informed consent, memory and age. *Gerontologist, 20,* 686–690.

Taub, H. A., Baker, M. T., & Sturr, J. F. (1986). Informed consent for research: Effects of readability, patient age, and education. *Journal of the American Geriatrics Society, 34,* 601–606.

Taub, H. A., Kline, G. E., & Baker, M. T. (1981). The elderly and informed consent: Effects of vocabulary level and corrected feedback. *Experimental Aging Research,* 137–146.

Triandis, H. C. (1995). *Individualism and collectivism.* New York: Simon & Schuster.

U.S. Bureau of the Census. (2001). *Projections of the total resident population by 5-year age groups, and sex with special age categories: Middle series, 2050 to 2070.* Washington, DC: Author.

U.S. Bureau of the Census. (2003). *Statistical abstract of the United States.* Washington, DC: Author.

U.S. Department of Health and Human Services. (2001). *Mental health: Culture, race and ethnicity—A supplement to mental health: A report of the surgeon general (SMA01–3613).* Rockville, MD: Department of Health and Human Services, Substance Abuse and Mental Health Services Administration, Center for Mental Health Services, National Institutes of Health, National Institute of Mental Health.

Unson, C. G., Dunbar, N., Curry, L., Kenyon, L., & Prestwood, K. (2001). The effects of knowledge, attitudes, and significant others on decisions to enroll in a clinical trial on osteoporosis: Implications for recruitment of older African-American women. *Journal of the National Medical Association, 93,* 392–401.

Whitbourne, S. K. (2005). *Adult development and aging: Biopsychosocial perspectives* (2nd ed.). New York: Wiley.

Williams, C. L., Tappen, R., Buscemi, C., Rivera, R., & Lezcano, J. (2001). Obtaining family consent for participation in Alzheimer's research in a Cuban-American population: Strategies to overcome the barriers. *American Journal of Alzheimer's Disease and Other Dementias, 16,* 183–187.

Yee, B. W. K. (1999a). Influence of traditional and cultural health practices among Asian women. In *Agenda for research on women's health for the 21st Century: Report of the task force on the NIH women's health research agenda for the 21st Century* (Differences Among Populations of Women, Vol. 6, NIH Publications No 99–4390, pp. 150–165). Washington, DC: Office of Research on Women's Health, National Institutes of Health.

Yee, B. W. K. (1999b). Life-span development of Asian and Pacific Islanders: Impact of gender and age roles. In B. W. K. Yee, N. Mokuau, & S. Kim (Eds.), *Developing cultural competence in Asian-American and Pacific Islander communities: Opportunities in primary health care and substance abuse prevention* (DHHS Pub. No. [SMA]98–3193, Special Collaborative Edition, Vol. 5, pp. 91–142). Washington DC: Center for Substance Abuse Prevention (SAMSHA), Bureau of Primary Health Care (HRSA), and Office of Minority Health (DHHS).

Yee, B. W. K. (1999c). Strategic opportunities and challenges for primary health care: Developing cultural competence in health promotion and disease prevention among Asian and Pacific Islander communities. In B. W. K. Yee, N. Mokuau, & S. Kim (Eds.), *Developing cultural competence in Asian American and Pacific Islander communities: Opportunities in primary health care and substance abuse prevention* (DHHS Pub. No. [SMA]98–3193, Special Collaborative Edition, Vol. 5, pp. 1–38). Washington, DC: Center for Substance Abuse Prevention (SAMSHA), Bureau of Primary Health Care (HRSA), and Office of Minority Health (DHHS).

Yee, B. W. K. (2004). Cultural factors and health. In N. Anderson (Ed.), *Encyclopedia of health and behavior* (Vol. 1, pp. 228–230). Thousand Oaks, CA: Sage.

Yee, B. W. K., Huang, L. N., & Lew, A. (1998). Families: Life-span socialization in a cultural context. In L. C. Lee & N. W. S. Zane (Eds.), *Handbook of Asian-American psychology* (pp. 83–135). Thousand Oaks, CA: Sage.

Yeo, G., & Hikoyeda, N. (2000). Cultural issues in end-of-life decision making among Asian and Pacific Islanders in the United States. In K. L. Braun, J. H. Pietsch, & P. L. Blanchette (Eds.), *Cultural issues in end-of-life decision making* (pp. 101–125). Thousand Oaks, CA: Sage.

CHAPTER 13

Changing Models of Research Ethics in Prevention Research Within Ethnic Communities

Fred Beauvais

If researchers and those researched have vastly different notions of what consti-
tutes social benefit and how it is achieved, the research is unlikely to satisfy the
needs and expectation of those on both sides of the divide.

—Marlene Brant Castellano, "Ethics of Aboriginal Research"

Prevention research encompasses two broad areas of inquiry: etiological studies and field interventions. Research conducted within the first area examines the relationships among individual and contextual predictors of social problems with the ultimate goal of using them to construct prevention interventions. These studies are also useful in educating parents and service providers about the nature and extent of the problems of interest. The second area of research assesses the efficacy of applying the knowledge gained from etiological studies to real-world interventions. For the last 25 years, I have been involved with both etiological and field intervention studies of substance abuse among rural ethnic minority youth, particularly American Indian and Mexican American adolescents. Although in one sense this is a fairly limited focus, I believe that what I have observed with regard to the ethical challenges in these areas of inquiry generalizes to other social and health contexts and to other ethnic populations. In addition to conducting laboratory and fieldwork, I have participated in many cross-cultural research meetings and conferences, and there appear to be common themes emerging among multicultural scientists when regarding ethical research issues. A number of these commonalities will be discussed in this chapter.

AUTHOR'S NOTE: The preparation of this chapter was supported in part by funds from the National Institute on Drug Abuse of the National Institutes of Health (Grant #DA03371). Appreciation is also expressed to Drs. Gene Oetting and Les Whitbeck for their review of the manuscripts and insightful comments.

COMMUNITY VULNERABILITY

The history of prevention research with ethnic minority populations has been inconsistent in regard to effectiveness and cultural sensitivity. Much has been written about the inequality of the value that communities have received vis-à-vis those conducting the research (Castellano, 2004; Duran & Duran, 1995; Fisher & Wallace, 2000; Mohatt, Hazel, Allen, Stachelrodt, Hensel, & Fath, 2004; Quinn, 2004; Sharp & Foster, 2000). There is a widespread perception that, primarily through grant-funded research projects, investigators have benefited far beyond the value that has accrued to community participants. To the extent that this is true, it is a serious breach of investigator-community trust and is unethical. What makes this particularly egregious is that the very need to develop a prevention program is evidence that a serious problem exists within a community. In such communities, there may be ongoing events occurring that lead to high levels of morbidity and mortality. When a prevention study fails to adequately address such problems in an ethical manner or fails to develop mechanisms for an empirically effective and sustainable intervention program, the community may experience irreversible losses.

When a community has experienced a major social crisis or perhaps a series of crises, the entire community may become vulnerable to external forces that normally would not present a problem. For example, a community that has been wracked with a number of adolescent suicides may be grieving and may exhibit desperation in their attempts to heal; any plausible solution will be considered. Furthermore, ethnic communities are often small and very close knit, and a tragedy in one family can have wide-ranging effects on the overall ability of the community to function effectively. Researchers approaching these communities should be aware that in

times of crisis, investigators may be attributed greater power to resolve community problems than they possess. Exaggerated expectations and trust, though flattering to the researcher, may set up the dynamics for letdown when a single intervention does not ameliorate the problem. Even when researchers are in a position to provide help, extra vigilance is needed to assure that their efforts are ethically sound and address the real needs of the community. Researchers are typically external to the community and may be tempted to tip the balance of their work to meet the needs of the research endeavor rather than the needs of the community. This is often easy to do because the researcher is free to leave the community and does not have to experience the day-to-day effects of the problems. One way to prevent this is to make sure that there is an active advisory board in the community, as discussed below, that can filter the research process through the community's experience. At times I have felt a need to supplement the knowledge provided by an advisory board by developing a trusting relationship with one or two community members with whom I can keep in close contact. These individuals are often able to provide critical information about dynamics in the community that may affect the conduct of research efforts.

A Case Example

I was scheduled to attend an advisory committee meeting in a community I was consulting with but was counseled to postpone the meeting by my contacts in the community. Earlier in the week a young father was killed in a car accident in which alcohol was involved, and cultural ceremonies involving a large number of community members were being conducted for the next several days. My presence during this time, although the intent of the project was to reduce alcohol abuse, would have been perceived as intrusive. Needless to say the meeting was cancelled.

COLLABORATIVE RESEARCH

Many of the ethical pitfalls involved in conducting research in ethnic communities can be addressed through the emerging paradigm of collaborative research.

Collaborative research is marked by equality in the relationship between researchers and community members in terms of both the conceptualization and the conduct of the research. This is clearly different from prevailing research models in which the research team maintains control over the process, and the community is only a passive participant. After reviewing several different models of collaborative research, Trickett and Espino (2004) concluded that, in addition to the issue of *local control* and *responsibility*, there are three key concepts that mark all of the models: *sustainability, utility,* and *validity* of information. Each of these will be discussed and illustrated.

LOCAL CONTROL

As a result of disappointment with past research relationships, communities are taking more control over the research in which they participate (Fisher & Ball, 2003). Increasingly these communities are asking to review and approve research proposals, to have a greater role in the conduct of the research, and to review and approve resulting publications. Although having grown out of unfortunate circumstances, this is a very promising turn of events for a number of reasons. Most prior research has been "top down" with the conceptualization and execution of projects originating in the academic

community and with the ethnic community having little input or control. There has been a gradual realization that this model has not led to much change in social or medical problems. For example, diabetes research has benefited significantly from research in ethnic communities over the past several decades. During this same time, however, the rates of diabetes in these communities have skyrocketed; in some places they have increased more than threefold. Had there been more community control in this situation, it is likely that this work would have focused at least as much on prevention research as on the gain in basic knowledge about diabetes.

Case Example

Several years back I was working with a group on a small reservation to collect data that would be useful in developing a prevention program for delinquency and substance abuse. A plan was devised and a series of interview questions was developed that would be asked of a random sample of tribal members. The plan was presented to the tribal counsel but was not approved. My immediate reaction was disappointment and confusion. This was not supposed to happen. But then again, I was at a transition from the old top-down model, and it occurred to me that I had not very often asked for tribal approval in the past and didn't entirely know what to expect. After some reflection on these events, I came to a disquieting realization that if one were going to ask for permission to engage in a piece of research, *no* is a legitimate answer. As it turns out, the tribal council had very sound reasons for their decision. Because the tribe was at a sensitive point in relationships among members, sending interviewers into the community, asking some very sensitive questions, could have set off some very negative reactions. As I reflect on this, one of my conclusions is that I did not spend nearly the amount of "up-front" time that was necessary to understand the community. In retrospect the reasons for the denial were obvious. Had I talked with a wider variety of community members and spent more informal time with them, I would probably have become aware of the various undercurrents that were affecting relationships in the community. At a minimum, I could have altered the types of questions that were included in the interviews to avoid sensitive topics within the community.

LONGEVITY AND SUSTAINABILITY

One of the things I have been struck with over the years is the sense of helplessness that I often feel within the communities with which I have worked. As might be expected, those who are willing to work with an outside resource to address a community problem are often those who are most heavily involved in community issues and are generally overworked. They are usually willing to share their sense of frustration over community problems, the lack of resources to address these problems, and sometimes even their sense of futility regarding any further efforts. Invariably, community members can relate a long list of prevention programs that have been implemented with a great deal of enthusiasm and outside support, only to be terminated over time when that support is withdrawn. This results in a strong pessimistic sense that any new program will be short-lived and have very little impact within the community. It is often with trepidation that I try to convey assurance that this time it will be different.

This sense of futility and distrust leads to an important ethical concern: the longevity of the proposed intervention. More and more, as researchers go into communities, they are asked, "How long will you be here?" Underlying this query is the need for some

assurance that the community/research team will continue to address the problem at hand until significant gains are made, not just until grant funding runs out. This has been a common complaint in the past; and again, resentment has ensued when the research team leaves while the community is still struggling with major problems. This may mean a commitment for the research team beyond the typical 3- to 5-year cycle of grant funding. It may not be realistic for an outside researcher to make an extended commitment, but there is an obligation to work toward building community capacity to continue whatever efforts are initiated in the short term. The response to this concern is to build in a sustainability plan that will carry the current efforts into the future. This includes the development of community capacity to develop and test future interventions.

Logical community structures need to be designated to be responsible for picking up the program once external research funds are no longer available. For instance, investigators could work with local or state health departments to ensure that drug abuse or other prevention programs will be continued beyond the initial intervention. Some drug prevention interventions in Indian communities have been sustained by tribes' modification of state block grant funds to include the intervention as part of ongoing social services programs. One of the main goals for bringing a research project to a close is a solid commitment on the part of the researchers to assist in the search for continuation of funds. This could include making the data available in forms that support applications for future funding from state or federal resources or even direct assistance in writing service grants.

Case Example

A recent example of the perils involved in long-term commitment occurred with a research project that I was consulting on that was attempting to develop effective alcohol prevention interventions with a group of Native Alaskan communities (Mohatt et al., 2004). The alcohol problems were very severe and were associated with a number of adolescent suicides. The funding agency worked hard with the research team to develop a successful proposal. After a federal grant was obtained to fund an intervention, 2 years of hard work went into developing a strong, collaborative relationship between the research team and community members. In particular, there was agreement among investigators and community members that this work would take more than the usual funding cycle, but it was also understood that such additional funding was not guaranteed. Some promising results were obtained over the next 3 years, and the communities were excited about the possibilities. The next proposal was submitted but did not survive after two reviews. The disappointment was palpable on both sides. The community was frustrated because the problem clearly had not abated appreciably, and despite the original understanding of the contingency on funding for continuation, there was a sense of once again being let down. The research team was disheartened that they were facing the possibility of reneging on their original commitment and feared resentment from the communities. Fortunately, a strong relationship had been built in the intervening years and work continues, albeit at a much reduced level and with lower expectations. There are no easy answers in these types of situations, although one avenue would be working with funding agencies to develop mechanisms that ensure support for long-term research efforts. An important step in that direction is to educate funding agencies that continued community trust and involvement is as much a measure of success as academic publications.

UTILITY OR BENEFIT TO THE COMMUNITY

The usefulness of the data at the local level should be a major goal of research projects in ethnic communities. It is not enough to gather data strictly for academic purposes or for publication in academic journals. Nor is it sufficient to assume that the community will benefit from a general increase in knowledge. Many ethnic communities are struggling with a number of social problems, and it is inequitable to simply use them as a participant pool without providing some tangible help. This is really nothing more than balancing the risk/benefit equation, with both risks and benefits jointly defined by investigator and prospective participants (Fisher, 1999). The tendency to exploit individuals and communities has lessened recently as communities exert more control and governing boards insist on substantive payback for their participation. One research group working with American Indians has handled this issue nicely by always providing copies of all academic publications emerging from the research project to their advisory board for review and approval (Les Whitbeck, personal communication, August 2002). In addition, the community is provided with a three-page summary of the article, written in nontechnical language that can be read and understood by the average community member. The summary also contains a series of practical implications derived from the article. These are possible actions that the community can immediately engage in, thus providing them with concrete benefits for project participation.

Prevention interventions that are tested in communities need to be practical, economical, and within the community's resources. If there are very high costs associated with evaluation of the program or obtaining information to test theory, they are generally not a problem because those costs will not have to be assumed if the program is continued. But the program itself cannot be unrealistically expensive, nor can it require skills, training, or credentials that are not available in the community. If a prevention intervention is being tested, then the payback to the community could be the development and continued funding for the program in the future. For basic or etiological research, the contribution back to the community is less clear but could take a number of directions, including providing training in basic research skills.

It has been my observation that most ethnic communities abound with competent, concerned, and caring professionals. The one thing these people have in common, however, is an enormous workload and strained resources. In these circumstances, it is incumbent on the research team to build the resources needed at the community level into their proposals and not add an even greater burden. For example, asking counselors to run prevention activities during their off-work hours, even if paid, could lead to untoward effects on the integrity of the program and stress for the individuals involved. Although this could be considered a general issue for good research, it takes on an ethical dimension within ethnic communities. The recent emphasis on the study of health disparities has made it clear that these communities bear a disproportionate burden, both in health problems and the resources to address these problems. Asking communities to stretch already thin resources to engage in research is not only impractical but unethical.

Case Example

In one of our projects, we utilize school-based surveys to track trends in drug use among Indian students as well as to conduct analyses on the causes and consequences of use. Although we hope that the gain in knowledge from this research will eventually benefit all Indian communities, we believe

there is a need to provide more immediate payback. When our surveys are completed, we prepare a very comprehensive 100-page report, including overhead transparencies and a presentation script, which is sent back to each school that participated in the survey. Most importantly, the data in the report are from the youth of that school and are not aggregate data from multiple sites. In this way, the schools have accurate information on their students that can be used in a number of ways including applying for grant funds, educating the community as to the nature of the local drug use situation, and evaluating prevention programs that may have been implemented in the community. We have found that aggregate data, even at the school district level, are not that helpful because they can easily be dismissed as not applying to "our kids."

VALIDITY OF KNOWLEDGE

Effective collaborative research in ethnic communities recognizes that there are multiple avenues to valid knowledge. Much social research to date has been under the hegemonic rule of Western science with little recognition that the communities themselves contain a wealth of wisdom, although its structure and content may not conform to the typical reductionistic approach of modern science (Duran & Duran, 1995). Communities and ethnic cultures have survived, and thrived, for millennia through the use of cultural forms and thought that may differ from that of the scientific community yet are a legitimate source of knowledge.

Social problems are enmeshed in the cultural and historic milieu of the community, and any data that is not interpreted through that lens will be incompletely understood (Duran & Duran, 1995; Fisher & Ball, 2003). Close collaboration with those knowledgeable of the local cultural context at all stages of the research process will make it more likely that the conclusions arrived at will more closely reflect the reality of the local community and thus lead to more effective prevention interventions (Mohatt et al., 2004). In short, close collaboration leads to better science. One example of this is the work of O'Nell and Mitchell (1996) who took an ethnographic approach to the meaning of pathological drinking among American Indian youth. Their analysis of interviews with a sample of community informants reached the following conclusion:

> Local norms suggest that pathological use lies not in the quantity or frequency of alcohol use but the degree to which drinking interferes with important tasks facing . . . adolescents: maintaining strong and respectful ties with family members and peers, and avoiding potentially shameful incidents for her family such as going to school with a hangover. (p. 575)

Without having the benefit of the cultural understanding of alcohol use, one might easily measure quantity and frequency of use and label adolescents deviant if they meet a certain criterion on this measure. In truth, it is not necessarily the amount one drinks (although there are clear limits to this) but whether one fulfills one's cultural role that marks one as deviant or conformant to community norms.

CULTURALLY SENSITIVE MEASURES

A consequence of accepting the value of cultural ways and knowledge is the realization of the need for and the development of culturally specific measures. This may involve the "cultural translation" of key prevention constructs as well as the identification and operationalization of culturally specific prevention constructs. Failure to culturally adapt and norm "off-the-shelf" psychological, social, and behavioral indexes that are typically used may result in inaccurate or incomplete information (Allen & Walsh, 2000). Furthermore, ignoring culturally specific risk and resiliency factors may mean missing a unique proportion of the variance in behaviors and the loss of knowledge of potential prevention resources.

Case Examples

The identification of culturally specific prevention resources comes through close collaboration of those most knowledgeable about the culture. A couple of examples might help to illustrate this. Among many American Indian tribes and communities, there traditionally has been a high level of reverence expressed toward elders by young people. In a program to improve the adjustment of adolescence, an important outcome might be to see an improvement in relationships between younger and older people. This could be operationalized by creating measures to assess the amount and quality of time spent with elders before and after the intervention, to assess attitudes toward elders, or to assess the relevance of advice from elders. A similar, important value in Hispanic culture is that of *respeto,* or respect. This is basically recognition of the dignity of others, especially those older than oneself, and displaying behavior that supports that dignity. In a program aimed at improving school adjustment of Hispanic youth, it would be possible to measure classroom and out-of-class behavior related to *respeto* and observe changes in the quality and types of the interactions between teachers and students.

Although pilot testing of instruments and debriefing of respondents is always good science, it is absolutely essential in cross-cultural research. There are often substantial discrepancies between what we think we are assessing and the meaning the respondent is assigning to the questions asked. One example of this is the difficulty we have in trying to assess spirituality among Indian populations. Most spirituality measures have a distinct "religious" basis to them, typically Christian, and do not assess the more traditional spiritual basis of most tribes. Further adding to the difficulty in this regard is that many Indian people adhere to traditional tribal beliefs and at the same time embrace a Christian religion. Developing questions that both distinguish between the two and assess each independently is a challenge, but the task is greatly aided by asking respondents what they are thinking when they respond to potential questions.

Trickett and Espino (2004) articulate another way in which validity is increased through collaborative research. The collaborative process clearly involves a trusting and respectful relationship between researchers and community members. When the community feels valued and not simply an object of study, the quality of data from respondents will improve. If respondents are seen as participating as equals in an effort to reduce social ills in their community, their motivation to provide accurate and in-depth information sharply increases.

COLLABORATIVE STEPS

Procedurally, collaborative research entails a number of elements and procedures that differ from the typical academic research approaches. A number of these will be discussed here.

Although collaborative research has tremendous advantages, it entails a lot more work than the type of university-driven research that has typically been approved in past years. This work starts with formal approval at the community level. Formal approval for research in ethnic communities is not a uniform process and will vary by location. In working with youth, the school

is typically the unit of measurement, and approval by school officials is a minimum requirement. If ethnic issues are being addressed, however, there is some onus on the researcher to obtain sanction from the ethnic community. What has happened in a number of instances is that researchers have made contact in a community and have proceeded to engage in research that has not been widely scrutinized for its cultural appropriateness or acceptability by the larger community. At some point during the conduct of the research, the nature of the work has come to light, disagreement has been expressed by community members, and the research has been halted. It should be recognized that obtaining community sanction is not always an easy process. Ethnic communities, like any others, are not always unanimous in how they view any particular issue. It is important for the research team to be cognizant of the different opinions in the community and to try to respond to and negotiate points of difference. The use of a community advisory group, described next, can often be useful in these negotiations.

In my work with American Indian tribes, research approval usually comes from the tribal council. With other ethnic groups, there may be no formal entity to provide this approval, and other means must be sought to make certain that the community is well represented and protected in the research effort. It is becoming more and more common in work with ethnic minority communities to convene an advisory committee that will guide the research (Quinn, 2004). Above all, this must be a very active group and not simply an empty gesture. Although the term *advisory* is often used to designate this type of group, a more appropriate term might possibly be *board of directors* to reflect the level of effort and control exerted by the group. The work of the advisory committee should be very detailed, and consensus should be sought on most issues, ranging from conceptualization to the wording of survey items and to the dissemination of findings. This is very time-consuming and difficult work because it is a matter of melding two worldviews and arriving at solutions satisfying to both (Beauvais, 1995). I have observed this process a number of times and, when done right, nearly half of the advisory committee's time is taken up clarifying points of misunderstanding and making sure that everyone is in agreement on the direction of the research.

A Precaution

It is important to have some knowledge of the community dynamics as advisory groups are formed. In one project, I consulted with an advisory group that consisted of a particular segment of the community that was often at odds with other segments on a variety of issues. The choice of this group was not intentional but resulted from the researcher having made initial contact with a very active group in the community, and it seemed logical that they should be the ones representing the community. The collaborative work struggled because there was not widespread support but, in fact, some active opposition. Once this was discovered, there was a successful effort to restructure the advisory committee to include a wider representation of community viewpoints. Had the community diversity been recognized initially, the entire research process would have moved more smoothly from the beginning. It has been my experience, however, that cleavages in a community can often be overcome when differing sides are brought together to resolve a common problem.

COMMUNITY CONTROL AND INDIVIDUAL AUTONOMY

The issue of obtaining permission to do research in ethnic communities presents a number of questions that are yet to be resolved.

One of these has to do with personal choice versus community control. It has been emphasized here and elsewhere that there is a growing call for community sanction to conduct research among ethnic populations. What does this mean, however, if an individual would like to be part of a research project but that project is not approved by the community leaders? Do these leaders have the ethical right to prevent an individual from making a personal choice?

A hypothetical example can be used to illustrate this. Suppose a writer is interested in collecting a series of stories about family life on Indian reservations. The information for a forthcoming book would come from a series of interviews with members from several families from a number of reservations, communities, or districts. The focus of these interviews would be on normal family functioning and how it may resemble or differ from family life for non-Indian families. Although the intent is not to study family problems, such problems and how they are resolved would probably come up in the course of the interviews and could be seen as sensitive material. Clearly, regardless of official approval, those families participating would only do so willingly, and any family member who did not want to would not have to.

The central question here is whether or not tribal approval would have to be obtained in order to conduct these interviews. On one hand, American Indian reservations are sovereign nations who exercise rights of access to their land. Interviews on reservation lands, therefore, could be prohibited. There have been instances in the past when sensitive information has been published and created controversy within the community leading to bans of future projects by the tribe (Foulks, 1989). On the other hand, there is the question of whether individuals have the right to decide for themselves what type of research, if any, they will participate in. If this project were to take place in a non-Indian community, it certainly would not have to have governmental approval. In an attempt to protect individuals, care must be taken that their autonomy is respected. These and similar issues will require sensitivity and dialogue in the coming years. Fortunately, there is an increasing willingness for researchers to discuss the rights of individuals and communities in the conduct of research and an increasing recognition that ethnic communities present special challenges in this regard.

FUNDING BARRIERS

A barrier to ethical collaborative research in ethnic communities lies in the structure of funding mechanisms. A typical grant application contains a thorough problem definition, a set of hypotheses to be tested, and a method for the testing of those hypotheses. When funding is awarded, the research proceeds according to that plan. In collaborative research on the other hand, the work involved in design and hypothesis construction is done in conjunction with the community and cannot be specified ahead of time. In fact, this up-front work needs to be considered an integral part of the research, and funding needs to be provided accordingly to engage in this work (Fisher & Ball, 2003). Without this initial step, the resulting research could have little value to the community, and asking them to participate in such an effort could be an ethical violation.

Case Examples

There is some beginning recognition by funding agencies to support this initial collaborative work. One example is provided by the recent support of a research program to address alcohol abuse prevention among several communities of native people. The overall theme of the research was to be "reducing alcohol problems," although the researcher wanted the specific problem definition to be left to the communities themselves. Advisory boards were convened in each of the communities and extended discussions were held within and between the communities. This was a laborious process that took nearly 18 months to complete with numerous visits to each community. Extensive travel was involved because the communities were widely scattered. The final research question that emerged was at once simple and profound: "What are the stories of our sober people?"

At first glance this may appear to be a very naïve question, but it is filled with cultural meaning. First, the use of stories is culturally meaningful because these communities operate from a cultural base of oral traditions. The important values, beliefs, and the meaning of rituals are passed down from one generation to the next through stories, both allegorical and historically factual. Secondly, if these stories could be clearly elucidated, they would provide critical information for both prevention (what kept people from beginning to drink) and treatment (what helped people stop drinking). This simple question presented the researcher with a challenging task: how could the question, and the search for its answer, be cast in a form that at once remained true to the cultural base from which it had sprung and yet was acceptable for scientific peer review? Without funding to do this up-front work, the resulting project probably would have reflected Western European worldview and have been of little relevance to the native communities.

Some years back I was approached by a prominent researcher who had been awarded a federal grant to study the causes and consequences of inhalant abuse. This was during a time when inhalant abuse was a particularly serious problem for Indian youth. The researcher was aware of this and his request of me was to "find some Indian communities where he could carry out his work." It was evident his concern was not for the welfare of the youth in these Indian communities but for the conduct of his scientific project. Nor was there any interest in examining this problem from the cultural perspective of the community. If I had agreed to do this, there would have been no community input, and it is unlikely that any benefit would have accrued to the community. Fortunately, this would probably not happen today because grant review committees are becoming more insistent that there be approval by the community and that there be more community participation, or at least some evidence that these potentially vulnerable populations would not be exploited.

PROTECTING THE COMMUNITY

Prevention research usually entails the collection of data, some of which could be quite sensitive and, if used inappropriately, reflect negatively on the reputation of the community. The most egregious occurrences of this have happened when rates of social problems have been used to reinforce stereotypes about ethnic populations. A few years back, in an unfortunate situation, a research group released data they had collected from a community that had a severe problem with alcoholism (Manson, 1989). The data were not only published in a journal with the community name attached but also released at a press conference. The story was picked up by the national media and the community experienced severe embarrassment and financial setbacks. In another instance, a researcher published accounts of life in a small community in a way that permitted the community and the individuals to be easily identified. The accounts in the book included personal disagreements among respondents and political controversy going back generations. Needless to say the

interpersonal dynamics in the community were negatively affected, and the extreme anger at the author and other community outsiders seeking information resulted. Loss of confidentiality during any research project involving sensitive data is a breach of ethics, yet it takes on particular importance with ethnic communities. A great deal of ethnic research in the past has been from a deficit model wherein ethnic populations are compared with the general population, and any differences are usually interpreted as a deficiency (Fisher et al., 2002). This is bad science, not only because cross-cultural differences are rarely accounted for but also because it perpetuates the stereotypes of ethnic groups as inferior.

COMMUNITY IDENTIFICATION AND DATA DISSEMINATION

Not only is the mishandling of data dissemination an ethical issue but it also leads to mistrust of the research enterprise, making future research all the more difficult. Prior to the initiation of a project, investigators and community members must address two critical questions: How will the research data be released publicly (if at all)? How will scientific publications be handled? Each of these questions should be answered very early in the research project so there are no misunderstandings when the data become available. Underlying these questions is the basic question of who owns the data. There has been discussion of this issue, but to date there is no single answer. Most likely the resolution will differ on a case-by-case basis. Perhaps the question itself is not as important as the careful negotiation as to how the rights and reputation of all parties involved will be assured. One of the specific issues that must be considered is whether or not the communities involved in a research project should be identified in any publication (Beauvais &

Trimble, 1992). Scientific rigor would normally dictate a complete sample description, needed for study replication and for understanding of the potential for, and limits to, population generalizability. Historically, however, this has often led to negative effects on the community. It is my view that before all else we must protect the reputation and integrity of the community. Consequently, I made the decision early in my work to always provide sufficient information to characterize the study population but to stop short of anything that would reveal its identity.

OBJECTIVITY VERSUS ACTIVISM

Research in ethnic communities requires a delicate balance between remaining objective and becoming involved in the social structure and politics. Extreme objectivity, in my experience, leads to poor science. One must have a sense for the culture of the community and some idea of the formal and informal power relations. The researcher must also demonstrate a respect for, and valuing of, the social and spiritual beliefs, values, and cultural practices. Participation in activities and ceremonies, if one is asked, is a legitimate way to gain the trust of community members and to gain a deeper understanding of cultural factors that may influence social problems. Invitations to the researcher to take part in community activities not only are an expression of respect toward the researcher but often serve as a barometer to determine the level of interest in, and commitment to, the cultural life of the community. The researcher who refuses these invitations is creating a barrier that may affect the quality of the work that is being planned. On the other hand, it is important for the researcher to judge the appropriate level of cultural participation, because there are limits to how closely

one can become affiliated with a traditional culture.

In prevention research, it is often tempting to become an advocate within the community for resolving social issues; however, becoming an active change agent could present a number of problems. First, although it is necessary to have some sense of the power relations in a community, they can never be fully understood by an outside researcher. Therefore, there is some ethical concern that an activist researcher may inadvertently disturb those power relations in ways that are harmful to the community. In their extensive monograph on collaborative research, Trickett and Espino (2004) warn against a "new tyranny" by which externally funded projects, especially those that can provide many resources, can co-opt the power structure in a community. In one project I was associated with, an ombudsman was hired by the research team to give voice to those being served by a prevention program. Through the work of the ombudsman, community members banded together and were ultimately successful in having the program director fired. Whether or not this firing was deserved, it led to very divisive feelings in the community, and there was no way for the research team to mediate the harsh feelings left in the aftermath.

Second, from a pragmatic perspective, the researcher's job is to uncover new information that will help the community engage in prevention. Close involvement with certain blocs within the community may close off access to other blocs, and with the possible loss of critical information.

Third, extreme community involvement could be taken as an indication that the researcher does not have confidence in the ability of the community to resolve its own problems. Again, the researcher's job is to provide information that the *community* can act on. If the prerogative for action is maintained by the researcher, sustainability of effort is undermined. Through years of frustration, many ethnic communities have come to rely on outside "experts" in the hopes that this time a particular problem can be resolved. Unless this dynamic is recognized, it is very easy for the researcher to usurp responsibility for community issues. The dictum that "knowledge is power" certainly applies here. There must be plans for research data to be woven back into the community structure or, as I learned very early in my work with small communities, the problem and the solution leave the minute the researcher leaves. This is another example of the value of solidly designed, collaborative research. There is no power hierarchy and there is a "buy in" from the community, an investment in the data derived from the research and a motivation to use it constructively.

SCIENCE AND COMMUNITY VALUES

At times the goals and methods of science appear to be at odds with participant protections with little chance of compromise. The use of control groups in the evaluation of the effectiveness of a prevention intervention is one example (Fisher et al., 2002). Many ethnic communities will not allow control groups to be used, yet many funding agencies insist on random assignment to treatment or control groups. A large number of ethnic community-based studies never make it past peer review for lack of a scientifically acceptable control group. Sometimes this is a matter of the community not understanding the need for a control group, in which case providing a basic explanation can often be useful. Still there may be resistance. Many ethnic communities are collectivist in nature, and it is the welfare of the entire community, rather than segments of

the community, that is of priority, and control groups are seen as withholding something of value from certain community members. There are certainly compromises that can be negotiated, such as wait-list control groups or comparing the new program with existing interventions that have been shown to have value; however, scientific review groups sometimes require an extended lag time (up to 2 years) between interventions, the intervention group, and the wait-list controls. Although this is good for scientific rigor, it may render prevention trials unacceptable to some ethnic communities. Compromises need to be found that assure good science, yet take into account novel or culturally based ways of designing and evaluating prevention trials.

One of the ways of resolving apparent conflicts between science and cultural knowledge is through a mixture of research approaches. Having been on grant application review committees for some time, I have seen an increasing number of well-designed research projects that use a combination of qualitative and quantitative methods. This strategy is often well received by both the scientific community and the ethnic community. It takes advantage of the epistemological basis of both science and the oral-based tradition of knowledge found in many ethnic cultures. The basis of this approach lies in the understanding that worldviews need not be seen as in opposition but rather as complementary (Beauvais, 1995).

CONCLUSION

For the last three decades, there has been increasing attention paid to the ethics of conducting research within ethnic communities. This is a highly significant movement in that it expresses a greater respect for diverse populations involved in research and leads to better science in the long run. The dialogue, of course, must go on. Ethical issues are rarely completely solved; rather they are the subject of continuing refinement and deeper understanding. Funding agencies, researchers, and ethnic communities must continue to come together for better understanding of how scientific knowledge and the knowledge of ethnic cultures can be melded to resolve social problems.

REFERENCES

Allen, J., & Walsh, J. A. (2000). A construct-based approach to equivalence: Methodologies for cross-cultural /multicultural personality assessment research. In R. H. Dana (Ed.), *Handbook of cross-cultural and multicultural personality assessment* (pp. 63–85). Mahwah, NJ: Lawrence Erlbaum.

Beauvais, F. (1995). Ethnic communities and research: Building a new alliance. In P. A. Langton (Ed.), *The challenge of participatory research: Preventing alcohol-related problems in ethnic communities* (CSAP Cultural Competence Series 3), (DHHS Publication No. SMA 95–3042, pp. 105–128). Rockville, MD: Department of Health and Human Services.

Beauvais, F., & Trimble, J. E. (1992). The role of the researcher in evaluating American Indian alcohol and other drug abuse prevention programs. In M. A. Orlandi (Ed.), *Cultural competence for evaluators: A guide for alcohol and other drug abuse prevention practitioners working with ethnic/racial communities* (CSAP Cultural Competence Series 1, DHHS Publication No. SMA 95–3066, pp. 173–201). Rockville, MD: Department of Health and Human Services.

Castellano, M. (2004). Ethics of aboriginal research. *Journal of Aboriginal Health, 1*(1), 98–114.

Duran, E., & Duran, B. (1995). *Native American postcolonial psychology.* Albany: State University of New York Press.

Fisher, C. B. (1999). *Relational ethics and research with vulnerable populations. Reports on research involving persons with mental disorders that may affect decision-making capacity* (Vol. 2, pp. 29–49). Rockville, MD: National Bioethics Advisory Commission.

Fisher, C. B., Hoagwood, K., Boyce, C., Duster, T., Frank, D. A., Grisso, T., et al. (2002). Research ethics for mental health science involving ethnic minority children and youths. *American Psychologist, 57,* 1024–1040.

Fisher, C. B., & Wallace, S. A. (2000). Through the community looking glass: Re-evaluating the ethical and policy implications of research on adolescent risk and psychopathology. *Ethics & Behavior, 10*(2), 99–118.

Fisher, P. A., & Ball, T. J. (2003). Tribal participatory research: Mechanisms of a collaborative model. *American Journal of Community Psychology, 32,* 207–216.

Foulks, E. F. (1989). Misalliances in the Barrow Alcohol Study. *American Indian and Alaskan Native Mental Health Research, 2*(2), 17.

Manson, S. (Ed.). (1989). American Indian and Alaska Native mental health research: *Journal of the National Center, 2*(3) [Entire Issue].

Mohatt, G., Hazel, K., Allen, J., Stachelrodt, M., Hensel, C., & Fath, R. (2004). Unheard Alaska: Culturally anchored participatory action research on sobriety with Alaska Natives. *American Journal of Community Psychology, 33,* 263–273.

O'Nell, T. D., & Mitchell, C. M. (1996). Alcohol use among American Indian adolescents: The role of culture in pathological drinking. *Social Science and Medicine, 42*(4), 565–578.

Quinn, S. (2004). Protecting human subjects: The role of community advisory boards. *American Journal of Public Health, 94,* 918–922.

Sharp, R., & Foster, M. (2000). Involving study populations in the review of genetic research. *Journal of Law and Medical Ethics, 28,* 41–51.

Trickett, E., & Espino, S. (2004). Collaboration and social inquiry: Multiple meanings of a construct and its role in creating useful and valid data. *American Journal of Community Psychology, 34,* 1–69.

CHAPTER 14

Ethnographic Research on Drugs and HIV/AIDS in Ethnocultural Communities

MERRILL SINGER

DELIA EASTON

The story of my project can join the literature on ethical dilemmas of fieldwork . . . what happens to the women [I interviewed] and my relationship with them as they become transformed into data? My social science training has taught me to keep the "I" out of things (i.e., leave the relationship out altogether), and besides, without data what do I analyze and interpret?

—Alisse Waterston, *Love, Sorrow and Rage*

Don't study the poor and powerless because everything you say about them will be used against them.

—Laura Nader, "Up the Anthropologist"

The American Anthropology Association's Code of Ethics (1998) states that "Anthropological researchers must expect to encounter ethical dilemmas at every stage of their work, and must make good-faith efforts to identify potential ethical claims and conflicts in advance when preparing proposals and as projects proceed." Since the publication of this code, which followed an earlier set of ethical guidelines issued by the Society for Applied Anthropology (1983), standards for assessing good-faith efforts have become more stringent, and the frustrations of communities and researchers over ethical questions and decisions have escalated significantly as well. Indeed, as government and community institutions have implemented ever more demanding review structures and sets of procedures intended to address the ethical issues that arise in studying humans, social and behavioral research has become increasingly complicated and often quite wearisome. Anthropologists, like their colleagues in other disciplines, have been forced to carefully think through all of the potential risks—however unlikely or improbable—that might be faced by study participants and their communities. Given the particular nature of ethnography as a research methodology, these risks are numerous. Additionally, they have had to confront a set ethical rules (midcourse changes in the research protocol must be approved by a human subject committee; informed consent should be provided by all study participants) that constrain some of the basic strengths of ethnographic research, for example the field discovery and exploration of unexpected findings and the observation of individuals in settings in which informed consent would be impossible to acquire.

THE ETHNOGRAPHER IN ETHNOCULTURAL COMMUNITIES

Based as it is on researcher immersion into the natural social and geographic space of research participants, those engaged in ethnographic research gain access to many arenas of individual and community life and behavior that often are closed to (or even actively hidden from) other kinds of researchers. Moreover, because ethnographers routinely seek to develop an insider's understanding and to comprehend the worldview of study participants, including their deepest feelings (day-to-day as well as most poignant experiences and heart-felt beliefs and ideas), they are pushed to dig ever deeper into the thoughts, sentiments, memories, and relationships of the ethnocultural groups they study. Additionally, as a result of the experience-near nature of their research method (being on hand when

things happen and immediately asking questions about what has happened, why it has happened, and how the participant feels about it), ethnographers are in a position (for protracted periods) of being able to see participants as they carry out their everyday lives, observe unexpected and even undesirable and upsetting events (from the participant's standpoint), and query the participant(s) about the significance of the event. In addition, ethnographers may meet and interact with individuals (encountered by the participant) with whom it may be difficult or impossible to obtain formal consent. For example, during a study in Israel the lead author was on hand when a youthful member of a religious sect that he was studying was caught shoplifting by a merchant. From the standpoint of the boy's community, this was a highly embarrassing occurrence that conflicted sharply with the public image of righteousness and perfection claimed by the group. Knowing that the ethnographer had witnessed the event was quite discomforting for group members. In contrast to their usual openness, they gruffly avoided answering questions for the rest of the day. In short, as discussed below, ethnography allows access to more intimate and private information, including information a group may not wish to be known by outsiders, while at the same time maintaining an informal style that actively weighs against constantly intruding and interrupting the natural flow of events to obtain informed consent.

On another occasion during this same study, while the ethnographer was with group members in one of the apartments they have in a southern Israeli town, a group of police arrived and demanded entrance, which was granted. The police proceeded to ask the ethnographer and members of the group various question (e.g., what was this person—the ethnographer—doing here?)

Although it was not possible to seek informed consent from them, certainly the realization that the police must be keeping very close watch on the group was an important research finding.

Immersion in Participants' Private Lives

Data collection in ethnography is interwoven with the sometimes confidential and quite intimate or highly emotionally charged activities of research subjects, including at times, illegal, unhealthy, and secret behaviors. Because of the extensive access ethnographers often gain to the "backstage" (or completely offstage) areas of participants' private lives, they are in a position to, and commonly do, learn about very guarded information (e.g., love affairs, theft, hidden resentments). Indeed, over time, ethnographers may hear, see, and learn about issues that neither the participant nor the researcher anticipated at the time of formal consent. This kind of access is propelled by the nature of ethnography, which not only exposes the lives of participants but those of ethnographers as well. Once in the field, ethnographers often do not go to work, per se, but rather live on the job, potentially around the clock as events warrant, and thus their personal lives are not (and cannot) be completely separated from those of research participants (Busier, Clark, Esch, Glesne, Pigeon, & Tarule, 1997).

Other behavioral researchers usually can remain snugly in professional roles in their interactions with study participants (e.g., during structured interviews in office settings at research centers) and pretend, at least, that the pathway of knowledge gathering is unidirectional. Ethnographers, however, know that they must open themselves to the gaze of community members and that the nature of their presentation of self will be under close

and continued scrutiny. In short, ethnographers know that the success of their project depends in no small measure on how they are judged. This situation is often complicated by the fact that ethnographers initially do not know how to act in ways that will met their host's approval. Often they stumble and sometimes they fall. Bourgois (1995), for example, reports inadvertently embarrassing a major crack dealer by exposing that he could barely read. All ethnographers make similar mistakes, especially early in their fieldwork experience. Ultimately, most ethnographers learn that being open (i.e., reasonably extroverted and chatty), honest (revealing about who you are personally and not giving the impression that you are hiding something), friendly and caring (sharing resources and assistance), and respectful (honoring the dignity of your hosts and their culture) will lead to acceptance in most settings. One consequence of this unique approach to understanding is that ethnographers often develop close personal relationships with at least some study participants (often called "key informants"), friendships that can outlive the period of research and can and sometimes do involve marriage or the establishment of fictive kinship. At the same time, anthropologists can develop enemies or have conflicts with people in the group under study, sometimes by inheriting the enemies of their friends but also because of unintended slights or fears people develop about the ethnographer as an outsider based on fanciful, and perhaps at times not so fanciful, interpretations of the ethnographer's real mission. Moreover, from the participants' perspective, the ethnographer as a distinct person with particular traits and resources often is of far greater interest to the community under study than the ethnographer as a scholarly researcher, a social role that participants may not fully understand or ultimately be much concerned about.

Community Description and Assessment: Contemporary Ethnographic Minefields

Finally, a completed ethnographic account stands as a public description and assessment of aspects of the group in question. Although anthropologists often attempt to hide the name or the location of the group through the use of pseudonyms, sometimes this is not possible, and some members of the group under study may learn about and be offended by how they feel their group is portrayed to the world. For example, a group of Latino undergraduate students in a New York university were assigned by the second author of this chapter to read an article by Singer (1996) on the biosocial entwinement of substance abuse, violence, and AIDS in the inner city and had unexpectedly negative reactions to what they read. One student commented, "My problem with this is that it says if you're Latina and a drug user, you're apt to get AIDS or be a victim of violence." This statement expressed a general unease among class members with seeing these three epidemics linked together as descriptive features of their community and, the students concluded, inherent community characteristics in the mind of the article's author. The students interpreted the author's argument as deterministic. They felt that Singer implied that being Latino/a, HIV positive, using injection drugs, and being victimized by violence were, in effect, inescapable attributes of people of color living in poor, urban neighborhoods.

In the article in question, Singer introduced the term *syndemic* to conceptualize the intimate relationship between multiple mutually reinforcing diseases and a set of social structural factors that increase the likelihood of there being numerous coterminous threats to health among the poor; however, calling focused attention to the critical importance of discrimination, racism, structural violence, and economic disadvantage in shaping abundantly documented indicators of comparatively poor health status among inner city populations did not lessen the students' indignation at what they perceived as an unfounded generalization, a stereotype of poor people, and a slight against Puerto Rican women imposed by an outsider. The second author attempted to clarify the utility of the concept of syndemics (Singer & Clair, 2003): It discourages the traditional public health focus on only one major health problem at a time and the biomedical tendency to look at health separate from the wider social relations that promote unhealthy conditions among the poor, which did help to move class discussion to an agreement that the term has some value. Still they asked, "How can you bring attention to health disparities without reinforcing them? How can you also point out community strengths and resiliency and not always emphasize a negative image?"

On another occasion, Singer and a colleague reported on the findings of a study of continued AIDS risk in Hartford to a community advisory group comprised primarily of members of ethnocultural and sociocultural minorities from around the state. In reporting the findings, Singer noted that a goal of the research was to identify practical changes that could be readily implemented without enormous cost. Thus, he commented, although eliminating poverty would help to fight the spread of AIDS in a city like Hartford where most people with AIDS are indeed poor, this was not a goal that could be achieved easily or rapidly. A member of the audience objected to this stance, not because it delayed the elimination of poverty but because to him it implied that only the poor get AIDS. Others in the room agreed with this interpretation, suggesting the keen sensitivity that exists about AIDS-related issues in ethnocultural communities.

Ethnographic Study of Illicit Drug Use and AIDS Risk

As these examples suggest, a further ethical complication is the fact that some arenas of ethnographic research are especially fraught with moral challenges and almost unavoidable ethical dilemmas, whatever the intentions of the ethnographer. Ethnographic study of illicit drug use and AIDS risk is one such arena because its focuses on behaviors that are at once illicit and stigmatized and because the behaviors of concern to such researchers have the potential for raising issues of community representation and public portrayal.

The cases cited in this chapter are based on research carried out through the Hispanic Health Council in Hartford, Connecticut, a community-based research, direct service, health education, and advocacy organization. As a research institution, the Hispanic Health Council has had an established Human Subject Committee to review all of its grant proposals for many years. Because most of our research grants have been submitted to the National Institutes of Health or the Centers for Disease Control and Prevention, all of our research proposals include a section on research with human subjects that discusses ethical issues that pertain to the study in question. Although this section of proposals broadly addresses the main types of ethical questions that are relevant to our research (getting subject consent, potential risks and how they will be handled, protecting confidentiality), the field of naturalistic human research is always unpredictable, changing, and filled with potential for both social and ethical dilemmas. We have been keenly aware of these issues in that since the late 1980s, a large body of our research has focused on illicit drug users, the majority of whom come from minority ethnocultural communities, who daily are engaged in activities that put them and others at high risk for disease, injury, and arrest.

Issues of concern in our research on drug use include ethical predicaments generated by existing drug prohibition laws (Buchanan, Khoshnood, Stopka, Santelices, & Singer, 2002), the need for guidelines to steer publicly funded research on illicit behaviors like drug use (Singer et al., 1999), the physical and ethical dangers inherent in the study of street violence as a factor in drug use behavior (Marshall et al., 2001; Singer, Scott, Wilson, Easton, & Weeks, 2001a), and the ethical challenges of research videography with active drug users. In this chapter, we review how the Hispanic Health Council has responded to some of these ethical challenges to research in light of its goals as a community-based health research, advocacy, and service organization.

DRUG LAWS AND ETHICAL RESEARCH

The starting point for any examination of ethical dilemmas encountered by researchers trying to study and understand mood-altering drug use is the criminalization of some (but not all) kinds of these drugs. A number of different types of ethical challenges for researchers are created by the existence of laws prohibiting drug possession and sales, including researcher actions that increase the potential for the arrest of research participants, disruptions of access to drug supply because of participation in research, risk of arrest for the research staff, threats to the confidentiality of the participants, and issues involving informed consent in working with people suffering from a criminalized addiction (Buchanan et al., 2002). Each of these will be discussed in turn.

Risk of Arrest

For illicit drug users, it is possible that participating in a research project may increase their risk of arrest. One way this can happen is through an increase in their visibility to police. Although addiction and the frequent need to acquire illicit drugs and paraphernalia often force drug users to be more visible than they would like, they commonly engage in strategies intended to hide from the criminal justice system both their actions (e.g., by using drugs in hidden places, by not carrying syringes or drugs on them for long periods, by avoiding locations with heightened police activity) and their identities (e.g., by avoiding the stereotypic appearance of a rundown, street drug user). Although it is not uncommon for the police to be aware of many of the regular, street-active drug users in a given locale, others may successfully hide their illicit drug use for long periods of time; however, when drug users enroll in a drug use study, some of these defenses may be inadvertently lowered. In light of the AIDS epidemic, this is doubly problematic, as incarceration might be perceived as a form of AIDS risk, given prison bans on access to condoms and sterile syringes, despite frequent illicit sex and injection drug use in prisons (Kane & Mason, 2001).

To avoid police harassment, field researchers conducting drug studies commonly introduce themselves and their research mission to police personnel, especially to those who walk the beat and are likely to see the researchers in certain places known for their role in the drug trade. Therefore, as a result, individuals seen spending time with researchers may be assumed by the police to be engaged in illicit drug use. Even if the police do not know the ethnographer, they are well aware that Whites who live in suburban areas travel to the inner city to buy drugs. From the police perspective, any ethnic minority person observed to be hanging out with a White person in certain neighborhoods is probably assumed to be buying drugs for them. As a result, if the ethnographer is White, the police may begin to pay greater attention to the activities of minority individuals seen with the ethnographer.

Additionally, the police may confiscate potentially incriminating research materials from drug users. For example, in one study, we enrolled drug users in a diary-keeping activity and asked them to record all instances of syringe acquisition, use, and discard for 1 week (Stopka, Springer, Khoshnood, Shaw, & Singer, 2004). The purpose of this method was to learn about the context of HIV risk as close to the actual event as possible. What do drug injectors actually do when a needle breaks in the middle of the night and they are forced to find another syringe in order to avoid the pains of withdrawal? Is this a moment when they are most likely to engage in risk? Despite instructions to avoid incriminating details, some participants included the places where drugs were acquired and the names of friends and acquaintances with whom they used drugs. On one known occasion, a participant was taken into custody by the police while in possession of his diary, which contained entries on drug use from several previous days. When booked at a local jail, the participant's diary was found by the arresting officer who began to flip through it. Throughout, the officer maintained a jocular conversation with the participant, implying that information in the diary might be used against him. In the end, the participant was released and not charged with a crime (he had only been loitering in front of the Hispanic Health Council building while awaiting an appointment to turn in his diary), and the diary was returned to him. Although we had dodged a bullet in this instance, the risks of this research method became abundantly clear. Subsequently, participants were given more explicit instructions to avoid including names, places, or other incriminating information and were required to turn in their diary every few days.

Risks From Drug Network Research

Another risk of research participation for drug users is that their drug supplier may notice that they are spending time with research staff, individuals who may not look like they are from the neighborhood. In the above-mentioned study, participants sometimes expressed concern that drug dealers might conclude that they were collaborating with the police and refuse to sell them drugs. For someone with a drug addiction, this is a frightening prospect. If their usual drug supplier refuses to sell to them, participants are forced to buy from other sellers, perhaps in other parts of the city. Searching for a new dealer, in turn, makes the participant visible to the police or might result in them being "burned" (sold highly adulterated "empty" drugs by an unfamiliar drug seller).

Risks to Research Staff

Risks associated with drug criminalization also extend to research staff. Drug scenes are the sites of heightened rates of violence of several sorts, including conflicts among dealers over selling areas ("turf"); attempts by drug users to "rip off" drug dealers for their drugs or money; retaliation by higher-level drug dealers for drug theft; short-tempered attitudes among addicted, drug-craving users; conflicts over fair distribution among individuals who pool their limited resources to buy drugs; and police harassment. The crack cocaine scene has been particularly violent, for example, because the trade is predicated on a low-profit-per-unit/high-volume business that puts a high premium on the best selling locations, which tend to be fought over by rival dealing organizations. It is possible for researchers to be unwittingly caught in any of the various types of violence that can break out suddenly in street drug scenes (Williams, Dunlap, Johnson, & Hamid, 1992).

Although such incidents involving injury to researchers are not common, researchers have, on occasion, been the targets of violence during the research process. Bourgois (1995), for example, was mugged along with others because of being in the wrong place at the wrong time, although he was not targeted because he was a researcher. Jacobs (1998), in contrast, was robbed at gunpoint by one of his key informants (Luther, a 17-year-old crack dealer) and later harassed by him with repeated baiting telephone calls (5–10 times a day for 6 weeks) precisely because he was a researcher. In this instance, after 40 interviews, the informant was offended and angered because Jacobs had moved on to interview other crack dealers (facilitated by Luther) and was no longer relying on him as his primary source of information about the crack scene. From a research standpoint, developing new research relationships and sources of information to broaden the scope of understanding was completely justified and scientifically appropriate. From the informant's point of view, however, it was a breach of personal relationship, a slap in the face to someone who had generously given a tremendous amount of information about crack dealing and provided contacts with other dealers and now felt used and taken for granted. From the informant's perspective, it was the relationship and not the research that was of primary importance, a lesson Jacobs learned the hard way at the point of a long-barrel .45 caliber pistol.

Risks to Confidentiality

Following federal guidelines and other precedents, our research team adheres to strict protocols for storing and retrieving all data and information collected from participants in order to protect their confidentiality. These procedures include the following:

- Informed and signed consent in the language of choice of participants prior to enrollment in a research project
- Voluntary participation, including the right of subjects to refuse to answer any questions, without risk of losing services offered by the Hispanic Health Council
- Use of arbitrarily constructed participant identification codes called unique identifiers on all questionnaires and interviews
- Storage of raw data in locked filing cabinets and password-protected computers
- Exclusion of any individually identifiable information from computerized data files and avoidance of participants' names in group discussions
- Storage of master identification lists in separate and locked facilities controlled by the project director
- Use of collected information for research purposes only

Although we believe that these procedures effectively protect study participants under most conditions, there are reasons to question whether this protection is universal.

We conduct interviews with drug users in various public buildings, like the Hispanic Health Council, a community health center, and a community center that houses other programs, as well as on the street or in "shooting galleries" and similar locations. Most of these settings have a normal flow of public traffic. As participants enter and exit these sites, it is always possible that they might run into or be seen by someone they know, including staff from other projects, and asked to explain, or rather more likely lie about, their reasons for being there. For many addicts, this is not an issue because everyone who is important to them already knows about their drug habit; however, for others, their addiction may remain a guarded secret or only be discussed with a few confidants. Because they participate in illegal behaviors, loss of confidentiality could mean a loss of a job, guardianship of children, insurance, or housing.

For example, at one site we have used for interviewing participants, the security guard is well known in the community. He is familiar with many of the drug addicts from the local neighborhood, greeting most by name. Under such circumstances, the possibility exists that unbeknownst to the guard, one of his children or some other relative, friend, or acquaintance who is addicted could show up at the site for an interview. Similarly, we have had cases in past studies in which we have interviewed both partners in a romantic relationship but one or both was unaware of the other's drug use. Conversely, on one occasion a relative of one of our outreach workers spotted him in the field talking with drug users and subsequently spread rumors about the individual, a recovering addict, having had a drug relapse.

As these examples suggest, the opportunities for loss of confidentiality are numerous and hard to completely avoid. Over time, research organizations like the Hispanic Health Council tend to learn from their own errors and those of others about the many ways confidentiality can be broken and implement measures to avoid known dangers (e.g., ensure that all staff, including nonresearchers like receptionists, bookkeepers, janitors, and security guards understand confidentiality and their responsibilities to maintain it).

PAYMENT TO DRUG USERS

It has become standard practice to pay drug users for their time to participate in research. Some have questioned the paying of research incentives to drug users because it is assumed that they will use the payment to buy more drugs (and potentially be put at HIV or other risk during drug consumption). Although far fewer drug users would participate in research if no monetary incentives were offered, there would be no fewer drug users nor any drop in drug use. Research is not the engine fueling drug use. Readily available addictive drugs combined with social misery, humdrum jobs, and thrill seeking are more likely causes of drug use; however, research does have the potential to lower risk and provide a link to a hard-to-reach population, a link that may serve eventually as a bridge to drug treatment.

Benefits of Research Stipends

Additionally, although it makes only limited impact in the larger scheme of things, it is likely that stipends paid to drug-using research participants may actually reduce crime, as the participants will not have to carry out their usual income-generating "hustle," which for some involves "boosting" (shop lifting), breaking and entering, opportunistic theft, or mugging, to raise the money needed to buy drugs that day. By asking drug users about their daily involvement in such crimes, it would be possible in any research project to roughly calculate the crime reduction benefits of participant incentives. Still the question can be raised: Are researchers complicit in assisting drug users in their self destruction?

Referrals. Almost all drug researchers would answer no to the question above because they are aware of the full set of interactions that constitute researcher/drug-user professional relationships. Although the risks noted above are both real and significant, it is also true that participation in research offers drug users a number of potential benefits. Participants are provided with HIV risk reduction information and materials, and their questions about risk are answered by trained staff. Staff are also trained to provide information about the drug treatment system (available providers, lengths of stay, admissions criteria, disqualifications, costs, etc.) and are expected to offer requested referral

assistance. If a participant wants to go into drug detoxification or treatment, our research staff make the necessary phone calls, collect needed information that providers will require, and even provide transportation and follow-up as needed. Additionally, for known participants who need a letter indicating that they have been using opiates (e.g., heroin) for a required period to qualify for methadone treatment, our staff provide certification. The Hispanic Health Council also operates a small emergency food bank and has an emergency fund to meet an immediate participant expense, for example, to pay money owed to the methadone clinic so that the participant will be able to enter drug treatment. As a general ethical rule of operation, the pressing health needs of study participants always take precedence over the needs of research.

Support systems. Moreover, because the decision to stop drug use does not come easily, the relationships that develop with project staff may play a role in the decision to seek help to enter into drug treatment. It is not unusual for an individual to start as participants in research, be assisted by research staff to enter into drug treatment, complete treatment, and subsequently be hired as a project outreach worker, a position that may be the first legal employment. Moreover, study participants regularly express appreciation concerning their involvement because of the attention they receive and the opportunity research participation provides for self-reflection—including realization that drug use exposes them to many risks and takes a heavy toll on their lives—suggesting that participation in research expands the opportunities for health-promoting change among drug users. The therapeutic benefits of research participation, at least for some study participants, is an aspect of research that is often overlooked, especially in critiques of research characterizing it as a system that takes away from, but does not give back to, the community being studied. Research that is fully based in a community by being implemented through, or in conjunction with, community agencies and driven by an authentic commitment to community service has the potential to reverse the usual direction of resource flow from the community to research (Singer 1993).

Justice. One additional factor contributes to researcher assertions that payment to drug-using research participants is ethical. Researchers assert that drug users over the age of 18 years are legal adults and should not automatically forfeit their right to be paid for their work and knowledge because they are addicted to drugs. To decide that drug users cannot be paid because of their disability, whereas non-drug-using participants in similar social science research can, would be both an insulting form of infantilization and discrimination against the disabled (National Institute on Drug Abuse defines drug addiction as a brain disease).

STUDYING ILLICIT BEHAVIORS WITH PUBLIC FUNDING

The ethical issues confronted in the study of illicit drug users are further complicated by the fact that most of this research is federally funded and supported by public monies. This source of funding raises issues of legality, responsibilities to employers (including protecting their access to future funding), responsibilities to colleagues, and responsibilities to the researcher's discipline (including protecting access to future funding). It also increase the possibility for public, governmental, and mass-media scrutiny because of the use of public funding. Although it is generally accepted that researchers' most fundamental ethical responsibility is to the

people who volunteer as participants in their research projects, we also have a strong responsibility to protect our sponsors from inappropriate condemnation, although it is recognized that our research findings may result in appropriate condemnation of our sponsors because of their failure to meet their own social obligations. Specific issues include the following:

• *Responsibility that arises when the researcher is aware of illegal behavior by subjects.* Is a federally funded researcher obligated to report this information to criminal justice authorities (Carey, 1972; Soloway & Walters, 1977)? Although there are those who might support this as reasonable researcher responsibility, such reporting would make illicit drug research impossible, as researchers would, in effect, become "snitches" and drug users would no longer talk to them.

• *Responsibility that arises when the researcher is aware of dangerous or unhealthy behavior by subjects (e.g., sharing syringes, sexual contact without condoms).* If, for example, a federally funded researcher knows the positive HIV status of one partner in a drug using dyad, is the researcher obligated to tell the other partner so that they can take actions to prevent infection?

• *Special responsibilities that arise from working with subjects like illegal immigrants, whose very presence is punishable by the government.* Are federally funded researchers obligated to report undocumented individuals who appear to be in the country illegally and, further, engaged in illicit drug use?

• *Special responsibilities that arise from working with highly vulnerable populations, including ethnocultural and sexual minorities and traditionally oppressed populations, as well as with individuals whose behavior* makes them subject to social opprobrium. What extra responsibilities do researchers have in working with these populations, including responsibility to address risks that present, but not as a result of participation in research?

• *Special responsibilities that arise from research awareness of highly intimate and confidential information about subjects, including information that, if disclosed, could cause harm to subjects or put them at risk (Wright, Klee, & Reid, 1998).* For example, researchers may learn that a drug-using participant has stolen money from a drug dealer and, as a result, has put at risk his or her own life or the lives of others, like family members. What is the responsibility of the researcher in possession of this information?

• *Need for standards for responding to participant requests and demands for involvement in problematic (including illegal) behavior by the researcher, as well as pressure to redirect research project resources in ways not intended in the study design.* Given that drug users may provide hours of interview or observation data to researchers, what are the boundaries of reciprocity vis-à-vis participants (as noted in the case of Jacobs above)?

Ethnographers studying drug users must confront all or most of these (sometimes burdensome) issues in terms of the well-established ethical standards of beneficence, respect, and justice, while simultaneously never losing sight of their responsibilities to their various constituencies (subjects, sponsors, employers, colleagues, the wider community). As these lists make clear, ethical issues place significant burdens and potentially contradictory demands on drug researchers, and, as noted below, this weight is magnified by ethnographic methods of knowledge generation.

Ethical Challenges of Ethnographic Immersion

Additionally, given the nature of drug use and the sociocultural survival and coping patterns that have emerged among drug users over the last 90 years when drugs like heroin and cocaine were first outlawed in the United States and elsewhere, a number of specific problematic behaviors and ethical dilemmas in federally funded research with drug users emerge (Singer et al., 1999), including the following examples of researcher participation:

• Sharing drugs with subjects, a not unknown nor unreported practice (Myerhoff, 1976) in ethnographic studies, especially outside of the United States or with specific ethnocultural populations (e.g., Native Americans)

• Procuring (through buying, trading, etc.) drugs for research participants, which a researcher might be tempted to do if a key research participant was badly "dope sick" (in drug withdrawal) or otherwise incapacitated

• Holding or transporting drugs for participants, which a researcher might be persuaded to do to protect a key research participant from arrest

• Transporting participants to acquire drugs, to assist them to avoid the police, or to help dope sick participants to "score" drugs more quickly

• Allowing participants to use drugs in a researcher's car, home, or other property, or on property belonging to the researcher's employer because the participant could not easily and quickly find another safe location to avoid police detection

• Giving/loaning subjects money to buy drugs in return for all the information the participant has provided to the researcher

• Helping prevent HIV or other blood-born infection by acquiring sterile syringes to give to subjects in a city without legal syringe exchange or legal over-the-counter purchase of syringes from pharmacies

- Holding syringes or other drug paraphernalia for participants, again to help them avoid detection or arrest by the police
- Assisting participants to avoid arrest for illegal activities, for example by serving as a lookout during illegal activities like drug purchase or use
- Having sex with participants (another behavior that is not unknown in other types of ethnographic research) (Bolton, 1992; Wolcott, 2002)

NIDA/Hispanic Health Council Workshop

In response to concerns about the lack of ethical standards in federally funded ethnographic research with drug users, in 1998 representatives of the National Institute on Drug Abuse (NIDA) requested that community-based researchers at the Hispanic Health Council convene a workshop to review the issues noted above and to formulate a set of guidelines. Drug researchers from several research projects around the country were invited to participate in the workshop. Using a methodology for confronting and resolving ethical issues in research developed by Patricia Marshall, the workshop was able to resolve a variety of issues and to propose a set of standards for ethical drug user research. These standards were subsequently published by NIDA (Singer et al., 1999). Although recognizing the social pressures that could lead ethnographers to engage in any of the bulleted items listed above, workshop participants found that all of these behaviors were problematic and ethnically unacceptable (except for legally acquiring sterile syringes to replace broken or potentially infected syringes). In each case, the behaviors in question (buying drugs for participants, sharing drug with participants, etc.) placed the study participant, the researcher, the research sponsor, the employer of the researcher, fellow researchers, science, or the community at large at risk in some fashion.

Workshop participants placed special importance on the *principle of good reputation*. This principle is described in the American Anthropological Association's *Principles of Professional Responsibility* as follows: "Anthropologists bear responsibility for the good reputation of the discipline and its practitioners. . . . They must not behave in ways that jeopardize either their own or other's future research or professional employment." For example, the sharing of drugs with study participants, it could be argued, could lead to a rapid loss of good reputation for the ethnography of drug use in the eyes of federal and other funders, as well as in the view of Congress, which provides the budgets for federal research institutions. Workshop members recognized that there may be occasions to challenge federal actions with regard to drug users, for example imprisonment of individuals for drug use in spite of NIDA's definition of addiction as a brain illness and ethical issues raised by judicial sentencing mandates for specific *forms* of drugs, like the significantly higher sentencing mandates for *crack* cocaine vs. *powder* cocaine, which has contributed to significantly greater numbers of individuals from minority ethnocultural communities being in prison. These issues, however, did not apply in the case of most of the bulleted items above.

Additional Aspects of Violence and Ethics in the Study of Drug Use

Although some like the New York students described earlier feel that social researchers overemphasize drug use and violence descriptions of inner city ethnocultural communities and ignore community resiliency, vitality, and creativity, the narratives of street drug users are replete with incidents of hostility, aggression, and even brutality (Duke, Teng, Simmons, & Singer, 2003). But they also hold acts of kindness and generosity (Singer, Scott,

Wilson, Easton, & Weeks, 2001). In fact, the ethnographic research on drug use did not until relatively recently focus particularly on violence. The inadequate attention given to violence as a factor in drug use and drug-involved sexual activities, including rape, is a notable shortcoming of qualitative drug use and AIDS risk research. Our research, however, and the work of various other researchers indicates that violence is a regular and frequent component of the lives of street drug users, commonly beginning during childhood and continuing throughout their drug careers (El Bassel, Gilbert, Wu, Go, & Hill, 2005; Romero-Daza, Weeks, & Singer, 2003). Although violence must be understood to fully understand drug use and HIV risk among drug users, it is also critical to the understanding of several ethical issues in drug research.

Payment for Peer Recruitment

Understanding the role of violence in the lives of drug users is important to understanding the issue of research incentives discussed above. One type of incentive drug researchers often use, one that is critical to a sample construction stratification commonly used in drug research (i.e., peer-driven sampling), is payment to drug users for the recruitment of friends and associates into the research sample. This approach allows drug researchers to reach layers of the drug-using population not effectively tapped by other methods, providing, as a result, a more accurate and complete picture of the complex and partially hidden world of drug use (Heckathorn, Broadhead, Grund, & Stern, 1995); however, this approach also opens up the possibility of coercion, for example when stronger or otherwise more socially powerful individuals force others to come in to be interviewed and then take some or all of the incentive that is paid, in addition to their "head hunter" fee.

In one such incident, a participant in one of our studies brought in a young woman whom he introduced as a member of his social network. The young woman, however, appeared to be reluctant to be interviewed and kept glancing nervously at the man who recruited her for the study. An appointment was made for an interview for her, but the woman missed the appointment and a subsequent appointment made for her through her alleged network member. Finally, on the third try, the woman and her recruiter came in. Taken to a one-on-one interview room, the woman admitted that she was afraid of the man who brought her in and did not want to participate in the interview (and, hence, did not participate) (Singer, Simmons, Duke, & Broomhall, 2001). The damage, however, was done. Because of the study, she had been coerced into doing something she did not want to do. The recruiter, in turn, was no longer allowed to bring in individuals for interviewing.

Reporting Lifetime Experiences: Effects on Participants and Investigators

As researchers have begun to explore the role of violence in both drug use and drug-related AIDS risk, they have started asking drug users about their lifetime experiences with violence. By raising this issue in a much more direct and detailed fashion than previously, the potential has been created for provoking, or at least exacerbating, emotional problems for participants. For example, during interviews on violence, especially violence experienced as a child, participants on occasion complain of painful memories or become emotionally upset and tearful. Even while providing an opportunity for informants to unburden themselves by talking (possibly for the first time) with an interested and concerned listener about painful experiences, interviews about violence have the potential to produce considerable emotional upset and distress for study participants.

Researchers who are not explicitly trained and experienced in addressing such upset in a supportive professional manner may be uncertain about how to handle the torment expressed by participants, leading to strong feelings of inadequacy for the researcher and frustration and confusion for the informant. For this reason, implementing prior arrangements for providing study participants with professional intervention is a critical component of study designs focused on negative experiences among participants. In interviewing on violence, clear and specific discussion of the topics to be covered and the potential for upset become especially important during the consent process.

Secondary trauma, emotional damage experienced by someone who is exposed to another's particularly intense description of traumatic events, is an additional potential outcome of ethnographic research on violence (Simmons & Koester, 2003). Interviewing a series of drug users and hearing about the level of violence in their lives, including the wrenching cruelties that they have suffered at the hands of partners, dealers, other drug users, the police, and sometimes street gang members, can become a significant emotional burden for interview staff. At times, we have implemented coworker support groups to address job-related stress issues while maintaining a contract with a mental health provider should staff need professional intervention. See Chapter 11 by Ana Mari Cauce and Richard H. Nobles for an account of a study in which both participant intervention and coworker support groups were used.

ETHICAL ISSUES IN VIDEOGRAPHY WITH DRUG USERS

One of the goals of street ethnographic research with drug users is the development of a detailed understanding of the precise technical processes and varied equipment used in drug consumption, with the intent of gaining insights about how these behaviors and implements create or prevent health risks for participants. Another goal of this research is the assessment of the role of particular kinds of social relationships in the acquisition, preparation, and use of drugs. Because of the conditions under which drug use often occurs, achieving these goals can strain the capacities of the single ethnographic researcher. Critical events may take place in concealed locations, occur rapidly, involve multiple actors and a shifting cast of participants, and contain complex and overlapping activities. Trying to merely watch what is happening and use these observations to develop a fine-grained and carefully contextualized description, a traditional task of ethnographic research, may prove to be a frustrating experience for the street ethnographer.

For example, while observing drug consumption by a group of injectors in which several syringes and "cookers" (containers used to mix drugs and water) are being passed back and forth, it may be impossible to accurately track the pathways of equipment transfer. As the ethnographer closely focuses on one part of a drug use scene, he or she may miss other behaviors that are of equal or even greater importance. In order to overcome some of these difficulties, a number of street ethnographers have videotaped drug use scenes (e.g., Finlinson, Colon, Robles, & Deren, 1998), thereby providing a permanent record of events that can be reobserved to identify previously unrecognized acts, social interactions, relevant features of the physical setting, and participant statements and conversations.

Appeals and Challenges of Video

The appeals of video are considerable. Better than any other approach, filming allows viewers to experience the feeling of what it was actually like in the field setting (Rosenberg, 1980, p. 5). Additionally, the introduction in recent years of low-cost, lightweight, and easy-to-operate equipment has made ethnovideography a practical research strategy. Indeed, videotaping has become a ubiquitous feature of modern life generally, one that can, as the Rodney King case suggests, have important impacts on society; however, as the debates that ensued from the King case indicate, there are an abundance of ethical questions that arise in the cinema verité filming of social events. From the anthropological standpoint, some of these issues involve the use of ethnographic films as educational tools (Piccini, 1996). Gonzalez (1975), for example, asserts that often ethnographic films only serve to confirm rather than debunk social stereotypes about those he called the "exotic other," whereas Williams, Steenveld, and Tomaselli (1986), conversely, point out the potential dangers of cinematic romanticism. Other issues stem from the act of producing a potentially accessible and enduring visual record. In the case of the ethnovideography of street drug use, this entails capturing images of illegal, socially condemned, and often risky behaviors.

The decision to videotape drug injection and crack cocaine smoking by our Hispanic Health Council research team grew out of our efforts to understand the actual processes and patterns of drug consumption, the social networks of drug users, and the social settings in which drug use and AIDS risk frequently occur. Videotaping offered our team an approach for the following:

- Identifying previously unknown pathways of HIV transmission through specific activities and the use of particular drug consumption equipment
- Closely examining the exact stages of the drug-using process and the AIDS and other health risks associated with each stage

(e.g., for assessing whether, before or after injection, drug injectors retain bleach in their syringes for a sufficient time to deactivate HIV)

- Determining the ways in which the social context of illicit drug consumption fosters particular patterns of use and associated risk

During 1998, we videotaped four drug use scenes: (a) a single drug injector injecting heroin in an abandoned building; (b) five drug injectors "shooting up" together in a city park; (c) a cocaine user smoking crack in the kitchen of his rented apartment; and (d) a cocaine user converting crack back into an injectable form by mixing it with vinegar on the hood of his car. These recordings have proven to be very useful in achieving our research objectives; for example, they have helped us to "see" the common and potentially important role of cigarette smoking during both illicit drug injection and drug smoking episodes. But in the course of making and showing these brief videos, our team encountered a number of difficult ethical challenges.

Case 1: Videotaping Bystanders

The first of these problems, and perhaps the one that has been the least difficult to handle, occurred during the filming of the lone heroin injector in a local abandoned building. Located not far from our organizational offices, this neglected and rapidly deteriorating (now leveled) building stood very near to a high-traffic "drug-copping" (drug-buying) area of the city. Access to the building through a doorless back entryway was somewhat hidden from passing cars and pedestrians on the adjacent busy street. These two factors, the ready availability of drugs and concealed entree, made this a popular "get off" site for local drug users. On the day of the filming, two project ethnographers visited the site, as they had on several previous occasions. The building was empty, save for the enormous accumulation of general garbage and injection-related litter scattered on the floor (discarded syringes, water bottles, bleach bottles, AIDS prevention literature, cigarette butts, soda cans, and crumpled tissues). The latter served as ample reminder of the frequent use of this site for illicit drug consumption. As arranged, the study participant (who had already signed an informed consent concerning the filming) joined the ethnographers after he had acquired a $10 bag of heroin. He quickly took a seat on a milk crate in a somewhat lighted corner of the main room and removed his newly acquired bag of heroin, injection equipment, and syringe cleaning supplies from his bag and set these on a small box. He was now ready to shoot up.

Over the next half hour, this project participant was filmed answering questions posed by the lead author of this chapter, mixing and shooting up heroin, and bleaching and rinsing his injection equipment. This process continued without interruption; but as the filming was coming to a close, two additional individuals arrived at the site intent on consuming drugs. These individuals were not known to the ethnographers. They did seem to recognize the project participant. An uneasy moment passed until these individuals reached the conclusion that we were not narcotics officers or some other threat to them. Although we did not know them personally, they were apparently quite aware of our research program on street drug use. Consequently, instead of running away (the most typical response) or resorting to violence (a less likely but not unimaginable response under certain conditions), these individuals pulled their jackets over their faces and laughingly implored us not to film them (which we had no intentions of doing anyhow). As the researchers left the building, the individuals went to a favorite corner to inject their drugs.

The incident described above was very brief and ended without negative consequences, but it did reveal the potential problems that could ensue from filming in a readily accessible and widely used drug site. However common, cameras are an understandable threat to street drug users, who are aware that the police use video cameras for surveillance. Although it is difficult for many of them to long protect their identities from the police, some report that they have never been arrested. Indeed accounts exist in the literature of drug users who go to considerable lengths to keep their activities a secret (e.g., Kane & Mason, 1992). Cameras have the potential to breach the walls around this hidden information. Further, using them in settings where drug users gather creates the possibility that some individuals may form incorrect impressions about the purpose and identities of the researchers. We sought to minimize these dangers by visiting the site beforehand to make sure that no one was present. In street ethnography, however, once the action begins, the researcher does not control the research setting. Although the presence of a stranger is unsettling for those engaged in illicit activities, a stranger with a camera is all the more cause for alarm. This incident alerted us to the need for considerable caution to minimize the potential for misunderstanding associated with videotaping in natural settings.

Case 2: Videotaping Minors in Illicit and Health-Endangering Behavior

Our next attempt at videotaping was with a group of drug injectors who told us that they shoot up together every day at a secluded location in a local park. As we got to know members of this network, which was self-named "the Super Seven," we inquired about the potential for videotaping its daily drug use ritual. The leader of this group, an enterprising individual who was always seeking ways to participate in our various research initiatives (and be paid for his participation), seemed open to this idea. When he learned that we were starting a new project focused on understanding the pathways of adolescent drug abuse, he told us that a 19-year-old was about to be initiated into his drug use network by being voluntarily injected with heroin for the first time. We were invited by the network leader to videotape the event.

Although this offer would allow us to view a previously unobserved occurrence, an individual's first injection of an illicit drug, and to videotape a network of drug users, it raised significant ethical questions as well. The individual to be inducted into the group was a minor. Moreover, based on interviews with participants, we knew that at least two members of the network were infected with HIV. If syringes were shared during the injection process, he could be exposed to HIV or other diseases, for example hepatitis.

After fully discussing this situation, research team members reached the conclusion that it would be unethical to be present at or film an adolescent's initiation into drug injection and possible exposure to HIV without trying to dissuade him from pursuing this risky course of action. This put team members in an awkward position because we could be in violation of the wishes of the Super Seven drug network and be seen by them as interfering with their group activities, something that we promised we would not do. As is common during ethnographic fieldwork with street drug users, we were forced to choose between two ethically flawed options.

Beneficence. The basis for our dilemma is found in the wording of the *National Commission for Protection of Human Subjects of Biomedical and Behavioral Research* (1978), specifically in the report's discussion of the enshrined ethical principle

of beneficence. The report reads: "Persons are treated in an ethical manner not only by respecting their decisions and protecting them from harm, but also by making efforts to secure their well-being" (p. 6). In this instance, respecting the decisions of group members could block us from making efforts to secure the well-being of the initiate member. Our decision to attempt to persuade the group that the initiation of a minor was wrong was based on our conclusion that in this instance, and with the information we had at hand (health risks of injection drug use and injection equipment sharing), the well-being of a minor superseded our commitment to nonjudgemental, nonintrusive interaction with study participants.

Limitations of ethical codes. Prioritization of potentially conflicting ethical standards is an unavoidable aspect of complex research contexts, a label that well fits the study of street injection drug use. The Belmont Report (p. 1) reads as follows with reference to various codes of proper conduct in research:

> The codes consist of rules, some general, other specific, that guide the investigators or the reviewers of research in their work. Such rules often are inadequate to cover complex situations; at times they come into conflict, and they are frequently difficult to interpret or apply.

In the end, we were rescued from this dilemma when it turned out that the initiation ritual was a ruse dreamed up by the drug network's leader to peak our interest in the group. Our interest, however, was already peaked because of the leader's assertion that group members gathered together each day at the same time to share drugs. If this was true, it constituted a behavior that we had not seen in various other loosely bounded networks of drug users that we were tracking in several of our street ethnographic studies. Consequently, we arranged to have the leader take us to this communal event for videotaping.

Case 3: Participant Identity

On the day this was to be carried out, two members of the network were arrested for shoplifting and were not present. The other five gathered together in a park in the seclusion of a clump of trees and proceeded, with little encouragement from two project ethnographers, to tell us about their drug-using patterns, AIDS risk prevention strategies, income generating efforts, group dynamics, and related matters. As they talked, they injected drugs into their arms, each individual in his/her own manner. We filmed the event without incident, although the presence of several police cars driving through the park gave us reason for discomfort in that we had in our possession the videotape showing each of the participants injecting drugs and signed consent forms agreeing to allow us to videotape drug injection. Our anxiety peaked when one of the police cars parked just down the hill from where the group was gathered; however, the police remained oblivious to the activities of the injecting group.

Is deidentification possible? To minimize the risk for the participants, a strong effort was made to avoid showing participants' faces; however, because of their movement during the filming process, this proved to be impossible and brief glimpses of several faces were recorded by the video camera.

When we subsequently showed part of the footage (in which no participant faces were exposed) as part of a university presentation about street ethnography, several members of our larger research team who had not yet seen it but who had contact with some of the participants expressed concern that the identities of participants could be detected, for example from an arm tattoo. Another individual who reviewed the video worried that the police might be able to determine the gathering site of the group and lay in wait to arrest them.

Natural or video-motivated behavior. Also expressed was the view that, given the initiation ruse, the whole gathering had been staged to gain the small cash incentives that we offered for allowing us to interview participants and videotape their activities. Other issues were aired as well, but these were not specifically about ethical issues per se (e.g., that the participants were probably much more careful to avoid AIDS risk during injection than they would have been were the camera not present and that they would not have been inclined to inject one at a time, which was not requested by the researchers but did facilitate filming each individual's injection behavior).

One-on-one interviews that we conducted with individuals who participated in the network videotaping affirmed to us that the group had not just been constituted for the purposes of making the videotape; however, these interviews suggested that the strength of group ties was not as great as suggested by comments made by the leader during the videotaping. This point was confirmed when the Super Seven subsequently disbanded. One of its pivotal members, the leader's wife whose earnings in commercial sex appeared to have supplied a disproportionate share of the drugs used by the group, was injured in a car accident.

Risk of video seizure. These issues aside, we were still left feeling uncertain as to whether we had put the participants at special risk by making the video. Compared with field notes, in which participants' names can be disguised and their identities kept confidential, a film record has a higher potential for the breach of confidentiality. Although our research records have never been subpoenaed, state child welfare officials once attempted (unsuccessfully) to force a staff member to testify as part of an effort to end the parental rights of one of our project participants. Consequently, our projects have sought and been awarded federal protection from the seizure of our research data, which would include our video recordings; however, any showing of the video does create some potential that a member of the viewing audience will recognize an individual. Although it is our intention to minimize this risk by having even partial glimpses of participants' faces digitally scrambled, in such research it is impossible to completely eliminate all risks.

Case 4: When Participants Must Deceive Others

The final example involves videotaping crack use. A participant in one of our studies who was a regular crack user agreed to being videotaped smoking several rocks of crack in his possession. The participant approved the videotaping in his apartment. When the ethnographers arrived at the apartment, the participant proposed filming in the kitchen; the camera was set up quickly and filming commenced. In the middle of the filming, however, two other individuals who lived in the apartment arrived and were clearly quite surprised to find their roommate being filmed using crack. As recorded by the video camera microphone, one of these individuals questioned whether the ethnographers were police; however, the participant, thinking quickly if dishonestly, responded that the ethnographers were from a drug treatment clinic and the filming was needed to verify drug use prior to treatment. The filming concluded without further incident, but from an ethics perspective the incident was regrettable.

As a result of his involvement in our study, the participant had been put into a situation in which he found dishonesty to be the only credible answer that came to mind

(because he wanted to hide from his roommates the fact that he was being paid for his involvement in the video). Had his roommates chosen to question his innovative if unusual answer, friction could have developed and gotten out of hand.

As these examples suggest, videotaping drug users, however appealing as a research strategy, cannot be entered into without considerable planning and a full consideration of the ethical traps inherent in this undertaking. Both the act of filming and the existence of a visual record generate their own ethical questions that require acceptable answers, for example deleting faces, ensuring that permission to film is clear, and devising concrete plans for how to use the video.

CONCLUSIONS

Addiction, overdose, disease, street violence, vulnerability to injury, and exposure to the elements constitute a set of grave threats to the lives and well-being of drug users and, in fact, are the cause of many drug user deaths each year (Singer, 2005). Additionally, and contrary to what some appear to believe, drug users are not an isolated population and can be a source of infection for other sectors of society. For all of these reasons, the study of drug use is a critical public health activity (Power, 2001). Since the beginning of the AIDS epidemic in particular, research focus on drug use has expanded considerably. As a result, the number and kinds of ethical issues raised in such research also has expanded. Although research and public focus on ethical issues in research have taken enormous leaps in recent years, illness, stigma, and illegality make the study of illicit drug use an especially important issue in the ethical-research discourse.

Given the many ethical challenges faced in studying active, not-in-treatment, illicit drug users, some might conclude that this line of research is too fraught with human-subject issues to be warranted. Additionally, in some cases, especially when multiple review panels are involved (e.g., in collaborative projects involving several research institutions), researchers have been pushed to the limit to address potential human-subject questions and quandaries; however, the critical need for research on drug use, which is an ever changing behavior and hence in continual need of restudy, demands that a fair balance be achieved between protecting human subjects and conducting critically important research. Although in the increasingly distant past the balance was tipped in the favor of anything-goes research, today social scientists—researchers who are not engaged in medical clinical trials or otherwise testing potentially harmful interventions—sometimes feel as if an inordinate amount of time is spent addressing minute human-subject issues like changing a word here and there on consent forms, explaining fairly straight forward procedures in microscopic detail, and resolving conflicting views across multiple initial review boards, rather than conducting vital public health research.

Ethnographers have been especially concerned about the application of human-subject protocols developed in biomedicine (in response to significant ethical violations) to the kinds of research procedures they employ (Fluehr-Lobban, 2003; Marshall, 1992; Marshall & Koenig, 1996). Currently, there is little in the social sciences in the way of human-subject protocol evaluation to determine if various decisions, requirements, procedures, and standards do, in fact, protect research subjects from harm or injury. Perhaps such evaluation is the new frontier in the field of research ethics.

REFERENCES

American Anthropological Association. (1998). *Code of ethics of the American Anthropological Association.* Washington, DC: Author.

Bolton, R. (1992). Mapping terra incognita: Sex research for AIDS prevention: An urgent agenda for the 1990s. In G. Herdt & S. Lindenbaum (Eds.), *In the time of AIDS* (pp. 124–158). Newbury Park, CA: Sage.

Bourgois, P. (1995). *In search of respect: Selling crack in El Barrio.* Cambridge, UK: Cambridge University Press.

Buchanan, D., Khoshnood, K., Stopka, T., Santelices, C., & Singer, M. (2002). Ethical dilemmas created by the criminalization of status behaviors: Case studies from ethnographic field research with injection drug users. *Health Education and Behavior, 29,* 30–42.

Busier, H., Clark, K., Esch, R., Glesne, C., Pigeon, Y., & Tarule, J. (1997). Intimacy in research. *Qualitative Studies in Education, 10,* 165–170.

Carey, J. (1972). Problems of access and risk in observing drug scenes. In J. Douglas (Ed.), *Research on deviance* (pp. 71–92). New York: Random House.

Duke, M., Teng, W., Simmons, J., & Singer, M. (2003). Structural and interpersonal violence among Puerto Rican drug users. *Practicing Anthropology, 25,* 28–31.

El Bassel, N., Gilbert, L., Wu, E., Go, H., & Hill, J. (2005). Relationship between drug abuse and initiate partner violence: A longitudinal study among women receiving methadone. *American Journal of Public Health, 95*(3), 465–470.

Finlinson, A., Colon, H., Robles, R., & Deren, S. (1998). *Access to sterile syringes by injection drug users in Puerto Rico.* Paper presented at the meeting of the Society for Applied Anthropology, San Juan, Puerto Rico.

Fluehr-Lobban, C. (2003). *Ethics and the profession of anthropology.* Walnut Creek, CA: AltaMira.

Gonzalez, N. (1975). Films for medical anthropology: Introductory remarks. *American Anthropologist, 77,* 170–172.

Heckathorn, D., Broadhead, R. S., Grund, J. C., & Stern, L. S. (1995). Drug users versus outreach workers in combating AIDS: Preliminary results of a peer-driven intervention. *Journal of Drug Issues, 25,* 531–564.

Jacobs, B. (1998). Researching crack dealers: Dilemmas and contradictions. In J. Ferrell & M. Hamm (Eds.), *Ethnography at the edge: Crime, deviance and field research* (p. 177). Boston: Northeastern University Press.

Kane, S., & Mason, T. (1992). "IV drug users" and "sex partners": The limits of epidemiological categories and the ethnography of risk. In G. Herdt & S. Lindenbaum (Eds.), *The time of AIDS* (pp. 199–224). Newbury Park, CA: Sage.

Kane, S., & Mason, T. (2001). AIDS and criminal justice. *Annual Reviews in Anthropology, 30,* 457–479.

Marshall, P. (1992). Anthropology and bioethics. *Medical Anthropology Quarterly, 6,* 49–73.

Marshall, P., Heimer, R., & Singer, M. (2001). Ethical considerations working with injection drug users. *CIRA Notes, 2,* 13–16.

Marshall, P., & Koenig, B. (1996). Bioethics and anthropology: Perspectives on culture, medicine, and mortality. In C. Sargent & T. Johnson (Eds.), *Medical anthropology: Contemporary method and theory* (Rev. ed., pp. 349–373). Westport, CT: Praeger.

Marshall, P., Singer, M., & Clatts, M. (Eds.). (1999). *Integrating cultural, observational, and epidemiological approaches in the prevention of drug abuse and HIV/AIDS.* Rockville, MD: National Institute on Drug Abuse.

Myerhoff, B. (1976). *Peyote hunt: The sacred journey of the Huichol Indians.* Ithaca, NY: Cornell University Press.

Nader, L. (1972). Up the anthropologist: Perspectives gained from studying up. In D. Hymes (Ed.) *Reinventing anthropology* (pp. 284–311). New York: Pantheon Books, p. 299.

National Commission for Protection of Human Subjects of Biomedical and Behavioral Research. (1978). The Belmont Report: Ethical principles and guidelines for the protection of human subjects research. (DHEW Publication No. (OS) 78–0012). Washington, DC: Government Printing Office.

Piccini, A. (1996). Filming through the mists. *Current Anthropology, 37*(Suppl. 1), 87–111.

Power, R. (2001). Reflections on participant observation in drugs research. *Addiction Research and Theory, 9,* 325–337.

Romero-Daza, N., Weeks, M., & Singer, M. (2003). "Nobody gives a damn if I live or die": Violence, drugs, and street-level prostitution in inner-city Hartford, CT. *Medical Anthropology, 22,* 233–259.

Rosenberg, A. (1980). *The documentary conscience: A casebook in film making.* Berkeley: University of California Press.

Simmons, J., & Koester, K. (2003). Hidden injuries of research on social suffering among drug users. *Practicing Anthropology, 25,* 53–57.

Singer, M. (1993). Knowledge for use: Anthropology and community-centered substance abuse research. *Social Science and Medicine, 37,* 15–26.

Singer, M. (1996). A dose of drugs, a touch of violence, a case of AIDS: Conceptualizing the SAVA syndemic. *Free Inquiry in Creative Sociology, 24,* 99–110.

Singer, M. (2005). *Something dangerous: The role of emergent and changing drug use in community health.* Prospect Heights, IL: Waveland Press.

Singer, M., Marshall, P., Trotter, R., Schensul, J., Weeks, M., Simmons, J., et al. (1999). Ethics, ethnography, drug use and AIDS: Dilemmas and standards in federally funded research. In P. Marshall, M. Singer, & M. Clatts (Eds.), *Cultural, observational, and epidemiological approaches in the prevention of drug abuse and HIV/AIDS* (pp. 198–222). Bethesda, MD: National Institute on Drug Abuse.

Singer, M., & Clair, S. (2003). Syndemics and public health: Reconceptualizing disease in bio-social context. *Medical Anthropology Quarterly, 17,* 423–441.

Singer, M., Scott, G., Wilson, S., Easton, D., & Weeks, M. (2001a). "War stories": AIDS prevention and the street narratives of drug users. *Qualitative Health Research, 11,* 589–611.

Singer, M., Simmons, J., Duke, M., & Broomhall, L. (2001b). The challenges of street research on drug use and AIDS risk. *Addiction Research and Theory, 9,* 365–402.

Society for Applied Anthropology. (1983). *Professional and ethical responsibilities* (Rev. ed.). Oklahoma City, OK: Author.

Soloway, I., & Walters, J. (1977). Workin' the Cordner: The ethics and legality of fieldwork among active heroin users. In R. Weppner (Ed.), *Street ethnography* (pp. 159–178). Beverly Hills, CA: Sage.

Stopka, T., Springer, K., Khoshnood, K., Shaw, S., & Singer, M. (2004). Writing about risk: Use of daily diaries in understanding drug-user risk behaviors. *AIDS and Behavior, 8,* 73–85.

Waterston, A. (1999). *Love, sorrow and rage: Destitute women in a Manhattan residence* (pp. 22–23). Philadelphia: Temple University Press.

Williams, A., Steenveld, L., & Tomaselli, R. (1986). *Myth, race and power: South Africans imaged on film and TV.* Bellville, South Africa: Anthropos.

Williams, T., Dunlap, E., Johnson, B., & Hamid, A. (1992). Personal safety in dangerous places. *Journal of Contemporary Ethnography, 21,* 344–369.

Wolcott, H. (2002). *Sneaky kid and its aftermath.* Walnut Creek, CA: Altamira.

Wright, S., Klee, H., & Reid, P. (1998). Interviewing illicit drug users: Observations from the field. *Addiction Research, 6,* 517–535.

Part IV

THE RIGHTS AND RESPONSIBILITIES OF INDIVIDUALS, COMMUNITIES, AND INSTITUTIONS

CHAPTER 15

Safeguarding Sacred Lives

The Ethical Use of Archival Data for the Study of Diverse Lives

COPELAND H. YOUNG

MONICA BROOKER

In unequal relationships, informed consent does not work.

—Annette Dula, "Yes, There Are African American
Perspectives on Bioethics"

INTRODUCTION
AND BACKGROUND

In this chapter, we will explore the advantages of preserving archival data about individuals and communities of color, as well as examine the ethical implications of data preservation through three critical discussions: (a) the distinction between primary and archival data sets; (b) the role of archival controls to promote individual and community protection; and (c) the contrasting ethical issues between the use of qualitative and quantitative archival data.

As we contemplate the emergence of these ethical challenges today, it is apropos to note the historical origins of our discussions, namely that social science research on

lives of color as well as the founding of the earliest data archive in the United States converged in the efforts of Howard W. Odum in the early 20th century (Brazil, 1988; Johnson & Johnson, 1980). In 1924, Odum founded the Institute for Research in Social Sciences through which he sought "to gather and organize immense amounts of raw data" (Brazil, 1988, pp. 489–490). Toward that end, Odum conducted a study of African American folklore, "to get a sort of habit of making descriptive or objective studies as opposed to the older philosophisings or opinionated dissertations" (Brazil, 1988, p. 490). Appropriately, Odum and his colleague, Guy Johnson, acknowledged the limitations of their folklore project as having been "conducted 'from the outside'" (Odum &

Johnson, 1925), and they urged black scholars "to press on with studies of their people's folk contributions" (Brazil, 1988, p. 491).

Nearly a century later, we find ourselves engaged in comparable deliberations, examining the importance of collecting and preserving data on the lives of individuals of color, distinguishing culturally valid quantitative and qualitative research methods, and defining the ethical responsibilities of researchers and data archivists. The use of archival social science data collected from individuals and communities of color poses intricate ethical challenges and concerns. Archival collections, such as the Murray's Diversity Archive, have become important agents for advancing discussions, not only about the advantages of data preservation but also about expanding research options through the use of qualitative and quantitative data for secondary analysis and about the potential role of archival data for enhancing research methods and designs.

Henry A. Murray and the Murray Archives

The Murray Archives represents a unique hybrid of two archival traditions. As a data archive, the Murray Archives follows in the tradition of such prestigious social science data archives in the United States as the Odum Institute's Data Archive (1924); the Roper Center (1947); the Inter-university Consortium of Political & Social Research (1962); the Steinmetz Archive (1962); and The Data Archive (1967) in Europe, among many others. Social science data archives predominantly preserve numeric data in electronic format. The Murray Archives is the only social science data archive in the United States, and one of only a few in the world, that preserves qualitative social science data in original record (paper) format and data in other formats *including* electronic numeric data. The Murray enjoys a second heritage

from those of traditional manuscript repositories which commonly manage paper archives and records (Ketelaar, 2001; Schellenberg, 1996; Thomassen, 2002). This dual heritage, along with Henry Murray's ideographic and interdisciplinary approach to research, sets a new course for the Murray Archives regarding social and behavioral science research resources and opportunities. The Murray's archival mission contrasts but also complements other data archives in focus (the study of lives) and format (i.e., nonelectronic data) and demonstrates similarities to, and differences from, mainstream humanities-oriented archival institutions as well.

Following in the tradition of Henry Murray's multidimensional approach to the study of lives (Elms, 1987), data sets maintained at the Murray Archives are multifaceted (Colby & Phelps, 1990; James, 2002; James & Malley, 1997; James & Sorensen, 2000; Phelps, 1990) with regard to formats (paper, audiotape, videotape, numeric, and electronic text); types of data collection instruments (Radcliffe Institute for Advanced Study, Henry A. Murray Research Center [Radcliffe], 2000); study designs (most notably qualitative and longitudinal); and disciplinary perspectives (e.g., psychology, sociology, history, nursing, anthropology, social work, political science, education). Drawing from the central mission of Radcliffe College (and later the Radcliffe Institute for Advanced Study), the archive's main focus has been the preservation of research on the lives of American women. This focus has more recently expanded to include the study of diverse lives. Murray's emphasis on "multiform" assessment for the study of lives rests at the heart of the Murray Archives' appraisal process and sets the background context for questions about the ethical use of archival data. The archival data to which we refer encompass a wide range of collection methods such as open-ended qualitative interviews, questionnaires, psychological tests, institutional records, behavioral observations, medical examinations, and atypical data sources (e.g., clinical summaries) defined as "other." These types of data contrast traditional closed-ended numeric survey questionnaire and structured interview data and avail themselves to users in a spectrum of formats as mentioned above.

Data Sharing

The contemporary research environment, with its assorted legal and ethical requirements, provides the relevant background to the salient concern about the ethical use of archival data on populations of color. The use of data for secondary analysis derives most broadly from data sharing of which several varieties exist (see National Institutes of Health, Office of Extramural Research, n.d., 2003). One sharing arrangement involves direct contact and/or collaboration with the principal investigator such as with national surveys (e.g., Panel Study of Income Dynamics). Another option involves accessing data through a "data enclave" in which data access is mediated through supervised onsite use (e.g., Melichar, Evans, & Bachrach, 2002; Nolte & Keller, 2001). A data archive, such as the Murray Archives, acquires data with the intention of preserving the data permanently and provides data access contractually mediated by a deed of gift known as a memorandum of agreement. Finally, the "mixed mode" option confers differing levels of access through the creation of multiple versions of a data set. Of the options mentioned, only a data archive intends to preserve data permanently for potential use in the future, whereas the other types of data sharing may have implicit "sunset" provisions if interest in a data set declines over time. As well, data sharing options other than a data archive often offer data from only a few data sets as opposed to a plethora of studies.

Ethical Codes

Underlying the practices of social science archives are mainstream ethical principles that have been shaped by biomedical models. The lineage of these modern bioethical principles originated with the Nuremberg Code of Ethics in Medical Research (Trials of War Criminals Before the Nuremberg Military Tribunals [Trials], 1949). This directive in conjunction with the World Medical Association's *Declaration of Helsinki* (World Medical Association, 1964) established the groundwork for institutional review boards (IRBs) to evaluate research in terms of potential harm to subjects in research (Pullman, 2002). In addition, the exposure of the 40-year Tuskegee Syphilis Study in 1972 (Jones, 1993) resulted in the creation of the National Commission for the Protection of Human Subjects of Biomedical and Behavioral Research in 1974 (Caplan, 1992). The commission's seminal document, known as the Belmont Report (U.S. Department of Health, Education, and Welfare [DHEW], 1979), set forth a federal code for the ethical protection of human subjects (U.S. Department of Health and Human Services, 2001) that is discernible in today's social science research practices: *respect for persons* (autonomy) as demonstrated by informed consent; *beneficence*, as reflected by evaluation of the risks and benefits of research; and *justice*, as demonstrated in fairness of subject selection. Beyond these fundamental issues lay the complex ethical concerns that arise when data are collected from individuals and communities of color and then made available for new researchers through an archive.

Advantages of Data Archives

Social science data archives serve as valuable allies and partners to research communities through the preservation of data that might otherwise be lost, by facilitating cost conscious research processes, and also by serving as a voice of advocacy for scholars conducting research. Although use of numeric quantitative archival data for secondary analysis has been well established in the fields of economics and sociology (Brooks-Gunn, Phelps, & Elder, 1991; Carlin, 1991; Duncan, 1991; Feinberg, Martin, & Straf, 1985; McCall & Applebaum, 1991), psychology and other behavioral sciences have more recently embraced the value of qualitative archival data such as those found at the Murray Archives (Johnson, 2001a, 2001b, 2001c, 2002; Melichar et al., 2002). The numerous advantages of preserving social science data have generated growing attention; notably archival research facilitates verification of findings through replication and reanalysis (Feinberg et al., 1985), reinforcing open and transparent scientific inquiry, and promoting scientific accuracy. Moreover, the awareness that one's data and subsequent published findings could become available for closer scrutiny can motivate added consideration of how theoretical, methodological, and operational procedures shape research design. The use of archival data promotes cost-effective research processes and also decreases the burden of reentry on researched communities.

Social science research findings affect individuals, communities, and societies, particularly through social policy. Without the availability of archival data, empirical research finds itself having to build from the more tenuous foundations of tabular findings from published reports of previous studies. Thus, some social science constructs, and perhaps especially those attributed to the lives of individuals of color, risk becoming "folk data," passed down from study to study without meaningful due diligence of a construct's foundations. With increased availability of quantitative and qualitative data on lives of color, new research (e.g., aggregated study) can verify or refute old paradigms.

The use of archival data sets can also contribute to research practices methodologically, and theoretically.

In an effort to promote expanded use of federally funded research efforts, federal funding entities are currently promoting or requiring that researchers share their data. The cost effectiveness of data sharing has reinforced such federal policies. The urgency for the preservation (or at least sharing) of data on people of color arises from the paucity of valid research on them (Sue & Sue, 2003) due to the costliness of high-quality studies and due to occurrences of poor funding (Sue, 1999). Scientifically valid research investigation in communities of color requires specialized and more costly customization of research methods rather than the use of standardized, "off-the-rack" research approaches (Sue & Sue, 2003). These methodological and financial realities, therefore, make such studies (to the extent that they exist) of vital interest for preservation.

DISTINCTIONS BETWEEN PRIMARY AND ARCHIVAL DATA SETS

The work of archival preservation of data ushers in meaningful qualitative and epistemological distinctions between primary and archival data sets. The main work for creating a primary data set involves data *collection*. By contrast, the central work undergirding the creation of an archival data set is data *processing*. Departing from the constricted parameters through which primary data come into being, archival data sets establish fresh foundations from which new researchers with alternative perspectives to those of the original researchers can encounter data (James & Malley, 1997; Phelps, 1990). Moreover, because many primary research studies include personal identifiers, they can be less amenable to sharing.

Data Durability and Preservation

The most prominent distinction between primary and archival data sets inheres in the durability of each. Because primary data sets are at greater risk for deterioration, physical maintenance and attention to issues of data preservation are central concerns in the creation of archival data sets. In general, data archives actively maintain and preserve data contributions for posterity. Making data available for long-term archival use requires extreme care in data preparation; this includes storage of data in environments that are optimal for their survival. An added complexity of data preservation, such as at the Murray Archives, concerns the varied formats in which data are acquired, such as audio, video, paper, microfiche, and electronic formats. Long-term preservation may include resource migration from outdated and obsolete formats to current format standards. Because archival data sets are maintained permanently, maintaining subject confidentiality becomes an ongoing aspect of archival concern and control. By contrast, subject confidentiality becomes increasingly susceptible to breaches in nonarchival primary data sets, in that data can become inadvertently misplaced, lost, forgotten about, or outright abandoned over time, thus risking unsanctioned discovery. Primary, nonarchival data sets also stand at greater risk for physical damage from de facto storage in basements, attics, garages, and in file cabinets in old offices and also at greater risk for accidental disposal due to inadequate labeling of records.

Scientific Verifiability

Another significant distinction concerns differences in scientific verifiability. In a primary data set, data claims and values may be unverifiable by outside audiences and may also lack internal consistency (Hammersley, 1997; Corti & Thompson, 2003). Archival data sets present data as "raw" and unfiltered, such that "what you see is what you get." After archival processing, data claims and values can be verified and data can be established as internally consistent through the reported findings contained in the generated reference information about each data set. Data from primary data sets are most often only available in tabular format whereby data claims are filtered and presented through publications, reports, and the like, or transformed through statistical analyses. One important caveat concerning archival data suggests that the quality of research generated from an archival data set is bound by the extent that primary research methods demonstrated ethical and scientific validity.

Multiple Uses/Multiple Data Sets

Contrasting the directed focus of primary research, archival data sets are designed for multiple uses (Corti & Thompson, 2003; Fielding, 2004; Hammersley, 1997). The amenability of an archival collection to new questions essentially results in a multiplicity of new studies, one for each new question from each new applicant; and as such, each data user essentially becomes a principal investigator of a new study. The ethical implications of each of these new questions require careful examination, particularly regarding risks and benefits to relevant communities in terms of physical, geographic community or social identities (e.g., gender, race, ethnogender, age, etc.). In reference to a subject's "community" of origin, we draw on the concept of "peoplehood" (Holm, Pearson, & Chavis, 2003). The term *peoplehood* invokes commonalities shared through "language, sacred history, religion, and land" (p. 12). Through "community" we conceive of common peoplehood.

The use and consultation of reference material generated about a given study (e.g., sample blank measures used in a study, detailed descriptions of sample and research design, technical reports, inventories and frequencies of available data, and/or codebooks) can facilitate replication studies, comparative analyses, follow-up studies and secondary analyses of the archival data themselves, pilot studies, or measures development. Generally, the ethical implications of each type of reanalysis vary according to the type of analysis. Comparative analyses, for example, raise ethical issues regarding the risk of resorting to deficit models in group comparisons (Fisher et al., 2002). Secondary analyses of archival data raise concerns about generating harmful conclusions about the primary community of origin. Ethical risks involved with developing new measures with archival data relate to how items from an archival measure are appropriated or incorporated into a new measure and to what extent such a new measure offers affirming or damaging assessments of a racial or ethnic group.

Additionally, primary data sets are designed to address problems in the here-and-now (e.g., Fielding, 2004), whereas archival data sets inherently exist for use in the future; although the facts remain the same, the meaning of the facts changes with time. Some of the ethical implications of this focus on the future relate to changing social, cultural, political definitions and meanings of race, ethnicity, culture, and gender. Specifically, social identities and community characteristics evolve over time; for instance, within the Murray holdings one finds a study of "Negro Professional Women Study" (Epstein, 1973), a study of "Black Women Attorneys" (Simpson, 1984), and a "Longitudinal Study of African-American Oldest Old" (Johnson, 1995) reflecting contemporary self-definitions. This has also been the case for many "Hispanic" identities of earlier times, which currently self-define as Latina, and many "Oriental" identities of earlier times, which now identify as Asian-American. Beyond race, contemporary individuals also self-identify in more specific ethnic terms such as Chicano, Puerto Rican, Korean-American, or Punjabi-American. The transformative nature of communities and the subsequent emergence of new social identities have proved to be critical for disenfranchised populations.

THE ROLE OF ARCHIVAL CONTROLS FOR INDIVIDUAL AND COMMUNITY PROTECTION

The uses of archival social science data, particularly ideographic archival data, raise a whole range of ethical issues (Tomilinson-Keasey, 1993). Establishment of archival control over a data set facilitates ethical oversight of a collection's use. An important aspect of the preparation of an archival data set that enables ethical access is the removal of personal identifiers, or "deidentification." The core component of converting data from a primary research study into an archival data set involves the transformation of data from personalized records to depersonalized archives. The decrease of potential risks for disclosure marks a key benefit of cleansing data of personal information about individual participants (Taube & Burkhardt, 1997).

Data Deidentification

Data deidentification (or "anonymization"), the process for securing and/or maintaining participant/individual confidentiality, enables wider potential for data circulation by substantially reducing the chances of identity disclosures (Dunn & Austin, 1997). Approaches to data anonymization vary according to format, the discussion of which would surpass the scope of our topic here;

however, working with original paper record data, the process of deidentification entails either the simple removal of personal identifiers (e.g., striking out names, addresses, etc.) without information substitution or the removal of personal names and addresses and the substitution of more general role designations (e.g., sister, supervisor, husband), geographic descriptors, and class/type of employment. This latter treatment of deidentified material works to retain as much of the original meaning and context as is possible without breaching the confidentiality of respondents. In this way, anonymization, a cornerstone for establishing the ethical use of archival social science data, facilitates access to data without compromising participant confidentiality.

In some cases, such as in an oral history project in which narrators intentionally identify themselves and offer their testimony and insights for posterity, attempts to deidentify transcripts are extremely difficult, susceptible to reidentification, or otherwise unnecessary. The onus of ethical oversight then inheres in the proposed *use* of the archival records for reanalysis and establishing the commitment to ethical use of records.

The value of data deidentification rests in its promotion of greater efficiency in the use of data resources already available. The use of deidentified data may also help to avert repeated intrusions into various communities by facilitating further research on an existing archival data set, thereby reducing the impetus for resampling (Fielding, 2004, p. 100; Hammersley, 1997, p. 137; Sieber, 1989). Reduction of research burdens on communities becomes especially desirable when considering that some researchers have gained much for themselves, yet offered little in return to the community of investigation. The ensuing ethical benefit of using archival data is also supported by the second principle of the Nuremberg Code which states, "The experiment should be such as to yield

fruitful results for the good of society, *unprocurable by other methods or means of study* [italics ours], and not random and unnecessary in nature" (Trials, 1949).

There are, however, some caveats to the mere removal of basic personal identifiers such as names and addresses. Additional precautionary steps are warranted in the case of longitudinal archival data sets to reduce the development of "mosaic effects" (Vijayan, 2004) whereby patterns from combinations of unrelated segments of information, which unfold over time, result in inadvertent identity disclosure. For example, in the case of research on individuals of color working in specialized occupations, where minority representation is nominal, one needs to strike an ethical balance. On one hand, the availability of data regarding the experiences of people of color in majority White occupations and/or work settings may increase understanding of significant sociological and psychological factors, and subsequently affect future policies and procedures. Yet, under such circumstances, individuals could be theoretically identified through the problem of mosaic effects despite basic deidentification. Thus, enabling such data to be used responsibly requires a more complex system of deidentification, in part due to more glaring mosaic effects: "Data elements that in isolation look relatively innocuous can amount to a privacy breach when combined" (Vijayan, 2004). Removal of personal identifiers, however, can create semantic shifts in focus from the individual level to the broader community level (both geographic and sociopolitical).

Data Deidentification and Detachment

A possible drawback of data deidentification is an attenuation of context along with shifts in meaning that could lead to distorted interpretations about a group of individuals' life experiences. Derived from, and directly related to, the study participants, primary data are personal documents about individuals. Archival data are impersonal documents the focus of which focus shifts from the individual to the class of individual in terms of gender, race, or sample membership (i.e., to the next facet/level of identification). Through the process of deidentification, data responses become dissociated from the original participants who authored the response, but data responses are not necessarily detached from the subjects' community. Only a subject's group identification remains after the process of removal of subject identifiers. Although data deidentification offers anonymity for the individual research subject, the process of detachment that ensues from deidentification prompts a shift of potential harm from the primary subjects to the subjects' community with implications, for better or for worse, that can reverberate, not only in a geographic community of origin but also among members of a broader sociopolitical identity (e.g., Japanese American women or Asian American women, Chicano men or Latino men).

In the case of the Tuskegee Syphilis Study, beyond the harm inflicted on participants in the study, the collective negative psychological impact of this infamous study on African American communities in the United States has been continual and manifests itself by the ongoing lack of African American participation in research studies. Within the strict context of an archival data set, the process of deidentification severs the organic professional and ethical bonds between researcher and participant shifting the relationship to that between data patrons and anonymized "data" (Corti & Thompson, 2003; Fielding, 2004; Leh, 2000; Richardson & Godfrey, 2003).

The need for careful oversight and archival control over research collections becomes clearer when one considers possible ethical consequences of deidentification.

Moreover, because ethical concerns embraced in the Belmont principles have less direct application with deidentified archival data, the "common rule" generally exempts archival research from IRB review (Wichman, Mills, & Sandler, 1996). These points taken together suggest that data archivists must don the role of ethical overseer concerning the uses of archival data. Thus, future analyses and findings based on archival data should receive additional attention and protection that takes into consideration the impact of economical, social, and psychological factors on the representative community.

Some of the ethical risks posed by archival research on communities of color involve the potential for data reanalysis resulting in "victimization or scapegoating," "blaming the victim," "stereotyping and adverse images" or the manipulation and control of data, thereby to strengthen "the power position of some groups and undermine that of others" (Warwick, 1982, p. 115). Nelkin (1982) cautioned about the "potential misuse of knowledge" generated from research and also observed that members of communities of color have now come to "view science as a commodity, indeed as a political resource that may be used to enhance the power and control of specific social groups" (p. 167). Through self-empowerment, communities have imposed "limits on research which they feel might have implications for social policy" and "have insisted that they must also derive tangible benefits from such research" (p. 167).

Contractual Controls

Other aspects of archival control for ethical oversight include the safeguard of using legal agreements between principal investigators and the data archive. Guidelines spelled out through a memorandum of agreement (or "memo") pertain to how future data users may or may not use data. In all cases, approved data users enter into contractual arrangements with the Murray Archives, ensuring a patron's commitment to follow all guidelines and to fulfill all requirements for use of data. A further safeguard is the requirement of a written proposal to evaluate proposed methods and intentions regarding the use of data. In its own way, this process provides additional ethical safeguards by requiring that an applicant declare his or her intentions through specifying research questions and hypotheses, how and why these data are relevant, and how these data will be used.

Legal mediation of data access provides ethically healthy solutions to the problem of access through the requirement that the data archive upholds the implicit ethical standards embraced during the primary research project. A memorandum of agreement provides a discernible code for access such that procedures are standardized for all prospective data users as part of the application process. Through this blend of legal and procedural evaluation, archival data access retains rigorous scrutiny while adopting greater regulatory features that facilitate equal opportunity access among qualified individuals. Legal mediation also intends to "level the playing field" in that, for qualified applicants, access to archival data doesn't hinge on who one knows, as much as whether one's proposal meets standard requirements and expectations. In this way, established requirements foster equal eligibility. A benefit of the ensuing equal opportunity access to data is that new researchers, whether from the same field or another discipline, coming with a fresh perspective, may tap into valuable new insights and interpretations. Other methods of access control at the Murray Archives include the use of screening committees in which several reviewers independently evaluate proposals to access data sets with especially sensitive data and the imposition of

access level restrictions based on level of professional education or competence.

The benefits of rigorous scrutiny and greater regulatory oversight of archival data provide for ongoing protection of both subjects and their community. Such ethical oversight places a mutual and shared onus of responsibility on the principal investigator as well as on archival custodians. Through the memo, the former is required to establish ethically sound guidelines for data access that are appropriate for the sample and community under investigation. The latter party is duty bound to enforce those guidelines, sometimes in perpetuity.

Archival Implications of Best Practice Recommendations

Although the acquisition and processing of data is of primary concern for archival institutions, the ultimate goal is to make data available for secondary analysis. To that end, a great deal of attention has been placed on processes that assure the ethically secure use of archival data emerging from populations of color. Although research preserved at a multidisciplinary archive such as the Murray Archives includes studies from numerous disciplines, few disciplines have actually presented systematic guidelines on best practices for research on communities of color. Although developed from the point of view of psychology, the Council of National Psychological Associations for the Advancement of Ethnic Minority Interests (CNPA-AEMI) has set forth some useful guidelines for research with individuals and communities of color, the direct implications of which point to potential archival practices that can further support ethical oversight of how data can be used.

CNPAAEMI comprises four organizations: the Society of Indian Psychologists; the Asian American Psychological Association; the Association of Black Psychologists;

and the National Hispanic Psychological Association. The recommendations of these organizations are as relevant for archival research as they are for primary research. CNPAAEMI's best practice recommendations for conducting ethical research offer implicit suggestions for the ethical handling of archival data. Such recommendations as community members assisting in the development of research design, methodology, and dissemination of findings could likewise serve as guidelines for research appraisal in a data archive's acquisition process, namely to pursue acquisition of studies that implement such suggestions. In this way, one can incorporate CNPAAEMI's recommendations in archival appraisal criteria.

CNPAAEMI further suggests that within specific communities, for example American Indian communities, written permission from tribal councils, tribal college research departments, or tribal oversight committees could be required before the start of a research project (Council of National Psychological Associations for the Advancement of Ethnic Minority Interests [CNPAAEMI], 2000). In an archival context, one could either prefer the acquisition of such studies in which community councils had been consulted or the data archive could set consultation with community councils as a procedural expectation before obtaining approval to use relevant data sets. The ethical value in such practices is that it affords an important protective function for communities (geographic or sociopolitical) and can also reduce the likelihood of misguided publication and dissemination of harmful and negatively stereotypical interpretations of findings (e.g., Atteneave, 1989).

Design of studies for primary and secondary research should incorporate cultural influences and experiences, attend to ethnic differences within cultural groups so as not to indiscriminately lump together distinct groups into meaningless categories, and avoid the use of deficit models for analysis and interpretations of community and group comparisons. A pervasive issue in research of communities of color is the avoidance of "ethnic gloss" (Trimble & Dickson, 2005), which confers sweeping generalizations across ethnicities toward composite portrayals of racial groups without regard to interethnic variations (Fisher et al., 2002; Fisher, Jackson, & Villarruel, 1997). The problem of ethnic gloss is specifically critical in light of the presence of hundreds of American Indian tribes and numerous Asian, Latino, and Black ethnicities, nationalities, and religious creeds.

The acquisition of research studies that attend to issues of measurement equivalencies is another way in which data archives can promote ethical use of archival data involving lives of color and filter out research with scientifically flawed methods that yield distortion-prone results. Similarly such acquisition efforts further the aim of promoting scientifically valid research. The acquisition of data collected through measures that have been developed using methods of measurement equivalency could facilitate highly meaningful future measure development or serve as a valuable teaching reference in research courses on measure construction.

There are several dimensions of measurement equivalence, the application of which enable scientifically and ethically valid data collection. Instruments used in research that are "indigenous from without," such that constructs, assessment tools, assumptions, and methods are Westernized through superficial translation (Enriquez, 1979, 1982; Pe-Pua & Protacio, 2000), require established validity in terms of "translation equivalence," "conceptual equivalence," and "metric equivalence." Translation equivalence entails translation of measure items by a bilingual translator from the original language into the language of the population for whom the measure is being developed, followed by back translation of the now translated materials to the original language by a second bilingual translation. Conceptual equivalence refers to "whether the psychological construct under investigation . . . holds the same meaning in two or more cultural groups" (Okazaki & Sue, 1995, p. 371). Metric equivalence refers to whether "the same metric can be used to measure the same concept in two or more cultures" (Okazaki & Sue, 1995, p. 371). The archival relevance of these issues arises particularly in appraising the quality of data acquired for preservation. If the data quality is poor and distortion-prone, then the promotion of the use of the data for future research raises ethical questions in the sense that in most cases additional analyses will only perpetuate misinformation.

Protecting the well-being of the community (both geographic and sociopolitical) studied should be foremost among research considerations (CNPAAEMI, 2000). Key questions that carry ethical underpinnings at the start of a research effort include inquiries into the basis for conducting research with a particular community of color, exploration of possible negative or positive impacts on the community being researched, and last, whether the research question/hypothesis is culturally relevant, sensitive, and appropriate. Beyond establishing an applicant's qualifications to access data, due diligence also involves querying applicants about their research intentions. Based on CNPAAEMI guidelines, social science data archives could initiate criteria for the use of data collected from samples of color and other unique or socially vulnerable populations. Whether such guidelines should apply to nonpsychological data raises other issues for further examination.

Again, it is important to note that the ideas put forth by CNPAAEMI represent those of psychologists and thus carry the most significance for ethical guidelines on the use of data sets generated on the lives of people of color using psychological methods. As well, the ethical and methodological recommendations of sociologists, political scientists, anthropologists, social workers, nurses, and psychiatrists, among others, should be incorporated in future writings.

Implications of Ethical Archival Acquisitions Policies: A Case in Point

In sharp contrast to best practice recommendations, the scarcity of valid research on people of color has been well established and points to the need for social science data archives to increase the acquisition of high-quality research studies with diverse samples. Studies that examine lives and experiences of populations of color in multiple contexts with multidimensional methods can significantly inform research communities and greater society. Deficit model research perniciously reinforces stereotypical conclusions about individuals and communities of color. Although sociopolitical and economic factors greatly affect the lives of people of color, many researchers have focused primarily on the negative impact of these factors.

Archival collection policies that advocate the acquisition and preservation of studies that diverge from stereotypical, and often prejudicial, perspectives on People of Color can work to indemnify misguided heuristic research by promoting high-quality research that challenges the countervailing impact of patronizing assumptions. In this way, ethical oversight to promote constructive archival research can responsibly inform research communities, policymakers, and the general public. The support and resources of social science archives facilitates the dynamic process of examining lives in authentic context. The more perspectives that are made available for researchers, the higher the likelihood that future research will endeavor to incorporate multiple perspectives.

Where a large portion of research on African American families has focused on negative attributes such as disenfranchisement, poverty, abuse, and failure, data sets that represent African American families from multiple perspectives and contexts, such as those found at the Murray's Diversity Archive, play a significant role in contradicting many of the presumptions and biases that often define People of Color in negative, one-dimensional terms. A case in point of best practice research, and of ethical best practice archival acquisitions, is Harriette Pipes McAdoo's *Study of Middle Class Urban and Suburban Black Families, 1976* (McAdoo, 1993; McAdoo & McAdoo, 1988). The study examined the impact of social mobility on the extended family relationship. McAdoo identified *supportive* components of Black life such as education, mobility patterns, socialization of children for achievement, the role of maternal employment, and *kin help networks over four generations of Black families*. Reflecting the U.S. Census, the sample comprised two-thirds two-parent households and one-third one-parent households. Data collection consisted of a combination of face-to-face interviews and self-administered questionnaires. All participants had graduate degrees, advanced professional degrees, or some college education. Eighty-five percent of the participating parents originated from working-class backgrounds, and 15% were born middle class. In many ways, the acquisition of McAdoo's family study illustrates an archival acquisition that promotes ethical archival research. This study also demonstrates that in contrast to the mainstream of deficit model research, theoretical approaches and perspectives of populations of color *can be changed*.

CONTRASTING ETHICAL ISSUES REGARDING QUALITATIVE AND QUANTITATIVE ARCHIVAL DATA

The collection and use of quantitative and qualitative data have numerous implications for individuals of color and communities.

Here the level of information becomes important in determining the necessary level of processing required to protect research subjects. Data sets within the Murray Archives holdings have drawn on seven approaches to data collection: interview; behavioral observation; medical examination; other measures including diaries, psychiatric evaluation, and clinical case notes; psychological test; questionnaire; and institutional record (Radcliffe, 2000, p. 249).

The actual data contained in a data set are qualitative, quantitative, or combinations of both. The qualitative type of data gathered through interview, behavioral observation, medical examination, and "other" data represent the most sensitive forms of data found at the Murray Archives due to the intimate nature of data collection that requires active interaction between researcher and participant. Depending on the data set, "Other" measure types can also refer to highly intimate information generated through case study methods such as clinical summaries or diaries. The latter three measure types, psychological test, questionnaire, and institutional record, usually manifest as quantitative data and are often available as numeric data files. These types of data generally require unilateral data generation and, as such, may result in more impersonal self-testimony.

As a category of psychological test, even projective tests such as Henry Murray's Thematic Apperception Test, Rorschach's Ink Blot Test, or Jane Loevinger's Washington University Sentence Completion Test tend to be thought of as revealing deeply personal insights about individuals. Yet the "meaning" of a response remains "encoded" until interpreted through a scoring method; ironically, "meaning" is somehow "projected" on to responses. In similar fashion, questionnaires and institutional records also provide passive, often close-ended, and/or indirect testimony from, and information about, a study participant.

Through such forms of data collection as a questionnaire or an institutional record, the connection between information provided and the individual to which it relates is less transparent than those collected through audiotaped and transcribed interviews, videotaped behavioral observations, or intimate medical examinations. This degree of transparency has ethical import regarding the degree of immediacy and intimacy of the information provided; the latter measure types provide information that is more personal and more intimately connected to the participants because one can hear and/or see the participants, or read transcripts of what the individuals actually and specifically said created out of their own volition but prompted or structured by research investigation. Struthers (2001) describes this intimacy: "The researcher and the participants interact with their whole beings in the research process. This includes their patterns, their knowledge, and their unknowns" (p. 132). The former type of information tends to be more constricted and mediated, and generally less directly attributable to a specific individual. The intimate or impersonal circumstances under which information is gathered from a study participant raises ethical issues for how this information can be shared with a future third party in an archival context. Such concerns are enhanced in the case of participants of color whose data responses and other information gathered about participants can be (and have been) used in harmful ways.

Ethically, these two levels of data collection point to two potential levels of access in the case of data sets generated from participants of color. Concerning interview data, one proposal for ethical safeguards is to obtain an additional informed consent from each interviewee within a data set consenting to their interview's being archived ("consent to archive") and made available to future researchers for secondary analysis (Corti,

Day, & Backhouse, 2000; Leh, 2000; Thompson, 2003), ideally at the time of primary data collection (Corti et al., 2000). An ethical flash point in the use of behavioral observation data is its potential for biased and subjective coding schemata (Burlew, 2003). Videotape data require permission from adult study participants. Videotape data involving participants under the age of consent require parental permission. All of these types of data can be transferred to an archive for eventual third-party archival use at the discretion of a study's principal investigator; however, especially in situations in which a study participant's responses have been passed on to a data archive unawares, as in the case of the acquisition of a study completed many years earlier, the imperative for ethical safeguards and mediations is paramount.

RECOMMENDATIONS FOR FUTURE RESEARCH

Future research in the field of library and information science would be helpful for comparative assessments of the "loss of meaning" and "loss of value" in deidentified data sets, as well as calibration of the relative loss of meaning and loss of value according to the removal of certain combinations of identifiers. This area of data archival exploration would be especially valuable concerning the possible impact of "mosaic effects" emerging from the content of qualitative or quantitative data. The extent of possible semantic and/or hermeneutic distortion arising from the analysis of data generated from assumptions framed by one discipline but interpreted through the lens of another discipline also warrants more systematic investigation.

As a result of the many disciplinary perspectives through which archival data may be interpreted, interdisciplinary analysis could potentially open the door for harmful misinterpretations. Richardson and Godfrey (2003) suggest that the development of "shared inter-disciplinary 'ethical' practices" (p. 347) is warranted in addition to developing new methodological strategies. From the standpoint of social science data archives and data management professionals, the contrast of ethical standards parallels the notion of an external imposition of values versus self-determination of values.

We suggest that a new standard calls for the integration of ethics and science, such that valid science presupposes and requires ethically sound underpinnings. Community self-determined ethical standards produce data quality with less susceptibility to malfeasance, disrespect, and injustice. In the archival context, applying similar standards promises to further enhance valid and meaningful scientific endeavors in the present, the future, and as permanent historical evidence.

Looking forward, the challenge is to build a new heritage of archival research for communities of color. The social sciences, in conjunction with social science data archives, have the theoretical, methodological, and operational tools to help societies overcome deficiencies in understanding current challenges and developing policies to meet them. Effective policy making requires a solid socioeconomic and cultural knowledge base and a huge demand for evidence from social science research (Kazancigil, 2003). Ultimately, the decision to ethically safeguard

research concerning people of color in social science data archives both affirms the contextualized lives and experiences while strengthening the development of scientifically valid research methods for the future.

CONCLUSIONS

Many contemporary researchers have sought to support study participants' empowerment and share Annette Dula's observation that "in unequal relationships, informed consent does not work" (Dula, 1992). The growing emphasis by researchers who work with populations of color on an autonomous as opposed to heteronomous (Colby, Kohlberg, & Abrahami, 1987, pp. 347–349) framing of ethical standards and deliberations underscores the common perspective the Murray Archives shares with scholars who advocate empowerment and liberatory transformation of research methodologies to promote ethical research in communities of color. The Murray Archives' focus on studies that utilize qualitative and/or multiple methods for examining lives derives from the basic concern for autonomous self-definition facilitated by these research methods and approaches. As Struthers (2001) observes from an Ojibwa perspective, "A qualitative research design is more conducive to a holistic worldview and oral tradition. It adds fluidity and flexibility to the research process and utilizes the art of traditional storytelling" (pp. 129–130).

REFERENCES

Atteneave, C. L. (1989). Who has the responsibility? An evolving model to resolve ethical problems in intercultural research. *American Indian and Alaska Native Mental Health Research, 2,* 18–24.

Brazil, W. D. (1988). *Howard W. Odum: The building years, 1884–1930.* New York: Garland.

Brooks-Gunn, J., Phelps, E., & Elder, G. (1991). Studying lives through time: Secondary data analyses in developmental psychology. *Developmental Psychology, 27*(6), 899–910.

Burlew, A. K. (2003). Research with ethnic minorities: Conceptual, methodological, and analytical issues. In G. Bernal, J. E. Trimble, A. K. Burlew, & F. T. L. Leong (Eds.), *Handbook of racial and ethnic minority psychology* (pp. 179–197). Thousand Oaks, CA: Sage.

Caplan, A. L. (1992). When evil intrudes. *Hastings Center Report, 22*(6), 29–32.

Carlin, A. P. (1991). On analyzing other people's data. *Developmental Psychology, 27*(6), 946–948.

Colby, A., Kohlberg, L., & Abrahami, A. (1987). *The measurement of moral judgment.* New York: Cambridge University Press.

Colby, A., & Phelps, E. (1990). Archiving longitudinal data. In D. Magnusson & L. R. Bergman (Eds.), *Data quality in longitudinal research* (pp. 249–262). New York: Cambridge University Press.

Corti, L., Day, A., & Backhouse, G. (2000). Confidentiality and informed consent: Issues for consideration in the preservation of and provision of access to qualitative data archives. *Forum Qualitatitive Sozialforschung/Forum: Qualitative Social Research,* [Online Journal], *1*(3). Retrieved May 3, 2004, from www.qualitative-research.net/fqs-texte/3–00/3–00cortietal-e.htm

Corti, L., & Thompson, P. (2003). Secondary analysis of archive data. In C. Seale, G. Gobo, J. F. Gubrium, & D. Silverman (Eds.), *Qualitative research practice* (pp. 327–343), London: Sage.

Council of National Psychological Associations for the Advancement of Ethnic Minority Interests. (2000). *Guidelines for research in ethnic minority communities.* Washington, DC: APA.

Dula, A. (1992). Yes, there are African-American perspectives on bioethics. In H. E. Flack & D. E. Pellegrino (Eds.), *African-American perspectives on biomedical ethics* (pp. 193–203). Washington, DC: Georgetown University Press.

Duncan, G. J. (1991). Made in Heaven: Secondary data analysis and interdisciplinary collaborators. *Developmental Psychology, 27*(6), 949–951.

Dunn, C. S., & Austin, E. W. (1997). Protecting confidentiality in archival data resources. *IASSIST Quarterly, 21*(2), 16–24.

Elms, A. C. (1987). The personalities of Henry A. Murray. *Perspectives in personality* (Vol. 2). Greenwich, CT: JAI Press.

Enriquez, V. G. (1979). Towards cross-cultural knowledge through cross-indigenous methods and perspective. *Philippine Journal of Psychology, 12*(1), 9–15.

Enriquez, V. G. (1982). *Towards a Filipino psychology: Essays and studies on language and culture.* University of Philippines Village, Quezon City: Philippine Psychology Research and Training House.

Epstein, C. F. (1973). Positive effects of the multiple negative: Explaining the success of Black professional women. *American Journal of Sociology, 78*(41), 913–935.

Feinberg, S. E., Martin, M. E., & Straf, M. L. (Eds.). (1985). *Sharing research data.* Washington, DC: National Academy Press.

Fielding, N. (2004). Getting the most from archived qualitative data: Epistemological, practical and professional obstacles. *International Journal of Social Research Methodology, 7*(1), 97–104.

Fisher, C. B., Hoagwood, K., Boyce, C., Duster, T., Frank, D. A., Grisso, T., et al. (2002). Research ethics for mental health science involving ethnic minority children and youths. *American Psychologist, 57*(12), 1024–1040.

Fisher, C. B., Jackson, J., & Villarruel, F. (1997). The study of African American and Latin American children and youth. In R. M. Lerner (Ed.), *Theoretical models of human development* (Handbook of Child Psychology, Vol. 1, 5th ed., pp. 1145–1207), Editor-in-Chief: W. Damon. New York: Wiley.

Hammersley, M. (1997). Qualitative data archiving: Some reflections on its prospects and problems: Sociology. *Journal of the British Sociological Association, 31*(1), 131–142.

Holm, T., Pearson, J. D., & Chavis, B. (2003). Peoplehood: A model for the extension of sovereignty in American Indian studies. *Wicazo Sa Review, 18*(1), 7–24.

James, J. B. (2002, September/October). *Acquisition criteria at the Murray Research Center: A center for the study of lives.* A paper prepared for presentation at the CODATA 18th International Conference, Montreal, Canada.

James, J. B., & Malley, J. E. (1997, August). *Reanalyzing qualitative data.* Paper presented at the American Psychological Association Annual Meeting, Chicago.

James, J. B., & Sorensen, A. (2000). Archiving longitudinal data for future research: Why qualitative data add to a study's usefulness. *Forum Qualitatitive Sozialforschung/Forum: Qualitative Social Research* [Online Journal], *1*(3). Retrieved May 3, 2004, from www.qualitative-research.net/fqs-texte/3–00/3–00 jamessorensen-e.htm

Johnson, C. L. (1995). Cultural diversity in the late-life family. In R. Blieszner & V. Bedford (Eds.), *Handbook of aging and the family* (pp. 307–331). Westport, CT: Greenwood Press.

Johnson, D. H. (2001a). Sharing data: It's time to end psychology's guild approach. *APS Observer* [Online Journal], *14*(8). Retrieved March 8, 2004, from www .psychologicalscience.org/observer/1001/data.html

Johnson, D. H. (2001b). Three objections to databases answered. *APS Observer* [Online Journal], *14*(9). Retrieved May 17, 2004, from www/psychologicalscience .org/observer/1101/database.html

Johnson, D. H. (2001c). Three ways to use databases as tools for psychological research. *APS Observer* [Online Journal], *14*(10). Retrieved March 8, 2004, from www/psychologicalscience.org/observer/1201/database.html

Johnson, D. H. (2002). The power of psychology's databases. *APS Observer* [Online Journal], *15*(1). Retrieved March 8, 2004, from www/psychologi-calscience.org/observer/0102/databases.html

Johnson, G. B., & Johnson, G. G. (1980). *Research in service to society: The first fifty years of the Institute for Research in Social Science at the University of North Carolina.* Chapel Hill: University of North Carolina Press.

Jones, J. H. (1993). *Bad blood: The Tuskegee syphilis experiment.* New York: Free Press.

Kazancigil, A. (2003). Strengthening the role of the social sciences in society: The World Social Science Initiative. *International Social Science Journal, 55*(177), 377–380.

Ketelaar, E. (2001). Tacit narratives: The meanings of archives. *Archival Science, 1,* 131–141.

Leh, A. (2000, December). Problems of archiving oral history interviews: The example of the C. S. Dunn & E. W. Austin (1998): Protecting confidentiality in archival data resources. *IASSIST Quarterly, 22,* 16–24.

McAdoo, H. P. (1993). Upward mobility and parenting in middle-income Black families. In A. K. H. Burlew, W. C. Banks, H. P. McAdoo, & D. A. Y. Azibo (Eds.), *African American psychology: Theory, research, and practice* (pp. 63–86). Newbury Park, CA: Sage.

McAdoo, H. P., & McAdoo, J. L. (1988). The dynamics of African American father's family roles. *Michigan Family Review: Fathers and Families in a Diverse and Changing World,* 7–15.

McCall, R. B., & Applebaum, M. I. (1991). Some issues of conducting secondary analyses. *Developmental Psychology, 27*(6), 911–917.

Melichar, L., Evans, J., & Bachrach, C. (2002). Data access and archiving: Options for the demographic and behavioral sciences branch. National Institute of Child Health and Human Development. Retrieved from March 8, 2004, from www.nichd.nih.gov/about/cpr/dbs/dbs.htm

National Institutes of Health, Office of Extramural Research. (2003, March 5). NIH data sharing policy and implementation guidance. Retrieved March 5, 2003, from http://grants.nih.gov/grants/policy/data_sharing/data_sharing_guidance.htm

National Institutes of Health, Office of Extramural Research. (n.d.). NIH data sharing policy. (DHHS Publication No. 03–5399). Retrieved March 5, 2003, from http://grants.nih.gov/grants/policy/data_sharing/data_sharing_brochure.pdf

Nelkin, D. (1982). Forbidden research: Limits to inquiry in the social sciences. In T. L. Beauchamp, R. R. Faden, R. J. Wallace, & L. Walters (Eds.), *Ethical issues in social science research* (pp. 163–174). Baltimore: Johns Hopkins University Press.

Nolte, M. A., & Keller, J. J. (2001). Access to restricted data in a controlled environment: The Michigan Center on the Demography of Aging Data Enclave. Retrieved 2004, May 12, from micda.psc.isr.umich.edu/enclave/Enclave JSM2001.pdf

Odum, H. W., & Johnson, G. B. (1925). *The Negro and his songs: A study of typical Negro songs in the South.* Chapel Hill: University of North Carolina Press.

Okazaki, S., & Sue, S. (1995). Methodological issues in assessment research with ethnic minorities. *Psychological Assessment, 7*(3), 367–375.

Pe-Pua, R., & Protacio, M. (2000). Sikolohiyang Pilipino (Filipino psychology): A legacy of Virgilio G. Enriquez. *Asian Journal of Social Psychology, 3,* 49–71.

Phelps, E. (1990). The Henry A. Murray Research Center: Alternative data sources: Unique, yet less visible archives and programs. *IASSIST Quarterly, 14*(3/4), 27–30.

Pullman, D. (2002). Conflicting interests, social justice and proxy consent to research. *Journal of Medicine and Philosophy, 27*(5), 523–545.

Radcliffe Institute for Advanced Study, Harvard University, Henry A. Murray Research Center. (2000). *A guide to the data resources of The Henry A. Murray Research Center: A center for the study of lives* [Annemette Sorensen, director]. Cambridge, MA: Author.

Richardson, J. C., & Godfrey, B. S. (2003). Towards ethical practice in the use of archived transcripted interviews. *International Journal of Social Research Methodology, 6*(4), 347–355.

Schellenberg, T. R. (1996). *Modern archives: Principles and techniques.* Chicago: Society of American Archivists.

Sieber, J. E. (1989). Sharing scientific data 1. *New problems for IRBs, 11*(6), 4–7.

Simpson, G. (1984). The daughters of Charlotte Ray: The career development process during the exploratory and establishment stages of Black women attorneys. *Sex Roles, 11*(1/2), 113–139.

Struthers, R. (2001). Conducting sacred research: An indigenous experience. *Wicazo Sa Review, 16*(1), 125–133.

Sue, S. (1999). Science, ethnicity, and bias: Where have we gone wrong? *American Psychologist, 54*(12), 1070–1077.

Sue, S., & Sue, L. (2003). Ethnic research is good science. In G. Bernal, J. E. Trimble, A. K. Burlew, & F. T. L. Leong (Eds.), *Handbook of racial and ethnic minority psychology* (pp. 198–207). Thousand Oaks, CA: Sage.

Taube, D. O., & Burkhardt, S. (1997). Ethical and legal risks associated with archival research. *Ethics & Behavior, 7*(1), 59–67.

Thomassen, T. (2002). A first introduction to archival science. *Archival Science, 1,* 373–385.

Tomilinson-Keasey, C. (1993). Opportunities and challenges posed by archival data sets. In D. C. Funder, R. D. Parke, C. Tomlinson-Keasey, & K. Widaman (Eds.), *Studying lives through time: Personality and development* (pp. 65–92). Washington, DC: APA.

Thompson, P. (2003). Towards ethical practice in the use of archived transcripted interviews: A response. *International Journal of Social Research Methodology, 6*(4), 357–360.

Trials of War Criminals Before the Nuremberg Military Tribunals. (1949). *Control Council Law, 2*(10), 181–182. Washington, DC: Government Printing Office.

Trimble, J. E., & Dickson, R. (2005). Ethnic Gloss. In C. B. Fisher & R. M. Lerner (Eds.), *Applied developmental science: An encyclopedia of research, policies, and programs* (pp. 412–415). Thousand Oaks, CA: Sage.

U.S. Department of Health, Education and Welfare. (1979). *The Belmont report: Ethical principles and guidelines for the protection of human subjects of research.* (DHEW Publication No. (05) 9–12065). Washington, DC: Government Printing Office.

U.S. Department of Health and Human Services. (2001, August). *Title 45 Public Welfare, Part 46, Code of Federal Regulations, Protection of Human Subjects.* Washington, DC: Author. (Original work published in 1991)

Vijayan, J. (2004). Sidebar: The mosaic effect. *Computerworld.* Retrieved June 16, 2004, from www.computerworld.com/securitytopics/security/story/0,10801,91109,00.html

Warwick, D. P. (1982). Types of harm in social research. In T. L. Beauchamp, R. R. Faden, R. J. Wallace, & L. Walters (Eds.), *Ethical issues in social science research* (pp. 101–124). Baltimore: Johns Hopkins University Press.

Wichman, A., Mills, D., & Sandler, A. L. (1996). Exempt research: Procedures in the Intramural Research Program of the National Institutes of Health. *IRB, 18*(2), 3–5.

World Medical Association. (1964). *Declaration of Helsinki.* Geneva: World Health Organization.

CHAPTER 16

Ethical Issues When White Researchers Study ALANA[1] and Immigrant People and Communities

JANET E. HELMS

KEVIN T. HENZE

JACKQUELYN MASCHER

ANMOL SATIANI

In the United States, White U.S. Americans and related immigrant groups conduct most of the published psychological, medical, and educational research in which African Americans, Latino/Latina Americans, Asian/Pacific Islander Americans, Native or Indigenous Americans (ALANAs) and related immigrant groups are the focus. Throughout their lifetimes, White American researchers develop and conduct their professional lives in arenas in which their racial group is the numerical majority in society generally and their research professions specifically. According to the most recent national census (U.S. Census Bureau [Census], 2000), Whites constitute just over 75% of the U.S. population, which means that in their daily lives, White researchers can choose not to associate with ALANA people and, consequently, may only come in contact with them when they need ALANA research participants.

By *associate* we mean joining together as friends or relationally connecting with another person. We differentiate *associate* from *encounter*. Whereas *associate* connotes a relational connection, *encounter* signifies a chance meeting in which a friendly relational exchange can ensue but in most cases does not. Arguably, even in metropolitan settings in which large percentages of ALANA people reside, White researchers can choose not to associate with them and may not regularly encounter ALANA people in their work or personal lives.

Moreover, White researchers receive their research training in settings in which most of their peers and professors are also White. For example, across disciplines, the percentage of Whites enrolled in doctoral and first professional degree (e.g., medicine) programs, the level of education at which most researchers are trained, ranges from 66.8% to 83% (National Center for Education Statistics [NCES], 2004). When White researchers graduate, assuming that most researchers are situated in universities and colleges, most (86%) of the researchers' faculty colleagues will be White (NCES, 2004). If the White researchers join professional research associations that bear the appellation *American* in their title, they will also be surrounded by a White membership, as more than 76.8% of the members of the American Psychological Association who self-reported their racial background were White in 2000 (APA, 2000); 78.7% of the members of the American Anthropological Association who in 1999 self-reported their racial background were White (AAA, 1999); 82% of the members of the American Sociological Association self-identified as White in 2003 (ASA, 2004); and at least 56% of the members of the American Educational Research Association (AERA, 2002) were White. Moreover, one suspects that most of the editors and reviewers of professional journals are also White in light of ongoing calls for "underrepresented groups" to apply for these positions (e.g., "Members of Underrepresented Groups," 2003).

Thus, regardless of which research domain one surveys, the obtained statistics indicate that Whites are by far the most numerous racial group in research-oriented arenas. Because of their numerical majority status and control of socioeconomic resources and political power, White researchers have the authority to define the critical research agendas for themselves and to set the research agendas for ALANA communities, in spite of the fact that many White researchers have probably had no personal contact with an ALANA person in their lifetime. Setting agendas means that White researchers may

decide which questions are important enough to address, which theoretical frameworks and methodologies may be used to address them, the nature of the populations to be studied, who is qualified to conduct the relevant research and interpret results, as well as which questions merit research funding or serious consideration in scholarly communities. Furthermore, it is only through their deftness in conforming to White research paradigms that ALANA researchers may be deemed qualified to study issues affecting their own racial or ethnic groups. Given their research omnipotence and the pervasiveness of Whiteness, there are many opportunities for White researchers to do harm to ALANA and immigrant individuals and communities without necessarily intending to do so.

In psychology, the *Ethical Principles of Psychologists and Code of Conduct* (APA, 2002), to some extent, and the *Guidelines on Multicultural Education, Training, Research, Practice, and Organizational Change for Psychologists* (APA, 2003), to a much greater extent, are intended to arouse psychological researchers' consciousness about the ways in which unacknowledged racial dynamics may result in harm to research participants; however, although it might be obvious to the relatively few ALANA psychological researchers that many of the guidelines are particularly germane to the common research practices of White researchers' studies of ALANA populations (e.g., Casas & Thompson, 1991), it is by no means certain that White researchers recognize themselves in these guidelines and principles or have read the relevant research sections of the two documents. Moreover, as is often the case with generic guidelines and principles, explicit examples seem to be needed to make them meaningful.

Therefore, in this chapter, we attempt to make explicit some ethical issues in the research process potentially faced by White researchers studying ALANA populations and provide some suggestions for how such issues might be recognized, prevented, redressed, or interpreted in subsequent research. In doing so, we supplement or elaborate on relevant aspects of the ethics code (APA, 2002) and multicultural guidelines (APA, 2003). Helms' (1993) White racial identity development (WRID) theory is used as a framework for recognizing the impact of internalized White racial socialization on White researchers' manners of conceptualizing the research process. The examples used to illustrate our points are real but have been altered to protect the identities of relevant parties, if necessary. Some are composites of our experiences and observations, whereas others are abstracted from published studies.

RESEARCHER SELF-EXAMINATION

In contrast to practitioners with respect to applied interventions (e.g., Thompson & Carter, 1997), White theorists and researchers have been oblivious to the fact that the nature of their own identification with Whites as a racial in-group is as intrinsic to their studies of their racial in-group as it is to their conceptions of ALANA and immigrant out-groups (Rowe, Behrens, & Leach, 1995); however, race and ethnicity are such emotionally laden themes in the history of the United States that it is important to recognize that just as racial attitudes and emotions influence White psychologists' practice of psychology, White researchers also engage in research processes that are influenced by specific attitudes and emotions about race and ethnic cultures (Zinn, 1999).

Principle E of the ethics code advises psychologists to "try to eliminate the effect on their work of biases based on those factors [e.g., race, ethnicity, culture]," and Standard 2.01 contends that psychologists "provide services, teach, and conduct research with

populations and in areas within their boundaries of competence" (APA, 2002, p. 4). White researchers generally have not understood such counsel to mean that they ought to examine themselves to ensure that they have the particular competencies and educational experiences required to study ALANA populations per se in an ethical manner, a manner that benefits rather than harms the populations under study. Perhaps because the ethics code does not explicitly describe race and culture as domains that require special knowledge, competencies, and training, White researchers may not be cognizant of the fact when they are functioning beyond their areas of competence.

The multicultural guidelines make the point more explicitly that self-examination, focused on one's own attitudes about racial and ethnic groups, is necessary by encouraging psychologists (e.g., White researchers) "to recognize that, as cultural [and racial] beings, they may hold attitudes and beliefs that can detrimentally influence their perceptions of and interactions with individuals who are ethnically and racially different from themselves" (APA, 2003, p. 382). Except for a tangential reference to research on White identity, the guidelines do not provide a conceptual framework for undertaking such self-examination if the researcher is White, although many conceptual models for studying people of color (i.e., ALANA groups) or minority status are referenced. Yet some consequences of obliviousness to the shared human condition of having one's definition of *self* develop in particular racial and/or cultural contexts are (a) White researchers may view the experiences of their racial group as "standard" or normal and those of ALANA groups as "deviant" with respect to the construct under study; (b) the researcher may not be aware that the assumptions on which his or her research is based are stereotypes; and (c) information that disconfirms the White researchers' stereotype(s) may never be collected or may be disregarded if it does not confirm the researcher's stereotype. WRID theory provides a conceptual framework for White researchers planning to conduct research on ALANA or immigrant samples to use to analyze their research for specific ethical concerns attributable to the researchers' differential use of White racial identity schemata.

White Racial Identity Theory

Helms (1990, 1995) theorized that in response to racial socialization in which Whiteness is pervasive, White people control the socioeconomic and political power structure and, thereby, are deemed the "best" racial group. Whites, as individuals, develop race-related cognitive-affective schemata for processing racial dynamics in their environments. *Race* in her framework is conceptualized as a social construction defined by societal customs, convention, and law. In explaining why Asian Indians were "Caucasians" but not "whites," the Supreme Court in *U.S. v. Bhagat Singh Thind* argued, "It may be true that the blond Scandinavian and the brown Hindu have a common ancestor in the dim reaches of antiquity, but the average man [sic] knows perfectly well that there are unmistakable and profound differences between them today . . . the words 'white persons' . . . are words of common speech and not of scientific origin" (*U.S. v. Bhagat Singh Thind* 261 U.S. 204 [1923], cited in Takaki, 1989, p. 299). Therefore, in our discussion, when we use the concepts of *Whites* and *Whiteness,* we also mean what the average man and the average woman understand the words *White researchers* to signify, which incidentally is the manner in which racial groups are defined in psychological research.

In Helms' theory, White identity schemata are intended to describe the processes by which White individuals construe and

interact with perceived racial in-group members (i.e., other White people) as well as ALANA group members individually or collectively. Interaction may be direct (e.g., collecting data) or vicarious (e.g., interpreting data). In the present discussion of her theory, the term *racial dynamics* refers to the general processes of perceiving others, construing meaning from one's perceptions, and reacting or interacting on the basis of the construed meaning. More specifically, the term refers to the manners in which White researchers potentially engage in these processes when studying ALANA and immigrant populations of color or nondominant cultural orientations.

Briefly, the six schemata described in Helms' (1993, 1995) identity model are as follows: (a) Contact (naïveté or obliviousness to racial dynamics); (b) Disintegration (confusion about the meaning of racial stimuli and, consequently, how one should respond to them); (c) Reintegration (idealization of White people and White culture—e.g., products and achievements—and denigration of ALANA people and culture; (d) Pseudoindependence (intellectualized understanding of racial dynamics combined with benevolent intentions); (e) Immersion-Emersion (quest for nonracist understanding of White racial dynamics; (f) Autonomy (affirmation and integration of various racial perspectives). The schemata reflect different levels of complexity in conceptualizing and reacting to racial dynamics, but use of one schema does not preclude use of the others; in fact, any particular action may be the result of a blend of more than one schema (Helms, 1984). For example, a researcher may engage in denigration of an ALANA sample (Reintegration) because he or she is naive about or oblivious to (Contact) the racial dynamics of the particular research situation; but alternatively, a researcher might engage in the same type of denigration because he or she consciously or not consciously believes that

Table 16.1 Summary of the Influence of Dominant Status of White Racial Identity on White Researchers' Cross-Racial and Cross-Cultural Research Activities

Identity Status	*Assumption*	*Implication*	Example
Contact	Universalism of White culture	If they are included at all, data from People of Color in predominantly White samples are not analyzed separately. Results are assumed to pertain to people regardless of race.	An anonymous reviewer rejected a manuscript that suggested a link between race-related psychological constructs and African Americans' performance on tests of cognitive abilities, knowledge, and skills (CAKS). The reviewer comments suggested a universalistic White cultural view informed by stereotypes, and obliviousness to racial dynamics in educational test policy propelled their rejection decision.
Disintegration	Ambivalence regarding study of race	Diversity research is permitted only if it conforms to standards of excellence of White research despite reality constraints.	A group of researchers conducted a study of a motivational intervention to reduce substance use. Though their sample contained 107 self-identified Hispanics, the authors did not discuss whether they made culturally responsive accommodations to informed consent procedures.
Reintegration	Ethnocentrism	Whites are the standard for normal behavior or behavioral norms. A study is deficient unless Whites are used as a control group.	In response to a study examining manifestations of depression in Haitian immigrant women, an anonymous reviewer noted that the exclusive study of Haitian women fails to reveal important differences between this population and normal [White] women.
Pseudoindependence	Liberalism	When racial-group differences are found, principles of cultural disadvantage are used to explain People of Color, but Whites are not explained.	White researchers published an article using racial and ethnic categories to explain test performance differences between White and ALANA students, despite admonishments from measurement experts regarding the misrepresentation of individual racial group members that can occur when using broad-based group categories to represent what is likely to be an individual difference phenomenon (i.e. racial identity development). The White researchers explain significant test score differences between Whites and Blacks as resulting from disproportionate poverty and deemphasis on educational success in Black communities.

(Continued)

Table 16.1 (Continued)

Identity Status	Assumption	Implication	Example
Immersion-Emersion	Reeducation	White culture and sociopolitical history is explicitly used to design studies and explain Whites' behavior.	A White graduate student conducted a dissertation study examining the relationship between White racial identity development and prejudice and racism in a sample of White heterosexual men, despite his mentor suggesting he study the efficacy of cognitive coping strategies employed by Black men dealing with racism. While acknowledging the importance of understanding how people of color cope with racism, the White graduate student deemed it equally important to understand White racism etiology.
Autonomy	Pluralism	Scholar recognizes inherent cultural assumptions of one's work and does not impose them on nongroup members.	A White researcher who planned to conduct research with a local Dominican population recognized that doing so required her to expand her boundaries of cultural competence. In addition to actively seeking out information about Dominican culture, this researcher involved a Dominican cultural consultant, as well as community-designated stakeholders from the local Dominican population, in all aspects of the study.

SOURCE: Adapted with permission of author from "I Also Said, 'White Racial Identity Influences White Researchers,'" by J. E. Helms, 1993, The *Counseling Psychologist, 21*(2), 243. Copyright 1993 by the Division of Counseling Psychology.

White people are superior to other racial or ethnic groups.

Helms (1993) discussed assumptions underlying use of each of the racial identity schemata in the research process. These are summarized in Table 16.1. In sum, White researchers are often socialized in White racially homogeneous environments where racial dynamics typically are not central concerns. Therefore, it is important for them to consider the possible effects of the researcher's use of White identity schemata in each phase of the research process, which for purposes of this chapter are (a) rationale, (b) method, (c) procedures, and (d) results. We discuss some ethical issues relevant to the tabled schemata and related assumptions in greater depth as they pertain to each of theses aspects of the research process.

Examples of Consequences of Failure to Self-Examine

It is impossible to know definitively from its published version what schemata influenced the researcher's conceptualization of a study at its inception; however, some examples from anonymous reviews of two rejected manuscripts and a not funded grant proposal illustrate how researchers' failure to examine their racial attitudes shaped their responses.[2]

Gatekeeping. Helms (2001) focused on the relative lack in traditional psychology outlets, with the exception of Steele and Aronson (1995), of the study of race-related psychological constructs in studies of ALANA test takers'—especially African Americans'—performance on tests of cognitive abilities, knowledge, and skills (CAKS). The reviewer uses quotations to imply that certain terminology or conceptualizations were present in the manuscript, but, in fact, they were not. For example, in the manuscript, the term *Whites* (but not *whites*) appeared only twice, once to describe the prototypical Black-White difference in test scores and once to describe the referent group in Helms' (2002) use of a Black identity measure. Otherwise, the manuscript focused explicitly on describing quantitative strategies for examining ALANA racial or cultural factors as explanations for the ALANA-White test score gap(s).

The irate reviewer opined,

> According to the author(s)' world view, cognitive testing is a morality play pitting 'whites' [sic] (who supposedly have a cultural advantage on CAT tests) against non-whites, or ALANA people (for whom CATs are possibly 'unfair' [sic]). Each group is treated as an undifferentiated, amorphous mass with no attention paid to important distinctions within groups. In reality, 'Whites' reflect a variety of ethnic groups, some of whom obtain higher average CAT scores than other 'white' groups (Eysenck, 1984). Asians are lumped together with groups that show average CAT scores that are lower than 'whites,' even though many Asian groups obtain *higher* average CAT scores than whites. In addition, many of the 'bias' [sic] issues for Hispanics involve non–English language issues, which bear

no relationship to explanations for the lower performance of African Americans." (Personal communication, anonymous reviewer A, 2002, p. 4, italics original)

Although there are a number of points within this segment of the reviewer's comments with which one might take exception, application of White racial identity theory suggests that the reviewer and (presumably) testing researcher is using a combination of Contact and Reintegration schemata in his or her review. Contact is apparent in the reviewer's seeming obliviousness to the facts that (a) national and statewide laws and testing movements, such as No Child Left Behind (U.S. Department of Education, 2002), require high-stakes decisions based on ALANA racial groups' average scores relative to the White *racial group's* average score, rather than ethnic-group comparisons; (b) the group that White researchers classify as "African American" consists of relatively large percentages of Black ethnic groups (e.g., Haitians, Brazilians, Dominicans) whose test performance also involves non–English language issues (El Nasser, 2003); (c) Asian Americans' average scores on tests of verbal knowledge and skills are typically lower than the average scores of their White American counterparts (cf. Sackett, Schmitt, Ellingson, & Kabin, 2001); and (d) Native Americans are invisible in the reviewers' analysis of racial-group testing behavior.

Ethnocentrism, or a White-centered orientation, and maintaining the racial hierarchy are the underlying themes of a Reintegration mind-set. Reintegration is apparent in the reviewer's discussion of "African Americans" and "Hispanics" as racially or linguistically homogenous out-groups that are different from White in-groups and "Asian" (almost) in-groups. To the extent that the reviewer uses the same racial identity schemata in reviewing other manuscripts, it is not likely that the contributions of other authors with alternative perspectives will gain credibility through the visibility and critique of ideas in widely read psychology journals.

Whites as normative. An assistant professor submitted a qualitative study of depression to a prestigious psychology journal that focuses on the psychology of women. It is a journal that routinely publishes small-sample qualitative studies of White women's psychological issues. The focus of the professor's study was symptoms, manifestations, and strategies for treating depression as manifested by Haitian immigrant women in the United States. Her sample consisted of 60 women being treated for depression in a community mental health center. It was a study that took more than a year to complete and submit for publication.

In advising against publication, one reviewer commented:

> Although understanding the different types of depression among Haitians is important [sic] it is not clear how this is different from *normal* women with depression. . . . We [sic] would recommend providing some comparative data, showing how this manifestation of depression is different from that of other women (i.e., Whites, African-Americans [sic], Asians, etc.). (Personal communication, anonymous, 2004, italics added)

Contact, Pseudoindependence, and Reintegration each seem to characterize this reviewer's reaction, although Reintegration seems to predominate. Contact is evident in the reviewer's naïveté about the process of collecting interview data focused on mental health concerns from the types of samples that she or he would like to use as comparison groups. This reviewer does acknowledge ethnic diversity within the "African-American" population and racial diversity in society, a perspective characteristic of Pseudoindependent liberalism; however,

the reviewer does not believe that Haitian women are "normal women" and are, therefore, worthy of study by themselves.

Some time ago, Korchin (1980) noted that reviewers devalue ethnic psychology by requiring that Whites be included as the standard for normal behavior against which all other groups are to be compared, even when the focus of the research is not germane to White people's life experiences. In addition to failing to recognize the racial-cultural vantage from which she or he evaluated the cultural content of the paper (APA multicultural guideline 1: Commitment to Cultural Awareness and Knowledge of Self and Others), the reviewer failed to recognize the importance of conducting culture-centered and ethical research with one of the largest Black ethnic groups in the United States (APA multicultural guideline 4: Conducting Culturally Sensitive Psychological Research).

Control of resources. Most large-scale studies of any population require external funding of some type (e.g., federal grants, contracts), but grant review panels often are comprised predominantly of White reviewers. Examination of rosters of reviewers and their publications, when they are made available to the public, suggests that most of these reviewers have had little or no professional training in racial or cultural psychology or experience conducting racially or culturally responsive research. A consequence of this lack of exposure is that grant reviewers often respond to proposals with a racial or cultural focus as if they are projective tests, responding to whichever part they choose.

For example, an ALANA clinical researcher submitted a proposal to study a manualized treatment for depression modified for a particular ALANA ethnic group. The grant agency's criteria for submission required that the researcher obtain a research mentor. The researcher obtained several mentors, only one of whom was local and helped the researcher design the study. In advising against funding the research, the reviewers noted that the proposal was quite strong and all of the distant mentors were "stellar." Yet the local ALANA research mentor was unsuitable because although he or she had supervised the research of 30 [sic] ALANA researchers and would provide sufficient attention to the researcher, the proposed mentor did not have "a history of external funding or expertise in interventions" or the manualized treatment being studied.

It is worth noting that virtually none of the "facts" obtained in the evaluation of the proposed mentor were contained in the researcher's proposal and most were not true. For example, the proposed mentor was a licensed psychologist whose training and practice had included the type of therapy that the mentor was judged incapable of doing, although capacity to do therapy is not ordinarily a criterion for research mentoring. Moreover, the mentor had received many awards (most not monetary) for "expertise" in interventions research, a topic that he or she had taught for almost 20 years. The automatic assumption that ALANA professionals must be unqualified in some significant way exemplifies use of the Reintegration schema and possibly accounts for the difficulty that ALANA researchers encounter in obtaining funds to conduct research with a racial or cultural focus.

Sometimes panels of 20 or so reviewers have one or two "minorities" whose roles are to be the "expert" on all ALANA and immigrant groups and to evaluate methodologies of studies with a racial or cultural focus, regardless of whether the ALANA reviewer has been trained in the methodology being proposed. For example, psychologists might be expected to evaluate sociological studies. It is often the case that standard research procedures ought to be modified to address the racial or cultural

dynamics of ALANA and immigrant samples; however, token ALANA reviewers have the intimidating task of explaining to White reviewers using the Reintegration and/or Contact schemata why and how unfamiliar methodologies should be modified to address racial and cultural concerns.

Summary

A researcher's expectancies about racial and ethnic group differences or similarities can affect every aspect of her or his research design from inception to interpretation of results. In the foregoing examples, it is unlikely that the anonymous reviewers could be receptive to information that was inconsistent with the reviewers' stereotypes about the groups being studied or the researchers conducting the studies. Therefore, research on ALANA samples, conducted under the reviewers' auspices, would likely "do harm" by maintaining the status quo with respect to race and ethnicity in the three illustrative research domains. Moreover, assuming that the action editors and administrative officers selected these reviewers because of the respective reviewers' expertise in testing and mental health, respectively, (but obviously not in racial or cultural psychology), and given that action editors and administrative officers let the reviews stand without refutation in either case, it is clear that the reviewers, action editors, and administrative officers in these examples used their power to prevent studies that challenged their racial and cultural belief systems from entering the scientific arena.

ETHICAL CONCERNS IN THE STUDY RATIONALE

A researcher's theory guides every phase of her or his research design but is most evident in the researcher's specification of a topic and related research questions or hypotheses. When using theory to study ALANA populations, it is useful to think about two levels of theorizing: focal theory and implicit racial and cultural dynamics. *Focal theory* is the formal or traditional psychological theory that researchers typically use to define the thematic focus of their study as reflected in their overall research design. *Racial* or *cultural dynamics* are the manners in which race and culture interact with focal theory in the research design. Racial or cultural theory could be focal theory, but rarely is.

Misuse of Formal Theory

Perhaps because of lack of awareness that alternative perspectives exist (Contact) or perhaps because these "ethnic" perspectives are not considered to be as "objective" as theories developed by White theorists and researchers (Reintegration), White researchers have applied White-centered theories to their samples regardless of their samples' racial compositions, even when such theories were clearly inadequate, inappropriate, or inaccurate (Korchin, 1980). The misfit is often documented in researchers' post hoc discussions of the limitations of their obtained results, but typically these are limitations that could have been avoided if the researchers had designed the study with explicit attention to racial and cultural dynamics.

When White researchers have used formal theories as if they were the only plausible rationales for studies of ALANA participants in their studies, universalism of White racial and cultural socialization experiences has been an underlying premise. In WRID theory, *universalism* is a White person's assumption that the White racial in-group's life experiences are necessarily the standard against which ALANA groups ought to be evaluated (Helms, 1993). It is the most primitive White identity schema for coping with racial dynamics. In the research context,

universalism refers to the belief that, or to the conducting of one's research as if one believes that, the experiences of White people and White socialization necessarily generalize to ALANA and immigrant populations. Perhaps because of White researchers' socialization in racially segregated research settings, this assumption frequently characterizes researchers' use of formal theories to formulate research questions.

Because formal theories generally are most relevant to researchers and participants from the cultural or racial contexts from which the theories emerge (Helms & Cook, 1999), White researchers typically have used theoretical perspectives that do not purposefully represent the life circumstances of People of Color. Perhaps because indigenous theories—other than those of European Americans—are not typically included in the research training that White researchers receive, they may not be aware that such theoretical frameworks exist. Alternatively, the researchers may devalue these theoretical frameworks because White research gatekeepers have prevented them from being published in first-tier outlets. Perhaps it is important to note that most of the race or ethnic group–specific theories were not first published in traditional psychology outlets. Consequently, even for White researchers who use advanced racial-identity schemata when conducting research on ALANA samples, it is relatively difficult to find relevant references. It is often the case that the literature most relevant to ALANA samples is not in stock in bookstores, cannot be located by public librarians, is not owned by private libraries, or has been destroyed.

Often, ALANA researchers and theorists, who may or may not be recognized as having made significant scientific contributions to the still White-dominated field of psychology (Korchin, 1980), have authored the studies most relevant to the life experiences of

ALANA samples. Also, some of the most important analyses of racial or ethnic characteristics have been conducted in countries outside of the continental United States. Finally, because Internet search engines are driven by feedback about the most popular searches and because Whites have disproportionate access to the Internet, search engines are not likely to provide equal amounts of content for each of the racial groups. Instead, Internet search engines are likely to supply information that is most relevant to the needs and interests of White Internet researchers. For all of these reasons, articles about ALANA psychological issues may not be included in literature reviews in traditional journals unless White researchers make a deliberate effort to seek them out and use them as formal theory in their research designs.

Typically, one of the primary steps in developing a research project is to review the relevant literature. Ethical practice with respect to the racial and cultural domains requires the White researcher to seek race- and culture-specific literature in sources that might not be esteemed by his or her colleagues or mentors. Undertaking such a search is the researcher's acknowledgment that the psychological interests of Whites should not preclude interests in other racial or ethnic groups, given that People-of-Color groups are the vast numerical majority of people in terms of the world population.

Using Whiteness as Theory

Other White researchers and theorists of equal or greater perceived status rarely challenge White researchers' and theorists' manners of making meaning from their own racial experiences, and such critiques are discounted if they are offered by People of Color (Rowe, Bennett, & Atkinson, 1994). Consequently, White theorists do not seem to recognize the extent to which they believe that comparisons of ALANA samples with White samples constitute a theory-based conceptualization of their research questions. This belief in "Whiteness" as theory is present in virtually all studies in which the research question has been conceptualized as a study of the effects of racial or ethnic characteristics on behavior, as psychologists define behavior. It is an ethical concern because, to the extent that the ALANA groups from which the researcher's sample will be selected have had racial or cultural lifetime socialization experiences different from those of their White counterparts in the intended study, the ALANA participants are necessarily "deviant," ipso facto, at the inception of the study.

Various authors have noted problems inherent in the dominant racial group's (e.g., White's) use of itself to define the standards for healthy functioning for ALANA samples (e.g., Akbar, 1991). One problem is that the automatic biases and negative stereotyping that are evoked when racial categories are used to differentiate people may be mistaken for theoretical explanations of observed between-group racial, ethnic, or cultural group differences. Consequently, when between-group differences are found that disfavor the ALANA study participants relative to the White participants, such differences are interpreted as empirical support for the stereotypes and biases that masquerade as theoretical explanations. The multicultural guidelines (APA, 2003) address the issue of quasi theory as follows:

> [People] make sense of their social world by creating categories of the individuals around them, a process that includes separating the categories into in-groups and out-groups. . . . This becomes problematic when one group holds much more power than the other group or when resources among in-groups are not distributed equitably, as is currently the case in the United States. . . . Thus, it is quite common to have

automatic biases and stereotypic attitudes about people in the out-group, and for the most [i.e., White] psychologists, individuals in racial/ethnic minority groups are in an out-group. (p. 383)

White researchers traditionally have conceptualized race, ethnicity, and culture as interchangeable constructs, which are all virtually always operationally defined by assigning research participants to either White in-group or ALANA "racial" or "ethnic" out-group categories on the basis of criteria that typically either are not specified or are nebulous at best. Racial categories are nominal variables, which means that they can vary between groups but not within groups and are stand-ins for more complex unspecified conceptual constructs. The unspecified constructs must be measured in order for racial categories to have meaning (Fisher et al., 2002). Yet researchers typically have treated the categories themselves as if they are naturally occurring "status" or "attribute" variables, that is, innate racial or cultural traits of study participants, rather than the mutable researcher conveniences that they are.

This reification of racial and ethnic categories means that, in their research designs, White researchers have treated racial or ethnic categories as true independent variables, predictor variables, or moderator variables. True independent, predictor, or moderator variables are supposed to evolve from theory and are the presumed causes of results involving them. Racial categories do not evolve from theory and, in fact, are not defined by specifiable inclusion or exclusion criteria. Yet researchers, regardless of racial-group membership, consistently have interpreted differences between racial or ethnic groups favoring White participants as having considerably more race- or culture-related conceptual meaning than logically can be inferred from racial categories (Akbar, 1991;

Brawley & Tejeda, 1995; Parham, 1993). In many cases, the consequences of doing so have been harmful to ALANAs.

Perhaps it is evident that researchers have no real theory or theories by which to explain obtained racial-group differences because the manner in which the same between-group variance is interpreted depends on the researchers' stereotype preference with some researchers opting for genetic explanations (e.g., Jensen, 1995; Rowe, Vazsonyi, & Flannery, 1994), others preferring environmental explanations (e.g., Eisenman, 1995), and others (typically ALANAs) preferring racial or cultural explanations (e.g., Steele & Aronson, 1995; Yee, Fairchild, Weizmann, & Wyatt, 1993). Stereotypic explanations of between-group differences might become theoretical constructs if they can be empirically supported, that is, if a researcher can demonstrate that his or her stereotype does explain or replace racial group as the explanations for differences on dependent or outcome measures. Empirically supported racial and cultural theoretical principles (not stereotypes) that can replace racial group as the cause of the relevant behavior in the researcher's interpretation of results become the foundations for meaningful racial and cultural dialogue and theory.

To bring about the movement, however, from use of Whiteness and racial stereotypes as theory to utilization of more substantive ALANA-focused theories, the White researcher needs to recognize that incessant searches for ALANA's deviations from nonspecific White models do not constitute theory (Helms & Cook, 1999). That is, White researchers need to become more astute at using more complex racial identity schemata (e.g., Immersion, Autonomy). Use of complex schemata would help the researcher deliberately focus on the racial or cultural aspects of specifying testable hypotheses, selecting relevant samples, choosing appropriate measures, and implementing relevant designs.

HIDDEN METHODOLOGICAL ISSUES

Ethnocentrism and denigration of ALANA research participants, characteristics of the Reintegration schema, occur in various aspects of the research design. Often these themes appear in response to the lack of formal race or cultural theory around which the research design can be structured.

Participants

Exclusion issues. The exclusion of ALANA and immigrant samples in psychological and health research has been an ongoing theme in critiques of behavioral and social science research (Akbar, 1991; Brawley & Tejeda, 1995; Parham, 1993). Concerns were fueled by critics' recognition that findings based on exclusively or predominantly White samples did not necessarily pertain to ALANA groups (Brawley & Tejeda, 1995; Miskimen, Marin, & Escobar, 2003). Federal funding requirements, such as the National Institute of Health (NIH) Revitalization Act of 1993 (Public Law 103–43), have attempted to address this concern by requiring clinical trial researchers to outreach to ALANA and immigrant communities as a means of increasing these community members' participation in health-related studies (Department of Health and Human Services, National Institutes of Health [NIH], 1994). Researchers indicate their conformance to these requirements by submitting a description of the numbers of each racial or ethnic group they intend to recruit and enroll. No fixed numbers are required, and no penalty results from failure to comply.

At their best, because inclusion requirements do not entail any conceptualization of

relevant racial or cultural concerns, they are indicative of an intellectualized, but naive approach (Pseudoindependent/Contact) to studying the relevant health concerns of ALANA populations. For their part, some White researchers have conformed to the spirit of the requirements by including some ALANA participants and theoretical conceptualizations relevant to them (Contact or Pseudoindependence); others have merely filled in enrollment tables with numbers of ALANA samples that they had no intention of recruiting once they had acquired research funding (Reintegration).

Addressing the need for theory-based participant selection strategies, Brawley and Tejeda (1995) advised clinical trial researchers to move beyond merely comparing racial categories with more conceptually complex delimiters of target populations, which take into consideration a community's specific needs, history, and concerns. They contended that "the history and needs of black [sic] populations in Virginia [for example] may be very different from black populations in Alabama or Louisiana" (p. 57).

Biased inclusion criteria. Biased or nonrepresentative sampling procedures have also been a longstanding criticism of ALANA samples used in studies of ALANA populations. Parham (1993) argued that White researcher's selection biases often lead to results obtained in studies of nonrepresentative samples of ALANA racial and cultural groups being generalized to the groups as a whole. Akbar (1991) noted another tendency of White researchers with respect to the African American community in particular:

> Those African Americans identified for sampling are those who typify the expectation of deviance from the [White] model. Disproportionate numbers of studies on African Americans look at prison inmates, delinquents, academic non-achievers, poor,

welfare recipients, single parents, etc. The focus on this population becomes a methodological self-fulfilling prophecy of the characteristics already implied in the model. (p. 714)

Thus, the implicit sampling model in such cases reinforces stereotypes of Whites as the healthy, universal standard with whom problematic ALANA and immigrant groups are compared (Hill, 1997; Toldson & Toldson, 2001). As previously discussed, the multicultural guidelines (APA, 2003) specifically describe this form of stereotyping as problematic.

Exploitation. Many critics have noted the exploitation inherent in primarily White researchers' propensity to conduct studies in ALANA and immigrant communities in which everyone involved benefits except the community under study (Casas & Thompson, 1991; Council of National Psychological Associations for the Advancement of Ethnic Minority Interests [CNPAAEMI], 2000; Goodman et al., 2004). Some ethical questions related to avoiding exploitative research concern where and when study results should be reported (e.g., Is it ethical to inform the general public about results before the ALANA community is informed?), data access and ownership (e.g., May a community withdraw its consent to participate and claim the data already collected?), and intended and unintended consequences of studying outgroup communities (e.g., Should ALANA participants be advised in advance when obtained results are likely to portray them in a negative light?). Casas and Thompson (1991) argue that it is not ethical to collect data from ALANA communities without involving them in conceptualizing research questions that are meaningful to their communities.

Answers to the foregoing questions that disregard the interests of ALANA communities clearly communicate to them that the White researcher believes that the needs and interests of the people under study are secondary to the researcher's educational pursuits and interests, a Reintegration perspective in WRID theory; however, sometimes the researcher's presumed intent to avoid exploitation of study participants may nevertheless result in exploitation.

For example, a group of researchers conducted a randomized trial of a motivational interviewing intervention with participants in outpatient and inpatient drug treatment. The central goal of their study was to replicate findings from previous randomized trials, which demonstrated the efficacy of motivational interviewing in reducing substance abuse. The average study participant was described as a Hispanic male in his mid-30s with a high school education, who had spent about 1 in 4 days working and 1 in 5 days (of the prior 90) in institutions. The researchers paid each participant $210. But the incentive available to participants in the study might have subtlety coerced their participation, particularly given that this amount of money offered might have represented more income than many participants had earned during the previous 3 months. Also, given the nature of participants' mental health issue (i.e., substance abuse), it is entirely possible that the incentive interacted with the researchers' intended treatment to make it more or less effective. After all, a person can purchase a lot of "substances" with $210, possibly more than many of their study participants could have purchased if they had not participated in that study.

Measurement Ethical Issues

The effects of the lack of explicit racial or cultural theory by which to guide the design of a study can contribute to many ethical issues when the researcher attempts to quantify the variables in his or her study. Some issues pertain to selection or use of existing measures, but most pertain to the manner in which measures of racial or cultural constructs in studies are quantified.

Quantification. For the most part, researchers have quantified the racial or ethnic cultural constructs in their studies by dividing their participants into supposedly mutually exclusive racial or ethnic groups that are dummy coded for use in subsequent statistical analyses. Dummy coding means that every individual within the same group receives the same score (e.g., one or zero). That is, race is a constant within groups. Consequently, individuals cannot differ from their in-group members with respect to racial-group membership. Given that racial-group categories are the sole operational definitions of race or ethnicity in most studies that purport to investigate racial or ethnic cultural factors, effects of racial or cultural factors on individuals' behaviors cannot be ascertained when race or culture is quantified as a categorical variable. Therefore, in the standard study of ALANA samples, conducted by researchers regardless of their race or ethnicity, racial, ethnic, or cultural constructs only exist relative to White groups, groups for whom White researchers typically do not acknowledge the relevance of racial or cultural factors.

Unlike most variables in psychology, racial categories can be assigned to participants and manipulated in the research design in a willy-nilly manner because the researcher is held to no standard in determining what constitutes the relevant racial groups in his or her study. Depending on the researcher's needs, ALANA participants may be assigned to a single group, collapsed across ALANA racial groups, or embedded in presumably predominantly White samples in which racial groups of the participants are barely mentioned, if they are mentioned at all (Graham, 1992). The flexibility that racial categories as "status variables" or "attributes"

gives researchers possibly accounts for why White researchers believe that they have actually measured racial or cultural theoretical constructs when they include racial categories as independent, predictor, or moderator variables in their research designs (e.g., Rowe et al., 1994).

A second anonymous reviewer of Helms' (2001) previously discussed manuscript on racial bias in intellectual testing chastised her as follows: "Racial categories are clearly limited, but they can be ascertain [sic] with a high degree of accuracy with self-reported data and they do not create an additional burden on respondents. . . . It is easy to critique racial categories, but why do you think they have been so widely used" (Personal communication, anonymous reviewer B, 2002)? Racial and ethnic categories have been so widely used because researchers, who use them to quantify race and culture as variables, do not have to conform to any of the measurement standards that are typically required of measures in psychology. These include conformance to standards of validity, reliability, and interpretation when racial categories are used as if they are veridical measures of racial or ethnic constructs (AERA, APA, & NCME, 1999). Perhaps the ultimate derogation of ALANA and immigrant samples, however, is that researchers seem to believe that they can capture the essence of the rich racial and cultural characteristics of ALANA peoples with single items (i.e., racial or cultural categories), which may be changed at the researcher's whim.

Use of measures. Innumerable problems arise when measures are used to study ALANA samples if the measures do not assess equivalent constructs across ALANA groups, problems that have been long standing (e.g., AERA et al., 1999; APA, 2002; Helms, 1992). For example, the *Standards for Educational and Psychological Testing* (AERA et al., 1999) devotes an entire chapter to psychometric issues related to development and use of tests for test takers whose first language is not English. Although White researchers, who use advanced racial identity schemata (e.g., Immersion, Autonomy), will recognize the standards chapter as only suggestive of the wide variety of racial and cultural characteristics of participants that potentially interact with their responses to "standardized" measures, it is at least more consideration than is often given to such matters in the typical study of ALANA samples conducted by White researchers.

In an effort to address the lack of equivalence of existing measures or the limited availability of measures suitable for addressing specific racial or cultural constructs, or simply because they devalue existing instruments, some White researchers develop their own measures. It is important for these scholars to recognize that constructs and the instruments by which they are measured are the socially constructed products of a particular culture (e.g., Whiteness) and worldview (APA, 2002). White researchers developing measures for ALANA or immigrant populations in the absence of cultural consultation and reflective practices likely develop measures that reflect White cultural values and norms (Helms, 1992). Using measures representative of White cultural values to assess ALANA and immigrant participants presents White researchers with another version of the cultural-equivalence ethical quandary, given the likelihood that misinformation and poor outcomes will still result if the researcher's self-developed measure does not match the realities of her or his ALANA and immigrants participants (APA, 2002; Helms, 1992).

Nevertheless, although researchers have been advised to evaluate the effects of the racial and cultural characteristics of study participants on their responses to standardized measures (e.g., Helms, 1992), few studies have examined these concerns empirically (cf. Satiani, Mascher, Henze, Perry, &

Helms, 2004). Instead, White psychologists continue to equate evidence of between-group differences on outcomes or dependent measures to evidence of cultural equivalence of the testing process from which participants' scores are obtained. Whereas inattention to cultural equivalence of measures is not a problem endemic to White researchers exclusively, it can be argued that this problem plagues research conducted by White researchers at a disproportionate rate in comparison with research conducted by ALANA scholars, given the White group's numerical majority status and pervasive influence in the field of psychology (APA, 2002). They, in fact, define what is and is not reality in psychology.

Procedures

The manners in which the various components of the study are implemented (i.e., procedures) also offer many opportunities for ethical concerns related to exploitation to occur. As previously noted, many White researchers do not speak the languages or dialects, interact comfortably with, or understand the customs and traditions of the ALANA samples that they study. Consequently, in violation of Ethical Standard 2.01 (APA, 2002), researchers are typically functioning beyond the boundaries of their competence with respect to race and culture. Although there are many adverse effects on research procedures resulting from the lack of racial and cultural competence and explicit racial and cultural theory, here we focus primarily on (a) data collection and (b) informed consent.

Data Collection

Typically, principal investigators do not collect data personally but rely on research assistants or research collaborators. When ALANA samples are the focus of the research,

White researchers often use students from these groups or community leaders to gain access to the relevant ALANA community. Often these research facilitators not only do not benefit personally from assisting the primary researcher, but they place themselves at risk for losing credibility in settings that are vital to their survival due to their naïveté about the research infrastructure.

During her first semester of graduate school, a Latina graduate student was asked by a White female faculty member to collect data for her in the local Latina/Latino community so that the faculty member could satisfy the terms of her federally funded grant. The faculty member supervised a research team of four White graduate students, but neither she nor they spoke Spanish. The student, feeling flattered that a faculty member asked for her help, threw herself wholeheartedly into the data collection task, but in doing so, she neglected her research responsibilities to her assigned advisor, an Asian American woman. At the end of her first year, the student found herself without an advisor for the coming year. The faculty member whose work the student had voluntarily done was too busy with her research grant to take on any new students, and her original advisor felt disrespected and did not want to continue their advisory relationship.

Clearly, the student in this situation had been used and placed in jeopardy by the help-seeking faculty member. The student was discredited in her academic environment because there was no one to attest to her research competence. She was discredited in her familial environment because she had to explain why the family's first woman graduate student was on academic probation. In the local Spanish-speaking community, she was discredited because the community gained nothing from supplying data for the study. Casas and Thompson (1991) point out that it is exploitative to use representatives from studied communities if they are

not permitted to insert real-life needs and priorities throughout the research process and are not appropriately compensated for their efforts.

Informed consent procedures. Informed consent procedures exist to protect "participants' autonomy and welfare by providing a description of the study with its benefits and harms" (Fisher et al., 2002, p. 1028). Use of appropriate informed consent procedures ensures that each potential individual participant's decision to participate in the study is rational and voluntary, which, given its focus on the individual, is an implicitly culture-bound decision-making strategy. Despite the seductive tendency to conceptualize informed consent procedures as universal across settings, research questions, and populations, some researchers and scholars have questioned the extent to which typical informed consent procedures are adequate or appropriate across social and cultural contexts (Fisher et al., 2002; Haney & Lykes, 2000; Jenkins & Parron, 1995; Patai, 1987).

Researchers' lack of understanding of ALANA and immigrant communities may contribute to inappropriate informed consent procedures. Inattention in informed consent procedures to values or conditions specific to ethnic communities can contribute to low participation rates of members of these communities (Fisher et al., 2002). It may also contribute to failure to adequately protect participants' confidentiality and anonymity. For example, when ALANA or immigrant participants are involved in a study, just as with White participants, it is crucial to exclude information in the data collection process, data coding and analysis, and reporting of results that would allow a participant(s) to be readily identified. For various reasons, ALANA group members typically are less numerous in research samples than are White participants. In research projects involving relatively small local communities and/or that focus on unique problems, it may be uncommonly easy for community members to specifically identify an ALANA participant.

Sometimes it will not be possible for the researcher to protect the confidentiality or anonymity of ALANA and immigrant participants. In such cases, it is mandatory that the researcher explains the risks of participating in the study in the preferred language of the participant and in doing so addresses issues that are relevant to the participants' racial and cultural circumstances. Sometimes it will be necessary for the researcher to abort the study in order to avoid doing harm to the research participant.

Participants' understandings of the research process may differ across cultural contexts. Therefore, it is necessary for the researcher to assume the responsibility of deconstructing the process for them. The multicultural guidelines (APA, 2003) and Fisher et al. (2002) provide thoughtful overviews of ethical considerations pertinent to use of informed consent procedures with ALANA and immigrant populations. Unfortunately, it is relatively easy to find examples of use of questionable informed consent procedures in the published social science literature (see for examples, Aharonovich, Nunes, & Hasin, 2003, and Miller et al., 2003).

In the previously discussed study of a motivational intervention to reduce substance abuse, the research sample consisted of 204 participants, 136 of whom were from ALANA groups, 107 of whom self-identified as Hispanic. The authors did not discuss whether they made culturally responsive accommodations to informed consent procedures, such as provision of a Spanish version of the informed consent form. Indeed, it seems that the researchers believed that minimal English proficiency (i.e., 8th-grade reading level) meant that Hispanic participants had assimilated to White cultural norms and were

proficient in written and spoken English, a belief that is suspect, given existing scholarship suggesting otherwise (AERA et al., 1999; Boulette, 1976, as cited in Kouyoumdjian, Zamboanga, & Hansen, 2003).

That the authors of the motivational intervention ostensibly gave limited attention to issues of linguistic and cultural diversity in their informed consent procedures is not unusual. More generally, one rarely finds discussions about how potential racial and cultural issues (e.g., collectivism, racial mistrust) were managed in White researchers' informed consent procedures. Nor does one find discussions of risks and benefits to the ALANA communities in which potential participants reside.

DATA ANALYSIS AND INTERPRETATION

Whether or not researchers are inclined to acknowledge it, the racial identity schemata that the researcher uses also may influence data analyses and interpretation of study results. Quintana, Troyano, and Taylor (2001, as cited in APA, 2003) urged psychological researchers, "to consider cultural hypotheses as possible explanations for their findings, to examine moderator effects, and to use statistical procedures to examine cultural variables" (p. 43). Yet many researchers in psychology do not even report the racial, cultural, or ethnic composition of their samples (Graham, 1992). It also appears to be the case that White researchers believe that because they can quantify racial categories and, therefore, analyze them statistically, it is permissible to interpret their results as if the categories reflect theory-driven constructs, which, of course, they do not (Frazier, Tix, & Barron, 2004).

In research design texts (e.g., Heppner, Kivlighan, & Wampold, 1999), ethnicity and occasionally race (if it is mentioned at all) are described as "status variables" because they supposedly cannot be manipulated or ethically assigned to participants (Heppner et al., 1999, p. 278), but the texts are often mute or wrong about the meaning of racial or ethnic categories. Pedhazur and Schmelkin (1991) come closest to advising researchers against the misuse of race and ethnicity, operationally defined as categorical *attribute* variables, in the following quotation:

> The decision whether to include attribute categorical variables in a study should not be made lightly. In particular, one should resist the temptation to include broad categorical variables [e.g., "sex," "race," "country of origin"], just because they are readily available, or because other researchers have included them in their studies. . . . Being broad, such variables are bound to be comprised of widely heterogeneous groups with respect to myriad variables. In the absence of a clear reason for doing so, inclusion of broad categorical variables in a study is likely to deflect attention from variable(s) that should be the focus of the study. Thus, it is easy to fall into the trap of "explaining" differences among people on some phenomenon of interest on the basis of sex [or race], say, when what is called for is to determine what specific variable(s) on which males and females [or racial groups] differ affect the phenomenon under study. (pp. 175–176)

Consider the implications of Pedhazur and Schmelkin's advice. If White researchers were to heed it, entire research areas in psychology would be discredited. Chief among these would be comparisons of the performance on intellectual tests of ALANA and White groups. Use of racial and ethnic categories to explain test performance has unquestionably resulted in harm to ALANA samples who differed from White standards in the testing domain. That this magnitude of misinterpretation has been allowed not only to persist for so long but has been the foundation of high-stakes decisions and interventions in society suggests the pervasiveness of the maintenance of the racial status quo that characterizes the Reintegration schema. It is worth investigating whether other research domains have been similarly defined by erroneous interpretations of racial or cultural attribute categories as causative.

DISSEMINATION OF RESULTS

Even if White researchers engage in ethical research with ALANA and immigrant samples, they might have difficulty disseminating their work through traditional channels because their work will challenge common research practices in White-oriented psychology (Helms, 1993). Action editors, grant administrative staff, and anonymous reviewers hold the power to alter and ultimately dismiss contributions from researchers that in their minds depart from standard practice in psychological research, although standard practice often has legitimized the racial and cultural oppression and suppression of research models other than those that support the cultural imperatives of White, heterosexual, middle-class men (i.e., "experts"). Yet these experts in psychology often lack the knowledge to realize that they need to self-examine their own racial and cultural orientations, and lack, as well, the skills to do so (Akbar, 1991; Graham, 1992; Hill, 1997; hooks, 1984; Parham, 1993; Stanfield, 1993, as cited in Young, 2000; Toldson & Toldson, 2001). The result is that White researchers who use Immersion/Emersion or Autonomy schemata to conduct their research are likely to be punished for their efforts by not having their manuscripts published and/or by having their character maligned (cf., Zuckerman, 1990).

In response to White psychology's rejection of their racial and cultural personhood and the racial and cultural realities of the communities that they reflect, ALANA psychologists have created a number of journals and newsletters friendly to research with explicit racial or cultural foci (e.g., *Journal of Black Psychology, Hispanic Journal of Behavioral Sciences*). Nevertheless, according to Parham (1993), new scholars, interested in remaining in academia, cannot afford to publish exclusively or even primarily in these venues because tenure and promotion committees do not accord these outlets and traditional journals the same level of respect when it is time to document one's expertise and contributions to one's specialty. Clearly, this issue could be addressed if senior scholars acquired the expertise in racial and cultural psychology to publish in these race and culture-focused outlets themselves and if the keepers of the gates of traditional journals would open them to the sophisticated study of racial and cultural constructs.

Helms (1993) argued that the significance of White researchers' gatekeeping role should not be underestimated, as social policy and knowledge creation often directly stem from research findings. Arguably, until White researchers at the gates of prestigious publication journals and other respected venues (e.g., granting agencies) become more welcoming of research that embodies the multicultural guidelines (APA, 2003), acquisition of meaningful knowledge in psychology and ethical research practice with ALANA and immigrant communities will continue to be sacrificed.

CONCLUSIONS AND RECOMMENDATIONS

Throughout the present chapter, we have raised some explicit racial and cultural concerns for White researchers to consider when engaging in research involving ALANA and immigrant samples, communities, and individuals at every level of the research process; however, some of our recommendations either were implicit or are so contrary to current research practice that it might be useful to reiterate and summarize them in a supplementary checklist (see Exhibit 16.1).

White researchers notice race and culture when they are not their own, but when White researchers study White samples or the focus of the research is not explicitly race or culture (which is most of the time), they assume that there are no racial or cultural contexts that pertain to the research underway. This obliviousness to racial and cultural dynamics in their samples parallels White researchers' lack of awareness of these issues as they pertain to themselves as members of the most powerful racial in-group in the United States. Given that this lack of consciousness potentially contributes to unethical practice throughout the research process, it behooves them to self-examine their racial and cultural belief systems before, during, and after the completion of each research project. White racial identity theory was offered as a conceptual framework that might be used to guide these self-examinations. Focus groups and arbiters from the communities represented in the study should also be used to clarify the relevant issues.

After identifying a research topic of interest, researchers specify questions that they want answered and put forth some hypotheses to be disproved. White researchers who study ALANA and immigrant samples need to consider the impact that research questions have on them, being certain that the problem is addressed in a manner that could potentially benefit members of all of the racial groups in the study or, at the least, that the hypotheses do not address the psychological concerns of Whites to the detriment of People of Color and those of immigrant status. Responsible and ethical White researchers will not only consider the impact

Exhibit 16.1   A Checklist of Ethical Research Practices for White Researchers Studying ALANA and Immigrant Samples

---

Researcher Self-Examination

Read the American Psychological Association (2002) *Ethical Principles of Psychologists and Code of Conduct* and (2003) "Guidelines on Multicultural Education, Training, Research, Practice, and Organizational Change for Psychologists."

Self-examine one's racial and cultural belief systems in light of WRID. This process may be best facilitated in a group format in which members' racial and cultural values and beliefs can be discussed and reflected on between members (cf. Running Wolf & Rickard, 2003; Sevig & Etzkorn, 2001).

Developing Research Questions, Hypotheses, and Study Design

Avoid use of Whiteness as formal theory (i.e. investigating ALANA's deviation from nonspecific White models).

Avoid inappropriate application of formal theories derived from a White cultural perspective with ALANA and immigrant samples.

Avoid conceptualization and measurement of race, culture, and experience of being an immigrant as categorical variables by enlisting racial, cultural, and immigrant identity theoretical frameworks and related measures.

Employ theoretical frameworks that purposefully represent life circumstances of immigrants and people of color. This may require conducting literature searches outside of traditional psychology outlets.

Include ALANA and immigrant community members in all aspects of study design and implementation via racial/cultural diversification of research teams and implementation of ALANA and immigrant community consultation groups.

Consider the impact of research on the population under study via solicitation of critical feedback from community consultation groups. Proactively incorporate such feedback into all aspects of study design.

Ensure that exploitation of the research team and consultation group members, as well as the community under study, does not occur by avoiding exploitative research team member assignments; offering culturally appropriate compensation; and making study participation useful and beneficial to all parties involved.

Conducting and Reporting Research

Implement ongoing strategies, such as community consultation groups, during the research process to monitor and address ethical concerns involving race and culture as they occur.

Report the racial composition of one's sample as well as one's research team.

Embed results in racial or cultural contexts.

of their research on these populations but will work actively to incorporate conceptualizations and critical analyses provided by members of these communities in every aspect of their research design (Casas & Thompson, 1992; Guba & Lincoln, 1989).

Ultimately, a primary concern for White psychologists ought to be that they lack credibility in many ALANA and immigrant communities (CNPAAEMI, 2000). Guba and Lincoln (1989) described credibility as the degree of convergence between the realities of study participants and involved researchers. Researchers might enhance their credibility by immersing themselves in the cultural contexts of participants as recommended by Guba and Lincoln, but Goodman et al. (2004) advise that the community under study does and ought to dictate the conditions under which such immersion should occur. Participating in focus groups with study participants, wherein feedback and reactions to the study are elicited, is another way of maximizing the credibility of the researcher and the researcher's findings.

When supervising research teams or collaborating with ALANA or immigrant professionals or community leaders, White psychologists should take special care to respect the racial and cultural knowledge, skills, and life experiences of members of these groups. Respect may be demonstrated by providing compensation suitable to the contributions of the research collaborator, as mutually agreed on, and by including collaborators from the relevant communities as advisors in every aspect of the research project. Formation of research teams should (a) include team members who can intimately and informatively address the racial and cultural concerns central to the groups under study rather than merely treat White or other skin colors as sufficient; (b) make use of consultation with "experts" about specific ALANA communities in a manner that is beneficial to both researchers and potential participants; (c) avoid exploitative assignment of supervisory tasks to research team members; and (d) implement ongoing strategies during the research process to monitor and address ethical concerns involving race and culture as they occur.

When White researchers limit themselves to conceptualizing racial and cultural dynamics as differences between members of different racial groups, race is likely to be viewed as an extraneous variable (Garcia-Coll, 1999) or falsely reified as a conceptual construct (Helms, 2004). It is important for researchers to report the racial or ethnic composition of their samples as well as their research team. That is, White researchers, in particular, should always embed their results in racial or cultural contexts, but they should not mistake racial or ethnic categories for theoretical constructs (Pedhazur & Schmelkin, 1991). When researchers enable themselves to use more advanced racial identity schemata to conceptualize their studies, it will be easier for them to give racial and cultural constructs a central place in the designs of their studies in ways that acknowledge the salience of such factors in the lives of study participants, collaborators, and White researchers.

NOTE

1.   The term ALANA refers to African Americans, Latino/Latina Americans, Asian/Pacific Islander Americans, and Native or Indigenous Americans.

2.   Given the nature of their comments, we are presuming that the anonymous reviewers discussed either are White or were mentored by White mentors primarily.

This presumption seems merited in light of recent calls for underrepresented groups to apply for editor and reviewer positions of professional journals and our own examination of grant review panels. Copies of anonymous reviews received by the first author and her responses are available from the first author on request.

REFERENCES

Aharonovich, E., Nunes, E., & Hasin, D. (2003). Cognitive impairment, retention and abstinence among cocaine abusers in cognitive-behavioral treatment. *Drug and Alcohol Dependence, 71,* 207–211.

Akbar, N. (1991). Paradigms of African American research. In R. L. Jones (Ed.), *Black psychology* (3rd ed., pp. 709–725). Berkeley, CA: Cobb & Henry.

American Anthropological Association. (1999). *American Anthropological Association section membership totals at December 31.* Retrieved August 1, 2004, from www.aaanet.org/faq/stats.pdf

American Educational Research Association. (2002, June 30). *AERA fact sheet.* Retrieved June 15, 2004, from www.aera.net/about/facts.htm

American Educational Research Association, American Psychological Association, & National Council on Measurement in Education. (1999). *Standards for educational and psychological testing.* Washington, DC: Author.

American Psychological Association. (2000). *Demographic characteristics of APA members by membership status, 2000.* Retrieved June 15, 2004, from http://research.apa.org/2000profiles.pdf

American Psychological Association. (2002). *Ethical principles of psychologists and code of conduct.* Washington, DC: Author.

American Psychological Association. (2003). Guidelines on multicultural education, training, research, practice, and organizational change for psychologists. *American Psychologist, 58,* 377–402.

American Sociological Association. (2004, January 29). *ASA membership by type and race/ethnicity 1999 to 2003 (percent of members).* Retrieved August 1, 2004, www.asanet.org/research/membership1.html

Brawley, O. W., & Tejeda, H. (1995). Minority inclusion in clinical trials issues and potential strategies. *Journal of the National Cancer Institute Monographs, 17,* 55–57.

Casas, J. M., & Thompson, C. E. (1991). Ethical principles and standards: A racial-ethnic minority research perspective. *Counseling and Values, 35,* 186–187.

Council of National Psychological Associations for the Advancement of Ethnic Minority Interests. (2000). *Guidelines for research in ethnic minority communities.* Washington, DC: APA.

Department of Health and Human Services, National Institutes of Health. (1994, March 28). National Institutes of Health guidelines on the inclusion of women and minorities as subjects in clinical research: Notice (Part 7). *Federal Register.*

Eisenman, R. (1995). Why psychologists should study race. *American Psychologist, 50,* 42–43.

El Nasser, H. (2003, February 17). Black America's new diversity. *USA Today,* p. A3.

Eysenck, H. (1984). Effect of race on abilities and test scores. In C. R. Reynolds & R. T. Brown (Eds.), *Perspectives on bias in mental testing* (pp. 253–291). New York: Plenum.

Fisher, C. B., Hoagwood, K., Boyce, C., Duster, T., Frank, D. A., Grisso, T., et al. (2002). Research ethics for the mental health science involving ethnic minority children and youths. *American Psychologist, 57*(12), 1024–1040.

Frazier, P. A., Tix, A. P., & Barron, K. E. (2004). Testing moderator and mediator effects in counseling psychology research. *Journal of Counseling Psychology, 51*, 115–134.

Garcia-Coll, C. (1999). Cultural influences on child development: Are we ready for a paradigm shift? In A. S. Masten (Ed.), *Cultural processes in child development: The Minnesota Symposium on Child Psychology* (pp. 1–24). Mahwah, NJ: Lawrence Erlbaum.

Goodman, L. A., Liang, B., Helms, J. E., Latta, R. E., Sparks, E., & Weintraub, S. R. (2004). Training psychologists as social justice agents: Feminist and multicultural principles in action. *Journal of Counseling Psychology, 32*(6), 793–837.

Graham, S. (1992). "Most of the subjects were White and middle class": Trends in published research on African Americans in selected APA journals, 1970–1989. *American Psychologist, 47*(5), 629–639.

Guba, E., & Lincoln, Y. (1989). *Fourth generation evaluation*. Beverly Hills, CA: Sage.

Haney, W., & Lykes, M. B. (2000). Practice, participatory research and creative research designs: The evolution of ethical guidelines for research. In F. T. Sherman & W. R. Torbert (Eds.), *Transforming social inquiry, transforming social action: New paradigms for crossing the theory/practice divide in universities and communities* (pp. 275–294). New York: Kluwer Academic/Plenum.

Helms, J. E. (1984). Toward a theoretical explanation of the effects of race on counseling. A Black and White model. *Counseling Psychologist, 12*(4), 153–165.

Helms, J. E. (1990). *Black and White racial identity: Theory, research, and practice*. Westport, CT: Greenwood.

Helms, J. E. (1992). Why is there no study of cultural equivalence in standardized cognitive ability testing? *American Psychologist, 47*(9), 1083–1101.

Helms, J. E. (1993). I also said, "White racial identity influences White researchers." *Counseling Psychologist, 21*(2), 240–243.

Helms, J. E. (1995). An update of Helms's White and People of Color racial identity models. In J. G. Ponterotto, J. M. Casas, L. A. Suzuki, & C. M. Alexander (Eds.), *Handbook of multicultural counseling* (pp. 181–198). Thousand Oaks, CA: Sage.

Helms, J. E. (2001). *Reports of the death of racial bias in high-stakes testing may be ill-founded: Simple strategies for detecting and removing irrelevant racial variance in testing*. Unpublished paper.

Helms, J. E. (2002). A remedy for the Black-White test-score disparity. *American Psychologist, 57*, 303–304.

Helms, J. E. (2004). Making race a matter of individual differences within groups. *Counseling Psychologist, 32*, 473–483.

Helms, J. E., & Cook, D. A. (1999). *Using race and culture in counseling and psychotherapy: Theory and process*. Needham Heights, MA: Allyn & Bacon.

Heppner, P. P., Kivlighan, D. M., & Wampold, B. E. (1999). *Research design in counseling* (2nd ed.). Boston: Brooks/Cole.

Hill, N. E. (1997). Does parenting differ based on social class? African American women's perceived socialization for achievement. *American Journal of Community Psychology, 2*(5), 675–697.

hooks, b. (1984). *Feminist theory from margin to center.* Boston: South End Press.

Jenkins, R. R., & Parron, D. (1995). Guidelines for adolescent health research: Issues of race and class. *Journal of Adolescent Health, 17,* 314–322.

Jensen, A. R. (1995). Psychological research on race differences. *American Psychologist, 50,* 41–42.

Korchin, S. J. (1980). Clinical psychology and minority problems. *American Psychologist, 35,* 262–269.

Kouyoumdjian, H., Zamboanga, B. L., & Hansen, D. J. (2003). Barriers to community mental health services for Latinos: Treatment considerations. *Clinical Psychology: Science and Practice, 10,* 394–422.

Members of underrepresented groups: Reviewers for journal manuscripts wanted. (2003). *Professional Psychology: Research and Practice, 34,* 209.

Miller, W. R., Yahne, C. E., & Tonigan, J. S. (2003). Motivational interviewing in drug abuse services: A randomized trial. *Journal of Consulting and Clinical Psychology, 71,* 754–763.

Miskimen, T., Marin, H., & Escobar, J. (2003). Psychopharmacological research ethics: Special issues affecting U.S. ethnic minorities. *Psychopharmacology, 171,* 98–104.

National Center for Education Statistics. (2004). *NCES fast facts.* Retrieved June 15, 2004, from http://nces.ed.gov/fastfacts/

Parham, T. A. (1993). White researchers conducting multicultural counseling research: Can their efforts be "mo betta"? *Counseling Psychologist, 21*(2), 260–256.

Patai, D. (1987). Ethical problems of personal narratives, or who should eat the last piece of cake? *International Journal of Oral History, 8*(1), 5–27.

Pedhazur, E. J., & Schmelkin, L. P. (1991). *Measurement, design, and analysis: An integrated approach.* Hillsdale, NJ: Lawrence Erlbaum.

Rowe, D. C., Vazsonyi, A. T., & Flannery, D. J. (1994). No more than skin deep: Ethnic and racial similarity in developmental process. *Psychological Review, 101,* 396–413.

Rowe, W., Behrens, J. T., & Leach, M. M. (1995). Racial/ethnic identity and racial consciousness: Looking backward and forward. In J. G. Ponterotto, J. M. Casas, L. A. Suzuki, & C. M. Alexander (Eds.), *Handbook of multicultural counseling* (pp. 218–233). Thousand Oaks, CA: Sage.

Rowe, W., Bennett, S. K., & Atkinson, D. R. (1994). White racial identity models: A critique and alternative proposal. *Counseling Psychologist, 22,* 129–146.

Running Wolf, P., & Rickard, J. A. (2003). Talking circles: A Native American approach to experiential learning. *Journal of Multicultural Counseling and Development, 31,* 39–43.

Sackett, P. R., Schmitt, N., Ellingson, J. E., & Kabin, M. B. (2001). High-stakes testing in employment, credentialing, and higher education: Prospects in a post-affirmative action world. *American Psychologist, 56,* 302–318.

Satiani, A., Mascher, J., Henze, K., Perry, J., & Helms, J. E. (2004). *Cultural equivalence in standardized tests of cognitive abilities, knowledge, and skills: A content analysis of empirical studies following Helms (1992).* Manuscript submitted for publication.

Sevig, T., & Etzkorn, J. (2001). Transformative training: A year-long multicultural counseling seminar for graduate students. *Journal of Multicultural Counseling and Development, 29,* 57–72.

Steele, C., & Aronson, J. (1995). Stereotype threat and the intellectual test performance of African Americans. *Journal of Personality and Social Psychology, 69,* 797–811.

Takaki, R. (1989). *Strangers from a different shore: A history of Asian Americans.* New York: Penguin.

Thompson, C. E., & Carter, R. T. (1997). *Racial identity theory: Applications to individual, group, and organizational interventions.* Mahwah, NJ: Lawrence Erlbaum.

Toldson, I. A., & Toldson, I. L. (2001). Biomedical ethics: An African-centered psychological perspective. *Journal of Black Psychology, 27*(4), 401–423.

U.S. Census Bureau. (2000). *All across the U.S.A.: Population distribution and composition, 2000.* Retrieved June 15, 2004, from www.census.gov/population/pop-profile/2000/chap02.pdf

U.S. Department of Education. (2002). *No child left behind: A desktop reference.* Retrieved February 20, 2004, from www.nochildleftbehind.gov

Yee, A. H., Fairchild, H. H., Weizmann, F., & Wyatt, G. E. (1993). Addressing psychology's problems with race. *American Psychologist, 48,* 1132–1140.

Young, M. D. (2000). Considering (irreconcilable?) contradictions in cross-group feminist research. *Qualitative Studies in Education, 13*(6), 629–660.

Zinn, H. (1999). *A people's history of the United States: 1492-present.* New York: HarperCollins.

Zuckerman, M. (1990). Some dubious premises in research and theory on racial differences: Scientific, social, and ethical issues. *American Psychologist, 45*(12), 1297–1303.

CHAPTER 17

Coda

The Virtuous and Responsible Researcher in Another Culture

JOSEPH E. TRIMBLE

GERALD V. MOHATT

> *Citizen participation means a horizontal, equal relationship. It means relating with the* other *at the same level. One understands one's usefulness as part of the solidarity produced within the relationship. Accepting the* otherness *involves admitting different modes of knowing and making possible the dialogue and the relation with the other in a plane of equality based on the acceptance of our own differences.*
>
> —Maritza Montero, "New Horizons for Knowledge"

Most researchers and scholars who write and advise about the conduct of research with populations other than their own devote most of their attention to the principles and codes of professional ethical standards and norms; that is, they are concerned about what is right and wrong, good or bad, harmless or harmful, intrusive or nonintrusive, and an assortment of other moral and humanistic moral considerations. Additionally, recently some notable scholars have expanded on normative professional standards to include often unstated ethical principles and guidelines that focus on the importance of establishing firm collaborative relationships with community leaders, especially in conducting research with ethnocultural groups (Fisher et al., 2002; Jason, Keys, Suarez-Balcazar, Taylor, & Davis, 2004; Mohatt, 1989). Trickett and Espino (2004) summarized the extensive literature in this growing subfield of inquiry and commented that, "It is time to place the collaboration concept in the center of inquiry and work out its importance for community research and intervention. Although some would see it as merely a tool or strategy to getting the 'real' work of behavioral science done, our strong preference is to view the research relationship in community research and intervention as a critical part of the 'real' work itself" (p. 62). Several contributors of chapters to this handbook emphasize the thrust, weight, and significance of Trickett and Espino's conditional advice and add in unison that without establishing and working through community partnerships, research ventures are doomed to failure at every stage of the research process. A relationship based research methodology also adds new challenges to conducting research.

In the opening quotation for this chapter, Maritza Montero emphasizes that to be successful and to establish a meaningful relationship with a community, one must view participants as equals, as well as recognize that the *others* have different worldviews. Recognizing and appreciating different worldviews does not mean that one has to embrace or adopt the views; indeed, as is often the case, some worldviews and belief systems may be at complete odds with those valued and cherished by the outsider to the point that they may present conflicts. When conflicts become apparent, the researcher must step back and reflect on the possibility that continued relationships might be intolerable and therefore unacceptable. At this point, the researcher may want to consider abandoning the research venture; regrettably, the literature is filled with stories of researchers who were not willing to abandon their mission because of the apparent conflicts in belief systems and consequently contributed to the negative reputation that research has generated among many ethnocultural communities. Let it be said that community acceptance and the establishment of collaborative relations and research partnerships begins with the acknowledgment that there are cultural differences and that they must be respected, tempered with active goodness, kindness, and justice as guiding moral principles for ethical decision making.

The majority of the information, advice, and recommendations contained in the preceding chapters in this handbook emphasize research procedures, methods, and evaluative approaches that promote collaborative relations in ethnocultural settings. Little attention has been given to the character of the researcher and how that can influence community relationships and assist in promoting the research agenda. In the coda, we give attention to the character and character development of the researcher, that is, one's moral and virtuous character, why that must be considered in establishing community partnerships, and how it may influence the overall success of the research. An emphasis on the virtues of the researcher is closely aligned with the "goodness-of-fit" model advocated in the first chapter by Fisher and Ragsdale. Along with several important considerations, the model and its proscriptions can create a circumstance in which one can "do good well." Doing good well implies that the researcher and the team are virtuous people and embody values and beliefs that community members and research participants find acceptable. Acceptability is a process of getting to know the researcher. It is a long process, one governed by the cultural rules for how the community will know if a person is trustworthy. One of the authors lived for 15 years in an indigenous community in which he raised his children, engaged in community and religious activities, taught, did clinical work, and conducted research. He moved after 15 years and as part of leaving was visiting with an elder who was very close to him and his family. When he told her that he was moving, her comment was, "Oh, that's too bad. We were just getting to know you." Fifteen years is brief when one resides in a face-to-face community. Our sense is that virtuous and principled ethics evolve out of a commitment to place and people that is needed in order for the community of concern to know us well enough to see if we have the virtue and moral character that will allow them to trust us with their personal knowledge.

VIRTUE AND PRINCIPLED ETHICS

What does it mean to be an ethical person when conducting research with ethnocultural communities? Does it imply that one must be a morally upstanding person who abides by a rigorous set of virtues that cannot be compromised? Does one approach ethical standards by viewing community-based dilemmas from a principled perspective, guided by the hard-and-fast rules of objectivity, reason, and impartiality? Is that approach likely to be acceptable to the community research partners? Is it possible that one's character, and thus moral and ethical standards, are incompatible with those likely to exist in the host research community? These are not mere academic and philosophical questions. The questions bear directly on the nature of relationships a researcher creates with community members, if for no other reason than the communities will want to know what kind of person they will be working with in due time. Many community residents may not fully comprehend the rigorous principles of the scientific method and the often elegant and sophisticated designs that drive research; however, they all understand what constitutes good character, although their standards indeed sometimes may not resonate with those of researchers (Beauvais & Trimble, 1992; Trimble, 1977).

Virtue ethics as originally conceptualized and espoused by Aristotle emphasizes the kind of person one should be or, more precisely, the *question,* "What kind of person should I be?" In more contemporary writings, the question emphasizes one's ethical and virtuous responsibilities and actions within a given context (Jordan & Meara, 1990).

According to Skeen (2002), Aristotle took the position that one's virtuous actions, and thus character, should strike a middle ground between extremes for one to be a successful and presumably happy, respectable person. The Aristotelian perspective has shaped Western, particularly Christian, views about attachment and detachment. The goal of a virtuous person was to achieve a sense of indifference so that one does not become so attached to one's views and desires that they cloud one's judgment. Discernment moves a person to become part of the decision-making process for determining what is good versus what is bad, to the extent that "I must be indifferent, without any inordinate attachment, so that I am not more inclined or disposed to accept the object in question than to relinquish it" (Puhl, 1951, p. 75). This also appears in some cultural communities, such as among Lakota healers who decide on whether they should accept a new patient based on whether they feel a neutrality when they are asked for help (Mohatt & Eagle Elk, 2000). They should not feel a desire to help or a sense of dread, but a sense of neutrality in order to effectively work with the client.

Until recently, however, the cultural context in which one enacts one's values and ethics has been largely overlooked. The importance of context comes into play within a community's habitat and therefore must be seriously considered as one assesses the fit between one's character and value ethics and community acceptance. On this point, Meara and Day (2003) suggested "that a substantial portion of behavior is a consequence of a person's internal attitudes or characteristics and this under the individual's control" (p. 472). This point is closely aligned to the incisive position taken by Boeree (1999) who maintained that "It is a virtuous person that creates good acts, not good acts that add up to a virtuous person" (p. 5).

Before embarking on field-based community research with ethnocultural populations, researchers would serve their purpose well to reflect on their character, values, and ethics to the point that they recognize the limitations and boundaries they have established for themselves. In the course of the self-reflection process, researchers must focus attention on the degree to which they are flexible because they are the ones who are ultimately responsible for their virtuous actions. Awareness of virtues implies that one constantly cultivates and practices them: The virtuous person creates good acts. Those who espouse the extreme form of virtuosity should recognize that their excessive commitments to the extremes could contribute to their inflexibility and erode their effectiveness with culturally unique populations.

A Researcher's Presence and Actions

One's deeds and actions are open to the assessment and evaluation of others, especially if one is a stranger to a community. In a fundamental sense, researchers who are new to the community are "other" to the community, and the community is "other" to them. Whose truth is, therefore, sanctioned or foreclosed by the researcher? To know this, one must become aware of how one is being represented in the community. Whatever the researcher's intention and research needs, their presence and actions will be scrutinized and assessed by community members. Is the researcher willing to be open to others' close and continuous observations, comments, and questions about her or his actions and beliefs? The question is more than speculative, as it speaks to one's willingness to be scrutinized, along with granting community residents permission and corresponding authority to question one's values, beliefs, and actions. Moreover, the questions may not stop with the assessment of character but focus, too, on the way research is being conducted and why the researcher is resorting to the use of procedures

and measures unfamiliar to residents and participants.

On arrival in the community, researchers become the main topic of attention, curiosity, conversation, and gossip. Consequently, they must have the courage to be open and free from reserve and pretense and expect to field questions about their character, wisdom, and personal convictions (Richardson, 2003). In effect, forthrightness and accessibility should be the principal trust on which one's value convictions are conveyed. Concealment of intentions and fraudulent character undoubtedly will be discovered. Confrontation will occur and with it the possibility of banishment if the deceit and screening continues.

Virtue Ethics in Psychology

In the past two decades, some noteworthy attention and scholarship has been given to the role of virtue ethics in psychology, especially its influence on providing professional clinical services (see Jordan & Meara, 1990; Meara & Day, 2003). For Jordan and Meara (2003) and Skeen (2002), virtue ethics provides the basis for one's character and corresponding professional development. Virtue ethics, therefore, involves our whole way of living. Yet researchers may experience conflict with their ethics and moral stances in settings where they are required to be value-free, such as in environments where research is occurring; the rules of the conventional tenets of valid scientific inquiry demand it. Is it possible for one to be truly neutral and value-free in field research settings? Does one set aside or minimize value convictions to assure objectivity? We believe these troubling philosophical questions may be illusory because community members will demand to know who the researcher is and why he or she is going about probing, questioning, manipulating, and measuring something about the people's lives and ways of believing and acting. And they have a right to do so because the researcher is an invited guest, and community residents are the stewards of the knowledge the researcher seeks to obtain. They have this right because they are subjects in the context of subjectivity, not subjects as the objects of positivism (Habermas, 2003).

Major Virtues for Consideration

What are the individual virtues that are likely to contribute to one's community acceptance? Skeen (2002) lists 13 of Aristotle's virtues that can guide one's responsible and virtuous behavior; they range from courage to indignation. According to Skeen (2002), Aristotle indicated that for one to behave virtuously, consideration must be given to the following: (1) "the social situation," where one is advised to avoid extreme circumstances; (2) "We must notice the errors into which we ourselves are liable to fall . . . and we must drag ourselves in the contrary direction"; and (3) "In every situation one must guard especially against pleasure and pleasant things because we are not impartial judges of pleasure" (p. 14). Aristotle's advice is well stated; however, Skeen (2002) cautions us to be mindful of the possibility that one may not be flexible enough to fully take the suggestions into consideration, as they may go against one's natural tendencies. Knowledge of one's natural tendencies comes from constant self-reflection and self-evaluation when one ventures into a culture that is distinctly different from one's ethnocultural background acquired through enculturative socialization. Accordingly, faced with unfamiliar cultural lifeways and thoughtways, one is advised to be attentive to one's natural tendencies and identify strategies to accommodate a fit within a new cultural milieu. More to the point, one must be flexible enough to compromise one's virtue ethics but only to the extent that the compromises are not contrived and outside the range of personal acceptability; compromises, if they're necessary, must remain within the levels of personal acceptance and tolerance where one's boundaries are within view. Much of the work of virtuous ethics in research is interpersonal and part of a process that is akin to the transference relationship in psychotherapy. Searles (1955) first brought attention to countertransference as a two-way communication in which the client draws from the therapist the therapist's strengths and weaknesses in order to heal him- or herself. Critical to the outcome is the ability of the therapist to know who she or he is and what is being asked of her or him at various points in the healing process. If not, the therapist will become lost and can do great harm to her- or himself and the client. Therapists are supposed to be trained to know the weaknesses that govern their desires and projections so that they can speak to what is needed for the client, to tolerate deep pain, and to discover secrets. In their training, therapists must learn enough about themselves so that with the advice of wise consultants, their weaknesses become avenues for understanding and empathy rather than resistances to the client's world. They do not confuse themselves with the client but know the person deeply. As researchers, we have the sense that the virtue that we work to achieve is analogous to this transferential process. We, too, need to know ourselves well, have this sense of detachment, be ruthless in seeking the truth, but steadfastly demonstrate empathy and respect for the other. We must know our interpersonal and personal biases as well as we know the methodological limitations of our designs and statistics.

Meara and Day (2003) take a more pragmatic approach to identifying virtues likely to guide professional judgment and actions. Lodged in the belief that the expression and enactment of virtues are influenced by contexts and relationships with others, Meara and Day offer four virtues for consideration, virtues that can ease tensions between the researcher and the community because they are framed according to the universal principles of civility, decency, and integrity.

Meara and Day (2003) propose that for one to be an effective, credible, and sensitive psychologist in academic settings, one should be trained in, and thus aware of the importance of, prudence, integrity, respectfulness, and benevolence. We want to add trustworthiness to the list, too. And taking our cues from Woodruff (2001), we suggest that reverence also be added to the list (see Richardson, 2003). According to Meara and Day (2003), *prudence* "emphasizes good judgment in the face of uncertainty" (p. 467). *Integrity* means that one should adhere to "a code of academic values" and professional codes of conduct. *Respectfulness* "means to embrace the concept that they are worthy of high regard and special attention as well as being sensitive to their needs and showing regard for them on their own terms" (p. 469). And *benevolence* "means being concerned about the welfare of others," where professionals act "in ways that put the common good and the welfare of others above personal gain or so-called guild issues" (p. 470). On *reverence*, Woodruff (2003) maintains that it is one's capacity for awe, respect, and shame in circumstances in which one recognizes one has little or no control over situations and events; here the emphasis is on one's awareness of one's limitations in the face of ambiguous and uncontrollable circumstances. *Trustworthiness* for us means that one is dependable, reliable, and therefore worthy of confidence. Not to be repetitive or truistic, but each of these six virtues implies reflexivity on the part of the researcher, the ability of the researcher to continually think about what he or she is feeling, thinking, and doing and, with humility, to submit it

to wise others who are part of the community of concern.

We are not certain the six virtues have been empirically substantiated through rigorous scientific inquiry; however, based on our collective 70 years of working and living in culturally different communities, we are reasonably confident that the virtues will equip one to be an effective and approachable participant in a collaborative research effort. At one level of reflection, the virtues appear to be idealistic and unattainable in settings where others don't value them. We would be remiss and irresponsible, though, not to remind researchers that not all community members subscribe to and live their lives according the six virtues. Indeed, there are social deviants and unsavory people just about everywhere who would seize an occasion to take advantage of and exploit outsiders; and in so doing, no doubt they would have a justification that at minimum made sense to them but to no one else. Richardson (2003) stated it well when he advised that "we understand that a healthy appreciation of human limitations does not undermine but is an essential component of cultivating and practicing the virtues" (p. 454). Social deviants and unsavory types provide occasion to test the strength of our virtuous convictions rather than an occasion to abandon or ease up on them in an attempt to counter untoward attempts at exploitation and manipulation.

There are egocentric, exploitative researchers, too, who have abused their relationships with numerous ethnocultural communities in the name of scientific inquiry and professional gain. Their self-serving forays into field-based research are the source of considerable criticism from numerous communities, many of whom refuse to permit any further research from occurring without explicit approval from a community-based governing body. The rules and dictates of a scientist-centered approach should not overshadow the importance of working in collaboration with a community. Beguiled approaches cloaked in deception and subtle manipulation will eventually betray the underlying motives and character of the self-centered researcher; such attempts undermine the dignity we must value for all people.

PUTTING VIRTUES TO WORK IN THE FIELD

Universal acceptance of the six virtues presented above can be debated from a relativist perspective. *Respect* and *trust*, for example, may have different meanings and expression across cultural groups. Their meaning for researchers may not coincide with their meaning within the worldview of a culture different and foreign to the outsider. Stated in slightly different terms, are there different meanings for what constitutes trust and respect? If there are differences in the meaning of the values, how does one earn trust and respect within the context of another culture? And, most important, how does one know one has earned and established trust and respect? Ibrahim (1996) and Vasquez (1996) remind us that all cultural groups have ethical standards often embedded in legends, traditions, and customs; these standards may not resonate with those of the researcher's cultural orientation (see Trickett & Espino, 2004). "To facilitate character and moral development in a multicultural system," maintains Ibrahim (1996), "we have to identify all the moral ideals that each (cultural) system subscribes to and find common ground" (p. 83). Learning the deep cultural meaning of what constitutes trust and respect, therefore, requires the researcher to spend time with the community. One will soon discover that community members will put the researcher through a sequence of "tests" to assess the researcher's level of commitment to working closely with them and learning about their cultural ways (Trickett & Espino, 2004). Discovering the meaning of these virtues must occur long before the research enterprise is set in motion.

Relational Methodology

The establishment of trust and respect occurs through the nature and depth of relationships researchers create and sustain in their host communities. Relationships of the kind we're recommending don't occur when one relies on a "safari" approach (also referred to as "helicopter research") for data collection, in which the researcher drops in for a short period of time to collect data and then leaves, in some instances never to be heard from again. Developing and nurturing relationships with community members and leaders takes a considerable amount of time, maybe years. It means spending precious time visiting with people at social functions such as community gatherings, celebrations, ceremonies, local school events, and related activities. It means spending time with community leaders such as elected officials and elders, as well as visiting with parents of school-aged youth as well as the youth themselves. It means being willing to engage in long conversations that have nothing at all to do with one's research interests. If a researcher wishes to establish and nurture a relationship with the community, the commitment must be authentic and born from a deep abiding interest in the ways, customs, and thoughts of the local people.

Community relationships can extend from the casual to those generated from the affectionate care that accompanies profound friendships. The nature of the relationship, in turn, can influence the quality of the information that a researcher seeks to obtain in the course of the study or investigation.

A short story may help to reify our contention. A few years ago one of us was visiting with tribal elders at their weekly luncheon at the community center, an occasion he attended with regularity for numerous years in succession. Up to that point, the researcher had involved community members in grant-sponsored research on a variety of mental health and substance abuse–related topics, some of which had been initiated by the tribe. The relationship he established with the community and certain families extended over 18 years; consequently, he and community members seemingly felt at ease with one another, to the point that they felt comfortable talking about a wide range of topics from local gossip to federal government politics. Toward the end of the luncheon, one of the elders took an empty seat next to him. They greeted one another and chatted about mundane matters for some time when without any apparent reason the elder said,

> You know, we have come to trust and respect you, not only because you're a college teacher but because you are our friend. You have been a true friend of ours for a long time. You really care about us. You are a spiritual friend, too. So I want to tell you that when you're doing your studies with our youth and us, we tell you what we really think and believe. We don't tell you what we tell other researchers. We tell them what we want them to know, but we don't go into much detail. And sometimes a few of us will make up stories so that they'll go away and we don't insult them by saying "No" to them. You can ask me anything, and I will really tell you what I'm really thinking or what I know. There are a lot of us who feel that way about you. We want you to know this.

The elder then shook the researcher's hand and slowly walked away over to another table to play a game of checkers with his buddies. The researcher thanked him profusely for his words and then sat there stunned by the sincerity and forthrightness of the elder's words. It was truly a humbling experience for him.

On the way home late that afternoon, he reflected on the meaning of "really think" compared with what one just *thinks* and what all of that meant for the validity, reliably, and quality of data collected from communities where researchers had impermanent, transient relationships. Of course, he wondered if the data he collected many years earlier in the community was based on what the elders "really thought" or on their need to be polite, hospitable, and kind. It didn't matter to him because there was nothing he could do about old findings; at the time, the results made sense so there was no need to question their integrity now. What mattered then and what matters now is the nature and quality of a relationship that one establishes with a community, a relationship built on trust, respect, integrity, prudence, benevolence, and reverence.

We have reason to believe that the elder's words, framed in the wisdom of his years and experiences, merits serious consideration. We contend that the nature and quality of a relationship and community partnership will wittingly and unwittingly influence the quality of the research findings. The relationship will determine whether or not one obtains data that gets to what people really think.

The importance of establishing and valuing relationships is the mainstay of the research and writings of Carol Gilligan (1982), especially as they apply to moral judgment and reasoning. Basically, Gilligan maintains that one component of morality is that people have responsibilities toward others: A truly moral person must care for the welfare and dignity of others. In one of her earlier writings, she draws attention to gender differences in moral reasoning. Men are prone to thinking about moral judgments through an emphasis on justice; women think in terms of their relationships with others and thus their responsibilities in those relationships. Gilligan also maintains that the nurturance of a responsible relationship will influence what people tell you; the deeper and more felt the relationship, the greater the likelihood that one will tell you what they "really think" (Carol Gilligan, personal communication, May 16, 2002; see Gilligan, 2003).

Thus, along with advocating the value and significance of the six virtues we lay out in this coda, we recommend that researchers seriously consider framing their field-based research around the formation and maintenance of responsible relationships; they form the major component of establishing community partnerships and collaborative arrangements. Relational methodology means that one takes the time to nurture relationships, not merely for the sake of expediting the research and gaining acceptance and trust but because one should care about the welfare and dignity of all people.

In closing out this small chapter, we rely on the wisdom of James Skeen to provide direction in understanding the value and role of virtuous thoughts and actions in research settings. Skeen (2002) maintained that "Virtuous behavior is a worthy objective for all of us. No one is perfect, or capable of being perfect, but each of us has a need-strength profile that makes the acquisition of certain virtuous traits difficult and others relatively easy. But merely knowing that it is possible to err in two directions—excess or deficiency—is valuable information" (p. 18).

REFERENCES

Beauvais, F., & Trimble, J. E. (1992). The role of the researcher in evaluating American Indian alcohol and other drug abuse prevention programs. In M. Orlandi (Ed.), *Cultural competence for evaluators working with ethnic minority communities: A guide for alcohol and other drug abuse prevention practitioners* (pp. 173–201). Rockville, MD: Office for Substance Abuse Prevention, Cultural Competence Series 1.

Boeree, C. G. (1999). *Ethics*. Retrieved March 14, 2005, from www.ship.edu/~cgboeree/ethics.html

Fisher, C. B., Hoagwood, K., Boyce, C., Duster, T., Frank, D. A., Grisso, T., et al. (2002). Research ethics for mental health science involving ethnic minority children and youths. *American Psychologist, 57,* 1024–1040.

Gilligan, C. (1982). *In a different voice: Psychological theory and women's development*. Cambridge, MA: Harvard University Press.

Gilligan, C. (2003). *The birth of pleasure: A new map of love*. New York: Vintage.

Habermas, J. (2003). *The future of human nature*. Cambridge, UK: Polity Press.

Ibrahim, F. A. (1996). A multicultural perspective on principle and virtue ethics. *Counseling Psychologist, 24*(1), 78–85.

Jason, L. A., Keys, C., Suarez-Balcazar, Y., Taylor, R. R., & Davis, M. I. (Eds.). (2004). *Participatory community research; Theories and methods in action*. Washington, DC: APA.

Jordan, A. E., & Meara, N. M. (1990). Ethics and the professional practice of psychologists: The role of virtues and principles. *Professional Psychology: Research and Practice, 21*(2), 107–144.

Meara, N. M., & Day, J. D. (2003). Possibilities and challenges for academic psychology: Uncertain science, interpretative conversation, and virtuous community. *American Behavioral Scientist, 47*(4), 459–478.

Mohatt, G. V. (1989). The community as informant and collaborator? *American Indian and Alaska Native Mental Health Research, 2*(3), 64–70.

Mohatt, G. V., & Eagle Elk, J. (2000). *The price of a gift: A Lakota healer's story.* Lincoln: University of Nebraska Press.

Montero, M. (2004). New horizons for knowledge: The influence of citizen participation. In L. Jason, C. Keys, Y. Suarez-Balcazar, & M. Davis (Eds.), *Participatory community research: Theories and methods in action* (pp. 251–261). Washington, DC: APA, p. 252.

Puhl, L. J. (1951). *The spiritual exercises of St. Ignatius.* Westminster, MD: Newman Press.

Richardson, F. C. (2003). Virtue ethics, dialogue, and "reverence." *American Behavioral Scientist, 47*(4), 442–458.

Searles, H. (1955). The informational value of the supervisor's emotional experiences. *Psychiatry, 18,* 135–146.

Skeen, J. W. (2002). Choice theory, virtue ethics, and the sixth need. *International Journal of Reality Therapy, 12*(1), 14–19.

Trickett, E. J., & Espino, S. (2004). Collaboration and social inquiry: Multiple meanings of a construct and its role in creating useful and valid knowledge. *American Journal of Community Psychology, 34*(1/2), 1–69.

Trimble, J. E. (1977). Research in American Indian communities: Methodological issues and concerns. *Journal of Social Issues, 33*(4), 159–174.

Vasquez, M. L. (1996). Will virtue ethics improve ethical conduct in multicultural settings? *Counseling Psychologist, 24*(1), 98–104.

Woodruff, P. (2001). *Reverence.* Oxford, UK: Oxford University Press.

Name Index

Subject Index

About the Editors

Joseph E. Trimble, PhD (University of Oklahoma, Institute of Group Relations, 1969), formerly a Fellow at Harvard University's Radcliffe Institute for Advanced Study, is Professor of Psychology at Western Washington University, a Senior Scholar at the Tri-Ethnic Center for Prevention Research at Colorado State University, and a Research Associate for the National Center for American Indian and Alaska Native Mental Health Research at the University of Colorado Health Sciences Center. He has held offices in the International Association for Cross-Cultural Psychology and the American Psychological Association. He holds Fellow status in three divisions in the APA (Divisions 9, 27, and 45). He is past-President of the Society for the Psychological Study of Ethnic Minority Issues (Division 45 of the APA) and a council member of the Society for the Psychological Study of Social Issues (Division 9 of the APA). He has generated over 100 publications on cross-cultural and ethnic topics in psychology, including 14 edited, coedited, and coauthored books; his most recent coedited *Handbook of Racial and Ethnic Minority Psychology* was selected one of CHOICE Magazine's Outstanding Academic Titles for 2004. The majority of his articles, book chapters, and books focus on the role of culture and ethnicity in psychology, with an emphasis on American Indian and Alaska Native populations. In the past decade, though, he has expanded his interests to include writing and research on ethnic and racial identity, cultural measurement equivalence, spirituality, and ethics, as well as contributing to the growth of ethnic psychology. He has received numerous excellence in teaching and mentoring awards for his work in the field of ethnic and cultural psychology, including the Excellence in Teaching Award and the Paul J. Olscamp Faculty Research Award from Western Washington University; APA's Division 45 Lifetime Achievement Award; the Janet E. Helms Award for Mentoring and Scholarship in Professional Psychology at Teachers College, Columbia University; the Washington State Psychological Association Distinguished Psychologist Award for 2002; and the Peace and Social Justice Award from APA's Division 48.

Celia B. Fisher, PhD, Marie Ward Doty Professor of Psychology and Director of the Fordham University Center for Ethics Education, is a member of the DHHS Secretary's Advisory Committee on Human Research Protections (SACHRP), Co-Chair of the SACHRP Subcommittee on Research Involving Children, Vice Chair of the APA Insurance Trust, and a founding editor of the journal *Applied Developmental Science*. She chaired the APA's Ethics Code Task Force, the New York State Board for Psychology, the Ethics Committee of the Society for Research in Child Development, and the National Task Force on Applied Developmental Science and is past member of the Ethics Working Group of the National Children's Study, the NIMH Data Safety and Monitoring Board, and the Institute of Medicine's Committee on Clinical Research Involving Children. She is author of *Decoding the Ethics Code: A Practical Guide for Psychologists* (Sage Publications); coeditor of five books including *Ethical Issues in Mental Health Research With Children and Adolescents* ((Lawrence Erlbaum) Erlbaum; author of over 100 publications in the areas of ethics and lifespan development, commissioned papers for the President's National Bioethics Advisory Commission on relational ethics and vulnerable populations, and ethics of suicide research for NIMH. With support from NICHD, she is studying how to assess and enhance research consent capacity of adults with developmental disabilities. With funding from NSF and NIH, she has developed research ethics instructional materials for undergraduates, graduate students, senior scientists, and IRBs. In July 2001, she co-chaired the APA, NIMH, and Fordham Ethics Center–sponsored national conference on Research Ethics for Mental Health Science Involving Ethnic Minority Children and Youth (*American Psychologist*, December 2002).

About the Contributors

Fred Beauvais, PhD, is a Senior Research Scientist with the Tri-Ethnic Center for Prevention Research at Colorado State University. He is Principal Investigator on a research project funded by the National Institute on Drug Abuse that examines the trends and patterns of drug abuse among American Indian adolescents with an emphasis on risk and protective factors and the impact of cultural identification on drug use patterns. This project has been ongoing since 1974. He also participates in a number of other research projects that are concerned with social and psychological problems confronting ethnic minority populations, including violence, victimization, delinquency, school dropout, and suicide. In addition to his interests in specific research topics, he has written extensively on the procedures and ethics of conducting research among ethnic minority populations with a special interest in the promotion of collaborative research models. He has served on the National Advisory Council for the National Institute on Alcohol Abuse and Alcoholism and is a member of several review panels.

Dina Birman, PhD, is an Assistant Professor of Psychology in the Community and Prevention Research Division at the University of Illinois at Chicago. Her expertise is in the area of acculturation, adaptation, and mental health of refugees and immigrants. Her research builds on 6 years of applied experience in refugee mental health. From 1991 to 1997, she worked in the Refugee Mental Health Program at the National Institute of Mental Health and Substance Abuse and Mental Health Services Administration (SAMHSA), where she provided consultation and technical assistance on mental health issues to the Office for Refugee Resettlement (DHHS) and to the state and local programs that they fund. Her research has focused on understanding the long-term acculturation and adaptation of adolescent, adult, and elderly refugees from the former Soviet Union, Somalia, and Vietnam and, more recently, mental health services for refugee youth and families. She is the author of about 30 papers in professional journals and edited books on these topics and has developed technical assistance documents for teachers working with refugee students published by the Spring Institute of Intercultural Learning in Denver.

Joshua R. Bringle, MS, is a doctoral candidate in psychology at the University of Massachusetts, Amherst. His research interests focus on normative aging and adult development, specifically psychosocial processes at the end of life. He anticipates finishing his PhD in spring 2006.

Monica Brooker is a member of the NIMH-funded Diversity Archive team at the Murray Archives. She graduated cum laude from Harvard University with an ALB in Psychology and is presently a Teaching Assistant. As President of the Harvard Extension Student Association, she cofounded the Harvard Extension Research Day, providing nontraditional students an opportunity to participate and think critically about research processes. Her primary research interests include coping, resilience, and protective behaviors among children of parents with mental illness;

resiliency in young adulthood; and measurement of subjective well-being.

Dedra S. Buchwald, MD, is a Professor of Medicine at the University of Washington. She has developed a program of culturally appropriate research that spans a wide range of topics, including physical and mental health, career development and training, and health care services and utilization in both urban and rural settings. She is involved in several program projects that address medical issues in native communities. She is the Director of the NIA-funded Native Investigator Faculty Development Program that trains native faculty to conduct health-related research in their own communities.

Nancy A. Busch-Rossnagel, PhD, is the Dean of the Graduate School of Arts and Sciences and Professor of Psychology at Fordham University. In past years, she has served as Consultant for the New York City Board of Education and the New York City Department of Heath, supervised standardization testing for the Bayley Scales of Infant Development for the Psych Corporation, and completed a term as Editor of the *Research Monographs in Adolescence.* Currently she is an Editorial Board Member for the journal *Applied Developmental Science* and on the executive committee for the Association of Graduate Schools in Catholic Colleges and Universities. Her specialty within psychology is human development. Her research focuses on parent–child relationships, particularly on socialization in Latino families and ethnic differences in parenting. In this area, she explores the relationship of maternal teaching behaviors to the development of mastery motivation and self-concept in young children and works to identify the best practices for the creation and validation of culturally centered measures of early child development and socialization. She has mentored more than 30 dissertations, and

her students are now on the faculties of universities and colleges and applied research psychologists in hospitals and research institutes.

Felipe González Castro, PhD, is Professor of Clinical Psychology at the Department of Psychology, Arizona State University. He received his master's degree in social work from the UCLA School of Social Welfare in 1976, and his PhD in clinical psychology from the University of Washington in 1981. Currently he is developing a methodology for conducting robust qualitative research that examines cultural issues with members of special populations. He is also a regular proposal reviewer for numerous federal and state institutes, including the NIDA Epidemiology of Drug Abuse Review Committee. He is especially interested in mentoring graduate students in clinical psychology to prepare them for the conduct of scientifically rigorous, yet culturally rich research with racial/ethnic minority populations.

Ana Mari Cauce, PhD, Earl R. Carlson Professor of Psychology and Professor of American Ethnic Studies, is Chair of the Department of Psychology at the University of Washington. For over 20 years, she has been conducting research focusing on normative and nonnormative development with ethnic minority adolescents and/or youth growing up in difficult circumstances. She was the 2003 recipient of the Distinguished Contribution Award from the Society for Community Research and Action for her contributions to research focusing on the prevention of negative behavioral and educational outcomes for at-risk youth. In 2002, she received the Distinguished Contribution Award from the American Psychological Association Minority Fellowship Program for her work on culture, ethnicity, and context. She has also served on numerous national panels including the

National Academies of Sciences Board on Family, Youth, and Children; the Advisory Board of the National Hispanic Science Network; the College Board's National Task Force on Minority High Achievement; and the West Coast Selection Committee for the Marshall Scholarship. She has received research grants from the National Institute of Mental Health, the National Institute of Child Health and Human Development, the National Institute of Drug Abuse, the National Institute on Alcohol Abuse and Alcoholism, and the W. T. Grant Foundation.

Stephanie Childs, PhD, is the Assistant Director for the School District of Philadelphia's 5,000-family Head Start Program. She received her doctoral training in Educational Leadership at the University of Pennsylvania. She has been honored by the University of Pennsylvania by receiving the Distinguished Alum Award. For the past three decades, she has made substantial contributions to early childhood education as an educator, administrator, and researcher. Her work has focused local and national attention on how family and community involvement enhances the quality of early childhood education. Her research on family involvement in education has been published in the leading journals in early childhood education.

Jean Lau Chin, PhD, is Systemwide Dean of California School of Professional Psychology at Alliant International University. She is a licensed psychologist with 30 plus years of experience including President of CEO Services providing clinical, educational, and organizational consulting services; Associate Professor at Boston University School of Medicine as core faculty for the Center for Multicultural Training in Psychology; Regional Director of Massachusetts Behavioral Health Partnership; Executive Director of South Cove Community Health Center; and Codirector of Thom Child Guidance Clinic.

She has two books released recently: She was Editor of *The Psychology of Prejudice and Discrimination,* a four-volume set on racism, ethnicity, gender, and all forms of discrimination; she authored *Learning From My Mother's Voice,* an oral history weaving mythology and legend as a healing and transformational journey for Chinese American immigrants. She is working on her upcoming book on feminist leadership and is currently Editor of the Race and Ethnicity Series of Praeger Press.

David A. Chiriboga, PhD, is Professor of Aging and Mental Health, Florida Mental Health Institute, University of South Florida. His research involves study of the influence of stress exposure on mental health; longitudinal study of acculturation and differential mental health issues in minority and majority populations; use of multimedia and distance technologies for health care and for training; and the use of large administrative data sets, such as Medicare and Medicaid, to study state-sponsored service initiatives and their efficacy in ethnic minority populations. He has served on two chartered NIMH review committees and is currently a member of a National Institute on Disability and Rehabilitation Research (NIDRR) chartered study section and of the Aging and Substance Abuse Task Force under the Substance Abuse and Mental Health Services Administration. He serves on the editorial boards of the *Journal of Gerontology: Psychological Sciences* and the *Journal of Health and Aging.* He is a Fellow in the Gerontological Society of America and in three divisions of the American Psychological Association.

Calvin Croy, PhD, is a Senior Instructor in the American Indian and Alaska Native Programs (AIANP) at the University of Colorado at Denver and Health Sciences Center where he provides statistical analysis support. He has coauthored papers about alcohol dependence and natural recovery at American Indian reservations and on statistical sample size determination. His current research interest is methods for data imputation. Prior to joining AIANP, he conducted research on the temporal stability of hobbies and leisure interests for National Demographics & Lifestyles and the Polk Company where he was Vice President of Research.

Delia Easton, a medical anthropologist, works as a qualitative researcher at the New York City Department of Health and Mental Hygiene. Her interests include the political economy of health, urban anthropology, the legacies of welfare reform, the development and applicability of structural interventions for HIV/AIDS, socioeconomic and ethnic disparities in health, the impact of institutionalized and internalized racism on health, and concern about HIV/AIDS, among competing health concerns among Puerto Rican youth. She teaches about racial/ethnic health disparities, community health, and the theory of health practice for the Hunter College Urban Public Health Program.

Katherine Ann Gilda Elliott, PhD, is a Psychologist at the Child and Adolescent Abuse Resources and Evaluation Diagnostic and Treatment Center of the University of California, Davis Medical Center in Sacramento, California. She provides bilingual assessment and psychotherapy services to children and families affected by family violence, focusing on parent–child interaction therapy with Spanish-speaking children in the Sacramento County Child Welfare System. In addition, she conducts training workshops for mental health providers throughout California.

John Fantuzzo, PhD, is the Diana Rausnitz Riklis Professor in the Graduate School of Education at the University of Pennsylvania. His research focuses on the design, implementation, and evaluation of school- and community-based strategies for young, low-income children in high-risk urban settings. In recent years, he has conducted longitudinal studies in Head Start that relate to the impact of community and family violence on school readiness, examine the development of approaches to learning, and investigate the effects of early social/ emotional adjustment problems and early school success. Also, he has been involved in population-based studies involving citywide, integrated databases across agencies serving young children.

Janet E. Helms, PhD, is the Augustus Long Professor in the Department of Counseling, Developmental, and Educational Psychology at Boston College. She is also the founding director of the Institute for the Study and Promotion of Race and Culture, a scholarly organization intended to conduct research and train researchers to value and respect racial and cultural diversity in their research and practice. She has authored many papers on the topics of racial identity and racial and cultural dynamics and assessment. More importantly, she has supervised the doctoral training of over 50 women and men who have made a positive difference in the world via their focus on diversity.

Jeffrey A. Henderson, MD, MPH, is an Assistant Professor in American Indian and Alaska Native programs at the University of Colorado at Denver Health Sciences Center. He is a Lakota and enrolled member of the Cheyenne River Sioux Tribe. After receiving his medicine and public health degrees at UC San Diego and the University of Washington, respectively, he worked as a clinician for the Indian Health Service. A board-certified Internist and Epidemiologist, in 1998 he founded the Black Hills Center for American Indian Health, a community-based, nonprofit organization whose mission is to enhance the wellness of American Indians living on the northern plains through research, service, education, and philanthropy.

Kevin T. Henze is a doctoral student in counseling psychology at Boston College. As a member of Dr. Janet E. Helms' Institute for the Study of Race and Culture (ISPRC) research and support team, he has coauthored several articles, revitalized ISPRC's website twice, and co-coordinated four ISPRC Diversity Challenge conferences. His dissertation research involves the interface of White racial identity development, gender identity, and intergroup relations. His passion for teaching was recognized in 2003 with a Boston College Donald J. White Teaching Excellence Award.

Gayle Y. Iwamasa, PhD, is an Associate Professor in Community-Clinical Psychology at DePaul University. She received her PhD in Clinical Psychology from Purdue University. Her research and clinical interests are in ethnic minority mental health, with a specific expertise in Asian American mental health. Her research on the mental health of Japanese American older adults has been funded by the National Institute of Mental Health. She is the editor of two books, 16 peer-reviewed journal articles, and 11 book chapters. She has presented her work in over 100 national and international presentations. She has served in many leadership roles in national organizations, including President, Asian American Psychological Association; Vice Chair, Committee on Women in Psychology, American Psychological Association; and Coordinator of Professional Issues and Coordinator of Membership for the Association for Advancement of Behavior Therapy.

Spero M. Manson PhD (Pembina Chippewa), is Professor of Psychiatry, and Head, American Indian and Alaska Native Programs at the University of Colorado Health Sciences Center. His research portfolio currently exceeds $60 million, involving 98 native communities. He has published 160 articles on the assessment, epidemiology, and prevention of alcohol, drug, mental, and physical health problems across the developmental life span of American Indian/Alaska Native people. He has received numerous awards for his work, including the Beverly Visiting Professorship, University of Toronto (1995); the Indian Health Service's Distinguished Service Award (1996, 2004); the Rema Lapouse Mental Health Epidemiology Award from the American Public Health Association (1998); the Walker-Ames Professorship at the University of Washington (1999–2000); Hammer Award from former Vice President Gore (1999), 10 Best TeleHealth Programs in the United States (2002); election to the prestigious Institute of Medicine (2002); and Stoklos Visiting Professorship at the University of Arizona (2004).

Jackquelyn Mascher is a doctoral candidate in counseling psychology at Boston College. Her research interests include racial identity development, issues of power and privilege, psychosocial colonization and trauma, the misreading and rereading of historical events, intersexuality, and unified theory. Her dissertation is a study on the relationship between White racial identity and the teaching beliefs of psychology professors. She continues to work closely with the staff of the Institute for the Study and Promotion of Race and Culture (ISPRC) founded by Dr. Janet E. Helms. She holds a bachelor's degree in Psychobiology from Yale University and two master's degrees from Lehigh University, one in social restoration and the other in counseling and human services.

Helen McGough has supported the human subjects review function at the University of Washington for over 19 years. She is a member of the board of directors for Public Responsibility in Medicine and Research (PRIM&R), a nonprofit organization devoted to the ethical conduct of research, and serves as a faculty member for PRIM&R's 101

On-The-Road Program. She is on the editorial board of the journal, *IRB*, and is a member of the board of directors of the Association for the Accreditation of Human Research Protection Programs. She edits the newsletter for the Applied Research Ethics National Association (ARENA).

Christine McWayne, PhD, is an Assistant Professor in the Department of Applied Psychology at New York University. She is currently involved in partnership- and community-based research within the Head Start community in New York City. Generally, her research interests include family involvement in children's education in low-income communities; helping to establish a whole-child understanding of low-income, preschool children's school readiness competencies; and validating assessment instruments and intervention for low-income, preschool children and their families. Her recent research has focused on the examination of multiple dimensions of school readiness within the context of classroom quality and the social and structural dimensions of urban neighborhoods.

Jeffery Scott Mio, PhD, is a Professor in the Psychology and Sociology Department at California State Polytechnic University, Pomona, where he also serves as the Director of the MS in Psychology program. He taught at California State University Fullerton in the Counseling Department from 1984 to 1986 and at Washington State University in the Department of Psychology from 1986 to 1994 before accepting his current position. His interests are in the teaching of multicultural issues, the development of allies, and how metaphors are used in political persuasion.

Gerald V. Mohatt, EdD, is Professor of Psychology and Director of the Center for Alaska Native Health Research at the University of Alaska Fairbanks. Throughout

his career, he has focused on building new settings in rural areas to increase opportunity for rural indigenous groups. His current work is to establish a permanent center to do interdisciplinary research on health disparities of Alaska Natives. He was raised in rural Iowa. He has two sons, their two partners, and a soon-to-be-born granddaughter. He has worked with American Indian, Canadian First Nations, and Alaska Natives since 1968.

Harry Montoya is President and CEO of Hands Across Cultures Corporation, an agency involved in community mobilization efforts and the promotion of educational, health, and social service programs. He has a master of arts degree in counseling psychology from New Mexico State University and a bachelor of arts in psychology from Westmar University in LeMars, Iowa. He served on the Pojoaque Valley School Board and as President of the New Mexico School Boards Association, as well as on various committees for the National School Boards Association. In June 2002, he was elected to the Santa Fe County Board of County Commissioners. Also in 2002, he was recognized by De Colores, Inc. when he was the recipient of the Business Leadership Award.

Richard H. Nobles is a graduate student in child clinical psychology at the University of Washington. He received his undergraduate degree in psychology from Yale University where his senior thesis focused on depression in young adults who identified as both ethnic and sexual minorities. His research interests include developmental psychopathology in at-risk adolescent populations and the prevention of internalizing disorders in adolescence.

Tim D. Noe, MDiv, is currently a doctoral candidate in the Graduate School of Public Affairs at the University of Colorado in Denver. He serves in several capacities at the American Indian and Alaska Native programs of the University of Colorado

Health Sciences Center in Denver including Project Director of a smoking cessation clinical trial for native elders and a project focusing on assessing Lakota attitudes toward health-related research. He is also Deputy Administrative Director for two federally funded program project grants focusing on health disparities. He was also the former Deputy Director of the National Program Office of the Healthy Nations Initiative, which focused on reducing the harm caused by substance abuse in AIAN communities. He has coauthored a number of publications on substance abuse prevention programming with youth and families, numerous journal articles, and a family-based substance abuse prevention curriculum.

Kathleen Ragsdale, PhD, is a Research Associate at the Fordham University Center for Ethics Education. Her academic and research interests include minority health disparities and HIV/AIDS, applied anthropology as it relates to public health, gender and power disparities, ethically relevant research, and health-related social justice for minority and vulnerable populations. She received a doctoral degree in anthropology with a specialization in medical anthropology and health communication from the University of Florida in 2002. While at the University of Florida, she received the Tinker Field Research Grant for Latin American Studies, the John M. Goggin Award for Outstanding PhD Research and Writing in Anthropology, and an International Population Studies Scholarship to attend the Population Fellows Programs, Summer Course in International Population at the University of Michigan. While an NIMH NRSA Fellow at CAIR, she was named a Health Disparities Scholar by the National Institutes of Health and competitively received a Health Disparities Research Loan Repayment Program Award through the National Center on Minority Health and Health Disparities. Her international field

experience among diverse ethnic groups has included research among the indigenous Kuna Yala of Panama, hurricane disaster recovery in the U.S. Virgin Islands, ethnobotanic research among first-generation immigrants in Miami, Florida, and other minority health-related projects in Belize, Costa Rica, and Milwaukee, Wisconsin.

Rebeca Rios is a first-year PhD student in clinical psychology at Arizona State University. Ms. Rios came to ASU from the University of California San Francisco where she worked for the Substance Abuse Research Program. Previously, as a Research Assistant at the American Institutes for Research in Washington, D.C., she worked on several federal contracts, including a project contracted by the Office of Minority Health to create teaching modules in cultural competence and a SAMHSA-funded contract to support community collaboration in children's mental health programs. Ms. Rios earned her BA in psychology from Georgetown University in 1999. Her current research interests include sociocultural aspects of resilience in health behaviors and community health psychology.

Anmol Satiani is a doctoral candidate in the counseling psychology program in the Carolyn A. and Peter S. Lynch School of Education at Boston College. She was a graduate assistant for 3 years in the Institute for the Study and Promotion of Race and Culture (ISPRC) founded and directed by Janet E. Helms. She is currently a predoctoral intern at the University of Illinois Chicago (UIC) Counseling Center. Her dissertation research is concerned with indigenous beliefs about suffering and healing among South Asian immigrant women.

Merrill Singer, PhD, is the Associate Director of the Hispanic Health Council and Director of the HHC's Center for Community Health Research in Hartford, Connecticut, as well as a scientist affiliated with the Yale University Center for Interdisciplinary Research on AIDS. He has been the Principal Investigator on a continuous series of applied federally funded drinking, drug use, and AIDS prevention projects since 1984 and currently is the Principal Investigator on a CDC-funded study designed to monitor emergent drug use trends and to build community health responses to identified public health risks. Additionally, he is the co-Principal Investigator on three studies: sexual communication and risk among inner-city young adults (CDC); assessing the implementation of oral HIV testing among injection drug users in Rio de Janeiro, Brazil (NIDA); and testing the implementation of hepatitis B vaccination of injection drug users in Hartford and Chicago (NIDA). He has over 150 published articles and chapters in health and social science journals and books, writes a regular column for the *Society for Applied Anthropology Newsletter,* and is author, coauthor, or coeditor of 10 books. His newest edited volume, *Unhealthy Health Policy* (AltaMira) was published in September 2004. Several additional volumes, *Something Dangerous: Emergent and Changing Illicit Drug Use Patterns and Their Public Health Implications* (Waveland), *Communities Assessing Their AIDS Risk* (Lexington Books), and *New Drugs on the Street: Changing Inner City Patterns of Illicit Consumption* (Haworth Books) are in press and will be available in 2005. In addition, he has served as the Associate Editor of the journal *Medical Anthropology,* is the current Book Editor of *Medical Anthropology Quarterly,* and is an editorial board member of the *Journal of Ethnicity and Substance Abuse* and the *International Journal of Drug Policy.* Recently, he was selected as the first recipient of the new Practicing Anthropology Award by the Society for Medical Anthropology.

Lisa R. Thomas, PhD, is a postdoctoral Fellow at the Alcohol and Drug Abuse Institute at the University of Washington and is Tlingit, Eagle, Dog Salmon. She has a doctorate in clinical psychology and has focused her work in American Indian and Alaska Native communities. She has a background in sobriety and wellness-oriented prevention and intervention programs. She has worked with the University of Washington and the Seattle Indian Health Board as part of a team that developed a bicultural life skills prevention/intervention program for native youth, the Journeys of the Circle Project. She has also worked with University of Alaska Fairbanks on a statewide research project with Alaska Natives, identifying individual, family, community, cultural, and spiritual factors in sobriety processes for Alaska Natives. She has worked as well with her tribe, Central Council Tlingit and Haida Indian Tribes of Alaska, on a multiyear wellness project with the goal of enhancing wellness in locally driven, culturally appropriate community programs. Currently, she is working with two reservation tribal communities in the Pacific Northwest to implement and test the Journeys of the Circle intervention with reservation-based native youth and is providing evaluation and consultation for tribal corporations and communities in Alaska. She is involved at the national level to work toward cultural competence and relevance at all levels of mental health research and service provision.

Anthony J. Urquiza, PhD, is a Clinical Associate Professor and Director of Mental Health Services at the CAARE Center, Department of Pediatrics, UC Davis Medical Center. During the last decade, he has been adapting parent–child interaction therapy (PCIT) to families involved in child welfare systems. His empirical research has supported the benefits of PCIT with both abusive families and foster families. In addition, he has been instrumental in developing PCIT as an intervention for Spanish-speaking families. He is currently involved in a PCIT dissemination training project, which is training 40 community mental health agencies throughout the state of California.

Scyatta A. Wallace, PhD, is an Assistant Professor in the Department of Preventive Medicine and Community Health at SUNY Downstate Medical Center, where she serves as faculty in the Masters of Public Health Program. Her research interests include examining cultural and contextual factors associated with health outcomes and the development of culturally relevant behavioral health interventions for Black populations. Currently, she is an Investigator on a study examining cultural and contextual influences associated with sexual risk reduction among ethnically diverse Black adolescents and a study examining attitudes towards HIV and HIV testing among urban and rural young-adult Black populations. She was a research fellow at the Division of HIV/AIDS Prevention, Centers for Disease Control and Prevention (CDC). She has been featured in the *APA Monitor* (2001). She is an NIH Health Disparities Scholar since 2002, received the first Dalamas A. Taylor Summer Policy Fellowship (2000) awarded by the American Psychological Association and Society for the Psychological Study of Social Issues, obtained a dissertation grant from the Center for Ethics Education (2000), and was selected as a member of the Graduate Research Ethics Education Training Program from the National Science Foundation and Association for Practical and Professional Ethics (1998–2001). She serves on the editorial boards of the scientific journals, *Applied Developmental Science* and *Journal of Black Psychology*.

Susan Krauss Whitbourne, PhD, is Professor of Psychology at the University of Massachusetts Amherst. A Fellow of the American Psychological Association (APA), she is Past President of Division 20 (Adult Development and Aging) and is serving as Council Representative and a member of the Policy and Planning Board. She is a Fellow of the Gerontological Society of America, serving as Chair of the Distinguished Mentorship Committee for the Behavioral and Social Sciences (BSS). Her teaching was recognized with a University Distinguished Teaching Award, and she has won the APA Division 20 Master Mentor Award and the GSA BSS Distinguished Mentorship Award. With research interests in psychosocial development in mid- and later life, she is currently completing a 34-year sequential study of college alumni through midlife. She serves on the editorial boards of the *Journals of Gerontology: Psychological Sciences and Developmental Psychology*.

Keith Whitfield, PhD, is Associate Professor and the Graduate Professor in Charge in the Department of Biobehavioral Health at the Pennsylvania State University. His research involves focuses on individual differences in the health of older minorities. He serves as Chair for the Gerontological Society of America's Task Force on Minority Issues. He was a member of the National Research Council/National Academy of Sciences Aging Mind Committee and currently serves on the Research Agenda for the Social Psychology of Aging Committee. He is a member of the NIA-Behavioral and Social Science Review Committee and also reviews regularly for the Alzheimer's Association. He is a member of the National Advisory Board for the Center for Urban African American Aging Research at the University of Michigan and the Institute on Aging at Wayne State University. He also serves as an Associate Editor for *Experimental Aging Research* and is on the editorial board for the *Journal of Applied Developmental Psychology.*

Barbara W. K. Yee, PhD, is Professor and Chair of the Department of Family and Consumer Sciences, College of Tropical Agriculture and Human Resources at the University of Hawaii at Manoa. She has taught at the University of Texas Medical Branch, University of Oklahoma, and University of South Florida. Since the fall of Saigon in 1975, she has been interested in how middle-aged and elderly Southeast Asian refugees adapt to the loss of homeland and culture. Her current research examines how acculturation influences health beliefs and lifestyle practices across three generations of Vietnamese adults living in the United States. She is a Fellow of the American Psychological Association and Gerontological Society of America. She serves on the Expert Panel of Minority Women's Health, Office of Women's Health, DHHS, and on the steering committee for the Bright Futures for Women's Health and Wellness, HRSA. She has served on editorial boards of the *Journals of Gerontology: Psychological Sciences, Psychology and Aging, Topics in Geriatric Rehabilitation,* and *Ethnicity and Aging.*

Copeland H. Young is an Archival Specialist on a Library of Congress–funded Data Preservation Alliance for the Social Sciences project to preserve born digital data and also oversees the Murray Virtual Data Center metadata digital conversion project. He participated in the initial phase of the groundbreaking Diversity Archive and coordinated the development of the Murray's Mental Health Archive. He is the lead author of *Inventory of Longitudinal Studies in the Social Sciences.* He is a graduate student in the Archives Management Program at Simmons College and graduated from Harvard College. He has worked at the Henry A. Murray Archives for 18 years.